SOUTH AMERICA

EUROPE

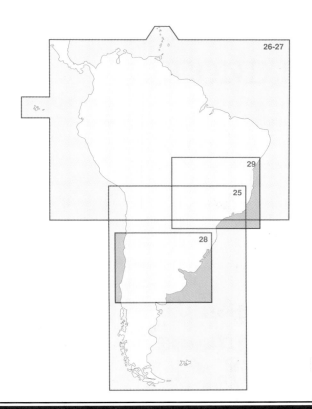

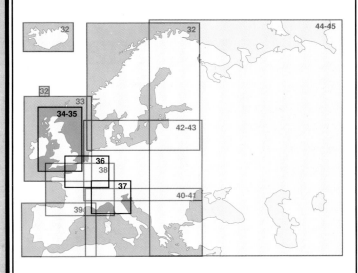

Bartholomew
A Division of HarperCollins Publishers
Duncan Street, Edinburgh EH9 1TA

First published by Bartholomew 1987
Revised edition 1994

© Bartholomew 1994

ISBN 0 89577 613 8

Printed in Great Britain by Bartholomew, The Edinburgh Press Limited.

Details included in this atlas are subject to change without notice. Whilst every effort is made to keep information up to date Bartholomew will not be responsible for any loss, damage or inconvenience caused by inaccuracies in this atlas. The publishers are always pleased to acknowledge any corrections brought to their notice, and record their appreciation of the valuable services rendered in the past by map users in assisting to maintain the accuracy of their publications.

GF7330

Acknowledgements

The Publishers acknowledge the assistance of the following in the preparation of material used in this publication: Dr Walter Stephen, Senior Adviser, Curriculum, Dean Education Centre, Edinburgh; Alister Hendrie, Assistant Headteacher, Portobello High School, Edinburgh; Andrew Grant, Principal Teacher, Geography, Wester Hailes Education Centre, Edinburgh; Stephen Hamilton, Principal Teacher, Geography, Broughton High School, Edinburgh.

The Publishers are grateful to the following for providing the photographs used in this atlas:
(picture number(s) shown in italics)
Travel Photo International: pages xxii-xxiii, savanna, rain forest, prairie, northern forest; page xxii, *7;* page xviii, *2;* page xv , *11;* page xvi , *4, 5, 13, 14;* page xx , *7;* page xxi , *2;* page vi , *3, 4;* page viii,*3,4.*
Photographers' Library: page xxii-xxiii, scrub *Chris Knaggs photograph,* desert *Oliver Martel photograph;* page x , *8 Clive Sawyer photograph;* page xiv, *8 Ian Wright photograph;* page xvii, *9 Tom Hustler photograph;* page xx , *4 Robyn Beeche photograph. Biofotos:* page x , *5 Heather Angel photograph;* page xx , *6 Andrew Henley photograph;* page xxi , *3 Soames Summerhays photograph. The Photo Source:* page xii ,*10;* page xviii, *4;* page xiv, *7. Wade Cooper Associates,* Edinburgh: page xvi , *12;* page xvii, *10;* page vi , *1. Pictor International:* page xiv, *6;* page vi , *2. B. and C. Alexander:* page xxii , tundra. *Bruce Coleman Ltd:* page viii, *6 WWF/Eugen Schuhmacher. Mepha:* page xviii, *1 C. Osborne photograph. Michael Scott:* page xxii , woodland and grass. *Yorkshire and Humberside Tourist Board:* page xi, *2. Spectrum Colour Library:* page xiii, *12, 14.*

CONTENTS

THE WORLD

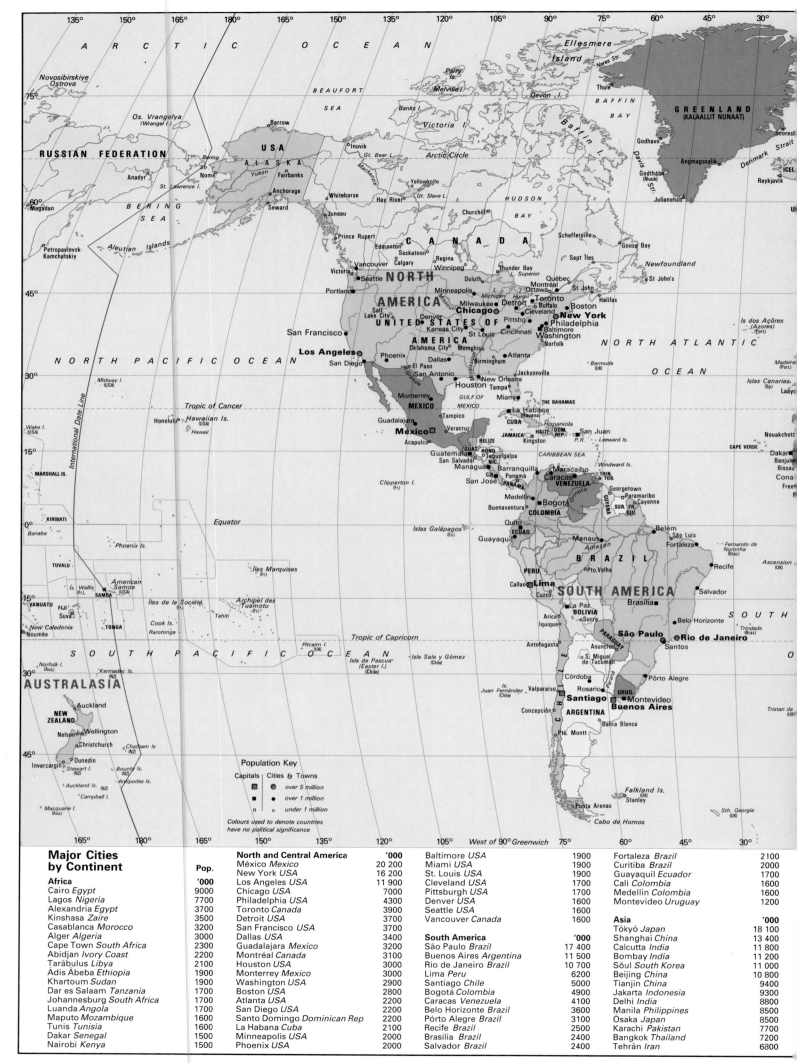

Population Key

Capitals	Cities & Towns	
■	●	over 5 million
▪	●	over 1 million
□	○	under 1 million

Colours used to denote countries
have no political significance

Major Cities by Continent

Africa	Pop. '000
Cairo *Egypt*	9000
Lagos *Nigeria*	7700
Alexandria *Egypt*	3700
Kinshasa *Zaire*	3500
Casablanca *Morocco*	3200
Alger *Algeria*	3000
Cape Town *South Africa*	2300
Abidjan *Ivory Coast*	2200
Tarābulus *Libya*	2100
Ādis Ābeba *Ethiopia*	1900
Khartoum *Sudan*	1900
Dar es Salaam *Tanzania*	1700
Johannesburg *South Africa*	1700
Luanda *Angola*	1700
Maputo *Mozambique*	1600
Tunis *Tunisia*	1600
Dakar *Senegal*	1500
Nairobi *Kenya*	1500

North and Central America	'000
México *Mexico*	20 200
New York *USA*	16 200
Los Angeles *USA*	11 900
Chicago *USA*	7000
Philadelphia *USA*	4300
Toronto *Canada*	3900
Detroit *USA*	3700
San Francisco *USA*	3700
Dallas *USA*	3400
Guadalajara *Mexico*	3200
Montréal *Canada*	3100
Houston *USA*	3000
Monterrey *Mexico*	3000
Washington *USA*	2900
Boston *USA*	2800
Atlanta *USA*	2200
San Diego *USA*	2200
Santo Domingo *Dominican Rep*	2200
La Habana *Cuba*	2100
Minneapolis *USA*	2000
Phoenix *USA*	2000

	'000
Baltimore *USA*	1900
Miami *USA*	1900
St. Louis *USA*	1900
Cleveland *USA*	1700
Pittsburgh *USA*	1700
Denver *USA*	1600
Seattle *USA*	1600
Vancouver *Canada*	1600

South America	'000
São Paulo *Brazil*	17 400
Buenos Aires *Argentina*	11 500
Rio de Janeiro *Brazil*	10 700
Lima *Peru*	6200
Santiago *Chile*	5000
Bogotá *Colombia*	4900
Caracas *Venezuela*	4100
Belo Horizonte *Brazil*	3600
Pórto Alegre *Brazil*	3100
Recife *Brazil*	2500
Brasilia *Brazil*	2400
Salvador *Brazil*	2400

	'000
Fortaleza *Brazil*	2100
Curitiba *Brazil*	2000
Guayaquil *Ecuador*	1700
Cali *Colombia*	1600
Medellin *Colombia*	1600
Montevideo *Uruguay*	1200

Asia	'000
Tōkyō *Japan*	18 100
Shanghai *China*	13 400
Calcutta *India*	11 800
Bombay *India*	11 200
Sŏul *South Korea*	11 000
Beijing *China*	10 800
Tianjin *China*	9400
Jakarta *Indonesia*	9300
Delhi *India*	8800
Manila *Philippines*	8500
Ōsaka *Japan*	8500
Karachi *Pakistan*	7700
Bangkok *Thailand*	7200
Tehrān *Iran*	6800

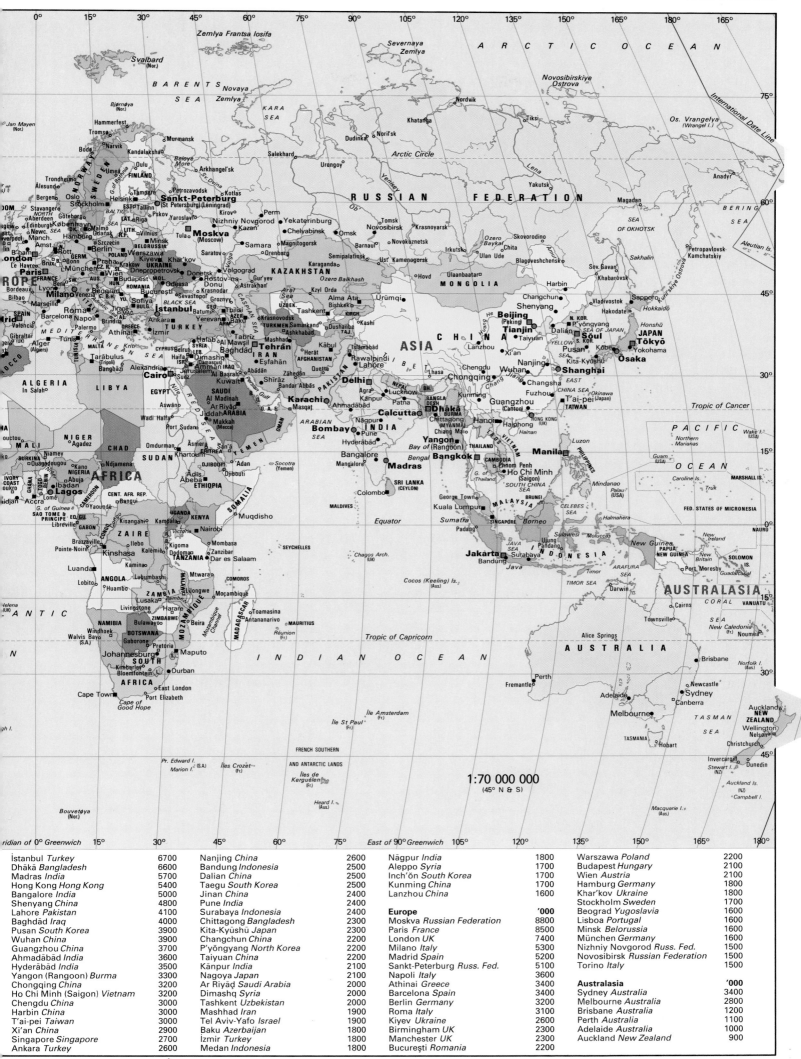

1:70 000 000
(45° N & S)

İstanbul *Turkey*	6700	Nanjing *China*	2600	Nägpur *India*	1800	Warszawa *Poland*	2200
Dhākā *Bangladesh*	6600	Bandung *Indonesia*	2500	Aleppo *Syria*	1700	Budapest *Hungary*	2100
Madras *India*	5700	Dalian *China*	2500	Inch'ŏn *South Korea*	1700	Wien *Austria*	2100
Hong Kong *Hong Kong*	5400	Taegu *South Korea*	2500	Kunming *China*	1700	Hamburg *Germany*	1800
Bangalore *India*	5000	Jinan *China*	2400	Lanzhou *China*	1600	Khar'kov *Ukraine*	1800
Shenyang *China*	4800	Pune *India*	2400			Stockholm *Sweden*	1700
Lahore *Pakistan*	4100	Surabaya *Indonesia*	2400	**Europe**	**'000**	Beograd *Yugoslavia*	1600
Baghdād *Iraq*	4000	Chittagong *Bangladesh*	2300	Moskva *Russian Federation*	8800	Lisboa *Portugal*	1600
Pusan *South Korea*	3900	Kita-Kyūshū *Japan*	2300	Paris *France*	8500	Minsk *Belorussia*	1600
Wuhan *China*	3900	Changchun *China*	2200	London *UK*	7400	München *Germany*	1600
Guangzhou *China*	3700	P'yŏngyang *North Korea*	2200	Milano *Italy*	5300	Nizhniy Novgorod *Russ. Fed.*	1500
Ahmadābād *India*	3600	Taiyuan *China*	2200	Madrid *Spain*	5200	Novosibirsk *Russian Federation*	1500
Hyderābād *India*	3500	Kānpur *India*	2100	Sankt-Peterburg *Russ. Fed.*	5100	Torino *Italy*	1500
Yangon (Rangoon) *Burma*	3300	Nagoya *Japan*	2100	Napoli *Italy*	3600		
Chongqing *China*	3200	Ar Riyāḍ *Saudi Arabia*	2000	Athinai *Greece*	3400	**Australasia**	**'000**
Ho Chi Minh (Saigon) *Vietnam*	3200	Dimashq *Syria*	2000	Barcelona *Spain*	3400	Sydney *Australia*	3400
Chengdu *China*	3000	Tashkent *Uzbekistan*	2000	Berlin *Germany*	3200	Melbourne *Australia*	2800
Harbin *China*	3000	Mashhad *Iran*	1900	Roma *Italy*	3100	Brisbane *Australia*	1200
T'ai-pei *Taiwan*	3000	Tel Aviv-Yafo *Israel*	1900	Kiyev *Ukraine*	2600	Perth *Australia*	1100
Xi'an *China*	2900	Baku *Azerbaijan*	1800	Birmingham *UK*	2300	Adelaide *Australia*	1000
Singapore *Singapore*	2700	İzmir *Turkey*	1800	Manchester *UK*	2300	Auckland *New Zealand*	900
Ankara *Turkey*	2600	Medan *Indonesia*	1800	Bucureşti *Romania*	2200		

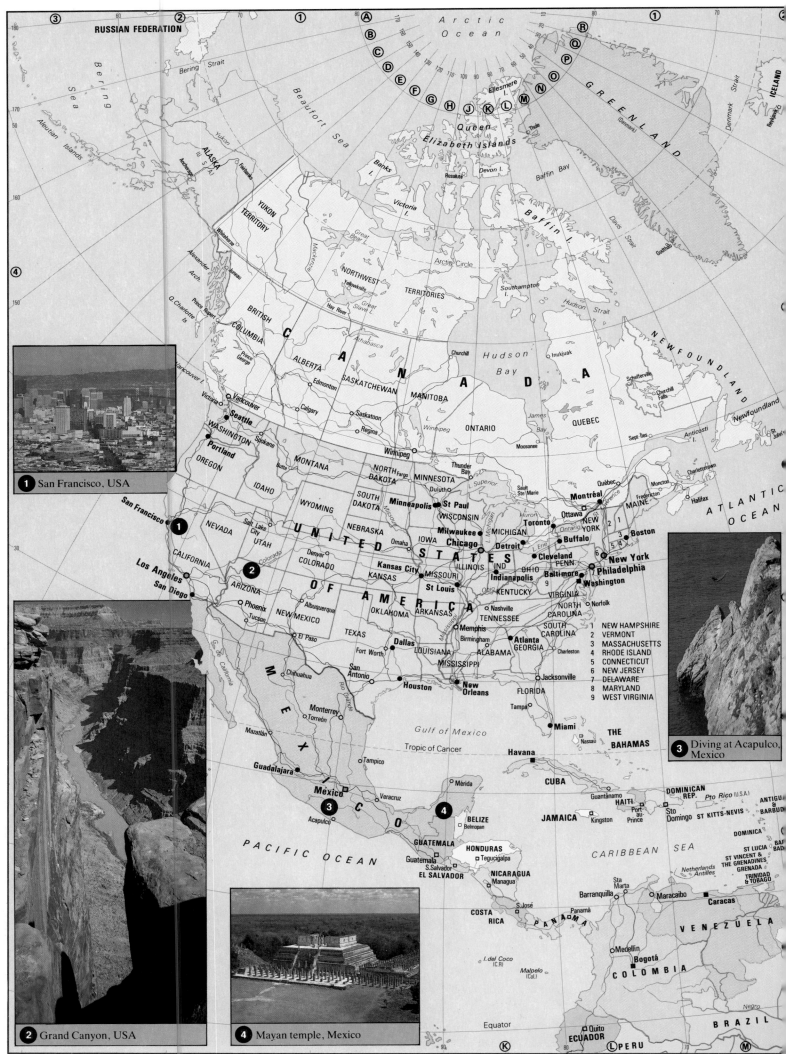

NORTH AMERICA

0   250   500   750   1000 km
0   250   500 mls

RUSSIAN FEDERATION

Arctic Ocean

GREENLAND (Denmark)

ICELAND

Bering Sea

Bering Strait

Beaufort Sea

Queen Elizabeth Islands

Baffin Bay

Denmark Strait

Aleutian Islands

ALASKA (U.S.A.)

Anchorage

Fairbanks

YUKON TERRITORY

Whitehorse

Banks I.

Victoria I.

Devon I.

Ellesmere I.

Thule

Resolute

Davis Strait

Godhåb

Reykjavik

Juneau

BRITISH COLUMBIA

Prince Rupert

Q. Charlotte Is

Vancouver I.

NORTHWEST TERRITORIES

Yellowknife

Great Bear L.

Great Slave L.

Hay River

Arctic Circle

Southampton I.

Hudson Strait

NEWFOUNDLAND

Baffin I.

Hudson Bay

C A N A D A

ALBERTA

Edmonton

Calgary

SASKATCHEWAN

Saskatoon

Regina

MANITOBA

Winnipeg

L. Winnipeg

Churchill

Inukjuak

James Bay

ONTARIO

Moosonee

QUEBEC

Schefferville

Churchill Falls

Sept-Îles

Anticosti I.

Newfoundland

St John's

Charlottetown

Moncton

Halifax

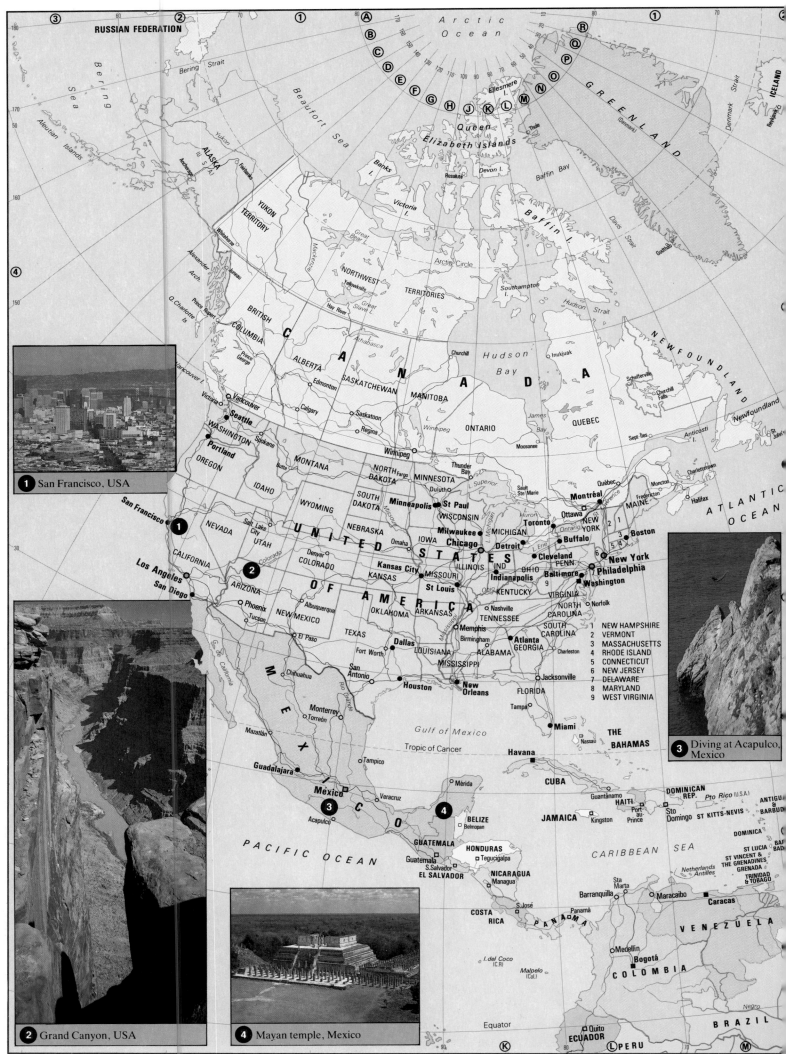
1 San Francisco, USA

Victoria

Vancouver

Seattle

WASHINGTON

Spokane

Portland

OREGON

Butte

MONTANA

IDAHO

WYOMING

NORTH DAKOTA

Fargo

SOUTH DAKOTA

NEBRASKA

Missouri

MINNESOTA

Duluth

L. Superior

Thunder Bay

Sault Ste Marie

WISCONSIN

Minneapolis

St Paul

Milwaukee

MICHIGAN

L. Michigan

L. Huron

Ottawa

Toronto

L. Ontario

Montréal

St Lawrence

MAINE

Fredericton

Québec

San Francisco

NEVADA

Salt Lake City

UTAH

Colorado

CALIFORNIA

Los Angeles

San Diego

ARIZONA

Phoenix

Tucson

NEW MEXICO

Albuquerque

El Paso

COLORADO

Denver

Omaha

IOWA

KANSAS

Kansas City

MISSOURI

St Louis

ILLINOIS

Chicago

Detroit

L. Erie

Cleveland

OHIO

IND

Indianapolis

KENTUCKY

Buffalo

NEW YORK

PENN

Baltimore

Washington

Philadelphia

New York

VIRGINIA

Norfolk

ATLANTIC OCEAN

Boston

UNITED STATES OF AMERICA

OKLAHOMA

ARKANSAS

TENNESSEE

Memphis

Nashville

Birmingham

NORTH CAROLINA

SOUTH CAROLINA

Charleston

TEXAS

Dallas

Fort Worth

San Antonio

Houston

LOUISIANA

New Orleans

MISSISSIPPI

ALABAMA

GEORGIA

Atlanta

Mississippi

FLORIDA

Jacksonville

Tampa

Miami

1 NEW HAMPSHIRE
2 VERMONT
3 MASSACHUSETTS
4 RHODE ISLAND
5 CONNECTICUT
6 NEW JERSEY
7 DELAWARE
8 MARYLAND
9 WEST VIRGINIA

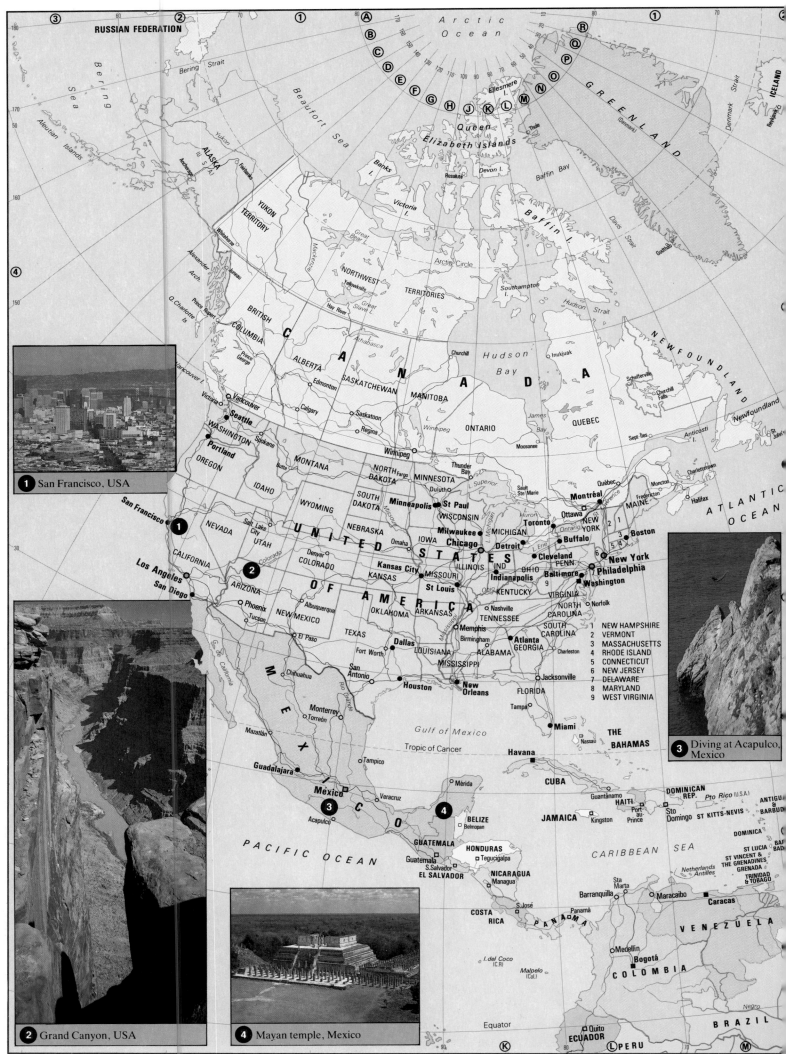
3 Diving at Acapulco, Mexico

M E X I C O

Chihuahua

Rio Grande

Monterrey

Torreón

Mazatlán

G. de California

Guadalajara

México

Veracruz

Acapulco

Tampico

Tropic of Cancer

Gulf of Mexico

Havana

Nassau

THE BAHAMAS

CUBA

Mérida

BELIZE
Belmopan

GUATEMALA

Guatemala

S.Salvador

EL SALVADOR

HONDURAS

Tegucigalpa

NICARAGUA

Managua

Guantánamo

HAITI

Kingston

JAMAICA

Port-au-Prince

DOMINICAN REP.

Sto Domingo

Pto Rico (U.S.A.)

ST KITTS-NEVIS

ANTIGUA & BARBUDA

DOMINICA

ST LUCIA

ST VINCENT & THE GRENADINES

GRENADA

TRINIDAD & TOBAGO

CARIBBEAN SEA

Netherlands Antilles

PACIFIC OCEAN

COSTA RICA

S.José

PANAMA

Panamá

Sta Marta

Barranquilla

Maracaibo

Caracas

VENEZUELA

I. del Coco (C.R)

Malpelo (Col.)

Medellín

Bogotá

C O L O M B I A

Equator

Quito

ECUADOR

PERU

Negro

B R A Z I L

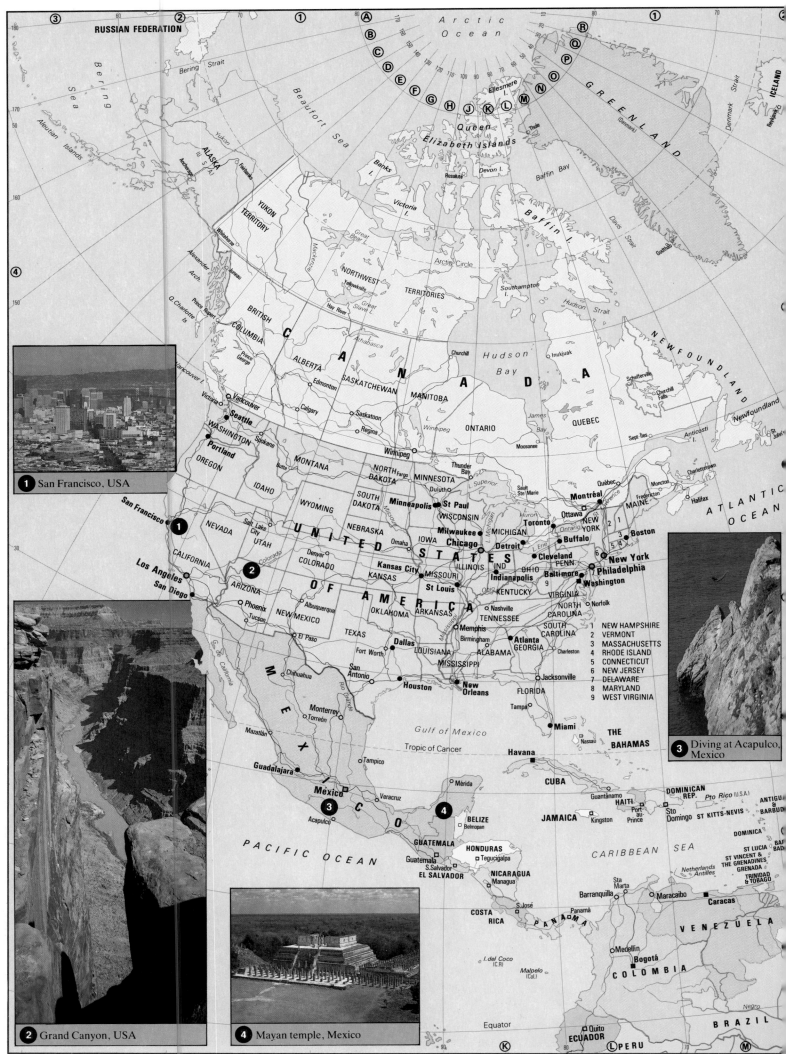
2 Grand Canyon, USA

4 Mayan temple, Mexico

FACTS ABOUT NORTH AMERICA

1 In 1906, the city of San Francisco was almost destroyed by the fires which resulted from an earthquake. The city was hit by another large earthquake in 1989. Beneath the city runs the San Andreas fault, where two of the 'continental plates' which make up the earth's crust slide against one another. When they get jammed together at any point, pressure builds up beneath them, until finally they are forced apart. This causes an earthquake because of the sudden release of so much energy. The longer the plates stay jammed together, the greater the build up of pressure and the greater the strength of the final earthquake: in 1906, land surfaces in San Francisco moved as much as 6 metres (20 feet).

2 The huge Grand Canyon in Arizona, USA, was gouged out of the rock by the Colorado River after the land was uplifted. It is as much as 1·6 kilometres (1 mile) deep, a maximum of 29 kilometres (18 miles) from rim to rim and no less than 446 kilometres (277 miles) long! The Grand Canyon is still being carved deeper (though very slowly) by the river.

3 At La Questrada, Acapulco Mexico, divers often swoop 36 m (118 feet) down into the sea. This is the highest dive which people do regularly.

4 The Maya were a people who lived in southern Mexico and Guatemala 1400 years ago. They built great cities with stone temples, public buildings and palaces. The picture shows one of their buildings which can be seen today. It was built without help from any modern machinery.

🐄 Cattle	🍎 Fruit	🌿 Wheat	⁶ Nickel
🐖 Hogs	🌾 Sugar cane	🌲 Maize	⁷ Lead
🍌 Bananas	🌲 Timber	⛏ Minerals	⁹ Silver
🍋 Citrus fruit	🍂 Tobacco	¹ Bauxite	¹¹ Uranium
🌸 Cotton	Coal	³ Copper	¹² Zinc
🐟 Fish	Oil	⁵ Iron	¹³ Asbestos

NATURAL VEGETATION/PRODUCTS

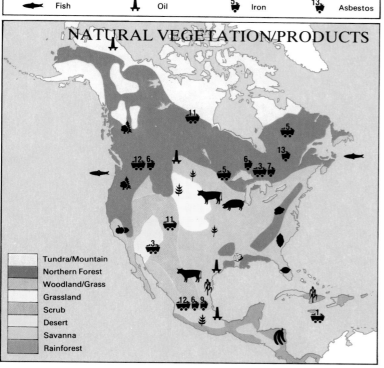

- Tundra/Mountain
- Northern Forest
- Woodland/Grass
- Grassland
- Scrub
- Desert
- Savanna
- Rainforest

POPULATION

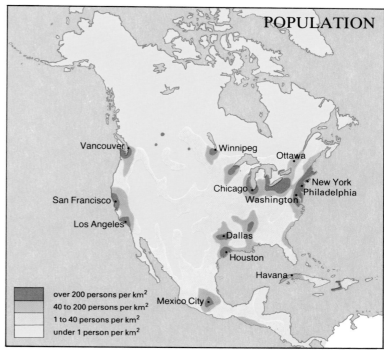

- over 200 persons per km²
- 40 to 200 persons per km²
- 1 to 40 persons per km²
- under 1 person per km²

CANADA

Area: 9 976 147 sq km (3 851 790 sq miles)
Population: 27 300 000
Capital: Ottawa
Languages: English, French
Currency: Canadian Dollar

CUBA

Area: 114 524 sq km (44 218 sq miles)
Population: 10 600 000
Capital: Havana
Language: Spanish
Currency: Cuban Peso

EL SALVADOR

Area: 20 865 sq km (8056 sq miles)
Population: 5 300 000
Capital: San Salvador
Language: Spanish
Currency: Colon

GUATEMALA

Area: 108 888 sq km (42 042 sq miles)
Population: 9 200 000
Capital: Guatemala
Language: Spanish
Currency: Quetzal

JAMAICA

Area: 11 424 sq km (4411 sq miles)
Population: 2 500 000
Capital: Kingston
Language: English
Currency: Jamaican Dollar

MEXICO

Area: 1 967 180 sq km (759 528 sq miles)
Population: 88 600 000
Capital: Mexico City
Language: Spanish
Currency: Mexican Peso

NICARAGUA

Area: 139 000 sq km (53 668 sq miles)
Population: 3 900 000
Capital: Managua
Language: Spanish
Currency: Cordoba

UNITED STATES OF AMERICA

Area: 9 363 130 sq km (3 615 104 sq miles)
Population: 248 700 000
Capital: Washington
Language: English
Currency: U.S. Dollar

SOUTH AMERICA

1:35M

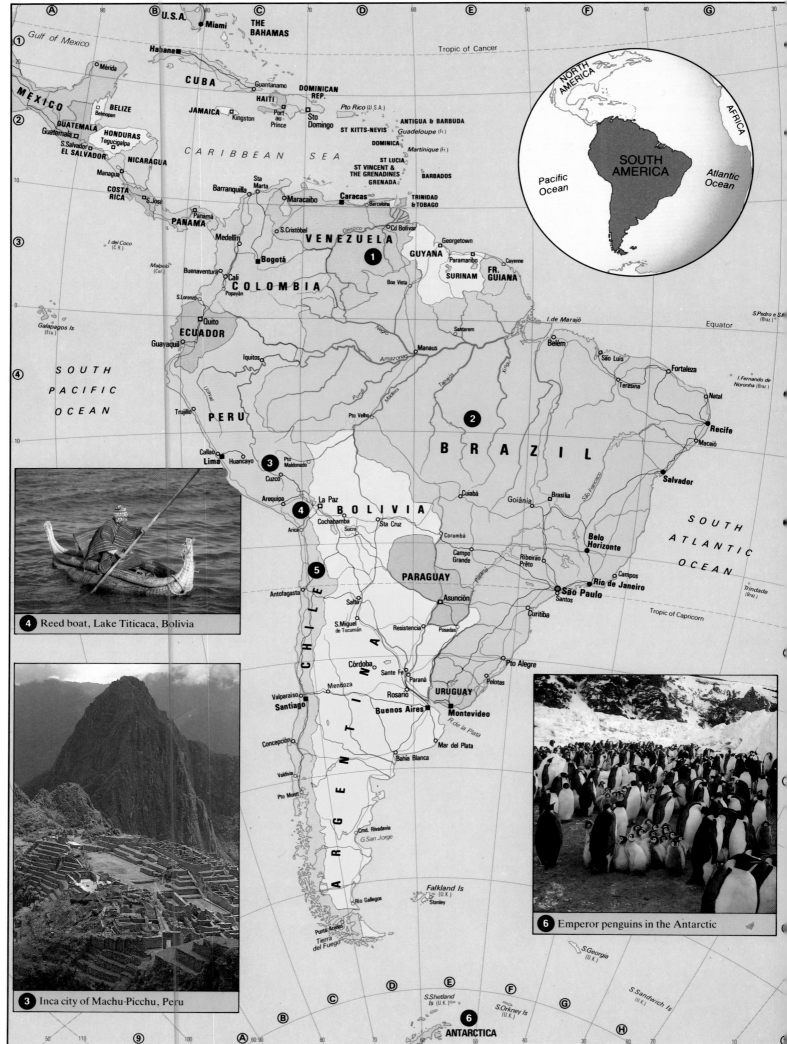

Gulf of Mexico

U.S.A.

THE BAHAMAS

Tropic of Cancer

Miami

Mérida

CUBA

Habana

MEXICO

BELIZE
Belmopan

GUATEMALA
Guatemala

HONDURAS
Tegucigalpa

EL SALVADOR
S.Salvador

HAITI

DOMINICAN REP.

Guantanamo

JAMAICA
Kingston

Port au Prince

Sto Domingo

Pto Rico (U.S.A.)

ST KITTS-NEVIS

ANTIGUA & BARBUDA

Guadeloupe (Fr.)

DOMINICA

Martinique (Fr.)

ST LUCIA

ST VINCENT &
THE GRENADINES

GRENADA

BARBADOS

NICARAGUA
Managua

COSTA RICA
S.José

PANAMA
Panamá

I. del Coco
(C.R.)

CARIBBEAN SEA

Barranquilla

Sta Marta

Maracaibo

Caracas

Barcelona

TRINIDAD
& TOBAGO

Malpelo
(Col)

Buenaventura

Cali

Popayán

S.Cristóbal

Medellín

Bogotá

VENEZUELA

COLOMBIA

Orinoco

Cd Bolívar

Georgetown

GUYANA

Paramaribo

SURINAM

Cayenne

FR. GUIANA

Boa Vista

Galapagos Is
(Ecu.)

S.Lorenzo

Quito

ECUADOR

Guayaquil

SOUTH

PACIFIC

OCEAN

Iquitos

PERU

Trujillo

Ucayali

Negro

Amazonas

Purús

Manaus

Santarem

I. de Marajó

Belém

São Luís

Fortaleza

Teresina

Equator

S.Pedro e S.
(Braz.)

I. Fernando de
Noronha (Braz.)

Natal

Recife

Maceió

Callao

Lima

Huancayo

Pto Velho

Madeira

Tapajós

Xingu

B R A Z I L

Cuiabá

Goiânia

Brasília

Salvador

S.Francisco

SOUTH

ATLANTIC

OCEAN

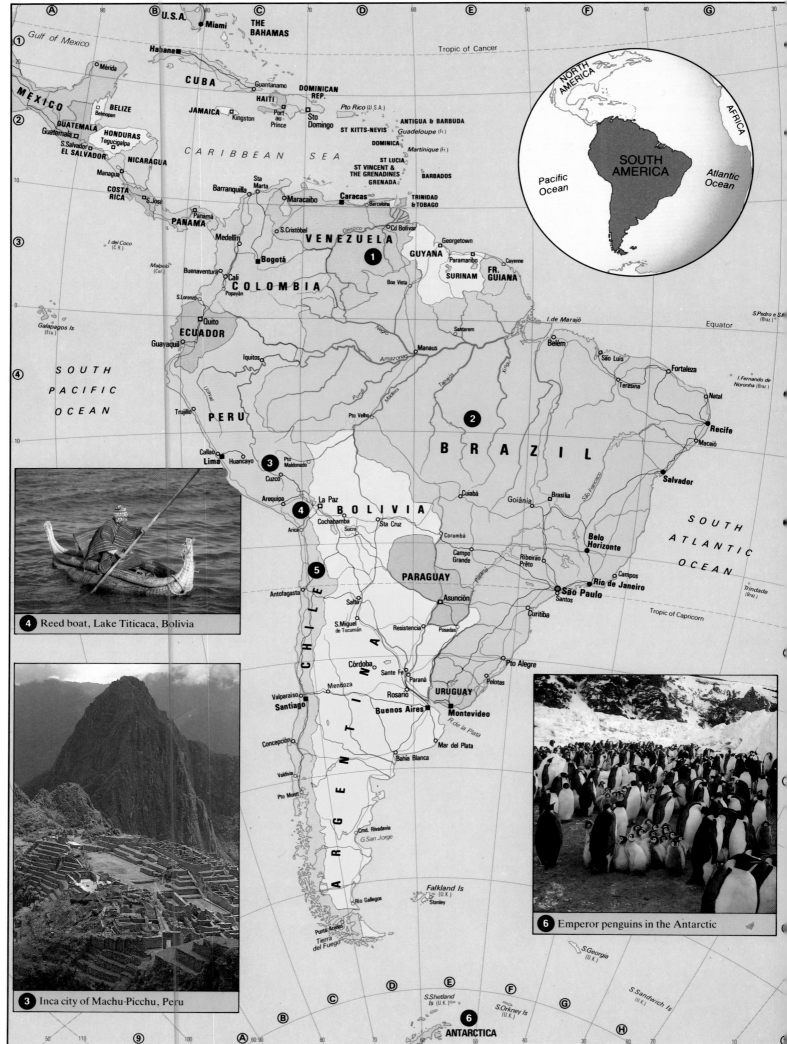

Cuzco

Pto Maldonado

Arequipa

La Paz

BOLIVIA

Cochabamba

Sucre

Sta Cruz

Corumbá

Campo Grande

Ribeirão Prêto

Belo Horizonte

Campos

Trindade
(Braz.)

Arica

Antofagasta

PARAGUAY

Asunción

Paraná

São Paulo

Santos

Rio de Janeiro

Curitiba

Tropic of Capricorn

Reed boat, Lake Titicaca, Bolivia

Salta

S.Miguel de Tucumán

Resistencia

Posadas

Pto Alegre

Pelotas

URUGUAY

Córdoba

Santa Fe

Paraná

Mendoza

Rosario

Buenos Aires

Montevideo

R. de la Plata

Valparaíso

Santiago

CHILE

A R G E N T I N A

Concepción

Mar del Plata

Bahía Blanca

Valdivia

Pto Montt

Cmd. Rivadavia

G. San Jorge

Falkland Is
(U.K.)

Stanley

Rio Gallegos

Punta Arenas

Tierra
del Fuego

Inca city of Machu-Picchu, Peru

S.Shetland
Is (U.K.)

S.Orkney Is
(U.K.)

S.Georgia
(U.K.)

S.Sandwich Is
(U.K.)

Emperor penguins in the Antarctic

ANTARCTICA

NORTH AMERICA

AFRICA

SOUTH AMERICA

Pacific Ocean

Atlantic Ocean

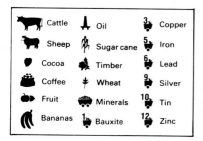

Cattle	Oil	3 Copper
Sheep	Sugar cane	5 Iron
Cocoa	Timber	6 Lead
Coffee	Wheat	9 Silver
Fruit	Minerals	10 Tin
Bananas	Bauxite	12 Zinc

FACTS ABOUT SOUTH AMERICA

1 The Angel Falls, Venezuela, are the highest waterfalls in the world, at 979 m (3212 feet).

2 Deforestation is a major problem in South America. About 1 per cent of the total area of forest is lost each year. Often trees are cut down to clear land for agriculture. On hillsides, the soil soon becomes too poor to grow crops and the land is abandoned. Trees cannot grow again, and so soil is eroded away by rain and wind. Trees are also lost when lakes are made for hydro-electric dams; when new towns are built; and as a result of the way people live – they take too much wood for fuel and timber, allow animals to graze on foliage, and light fires which get out of control.

3 In the Andes Mountains, in the north-west of South America, there are ruins of cities built by the Incas. They ruled the Indians in the area 500 years ago. The Incas had well-developed political and religious systems. They built their cities on terraces engineered from the mountain side. The Spanish, the first Europeans to discover these cities, killed the Incas to seize the gold and silver which they had mined, and their cities were abandoned.

4 The highest navigable lake in the world is Lake Titicaca, on the Peru/Bolivia border. It is no less than 3811 m (12 503 feet) above sea level. The local Indian people make boats from bundles of reeds tied together, to use for fishing. The reeds grow around the edge of the lake.

5 Although in the rain forests of the Amazon Basin it rains every day, in the Atacama Desert, Chile, hundreds of years can pass between one rain storm and the next. A storm in 1971 was the first for 400 years. The desert is the driest place in the world.

6 The Emperor Penguin, found in the Antarctic, does not make a nest. Instead, a single egg is carried on top of the male penguin's feet. It is kept warm by a fold of skin which hangs down and covers it. The penguin does not eat during the two months it takes for the egg to hatch out.

NATURAL VEGETATION/ PRODUCTS

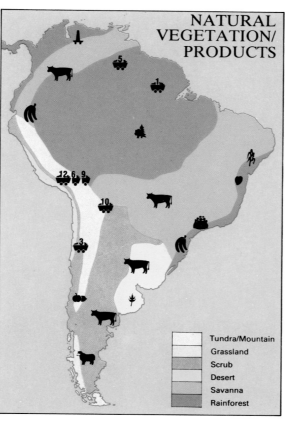

Tundra/Mountain
Grassland
Scrub
Desert
Savanna
Rainforest

POPULATION

over 200 persons per km²
40 to 200 persons per km²
1 to 40 persons per km²
under 1 person per km²

ARGENTINA

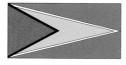

Area: 2 777 815 sq km (1 072 514 sq miles)
Population: 32 300 000
Capital: Buenos Aires
Language: Spanish
Currency: Argentine Peso

BOLIVIA

Area: 1 098 575 sq km (424 160 sq miles)
Population: 7 300 000
Capital: La Paz
Languages: Spanish, Aymara, Quechua
Currency: Bolivian Peso

BRAZIL

Area: 8 511 968 sq km (3 286 471 sq miles)
Population: 150 400 000
Capital: Brasilia
Language: Portuguese
Currency: Cruzeiro

CHILE

Area: 756 943 sq km (292 256 sq miles)
Population: 13 200 000
Capital: Santiago
Language: Spanish
Currency: Chilean Peso

COLOMBIA

Area: 1 138 907 sq km (439 732 sq miles)
Population: 33 000 000
Capital: Bogota
Language: Spanish
Currency: Colombian Peso

ECUADOR

Area: 455 502 sq km (175 869 sq miles)
Population: 10 600 000
Capital: Quito
Language: Spanish
Currency: Sucre

GUYANA

Area: 214 969 sq km (83 000 sq miles)
Population: 800 000
Capital: Georgetown
Language: English
Currency: Guyanese Dollar

PERU

Area: 1 285 215 sq km (496 222 sq miles)
Population: 21 600 000
Capital: Lima
Languages: Spanish, Aymara, Quechua
Currency: Sol

VENEZUELA

Area: 912 047 sq km (352 141 sq miles)
Population: 19 700 000
Capital: Caracas
Language: Spanish
Currency: Bolivar

1:15M

| 0 | 200 | 400 | 600 km |

0   100   200   300 mls

8 Venice, Italy

5 Cork stack and cork oak tree, Portugal

ARCTIC OCEAN

ICELAND
1

Reykjavik

Murmansk

Narvik

Arctic Circle

N O R W A Y

S W E D E N

FINLAND

Trondheim

Umeå

Vaasa

Oulu

Sundsvall

Tampere

Bergen

Åland

Helsinki

Stavanger

Vänern

Oslo

Stockholm

St Petersb
(Leningra

Tallinn

ESTONIA

Göteborg

Jönköping

Gotland

Riga
LATVIA

Ålborg

Öland

LITHUANIA

DENMARK
Copenhagen

Malmö

Bornholm

B a l t i c   S e a

Vilnius

Kaliningrad   RUS. FED.

Minsk

BELOR

Rostock

Gdańsk

UNITED KINGDOM
OF GREAT BRITAIN AND
NORTHERN IRELAND

12

Orkney

Shetland

Glasgow

Edinburgh

Aberdeen

NORTH
SEA

Hamburg

Berlin

Warsaw

Poznań

Łódź

Belfast

Newcastle

2

IRELAND

Dublin

Liverpool

Manchester

Hannover

G E R M A N Y

P O L A N D

Wrocław

Cork

Birmingham

Amsterdam

's-Gravenhage

Essen

Leipzig

Dresden

Prague

Kraków

L'vov

Cardiff

Bristol

London

Rotterdam

NETHERLANDS

Cologne

Bonn

CZECH
REPUBLIC

Brno

SLOVAKIA

13

Brussels

BELGIUM

Frankfurt

LUXEMBOURG

Nürnberg

English Channel

Le Havre

Lille

Rouen

Seine

Paris

Strasbourg

Stuttgart

Vienna

Bratislava

Budapest

Cluj

ATLANTIC

OCEAN

Nantes

Tours

Loire

F R A N C E

Rhine

Munich

Salzburg

A U S T R I A

Graz

H U N G A R Y

Szeged

R O M A N I

La Coruña

Bordeaux

Clermont-
Ferrand

Bern

Zurich

SWITZERLAND

Geneva

LIECHTENSTEIN

Ljubljana

Trieste

SLOVENIA

Zagreb

Timişoara

Bay of
Biscay

Bilbao

Lyon

Rhône

Turin

Milan

Venice

CROATIA

Porto

PORTUGAL

Valladolid

Toulouse

6

ANDORRA

Marseille

7

MONACO

Genoa

Florence

SAN
MARINO

8

A D R I A T I C   S E A

Split

BOSNIA-
HERZEGOVINA

Sarajevo

Belgrade

Bucharest

Lisbon

Madrid

S P A I N

Zaragoza

Ebro

Barcelona

Corsica

Ajaccio

Bastia

I T A L Y

YUGOSLAVIA

Danube

Sofia

BULGAR

Tajo

Toledo

5

Valencia

Balearic   Islands

Menorca

Sardinia

Olbia

Rome

Skopje

MACEDONIA

Plovdiv

Faro

Seville

Murcia

Ibiza

Mallorca

TYRRHENIAN
SEA

Naples

Taranto

ALBANIA

Tirana

Thessaloniki

Málaga

14

Tangier

Gibraltar (U.K.)

Ceuta (Sp.)

M E D I T E R R A N E A N

Cagliari

Palermo

Messina

Reggio di Calabria

Sicily

9

10
GREECE

Pátrai

Athens

Rabat

Melilla
(Sp.)

Oran

Algiers

S E A

MALTA

Kalámai

Cyclades

11

Casablanca

M O R O C C O

A L G E R I A

TUNISIA

Tunis

Khania

Marrakech

POPULATION

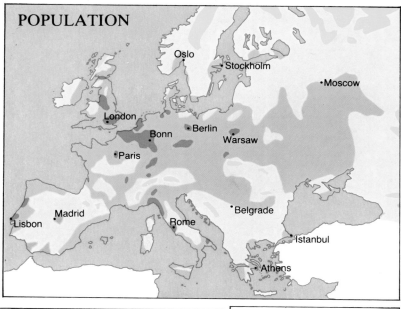

NATURAL VEGETATION/ PRODUCTS

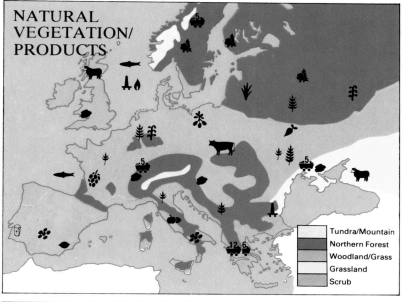

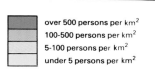

	over 500 persons per km²
	100-500 persons per km²
	5-100 persons per km²
	under 5 persons per km²

Cattle		Oil
Sheep		Coal
Fish		Gas
Fruit		Oats
Citrus fruit		Wheat
Grapes		Maize
Yams		Rye
Sugar beet		Barley
Potatoes	5	Iron
Timber	6	Lead
Cork	12	Zinc

	Tundra/Mountain
	Northern Forest
	Woodland/Grass
	Grassland
	Scrub

FACTS ABOUT EUROPE

1 In Iceland, ice and fire exist side by side. Many active volcanoes and geysers (hot springs which shoot a column of water into the air at intervals) can be seen, while glaciers (continually moving 'rivers' of ice) and ice sheets cover much of the land. One volcano – Vatnajokull – is particularly dangerous for an unusual reason: it is underneath a glacier and when it erupts, the ice melts very quickly, causing terrible floods.

2 The Humber Bridge, England, has one of the longest single spans of any bridge in the world. It stretches for 1410 m (4626 feet).

3 More than a third of the land area of the Netherlands has been reclaimed from the sea. These lands (the *polders*) are below sea level and the sea is kept out by dykes. Drainage ditches divide the fertile fields. The water from them is pumped into canals and rivers, then out to sea.

4 The longest river in Europe is the Volga, which runs for 3690 km (2292 miles) from the forests north west of Moscow in Russia all the way to the Caspian Sea.

5 Portugal is an important source of cork, which is actually the bark of a tree. The cork oak produces cork bark up to 15 cm (6 inches) thick and this is stripped off the trees every 10 to 15 years. Cork oaks grow throughout the western and central Mediterranean region.

6 The Pierre Saint Martin Cavern in the Pyrenees mountains, France, is the deepest cave system yet discovered in the world. It goes 1330 m (4364 feet) into the heart of the mountains.

7 The principality of Monaco is one of the most crowded countries in the world: 28 000 people live on 1.9 sq km (467 acres) of land! By contrast, most of Scandinavia has fewer than 40 people per square kilometre.

8 Venice, Italy, is built on no less than 118 islands. Instead of roads, there are canals, and boats are used for transport. Venice is sinking at a rate of 12 inches each century. Some of the reasons for this include water being extracted from wells, and the compression of the mud on the floor of the lagoon.

9 Mount Etna, Sicily, is the highest volcano in Europe (about 3323 m, 10 902 ft) and is still very active. Despite this, many people live on its lower slopes. This is because the soil there is very fertile and grows good produce.

2 The Humber Bridge, England

ALBANIA

Area: 28 748 sq km
(11 079 sq miles)
Population: 3 200 000
Capital: Tirana
Language: Albanian
Currency: Lek

AUSTRIA

Area: 83 848 sq km
(32 374 sq miles)
Population: 7 600 000
Capital: Vienna
Language: German
Currency: Schilling

BELGIUM

Area: 30 512 sq km
(11 781 sq miles)
Population: 9 900 000
Capital: Brussels
Languages: Flemish, French
Currency: Belgian Franc

BELORUSSIA

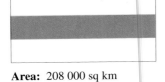

Area: 208 000 sq km
(80 309 sq miles)
Population: 10 278 000
Capital: Minsk
Language: Belorussian
Currency: Rouble

BULGARIA

Area: 110 911 sq km
(42 822 sq miles)
Population: 9 000 000
Capital: Sofia
Language: Bulgarian
Currency: Lev

CZECH REPUBLIC

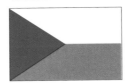

Area: 78 864 sq km
(30 449 sq miles)
Population: 10 300 000
Capital: Prague
Language: Czech
Currency: Koruna

DENMARK

Area: 43 030 sq km
(16 614 sq miles)
Population: 5 100 000
Capital: Copenhagen
Language: Danish
Currency: Krone

ESTONIA

Area: 45 100 sq km
(17 413 sq miles)
Population: 1 600 000
Capital: Tallinn
Language: Estonian
Currency: Kroon

FINLAND

Area: 337 032 sq km
(130 128 sq miles)
Population: 5 000 000
Capital: Helsinki
Languages: Finnish, Swedish
Currency: Markka

FRANCE

Area: 543 965 sq km
(210 025 sq miles)
Population: 56 100 000
Capital: Paris
Language: French
Currency: French Franc

GERMANY

Area: 356 854 sq km
(137 781 sq miles)
Population: 79 000 000
Capital: Berlin
Language: German
Currency: Deutschmark

GREECE

Area: 131 955 sq km
(50 948 sq miles)
Population: 10 000 000
Capital: Athens
Language: Greek
Currency: Drachma

HUNGARY

Area: 93 030 sq km
(35 919 sq miles)
Population: 10 600 000
Capital: Budapest
Language: Magyar
Currency: Forint

ICELAND

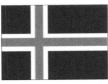

Area: 102 828 sq km
(39 702 sq miles)
Population: 259 577
Capital: Reykjavik
Language: Icelandic
Currency: Króna

IRELAND

Area: 70 282 sq km
(27 136 sq miles)
Population: 3 700 000
Capital: Dublin
Language: Irish (Gaelic),
English
Currency: Irish Pound (Punt)

10 Monasteries on rock pillars, Greece

10 Near Kalabaka, Greece, are a group of monasteries built for monks with no fear of heights! They are perched on top of pillars of rock, called meteora, 300 m (1 000 ft) high. The only way up was by ladders or baskets slung on the end of ropes. Now stairways have been constructed so that tourists can visit the buildings.

11 The island of Santorini (Thira) in Greece is the site of the world's largest natural disaster. About 1500 BC this volcanic island erupted leaving a *caldera* (hollow basin shape where the top of the volcano had been) about 13 km (8 miles) across. Many people believe that the destruction of this island is the origin of the story of Atlantis. The people of Atlantis are mentioned by the Greek writer Plato. Crime and corruption spread throughout their island as they became wealthier, until finally the Athenians conquered them. Later the island disappeared into the sea in a single day and night.

7 Monte Carlo, Monaco

12 Loch Ness, in the Highlands of Scotland, is one of the most famous freshwater expanses in the world. Its length and depth are so great that it could accommodate the population of the earth three times over. Its greatest mystery is the world-famous Loch Ness Monster which was first recorded in the 6th century by the Abbot of Iona. 'Nessie', as the monster is affectionately known, has been sighted by many people but evidence of the monster's existence is inconclusive. If it does exist, the most popular theory is that the monster is one of a small colony of unknown creatures which have descended from marine animals trapped in the loch at the end of the last Ice Age 12,000 years ago.

12 Loch Ness, Scotland

13 The stalactite caves of Aggtelek in Hungary form one of the largest cave systems in Europe. They are 23km (14 miles) long and extend over the border into Slovakia. The stalactites and stalagmites in the cave make a spectacular impact. Stalagmites on the floor of the Aggtelek caves bear a clear resemblance to the human form. Others resemble animals, temples, waterfalls, a 'Great Organ' and even a 'Butcher's Shop'.

14 The spectacularly beautiful Alhambra in Spain is situated on a hill overlooking Granada. From the outside, the fortress walls look plain but they belie the complex and colourful interior. Visitors find the intricate stonework, the sumptuous halls and the attractive gardens with their many fountains quite breathtaking. The Palace of the Alhambra was built as a home for the Moorish rulers in the 14th century and is a well-preserved example of the very best of Moorish art.

14 The Alhambra, Spain

ITALY

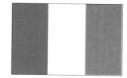

Area: 301 245 sq km (116 311 sq miles)
Population: 57 100 000
Capital: Rome
Language: Italian
Currency: Lira

LATVIA

Area: 63 700 sq km (24 595 sq miles)
Population: 2 700 000
Capital: Riga
Language: Latvian
Currency: Lat

LITHUANIA

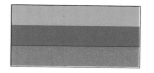

Area: 65 200 sq km (25 170 sq miles)
Population: 3 700 000
Capital: Vilnius
Language: Lithuanian
Currency: Litas

NETHERLANDS

Area: 33 940 sq km (13 104 sq miles)
Population: 15 000 000
Capital: Amsterdam & The Hague
Language: Dutch
Currency: Guilder

NORWAY

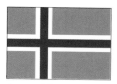

Area: 324 218 sq km (125 180 sq miles)
Population: 4 200 000
Capital: Oslo
Language: Norwegian
Currency: Krone

POLAND

Area: 312 683 sq km (120 727 sq miles)
Population: 38 400 000
Capital: Warsaw
Language: Polish
Currency: Zloty

PORTUGAL

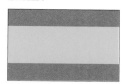

Area: 91 671 sq km (35 394 sq miles)
Population: 10 300 000
Capital: Lisbon
Language: Portuguese
Currency: Escudo

ROMANIA

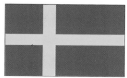

Area: 237 500 sq km (91 699 sq miles)
Population: 23 300 000
Capital: Bucharest
Language: Romanian
Currency: Leu

RUSSIAN FEDERATION

Area: 17 078 000 sq km (6 593 816 sq miles)
Population: 148 263 000
Capital: Moscow
Language: Russian
Currency: Rouble

SPAIN

Area: 504 745 sq km (194 882 sq miles)
Population: 39 200 000
Capital: Madrid
Language: Spanish
Currency: Peseta

SWEDEN

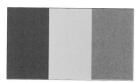

Area: 449 791 sq km (173 664 sq miles)
Population: 8 400 000
Capital: Stockholm
Language: Swedish
Currency: Krona

SWITZERLAND

Area: 41 287 sq km (15 941 sq miles)
Population: 6 600 000
Capital: Bern
Languages: German, French Italian, Romansch
Currency: Swiss Franc

UKRAINE

Area: 603 700 sq km (233 089 sq miles)
Population: 51 857 000
Capital: Kiev
Languages: Ukrainian, Russian
Currency: Rouble

UNITED KINGDOM

Area: 244 104 sq km (94 249 sq miles)
Population: 57 200 000
Capital: London
Language: English
Currency: Pound Sterling

YUGOSLAVIA

Area: 91 285 sq km (35 245 sq miles)
Population: 10 300 000
Capital: Belgrade
Language: Serbo-Croatian
Currency: Dinar

1:40M

0   400   800   1200   1600 km
0   400   800 mls

6 The bullet train and Mount Fuji-san, Japan

7 The Taj Mahal, India

8 Mount Everest, Nepal

PORT.
SPAIN
IRELAND
London
UNITED KINGDOM
FRANCE
Paris
NETH.
BEL.
LUX.
GERMAN
DENMARK
NORWAY
SWEDEN
Edinburgh
Dublin
Stockholm
Copenhagen
Helsinki
FINLAND
Oslo
SWITZ.
ITALY
Corse (Fr.)
Marseille
Rome
Sardegna
Sicily
AUSTRIA
CZECH REPUBLIC
SLOV.
HUNGARY
POLAND
CROATIA
B.-H.
YUGOS.
ALB.
MAC.
SLOVENIA
ROMANIA
BULGARIA
GREECE
Athens
Warsaw
Kiev
UKRAINE
BELORUSSIA
Minsk
Vilnius
Riga
LAT.
LITH.
EST.
Tallinn
St Petersburg (Leningrad)
Moscow
RUS. FED.
Bucharest
MOLD.
Odessa
Khar'kov
Nizhniy Novgorod
Rostov
Astrakhan'
Samara
Volga
Black Sea
TURKEY
Istanbul
Ankara
GEORGIA
Tbilisi
ARM.
AZER.
Yerevan
Baku
Caspian Sea
TUNIS
LIBYA
Alexandria
Cairo
EGYPT
Nile
Aswân
RED SEA
SUDAN
Khartoum
ERITREA
Asmara
ÂDIS ÂBEBA
ETHIOPIA
DJIBOUTI
G. of Aden
Adan
YEMEN
San'a
Socotra (Yemen)
SAUDI ARABIA
Makkah
Ar Riyâd
BAHRAIN
QATAR
Abu Dhabi
U.A.E.
OMAN
Muscat
KUWAIT
The Gulf
IRAQ
Basra
Abādān
Baghdâd
Al Mawşil (Mosul)
SYRIA
Halab
Damascus
Beirut
LEB.
ISRAEL
JOR.
Jerusalem
Amman
CYPRUS
IRAN
Tehrân
Tabrîz
Esfahân
Kerman
Mashhad
TURKMENISTAN
Ashkhabad
UZBEKISTAN
Tashkent
KIRGHIZIA (KRYGYZSTAN)
Bishkek
Alma Ata
TAJIKISTAN
Dushanbe
AFGHANISTAN
Herat
Kabul
Islamabad
Kashmir
PAKISTAN
Lahore
Karachi
Hyderābād
Indus
INDIA
Delhi
Kanpur
Lucknow
Ahmadābād
Jabalpur
Nāgpur
Bombay
Hyderabad
Godavari
Krishna
Bangalore
Madras
Madurai
SRI LANKA
Colombo
Kandy
ARABIAN SEA
KAZAKHSTAN
Aral Sea
RUSSIAN FEDERATION
Murmansk
Arkhangel'sk
Vorkuta
Yekaterinburg
Chelyabinsk
Omsk
Ob'
Yenisey
Novosibirsk
Krasnoyarsk
Irkutsk
Yakutsk
Lena
Ürümqi
SINKIANG
MONGOLIA
Ulaanbaatar
INNER MONGOLIA
CHINA
TIBET
Lhasa
NEPAL
Kathmandu
BHUTAN
Thimphu
Brahmaputra
BANGLA-DESH
Dhākā
Ganga
Patna
Calcutta
Chittagong
Imphal
Mandalay
BURMA (MYANMA)
Irrawaddy
Rangoon (Yangon)
Moulmein
Chiang Mai
THAILAND
Vientiane
LAOS
Bangkok
Surat Thani
CAMBODIA (KAMPUCHEA)
Phnom Penh
Ho Chi Minh (Saigon)
VIETNAM
Hanoi
Haiphong
Da Nang
Lanzhou
Chengdu
Chongqing
Wuhan
Changsha
Chang Jiang
Guiyang
Kunming
Guangzhou
Zhengzhou
Xi'an
Taiyuan
Tientsin
Beijing
Mekong
George Town
Kuala Lumpur
SINGAPORE
MALAY
SUMATRA
Padang
Palembang
Jakarta
Bay of Bengal
Andaman Is (Ind.)
Nicobar Is (Ind.)
INDIAN OCEAN
Cocos Is (Aust.)
Christmas (Aust.)
KENYA
SOMALIA
Muqdisho
Mombasa
TANZANIA
Dar es Salaam
COMOROS
MOZAMBIQUE
MADAGASCAR
Antananarivo
Aldabra Is (Sey.)
Equator
ARCTIC OCEAN
Arctic Circle
Novosibirskye Ostrova
ICELAND
Færøerne (Den.)

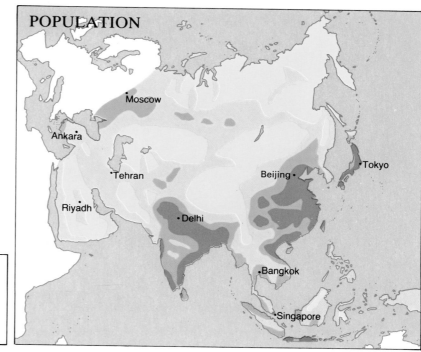

over 500 persons per km²
100-500 persons per km²
5-100 persons per km²
under 5 persons per km²

Cattle		Oil	
Citrus fruit		Barley	
Coconut		Wheat	
Cotton		Minerals	
Fish	3	Copper	
Rice	4	Gold	
Rubber	5	Iron	
Spices	6	Lead	
Tea	7	Nickel	
Timber	11	Uranium	
Coal	12	Zinc	

NATURAL VEGETATION/PRODUCTS

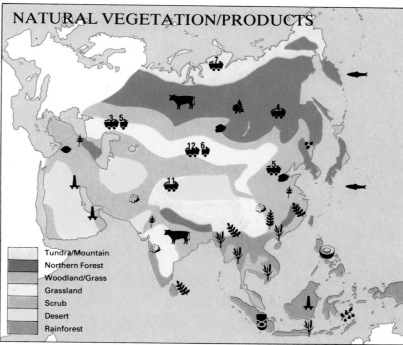

Tundra/Mountain
Northern Forest
Woodland/Grass
Grassland
Scrub
Desert
Rainforest

FACTS ABOUT ASIA

1 The Chang Jiang river (formerly known as the Yangtze Kiang) is the longest river in Asia. Rising in the Tibetan hills, it flows across southern China to the East China Sea. The river has a length of over 5550 km (3450 miles).

2 In Siberia, there is a huge forest called the *taiga*, which makes up a quarter of the total area of forest in the world. The trees are mostly coniferous - pine and larch. Few people used to live in the taiga, as it is a very cold area, but because it is rich in minerals more people are moving into the forest. They live in industrial towns being built deep in its heart, to exploit the minerals.

3 The huge Gobi Desert covers much of Mongolia. The Gobi is a cold, barren region of rocky plains and hills. Water is very scarce and only a few nomads live here. They exist mainly by cattle raising and live in an unusual tent called a *yurt*, which is shaped like an upside-down bowl.

4 The Great Wall of China stretches for 3460 km (2150 miles), making it the longest in the world. It was built for defence in the 3rd century BC and kept in good repair until 400 years ago. Although part of the wall was blown up to make a dam in 1979, the many remaining sections of the wall are still impressive.

11 Floating vegetable market, Thailand

14 Singapore

12 Bangkok, Thailand

5 Cliff dwellings in Cappadocia, Turkey

13 Water buffalo ploughing Chinese paddy fields

FACTS ABOUT ASIA

5 In central Turkey, near Urgup in the region called Cappadocia, an extraordinary landscape can be seen. There was once a plateau here, made up of layers of rock, some hard and some much softer. Over thousands of years the softer rocks have been eroded by the weather, by streams and even by men digging out caves to live in. The rocks are now shaped into strange cones, towers and 'mushrooms', with 'hats' of harder rock balancing on top. There are also complete 'villages' of caves connected to each other by passageways cut through the rock. Each cave has 'cupboards' and 'shelves' cut into its walls. Here many centuries ago people hid from religious persecution. Over 300 churches which they dug out of the rock have been found. Some people still live in caves in this region, today.

6 The Seikan Tunnel in Japan is the longest tunnel in the world. It is an underwater tunnel, stretching for 54 km (34 miles). It was built for Japan's famous *bullet train*, the first passenger train to travel at 200 kph.

7 There should have been two Taj Mahals in India – a black one and a white one. In 1648, Emperor Shah Jahan completed the present Taj Mahal. It was a tomb for his wife, and made of white marble. He then began building a tomb of black marble for himself. Before work had got very far, he was overthrown.

8 At 8848 m (29 028 ft) the peak of Mt Everest in the Himalayas is the Earth's highest point. In May 1953, New Zealander Sir Edmund Hillary was the first man to climb Everest. Twenty two years later, in 1975, the first woman to reach the summit was Junko Tabei of Japan.

9 In India cows are sacred animals and are allowed to wander freely, even in the centre of big cities! Drivers are used to going round cows lying peacefully in the middle of the road.

10 Banyan trees can be seen in India and Sri Lanka. They are very unusual to look at, because what seems to be several trees growing close together, is actually just one tree! Aerial roots grow down from the banyan's branches and root in the ground. They become extra 'trunks' and support a huge canopy of leaves, which gives a lot of shade, very useful in such a hot climate.

11 Throughout Asia there are areas where many people live on boats – because there is not enough room for them to live in houses on land (or they cannot afford to) or because they just prefer to live on water. In these places, even the shops are on boats.

4 The Great Wall, China

10 Banyan tree, India

9 Street in India

12 Bangkok, Thailand, once had many canals, called *klongs*, instead of roads. (The city was called the 'Venice of the East' because the klongs reminded visitors of the canals in Venice, Italy.) They were used for transport and also helped to drain the land during the rainy season. After cars and lorries began to be used for transport, many of the klongs were filled in to make roads. Now Bangkok has problems with flooding when the monsoons come.

13 Paddy fields, the irrigated fields in which rice is grown, get their name from *padi*, the Malayan word for rice. Rice is grown throughout Asia in the fertile lowlands near the equator. Millions of people live in these areas, and rice is very important to them as it yields more food per acre than any other crop.

14 Over half the population of the world lives in Asia – that is 3 113 000 000 people. Some parts of Asia have many people living in a small area. One of the most densely populated countries is Singapore, which has an average of 4 420 people for each square kilometre of ground.

AFGHANISTAN

Area: 674 500 sq km
(260 424 sq miles)
Population: 16 600 000
Capital: Kabul
Languages: Pashtu, Dari, Uzbek
Currency: Afghani

CHINA

Area: 9 561 000 sq km
(3 691 502 sq miles)
Population: 1 118 800 000
Capital: Beijing
Language: Chinese (Mandarin)
Currency: Yuan

INDIA

Area: 3 287 593 sq km
(1 269 340 sq miles)
Population: 853 100 000
Capital: Delhi
Languages: Hindi, English
Currency: Indian Rupee

INDONESIA

Area: 1 919 263 sq km
(741 027 miles)
Population: 185 000 000
Capital: Jakarta
Language: Bahasa (Indonesian)
Currency: Rupiah

IRAN

Area: 1 648 184 sq km
(636 364 sq miles)
Population: 54 600 000
Capital: Tehran
Language: Persian (Farsi)
Currency: Rial

IRAQ

Area: 434 924 sq km
(167 924 sq miles)
Population: 18 900 000
Capital: Baghdad
Language: Arabic
Currency: Iraqi Dinar

ISRAEL

Area: 20 770 sq km
(8019 sq miles)
Population: 4 600 000
Capital: Jerusalem
Languages: Hebrew, Arabic
Currency: Shekel

JAPAN

Area: 371 000 sq km
(143 243 sq miles)
Population: 123 500 000
Capital: Tokyo
Language: Japanese
Currency: Yen

MALAYSIA

Area: 330 669 sq km
(127 671 sq miles)
Population: 17 900 000
Capital: Kuala Lumpur
Language: Malay
Currency: Ringgit (Malaysian Dollar)

PAKISTAN

Area: 803 941 sq km
(310 402 sq miles)
Population: 122 600 000
Capital: Islamabad
Language: Urdu
Currency: Pakistan Rupee

PHILIPPINES

Area: 299 765 sq km
(115 739 sq miles)
Population: 62 400 000
Capital: Manila
Language: Philipino
Currency: Philippine Peso

SAUDI ARABIA

Area: 2 400 930 sq km
(927 000 sq miles)
Population: 14 100 000
Capital: Riyadh
Language: Arabic
Currency: Riyal

SINGAPORE

Area: 616 sq km
(238 sq miles)
Population: 2 700 000
Capital: Singapore
Languages: Chinese, Malay, Tamil, English
Currency: Singapore Dollar

THAILAND

Area: 513 517 sq km
(198 269 sq miles)
Population: 55 700 000
Capital: Bangkok
Languages: Thai, Chinese
Currency: Baht

TURKEY

Area: 780 576 sq km
(301 380 sq miles)
Population: 55 900 000
Capital: Ankara
Language: Turkish
Currency: Turkish Lira

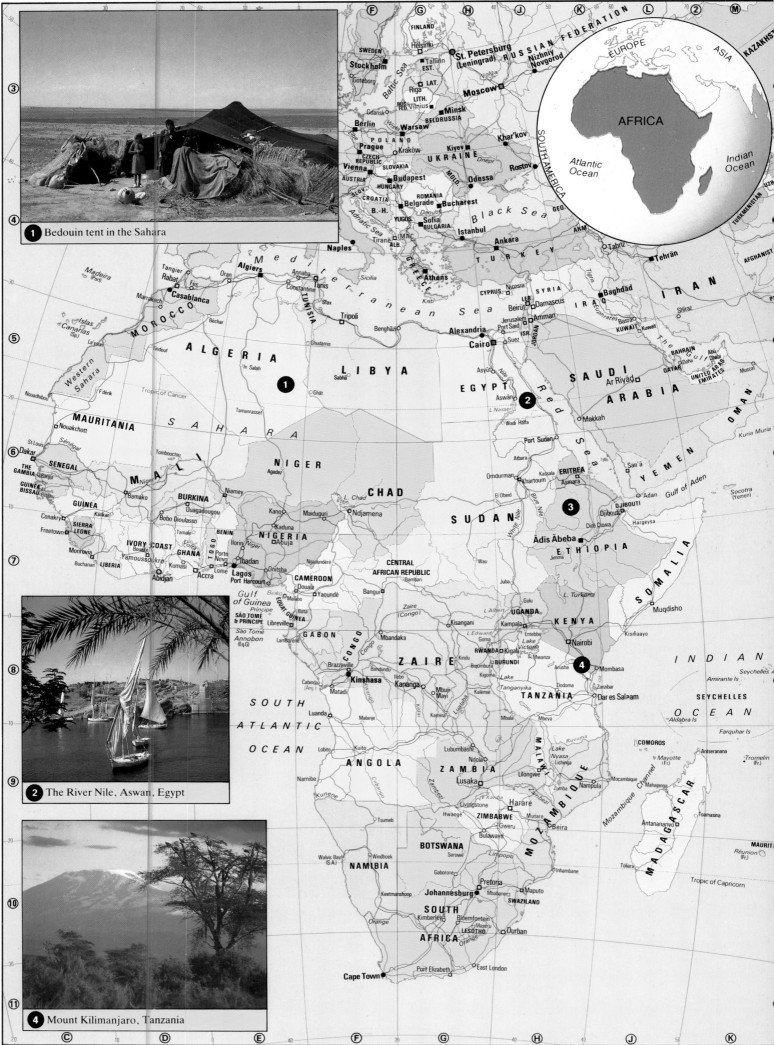

1 Bedouin tent in the Sahara

2 The River Nile, Aswan, Egypt

4 Mount Kilimanjaro, Tanzania

POPULATION

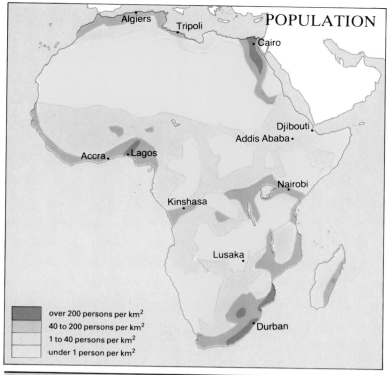

- over 200 persons per km²
- 40 to 200 persons per km²
- 1 to 40 persons per km²
- under 1 person per km²

NATURAL VEGETATION/ PRODUCTS

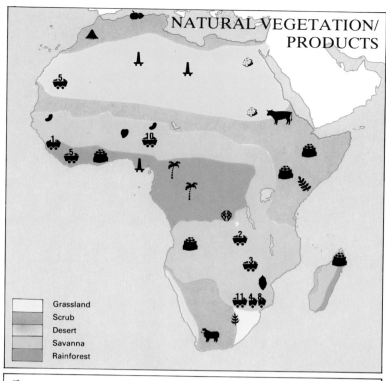

- Grassland
- Scrub
- Desert
- Savanna
- Rainforest

Cattle	Peanuts	Phosphates	4 Gold
Sheep	Palm oil	Maize	5 Iron
Cocoa	Tea	Minerals	8 Platinum
Coffee	Tobacco	1 Bauxite	10 Tin
Cotton	Diamonds	2 Cobalt	11 Uranium
Fruit	Oil	3 Copper	

FACTS ABOUT AFRICA

1 The largest desert in the world is the Sahara, but only about 30% of it is sand. The rest is rocky waste. People live mainly near oases, where the land is watered by springs rising to the surface and crops can be grown. The desert is very hot and dry, but there are a few plants and animals (like camels) specially adapted to these conditions.

2 The Nile is the longest river in the world and flows for 6650 km (4160 miles) through North Africa to the Mediterranean Sea.

The Nile used to flood its banks each year, but now the High Dam at Aswan controls the floods. When the dam was built, the temples of Abu Simbel (3000 years old) were moved to a higher site to stop them being flooded.

3 Some parts of Africa have had no rain, or very little, for several years. Food crops have failed and many people have died from malnutrition and starvation. A further problem has been wars, which have driven many people from their homes and fields. Even if part of a country can grow food, it is difficult to move that food into areas where none can be grown. There are few lorries and, where people are at war, transporting food may be dangerous. Although western countries have sent food supplies, there is still not enough to feed the hundreds of thousands of people who are starving. Governments are trying to find ways of growing more food and distributing it more quickly.

4 Kilimanjaro (now renamed Uhuru, meaning 'freedom') is the highest mountain in Africa (5895 m; 19 340 feet) and its peaks are always covered in snow.

EGYPT

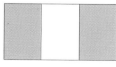

Area: 1 000 250 sq km (386 197 sq miles)
Population: 52 400 000
Capital: Cairo
Language: Arabic
Currency: Egyptian Pound

ETHIOPIA

Area: 1 104 318 sq km (426 377 sq miles)
Population: 46 626 000
Capital: Addis Ababa
Language: Amharic
Currency: Birr

KENYA

Area: 582 644 sq km (224 959 sq miles)
Population: 24 000 000
Capital: Nairobi
Languages: English, Swahili
Currency: Kenya Shilling

LIBYA

Area: 1 759 530 sq km (679 355 sq miles)
Population: 4 500 000
Capital: Tripoli
Language: Arabic
Currency: Libyan Dinar

NIGERIA

Area: 923 769 sq km (356 667 sq miles)
Population: 108 500 000
Capital: Lagos
Language: English
Currency: Naira

SOUTH AFRICA

Area: 1 221 038 sq km (471 443 sq miles)
Population: 35 300 000
Capital: Pretoria
Languages: Afrikaans, English
Currency: Rand

SUDAN

Area: 2 505 792 sq km (967 486 sq miles)
Population: 25 200 000
Capital: Khartoum
Language: Arabic
Currency: Sudanese Pound

ZAIRE

Area: 2 344 885 sq km (905 360 sq miles)
Population: 35 600 000
Capital: Kinshasa
Language: French
Currency: Zaire

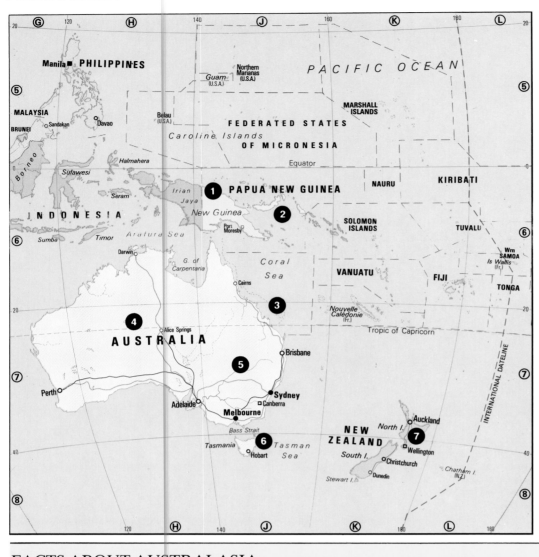

⑦ Geysers at Whakarewarewa, New Zealand

FACTS ABOUT AUSTRALASIA

❶ Over 700 languages are spoken in Papua New Guinea. That is more than a quarter of all the languages spoken in the world. Papua New Guinea's mountains, thick forests and islands meant that different tribes did not mix, so they did not share a common language, but instead each developed its own. Today, Pidgin English and Police Motu have become the languages which the different tribes use to talk to each other.

❷ No less than 38 different species of the beautiful Bird of Paradise are to be seen in Papua New Guinea. Another 5 species are found on neighbouring islands and in northern Australia. Their tail feathers are a traditional part of Papua New Guinea tribal costume, although the birds are now protected from hunting to a great extent.

❸ Australia's Great Barrier Reef is formed from the shells of millions of tiny sea creatures. It is 2300 km (1430 miles) long and is the world's biggest coral reef. There are many thousands of coral islands or *atolls* in the Pacific region.

❹ Ayers Rock is a huge sandstone rock formation which rears up abruptly from the desert in central Australia. The rock is special because it changes colour with the light. To Australia's native *aborigine* people the rock has a very deep spiritual meaning.

❺ Australia is a very dry continent. Rainfall is also very unevenly distributed throughout the island: even though some parts of the tropical north receive about 2000 millimetres (79 inches) a year, the central deserts receive less than 150 millimetres (6 inches). Irrigation is very important for agriculture, with rivers and artesian wells being used as sources of water. The Snowy Mountains reservoir and irrigation scheme has brought water from the mountains to irrigate farmland in the east of Australia.

❻ A Tasmanian Devil is a little bear-like creature found only in Tasmania. It is just 60 cm (2 ft) long, with a big bushy tail. It has very sharp teeth and eats other

❹ Ayers Rock, Australia

❻ Tasmanian Devil

POPULATION

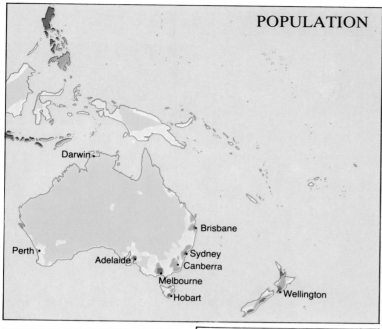

NATURAL VEGETATION/PRODUCTS

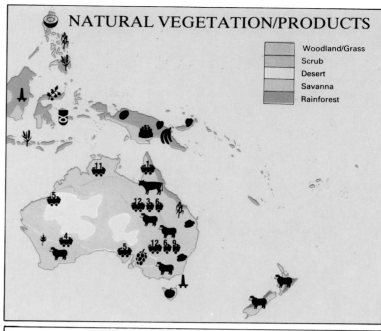

Woodland/Grass
Scrub
Desert
Savanna
Rainforest

over 500 persons per km²		
100-500 persons per km²		
5-100 persons per km²		
under 5 persons per km²		

🐑 Sheep	☕ Coffee	Coal	Minerals	6 Lead
🍎 Apples	Cocoa	Oil	1 Bauxite	9 Silver
🍌 Bananas	Rubber	Spices	3 Copper	11 Uranium
🍇 Grapes	Yams	Sugar cane	4 Gold	12 Zinc
Coconut	Rice	Wheat	5 Iron	

2 Traditional dress, Papua New Guinea

animals and small birds when it comes out at night. The Tasmanian Devil is a *marsupial*. This means it carries its young in a pouch.

7 The tallest geyser ever to have erupted was the Waimangu Geyser in New Zealand. Waimangu geyser played to a height of 490 m (1608 ft) between 1900 and 1904. Today, steam from New Zealand's hot springs and geysers is harnessed to generate electricity.

3 The Great Barrier Reef, Australia

AUSTRALIA

Area: 7 682 300 sq km (2 966 136 sq miles)
Population: 17 658 700
Capital: Canberra
Language: English
Currency: Australian Dollar

NEW ZEALAND

Area: 268 675 sq km (103 735 sq miles)
Population: 3 450 000
Capital: Wellington
Language: English
Currency: New Zealand Dollar

TONGA

Area: 699 sq km (270 sq miles)
Population: 100 000
Capital: Nuku'alofa
Languages: English, Tongan
Currency: Pa'anga

FIJI

Area: 18 272 sq km (7055 sq miles)
Population: 800 000
Capital: Suva
Languages: English, Fijian
Currency: Fiji Dollar

PAPUA NEW GUINEA

Area: 461 692 sq km (178 259 sq miles)
Population: 3 900 000
Capital: Port Moresby
Languages: English, Melanesian Pidgin
Currency: Kina

VANUATU

Area: 14 763 sq km (5700 sq miles)
Population: 160 000
Capital: Vila
Languages: Bislama, English, French
Currency: Australian Dollar, Vatu

KIRIBATI

Area: 800 sq km (309 sq miles)
Population: 66 000
Capital: Tarawa
Languages: English, I Kiribati
Currency: Australian Dollar

SOLOMON ISLANDS

Area: 29 785 sq km (11 500 sq miles)
Population: 320 000
Capital: Honiara
Languages: English, Pidgin
Currency: Solomon Islands Dollar

WESTERN SAMOA

Area: 2831 sq km (1093 sq miles)
Population: 170 000
Capital: Apia
Languages: Samoan, English
Currency: Tala

WORLD ENVIRONMENT

The world can be divided into 8 broad 'climatic zones' (these are areas with a particular sort of weather). The natural types of plants and animals found in each zone are different and depend on the weather the zone has. This map shows which parts of the world are in each zone. The colour of the strip at the top of each zone description (for example, Desert, Rainforest) is the same as the colour used for the zone on the big map. The little map beside each zone description pinpoints where that type of habitat is found in the world. (For example, the Desert strip is orange/yellow. The little sketch map shows you where on the big map to look for this colour. You will find this colour in the north of Africa, the west of North America and in parts of Asia and Australia. All these places have deserts. The description tells you what the natural countryside looks like and what plants and animals live there.)

SCRUB OR MEDITERRANEAN

 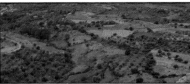

Areas of long, hot, dry summers and short, warm winters. The land used to be covered with trees, but man cleared it for crops and grazed his animals on it. Now there is evergreen scrub – vines and olive trees.

TUNDRA OR MOUNTAIN

Polar areas which are usually frozen over. During the short summers the top layer of soil thaws, creating vast marshes. Compact, wind-resistant plants and lichens and mosses are found here. Animals include lemmings and reindeer.

NORTHERN FOREST (TAIGA)

Forests of conifers growing over a large area. Winters are very cold and long. Summers are short. Trees include spruce and fir. Animals found here include beavers, squirrels and red deer.

WOODLAND AND GRASS

Temperate areas (where the weather is seldom very cold or very hot). Deciduous trees (which lose their leaves in winter) grow in the woodlands. They include oak, beech and maple. Man uses these areas most of all, for farming, building towns and villages, and industry.

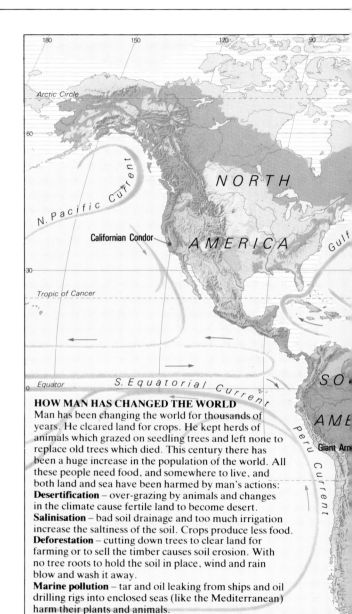

HOW MAN HAS CHANGED THE WORLD

Man has been changing the world for thousands of years. He cleared land for crops. He kept herds of animals which grazed on seedling trees and left none to replace old trees which died. This century there has been a huge increase in the population of the world. All these people need food, and somewhere to live, and both land and sea have been harmed by man's actions:

Desertification – over-grazing by animals and changes in the climate cause fertile land to become desert.

Salinisation – bad soil drainage and too much irrigation increase the saltiness of the soil. Crops produce less food.

Deforestation – cutting down trees to clear land for farming or to sell the timber causes soil erosion. With no tree roots to hold the soil in place, wind and rain blow and wash it away.

Marine pollution – tar and oil leaking from ships and oil drilling rigs into enclosed seas (like the Mediterranean) harm their plants and animals.

GRASSLAND

Hot summers, cold winters and moderate rainfall. Huge area of grassland and 'black' (very fertile) soils. Grain crops grow well, and so does rich pasture for beef cattle. Names for this kind of grassland include steppe, veld, pampas and prairie.

SAVANNA

Tall grasses with thick stems, and flat-topped thorny trees grow here. Animals grazing here include giraffes and zebras. There is a short rainy season. Often it does not rain for a long time (a drought). Fires burn the dried out plants but they have adapted to survive this and grow again.

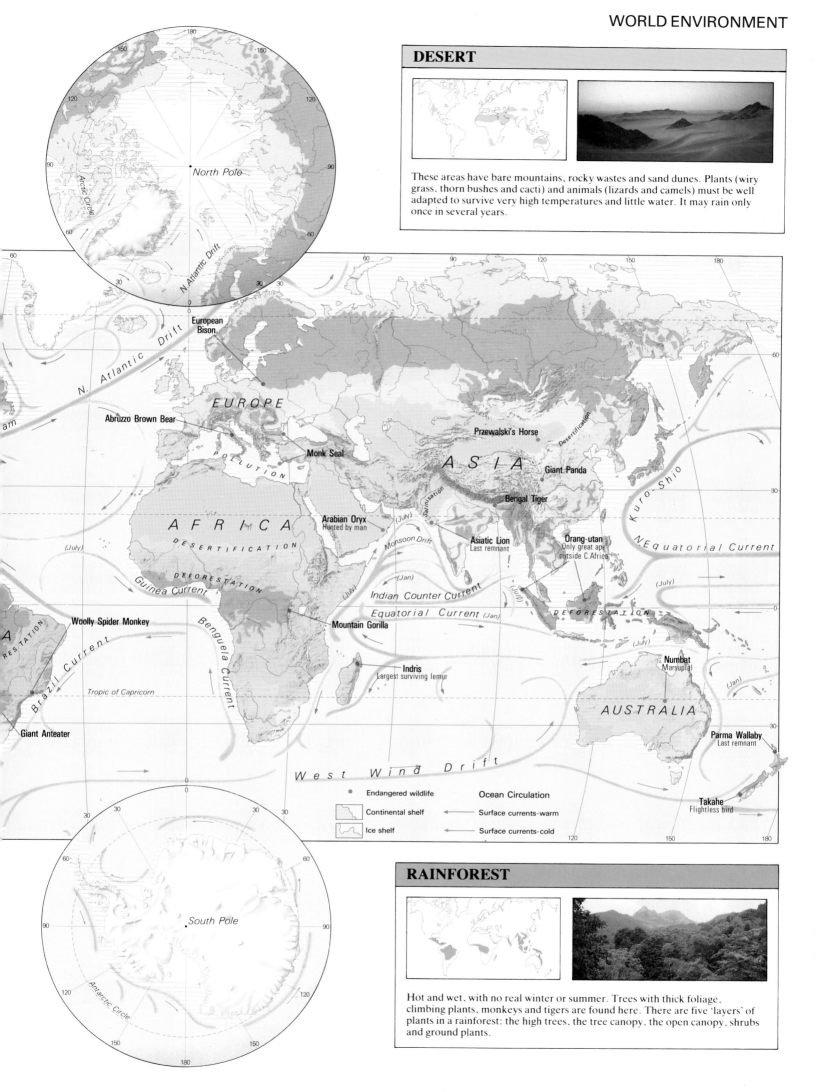

DESERT

These areas have bare mountains, rocky wastes and sand dunes. Plants (wiry grass, thorn bushes and cacti) and animals (lizards and camels) must be well adapted to survive very high temperatures and little water. It may rain only once in several years.

North Pole

Arctic Circle

N. Atlantic Drift

N. Atlantic Drift

European Bison

EUROPE

Abruzzo Brown Bear

Monk Seal

POLLUTION

Przewalski's Horse

ASIA

Desertification

Giant Panda

AFRICA

DESERTIFICATION

Arabian Oryx
Hunted by man

(July)

Salinisation

Bengal Tiger

Kuro-Shio

DEFORESTATION

(July)

Asiatic Lion
Last remnant

Orang-utan
Only great ape
outside C.Africa

N Equatorial Current

Guinea Current

(July)

Monsoon Drift

(Jan)

Indian Counter Current

(Jan)

DEFORESTATION

Woolly Spider Monkey

Benguela Current

Mountain Gorilla

Equatorial Current (Jan)

(July)

(July)

RESTATION

Brazil Current

Indris
Largest surviving lemur

Numbat
Marsupial

Tropic of Capricorn

AUSTRALIA

(Jan)

Giant Anteater

Parma Wallaby
Last remnant

West Wind Drift

0

Takahe
Flightless bird

● Endangered wildlife

Ocean Circulation

Continental shelf

Surface currents-warm

Ice shelf

Surface currents-cold

South Pole

Antarctic Circle

RAINFOREST

Hot and wet, with no real winter or summer. Trees with thick foliage, climbing plants, monkeys and tigers are found here. There are five 'layers' of plants in a rainforest: the high trees, the tree canopy, the open canopy, shrubs and ground plants.

WORLD CLIMATE

World climate has a profound influence upon mankind. Everything is affected by it, from our environment and ability to grow food to our mobility and health. The most important characteristics of climate are rainfall patterns and temperature variations. As the earth revolves around the sun the tilt of its axis causes each hemisphere in turn to be closer than the other to the sun for half a year. The hemisphere facing the overhead sun enjoys a warm summer season while the other experiences winter. Solar radiation, winds, ocean currents, latitude, altitude and land relief also determine types of climate, examples of which are illustrated by the graphs below.

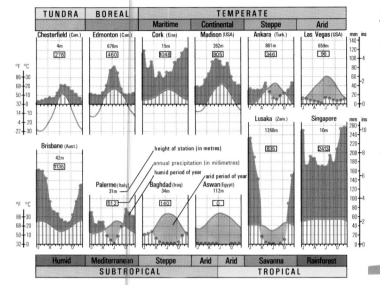

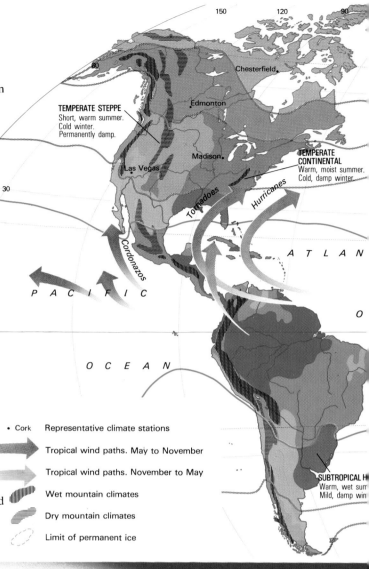

TEMPERATE STEPPE
Short, warm summer.
Cold winter.
Permanently damp.

TEMPERATE CONTINENTAL
Warm, moist summer.
Cold, damp winter.

SUBTROPICAL H
Warm, wet sum
Mild, damp win

- Cork   Representative climate stations

Tropical wind paths. May to November

Tropical wind paths. November to May

Wet mountain climates

Dry mountain climates

Limit of permanent ice

THE RESTLESS ATMOSPHERE

As people who travel by aeroplane at altitude soon discover, all weather is confined to the lower part of the atmosphere, where the air is in a continuous state of unrest. This movement can have tremendous force, eroding land and depositing rain and snow. The map shows the intertropical convergence zone which is where trade winds meet, forcing air to rise upwards and causing torrential rainfall. Circulation of air forms three separate 'cells' in each hemisphere where warm air rises and cold air sinks. These are called the Polar, Ferrel and Hadley cells.

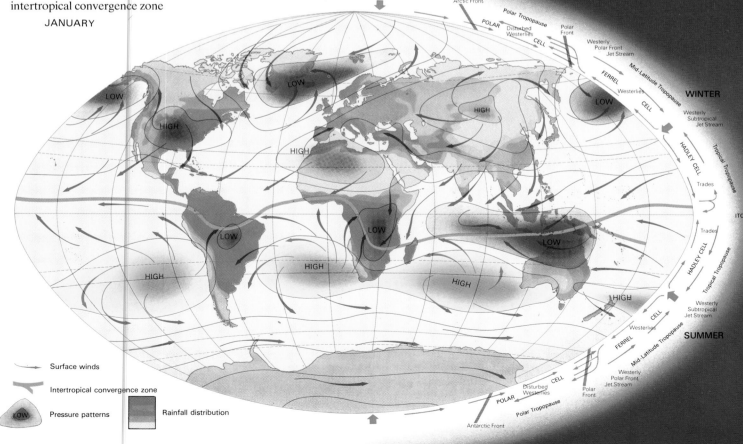

JANUARY

Surface winds

Intertropical convergence zone

Pressure patterns

Rainfall distribution

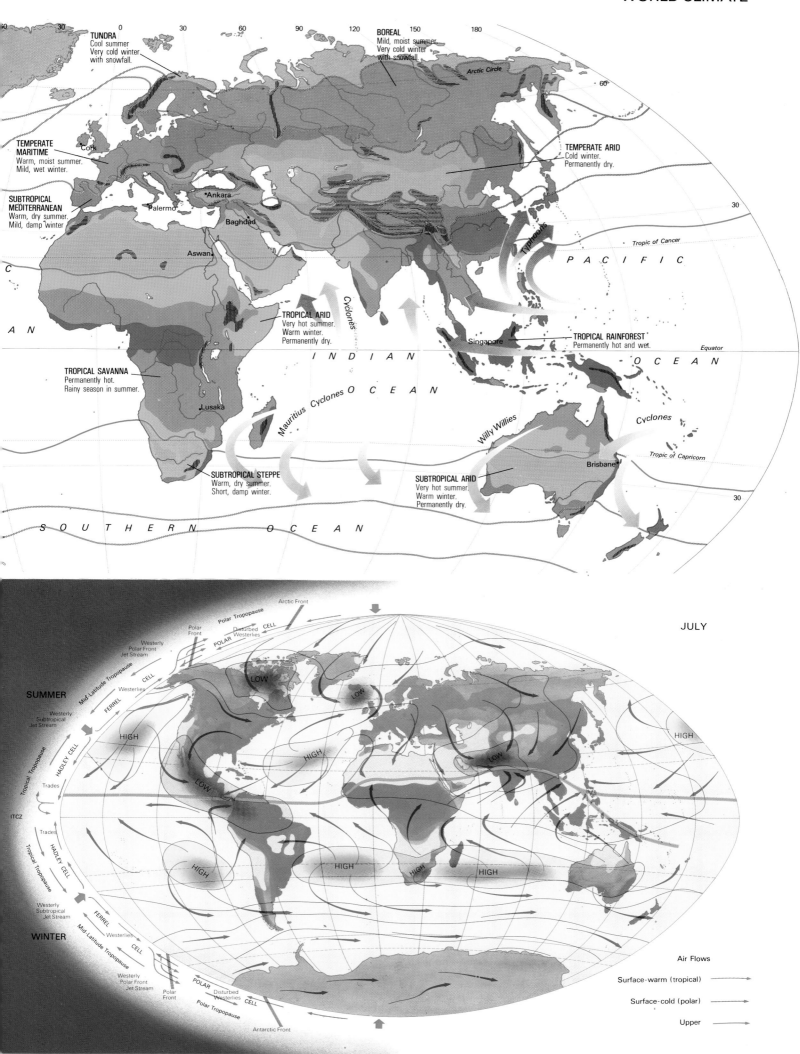

TUNDRA
Cool summer
Very cold winter
with snowfall.

BOREAL
Mild, moist summer.
Very cold winter
with snowfall.

Arctic Circle

TEMPERATE
MARITIME
Warm, moist summer.
Mild, wet winter.

Cork

TEMPERATE ARID
Cold winter.
Permanently dry.

SUBTROPICAL
MEDITERRANEAN
Warm, dry summer.
Mild, damp winter.

Palermo

Ankara

Baghdad

Aswan

Tropic of Cancer

P A C I F I C

Typhoons

TROPICAL ARID
Very hot summer.
Warm winter.
Permanently dry.

Cyclones

TROPICAL RAINFOREST
Permanently hot and wet.

Singapore

Equator

I N D I A N

O C E A N

TROPICAL SAVANNA
Permanently hot.
Rainy season in summer.

Lusaka

Mauritius Cyclones O C E A N

Willy Willies

Cyclones

Brisbane

Tropic of Capricorn

SUBTROPICAL STEPPE
Warm, dry summer.
Short, damp winter.

SUBTROPICAL ARID
Very hot summer.
Warm winter.
Permanently dry.

S O U T H E R N   O C E A N

JULY

Arctic Front

Polar Tropopause

Polar Front

Disturbed CELL
POLAR Westerlies

Westerly
Polar Front
Jet Stream

Mid-Latitude Tropopause

LOW

LOW

SUMMER

Westerlies

CELL

FERREL

Westerly
Subtropical
Jet Stream

HIGH

HIGH

HADLEY CELL

Tropical Tropopause

HIGH

LOW

HIGH

Trades

LOW

ITCZ

Trades

HADLEY CELL

Tropical Tropopause

HIGH

HIGH

HIGH

HIGH

Westerly
Subtropical
Jet Stream

FERREL

Mid-Latitude Tropopause

WINTER

Westerlies

CELL

Westerly
Polar Front
Jet Stream

Polar
Front

POLAR

Disturbed
Westerlies CELL

Polar Tropopause

Antarctic Front

Air Flows

Surface-warm (tropical) →

Surface-cold (polar) →

Upper →

CLIMATE INDICATORS

Listed from north to south, is selection of places from different climate zones of the world (see p xxiv/xxv), indicating their mean monthly temperatures (in °C and °F) and precipitation (in mm and inches). Also shown are their average temperatures and total precipitation for the year.

REYKJAVIK Iceland 64·1°N 21·9°W *TUNDRA*

	J	F	M	A	M	J	J	A	S	O	N	D	Year
°C	-0·2	0·2	1·5	3·5	6·7	9·7	11·3	10·8	8·5	5·2	3·0	0·4	5·0
°F	32	32	35	38	44	49	52	51	47	41	37	33	41
mm	89	64	62	56	42	42	50	56	67	94	78	79	779
ins	3·5	2·5	2·4	2·2	1·6	1·6	2·0	2·2	2·6	3·7	3·1	3·1	30·7

ANCHORAGE U.S.A. 61·2°N 150·0°W *BOREAL*

	J	F	M	A	M	J	J	A	S	O	N	D	Year
°C	-10·4	-7·6	-4·8	2·0	7·7	12·2	14·1	13·1	8·7	1·8	-5·6	-10·2	1·7
°F	13	18	23	36	46	54	57	56	48	35	22	14	29
mm	20	18	13	11	13	25	47	65	63	47	26	24	372
ins	0·8	0·7	0·5	0·4	0·5	1·0	1·8	2·6	2·5	1·8	1·0	0·9	14·6

STOCKHOLM Sweden 59·3°N 18·1°E *TEMPERATE Continental*

	J	F	M	A	M	J	J	A	S	O	N	D	Year
°C	-3·0	-3·1	-0·5	4·6	10·2	15·0	18·5	16·6	12·3	7·1	2·7	0·0	6·6
°F	27	26	31	40	50	59	65	62	54	45	37	32	44
mm	43	30	25	31	34	45	61	76	60	48	53	48	554
ins	1·7	1·2	1·0	1·2	1·3	1·8	2·4	3·0	2·4	1·9	2·1	1·9	21·8

EDINBURGH U.K. 55·9°N 3·2°W *TEMPERATE Maritime*

	J	F	M	A	M	J	J	A	S	O	N	D	Year
°C	3·3	3·5	5·1	7·4	9·9	12·9	14·8	14·4	12·5	9·4	6·4	4·6	8·6
°F	38	38	41	45	50	55	59	58	54	49	43	40	47
mm	57	39	39	39	54	47	83	77	57	65	62	57	676
ins	2·2	1·5	1·5	1·5	2·1	1·8	3·3	3·0	2·2	2·6	2·4	2·2	26·6

MOSKVA Russian Federation 55·7°N 37·6°E *TEMPERATE Continental*

	J	F	M	A	M	J	J	A	S	O	N	D	Year
°C	-12·7	-9·6	-3·8	5·7	13·3	15·8	17·8	16·9	11·8	5·9	-0·9	-7·0	4·4
°F	9	15	25	42	56	60	64	62	53	43	30	19	40
mm	39	38	36	37	53	58	88	71	58	45	47	54	624
ins	1·5	1·5	1·4	1·5	2·1	2·3	3·5	2·8	2·3	1·8	1·8	2·1	24·6

VANCOUVER Canada 49·2°N 123·2°W *TEMPERATE Maritime*

	J	F	M	A	M	J	J	A	S	O	N	D	Year
°C	2·8	4·1	6·4	9·4	12·6	15·5	17·8	17·2	14·4	10·3	6·3	4·2	10·0
°F	37	39	43	49	55	60	64	63	58	50	43	40	50
mm	214	161	151	90	69	65	39	44	83	172	198	243	1529
ins	8·4	6·3	5·9	3·5	2·7	2·6	1·5	1·7	3·3	6·8	7·8	9·6	60·2

PARIS France 48·8°N 2·3°E *TEMPERATE Maritime*

	J	F	M	A	M	J	J	A	S	O	N	D	Year
°C	3·4	4·3	7·9	11·0	14·6	17·8	19·5	19·1	16·5	11·7	7·2	4·3	11·5
°F	38	40	46	52	58	64	67	66	62	53	45	40	53
mm	56	46	35	42	57	54	59	64	55	50	51	50	619
ins	2·2	1·8	1·4	1·6	2·2	2·1	2·3	2·5	2·2	2·0	2·0	2·0	24·3

BUCUREŞTI Romania 44·5°N 26·0°E *TEMPERATE Steppe*

	J	F	M	A	M	J	J	A	S	O	N	D	Year
°C	-4·2	-1·5	6·2	12·4	17·3	21·2	23·5	22·9	18·2	13·0	6·4	0·6	8·2
°F	24	29	43	54	63	70	74	73	65	55	43	33	47
mm	46	26	28	59	77	121	53	45	45	29	36	27	592
ins	1·8	1·0	1·1	2·3	3·0	4·8	2·1	1·8	1·8	1·1	1·4	1·1	23·4

NEW YORK U.S.A. 40·7°N 74·0°W *TEMPERATE Continental*

	J	F	M	A	M	J	J	A	S	O	N	D	Year
°C	0·7	0·8	4·7	10·5	16·3	21·2	24·1	23·3	19·8	14·3	8·1	2·2	12·2
°F	33	33	40	51	61	70	75	74	68	58	47	36	54
mm	89	74	104	89	91	86	102	119	89	84	89	84	1100
ins	3·5	2·9	4·1	3·5	3·6	3·4	4·0	4·7	3·5	3·3	3·5	3·3	43·3

TŌKYŌ Japan 35·7°N 139·8°E *TEMPERATE Continental*

	J	F	M	A	M	J	J	A	S	O	N	D	Year
°C	3·3	4·2	7·2	12·5	16·9	20·8	24·7	26·1	22·5	16·7	10·8	5·8	14·4
°F	38	40	45	54	62	69	76	79	72	62	51	42	58
mm	48	74	107	135	147	165	142	152	234	208	96	56	1565
ins	1·9	2·9	4·2	5·3	5·8	6·5	5·6	6·0	9·2	8·2	3·8	2·2	61·6

TANGER Morocco 35·8°N 5·8°W *SUBTROPICAL Mediterranean*

	J	F	M	A	M	J	J	A	S	O	N	D	Year
°C	11·9	12·5	13·6	14·4	17·2	20·0	22·2	23·0	21·4	18·6	14·7	12·4	16·7
°F	53	54	56	58	63	68	72	73	70	65	58	54	62
mm	114	107	122	89	43	15	2	2	23	99	147	137	897
ins	4·5	4·2	4·8	3·5	1·7	0·6	0·1	0·1	0·9	3·9	5·8	5·4	35·3

JERUSALEM Israel 31·8°N 35·2°E *SUBTROPICAL Steppe*

	J	F	M	A	M	J	J	A	S	O	N	D	Year
°C	8·9	9·4	13·0	16·4	20·5	22·5	23·9	24·1	23·0	21·1	16·4	11·1	17·2
°F	48	49	55	61	69	72	75	75	73	70	61	52	63
mm	132	132	63	28	2	1	0	0	1	13	71	87	528
ins	5·2	5·2	2·5	1·1	0·1	0·1	0·0	0·0	0·1	0·5	2·8	3·4	20·8

NEW ORLEANS U.S.A. 30·0°N 90·2°W *SUBTROPICAL Humid*

	J	F	M	A	M	J	J	A	S	O	N	D	Year
°C	12·5	13·9	16·3	19·9	23·5	26·7	27·6	27·7	25·7	21·3	15·5	13·0	20·3
°F	54	57	61	68	74	80	82	82	78	70	60	55	68
mm	97	102	135	114	112	112	170	135	127	71	84	104	1363
ins	3·8	4·0	5·3	4·5	4·4	4·4	6·7	5·3	5·0	2·8	3·3	4·1	53·7

BAHRAIN 26·2°N 50·5°E *SUBTROPICAL Arid*

	J	F	M	A	M	J	J	A	S	O	N	D	Year
°C	16·9	18·0	20·5	25·0	29·4	31·7	33·3	33·6	31·4	28·0	24·2	18·6	25·8
°F	62	64	69	77	85	89	92	92	88	82	75	65	78
mm	8	18	13	8	1	0	0	0	0	0	18	18	79
ins	0·3	0·7	0·5	0·3	0·1	0·0	0·0	0·0	0·0	0·0	0·7	0·7	3·2

HONG KONG 22·3°N 114·2°E *SUBTROPICAL Humid*

	J	F	M	A	M	J	J	A	S	O	N	D	Year
°C	15·5	15·0	17·5	21·7	25·5	27·5	28·0	28·0	27·2	25·0	20·8	17·5	22·5
°F	60	59	63	71	78	81	82	82	81	77	69	63	72
mm	33	46	74	137	292	394	381	361	256	114	43	30	2161
ins	1·3	1·8	2·9	5·4	11·5	15·5	15·0	14·2	10·1	4·5	1·7	1·2	85·1

MIAMI U.S.A. 25·8°N 80·3°W *TROPICAL Savanna*

	J	F	M	A	M	J	J	A	S	O	N	D	Year
°C	19·3	19·9	21·4	23·4	25·3	27·1	27·6	27·9	27·4	25·4	22·4	20·1	23·9
°F	67	68	70	74	77	81	82	82	81	78	72	68	75
mm	51	48	58	99	163	188	170	178	241	208	71	43	1518
ins	2·0	1·9	2·3	3·9	6·4	7·4	6·7	7·0	9·5	8·2	2·8	1·7	59·8

BANGKOK Thailand 13·7°N 100·5°E *TROPICAL Savanna*

	J	F	M	A	M	J	J	A	S	O	N	D	Year
°C	25·8	27·5	28·9	30·0	29·4	28·6	28·3	28·3	28·0	27·5	26·4	25·3	27·7
°F	78	81	84	86	85	83	83	83	82	81	79	77	82
mm	8	20	36	58	198	160	160	175	305	206	66	5	1397
ins	0·3	0·8	1·4	2·3	7·8	6·3	6·3	6·9	12·0	8·1	2·6	0·2	55·0

COLOMBO Sri Lanka 6·9°N 79·9°E *TROPICAL Rainforest*

	J	F	M	A	M	J	J	A	S	O	N	D	Year
°C	26·1	26·4	27·2	27·7	28·0	27·2	27·2	27·2	27·2	26·6	26·1	25·8	26·9
°F	79	80	81	82	82	81	81	81	81	80	79	78	80
mm	89	69	147	231	371	223	135	109	160	348	315	147	2344
ins	3·5	2·7	5·8	9·1	14·6	8·8	5·3	4·3	6·3	13·7	12·4	5·8	92·3

NAIROBI Kenya 1·3°S 36·8°E *TROPICAL Savanna*

	J	F	M	A	M	J	J	A	S	O	N	D	Year
°C	18·6	19·4	19·4	19·2	17·7	16·4	15·5	16·1	17·5	18·6	18·3	18·0	18·0
°F	65	67	67	67	64	61	60	61	63	65	65	64	64
mm	38	63	124	211	157	46	15	23	30	53	109	86	958
ins	1·5	2·5	4·9	8·3	6·2	1·8	0·6	0·9	1·2	2·1	4·3	3·4	37·7

LIMA Peru 12·1°S 77·0°W *TROPICAL Arid*

	J	F	M	A	M	J	J	A	S	O	N	D	Year
°C	23·3	23·8	23·6	21·9	19·4	17·2	16·7	16·1	16·9	18·0	19·4	21·1	20·0
°F	74	75	74	71	67	63	62	61	62	64	67	70	68
mm	1	1	1	1	5	5	8	8	8	2	2	1	41
ins	0·1	0·1	0·1	0·1	0·2	0·2	0·3	0·3	0·3	0·1	0·1	0·1	1·6

RIO DE JANEIRO Brazil 22·9°S 43·2°W *TROPICAL Savanna*

	J	F	M	A	M	J	J	A	S	O	N	D	Year
°C	25·8	26·1	25·3	23·6	21·9	21·1	20·5	21·1	21·1	21·9	23·0	24·7	23·0
°F	78	79	77	74	71	70	69	70	70	71	73	76	73
mm	124	122	130	107	79	53	41	43	66	79	104	137	1085
ins	4·9	4·8	5·1	4·2	3·1	2·1	1·6	1·7	2·6	3·1	4·1	5·4	42·6

JOHANNESBURG S. Africa 26·2°S 28·1°E *SUBTROPICAL Steppe*

	J	F	M	A	M	J	J	A	S	O	N	D	Year
°C	20·0	19·7	18·3	16·1	12·5	10·3	10·5	13·0	15·8	18·3	18·9	19·7	16·1
°F	68	67	65	61	54	50	51	55	60	65	66	67	61
mm	114	109	89	38	25	8	8	8	23	56	107	124	709
ins	4·5	4·3	3·5	1·5	1·0	0·3	0·3	0·3	0·9	2·2	4·2	4·9	27·9

PERTH Australia 31·9°S 115·8°E *SUBTROPICAL Mediterranean*

	J	F	M	A	M	J	J	A	S	O	N	D	Year
°C	23·3	23·3	21·7	19·2	16·1	13·9	13·0	13·3	14·7	16·4	19·2	21·7	17·8
°F	74	74	71	66	61	57	55	56	58	61	66	71	64
mm	8	10	20	43	130	180	170	145	86	56	20	13	881
ins	0·3	0·4	0·8	1·7	5·1	7·1	6·7	5·7	3·4	2·2	0·8	0·5	34·7

WELLINGTON New Zealand 41·3°S 174·8°E *TEMPERATE Maritime*

	J	F	M	A	M	J	J	A	S	O	N	D	Year
°C	16·9	16·9	15·8	13·9	11·4	9·7	8·6	9·2	10·8	12·2	13·6	15·8	12·8
°F	62	62	60	57	52	49	47	48	51	54	56	60	55
mm	81	81	81	97	117	117	137	117	97	102	89	89	1205
ins	3·2	3·2	3·2	3·8	4·6	4·6	5·4	4·6	3·8	4·0	3·5	3·5	47·4

Civilisation depends on trade for growth and travel makes this possible. Shipping is the most important method of world transport but economic progress and moblity are constantly being improved by the development of new routes and new modes of transport.

ROAD AND RAIL

Integrated road and rail networks are the basis of industrial society. Extended highway systems and improved containerisation techniques have made the whole road and rail system much more flexible.

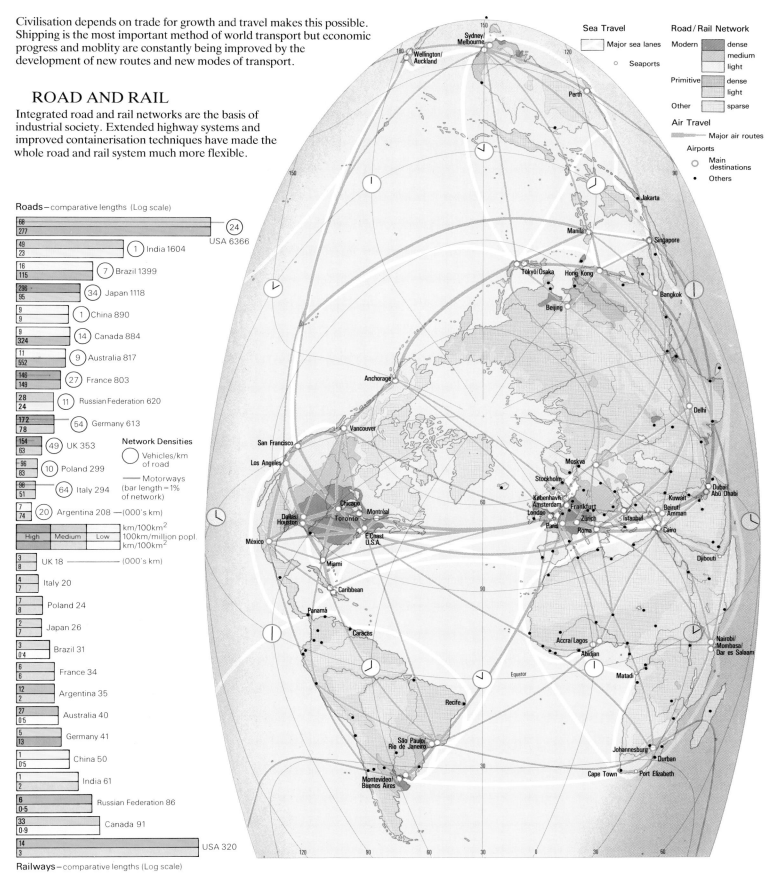

Sea Travel
- Major sea lanes
- ○ Seaports

Road / Rail Network

Modern	dense
	medium
	light
Primitive	dense
	light
Other	sparse

Air Travel
- Major air routes

Airports
- ○ Main destinations
- • Others

Roads – comparative lengths (Log scale)

- 68/277 (24) USA 6366
- 49/23 (1) India 1604
- 16/115 (7) Brazil 1399
- 296/95 (34) Japan 1118
- 9/9 (1) China 890
- 9/324 (14) Canada 884
- 11/552 (9) Australia 817
- 146/149 (27) France 803
- 28/24 (11) Russian Federation 620
- 172/78 (54) Germany 613
- 154/63 (49) UK 353
- 96/83 (10) Poland 299
- 98/51 (64) Italy 294
- 7/74 (20) Argentina 208 — (000's km)

Network Densities
- ○ Vehicles/km of road
- — Motorways (bar length = 1% of network)

| High | Medium | Low |

km/100km^2
100km/million popl.
km/100km^2

Railways – comparative lengths (Log scale)

- 3/8 UK 18 — (000's km)
- 4/7 Italy 20
- 7/8 Poland 24
- 2/7 Japan 26
- 3/0·4 Brazil 31
- 6/6 France 34
- 12/2 Argentina 35
- 27/0·5 Australia 40
- 5/13 Germany 41
- 1/0·5 China 50
- 1/2 India 61
- 6/0·5 Russian Federation 86
- 33/0·9 Canada 91
- 14/3 USA 320

JOURNEY TIME

The Suez canal cuts 3600 miles off the London-Singapore route, while Concorde halves the London-New York journey time.

AIR AND SEA ROUTES

A complex network of primary air routes centred on the Northern Hemisphere provides rapid transit across the world for mass travel, mail and urgent freight. Ships also follow these principal routes, plying the oceans between major ports and transporting the commodities of world trade in bulk.

Sail (via Cape) 164 days
Steam (via Cape) 43 days
Steam (via Suez) 30 days
Supertanker (via Cape) 28 days
Diesel (via Suez) 15 days

Concorde 3½ hours
Jet 7 hours
Propeller 12 hours
First Flight 4½ days

Singapore ◄— London —► New York

1:60M

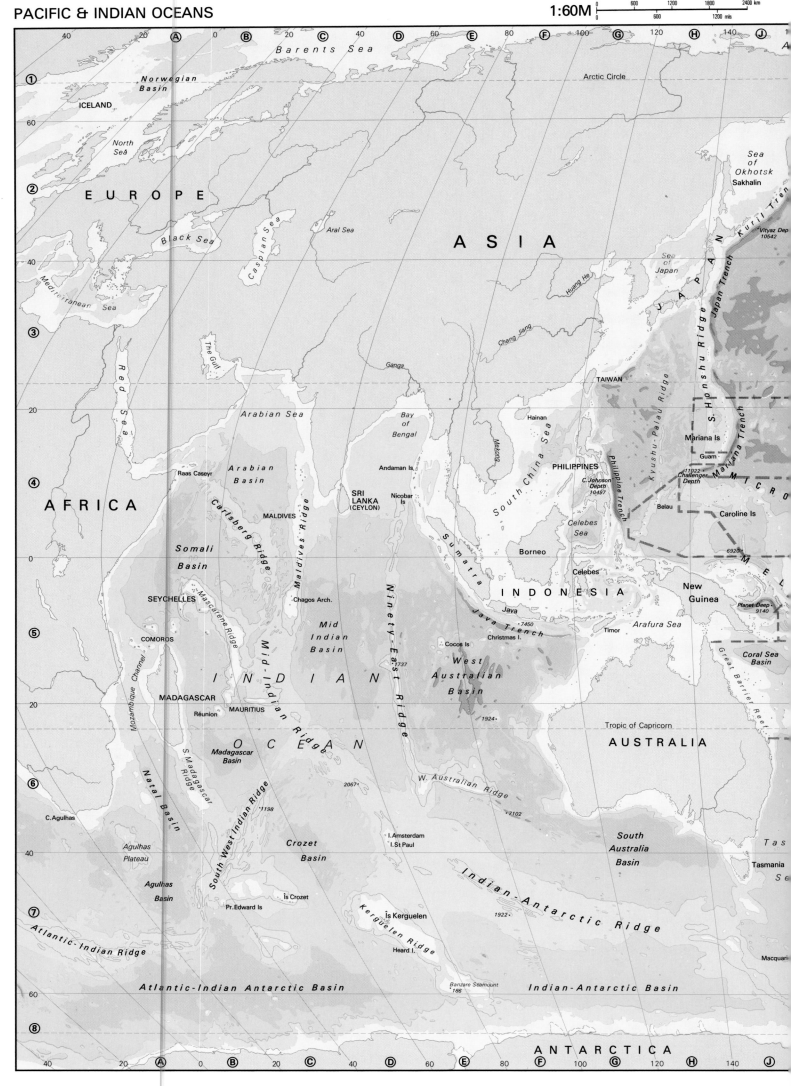

Barents Sea

Norwegian Basin

ICELAND

North Sea

Arctic Circle

EUROPE

Mediterranean Sea

Black Sea

Caspian Sea

Aral Sea

ASIA

Sea of Okhotsk

Sakhalin

Sea of Japan

JAPAN

Kuril Trench

Vityaz Dep 10542

Japan Trench

Red Sea

The Gulf

Huang He

Chang Jiang

Ganga

TAIWAN

S. Honshu Ridge

Kyushu-Palau Ridge

Arabian Sea

Bay of Bengal

Hainan

Mariana Is

Mariana Trench

AFRICA

Raas Caseyr

Arabian Basin

Carlsberg Ridge

MALDIVES

Maldives Ridge

Andaman Is

SRI LANKA (CEYLON)

Nicobar Is

Mekong

South China Sea

PHILIPPINES

C. Johnson Depth 10497

Philippine Trench

Guam

11022 Challenger Depth

MICRO

Belau

Caroline Is

6920

Somali Basin

SEYCHELLES

Mascarene Ridge

Chagos Arch.

Mid Indian Basin

Ninety-East Ridge

Sumatra

Celebes Sea

Borneo

Celebes

INDONESIA

New Guinea

Planet Deep 9140

MEL

COMOROS

MADAGASCAR

Réunion

MAURITIUS

S. Madagascar Ridge

Madagascar Basin

INDIAN

Mid-Indian Ridge

OCEAN

7450

West Australian Basin

Java

Java Trench

Christmas I.

Cocos Is

1737

Timor

Arafura Sea

Coral Sea Basin

Tropic of Capricorn

AUSTRALIA

Great Barrier Reef

1924

C. Agulhas

Natal Basin

Agulhas Plateau

Agulhas Basin

South West Indian Ridge

1198

Crozet Basin

2067

W. Australian Ridge

2102

South Australia Basin

Tas

Tasmania

Se

Atlantic-Indian Ridge

Pr. Edward Is

Îs Crozet

Îs Kerguelen

Kerguelen Ridge

I. Amsterdam
I. St Paul

Indian-Antarctic Ridge

1922

Macquari

Heard I.

Atlantic-Indian Antarctic Basin

Banzare Seamount 186

Indian-Antarctic Basin

ANTARCTICA

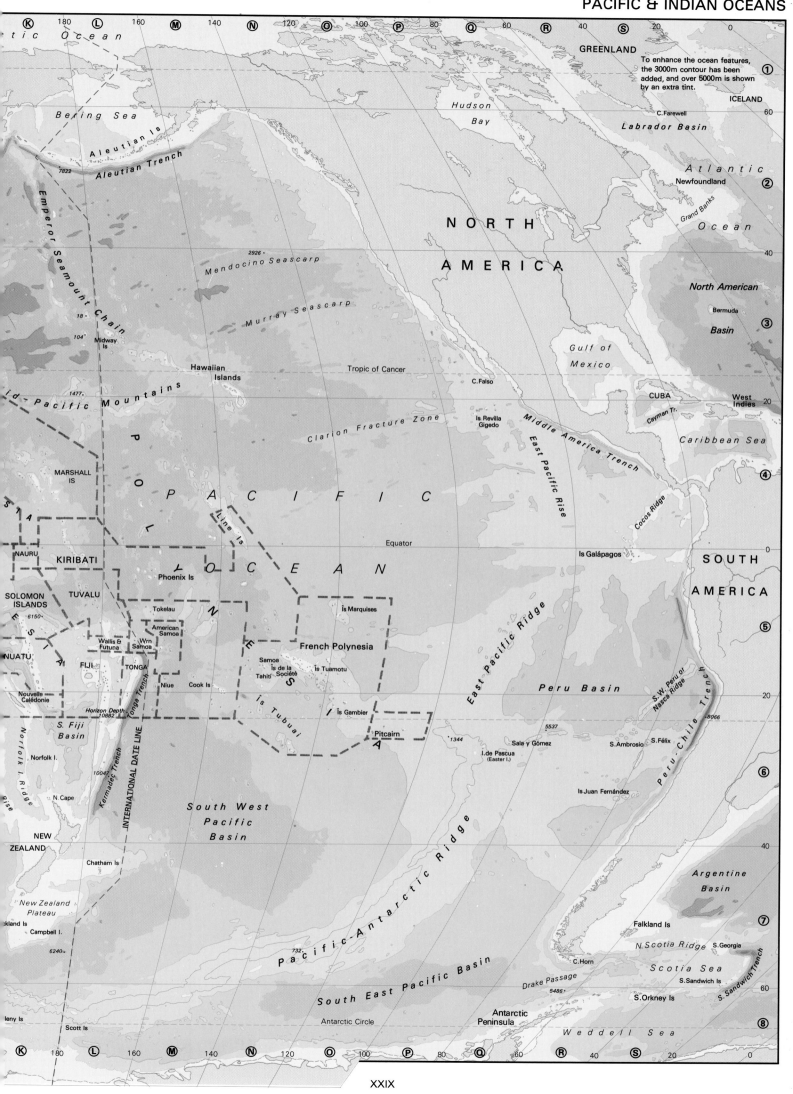

1:60M

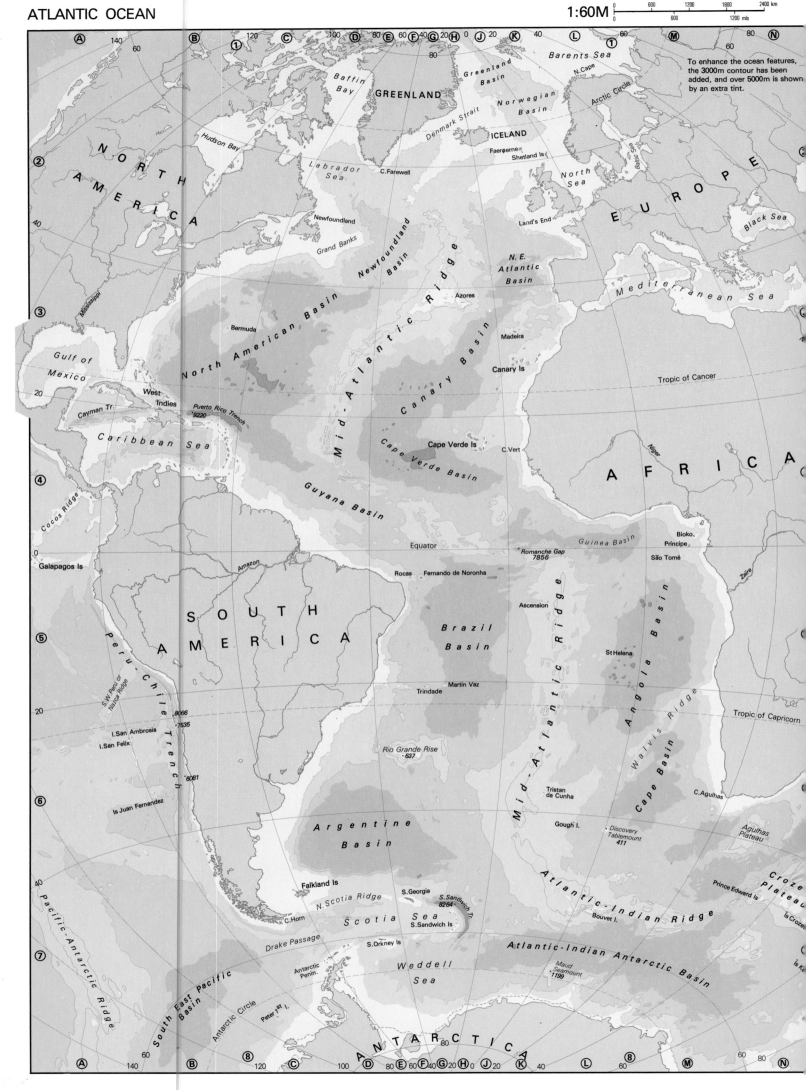

600   1200   1800   2400 km

600   1200 mls

To enhance the ocean features,
the 3000m contour has been
added, and over 5000m is shown
by an extra tint.

Ⓐ   140   Ⓑ   120   Ⓒ   ①   100   Ⓓ   80   Ⓔ   60   Ⓕ   40   Ⓖ   20   Ⓗ   0   Ⓙ   20   Ⓚ   40   Ⓛ   60   ①   Ⓜ   60   Ⓝ

Barents Sea

Baffin
Bay

Greenland
Basin

GREENLAND   N.Cape

Norwegian
Basin   Arctic Circle

②   NORTH

Denmark Strait   ICELAND

Hudson Bay   Faeroerne
Shetland Is

Labrador
Sea   C.Farewell   North
Sea   EUROPE

AMERICA

40   Newfoundland   Land's End   Black Sea

Grand Banks   N.E.
Atlantic
Basin   Mediterranean Sea

Newfoundland
Basin

③   North American Basin   Azores

Bermuda   Madeira

Gulf of
Mexico   Canary Basin   Canary Is   Tropic of Cancer

20   West
Indies   Puerto Rico Trench
•9220   Canary Basin

Cayman Tr.   Cape Verde Is   C.Vert

Caribbean Sea   Cape Verde Basin   AFRICA

④   Guyana Basin

Cocos Ridge   Bioko
Príncipe

Guinea Basin   São Tomé

Galapagos Is   Equator   Romanche Gap
7856   Zaïre

0   Amazon   Rocas   Fernando de Noronha

SOUTH   Ascension   Mid-Atlantic Ridge   St Helena   Angola Basin

⑤   AMERICA   Brazil
Basin

Peru-Chile Trench   Martin Vaz   Walvis Ridge   Tropic of Capricorn

20   S.W.Peru or
Nazca Ridge   •8066   Trindade
•7635   Cape Basin

I.San Ambrosia   Rio Grande Rise
•637
I.San Felix   •6081   Tristan
da Cunha   C.Agulhas

⑥   Is Juan Fernandez   Argentine
Basin   Agulhas
Plateau

Gough I.   Discovery
Tablemount
411   Mid-Atlantic Ridge

40   Falkland Is   Prince Edward Is   Crozet
Plateau

Pacific-Antarctic Ridge   S.Georgia   S.Sandwich Tr.
8264   Atlantic-Indian Ridge

N.Scotia Ridge   C.Horn   Scotia Sea   S.Sandwich Is   Bouvet I.   Is Crozet

⑦   Drake Passage   S.Orkney Is   Atlantic-Indian Antarctic Basin   Is Ke

South East Pacific   Maud
Basin   Weddell   Seamount
1195

Antarctic
Penin.   Sea

Antarctic Circle   Peter I st I.   80

⑧   ANTARCTICA

Ⓐ   140   Ⓑ   120   Ⓒ   100   Ⓓ   80   Ⓔ Ⓕ 40 Ⓖ 20 Ⓗ 0   Ⓙ 20   Ⓚ   40   Ⓛ   60   Ⓜ   60   80   Ⓝ

MOUNTAIN HEIGHTS

Metres	Feet		Metres	Feet	
8848	29 028	Everest (Qomolangma Feng) Nepal-Tibet	6870	22 541	Bonete Bolivia
8611	28 250	K2 (Godwin Austen) Kashmir-Sinkiang	6800	22 310	Tupungato Argentina-Chile
8586	28 168	Kangchenjunga Nepal-India	6770	22 211	Mercedario Argentina
8475	27 805	Makalu Tibet-Nepal	6768	22 205	Huascarán Peru
8172	26 810	Dhaulagiri Nepal	6723	22 057	Llullaillaco Argentina-Chile
8126	26 660	Nanga Parbat Kashmir	6714	22 028	Kangrinboqê Feng (Kailas) Tibet
8078	26 504	Annapurna Nepal	6634	21 765	Yerupaja Peru
8068	26 470	Gasherbrum Kashmir	6542	21 463	Sajama Bolivia
8013	26 291	Xixabangma Feng (Gosainthan) Tibet	6485	21 276	Illampu Bolivia
7890	25 885	Distaghil Sar Kashmir	6425	21 079	Coropuna Peru
7820	25 656	Masherbrum Kashmir	6402	21 004	Illimani Bolivia
7817	25 645	Nanda Devi India	6388	20 958	Ancohuma Bolivia
7780	25 550	Rakaposhi Kashmir	6310	20 702	Chimborazo Ecuador
7756	25 447	Kamet India-Tibet	6194	20 320	McKinley USA
7756	25 447	Namcha Barwa Tibet	6050	19 850	Logan Canada
7728	25 355	Gurla Mandhata Tibet	5895	19 340	Kilimanjaro Tanzania
7723	25 338	Muztag (Ulugh Muztagh) Sinkiang	5700	18 700	Citlaltepetl Mexico
7719	25 325	Kongur Shan (Kungur) Sinkiang	5642	18 510	El'bruz Russian Federation
7690	25 230	Tirich Mir Pakistan	5452	17 887	Popocatepetl Mexico
7590	24 903	Gongga Shan (Minya Konka) China	5199	17 057	Kirinyaga (Kenya) Kenya
7546	24 757	Muztagata (Muztagh Ata) Sinkiang	5165	16 946	Ararat Turkey
7495	24 590	Pik Kommunizma Tajikistan	5140	16 864	Vinson Massif Antarctica
7439	24 407	Pik Pobedy (Tomur Feng) Kirghizia-Sinkiang	5110	16 763	Stanley Zaire-Uganda
7313	23 993	Chomo Lhari Bhutan-Tibet	5030	16 500	Jaya (Carstensz) Indonesia
7134	23 406	Pik Lenina Kirghizia-Tajikistan	4808	15 774	Mont Blanc France
6960	22 834	Aconcagua Argentina	4508	14 790	Wilhelm Papua New Guinea
6908	22 664	Ojos del Salado Chile-Argentina	4201	13 784	Mauna Kea USA

RIVER LENGTHS

Km	Miles		Km	Miles	
6695	4160	Nile Africa	2850	1770	Danube Europe
6570	4080	Amazon South America	2820	1750	Salween Asia
6380	3964	Yangtze Asia	2780	1730	São Francisco South America
6020	3740	Mississippi-Missouri North America	2655	1650	Zambezi Africa
5410	3360	Ob-Irtysh Asia	2570	1600	Nelson-Saskatchewan North America
4840	3010	Huang He (Yellow River) Asia	2510	1560	Ganges Asia
4630	2880	Zaïre (Congo) Africa	2430	1510	Euphrates Asia
4500	2796	Paraná South America	2330	1450	Arkansas North America
4440	2760	Irtysh Asia	2330	1450	Colorado North America
4416	2745	Amur Asia	2285	1420	Dnieper Europe
4400	2730	Lena Asia	2090	1300	Irrawaddy Asia
4240	2630	Mackenzie North America	2060	1280	Orinoco South America
4180	2600	Mekong Asia	2000	1240	Negro South America
4100	2550	Niger Africa	1870	1160	Don Europe
4090	2540	Yenisey Asia	1859	1155	Orange Africa
3969	2466	Missouri North America	1799	1118	Pechora Europe
3779	2348	Mississippi North America	1609	1000	Marañón South America
3750	2330	Murray-Darling Australia	1410	876	Dniester Europe
3688	2292	Volga Europe	1320	820	Rhine Europe
3240	2013	Madeira South America	1183	735	Donets Europe
3058	1900	St. Lawrence North America	1159	720	Elbe Europe
3030	1880	Rio Grande North America	1094	680	Gambia Africa
3020	1870	Yukon North America	1080	671	Yellowstone North America
2960	1840	Brahmaputra Asia	1014	630	Vistula Europe
2896	1800	Indus Asia	1006	625	Tagus Europe

LAKE AND INLAND SEA AREAS

Areas are average and some are subject to seasonal variations.

Sq. Km	Sq. Miles		Sq. Km	Sq. Miles	
371 000	142 240	Caspian Central Asia (salt)	22 490	8680	Nyasa (Malawi) Malawi-Mozambique
82 900	32 010	Superior USA-Canada	19 400	7490	Ontario USA-Canada
68 800	26 560	Victoria Kenya-Uganda-Tanzania	18 390	7100	Ladoga Russian Federation
59 580	23 000	Huron USA-Canada	17 400	6700	Balkhash Kazakhstan
58 020	22 480	Michigan USA	10-26 000	4-10 000	Chad Nigeria-Niger-Chad-Cameroon
36 500	14 100	Aral Central Asia (salt)	9600	3710	Onega Russian Federation
32 900	12 700	Tanganyika Tanzania-Zambia-Zaire-Burundi	0-8900	0-3430	Eyre Australia
31 330	12 100	Great Bear Canada	8340	3220	Titicaca Peru-Bolivia
30 500	11 800	Baykal Russian Federation	8270	3190	Nicaragua Nicaragua
28 570	11 030	Great Slave Canada	6410	2470	Turkana (Rudolf) Kenya-Ethiopia
25 680	9910	Erie USA-Canada	5780	2230	Torrens Australia (salt)
24 390	9420	Winnipeg Canada	5580	2160	Vänern Sweden

GREATEST OCEAN DEPTHS

Metres	Feet	Location	Metres	Feet	Location
		PACIFIC OCEAN			ATLANTIC OCEAN
11 022	36 160	Marianas Trench	9220	30 249	Puerto Rico Trench
10 882	35 702	Tonga Trench	8264	27 113	South Sandwich Trench
10 542	34 586	Kuril Trench	7856	25 774	Romanche Gap
10 497	34 439	Philippine Trench	7500	24 600	Cayman Trench
10 047	32 962	Kermadec Trench			
9810	32 185	Izu-Bonin Trench			INDIAN OCEAN
9165	30 069	New Hebrides Trench	7450	24 442	Java Trench
9140	29 987	South Solomon Trench	7440	24 409	Weber Basin
8412	27 598	Japan Trench	7102	23 300	Diamantina Trench
8066	26 463	Peru-Chile Trench			
7822	25 662	Aleutian Trench			ARCTIC OCEAN
6662	21 857	Middle America	5570	18 274	Nansen Fracture Zone

STATES AND DEPENDENCIES

COUNTRY	Area (sq. km)	Population ('000)	Capital
North and Central America			
Anguilla (UK)	91	7	The Valley
Antigua and Barbuda	442	76	St. John's
The Bahamas	13 864	253	Nassau
Barbados	430	255	Bridgetown
Belize	22 965	187	Belmopan
Bermuda (UK)	53	58	Hamilton
Canada	9 976 147	27 296	Ottawa
Cayman Is. (UK)	259	25	George Town
Costa Rica	50 899	3 015	San José
Cuba	114 524	10 608	La Habana (Havana)
Dominica	751	82	Roseau
Dominican Republic	48 441	7 170	Santo Domingo
El Salvador	20 865	5 252	San Salvador
Grenada	344	85	St. George's
Guadeloupe (Fr.)	1 779	343	Basse Terre
Guatemala	108 888	9 197	Guatemala
Haiti	27 749	6 513	Port-au-Prince
Honduras	112 087	5 138	Tegucigalpa
Jamaica	11 425	2 456	Kingston
Martinique (Fr.)	1 101	341	Fort-de-France
Mexico	1 967 180	107 233	Mexico
Montserrat (UK)	102	12	Plymouth
Netherlands Antilles (Neth.)	993	188	Willemstad
Nicaragua	139 000	3 871	Managua
Panama	75 648	2 418	Panamá
Puerto Rico (USA)	8 897	3 480	San Juan
St. Kitts-Nevis	260	44	Basseterre
St. Lucia	616	150	Castries
St. Vincent	389	116	Kingstown
Trinidad and Tobago	5 128	1 281	Port of Spain
United States of America	9 363 130	248 700	Washington
South America			
Argentina	2 777 815	32 322	Buenos Aires
Bolivia	1 098 575	7 314	La Paz
Brazil	8 511 968	150 368	Brasília
Chile	756 943	13 173	Santiago
Colombia	1 138 907	32 978	Bogotá
Ecuador	455 502	10 587	Quito
French Guiana (Fr.)	91 000	98	Cayenne
Guyana	214 969	796	George Town
Paraguay	406 750	4 277	Asunción
Peru	1 285 215	21 550	Lima
Surinam	163 820	422	Paramribo
Uruguay	186 925	3 094	Montevideo
Venezuela	912 047	19 735	Caracas
Europe			
Albania	28 752	3 245	Tiranë (Tirana)
Andorra	453	47	Andorra-la-Vella
Austria	83 848	7 583	Wien (Vienna)
Belgium	30 512	9 845	Bruxelles (Brussels)
Belorussia (Belarus)	207 600	10 278	Minsk
Bosnia-Herzegovina	51 130	4 400	Sarajevo
Bulgaria	110 911	9 010	Sofiya (Sofia)
Croatia	56 540	4 700	Zagreb
Cyprus	9 251	701	Nicosia
Czech Republic	78 864	10 300	Praha (Prague)
Denmark	43 030	5 143	København (Copenhagen)
Estonia	45 100	1 573	Tallinn
Faroes (Den.)	1 399	47	Tórshavn
Finland	337 032	4 975	Helsinki
France	551 000	56 138	Paris
Germany	356 854	79 070	Berlin
Gibraltar (UK)	6	30	Gibraltar
Great Britain and N. Ireland, see United Kingdom			
Greece	131 955	10 047	Athinai (Athens)
Greenland (Den.)	2 175 600	56	Godthåb
Hungary	93 030	10 552	Budapest
Iceland	102 828	260	Reykjavik
Ireland	70 282	3 720	Dublin
Italy	301 245	57 061	Roma (Rome)
Latvia	63 700	2 681	Riga
Liechtenstein	161	28	Vaduz
Lithuania	65 200	3 690	Vilnius
Luxembourg	2 587	373	Luxembourg
Macedonia	25 713	2 090	Skopje
Malta	316	353	Valletta
Moldova	33 700	4 341	Kishinev
Monaco	1.8	28	Monaco
Netherlands	33 940	14 951	Amsterdam/'s-Gravenhage
Norway	324 218	4 212	Oslo
Poland	312 683	38 423	Warszawa (Warsaw)
Portugal	91 671	10 285	Lisboa (Lisbon)
Romania	237 500	23 272	Bucuresti (Bucharest)
Russian Federation	17 075 000	148 263	Moskva (Moscow)
San Marino	61	23	San Marino
Slovakia	49 035	5 300	Bratislava
Slovenia	7 815	1 900	Ljubljana
Spain	504 745	39 187	Madrid
Sweden	449 791	8 444	Stockholm
Switzerland	41 287	6 609	Bern
Ukraine	603 700	51 857	Kiyev
United Kingdom	244 104	57 237	London
Vatican City	.4	1	Vatican City
Yugoslavia	255 803	23 807	Beograd (Belgrade)
Asia			
Afghanistan	674 500	16 557	Kabul
Armenia	29 800	3 283	Yerevan
Azerbaijan	86 600	7 029	Baku
Bahrain	660	516	Al Manāmah
Bangladesh	144 020	115 593	Dhaka (Dacca)
Bhutan	46 620	1 516	Thimphu
Brunei	5 765	266	Bandar Seri Begawan
Burma (Myanma)	678 031	41 675	Yangon (Rangoon)
Cambodia	181 035	8 246	Phnom Penh
China	9 561 000	1 118 760	Beijing (Peking)
Georgia	69 700	5 449	Tbilisi
Hong Kong (UK)	1 062	5 851	
India	3 287 593	853 094	New Delhi
Indonesia	1 919 263	185 020	Jakarta
Iran	1 648 184	54 607	Tehrän
Iraq	434 924	18 920	Baghdäd
Israel	20 770	4 600	Jerusalem
Japan	371 000	123 460	Tökyö
Jordan	97 740	4 009	Amman
Kazakhstan	2 717 300	16 538	Alma Ata
Kirghizia (Kyrgyzstan)	198 500	4 291	Bishkek (Frunze)
Korea, North	121 248	21 773	P'yöngyang
Korea, South	98 447	42 793	Sŏul (Seoul)
Kuwait	24 300	2 039	Kuwait
Laos	236 798	4 139	Vientiane
Lebanon	10 399	2 701	Beirut
Macau (Port)	16	479	Macao
Malaysia	330 669	17 891	Kuala Lumpur
Maldives	298	215	Malé
Mongolia	1 565 000	2 190	Ulaanbaatar (Ulan Bator)
Nepal	141 414	19 143	Kathmandu
Oman	212 379	1 502	Masqat (Muscat)
Pakistan	803 941	122 626	Islamabad
Philippines	299 765	62 413	Manila
Qatar	11 437	368	Ad Dawḥah
Saudi Arabia	2 400 930	14 134	Ar Riyāḍ
Singapore	616	2 723	Singapore
Sri Lanka	65 610	17 217	Colombo
Syria	185 179	12 530	Dimashq (Damascus)
Taiwan	35 980	20 300	T'ai-pei
Tajikistan	143 100	5 112	Dushanbe
Thailand	513 517	55 702	Bangkok
Turkey	780 576	55 868	Ankara
Turkmenistan	488 100	3 534	Ashkhabad
United Arab Emirates	83 600	1 589	Abū Ẓabī
Uzbekistan	447 400	19 906	Tashkent
Vietnam	329 566	66 693	Hanoi
Yemen	528 038	11 687	San'ä'
Africa			
Algeria	2 381 731	24 960	Alger (El Djezair)
Angola	1 246 694	10 020	Luanda
Benin	112 622	4 630	Porto Novo
Botswana	582 000	1 304	Gaborone
Burkina	274 122	8 996	Ouagadougou
Burundi	27 834	5 472	Bujumbura
Cameroon	475 499	11 833	Yaoundé
Cape Verde	4 033	370	Praia
Central African Republic	622 996	3 039	Bangui
Chad	1 284 000	5 678	N'Djamena
Comoros	1 862	550	Moroni
Congo	342 000	2 271	Brazzaville
Djibouti	21 699	409	Djibouti
Egypt	1 000 250	52 426	Cairo
Equatorial Guinea	28 051	352	Malabo
Eritrea	117 600	2 614	Åsmera (Asmara)
Ethiopia	1 104 318	46 626	Ådis Ábeba
Gabon	267 667	1 172	Libreville
The Gambia	10 688	861	Banjul
Ghana	238 538	15 028	Accra
Guinea	245 855	5 755	Conakry
Guinea-Bissau	36 125	964	Bissau
Ivory Coast	322 463	11 997	Yamoussoukro
Kenya	582 644	24 031	Nairobi
Lesotho	30 344	1 774	Maseru
Liberia	111 370	2 575	Monrovia
Libya	1 759 530	4 545	Tripoli
Madagascar	587 042	12 004	Antananarivo
Malawi	94 100	8 754	Lilongwe
Mali	1 240 142	9 214	Bamako
Mauritania	1 030 700	2 024	Nouakchott
Mauritius	1 865	1 082	Port Louis
Morocco	459 000	25 061	Rabat
Mozambique	784 961	15 656	Maputo
Namibia	824 293	1 781	Windhoek
Niger	1 267 000	7 731	Niamey
Nigeria	923 769	108 542	Abuja
Réunion (Fr.)	2 510	598	Saint-Denis
Rwanda	26 338	7 237	Kigali
São Tomé and Principe	964	121	São Tomé
Senegal	196 722	7 327	Dakar
Seychelles	443	69	Victoria
Sierra Leone	71 740	4 151	Freetown
Somalia	637 539	7 497	Muqdisho (Mogadishu)
South Africa	1 221 038	35 282	Pretoria/Cape Town
Sudan	2 505 792	25 203	Khartoum
Swaziland	17 366	788	Mbabane
Tanzania	942 000	27 318	Dodoma
Togo	56 785	3 531	Lomé
Tunisia	164 148	8 180	Tunis
Uganda	236 036	18 794	Kampala
Western Sahara	266 000	178	-
Zaire	2 344 885	35 568	Kinshasa
Zambia	752 617	8 452	Lusaka
Zimbabwe	390 308	9 709	Harare
Oceania			
American Samoa (USA)	197	38	Fagatogo
Australia	7 682 300	17 659	Canberra
Fiji	18 272	764	Suva
French Polynesia (Fr.)	4 198	206	Papeete
Guam (USA)	549	118	Agaña
Kiribati	800	66	Tarawa
Marshall Islands	181	40	Dalap-Uliga-Darrit
Nauru	21	9	Yaren
New Caledonia (Fr.)	19 104	167	Nouméa
New Zealand	268 675	3 450	Wellington
Niue (NZ)	259	3	Alofi
Federated States of Micronesia	1 300	99	Kolonia
Papua New Guinea	461 692	3 874	Port Moresby
Solomon Islands	29 785	320	Honiara
Tonga	699	95	Nuku'alofa
Tuvalu	25	9	Funafuti
Vanuatu	14 763	158	Vila
Western Samoa	2 831	168	Apai

This page explains the main symbols, lettering style and height/depth colours used on the reference maps on pages 2 to 79. The scale of each map is indicated at the top of each page. Abbreviations used on the maps appear at the beginning of the index.

BOUNDARIES

———————	International
— — — —	International under Dispute
· · · · · · · ·	Cease Fire Line
———————	Autonomous or State
———————	Administrative
— ·· — ·· —	Maritime (National)
— — — —	International Date Line

COMMUNICATIONS

———————	Motorway/Express Highway
=========	Under Construction
———————	Major Highway
———————	Other Roads
— — — —	Under Construction
· · · · · · · ·	Track
→===←	Road Tunnel
— — — —	Car Ferry
———————	Main Railway
———————	Other Railway
— — — —	Under Construction
→---←	Rail Tunnel
— — — —	Rail Ferry
—— +——+——	Canal
⊕	International Airport
✦	Other Airport

LAKE FEATURES

	Freshwater
	Saltwater
	Seasonal
	Salt Pan

LANDSCAPE FEATURES

	Glacier, Ice Cap
	Marsh, Swamp
	Sand Desert, Dunes

OTHER FEATURES

	River
	Seasonal River
≍	Pass, Gorge
	Dam, Barrage
	Waterfall, Rapid
	Aqueduct
	Reef
▲ 4231	Summit, Peak
· 217	Spot Height, Depth
⌣	Well
∆	Oil Field
▲	Gas Field
Gas / Oil	Oil/Natural Gas Pipeline
Gemsbok Nat. Pk	National Park
∴ UR	Historic Site

LETTERING STYLES

CANADA	Independent Nation
FLORIDA	State, Province or Autonomous Region
Gibraltar (U.K.)	Sovereignty of Dependent Territory
Lothian	Administrative Area
LANGUEDOC	Historic Region
Loire ***Vosges***	Physical Feature or Physical Region

TOWNS AND CITIES

Square symbols denote capital cities. Each settlement is given a symbol according to its relative importance, with type size to match.

▣	◉	**New York**	Major City
■	●	**Dallas**	City
▢	○	Memphis	Small City
■	●	Oakland	Large Town
□	○	Boise	Town
□	○	Durango	Small Town
□	○	Marshfield	Village
			Built-up-area

Height

| 6000m |
| 5000m |
| 4000m |
| 3000m |
| 2000m |
| 1000m |
| 500m |
| 200m |

0 — 0 Sea Level

| 200m |
| 2000m |
| 4000m |
| 6000m |
| 8000m |

Depth

1:35M

0 250 500 750 1000 1250 km
0 250 500 750 mls

③ RUS. FED. ② ① Ⓐ 170 160 150 140 130 120 110 100 90 80 70 60 50 40 30 20 10

Arctic Ocean

Ⓑ Ⓒ Ⓓ Ⓔ Ⓕ Ⓖ Ⓗ Ⓙ Ⓚ Ⓛ Ⓜ Ⓝ Ⓞ Ⓟ Ⓠ Ⓡ

Bering Strait
Bering Sea
Aleutian Islands

Beaufort Sea

Ellesmere I.
Thule

G R E E N L A N D
(KALAALLIT NUNAAT)
(Denmark)

Denmark Strait

ICELAND
Reykjavik

Queen Elizabeth Islands

Banks I.
Resolute
Devon I.

Baffin Bay
Baffin I.

Davis Strait

Godthåb (Nuuk)

A L A S K A
Yukon
Anchorage
Fairbanks
Juneau

Whitehorse
Alexander Arch.
Q. Charlotte Is
Prince Rupert
Prince George
Vancouver I.
Victoria
Vancouver
Seattle
Portland
Spokane
Butte

Great Bear L.
Mackenzie
Yellowknife
Hay River
Great Slave L.
Athabasca

C A N A D A

Churchill
Hudson Bay
Inukjuak

Southampton I.

Hudson Strait

Schefferville
Churchill Falls

James Bay
Moosonee

Sept-Iles
Anticosti I.
Newfoundland
St. John's

Edmonton
Calgary
Saskatoon
Regina
L. Winnipeg

Winnipeg
Thunder Bay
Fargo
Duluth
L. Superior
Sault Ste Marie

Québec
Moncton
Fredericton
Charlottetown
Halifax

San Francisco
Salt Lake City

U N I T E D   S T A T E S   O F   A M E R I C A

Minneapolis St Paul
Milwaukee
Chicago
L. Michigan
Omaha
Denver
Colorado
Kansas City

Detroit
L. Huron
L. Erie
Cleveland
Ontario
Toronto
Ottawa
Montréal
St. Lawrence

Buffalo
Boston
New York
Philadelphia
Baltimore
Washington

ATLANTIC OCEAN

Los Angeles
San Diego
Phoenix
Tucson

St Louis
Indianapolis
Ohio
Nashville
Norfolk

Missouri
Albuquerque
El Paso

Mississippi

Guadalupe (Mex.)

Tropic of Cancer

G. de California

M E X I C O

Dallas
Fort Worth
Birmingham
Memphis
Atlanta
Charleston

Bermuda (U.K)

San Antonio
Houston
New Orleans
Jacksonville
Tampa
Miami

Chihuahua
Rio Grande
Monterrey
Torreón
Mazatlán

Gulf of Mexico

THE BAHAMAS
Nassau

Habana
CUBA
Guantánamo

DOMINICAN REP.
Pto Rico (U.S.A.)
HAITI
Port-au-Prince
Sto Domingo

ANTIGUA & BARBUDA
DOMINICA
ST KITTS-NEVIS
ST LUCIA

Is Revilla Gigedo (Mex.)

Guadalajara
México
Veracruz
Tampico
Mérida

Acapulco

BELIZE
Belmopan
GUATEMALA
Guatemala
S.Salvador
EL SALVADOR

HONDURAS
Tegucigalpa

NICARAGUA
Managua

JAMAICA
Kingston

CARIBBEAN SEA

Netherlands Antilles

ST VINCENT & THE GRENADINES
GRENADA
TRINIDAD & TOBAGO

P A C I F I C   O C E A N

Clipperton (Fr.)

COSTA RICA
S.José
PANAMA
Panamá

Sta Marta
Barranquilla
Maracaibo
Caracas

VENEZUELA

I.del Coco (C.R)

Medellín
Bogotá
COLOMBIA

Malpelo (Col.)

Negro

Equator

Galapagos Is (Ecu.)

Quito
ECUADOR
PERU

BRAZIL

Ⓖ 110 Ⓗ 100 Ⓙ 90 Ⓚ 80 Ⓛ 70 Ⓜ

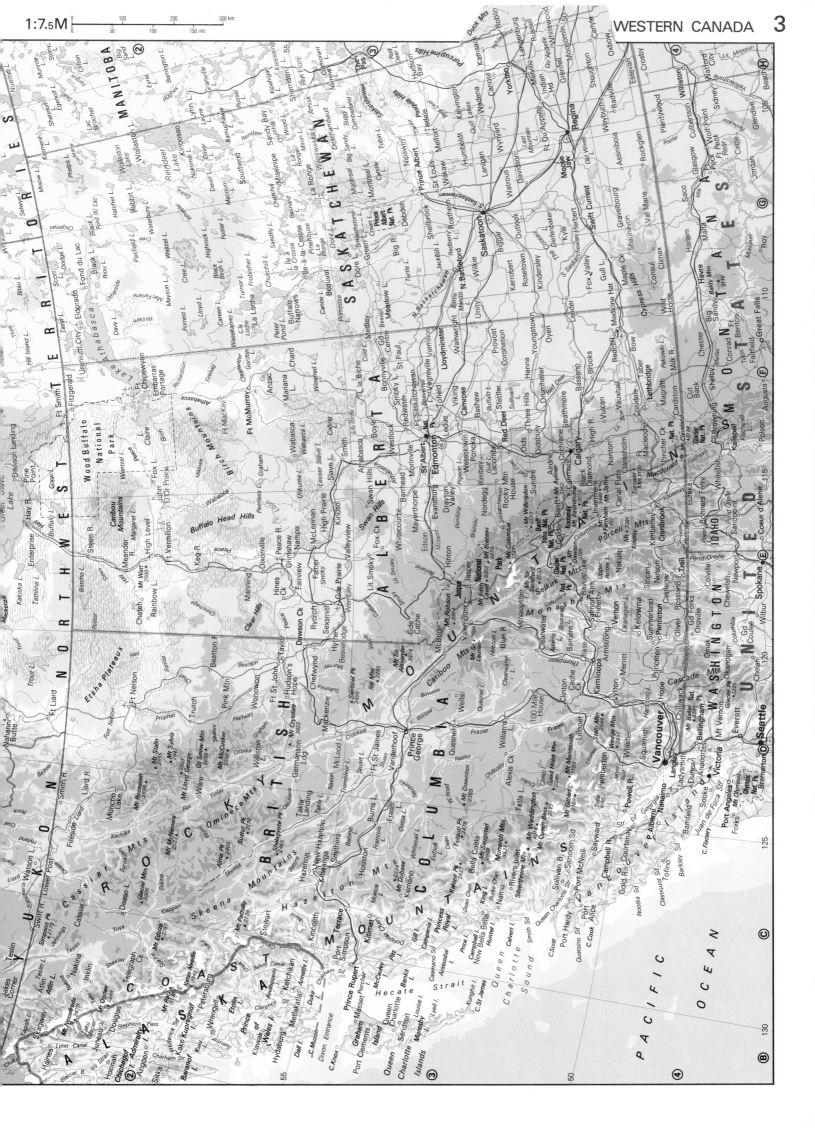

1:7.5M

100 · 95 · 90 · 85 · 80

Smith I.
Akulivik

HUDSON BAY

Povungnituk
Ottawa Is.
B. Kogaluc
Inukjuak
R. Innuksuac

Sleeper Islands
King George Islands
Belcher Islands
Nastapoka Islands

C. Churchill
Churchill
Cromarty
M'Clintock
Silcox
Port Nelson
Bird Nelson
York Factory
C. Tatnam
Kaskattama

MANITOBA

Brochet
Reindeer Lake
Goldsand L.
Wells L.
Southern Indian L.
Big Sand L.
N. Knife
S. Knife
Caribou
Seal
Tadoule L.
Churchill

Lynn Lake
Russell L.
Sipiwesk L.
S. Seal
Northern Indian L.
High Hill
Stupart
Hayes
Gods
Shamattawa

Pukatawagan
Highrock
Thompson
Ilford
Arnot
Niskibi
Beaver
Fort Severn
Winisk

Sherridon
Thicket Portage
Sipiwesk L.
Split L.
Kettle
Black Duck
Fawn
Severn
Winisk

Flin Flon
Wekusko
Cormorant
The Pas
Cedar Lake
Grand Rapids
Easterville
Lake Winnipegosis

Polar Bear Provincial Park
Winisk
Sutton
C. Henrietta Maria
Lake River
Kuujjuarapik
Long Island
Pointe Louis XIV

ONTARIO

Bearskin Lake
Big Trout Lake
Big Trout L.
Shibogama L.
Sandy Lake
Opasquia
Cobham
Sachigo L.
Wunnummin L.
Winisk L.
Attawapiskat
Ekwan
Opinnagau

James Bay
N. Twin I.
S. Twin I.
Akimiski Island
C. Duncan
Fort Albany
Chisasibi
Radisson
La Grande Résr. 2
Eastmain
Wemindji

Cat Lake
Pickle Lake
Lansdowne House
Attawapiskat L.
Kapiskau
Albany
Ogoki
Charlton Island
Hannah Bay
Moosonee
Waskaganish
Rupert

Red Lake
Goldpines
Sioux Lookout
Savant Lake
Lac Seul
Albany
Fort Hope
Ogoki
Little Current
Chipie
Strooping
Eastmain

Lake Winnipeg
Berens River
Little Grand Rapids
Pikangikum
Sandy L.
Trout L.
Ebamet L.
Miminiska L.
Fawcett L.

Portage la Prairie
Winnipeg
St. Boniface
Steinbach
Selkirk
Beausejour
Whiteshell Prov. Park
Minaki
Keewatin
Kenora
Lake of the Woods
Sioux Narrows
Fort Frances
Emerson
Roseau

Dryden
Ignace
Sesaganaga
Savant Lake
Nakina
Auden
Lynx
Pagwa River
Kenogami
Missinaibi
Otter Rapids
Kesagami L.
Kitchigama

Lake Nipigon
Geraldton
Longlac
Hearst
Mattice
Kapuskasing
Opasatika
Groundhog
Cochrane
Driftwood
Iroquois Falls
L. Abitibi
Amos
Barraute
Senneterre

Thunder Bay
Nipigon
Schreiber
Coldwell
White River
Franz
Elsas
Timmins
Foleyet
Matheson
Kirkland Lake
Noranda
Rouyn
Val d'Or

Quetico Provincial Park
International Falls
Rainy L.
Atikokan
Heron Bay
Pukaskwa Nat. Park
Wawa
Lake Superior Provincial Park
Chapleau
Gogama
New Liskeard
Cobalt
Temiscaming

LAKE SUPERIOR
Isle Royale
Copper Harbor
Keweenaw Pen.
Keweenaw B.
Michipicoten
Sault Ste. Marie
Sault Ste. Marie
Espanola
Sudbury
North Bay

MINNESOTA
Duluth
Superior
Bemidji
Grand Rapids
Hibbing
Virginia
Ely
Grand Marais
Two Harbors
Ashland
Ironwood
Marquette

Moorhead
Detroit Lakes
Brainerd
Little Falls
St. Cloud
Minneapolis
St. Paul
Bloomington

WISCONSIN
Eau Claire
Wausau
Green Bay
Appleton
Oshkosh
Madison
Milwaukee
Racine
Kenosha

MICHIGAN
LAKE MICHIGAN
Menominee
Marinette
Escanaba
Manistique
St. Ignace
Mackinaw City
Cheboygan
Petoskey
Traverse City
Cadillac
Ludington
Muskegon
Grand Rapids
Lansing
Flint
Detroit
Ann Arbor

LAKE HURON
Georgian Bay
Manitoulin
Tobermory
Owen Sound
Collingwood
Barrie
Orillia
Midland

Algonquin Prov. Park
Pembroke
Renfrew
Arnprior
Ottawa
Hull
Mont-Laurier

IOWA
Des Moines
Cedar Rapids
Iowa City
Davenport
Dubuque

ILLINOIS
Rockford
Chicago
Joliet
Gary
Peoria

UNITED STATES

LAKE ERIE
Toledo
Cleveland
Sandusky
Erie
Sarnia
London
St. Thomas
Chatham
Windsor
Detroit

LAKE ONTARIO
Toronto
Hamilton
Burlington
Oakville
St. Catharines
Niagara Falls
Buffalo
Rochester
Syracuse
Kitchener
Guelph
Oshawa
Whitby
Cobourg
Trenton
Kingston
Belleville
Peterborough
Brockville

NEW YORK
Watertown
Oswego
Geneva
Binghamton
Elmira

1:15M

200   400   600 km
100   200   300 mls

ARCTIC OCEAN

BEAUFORT SEA

PACIFIC OCEAN

Gulf of Alaska

BERING SEA

RUS. FED.

ALASKA

YUKON TERRITORY

NORTHWEST TERRITORIES

BRITISH COLUMBIA

ALBERTA

SASKATCHEWAN

MANITOBA

Banks Island

Victoria Island

Kitikmeot

Prince of Wales Island

Parry Islands

Melville Island

Aleutian Ra.

Kodiak Island

Queen Charlotte Islands

Vancouver Island

WASHINGTON

OREGON

IDAHO

MONTANA

WYOMING

NORTH DAKOTA

SOUTH DAKOTA

U. S.

ROCKY MOUNTAINS

Mackenzie Mountains

Selwyn Mountains

Brooks Range

Alaska Range

Caribou Mountains

Great Bear Lake

Great Slave Lake

Lake Athabasca

Reindeer Lake

Wollaston Lake

Anchorage

Fairbanks

Whitehorse

Dawson

Yellowknife

Fort Smith

Edmonton

Calgary

Red Deer

Saskatoon

Regina

Winnipeg

Prince Albert

Vancouver

Victoria

Seattle

Tacoma

Olympia

Portland

Salem

Spokane

Boise

Helena

Great Falls

Billings

Bismarck

Pierre

Wood Buffalo Nat. Pk.

Names underlined indicate Province/State capitals

1:12.5M

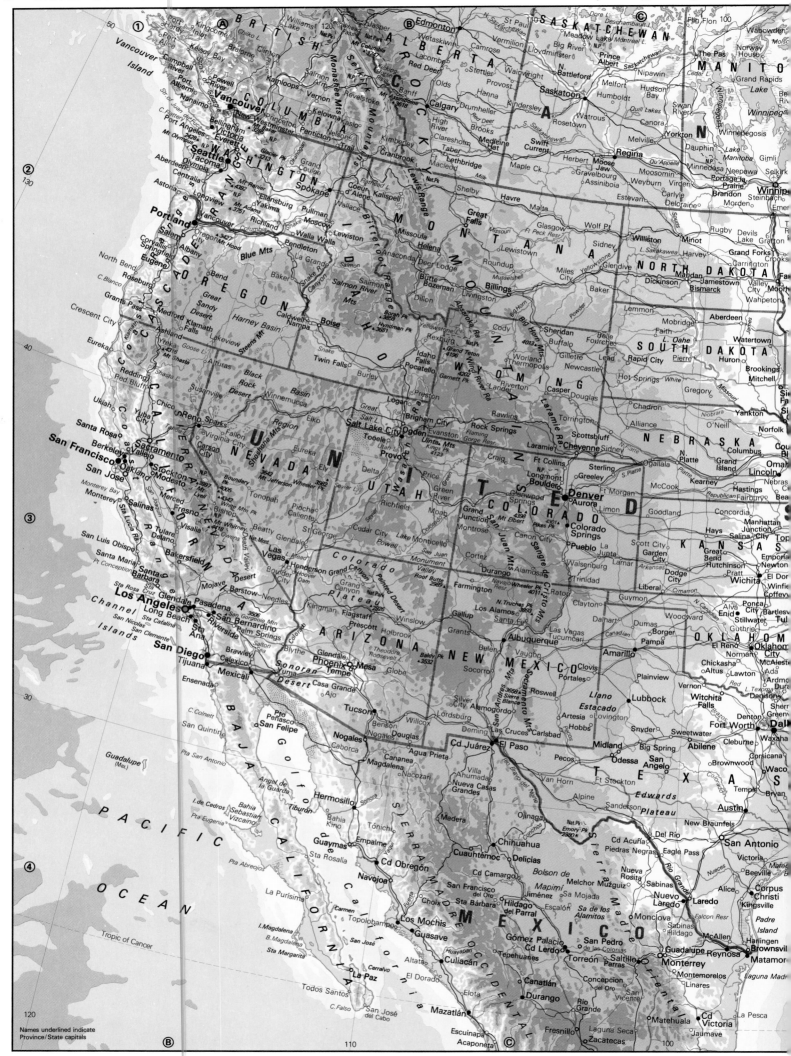

1:10M

100 200 300 400 km
100 200 mls

RUSSIAN FEDERATION

Beaufort Sea

NORTH WEST TERRITORIES

Melville Hills

YUKON TERRITORY

Mackenzie Mountains

BRITISH COLUMBIA

Brooks Range

North Slope

Arctic Ocean

Chukchi Sea

Bering Strait

Seward Peninsula

Norton Sound

Bering Sea

Gulf of Alaska

Alexander Archipelago

Aleutian Islands

Near Islands

Rat Islands

Fox Islands

Shumagin Islands

Kodiak I.

Fairbanks

Anchorage

Cook Inlet

Bristol Bay

Kuskokwim Mts

Alaska Range

Wrangell Mts

Chugach Mountains

St Elias Mountains

Trans Alaska Pipeline

Nome

Barrow

Prudhoe Bay

Nunivak I.

St Lawrence I.

Pribilof Is
St Paul
St George

Kenai Peninsula

Unimak I.

Unalaska

1:5M

50 100 150 200 km
50 100 mls

States/Provinces: ONTARIO, MANITOBA, SASKATCHEWAN, MINNESOTA, WISCONSIN, IOWA, NORTH DAKOTA, SOUTH DAKOTA, NEBRASKA, MONTANA, WYOMING

Water bodies: L. SUPERIOR, Lake of the Woods, Lake Winnipeg, Lake Manitoba, Lake Sakakawea, Lake Oahe, Fort Peck Reservoir, Upper Red L., Lower Red L., Leech L., Mille Lacs L., Devils Lake

Major cities: Thunder Bay, Winnipeg, St Boniface, Regina, Duluth, Superior, Minneapolis, St Paul, Bloomington, Fargo, Moorhead, Bismarck, Mandan, Sioux Falls, Sioux City, Des Moines, Rapid City, Dubuque, Davenport, Rock Island, Cedar Rapids

Other place names (selected):
Kenora, Dryden, Sioux Lookout, Savant Lake, Atikokan, Fort Frances, International Falls, Baudette, Warroad, Bemidji, Grand Rapids, Hibbing, Virginia, Two Harbors, Ashland, Hayward, Chippewa Falls, Eau Claire, Menomonie, La Crosse, Winona, Rochester, Austin, Albert Lea, Mason City, Waterloo, Marshalltown, Ames, Boone, Fort Dodge, Spencer, Storm Lake, Le Mars, Cherokee, Orange City, Yankton, Norfolk, Vermillion, Crofton, O'Neill, Valentine, Ainsworth, Chadron, Alliance, Scottsbluff, Gering, Bridgeport, Torrington, Douglas, Casper, Sheridan, Buffalo, Gillette, Newcastle, Lusk, Spearfish, Lead, Deadwood, Custer, Hot Springs, Edgemont, Pierre, Fort Pierre, Chamberlain, Mitchell, Huron, Aberdeen, Watertown, Brookings, Madison, Redfield, Miller, Gettysburg, Mobridge, Eagle Butte, Faith, Lemmon, Bowman, Dickinson, Hettinger, Williston, New Town, Minot, Devils Lake, Grand Forks, Crookston, Detroit Lakes, Fergus Falls, Alexandria, St Cloud, Brainerd, Willmar, Mankato, New Ulm, Marshall, Worthington, Fairmont, Jackson, Windom, Pipestone, Luverne

Montana towns: Wolf Point, Glasgow, Malta, Glendive, Miles City, Forsyth, Hardin, Ashland, Broadus, Baker, Ekalaka

Saskatchewan: Moose Jaw, Swift Current, Weyburn, Estevan, Assiniboia

Wyoming: Medicine Bow Pk. 3661, Laramie Mts, Bighorn Mts, Cloud Peak 4016

National Parks: Voyageurs Nat. Pk., Riding Mountain Nat. Park, Wind Cave Nat. Pk.

50   100   150   200 km
50   100 mls

Major labels and regions:

LAKE SUPERIOR

MINNESOTA

WISCONSIN

MICHIGAN

LAKE MICHIGAN

LAKE HURON

ONTARIO

CANADA

IOWA

ILLINOIS

INDIANA

OHIO

MISSOURI

KENTUCKY

TENNESSEE

ARKANSAS

WEST VIRGINIA

CUMBERLAND PLATEAU

ALLEGHENY

Georgian Bay

LAKE ERIE

Selected place names:

Littlefork, Pelican L., Little Fork, Chisholm, Keewatin, Hibbing, Buhl, Babbitt, Virginia, Birch L., Ely, Kakabeka Falls, Thunder Bay, Pie I., Isle Royale Nat. Pk., Nipigon, Nipigon B., Schreiber, St Ignace I., Terrace Bay, Marathon, White River, Wabatongushi L., Kabinakagami L., Timmins, S. Porcupine, Nighthawk L., Iroquois Falls, Ansonville

Grand Rapids, Hoyt, Floodwood, Silver Bay, Apostle Is., Duluth, Superior, Cloquet, Proctor, Two Harbors, Bayfield, Washburn, Ashland, Grand Marais, Michipicoten I., Michipicoten, Wawa, Manitowik L., Coppermine Pt., Bathawana Mtn 653, Rocky I. L., Onaping, L. Temagami

Moose Lake, Sandstone, Hinckley, Mora, Pine City, Cambridge, Spooner, Hayward, Glidden, Chequamegon, Bessemer, Wakefield, Ironwood, Watersmeet, Iron River, Marquette, Munising, Keweenaw Pen., Copper Harbor, Houghton, Hancock, Keweenaw Bay, Whitefish Pt., Sault Ste Marie, Echo Bay, Thessalon, Blind River, Webbwood, Elliot Lake, Massey, Espanola, Copper Cliff, Sudbury, Conisto

St Paul, Hastings, Red Wing, Lake City, Zumbrota, Rochester, Stewartville, Winona, Onalaska, La Crosse, Sparta, Tomah, Wisconsin Rapids, Stevens Point, Wausau, Mosinee, Merrill, Antigo, Shawano, Green Bay, Marinette, Menominee, Escanaba, Gladstone, Manistique, Straits of Mackinac, St Ignace, Cheboygan, Bois Blanc I., Beaver I., Petoskey, Charlevoix, Rogers City, Gaylord, Atlanta, Harrisville, Tobermory, Manitoulin I., Wiarton, Owen Sound, Southampton, Port Elgin

St Paul, Dubuque, Madison, Milwaukee, Waukesha, Racine, Kenosha, Rockford, Chicago, Oak Lawn, Gary, Hammond, Joliet, Aurora, Elgin, Evanston, Waukegan, Grand Rapids, Holland, Muskegon, Kalamazoo, Battle Creek, Lansing, Flint, Detroit, Windsor, Sarnia, London, Kitchener, Stratford, Woodstock, Ingersoll

Cedar Rapids, Iowa City, Davenport, Rock Island, Moline, Clinton, Galesburg, Peoria, Bloomington, Champaign, Urbana, Danville, Lafayette, Frankfort, Kokomo, Marion, Fort Wayne, Muncie, Anderson, Toledo, Cleveland, Akron, Canton, Youngstown, Warren, Mansfield

Indianapolis, Terre Haute, Columbus, Dayton, Springfield, Cincinnati, Columbus, Zanesville, Newark, Marietta, Parkersburg, Clarksburg

St Louis, East St Louis, Belleville, Collinsville, Alton, Vandalia, Effingham, Mt Vernon, Vincennes, Evansville, Owensboro, Henderson, Bowling Green, Louisville, Jeffersonville, New Albany, Lexington, Frankfort, Ashland, Huntington, Charleston, St Albans

Cape Girardeau, Paducah, Mayfield, Fulton, Murray, Clarksville, Nashville, Hendersonville, Lebanon, Cookeville, Mammoth Cave Nat. Pk., Glasgow, Campbellsville, Somerset, Corbin, Middlesboro, Kingsport, Bristol, Johnson City, Elizabethton, Mt Rogers 1743

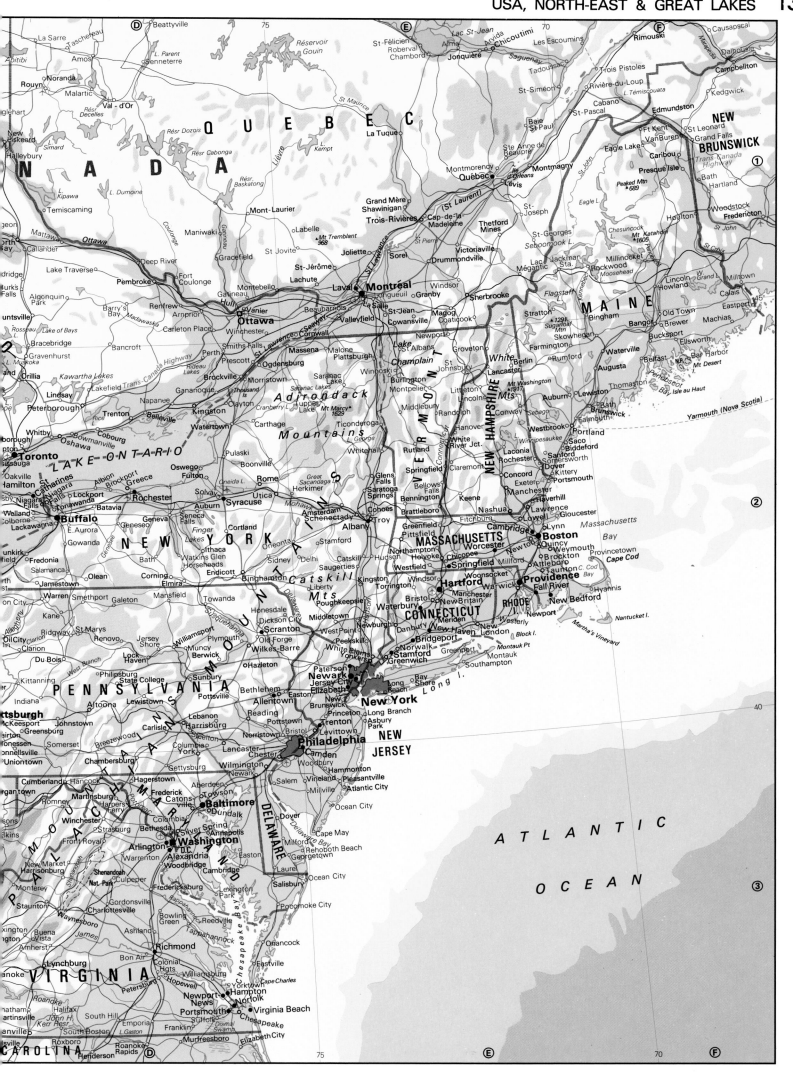

1:2.5M

0 25 50 75 100 km
0 25 50 mils

A T L A N T I C   O C E A N

NEW HAMPSHIRE
VERMONT
MASSACHUSETTS
CONNECTICUT
RHODE ISLAND
NEW YORK
PENNSYLVANIA
NEW JERSEY
DELAWARE
MARYLAND
VIRGINIA
W. VIRGINIA

Boston
Cambridge
Providence
Worcester
Springfield
Hartford
New Haven
Bridgeport
Stamford
New York
Newark
Jersey City
Elizabeth
Paterson
Yonkers
Albany
Schenectady
Troy
Syracuse
Rochester
Buffalo
Utica
Binghamton
Scranton
Wilkes-Barre
Harrisburg
Philadelphia
Camden
Trenton
Allentown
Bethlehem
Reading
Lancaster
York
Baltimore
Washington
Arlington
Annapolis
Atlantic City
New Bedford
Fall River
Pawtucket

Cape Cod
Cape Cod Bay
Nantucket Island
Martha's Vineyard
Long Island
Long Island Sound
Block Island
Lake Ontario
Lake Erie
Finger Lakes
Catskill Mountains
Adirondack
Chesapeake Bay
Delaware Bay
Cape May
Montauk

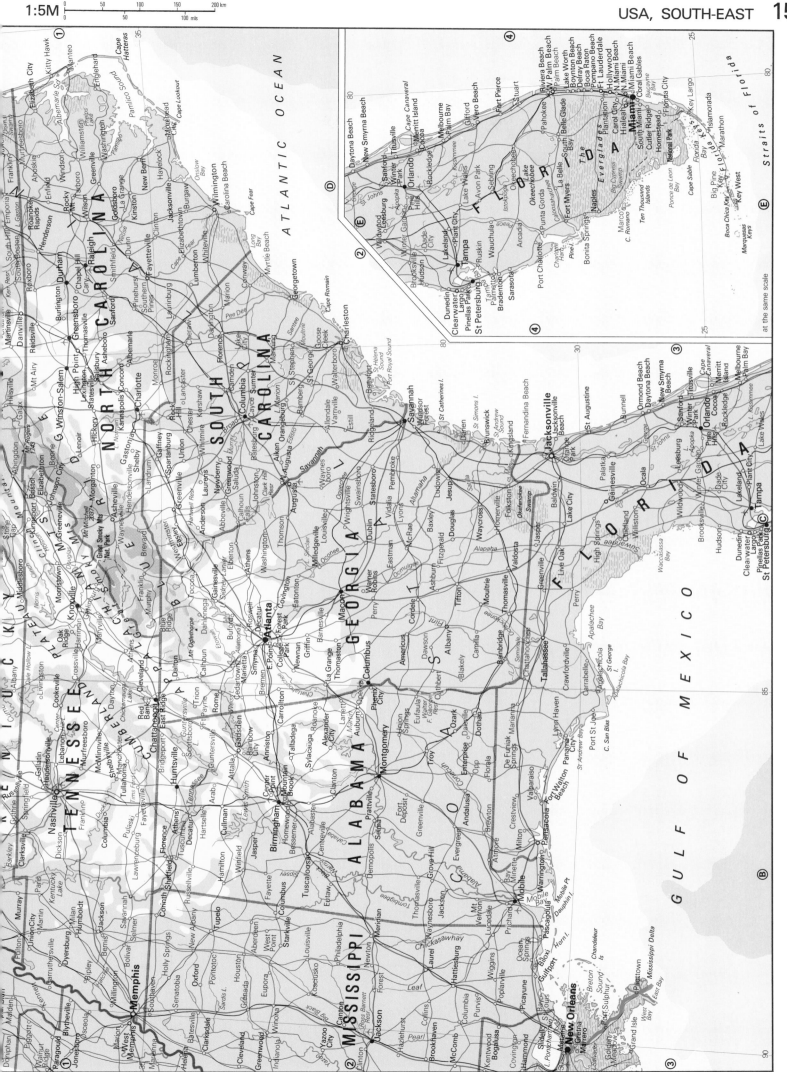

Scale: 0 50 100 150 200 km / 0 50 100 mls

States and regions: COLORADO, NEW MEXICO, NEBRASKA, KANSAS, OKLAHOMA, TEXAS, MEXICO, CHIHUAHUA, COAHUILA

Mountains and features: Uinta Mts, Roan Plateau, Medicine Bow Mts, Sangre de Cristo Mts, San Juan Mts, Uncompahgre Plateau, Sawatch Mts, Sacramento Mts, San Andres Mts, Abajo Mts, Zuni Mts, Llano Estacado, Red Hills, Smoky Hills, Edwards Plateau, PLATEAU

Peaks:
- Kings Peak 4114
- Medicine Bow Pk 3661
- Bridger Peak 3662
- Longs Peak 4345
- Mt Evans 4348
- Mt Elbert 4399
- Mt Harvard 4378
- Pikes Peak 4301
- Mt Peale 3857
- Mt Wilson 4342
- Blanca Peak 4364
- Wheeler Peak 4011
- Mt Taylor 3444
- South Baldy 3288
- Salinas Peak
- Animas Peak 2597
- Guadalupe Pk 2667
- Mt Livermore 2554
- Chinati Pk 2357
- Emory Pk 2389

Major cities: Denver, Aurora, Englewood, Lakewood, Littleton, Colorado Springs, Pueblo, Boulder, Fort Collins, Cheyenne, Laramie, Grand Junction, Albuquerque, Santa Fe, Amarillo, Lubbock, El Paso, Ciudad Juárez, Odessa, Midland, Abilene, San Angelo, Grand Island, Dodge City, Garden City, North Platte, Chihuahua

Colorado towns: Manila, Vernal, Roosevelt, Dinosaur, Rangely, Meeker, Craig, Hayden, Steamboat Springs, Kremmling, Granby, Idaho Springs, Estes Park, Loveland, Longmont, Greeley, Lafayette, Arvada, Byers, Eagle, Minturn, Leadville, Buena Vista, Salida, Canon City, Florence, Castle Rock, Simla, Limon, Burlington, Mack, Fruita, Grand Valley, Rifle, Glenwood Springs, Palisade, Delta, Montrose, Gunnison, Saguache, Monte Vista, Alamosa, Walsenburg, Trinidad, Las Animas, Lamar, La Junta, Rocky Ford, Ordway, Boone, Fowler, Wiley, Holly, Springfield, Ouray, Silverton, Durango, Cortez, Dove Creek, Monticello, Blanding, Bluff, Mexican Hat, Shiprock, Pagosa Springs, South Fork, Wolf Creek Pass, Tennessee Pass, Monarch Pass, Berthoud Pass, Loveland Pass, Fall River Pass, Fort Morgan, Brush, Otis, Sterling, Holyoke, Wray, Cope, Arikaree, Kit Carson, Cheyenne Wells

New Mexico towns: Raton, Des Moines, Clayton, Springer, Cimarron, Taos, Caliente, Canjilon, Tierra Amarilla, Chama, Aztec, Bloomfield, Farmington, Gallup, Thoreau, Grants, Zuni, Laguna, Bernalillo, Los Lunas, Belen, Moriarty, Santa Rosa, Newkirk, Tucumcari, San Jon, Logan, Vaughn, Corona, Fort Sumner, Clovis, Portales, Hereford, Friona, Roswell, Dexter, Hondo, Carrizozo, Tularosa, Alamogordo, Mayhill, Artesia, Hobbs, Lovington, Tatum, Kenna, Socorro, San Antonio, Truth or Consequences, Magdalena, Polvadera, Glenwood, Alpine, Springerville, Quemado, Hillsboro, Silver City, Tyrone, Central, Bayard, Lordsburg, Deming, Las Cruces, University Park, Anthony, Columbus, Fairacres, Malaga, Carlsbad, Eunice, Jal, Espanola, Los Alamos, Jemez Pueblo, Las Vegas, Watrous, Mosquero, St Johns, Ganado, Tohatchi, Menmore, Ft Wingate

Nebraska/Kansas towns: Broadwater, Oshkosh, Stapleton, Broken Bow, Ansley, St Paul, Kimball, Sidney, Potter, Paxton, Sutherland, Gothenburg, Cozad, Lexington, Kearney, Gibbon, Hastings, Ogallala, Big Springs, Maywood, Arapahoe, Holdrege, Alma, Red Cloud, Chappell, Ovid, Julesburg, Imperial, McCook, Culbertson, Benkelman, Oberlin, Norton, Phillipsburg, Lebanon, St Francis, Colby, Hill City, Stockton, Russell, Hays, WaKeeney, Goodland, Oakley, Scott City, Tribune, Syracuse, Lakin, Ulysses, Hugoton, Liberal, Meade, Ashland, Medicine Lodge, Greensburg, Pratt, Lewis, Kinsley, Larned, Jetmore, Ness City, Great Bend, Montezuma, Plains

Oklahoma/Texas Panhandle: Boise City, Hooker, Guymon, Texhoma, Forgan, Fort Supply, Cherokee, Alva, Stratford, Dalhart, Hartley, Dumas, Cactus, Stinnett, Borger, Spearman, Perryton, Woodward, Fairview, Seiling, Arnett, Canadian, Pampa, Panhandle, Canyon, Hereford, Vega, Adrian, Groom, Shamrock, Wellington, Memphis, Childress, Quanah, Mangum, Hollis, Altus, Frederick, Hobart, Lawton, Clinton, Anadarko, Weatherford, Sayre

Texas towns: Farwell, Muleshoe, Earth, Littlefield, Plainview, Morton, Levelland, Brownfield, Seminole, Andrews, Tatum, Floydada, Dickens, Guthrie, Paducah, Vernon, Seymour, Olney, Jacksboro, Haskell, Stamford, Anson, Breckenridge, Post, Tahoka, Lamesa, Snyder, Aspermont, Colorado City, Sweetwater, Merkel, Abilene, Cisco, Stephenville, Brownwood, Goldthwaite, Eden, Brady, Mason, Llano, San Saba, Lampasas, Big Spring, Midland, Odessa, Kermit, Monahans, Crane, Pecos, McCamey, Big Lake, Barnhart, Eldorado, Sonora, Ozona, Sterling City, San Angelo, Ballinger, Coleman, Santa Anna, Comanche, Van Horn, Kent, Toyah, Balmorhea, Fort Stockton, Sheffield, Sanderson, Marathon, Alpine, Marfa, Valentine, Sierra Blanca, Fort Hancock, Fort Davis, Langtry, Del Rio, Rocksprings, Junction, Kerrville, Comfort, Leakey, Uvalde, Brackettville, Eagle Pass

Mexico towns: Nueva Casas Grandes, Buenaventura, Madera, Matachic, Galeana, El Sueco, Gallego, Aldama, Ojinaga, Presidio, Boquillas, Manuel Benavides, San Antonio de Bravo, Villa Ahumada, Guadalupe, El Porvenir, Lucero, Senecu, Ciudad Acuña, Jiménez, Amistad Resr, Big Bend Nat. Park

Rivers and water features: Green River, White, Yampa, Colorado, Gunnison, Dolores, Animas, San Juan, Rio Grande, Pecos, Canadian, N. Canadian, Arkansas, Purgatoire, Smoky, Saline, Republican, S. Platte, Platte, Red, Wichita, Double Mtn Fork, Prairie Dog Town Fork, Rio Bravo del Norte, Conchos, Flaming Gorge Resr, Navajo Resr, Elephant Butte Resr, Caballo Resr, John Martin Resr, Conchas L., Meredith L., L. McMillan, Red Bluff L., Lag. de Guzmán, Lag. de Sta Maria, Twin Buttes Resr, L. Buchanan, Amistad Resr

National Parks: Rocky Mtn Nat. Park, Mesa Verde N.P., Carlsbad Caverns N.P., Guadalupe Mtns N.P., Big Bend Nat. Park

Grid references: ① ② ③ ④ (left margin), Ⓐ Ⓑ (top and bottom)

Longitude/latitude marks: 110, 105, 100 / 40, 35, 30

TEXAS

MISSOURI

KENTUCKY

TENNESSEE

OKLAHOMA

ARKANSAS

MISSISSIPPI

ALABAMA

LOUISIANA

Boston Mts

Ouachita Mts

Plateau

Major cities: Omaha, Council Bluffs, Lincoln, Des Moines, Kansas City, Independence, Topeka, Lawrence, Wichita, Tulsa, Oklahoma City, Springfield, St Louis, Little Rock, Fort Smith, Memphis, Nashville, Dallas, Fort Worth, Houston, Shreveport, Jackson, Baton Rouge, New Orleans, Birmingham, Tuscaloosa, Mobile, Pensacola, San Antonio, Corpus Christi, Brownsville, Matamoros, Laredo, Nuevo Laredo, Reynosa, Evansville, Owensboro, Bowling Green

Rio Grande / Rio Bravo del Norte

L. Corpus Christi

Baffin Bay

Laguna Madre

Matagorda I.

Gulf of Mexico

Mississippi Delta

at the same scale

1:2.5M

25   50   75   100 km
25   50 mls

NEVADA

PACIFIC OCEAN

SIERRA NEVADA

San Francisco
Oakland
Berkeley
Sacramento
Stockton
Modesto
San Jose
Fresno
Santa Cruz
Monterey
Bakersfield
San Luis Obispo
Santa Barbara
Los Angeles
Long Beach
San Diego

Yosemite National Park
Kings Canyon National Park
Sequoia National Park
Death Valley National Monume
Mojave Desert

Mt Whitney 4418

COAST RANGES
Santa Lucia Range
Gabilan Ra.
San Joaquin Valley
Temblor Range
Santa Ynez Mts
San Gabriel Mts

Channel Islands
San Miguel, Santa Rosa, Santa Cruz, Anacapa Is
Santa Catalina
San Clemente

USA, HAWAII

1:5M

50   100   150   200 km
50   100 mls

Kauai
Hanalei, Kapaa, Lihue, Koloa
Niihau
Oahu
Honolulu, Waialua, Wahiawa, Kaneohe, Kailua, Pearl City, Nanakuli
Molokai, Kaunakakai
Lanai, Lanai City
Maui, Wailuku, Kahului, Hana, Haleakala Nat. Pk. 3055
Kahoolawe
Hawaii, Hilo, Kailua, Waimea, Mauna Kea 4201, Mauna Loa 4169, Kilauea Crater, Hawaii Volcanoes Nat. Park, Naalehu

PACIFIC OCEAN

1:15M

200 400 600 km
100 200 300 mls

THE BAHAMAS

CUBA

Habana (Havana)

CARIBBEAN SEA

JAMAICA

GULF OF MEXICO

M E X I C O

Bahía de Campeche

UNITED STATES

TEXAS

FLORIDA

GEORGIA

ALABAMA

MISSISSIPPI

LOUISIANA

OKLAHOMA

NEW MEXICO

ARIZONA

New Orleans

Dallas

Houston

Monterrey

Guadalajara

México

Yucatan

BELIZE

GUATEMALA

EL SALVADOR

HONDURAS

NICARAGUA

COSTA RICA

PANAMA

Golfo de Panamá

PACIFIC OCEAN

Baja California

Golfo de California

Sierra Madre Occidental

Sierra Madre Oriental

Sierra Madre del Sur

Tropic of Cancer

GULF OF MEXICO

Bahia de Campeche

Golfo de Tehuantepec

Tropic of Cancer

DURANGO

ZACATECAS

SAN LUIS POTOSI

NUEVO LEON

TAMAULIPAS

JALISCO

GUANAJUATO

QUERETARO

HIDALGO

MICHOACAN

COLIMA

GUERRERO

MORELOS

TLAXCALA

PUEBLA

VERACRUZ

OAXACA

TABASCO

México F.D.

Guadalajara

Monterrey

Durango

Zacatecas

San Luis Potosí

Aguascalientes

León

Morelia

Querétaro

Pachuca

Toluca

Cuernavaca

Puebla

Veracruz

Jalapa

Orizaba

Córdoba

Oaxaca

Acapulco

Tampico

Cd Madero

Cd Victoria

Poza Rica

Coatzacoalcos

Minatitlán

Tuxtla Gutiérrez

Mazatlán

Tepic

Colima

Manzanillo

Sierra Madre Oriental

Sierra Madre Occidental

Sierra Madre del Sur

Rio Grande de Santiago

1:10M

100 200 300 400 km
100 200 mls

DOMINICA 1:2.5 M
C. Melville
Portsmouth
Rosalie
Roseau

BARBADOS 1:2.5 M
North Pt
Speightstown
Holetown
Bridgetown
Blackman's
Ragged Pt
South Pt
Mt Hillaby 340

ST. LUCIA 1:2.5 M
Gros Islet Cap Pt
Castries
Soufrière 950
Vieux Fort C. Moule
à Chique
Dennery

ST. VINCENT 1:2.5 M
Porter Pt
Georgetown
Soufrière 1234
Barrouallie
Kingstown
Johnston Pt

GRENADA 1:2.5 M
Bedford Pt
Sauteurs
Mt St Catherine 840
St
George's
Grenville
Prickly Pt
Pt Salines

Pt of Spain
San Juan
Arima
Tunapuña
Princes Town
Upper Manzanilla
San Fernando
Point Fortin
Fullarton
Galera Pt
Matura Bay
Pt Radix
St Joseph
Galeota Pt
Mt Aripo 940
Northern Range
Guayaguayare
Moruga
Debé
Siparia
Río Claro
Chaguanas
Chupara Pt
Matelot
Cocos Bay
Gulf of Paria
Guava

Speyside
Crown
Pt
Scarborough
Canaan

JAMAICA
Montego Bay
Port Antonio
Annotto Bay
Morant Pt
Morant Bay
Kingston
Port Royal
Spanish Town
Blue Mtn Pk 2256
Blue Mts
St Ann's Bay
Ocho Rios
Moneague
Chapelton
May Pen
Salt River
Mandeville
Mt Denham 966
Dry Harbour Mts
Cambridge
The Cockpit Country
Wakefield
Falmouth
Black River
Southfield
Long Bay
Portland Pt
Portland Bight
Savanna la Mar
Negril
S. Negril Point
Galina Pt

Miami
Naples
Key West
Marquesas Keys
Florida Keys
Florida Bay
FLORIDA
Glade
L. Worth
Delray Beach
Pompano Beach
Hollywood
Ft. Lauderdale
Freeport
Marsh Harbour
Great Abaco
Nicholl's Town
New Providence
Nassau
Dunmore Town
Eleuthera
Cat
Andros
Great Bahama Bank
Kemps Bay
Great Exuma
Anguilla Cays
Cay Sal
Cay Sal Bank
Straits of Florida
Tropic of Cancer
Havana
Habana
Guanabacoa
S. Antonio de los Baños
Güines
Matanzas
Cárdenas
Cienfuegos
Santa Clara
Sagua la Grande
Pinar del Río
C. San Antonio
G. de Batabanó
Nueva Gerona
I. de la Juventud
(I. de Pinos)
CUBA
Moron
Ciego de Avila
Jardines de la Reina
Sta Cruz del Sur
Camagüey
Victoria de las Tunas
Nuevitas
Esmeralda
Arch. de Camagüey
Banes
Holguín
Santiago de Cuba
Manzanillo
Bayamo
Palma Soriano
Sagua de Tánamo
Baracoa
G. de Guacanayabo
C. Cruz
Swan I. (Hond.)
Cayman Brac
Grand Cayman
Little Cayman
Cayman Islands (U.K.)

THE BAHAMAS
New Bight
Cat
Long
Great Exuma
Rum Cay
San Salvador
Deadman's Cay
Acklins
Crooked
Mayaguana
Caicos Is (U.K.)
Turks Is. (U.K.)
Lt. Inagua
Great Inagua
Matthew Town

ATLANTIC OCEAN

Cap-Haïtien
Port-de-Paix
Môle St Nicolas
Monte Cristi
Puerto Plata
Santiago
S. Francisco
Pico Duarte 3175
Cordillera Central
HAITI
I. de la Gonâve
Port-au-Prince
La Selle 2660
Jacmel
Les Cayes
Massif de la Hotte
Anse d'Hainault
Jérémie
Miragoâne
Gonaïves
St-Marc
DOMINICAN REPUBLIC
Santo Domingo
San Cristóbal
La Romana
C. Beata
I. Beata
Samaná
Miches
Hispaniola

Windward Passage
Windward Passage

JAMAICA
Montego Bay
Savanna la Mar
Mandeville
Spanish Town
Kingston
Port Antonio
Blue Mts 2256
Pedro Cays (Jam.)

PUERTO RICO (U.S.A.)
San Juan
Arecibo
Aguadilla
Mayagüez
Ponce
Caguas
Mona Passage
Humacao
Guayama

Virgin Is. (U.S.A. & U.K.)
St Croix (U.S.A.)
Anguilla (U.K.)
St Martin (Fr. & Neth.)
St. Barthélémy

ANTIGUA & BARBUDA
St Kitts
Nevis
Montserrat (U.K.)
Guadeloupe (Fr.)
Basse Terre
Pointe-à-Pitre
Marie Galante
DOMINICA
Roseau
Martinique (Fr.)
Fort-de-France
ST LUCIA
Castries
ST VINCENT & THE GRENADINES
Kingstown
GRENADA
St George's
BARBADOS
Bridgetown

TRINIDAD AND TOBAGO
Tobago
Scarborough
Port of Spain
Trinidad
San Fernando

Leeward Islands
Windward Islands
Lesser Antilles

Los Testigos
La Asunción
Isla Margarita
I. Blanquilla (Ven.)
I. la Tortuga
Islas los Roques (Ven.)
Isla de Aves (Ven.)
La Orchila
Bonaire (Neth.)
Curaçao (Neth.)
Aruba (Neth.)

PUERTO RICO TRENCH

CARIBBEAN SEA

CAYMAN TRENCH

LESSER ANTILLES

VENEZUELA
Caracas
Maracay
Valencia
Barcelona
Cumaná
Carúpano
Güiria
Maturín
El Tigre
Anaco
Cd Bolívar
Cd Guayana
Barquisimeto
Coro
Maracaibo
Cabimas
Lago de Maracaibo
Mérida
Valera
Barinas
Trujillo
San Cristóbal
Pto Cabello
San Felipe
Acarigua
Guanare
Calabozo
El Baúl
V. de la Pascua
Altagracia de Orituco
Pto la Cruz
Maiquetía
Barquisimeto
Orinoco
Barrancas
Tucupita
Temblador
Río Coloradito
Pto Fijo
San Juan de los Morros
San Juan de los Cayos
Pen. de la Guajira
Guanta

COLOMBIA
Barranquilla
Cartagena
Sta Marta
Ciénaga
Valledupar
Riohacha
Montería
Sincelejo
Sabanalarga
Soledad
El Banco
Plato
Magangué
S. Onofre

PANAMA
Panamá
Colón
Panama Canal
La Chorrera
Penonomé
Arch. de las Perlas
G. de los Mosquitos
Golfo del Darién

COSTA RICA
San José
Cartago
Alajuela
Heredia
Limón
Pto Armuelles
David
Chiriquí

NICARAGUA
Bluefields
Rama
Río Grande
Prinzapolca
Puerto Cabezas
Cabo Gracias à Dios
Cayos Miskito
I. del Maíz (Nic. & U.S.A.)

HONDURAS
Caratasca
La. de Caratasca
Waspán
Brus Laguna
Bonanza

250 500 750 1000 1250 km
250 500 750 mls

Ⓐ 90 Ⓑ U.S.A. 80 Ⓒ THE BAHAMAS 70 Ⓓ 60 Ⓔ 50 Ⓕ 40 Ⓖ 30

① Gulf of Mexico
Tropic of Cancer
Miami

Habana
Mérida
CUBA
MEXICO
BELIZE
Belmopan
② GUATEMALA
Guatemala
S.Salvador Tegucigalpa
EL SALVADOR HONDURAS
NICARAGUA
Managua
COSTA RICA
S.José
Panamá
PANAMA

Guantanamo
HAITI
JAMAICA Kingston
Port au Prince
DOMINICAN REP.
Sto Domingo
Pto Rico (U.S.A.)

CARIBBEAN SEA

ANTIGUA & BARBUDA
ST KITTS-NEVIS
Guadeloupe (Fr.)
DOMINICA
Martinique (Fr.)
ST LUCIA
ST VINCENT & THE GRENADINES
GRENADA
BARBADOS

Barranquilla
Sta Marta
Maracaibo
Caracas
Barcelona
TRINIDAD & TOBAGO

I.del Coco (C.R.)
Medellín
S.Cristóbal
VENEZUELA
Cd Bolivar
Orinoco
Georgetown
GUYANA
Paramaribo
SURINAM
FR. GUIANA
Cayenne

③ Malpelo (Col.)
Buenaventura
Bogotá
Cali
Popayán
COLOMBIA
Boa Vista

S.Lorenzo
Quito
ECUADOR
Guayaquil

Negro
S.Pedro e S. (Braz.)
Equator

Galapagos Is (Ecu.)

I. de Marajó
Santarem
Belém
São Luis
Fortaleza
Teresina
I.Fernando de Noronha (Braz.)
Natal

④ Iquitos
Manaus
Amazonas
Purús
Madeira
Tapajós
Xingu

Trujillo
PERU
Pto Velho

⑤ Callao
Lima Huancayo
Pto Maldonado
Cuzco
Arequipa
La Paz
BOLIVIA
Cochabamba
Sucre
Sta Cruz
Arica
Corumbá
Campo Grande

BRAZIL
Recife
Maceió
Salvador
Cuiabá
Goiânia
Brasília
São Francisco
Belo Horizonte

SOUTH PACIFIC OCEAN

Tropic of Capricorn

PARAGUAY
Asunción
Campos
Ribeirão Prêto
Rio de Janeiro
São Paulo
Santos
Curitiba
Trindade (Braz.)

S.Félix (Chi.)
Antofagasta
Salta
S.Miguel de Tucumán
Resistencia
Posadas
Paraná

⑥ CHILE
Córdoba
Sante Fe
Paraná
Mendoza
Rosario
URUGUAY
Valparaíso
Santiago
Buenos Aires
Montevideo
R.de la Plata
Pto Alegre
Pelotas

SOUTH ATLANTIC OCEAN

Is Juan Fernández (Chi.)

Concepción
ARGENTINA
Mar del Plata
Bahía Blanca
Valdivia
Pto Montt

⑦ Cmd. Rivadavia
G.San Jorge

Falkland Is (U.K.)
Stanley

Río Gallegos
Punta Arenas
Tierra del Fuego

S.Georgia (U.K.)

⑧ Ⓓ Ⓔ Ⓕ
Ⓒ S.Shetland Is (U.K.) S.Orkney Is (U.K.) Ⓖ S.Sandwich Is (U.K.)
Ⓑ
ANTARCTICA Ⓗ

⑨ 50 110 100 Ⓐ 60 90 80 70 60 50 40 30 20 10

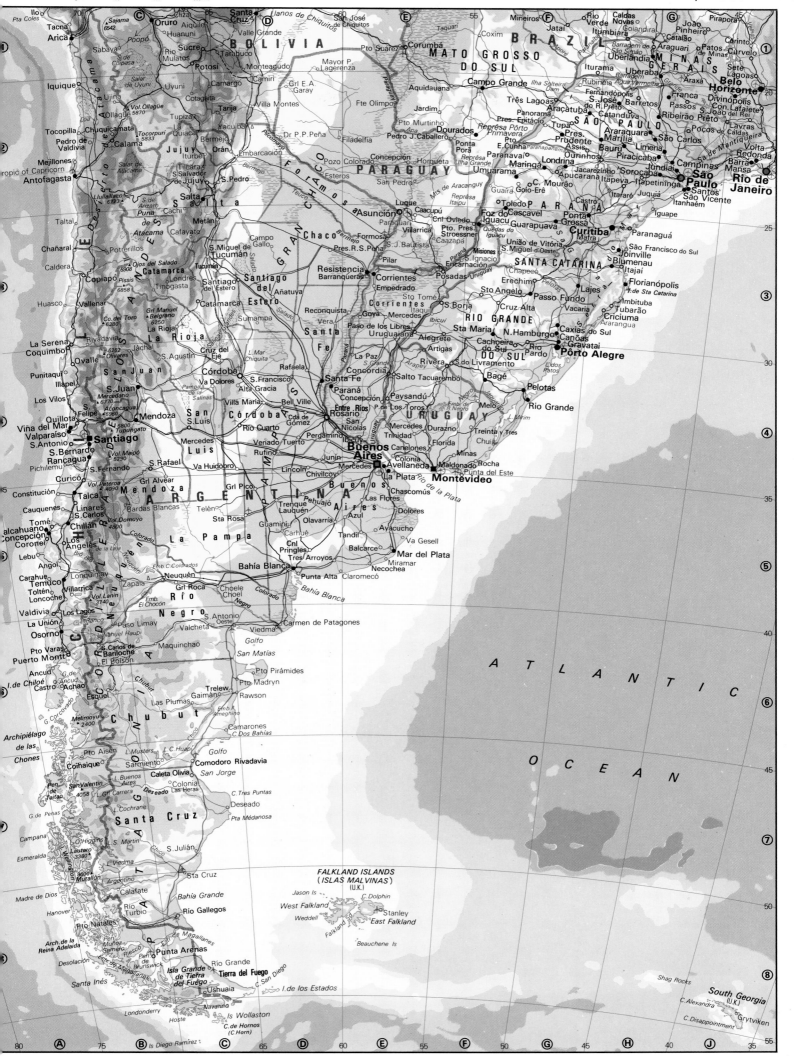

1:15M

1:15M

200 400 600 km
0 100 200 300 mls

Roseau
Fort-de-France
Martinique (Fr.)
ST LUCIA
Castries
Kingstown
ST VINCENT &
THE GRENADINES
GRENADA
St Geor
Port Sp

PACIFIC OCEAN

NICARAGUA
Siguatepeque
Comayagua
Tegucigalpa
San Miguel
Somoto
La Unión
Chinandega
Matagalpa
Estelí
León
Managua
Masaya
Granada
L. de Nicaragua
Rivas
S. Carlos
San Juan
Alajuela
Heredia
Limón
Puntarenas
San José
Cartago
COSTA RICA
Pen. de Nicoya
G. del Papagaya
Pto Armuelles
G. Dulce
Pto Coronado
David
Santiago
Chitré
Pen. de Azuero
I. Coiba
PANAMÁ
La Chorrera
Colón
La Palma
Arch. de las Perlas
G. de Panamá

Pto Cabezas
I. de Providencia (Col.)
I.de Perlas
I. de San Andrés (Col.)
Bluefields

Pta Gallinas
Ríohacha
Sta Marta
Ciénaga
Maicao
Barranquilla
Cartagena
Valledupar
S. Jacinto
Sincelejo
El Banco
Magangué
Montería
Turbo
Caucasia
Barrancabermeja
Yarumal
Bello
Pto Berrío
Barbosa
Itagüí
Medellín
Quibdó
Manizales
Pereira
Cartago
Armenia
Ibagué
Buga
Palmira
Cali
Buenaventura
Santander
Popayán
Neiva
Pitalito
Tumaco
El Diviso
Pasto
Ipiales
Mocoa
Tulcán
Pto Asís
Esmeraldas
Ibarra
Otavalo
Lago Agrio
Quito
Coca
Cotopaxi
Chone
Ambato
Tena
Manta
Jipijapa
ECUADOR
Guaranda
Chimborazo 6310
Guayaquil
Babahoyo
Riobamba
Milagro
Macas
Cuenca
Azogues
Gualaceo
G. de Guayaquil
Machala
Tumbes
Zaruma
Loja
Zamora
Talara
Negritos
Paita
Sullana
Chulucanas
Piura
Catacaos
Huancabamba
Jaén
Moyobamba
Tarapoto
Lambayeque
Ferreñafe
Chachapoyas
Chiclayo
Chepén
Cajamarca
Pacasmayo
Cajabamba
Huamachuco
Otusco
Trujillo
Pucallpa
Pomabamba
Huascarán 6768
Chimbote
Huaraz
La Unión
Casma
Huánuco
Huarmey
Oxapampa
Cerro de Pasco
La Merced
Pativilca
Barranca
Huacho
La Oroya
Tarma
Ancón
Jauja
Callao
Lima
Huancayo
Huancavelica
Ayacucho
Chincha Alta
Pisco
Andahuaylas
Ica
Pen. de Paracas
Nazca
Chala
Coropuna 6425
Arequipa
Misti 5822
Camaná
Matarani
Mollendo
Ilo
Moquegua
Tacna
Arica

COLOMBIA
Ocaña
Cúcuta
Pamplona
Bucaramanga
Málaga
Sogamoso
Tunja
Chocontá
Bogotá
Girardot
Villavicencio
Granada
Puerto Rico
Florencia
Belén
Leguizamo

VENEZUELA
Riohacha
Maracaibo
Cabimas
Cd Ojeda
Machiques
Valera
Trujillo
Mérida
Barquisimeto
Acarigua
Guanare
Barinas
V. de la Pascua
El Tigre
Cd Bolívar
Upata
Cd Guayana
Maturín
Caracas
Valencia
Maracay
Barcelona
Anaco
Cumaná
Carúpano
Güiria
Caripito
Tucupita
Barrancas
Cd Piar
Emb. de Guri
El Dorado
Salto del Angel
Pto Ayacucho
Pto Carreño

RORAIMA
Boa Vist
Sa Pacaraima
Sta Elena
La Gran Sabana

AMAZONAS
SELVAS
Iquitos
Leticia
Tabatinga
Caxias
Elvira
Tefé
Manacapur
Cruzeiro do Sul
Feijó
ACRE
Sena Madureira
Rio Branco
Brasiléia
Cobija
Porto Velho
Guajará-Mirim
RONDÔNIA
Porvenir
Riberalta
Abunã
Pto Maldonado
Pto Heath
Rurrenabaque
Trinidad
BOLIVIA
La Paz
Cochabamba
Santa Cruz
Quillacollo
Oruro
Sucre
Potosí
Titicaca
Puno
Juliaca
Ayaviri
Sicuani
Cuzco
MACHU PICCHU
Abancay
Quillabamba
Parque Nac. de Manú

CHILE
Iquique
Tocopilla
Chuquicamata
Calama
Mejillones
Antofagasta
Tropic of Capricorn
ARGENTINA
Jujuy
Orán
Salta

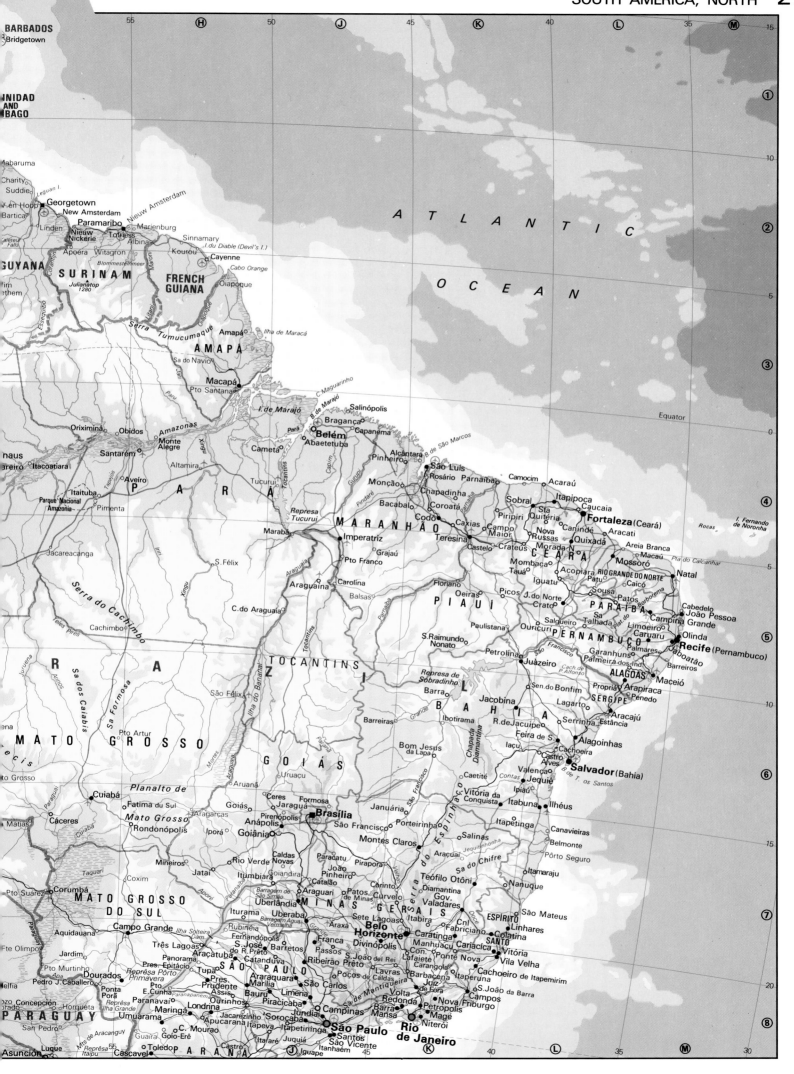

0 100 200 300 km
0 50 100 150 mls
ATLANTIC OCEAN
PACIFIC OCEAN
BRAZIL
URUGUAY
ARGENTINA
CHILE
Buenos Aires
Montevideo
Santiago
Pôrto Alegre
Córdoba
Rosario
Mendoza
Mar del Plata
Bahía Blanca
Concepción
Valparaiso
La Plata
Santa Fe
Paraná
Corrientes
Resistencia
Neuquén
Temuco
Valdivia
Osorno
San Juan
San Luis
La Rioja
Santa Rosa
Pelotas
Rio Grande
Caxias do Sul
Passo Fundo
Santa Maria
Bagé
Salto
Paysandú
Melo
Rivera
Mercedes
La Serena
Coquimbo
Talca
Chillán
Rancagua
Viña del Mar
Talcahuano
Buenos Aires
Entre Ríos
Córdoba
Santa Fe
La Pampa
Río Negro
Neuquén
Corrientes
Misiones
Chaco
Catamarca
Mendoza

1:7.5M

ATLANTIC OCEAN

Tropic of Capricorn

Major cities and places:

Salvador (Bahia), Ilhéus, Itabuna, Vitória da Conquista, Jequié, Teófilo Otoni, Governador Valadares, Vitória, Vila Velha, Colatina, Linhares, Campos, Rio de Janeiro, Niterói, Nova Friburgo, Petrópolis, Teresópolis, Juiz de Fora, Barbacena, Belo Horizonte, Ouro Prêto, Montes Claros, Pirapora, Brasília, DISTRITO FEDERAL, Anápolis, Goiânia, Uberlândia, Uberaba, Ribeirão Prêto, Franca, São Paulo, Santos, São Vicente, Campinas, Sorocaba, Bauru, Marília, Presidente Prudente, Curitiba, Ponta Grossa, Londrina, Maringá, Campo Grande, Corumbá, Cuiabá, Dourados, Foz do Iguaçu, Cáceres

States: BAHIA, MINAS GERAIS, ESPÍRITO SANTO, RIO DE JANEIRO, SÃO PAULO, GOIÁS, MATO GROSSO, MATO GROSSO DO SUL, PARANÁ

Countries: BOLIVIA, PARAGUAY, ARGENTINA (ARG.)

Rio São Francisco, Rio Paraná, Rio Paranaíba, Rio Grande, Pantanal de Mato Grosso, Serra do Roncador, Planalto do Mato Grosso, Serra Geral de Goiás

1:15M

200 400 600 km
0 100 200 300 mls

ATLANTIC

OCEAN

Greenland
(Den.)
Kap Farvel

ICELAND

Reykjavík

Arctic Circle

ARCTIC

Jan Mayen
(Nor.)

NORWEGIAN

SEA

Vesterålen
Lofoten
Nar

Faerøerne
(Den.)

Trondheim

N O R W A Y

S W E D E N

Bergen
Stavanger
Oslo
Göteborg
Jönköping
Stockholm
Öland
Värnern

Shetland

Orkney

Aberdeen

UNITED KINGDOM
OF GREAT BRITAIN AND
NORTHERN IRELAND

Glasgow
Edinburgh

NORTH

SEA

Ålborg
DENMARK
København
Malmö
Bornholm

Belfast

Newcastle

IRELAND

Dublin
Liverpool
Manchester

Cork

Birmingham

Cardiff
Bristol
London

English Channel

Rostock
Poznań

Hamburg
Hannover
Berlin
PO

Amsterdam
's-Gravenhage
Rotterdam
NETHERLANDS

GERMANY

Bruxelles
BELGIUM
Lille
Essen
Köln
Bonn
Frankfurt
Leipzig
Dresden
Wrocław

LUXEMBOURG

Praha
CZECH
REPUBLIC
Brno

Le Havre
Rouen
Seine

Paris

Nürnberg
Strasbourg
Stuttgart

Wien
Bratislava

Nantes
Tours
Loire

F R A N C E

München
Salzburg
AUSTRIA
Graz
HU

La Coruña

Bay of
Biscay

Bordeaux

Clermont-
Ferrand

Genève
SWITZERLAND
Bern
Zürich
LIECHTENSTEIN

Ljubljana
SLOVENIA
Trieste
Zagreb
CROATIA

Lyon
Rhône

Porto

PORTUGAL

Valladolid
Bilbao

S P A I N

Ebro

Zaragoza

ANDORRA

Marseille

Torino
Milano

Venezia

BOSNIA
HERZEGOV
Sara

Genova

Rhein

MONACO

I T A L Y

Firenze
SAN
MARINO

Bastia
Corse

Split

ADRIATIC SEA

Madrid
Toledo
Tajo

Barcelona

Ajaccio

Lisboa

Faro
Sevilla

Valencia

Murcia

Balearic Islands

Menorca

Ibiza
Mallorca

Sardegna

Olbia

Roma

Napoli
Taran

Cagliari

TYRRHENIAN
SEA

Málaga

Tanger
Gibraltar (U.K.)
Ceuta (Sp.)

Madeira
(Port.)

M E D I T E R R A N E A N

Palermo
Messina
Reggio di Calabria

Melilla
(Sp.)
Oran

Alger

Sicilia

Casablanca
Rabat

Tunis

Islas Canarias
(Sp.)

M O R O C C O

Marrakech

A L G E R I A

T U N I S I A

MALTA

SE

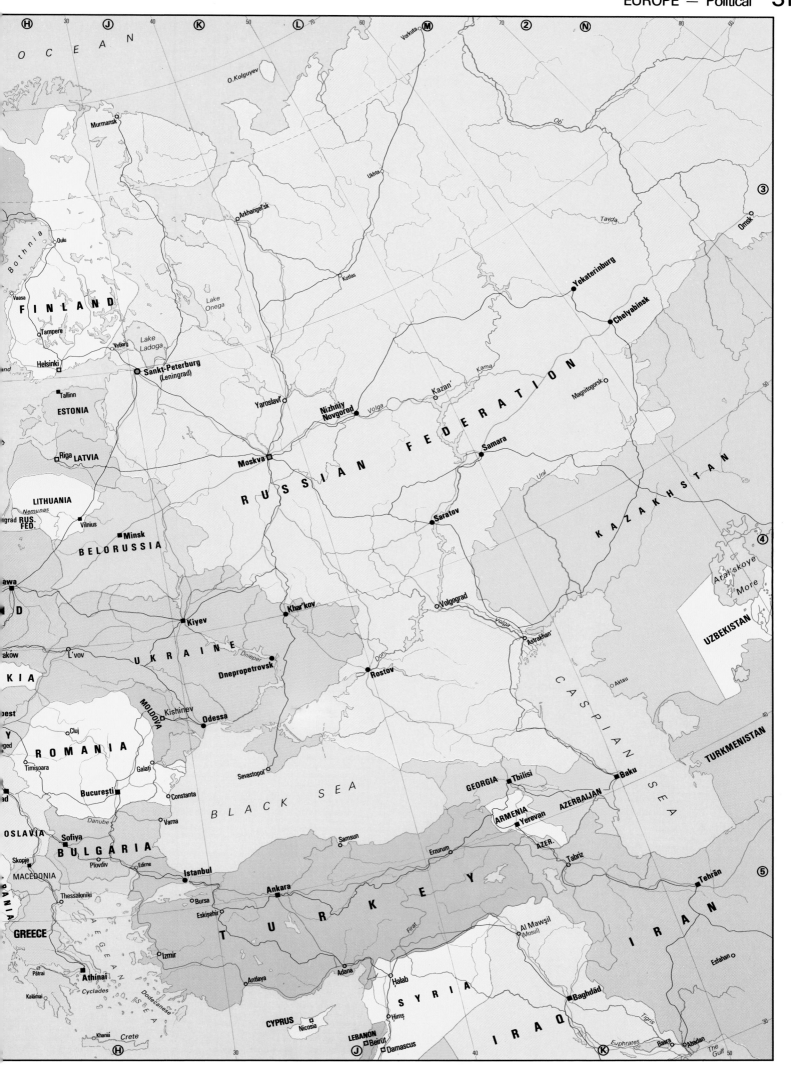

100 200 300 km
50 100 150 mls

Iceland inset (at the same scale)

Arctic Circle

Bolungarvik Drangajökull Grimsey
Ísafjörður Siglufjörður Ólafsfjörður Bakkaflói
Biargtangar Húsavík
Breiðafjörður Glama 845 Dalvík Njarðvík
Húnaflói Sauðárkrókur Akureyri Seyðisfjörður
Stykkishólmur Blönduós Neskaupstaður
Hofsjökull Eskifjörður
ICELAND Langjökull Óðáðahraun Tungnafells-
jökull Snæfell 1833
Faxaflói Akranes Vatnajökull
Reykjavík Kópavogur Öræfajökull 2119
Keflavík Hafnarfjörður
Grindavík Selfoss
Vestmannaeyjar Myrdalsjökull Ingólfshöfði
Surtsey

Føroyar (Den.) inset (at the same scale)
Streymoy
Vágar Tórshavn
Sandoy
Suðuroy

NORWEGIAN SEA

Arctic Circle

ARCTIC OCEAN

BARENTS SEA

Nordkapp Honningsvåg
Hammerfest Vardø
Sørøya Vadsø
Tromsø Varangerhalvøya
Alta Kirkenes Nikel
Narvik Murmansk
Kiruna
Bodø Gällivare
Luleå
Rovaniemi
Kemi
Oulu

FINLAND

Vaasa
Tampere
Turku Helsinki (Helsingfors)
Sankt-Peterburg (Lening...)

ESTONIA
Tallinn Narva
RUSSIAN FEDERATION
Pskov

LATVIA
Riga

LITHUANIA
Šiauliai Panevėžys
Klaipėda
Kaunas Vilnius
Kaliningrad (RUS. FED.)

BELORUSSIA
Minsk

NORWAY
Trondheim
Ålesund
Bergen
Oslo Drammen
Stavanger
Kristiansand

SWEDEN
Östersund
Sundsvall
Gävle
Uppsala
Västerås Stockholm
Örebro Norrköping
Göteborg Jönköping Linköping
Borås Kalmar
Malmö
Gotland Visby

DENMARK
København
Ålborg Århus
Odense
Esbjerg

GERMANY
Hamburg Bremen
Hannover Berlin

POLAND
Gdańsk Gdynia
Szczecin Bydgoszcz
Poznań
Warszawa

BALTIC SEA
Bornholm (Den.)
Öland

Gulf of Bothnia
Gulf of Finland
Gulf of Riga
Kattegat
Skagerrak
North Sea

1:5M

50 100 150 200 km
50 100 mls

NORWAY
Nordhordland
Dale
Bergen
Sotra
Sunnhordland Stord
Leirvik
Bømlo
Skjold
Haugesund
Karmøy
Stavanger
Sandnes

60

Shetland
Herma Ness
Unst
Isbister
Fetlar
St Magnus B.
Yell
Whalsay
Foula
Lerwick
Sumburgh Hd

Fair Isle

Orkney
Westray
Rousay
Sanday
Sule Skerry
Stromness
Stronsay
Stack Skerry
Kirkwall
Hoy
Scapa Flow

N. Rona
Sula Sgeir

SCOTLAND
Flannan Is
Butt of Lewis
Stornoway
Lewis
St Kilda
Harris
N. Uist
The Minch
S. Uist
Barra

C. Wrath
Thurso
Duncansby Hd
Wick
Ben Hope 927
Ben More Assynt 996
Helmsdale
Ullapool
Dornoch
Dornoch Firth
Dingwall
Moray Firth
Elgin
Banff
Fraserburgh
Peterhead
Buchan Ness
L. Ness
Inverness
Portree
Skye
Kyle of Lochalsh
Spey
Ben Macdui 1309
Don
Aberdeen
Fort Augustus
Braemar
Dee
Stonehaven
Mallaig
Fort William
Ben Nevis 1344
Rum
Ben Lawers 1214
Pitlochry
Montrose
Coll
Grampian Mts
Perth
Arbroath
Tiree
Mull
Oban
L. Awe
Dundee
St Andrews
F. of Lorn
L. Lomond
Kirkcaldy
F. of Forth
Colonsay
Jura
Stirling
Greenock
Paisley
Glasgow
Edinburgh
St Abbs Hd
Islay
Motherwell
Berwick-upon-Tweed
Holy I.
Irvine
Kilmarnock
White Coomb 822
Galashiels
Campbeltown
Arran
Ayr
Alnwick
Merrick 843
Moffat
Hawick
Cheviots
Morpeth
Blyth

NORTH SEA

55

N. IRELAND
Tory I.
Malin Hd
Coleraine
Errigal 752
Londonderry
Rathlin I.
Rossan Pt
Ballymena
Larne
Donegal
L. Foyle
Omagh
Belfast
Bangor
Stranraer
Kirkcudbright
Carlisle
Gateshead
Newcastle upon Tyne
S. Shields
Sunderland
Durham
Hartlepool
Darlington
Middlesbrough
Scarborough
Erris Hd
Sligo B.
Enniskillen
L. Erne
Monaghan
Armagh
Newry
Luce B.
Solway Firth
Penrith
Scafell Pike 977
Pennines
Yorkshire Moors
Flamborough Hd
Achill I.
Ballina
Castlebar
L. Conn
L. Allen
Cavan
Dundalk
Isle of Man
Kendal
Barrow-in-Furness
Morecambe
Lancaster
Harrogate
Ouse
York
Hull

IRISH SEA

Clew B.
Boyle
Roscommon
L. Ree
Longford
Mullingar
Drogheda
Douglas
Blackpool
Preston
Bradford
Huddersfield
Leeds
Doncaster
Grimsby
Spurn Hd
Humber
L. Mask
L. Corrib
Galway
Athlone
Dublin
(Baile Atha Cliath)
Holyhead
Liverpool
Bolton
Manchester
Sheffield
Lincoln
Ne Hd
Galway Is
Aran Is
Monasterevan
Dun Laoghaire
Birkenhead
Warrington
Chester
Warrington
Stoke on-Trent
Nottingham
The Wash
Ennis
Shannon
REP. OF IRELAND
Port Laoise
Carlow
Wicklow Mts
Bray
Anglesey
Crewe
Dee
Derby
King's Lynn
Norwich
Great Yarmouth
Kilrush
L. Derg
Nenagh
Kilkenny
Wicklow
Snowdon 1085
Shrewsbury
Leicester
Coventry
Peterborough
Lowestoft
Limerick
Tipperary
Clonmel
Arklow
Pwllheli
Cambrian Mts
Wolverhampton
Birmingham
ENGLAND
Northampton
Cambridge
Ipswich
Tralee
Blackwater
Waterford
Wexford
Cardigan Bay
Aberystwyth
WALES
Worcester
Bedford
Felixstowe
Harwich
Killarney
Carrauntoohill 1041
Clonmel
Dungarvan
Rosslare
Nene
Ouse
Newmarket
Colchester
Kilkenny
Cork
Youghal
St George's Chan.
St David's Hd
Fishguard
Builth Wells
Brecon
Wye
Gloucester
Milton Keynes
Luton
Chelmsford
Southend-on-Sea
Bantry
Bantry B.
C. Clear
Old Hd of Kinsale
Carmarthen
Pembroke
Swansea
Newport
Cardiff
Oxford
Swindon
London
Thames
Bristol Chan.
Bristol
Bath
Reading
Windsor
Maidstone
Canterbury
Dover
Lundy I.
Weston-super-Mare
Guildford
Crawley
Folkestone
Barnstaple
Taunton
Salisbury
Winchester
Hastings
Eastbourne
Bude
Exeter
Bournemouth
Southampton
Brighton
Portsmouth
Isle of Wight
Weymouth
Dartmoor
Torquay
Newquay
Plymouth
Truro
Penzance
Falmouth
Land's End
Isles of Scilly
Lizard Pt
Prawle Pt

English Channel

NETHERLANDS
Den Helder
Alkmaar
Texel
Vlieland
Haarlem
Leiden
's-Gravenhage (Den Haag)
Rotterdam
Dordrecht
Esberg
Vlissingen
Zeebrugge
Oostende
Antwerpen
Brugge
Gent
Bruxelles (Brüssel)
BELGIUM
Mechelen
St-Omer
Calais
Dunkerque
Kortrijk
Tourcoing
Roubaix
Soignies
Tournai
Mons
Lille
Boulogne
Béthune
Lens
Valenciennes
Charleroi
Douai
Denain
Maubeuge
Montreuil
Arras
Cambrai
Fourmies
Abbeville
St-Quentin
Le Tréport
Dieppe
PICARDIE
Amiens
Laon
C. de la Hague
Neufchâtel
Montdidier
Compiègne
Oise
Aisne
Alderney
Pte de Barfleur
Beauvais
Soissons
Reims
Guernsey
Sark
Cherbourg
Fécamp
Bolbec
Senlis
Château-Thierry
Jersey
Valognes
Le Havre
Rouen
Epernay
St-Lô
Bayeux
Deauville
Elbeuf
Louviers
Seine
Cergy
Pontoise
Meaux
Coutances
Caen
Lisieux
Mantes
Melun
Golfe de St-Malo
Granville
Paris
Versailles
Dreux
Evreux
Eure
Provins
Romilly-s-S
Roscoff
Morlaix
St-Malo
Dinan
Argentan
Rambouillet
Etampes
Fontainebleau
Sézanne
Brest
St-Brieuc
Carhaix-Plouguer
Mayenne
Domfront
Mont-St-Michel
Fougères
Alençon
Chartres
Sens
Troyes
FRANCE
NORMANDIE
I. d'Ouessant

25 50 75 100 km
25 50 mls

at the same scale

North Sea

Shetland
Herma Ness, Unst, Yell, Fetlar, Whalsay, Bressay, Noss, Lerwick, Scalloway, St Magnus Bay, Brae, Hillswick, Isbister, The Faither, Papa Stour, Muckle Roe, Gruthess, Fitful Hd, Sumburgh Hd, Fair Isle, Foula

Tórshavn-Seydisfjördur
Hanstholm-Bergen
Bergen-Stavanger
Norway
U.K.
Esbjerg-Göteborg
Torshavn
Stromness
Aberdeen
Lerwick

DOGGER

Cod
Lomond, Josephine, Fulmar, Auk, Clyde, Albuskjell, Nat. Gas, Duncan, Argyll

Montrose, Forties, S.E. Forties, Buchan, Piper, Tartan, Claymore, Highlander, Scapa, Petronella, Beatrice

Long Forties, Devil's Hole, Buchan Deep, Farne Deep

Little Halibut Bank, Nat. Gas

Orkney
N Ronaldsay, Sanday, Stronsay, Shapinsay, Eday, Westray, Papa Westray, Rousay, Kirkwall, Mainland, Stromness, Scapa Flow, Hoy, S. Ronaldsay, Duncansby Hd, Pentland Firth

Scotland

C. Wrath, Durness, Tongue, Thurso, John O'Groats, Dunnet Hd, Wick, Lybster, Helmsdale, Brora, Golspie, Dornoch, Dornoch Firth, Tain, Tarbat Ness, Lossiemouth, Elgin, Forres, Nairn, Inverness, Moray Firth, Cromarty, Black Isle, Dingwall, Beauly

Ben Kilbreck 961, Ben Hope 927, Ben More Assynt 998, Ben Dearg 1081, Ben Wyvis 1045, Lochinver, Ullapool, Loch Shin, Lairg, Oykel, Farrar, Highland, Ben Attow 1031, Ben Nevis 1344, Fort Augustus, Fort William, Mallaig, Arisaig

Monadhliath Mts, Kingussie, Aviemore, Grantown-on-Spey, Dufftown, Keith, Huntly, Banff, Kinnairds Hd, Fraserburgh, Peterhead, Buchan Ness, Aberdeen, Girdle Ness, Stonehaven, Banchory, Dee, Ballater, Braemar, Ben Macdui 1310, Cairngorm Mts, Cairngorms 1245, Lochnagar 1155

Grampian

Highland

Tayside, Blair Atholl, Pitlochry, Forfar, Brechin, Montrose, Arbroath, Dundee, Perth, Crieff, Callander, Stirling, Dunfermline, Edinburgh

Central
Fife, St Andrews, Fife Ness, Firth of Forth, North Berwick, Glenrothes, Methil, Kirkcaldy, Leven, Kinross, Loch Leven

Lothian
Haddington, Dunbar, St Abb's Hd, Eyemouth, Berwick-upon-Tweed, Duns, Galashiels, Kelso, Jedburgh, Hawick, Selkirk, Peebles

Borders

Strathclyde
Glasgow, Coatbridge, Motherwell, Hamilton, Lanark, Paisley, Dumbarton, Helensburgh, Greenock, Largs, Arrochar, Inveraray, Oban, Ballachulish

Firth of Clyde, Isle of Arran, Brodick, Ardrossan, Irvine, Troon, Prestwick, Ayr, Maybole, Girvan, Kilmarnock, Cumnock, New Galloway, Newton Stewart, Merrick 843, Wigtown, Galloway, Ballantrae, Corsewall Pt

Dumfries and Galloway
Dumfries, Castle Douglas, Kirkcudbright, Thornhill, Moffat, Lockerbie, Langholm, Annan, Gretna, Carlisle

Kintyre, Mull of Kintyre, Campbeltown, Tarbert, Gigha, Islay, Port Ellen, Port Askaig, Jura, Sd of Jura, Colonsay, Oa, Rathlin I.

Isle of Skye, Portree, Broadford, Cuillin Hills, Kyle of Lochalsh, Raasay, Sd of Raasay, L. Torridon, Gairloch, L. Maree, Rubha Hunish, L. Snizort

Western Isles
Lewis, Stornoway, Butt of Lewis, Broad B., N. Rona, Sula Sgeir, Flannan Is, Harris, Tarbert, Scarp, Taransay, Pabbay, Sd of Harris, North Uist, Benbecula, Lochmaddy, Lochboisdale, South Uist, Monach Is, Barra, Castlebay, Barra Hd, Eriskay, Sd of Barra

Outer Hebrides

Little Minch, The Minch, North Minch

Rum, Eigg, Muck, Canna, Coll, Tiree, Ardnamurchan Pt, Tobermory, **Mull**, Ulva, Staffa, Iona, Morvern, Loch Linnhe, Firth of Lorn

St Kilda, Stanton Banks

North Channel
Larne, Ballymena, Antrim, Antrim Hills, Coleraine, Ballymoney, Ballycastle, Portrush, Portstewart, Limavady, Londonderry, Strabane, Lifford, Stranorlar, Donegal, L. Swilly, L. Foyle, Malin Hd, Inishowen, Carndonagh, Buncrana, Sheep Haven, Errigal 752, Derryveagh Mts, Bloody Foreland, Bunbeg

Northumberland, Alnwick, Morpeth, Amble, Blyth, Tynemouth, Newcastle upon Tyne, Sth Shields, Gateshead, **Tyne and Wear**, Sunderland, Hexham, Haltwhistle, Alston, Consett, Durham

Holy I., Farne Is, Bamburgh, Belford, Cheviot Hills, The Cheviot 816, Wooler, Rothbury, Kielder, Nat. Park, Redesdale, Carter Bar, Tweed, Teviot

Sule Skerry, Stack Skerry

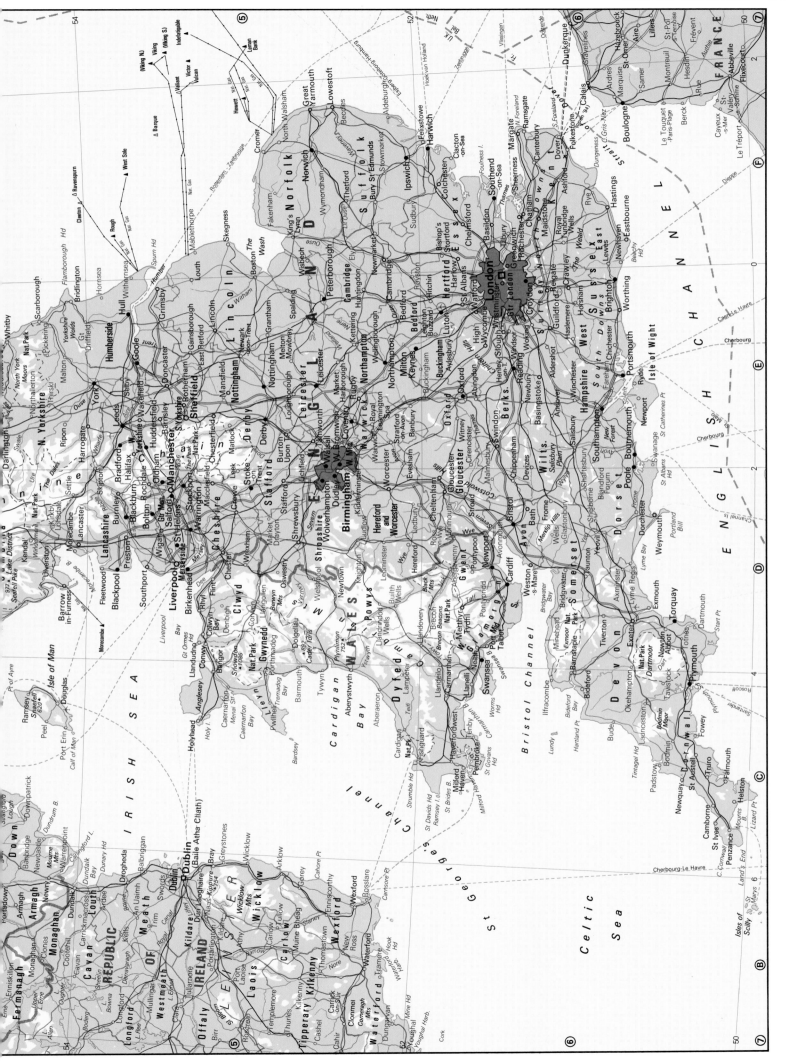

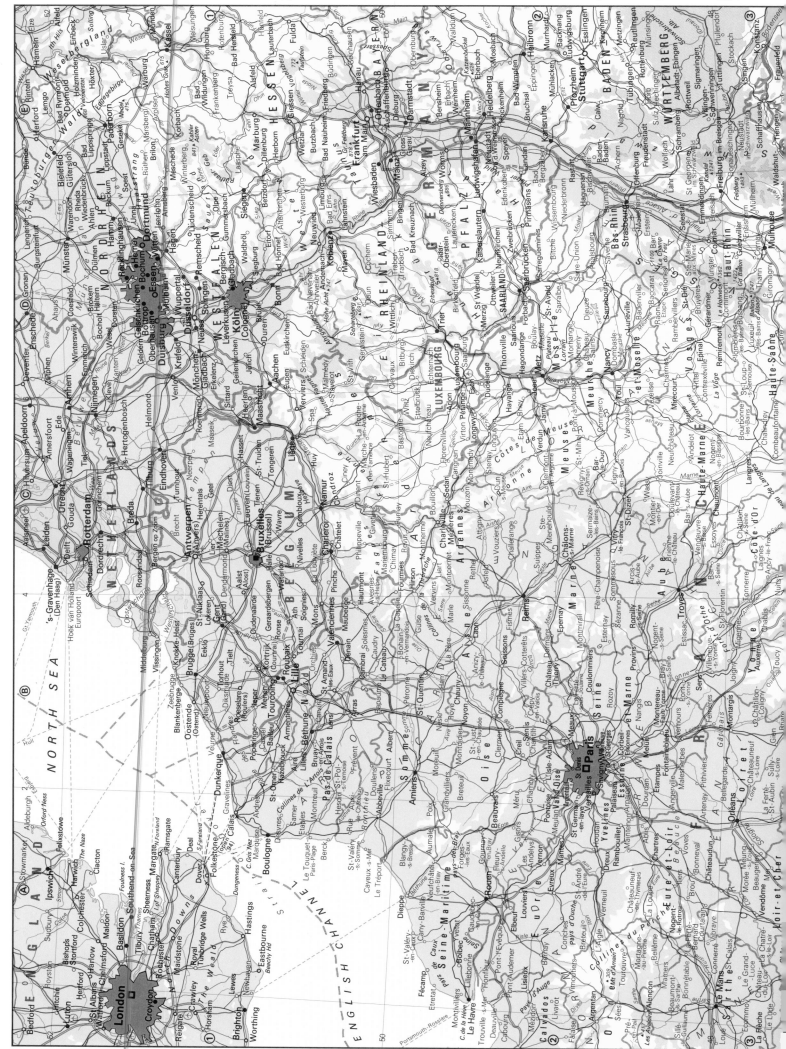

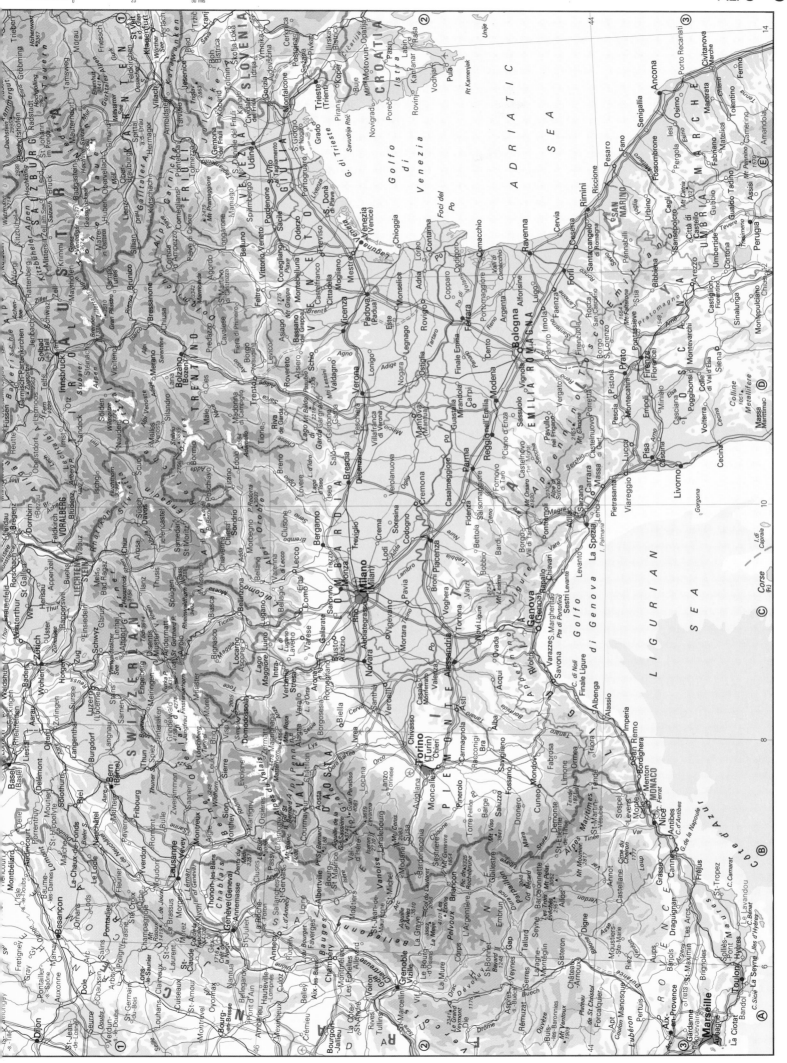

1:5M

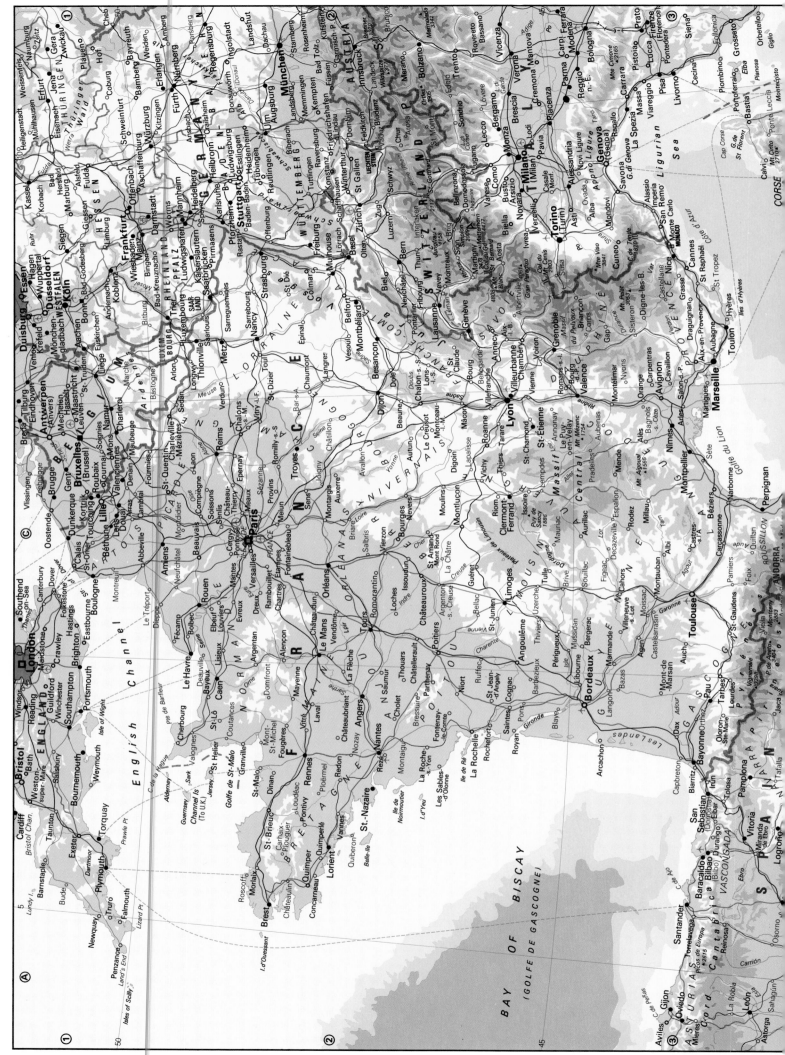

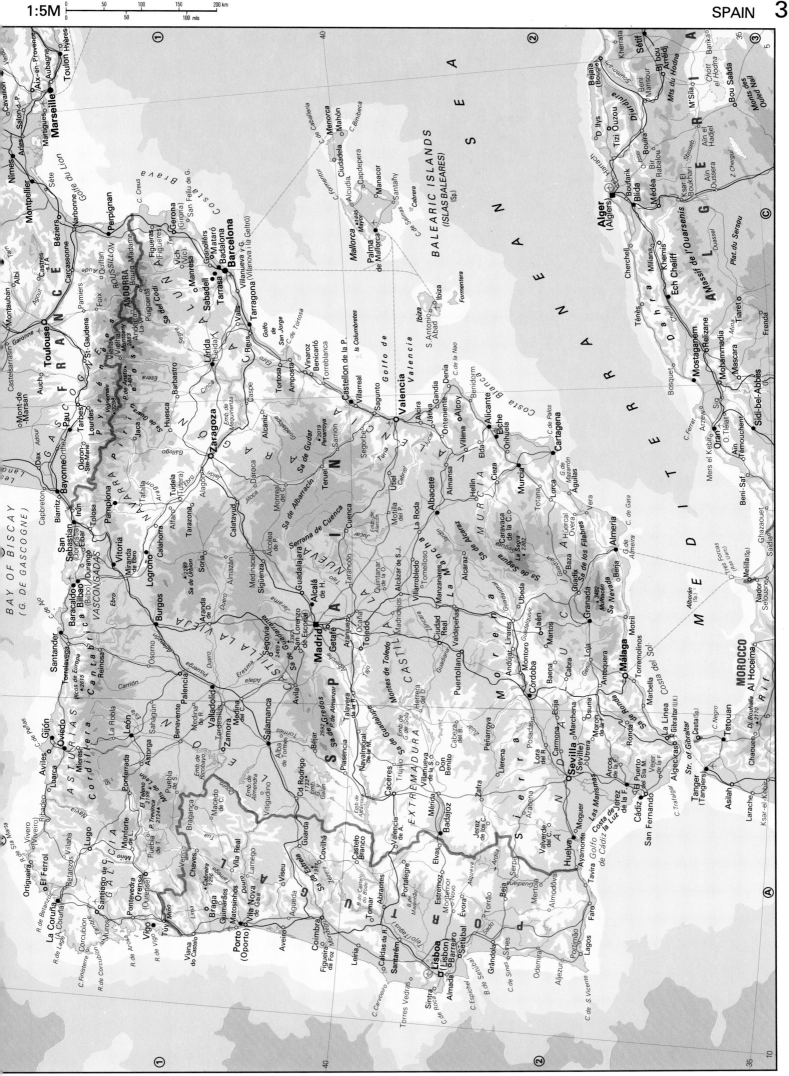

1:5M

50 100 150 200 km
50 100 mls

GERMANY

SWITZERLAND

AUSTRIA

FRANCE

SLOVENIA

CROATIA

BOSNI

Lyon
St-Étienne
Grenoble
Valence
Marseille
Toulon
Nice
MONACO
Monte Carlo

München
Salzburg
Wien
Innsbruck
Zürich
Bern
Genève
Graz
Klagenfurt
Maribor
Zagreb
Ljubljana
Trieste
Rijeka (Fiume)
Pula
Zadar
Split (Spalato)
Šibenik

TORINO (Turin)
MILANO (Milan)
Genova (Genoa)
La Spezia
Brescia
Verona
Padova
Venezia (Venice)
Bologna
Ravenna
Rimini
Ancona
Pescara

Firenze (Florence)
Pisa
Livorno
Siena
Perugia
Terni

CORSE (CORSICA)
Ajaccio
Bastia
Mt Cinto 2710

Città del Vaticano
Roma (Rome)
Ostia
Civitavecchia
Latina
Foggia
Napoli (Naples)
Salerno
Vesuvio 1277
Avellino
Potenza
Bari
Barletta
Andria

SARDEGNA (SARDINIA)
Sassari
Oristano
Cagliari
Alghero
Nuoro

TYRRHENIAN SEA

LIGURIAN SEA

ADRIATIC

MEDITERRANEAN

Cosenza
Catanzaro
Vibo Valentia
Reggio di Calabria
Messina
Palermo
Trapani
Marsala
Agrigento
Catania
Siracusa (Syracuse)
Ragusa

SICILIA (SICILY)
Etna 3323

ALGERIA
TUNISIA
Constantine
Skikda
Annaba (Bône)
Tunis
Bizerte
Sousse
Kairouan

MALTA
Valletta

Malta Channel
Sicilian Channel

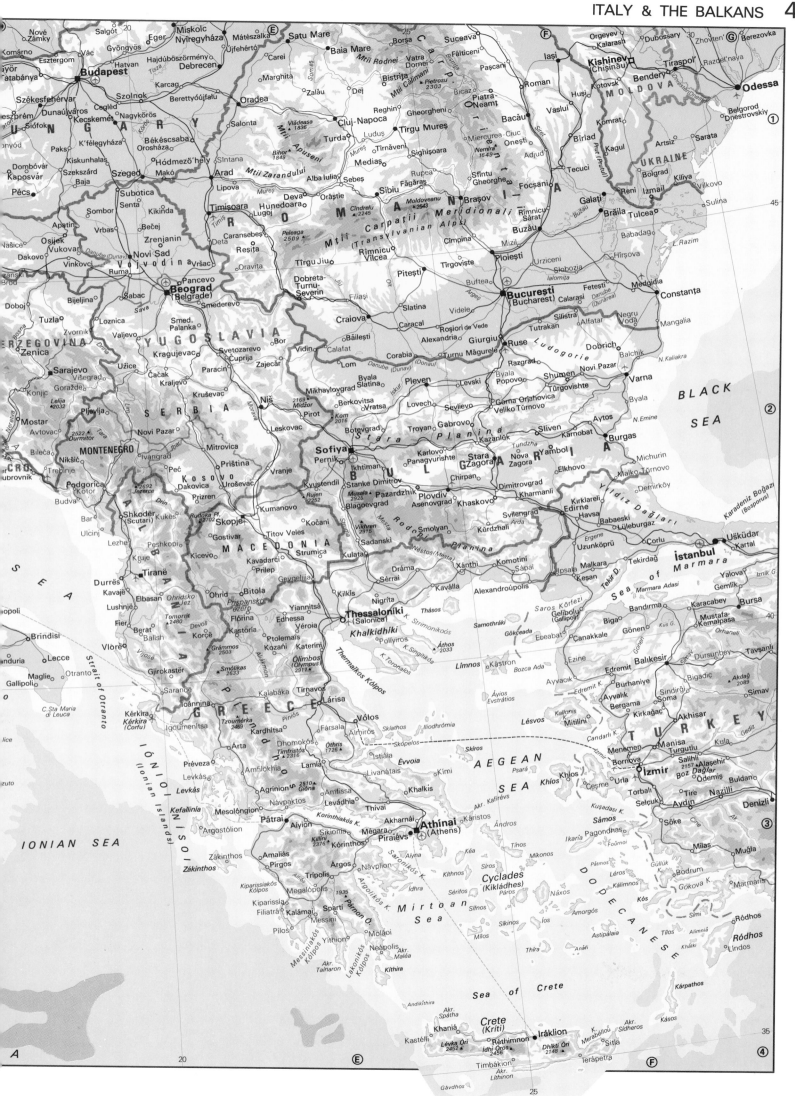

1:5M

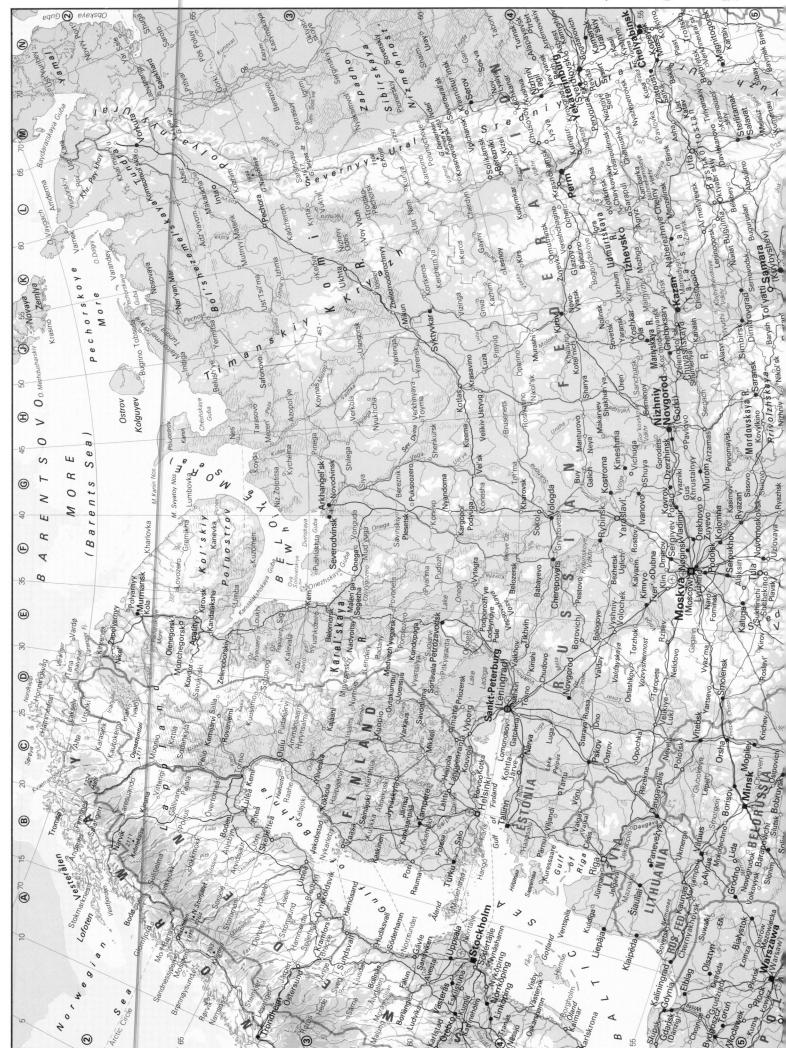

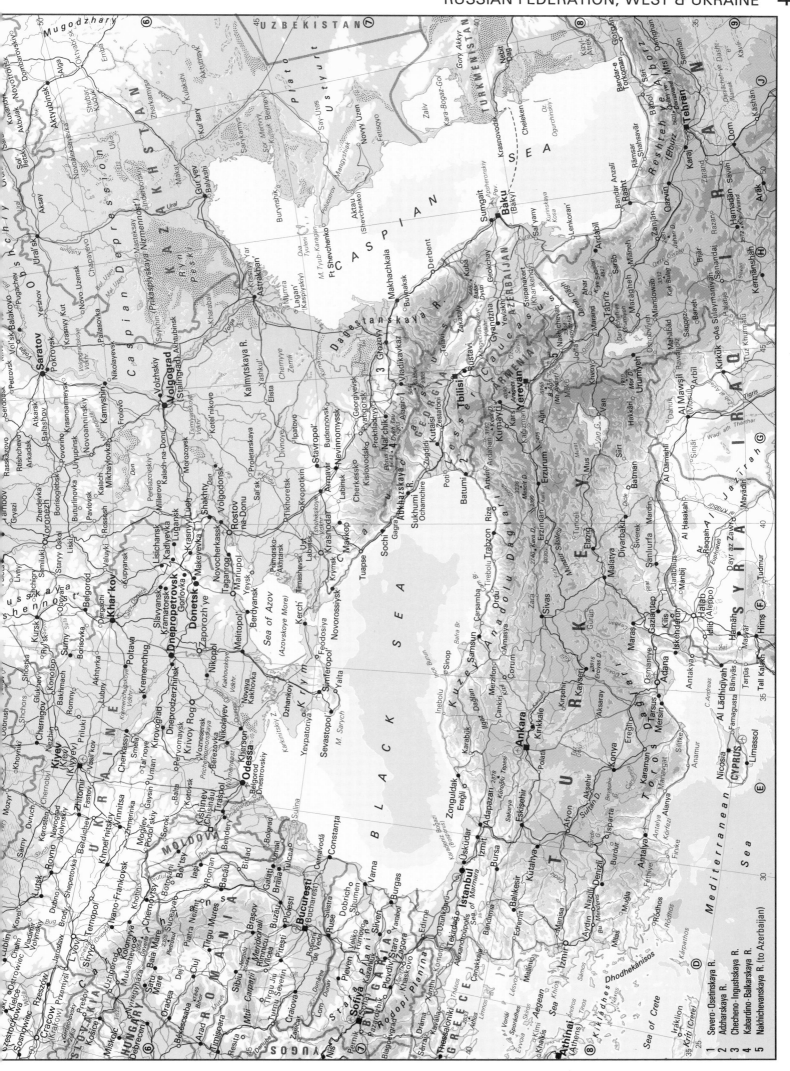

1 Severo-Osetinskaya R.
2 Adzharskaya R.
3 Checheno-Ingushskaya R.
4 Kabardino-Balkarskaya R.
5 Nakhichevanskaya R. (to Azerbaijan)

1:40M

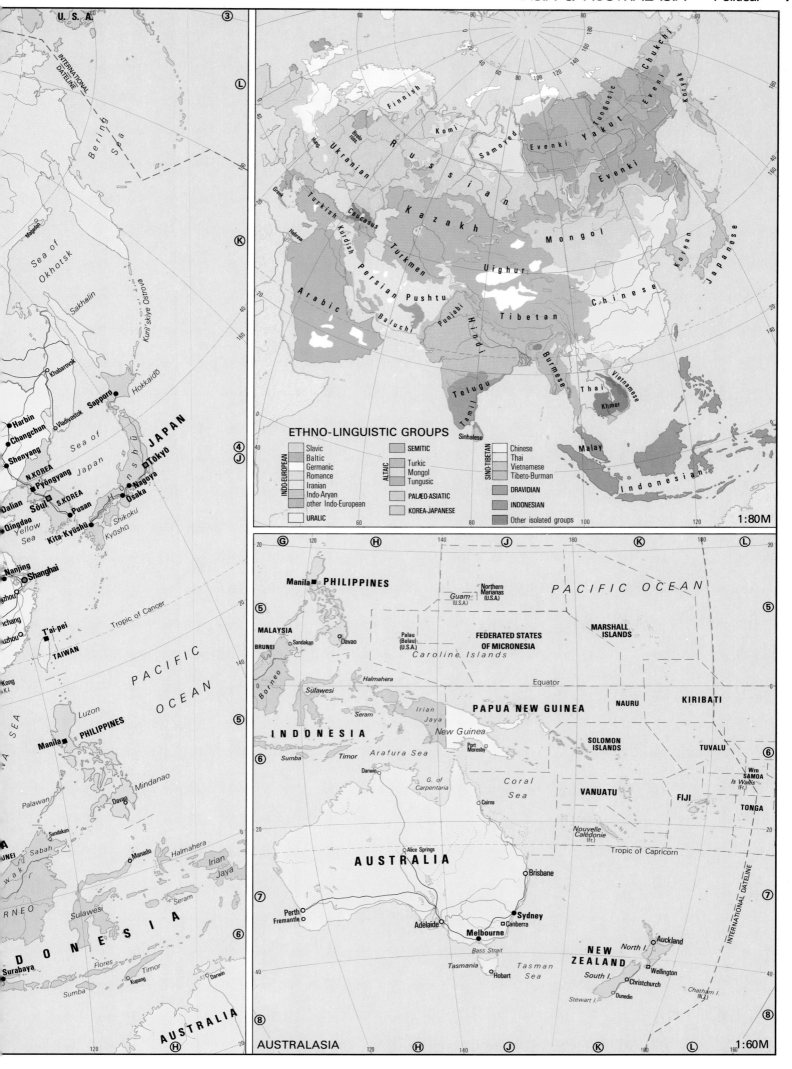

Main map (top left)

U.S.A.
③
INTERNATIONAL DATELINE
Ⓛ
Bering Sea
Ⓚ
Sea of Okhotsk
Magadan
Sakhalin
Kuril'skiye Ostrova
Khabarovsk
④
Ⓙ
Sapporo
Hokkaidō
Harbin
Vladivostok
Changchun
Shenyang
JAPAN
Sea of Japan
Honshū
Tokyo
N.KOREA
Pyŏngyang
Nagoya
Dalian
S.KOREA
Osaka
Sŏul
Pusan
Qingdao
Shikoku
Yellow Sea
Kita-Kyūshū
Kyūshū
Nanjing
Shanghai
Tropic of Cancer
②
T'ai-pei
TAIWAN
Hong Kong
PACIFIC OCEAN
⑤
Luzon
Manila
PHILIPPINES
Mindanao
Palawan
Davao
Sandakan
Sabah
Manado
Halmahera
Sulawesi
Irian Jaya
BRUNEI
Seram
BORNEO
INDONESIA
Flores
Timor
Surabaya
Sumba
Kupang
Darwin
AUSTRALIA
⑥
Ⓗ

ETHNO-LINGUISTIC GROUPS

Finnish
Komi
Nenets
Ukranian
Russian
Samoyed
Evenki
Yakut
Tungusic
Eveni
Chukchi
Koryak
Greek
Turkish
Caucasus
Evenki
Evenki
Hebrew
Kurdish
Turkmen
Kazakh
Mongol
Korean
Japanese
Arabic
Persian
Pushtu
Uighur
Baluchi
Punjabi
Tibetan
Chinese
Hindi
Telugu
Burmese
Vietnamese
Thai
Tamil
Khmer
Sinhalese
Malay
Indonesian

ETHNO-LINGUISTIC GROUPS

INDO-EUROPEAN		ALTAIC		SINO-TIBETAN	
Slavic		SEMITIC		Chinese	
Baltic		Turkic		Thai	
Germanic		Mongol		Vietnamese	
Romance		Tungusic		Tibeto-Burman	
Iranian		PALÆO-ASIATIC		DRAVIDIAN	
Indo-Aryan		KOREA-JAPANESE		INDONESIAN	
other Indo-European				Other isolated groups	
URALIC					

1:80M

Australasia map (bottom)

G 120 H 140 J K 160 L 180
Manila ■ PHILIPPINES
PACIFIC OCEAN
Guam (U.S.A.)
Northern Marianas (U.S.A.)
⑤
MALAYSIA
Sandakan
Davao
Palau (Belau) (U.S.A.)
FEDERATED STATES OF MICRONESIA
MARSHALL ISLANDS
BRUNEI
Caroline Islands
Borneo
Halmahera
Equator
Sulawesi
Seram
PAPUA NEW GUINEA
NAURU
KIRIBATI
INDONESIA
Irian Jaya
New Guinea
⑥
Sumba
Timor
Arafura Sea
Port Moresby
SOLOMON ISLANDS
TUVALU
Darwin
Wm SAMOA
Is Wallis (Fr.)
G. of Carpentaria
Coral Sea
VANUATU
FIJI
Cairns
TONGA
Nouvelle Calédonie (Fr.)
Tropic of Capricorn
Alice Springs
AUSTRALIA
⑦
Brisbane
Perth
Fremantle
Sydney
Adelaide
Canberra
Melbourne
Auckland
North I.
NEW ZEALAND
Bass Strait
Tasmania
Tasman Sea
Wellington
Hobart
South I.
Christchurch
Chatham I. (N.Z.)
Stewart I.
Dunedin
⑧
AUSTRALASIA
1:60M

200   400   600   800 km
200   400 mls

RUSSIAN FEDERATION
1 Chuvashkaya R.
2 Checheno-Ingushskaya R.
3 Severo-Osetinskaya R.
4 Kabardino- Balkarskaya R.
GEORGIA
5 Abkhazskaya R.
6 Adzharskaya R.
AZERBAIJAN
7 Nakhichevanskaya R.

ARCTIC
NORWEGIAN SEA
BARENTS SEA
KARA SEA
NOVAYA ZEMLYA
ZEMLYA FRANTSA JOSIFA (FRANZ-JOSEF-LAND)
SVALBARD (SPITSBERGEN)

RUSSIAN FEDERATION
Zapadno Sibirskaya

Glasgow
Edinburgh
Aberdeen
U.K.
SCOTLAND
Inverness
Wick
NORTH SEA
DENMARK
København
Hamburg
Berlin
GERMANY
POLAND
Warszawa
Kraków
BALTIC SEA
Stockholm
Oslo
NORWAY
SWEDEN
FINLAND
Helsinki
Sankt-Peterburg (Leningrad)
Murmansk
Arkhangel'sk
Moskva (Moscow)
Nizhniy Novgorod
Kazan'
Samara (Kuybyshev)
Saratov
Volgograd
Rostov-na-Donu
Odessa
Kyiv
Kharkov
Donetsk
Dnepropetrovsk
Minsk
BLACK SEA
CASPIAN SEA
TURKEY
Yerevan
Tbilisi
Baku (Baky)
GEORGIA
AZERBAIJAN
ARMENIA
IRAN
Tehrān
IRAQ
Yekaterinburg (Sverdlovsk)
Chelyabinsk
Omsk
Novosibirsk
Novokuznetsk
Barnaul
KAZAKHSTAN
Karaganda
Tashkent (Toshkent)
UZBEKISTAN
TURKMENISTAN
Ashkhabad
TAJIKISTAN
Dushanbe
AFGHANISTAN
KIRGHIZIA (KYRGYZSTAN)
Bishkek
Alma Ata (Almaty)
SINKIANG
Tien Shan
Tarim Pendi

ARCTIC OCEAN

SEVERNAYA ZEMLYA (NORTHLAND)
Ostrov Komsomolets
Ostrov Bol'shevik
O. Malyy Taymyr
O. Petra

NOVOSIBIRSKYE OSTROVA (NEW SIBERIAN ISLANDS)
Ostrova De Longa
O. Bennetta
O. Novaya Sibir'
O. Bol'shoy Lyakhovskiy
O. Malyy Lyakhovskiy

LAPTEV SEA

EAST SIBERIAN SEA

CHUKCHI SEA

Bering Str.

BERING SEA

KAMCHATKA
Petropavlovsk-Kamchatskiy

Gory Byrranga
Poluostrov Taymyr
Ozero Taymyr
Khatanga
Nordvik
Tiksi
Chokurdakh

SEA OF OKHOTSK

Magadan

SAKHALIN
Yuzhno-Sakhalinsk
Kuril'skiye Ostrova (Kurii Islands)

FEDERATION

Yakutsk
Vilyuysk
Verkhnevilyuysk
Namtsy
Pokrovsk
Aldan
Tommot
Olekminsk

Mirnyy
Suntar
Lensk

Yakut Khrebet
Verkhoyanskiy Khrebet
Khrebet Cherskogo
Stanovoy Khrebet

Sredne Sibirskoye Ploskogor'ye

Bratsk
Kansk
Krasnoyarsk
Abakan
Minusinsk
Kyzyl
Tuvinskaya R.

Irkutsk
Angarsk
Ulan Ude
Chita
Ozero Baykal

Ust' Kut
Kirensk
Bodaybo

Skovorodino
Tynda
Zeya
Svobodnyy
Blagoveshchensk
Belogorsk

Komsomol'sk na Amure
Khabarovsk
Birobidzhan

Sovetskaya Gavan'
Nikolayevsk na Amure

HOKKAIDO
Sapporo
Otaru
Hakodate
Asahikawa
Muroran
Wakkanai

Ust'-Kamchatsk

Vladivostok
Ussuriysk
Nakhodka

MONGOLIA
Ulaanbaatar
Bayanzürh
Darhan
Erdenet
Choybalsan
Altanbulag
Sühbaatar

Dzüylen
Altay
Uliastay
Arvayheer
Mandalgovi
Saynshand
Dalandzadgad

SEA OF JAPAN

Manzhouli
Hailar
Qiqihar
Harbin
Changchun
Shenyang
Fushun
Anshan
Jilin
Mudanjiang
Jiamusi
Hegang
Baicheng
Tongliao

MANCHURIA

INNER MONGOLIA
Hohhot
Baotou
Datong
Zhangjiakou

Beijing (Peking)
Tianjin (Tientsin)
Tangshan
Qinhuangdao
Chengde

NORTH KOREA
P'yŏngyang
Namp'o
Kaesŏng
Sinŭiju
Hamhŭng
Wŏnsan
Ch'ŏngjin

SOUTH KOREA
Seoul
Inch'ŏn
Taejŏn
Taegu
Pusan
Kwangju
Mokp'o

Chejudo

YELLOW SEA

Jinan
Qingdao
Yantai
Weifang
Zibo
Tai'an

Shijiazhuang
Taiyuan
Handan
Anyang
Xuzhou
Jining

Yinchuan
Hami
Dunhuang

HONSHU
TOKYO
Yokohama
Nagoya
Kyoto
Osaka
Kobe
Hiroshima
Fukuoka
Nagasaki
Kagoshima
Sendai
Niigata
Akita
Aomori
Morioka
Yamagata
Fukushima
Matsuyama
Kochi
Kita Kyushu
KYUSHU
SHIKOKU
JAPAN

GREAT WALL

CHINA

Qilian Shan
Altun Shan

1:20M

200 400 600 800 km
0 200 400 mls

KAMCHATKA

SEA OF OKHOTSK

Kuril'skiye Ostrova (Kuril Islands)

SAKHALIN

HOKKAIDŌ

Sapporo

SEA OF JAPAN

U.S.S.R.

MANCHURIA

MONGOLIA

INNER MONGOLIA

Novosibirsk
Krasnoyarsk
Irkutsk
Ulaanbaatar

Harbin
Changchun
Shenyang
Dalian

NORTH KOREA
P'yŏngyang
SOUTH KOREA
Sŏul (Seoul)
Pusan
Taegu

Tōkyō
Yokohama
Ōsaka
Kyōto
Kōbe
Nagoya
Kyūshū
Shikoku

Beijing (Peking)
Tianjin (Tientsin)
Jinan
Qingdao

YELLOW SEA

Shanghai

EAST CHINA SEA

CHINA

Xi'an
Wuhan
Nanjing
Chengdu
Chongqing
Guangzhou (Canton)
Kunming
Guiyang
Nanning

TAIWAN (FORMOSA)
T'ai-pei
Kao-hsiung

HONG KONG (U.K.)
Kowloon

RYUKYU RETTO

Okinawa

PACIFIC OCEAN

Tropic of Cancer

SINKIANG

TIBET

BURMA (MYANMAR)
Mandalay

INDIA

Hanoi

Nanhai

Seas and Oceans

PACIFIC OCEAN
SOUTH CHINA SEA
PHILIPPINE SEA
CELEBES SEA
SULU SEA
MOLUCCA SEA
CERAM SEA
BANDA SEA
FLORES SEA
JAVA SEA
ARAFURA SEA
TIMOR SEA
CORAL SEA
ANDAMAN SEA
INDIAN OCEAN
CAROLINE ISLANDS
FEDERATED STATES OF MICRONESIA

Regions and Countries

PHILIPPINES
LUZON
MINDANAO
MALAYSIA
PENINSULAR MALAYSIA
INDONESIA
BORNEO
KALIMANTAN
SABAH
SARAWAK
BRUNEI
SULAWESI (CELEBES)
SUMATRA
JAWA (JAVA)
THAILAND
CAMBODIA
VIETNAM
INDO-CHINA
PAPUA NEW GUINEA
IRIAN JAYA
AUSTRALIA
Arnhem Land

Cities and Towns

Manila, Quezon City, San Pablo, Batangas, Santa Cruz, Cabanatuan, Tarlac, Lingayen, Dagupan, San Fernando, Baguio, Vigan, Laoag, Aparri, Tuguegarao, Ilagan, Baler, Daet, Naga, Legazpi, Bulan, Masbate, Catarman, Catbalogan, Tacloban, Roxas, Iloilo, Bacolod, Cebu, Tagbilaran, Surigao, Butuan, Cagayan de Oro, Malaybalang, Ozamiz, Marawi, Cotabato, Davao, Digos, General Santos, Zamboanga, Jolo, Puerto Princesa, Taytay

Bangkok (Krung Thep), Ayutthaya, Nakhon Sawan, Phitsanulok, Nakhon Si Thammarat, Surat Thani, Songkhla, Hat Yai, Trang, Phuket, Chumphon, Nakhon Ratchasima, Ubon Ratchathani, Khon Kaen, Udon Thani, Nong Khai, Vientiane, Savannakhet, Pakse

Phnom Penh, Battambang, Kompong Cham, Kratie, Kompong Som (Sihanoukville)

Ho Chi Minh (Saigon), My Tho, Can Tho, Long Xuyen, Vinh Long, Phan Thiet, Phan Rang, Nha Trang, Da Lat, Qui Nhon, Pleiku, Da Nang, Hue, Quang Tri, Dong Hoi, Vinh, An Nhon

Kuala Lumpur, Kelang, Melaka, Johor Bharu, Singapore, Kota Bharu, Kuala Trengganu, Kuantan, Ipoh, George Town, Taiping, Alor Setar

Kuching, Sibu, Bintulu, Miri, Bandar Seri Begawan, Kota Kinabalu, Sandakan, Lahad Datu, Tawau, Tarakan, Balikpapan, Samarinda, Banjarmasin, Palangkaraya, Pontianak, Singkawang, Sambas

Medan, Padang, Pekanbaru, Jambi, Palembang, Bengkulu, Bandar Lampung (Telukbetung), Bukittinggi, Sibolga, Banda Aceh

Jakarta, Tanjung Priok, Bogor, Bandung, Cirebon, Semarang, Surakarta, Yogyakarta, Surabaya, Malang, Kediri, Probolinggo, Jember, Banyuwangi, Cilacap, Purwokerto, Tegal

Ujung Pandang (Makassar), Manado, Gorontalo, Palu, Kendari, Parepare, Pinrang, Majene

Ternate, Tobelo, Ambon, Piru

Denpasar, Mataram, Sumbawa Besar, Kupang, Dili, Ende

Jayapura, Manokwari, Sorong, Fakfak, Merauke, Nabire

Port Moresby, Wewak, Madang, Lae, Morobe, Wau

Darwin, Katherine, Cairns, Cooktown, Normanton, Burketown

Physical Features

Equator
Great Barrier Reef
Spratly Islands
Paracel Islands
Isthmus of Kra
Mouths of the Mekong
Mouths of the Irrawaddy
Gulf of Papua
Gulf of Carpentaria
Torres Strait
Makassar Strait
Malacca Strait
Mindoro Strait
Pegunungan Maoke
Pegunungan Barisan
Mentawai Kepulauan

MONGOLIA

NEI MONGOL

GOBI

Beijing (Peking)

Hebei

Tianjin (Tientsin)

Shanxi

Shaanxi

Ningxia

Qinghai

Shandong

Jinan (Tsinan)

Qingdao (Tsingtao)

Henan

Jiangsu

Nanjing (Nanking)

Shanghai

Anhui

CHINA

Hubei

Wuhan

Zhejiang

Sichuan

Chengdu

Chongqing (Chungking)

Hunan

Jiangxi

Fujian

Guizhou

Guiyang

Guangxi

Guangdong

Guangzhou (Canton)

Hong Kong (U.K.)

Macao (Port.)

Yunnan

Kunming

VIETNAM

LAOS

Hanoi

Haiphong

GULF OF TONGKIN

Hainan

SOUTH CHINA SEA

YELLOW SEA (HUANG HAI)

BO HAI

KOREA BAY

Shenyang

Liaoning

Dalian

TAIWAN

T'ai-pei

Kao-hsiung

FORMOSA STRAIT

1:5M

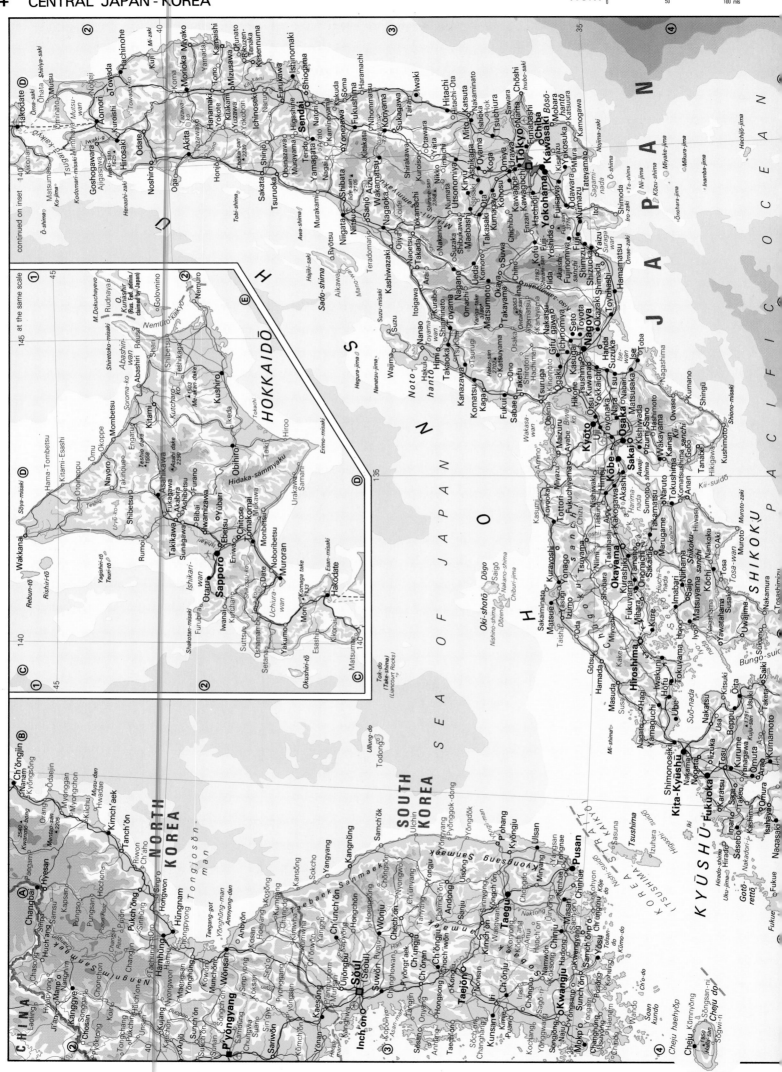

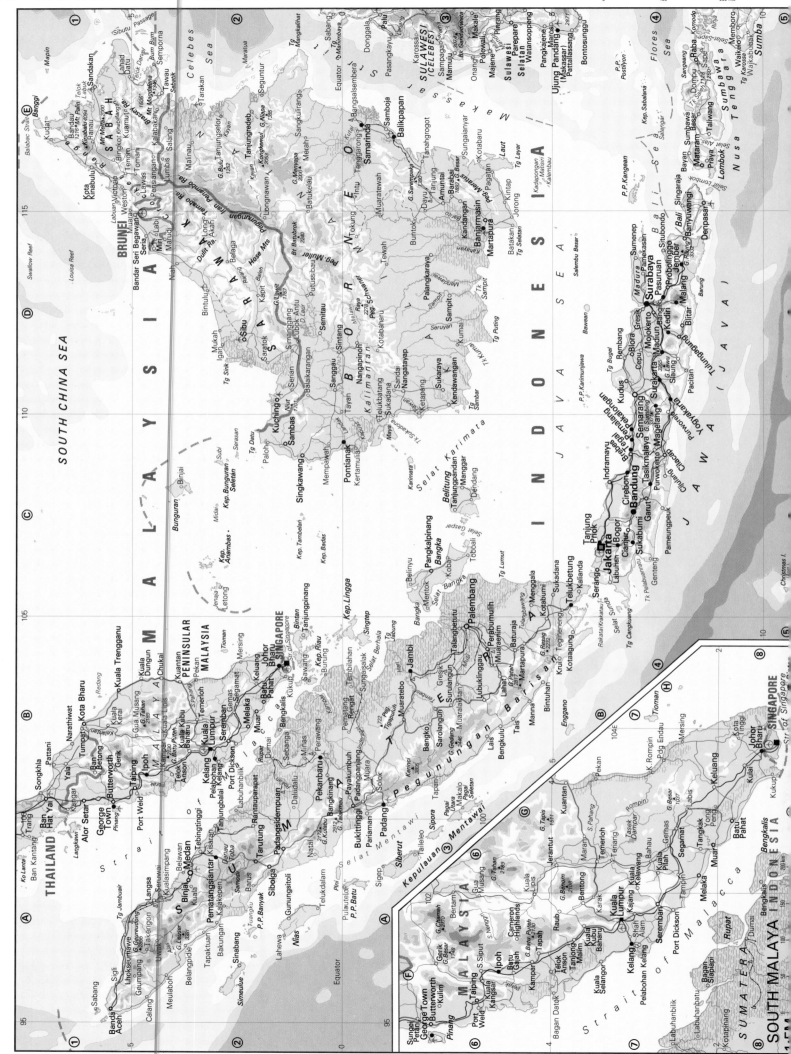

200 400 600 800 km
200 400 mls

Countries and regions:
YUGOS. (Yugoslavia), ROMANIA, MOLDOVA, BULGARIA, MACEDONIA, ALBANIA, GREECE, TURKEY, CYPRUS, SYRIA, LEBANON, ISRAEL, JORDAN, IRAQ, IRAN, SAUDI ARABIA, KUWAIT, BAHRAIN, QATAR, UNITED ARAB EMIRATES, OMAN, YEMEN, EGYPT, LIBYA, SUDAN, ERITREA, ETHIOPIA, DJIBOUTI, SOMALIA, KENYA, UGANDA, TANZANIA, RWANDA, BURUNDI, ZAIRE, RUS. FED. (Russian Federation), GEORGIA, ARMENIA, AZERBAIJAN, TURKMENISTAN, UZBEKISTAN, KAZ (Kazakhstan), AFGHANISTAN, PAKISTAN

Seas and water bodies:
BLACK SEA, MEDITERRANEAN SEA, CASPIAN SEA, Aral Sea (Aral'skoye More), The Gulf, Gulf of Oman, Gulf of Aden, ARABIAN SEA, Sea of Marmara, Aegean Sea, L. Nasser, L. Tana, L. Victoria, L. Rudolf, L. Albert, L. Kyoga, L. Turkana

Cities and towns (selection):
Beograd, Sarajevo, Split, Dubrovnik, Skopje, Sofiya, Tiranë, Thessaloniki, Athínai, Pátrai, Bucuresti, Ploiesti, Ruse, Varna, Burgas, Plovdiv, Istanbul, Bursa, Ankara, Konya, Adana, Izmir, Denizli, Antalya, Nicosia, Halab, Hamah, Hims, Beirut, Damascus, Tel Aviv, Jerusalem, Amman, Baghdad, Karbalā, An Najaf, Al Başrah, Kuwait, Tehrān, Esfahān, Shīrāz, Kermān, Mashhad, Herat, Kandahār, Cairo, Alexandria, Port Said, Suez, Aswân, Luxor, Asyût, El Minya, Khartoum, Omdurman, Port Sudan, Atbara, Medina, Makkah, Jiddah, At Ta'if, Ar Riyâd, Manāmah, Doha, Abū Dhabi, Dubai, Muscat, San'ā, Al Hudaydah, Ta'izz, Adan (Aden), Djibouti, Ādīs Ābeba, Dirē Dawa, Harēr, Hargeysa, Muqdisho (Mogadishu), Marka, Kismaayo, Nairobi, Kampala, Kigali, Bujumbura, Moshi, Baku (Baky), Tbilisi, Yerevan, Tabriz, Rasht, Ashkhabad (Ashgabat), Chardzhou, Bukhara, Karshi, Mary, Nukus, Tashauz, Urgench, Volgograd, Astrakhan', Donetsk, Odessa, Rostov-na-Donu, Krasnodar, Sochi, Groznyy, Makhachkala

Tropic of Cancer
Equator

Socotra (Suqutra) (Yemen)
Maşīrah
Rub' al Khālī
An Nafūd
Ad Dahnā
Nubian Desert
Libyan Desert
Qattâra Depression
Sinai
Dasht-e Kavir
Dasht-e Lūt
Elburz
Zagros
Makran
Baluchistan
Hadramawt
Carlsberg Basin
Somali Basin
INDIAN OCEAN

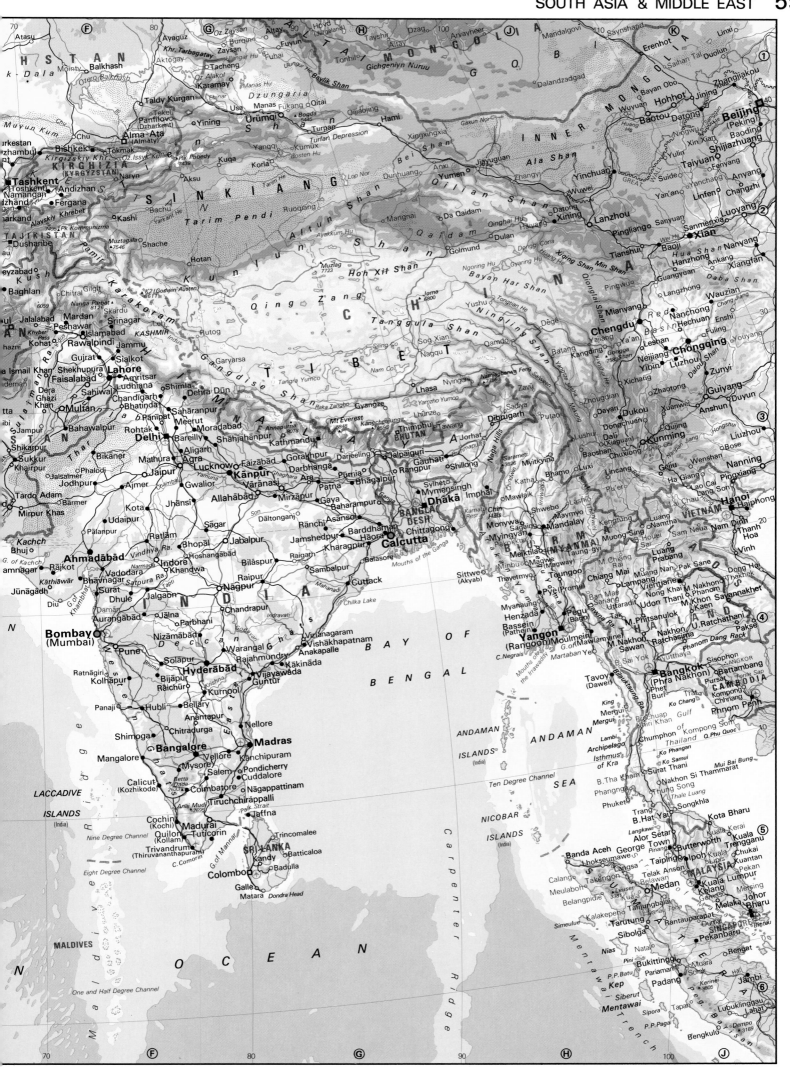

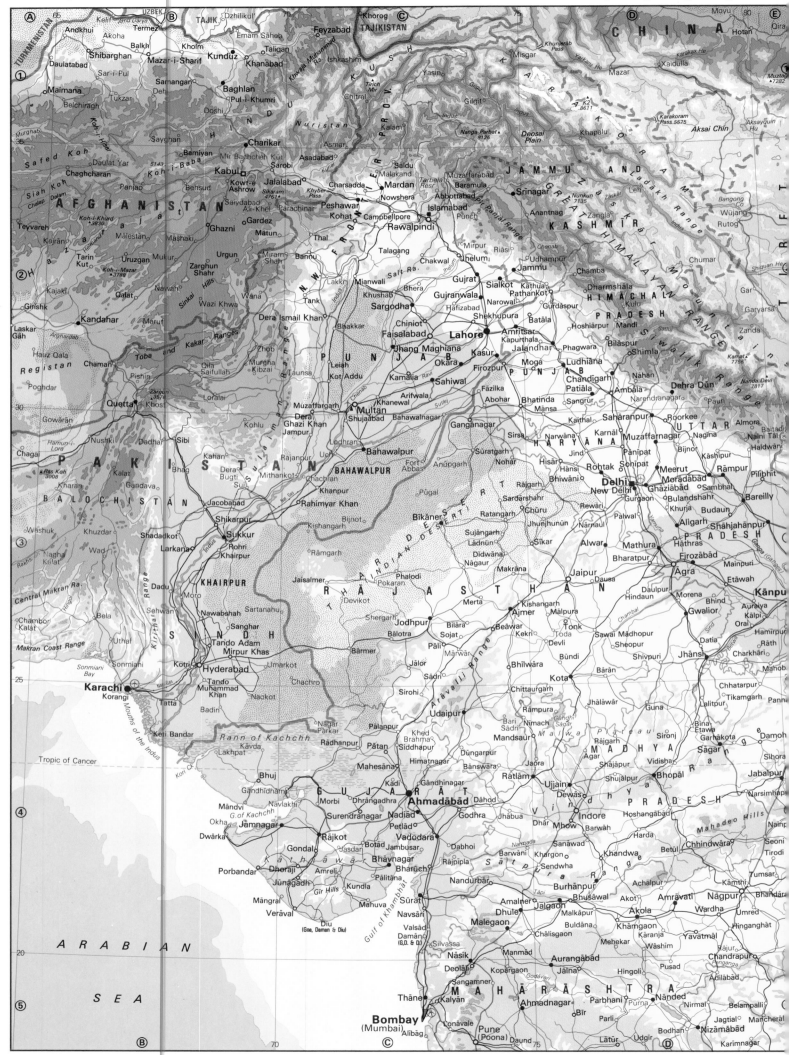

1:7.5M

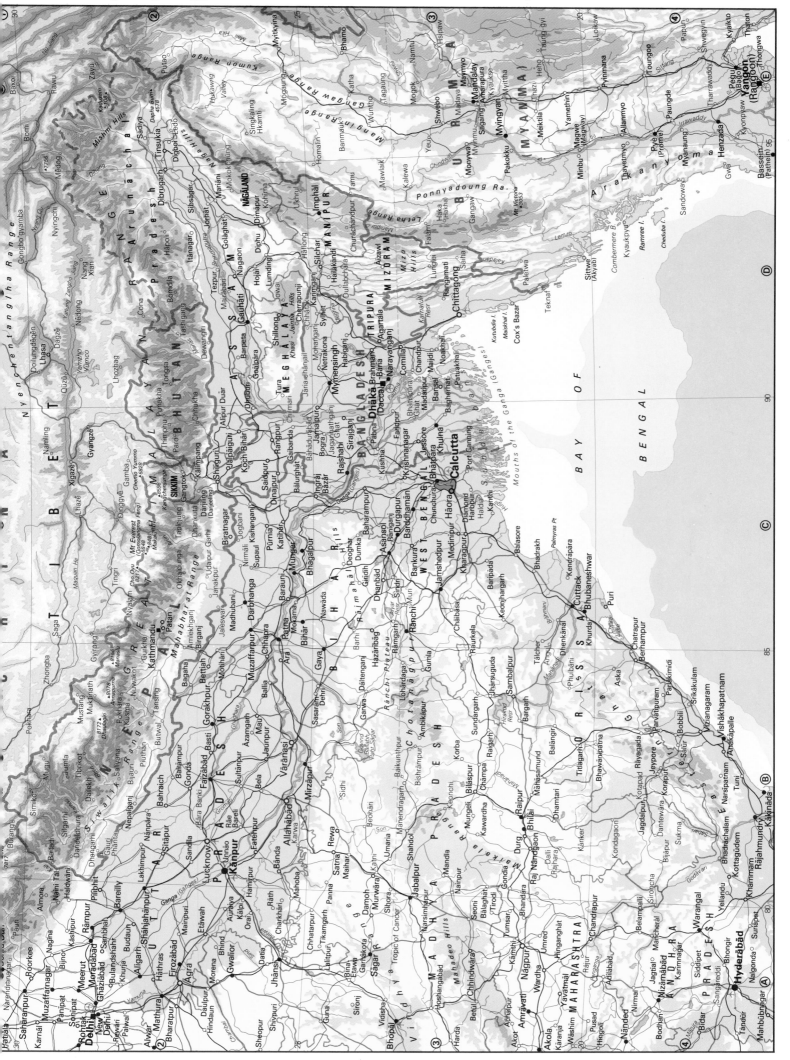

1:7.5M

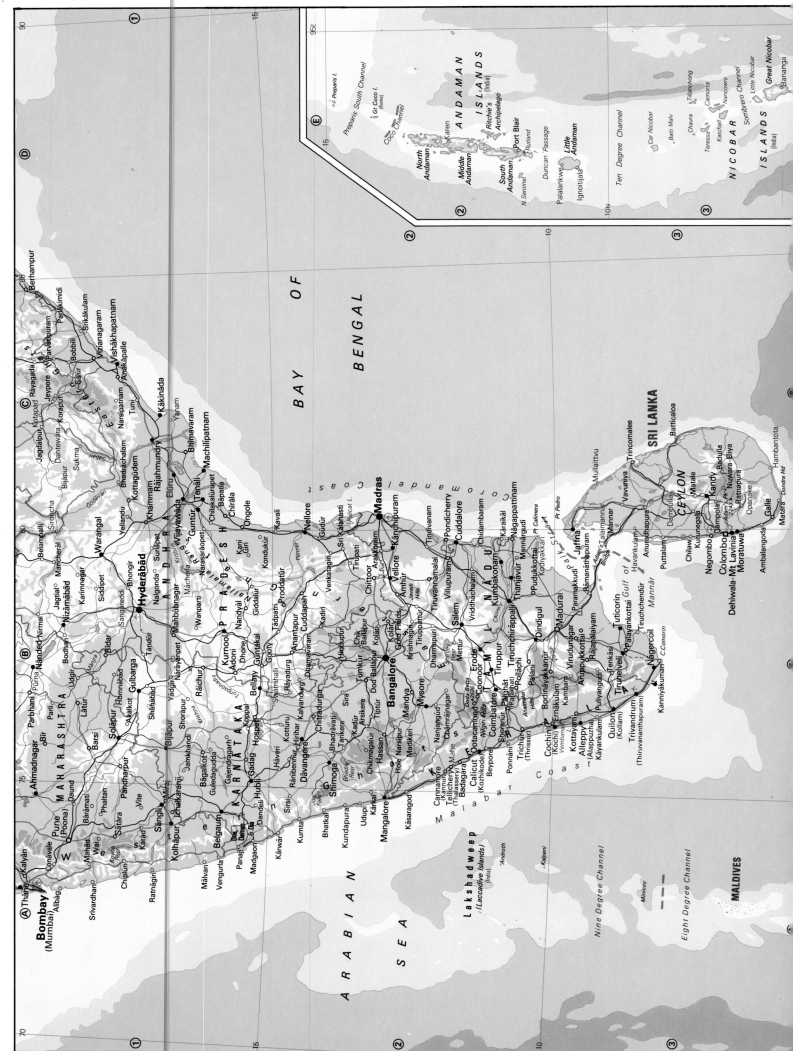

1:7.5M

100 200 300 km
50 100 150 mls

TURKMENISTAN

AFGHANISTAN

PAKISTAN

IRAN

SAUDI ARABIA

KUWAIT

QATAR

BAHRAIN

Caspian Sea

The Gulf

Strait of Hormuz

Gulf of Oman

Dasht-e Kavir

Dasht-e Lut

Zagros Mountains

Reshteh-ye Alborz (Elburz Mts)

Paropamisus

Bandi-Turkestan

Central Makran Range

Makran Coast Range

Baluchistan

Kopet Dag

Kavir-i-Namak

Dasht-e Naomid

Namakzar-e Shaded

Gaud-i-Zirreh

Registan

Dasht-i-Margo

Major cities and towns:

Baghdad · Tehrān · Mashhad · Kandahar · Herat · Kermān · Esfahān · Shirāz · Yazd · Tabrīz · Rasht · Qom · Hamadān · Arāk · Ahvāz · Abādān · Khorramshahr · Basra · Kuwait · Manāmah · Doha · Bandar Abbās · Zāhedān · Zābol · Girishk · Maimana · Shibarghān · Mary · Ashkhabad

100   200   300 km
50   100   150 mls

Countries / Regions: AZERBAIJAN, ARMENIA, GEORGIA, IRAN, IRAQ, SYRIA, TURKEY, JORDAN, ISRAEL, LEBANON, CYPRUS, SAUDI ARABIA, KUWAIT, EGYPT, GREECE

Seas: BLACK SEA, Mediterranean Sea, Sea of Marmara, Caspian Sea, Gulf of Aqaba, Gulf of Suez

Selected cities and towns:
Baku, Sumgait, Tbilisi, Rustavi, Yerevan, Gyandzha, Tabriz, Zanjan, Hamadan, Kermanshah, Khorramabad, Borujerd, Dezful, Ahvaz, Abadan, Khorramshahr, Basra, Kuwait, Al Ahmadi

Baghdad, Kirkuk, Al Mawsil (Mosul), Arbil, As Sulaymaniyah, Samarra, Ar Ramadi, Fallujah, Karbala, An Najaf, Ad Diwaniyah, As Samawah, An Nasiriyah, Al Hillah

Aleppo (Halab), Hamah, Hims, Dayr az Zawr, Ar Raqqah, Al Hasakah, Al Qamishli, Tudmur, Damascus (Dimashq), As Suwayda, Dar'a

Beirut (Beyrouth), Tripoli (Tarabulus), Saida, Tyr

Amman, Irbid, Az Zarqa, Ma'an, Al Aqaba

Jerusalem, Tel Aviv Yafo, Haifa, Beersheba, Gaza, Ashdod, Netanya, Nazareth, Hebron

Nicosia, Limassol, Larnaca, Famagusta

Istanbul, Ankara, Izmir, Bursa, Adana, Konya, Kayseri, Antalya, Samsun, Trabzon, Erzurum, Diyarbakir, Gaziantep, Sanliurfa, Malatya, Sivas, Eskişehir, Kütahya, Denizli, Mersin, Tarsus, Iskenderun, Antakya, Kahramanmaraş, Van, Kars, Erzincan, Elazig, Batman, Mardin, Nusaybin

Cairo (El Qâhira), Alexandria (El Iskandarîya), El Giza, Suez, Port Said, Ismâ'ilîya, El Mansûra, Tanta, Damanhûr, Beni Suef, El Faiyûm, El Minya

Physical features: Anadolu Dağları, Toros Dağları, Kuzey Anadolu Dağları, Munzur Silsilesi, Tigris, Euphrates, Nile, Suez Canal, Sinai (Sinâ), Libyan Plateau, An Nafud, Jazira, Badiyat ash Sham, Al Widyan al Hijarah, Wadi as Sirhan

1:2.5M

| 0 | 25 | 50 | 75 | 100 km |
| 0 | 25 | 50 mils | | |

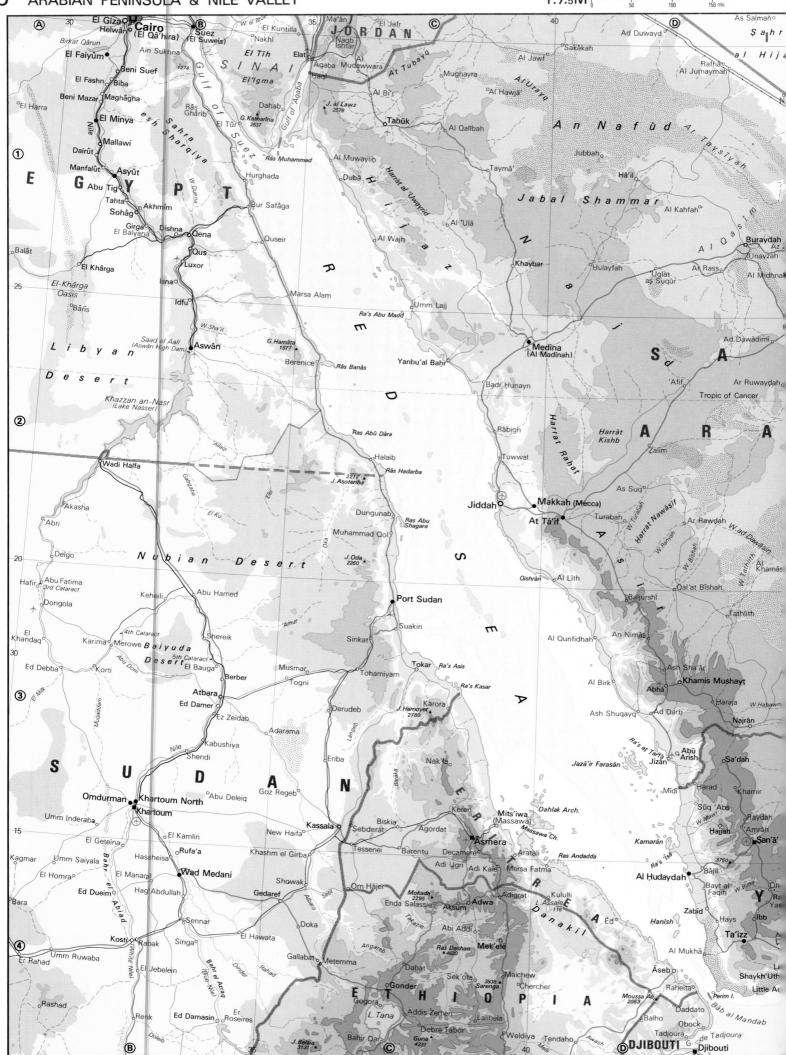

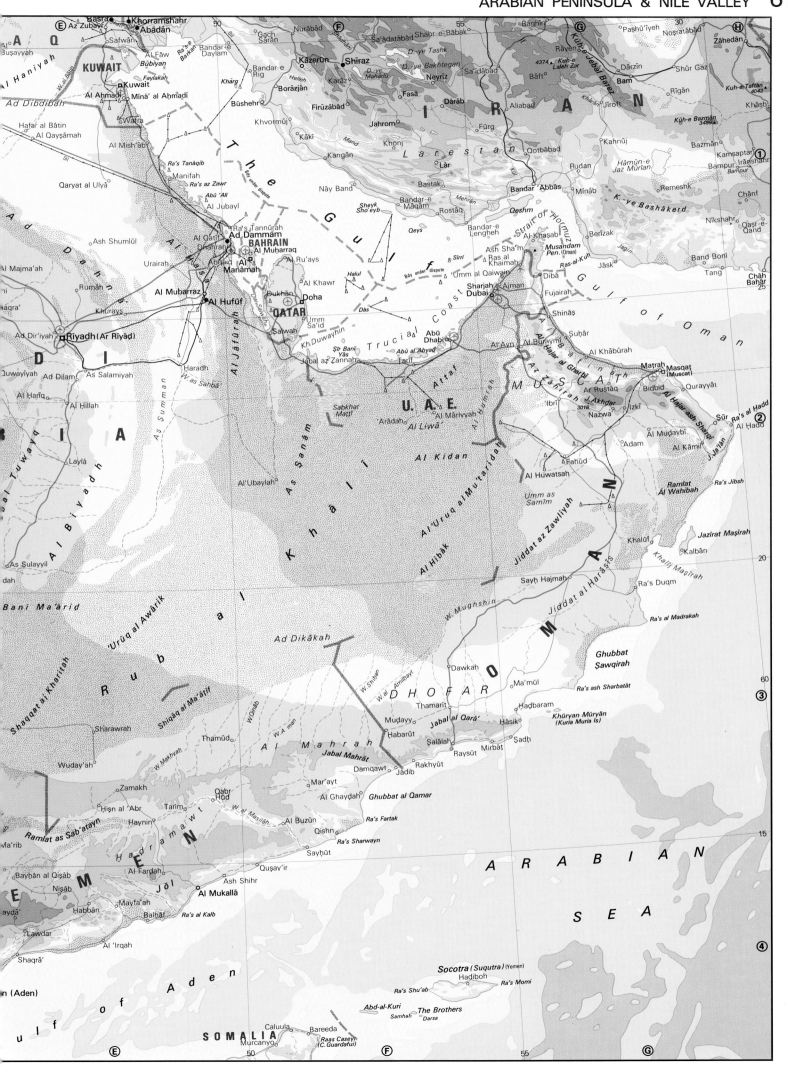

400 800 1200 1600 km
400 800 mls

A 2 30 B 20 60 C 10 D E F G H 40 J 50 K 60 L 70 2 M

NORWAY FINLAND
Helsinki
Oslo SWEDEN Tallinn Sankt Peterburg Nizhniy Magnitogorsk
Stockholm EST. (Leningrad) Novgorod
Göteborg Riga LAT. Volga
UNITED North DENMARK Baltic Sea LITH. Moskva RUSSIAN FEDERATION Samara
KINGDOM Sea København R.F. Vilnius Minsk
IRELAND Edinburgh Hamburg Gdansk BELORUSSIA Ural Oz. Balkhash
Dublin London NETH. Berlin Warszawa Khar'kov Volgograd KAZAKHSTAN
s'Gravenhage GERMANY POLAND Kiyev Volga
BELG. Bonn Kraków UKRAINE Don Aral Syr-Darya
Bruxelles Praha Rostov Sea UZBEKISTAN
Paris LUX. CZECH Odessa Volgograd Tashkent
FRANCE Bern München REPUBLIC MOLD. Amu-Darya
Bay of SWITZ. AUSTRIA Budapest ROMANIA GEORGIA Tbilisi TURKMENISTAN
Biscay Milano SLOV. HUNGARY Bucureşti Baku Ashkhabad
Bordeaux CROATIA Beograd ARM. AZER. Caspian
Marseille BOSNIA- Sofia Black Sea Mashhad
Porto Corse HERZ. YUGOS. BULGARIA Istanbul Ankara Tabriz
Madrid Roma Tirana MAC. TURKEY Tehrān
Lisboa Barcelona Napoli ALB. Athinai AFGHANIST
PORTUGAL Tajo SPAIN Balearic Sardegna GREECE Damascus Shiraz
Islands CYPRUS Nicosia SYRIA IRAN
Madeira Tanger Oran Sicilia Crete Beirut Baghdad
(Port) Rabat Fès Alger Annaba LEB. IRAQ Basra
Marrakech Casablanca Tunis Mediterranean Sea Jerusalem Amman Kuwait
Islas TUNISIA Constantine Port Said ISR. KUWAIT Kuwait
Canarias MOROCCO Sfax Tripoli Benghazi JORDAN BAHRAIN Abu
(Sp.) Béchar Alexandria Suez SAUDI Doha Dhabi
La'youn Cairo QATAR UNITED ARAB
Western ALGERIA Ghadamis Asyût Nile ARABIA EMIRATES Muscat
Sahara Tindouf In Salah LIBYA EGYPT Ar Riyād OMAN
Nouadhibou Tropic of Cancer Sabha Aswân Red The Gulf
Ghät L. Nasser Sea Makkah Muscat
F'dérik Tamanrasset Wadi Halfa YEMEN Kuria Muria I
MAURITANIA SAHARA Port Sudan San'a Socotra
Nouakchott Atbara ERITREA Adan Gulf of Aden (Yemen)
Dakar Tombouctou NIGER Omdurman Khartoum Kassala Asmera DJIBOUTI
SENEGAL Sénégal Agadez El Obeid Djibouti Hargeysa
THE Banjul Niger L. Chad CHAD SUDAN Blue Nile Diré Dawa
GAMBIA Bamako Niamey Kano Ndjamena Ādis Ābeba
GUINEA MALI BURKINA Maiduguri Wau ETHIOPIA
BISSAU Bissau Ouagadougou Kaduna White Nile Jimma SOMALIA
GUINEA Kankan Bobo Dioulasso NIGERIA Juba Gulu Muqdisho
Conakry SIERRA Tamale BENIN Abuja CENTRAL L. Turkana
LEONE IVORY COAST GHANA Ilorin Niger AFRICAN REPUBLIC UGANDA KENYA
Freetown Yamoussoukro TOGO Ibadan Ngaoundéré Bambari L. Albert
Monrovia Kumasi Porto Onitsha CAMEROON Bangui Kisangani Kampala Nairobi
Buchanan LIBERIA Novo Lagos Douala ZAIRE L. Edward Entebbe
Abidjan Accra Lomé Port Harcourt Yaoundé (Congo) Goma Lake Mombasa
Gulf of Guinea Bioko Malabo Bata Mbandaka RWANDA Kigali Victoria INDIAN
Principe EQUAT. Libreville Congo Kindu BURUNDI Mwanza Seychelles
SÃO TOMÉ GUINEA GABON Bujumbura Arusha SEYCHELLES
& PRINCIPE Lambaréné CONGO Kananga Kigoma Lake Dodoma OCEAN Amirante Is
São Tomé Brazzaville Kisangani Lake Zanzibar
Annobon Kinshasa Ilebo Mbuji- Tanganyika TANZANIA Dar es Salaam Aldabra Is
(Eq.G) Cabinda Matadi Bandundu Mayi Kalémié Mbala Farquhar Is
(Ang.) Kwango Kasai Kamina Mbeya COMOROS
Luanda Malanje Lulaburg Mbala Antserana
Ascension Lobito ANGOLA Lubumbashi MALAWI Lake Mayotte (Fr.)
(U.K.) Kuito Ndola Nyasa Lichinga Tromelin
Benguela Cubango ZAMBIA Lilongwe Zomba Nampula (Fr.)
St Helena Namibe Lusaka Zambezi MOZAMBIQUE Mozambique MADAGASCAR
(U.K.) Kunene L. Kariba Harare Mahajanga
Tsumeb Livingstone ZIMBABWE Mutare Beira Antananarivo Toamasina
Walvis Bay Hwange Gweru Limpopo Inhambane MAURITI
(S.A.) Windhoek Bulawayo Réunion (Fr.)
BOTSWANA Serowe Toliara
NAMIBIA Tropic of Capricorn Gaborone Maputo
Keetmanshoop Pretoria Mbabane SWAZILAND
Johannesburg LESOTHO Maseru Durban
SOUTH Kimberley Bloemfontein
AFRICA Orange East London
Cape Town Port Elizabeth

NORTH ATLANTIC OCEAN
SOUTH ATLANTIC OCEAN
Açores (Port)

Tristan da Cunha (U.K.)

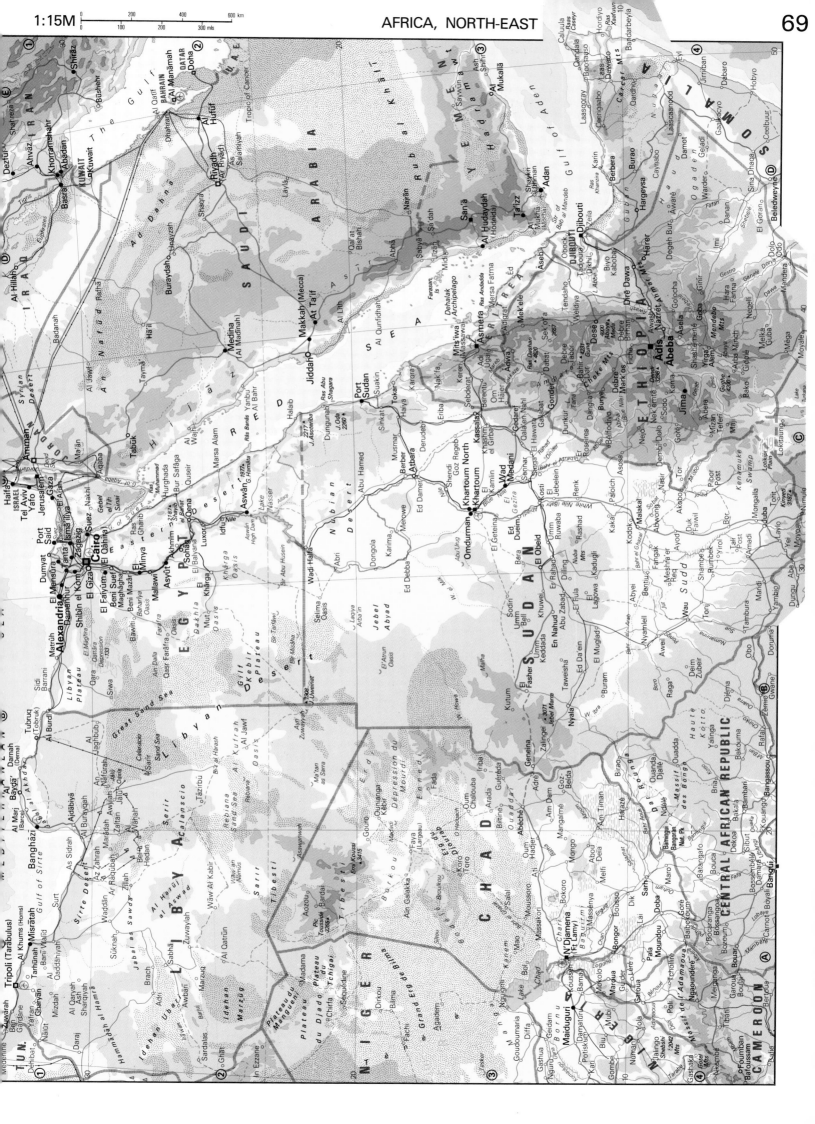

0   200   400   600 km
0   100   200   300 mils

Inset (top left): Açores / Madeira / Canary Islands

40 N   30 W
Corvo
Flores
São Jorge   Angra Do Heroismo
Faial   Pico   Terceira
Açores
(Azores)
(Portugal)
Ponta Delgada   São Miguel
Formigas
Santa Maria
at the same scale

20
Madeira (Portugal)   Porto Santo
Funchal   Deserta Grande

30
Ilhas Selvagens (Port.)
Islas Canarias (Canary Islands) (Spain)
Lanzarote
Santa Cruz De La Palma   Arrecife
La Palma   Pio Del Rosario   Fuerteventura
Gomera   Santa Cruz De Tenerife   Tenerife
Hierro   Gran Canaria   Las Palmas De Gran Canaria

PORTUGAL / SPAIN
Lisboa (Lisbon)   Badajoz   Ciudad Real   Albacete
Beja   Sierra Morena   Murcia   Alicante
C. de S. Vicente   Faro   Huelva   Córdoba   Granada   Cartagena
Sevilla (Seville)   Málaga   Almería
Cádiz   Str. of Gibraltar   Gibraltar (U.K.)
Tanger (Tangier)   Ceuta (Sp.)   Melilla (SP.)

MEDITERRANEAN SEA
Ibiza   Islas Baleares (Balearic Is)
Sardegna (Sardinia)   Cagliari
Alger (Algiers)   Tizi Ouzou   Bejaïa (Bougie)   Skikda (Philippeville)   Annaba (Bône)   Bizerte   Tunis
Cherchell   Blida   Constantine   Sétif   Souk Ahras   Tébessa   El Kef   Sousse
Mostaganem   Ech Cheliff   Ksar   Batna   Kairouan   Sfax
Oran   Mascara   Saïda   Bou Saâda   Biskra   Gafsa   Gabès
Tetouan   Oujda   Tlemcen   Sidi-bel-Abbès   Laghouat   Touggourt   TUNISIA

MOROCCO
Kenitra   Rabat   Fès   Taza   Meknès
Casablanca (Dar-el-Beida)   El Jadida   Azrou
Safi   Marrakech   Beni Mellal
Essaouira   Haut Atlas   Toubkal 4165   Ouarzazate
Agadir   Taroudannt   Anti Atlas   Zagora
Tiznit   Tata
Tan-Tan   Tarfaya
Laâyoune   Smara

Western Sahara
C. Bojador   Dakhla   B. de Rio de Oro
Tropic of Cancer

MAURITANIA
Nouadhibou   Ras Nouadhibou
Atar   Chinguetti   Tichla
Akjoujt
Nouakchott
Tidjikja   Tichitt   Néma   Oualata
Boutilimit   Aleg   Kaédi   Kiffa   Tamchaket   Aïoun El Atrouss

ALGERIA / SAHARA
El Golea   El Gassi   Ghardaïa   Ouargla   Hassi-Messaoud
Béchar   Abadla   Timimoun   In Salah   Ghadames
Tindouf   Adrar   Reggane   Aoulef   Arak   Tamanrasset (Ahaggar)   Djanet   Ghāt
Bidon 5 (Ruins)   Silet   Mts du Mouydir   In Ecker   Hoggar
Tanezrouft   Tessalit   Tin Zaouaten   In Guezzam

MALI
Tombouctou   Gourma Rharous   Gao   Ansongo   Ménaka   Kidal   Gao
Goundam   Niafounké   Bourem
Nara   Nampala   Mopti   Douentza   Bandiagara   Gossi
Nioro Du Sahel   Diéma   Goumbou   Sokolo   Ke Macina   Djenné   Ségou   San   Tougan
Kayes   Bafoulabé   Kolokani   Banamba   Koulikoro   Bamako
Kita   Kangaba   Sikasso   Bougouni

NIGER
Agadez   Ingal   Tahoua   Tchin Tabaradene   Tanout   Zinder
Birnin N'Konni   Madaoua   Dogondoutchi   Maradi   Gouré
Niamey   Tillabéri   Dosso   Sokoto   Katsina   Kano   Kaduna

SENEGAL
St-Louis   Louga   Dagana   Matam   Linguère
Thiès   Dakar   Diourbel   Touba   Kébémer
Kaolack   Kaffrine   Tambacounda   Bakel
THE GAMBIA   Banjul   Georgetown

GUINEA-BISSAU
Bissau   Bafatá   Gabú   Bolama   Catio
Arquipélago dos Bijagós

GUINEA
Conakry   Forécariah   Boké   Fria   Kindia   Mamou   Labé   Dalaba   Dabola   Kankan   Kouroussa   Siguiri   Kissidougou   Faranah   Beyla   Macenta   Nzérékoré

SIERRA LEONE
Freetown   Port Loko   Makeni   Bo   Kenema

LIBERIA
Monrovia   Buchanan   Greenville   Harper   Robertsport   Yamoussoukro

IVORY COAST
Abidjan   Man   Daloa   Bouaké   Korhogo   Odienné   Séguéla   Bondoukou   Agboville   Grand Bassam   Sassandra   San Pédro   Tabou   C. Palmas

GHANA
Accra   Kumasi   Sekondi   Takoradi   Cape Coast   Sunyani   Tamale   Wa   Bolgatanga   Bawku   Yendi   Winneba   Koforidua

BURKINA
Ouagadougou   Bobo Dioulasso   Koudougou   Kaya   Fada N'Gourma   Tenkodogo   Dori   Gaoua   Banfora

TOGO / BENIN
Lomé   Cotonou   Porto Novo   Abomey   Parakou   Natitingou   Djougou   Kandi   Malanville

NIGERIA
Lagos   Ibadan   Abeokuta   Ilorin   Oshogbo   Ife   Ogbomosho   Oyo   Benin City   Onitsha   Enugu   Abuja   Minna   Kaduna   Zaria   Kano   Katsina   Sokoto   Maradi   Bauchi   Jos   Makurdi   Calabar   Port Harcourt   Owerri   Aba   Warri   Sapele

CAMEROON
Douala   Yaoundé   Kumba   Buea   Mamfé   Bamenda   Foumban   Bafoussam   Ngaoundéré

EQUATORIAL GUINEA
Malabo   Bioko (Fernando Poo)   Bata   Ebebiyin   Evinayong   Mbini

S. TOME & PRINCIPE
São Tomé   Principe

GULF OF GUINEA
Bight of Benin   Bight of Biafra   Annobon (Equat. Guinea)   Equator

Inset (bottom left): Cape Verde
25 W
Sto Antão   Sta Luzia   Sal
S Vicente   S Nicolau
Boa Vista
CAPE VERDE
S Tiago   Maio
Praia
Fogo   Brava
15 N
at the same scale

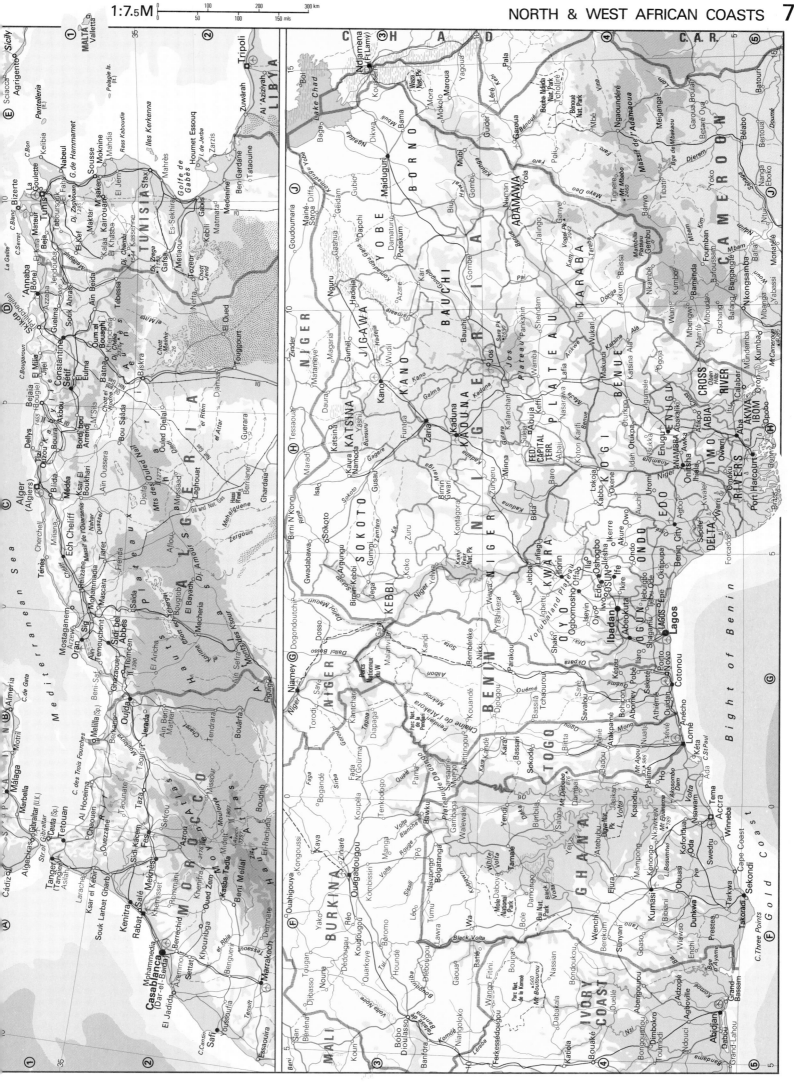

1:7.5M

100   200   300 km
50   100   150 mls

1:15M

0 200 400 600 km
0 100 200 300 mls

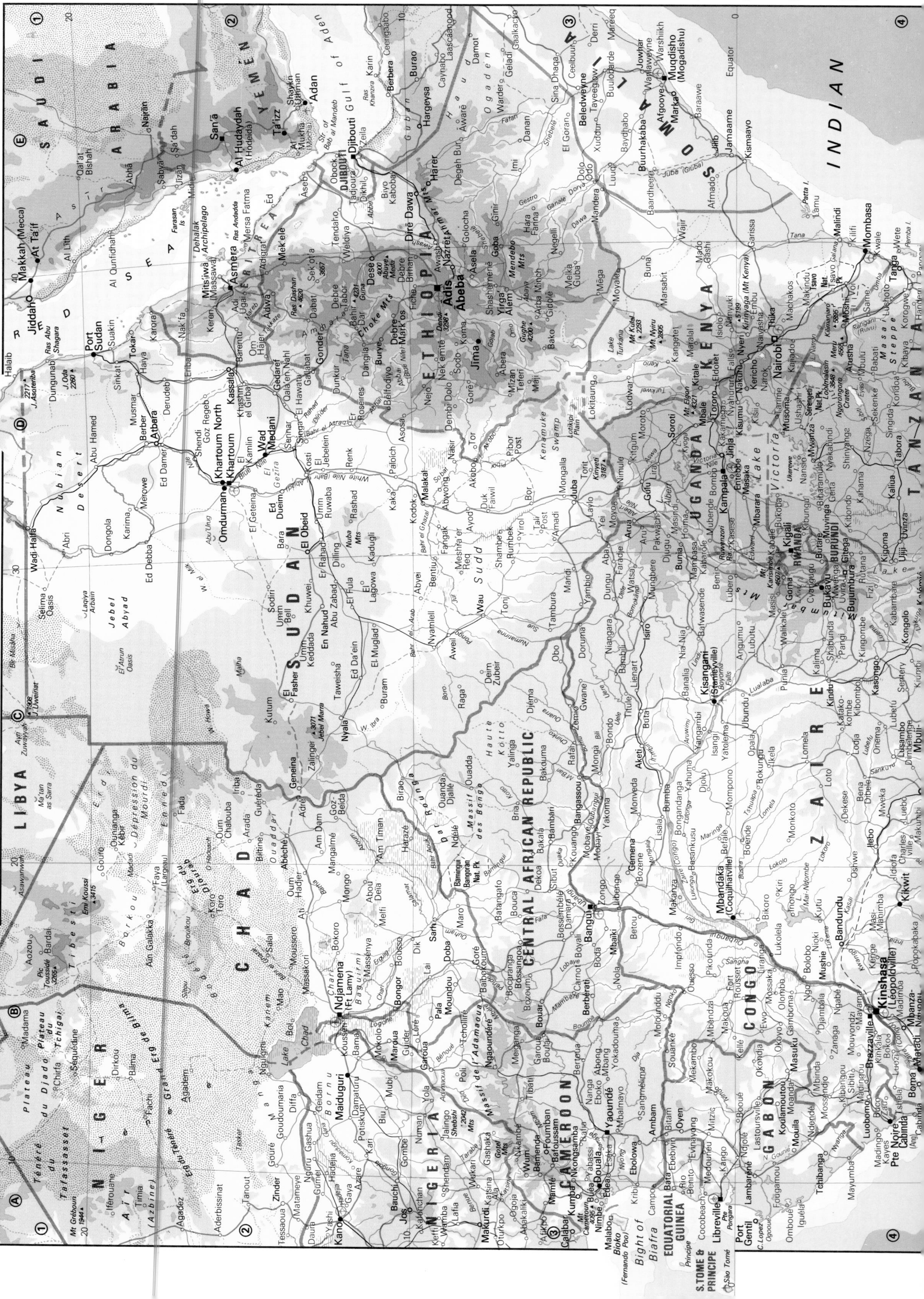

1:7.5M

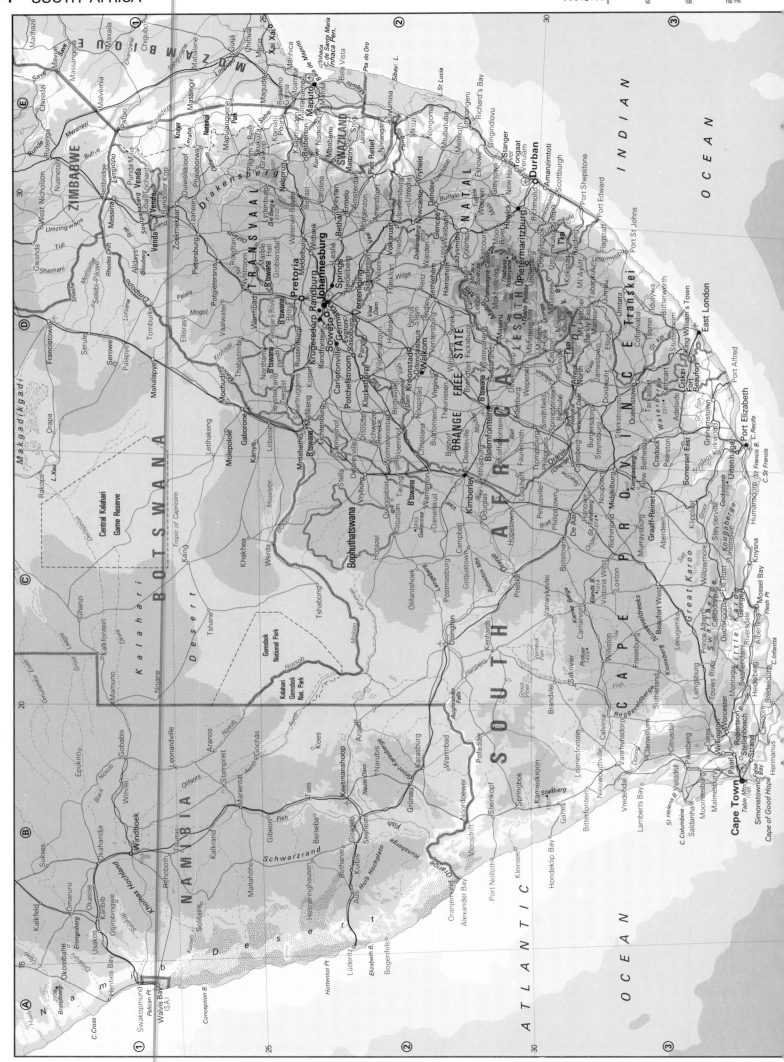

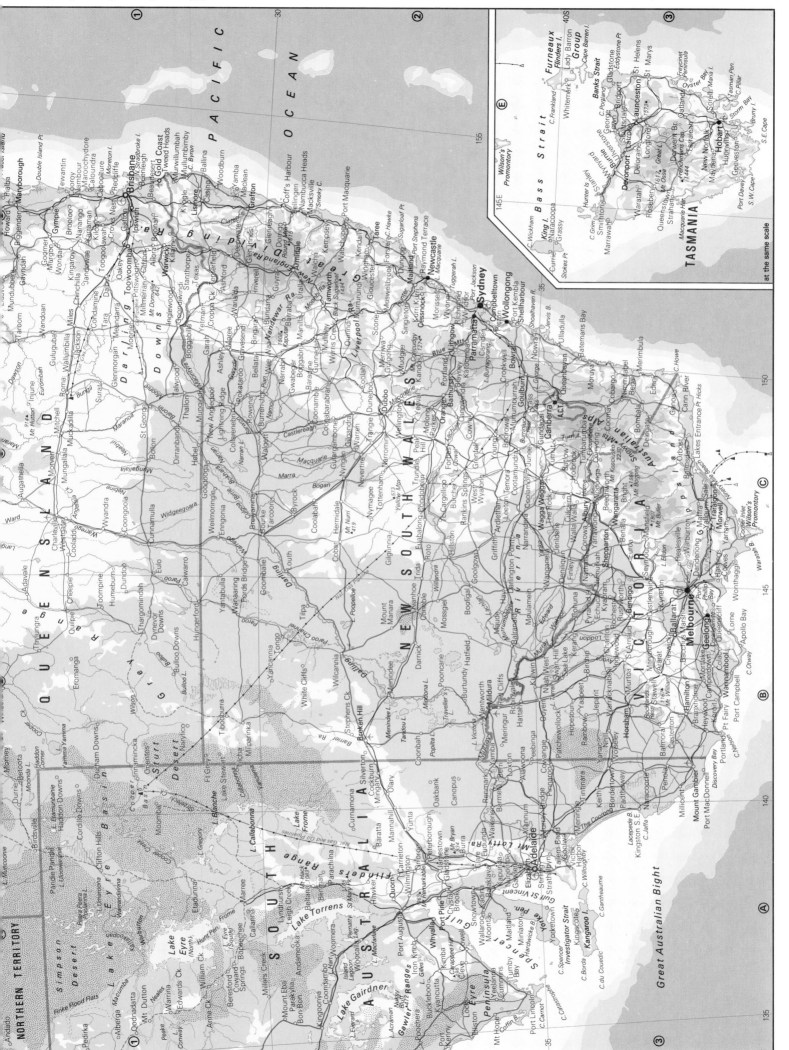

1:7.5M

200 400 600 800 km
200 400 mls

120 130 140 150

BORNEO

Tajungselor
Tanjungredeb
Kelolokan
Toliton
Manado
Minahassa Peninsula
Gorontalo
Belang Sea
Molucca Sea
Ternate
Weda
Teluk Weda
Tubelo
Halmahera
Morotai
Kep. Asia
Kep. Ayu
P.P. Mapia
Ninigo Is
Hermit Is
Admiralty Is
Mussau
Saint Matthias Group
New Hanover
Manus
Kavieng

Samarinda
Balikpapan
Donggala
Samboja
Palu
Poso
Luwuk
Peleng
Taliabu
Kep. Togian
Teluk Tomini
Kep. Sula
Obi
Ceram Sea
Piru
Bula
Seram
Ambon
Kep. Banda
Salawati
Misool
Sorong
Fakfak
Kaimana
Babo
Teluk Berau
Kokonau
Manokwari
Biak
Numfoor
Yapen
Cendrawasih
Sarmi
Jayapura
Aitape
Wewak
IRIAN JAYA
Pegunungan Maoke
Pk. Jaya 5029
Tanahmerah
Madang
Mt Hagen
Goroka
Mt Wilhelm
Sepik
Central Ra.
Bismarck Archipelago
Bismarck Sea
PAPUA NEW GUINEA
Umboi
Lae
Morobe

Kintap
Banjarmasin
Tg Selatan
Majene
Parepare
Bone
Watampone
Butung
Bonthain
Kabaena
Kendari
Kabia
Buru
Namlea
INDONESIA
Kep. Barat Daya
Damar
Romang
Kep. Babar
Kep. Tanimbar
Kep. Kai
Dobo
Kep. Aru
Dolak
Digul
Merauke
Daru
Kikori
Kerema
Mt St Mary
Popondetta
Kokoda
Owen Stanley Ra.
D Entrec
Port Moresby
Kupiano
Samarai

Ujung Pandang (Makassar)
P.P. Macan
P.P. Kangean
Flores Sea
Bali
Denpasar
Mataram
Lombok
Sumbawa
Raba
Sumba
Memboro
Reo
Ruteng
Flores
Ende
Lomblen
Alor
Wetar
Kep. Leti
Kep. Sermata
Wangapu
Sawu
Roti
Kupang
Timor
Dili

INDIAN OCEAN
Java Trench
Cartier I.
Scott Reef
Rowley Shoals
Timor Sea
Arafura Sea
Torres Strait
Pr. of Wales
C. York
Somerset
Saibai I.

Melville I.
Bathurst I.
Van Diemen G.
Clarence
Cobourg Pen.
Croker I.
Wessel Is
C. Arnhem
Nhulunbuy
Groote Eylandt
Gulf of Carpentaria
Weipa
Cape York
Iron Range
C. Grenville
Princess Charlotte B.

Darwin
Rum Jungle
Adelaide River
Joseph Bonaparte Gulf
C. Londonderry
Pago Mission
Wyndham
Adelaide River
Burrundie
Pine Creek
Katherine
Daly
Roper
Limmen Bight
Sir Edward Pellew Group
Mornington
Wellesley Is
Coen
Peninsula
Mitchell River
Laura
Cooktown

Cartier I.
C. Lévêque
King Sound
Derby
Fitzroy
Halls Creek
Broome
Lagrange
Eighty Mile Beach
Victoria River Downs
L. Argyle
Kimberley Plateau
Mt Ord 936
King Leopold Ra.
Fitzroy Crossing
Wave Hill
Powell Creek
Daly Waters
Borroloola
Newcastle Waters
Burketown
Normanton
Croydon
Forsayth
Gilbert
Mt Bartle Frere 1611
Cairns
Innisfail
Ravenshoe
Palm Is
Ingham
Townsville
Ayr
Charters Towers
Bowen
Proserpine
Mackay

NORTHERN TERRITORY
Tennant Creek
Barrow Creek
Barkly Tableland
Camooweal
Mount Isa
Cloncurry
Hughenden
Richmond
Collinsville
Sarina

Port Hedland
Dampier
Roebourne
Monte Bello Is
Barrow I.
Onslow
North West C.
Fortescue
Nullagine
Whittenoom
Marble Bar
Shay Gap
De Grey
Great Sandy Desert
L. Mackay
L. Disappointment
WESTERN AUSTRALIA
Gibson Desert
Macdonnell Ranges
Mt Ziel 1510
Alice Springs
Simpson Desert
Birdsville
QUEENSLAND
Selwyn
Dajarra
Winton
Longreach
Barcaldine
Blackall
Clermont
Emerald
Rockhampton
Barcoo
Windorah
Thomson
Diamantina
Georgina
Leichhardt
Flinders

Hamersley Ra.
Mt Bruce 1226
Paraburdoo
Newman
Ashburton
Barlee Ra.
Lyons
Gascoyne
Carnarvon
Shark B.
Dirk Hartog I.
Murchison
Mt McLeod
Mt Augustus 1106
Carnegie
Wiluna
Meekatharra
L Wells
Mt Aloysius 987
Tomkinson Ra.
Petermann Ra.
Musgrave Ra.
Mt Woodroffe 1440
Lake Eyre Basin
Oodnadatta
L. Eyre
Cooper Ck
Great Victoria Desert
Coober Pedy
Marree
SOUTH AUSTRALIA
Diamantina
Grey Range
Charleville
Quilpie
Roma
Miles
Toowoomba
St George
Cunnamulla
Bourke
Warrego
Walgett
Narrabri
Tamworth

Cue
Sandstone
Mt Magnet
Leonora
Laverton
Barlee
Moore
Wiluna
Meekatharra
Northampton
Mullewa
Geraldton
Dongara
Houtman Abrolhos
Moora
Bencubbin
Southern Cross
Coolgardie
Kalgoorlie
Norseman
Rawlinna
Forrest
Nullarbor Plain
Ooldea
Tarcoola
Penong
Ceduna
Great Australian Bight
Eyre
Gawler Ranges
L. Everard
L. Gairdner
Woomera
St Mary Pk 1189
L. Torrens
L. Frome
Leigh Ck
Wilcannia
Cobar
Menindee
Broken Hill
Ivanhoe
Nyngan
Dubbo
Orange
NEW SOUTH WALES
Darling

Perth
Fremantle
Pinjarra
Bunbury
Busselton
Collie
Narrogin
Wagin
Katanning
Manjimup
Albany
C. Naturaliste
C. Leeuwin
Bluff Knoll 1110
Esperance
C. Pasley
Arch. of the Recherche
Norseman
Kingoonya
Port Augusta
Whyalla
Port Pirie
Peterborough
Quorn
Iron Knob
Spencer Gulf
Eyre Pen.
Port Lincoln
Kangaroo I.
Investigator Str.
Adelaide
Murray Bridge
Victor Harbour
Kingston
Naracoorte
Mount Gambier
Hamilton
Ballarat
Geelong
Melbourne
Morwell
Sale
Bairnsdale
VICTORIA
Bendigo
Shepparton
Echuca
Wagga Wagga
Albury
Wangaratta
Australian Alps
Mt Kosciusko 2230
Canberra
Sydney
Wollongong
Goulburn
Cootamundra
Griffith
Hay
Deniliquin
Balranald
Mildura
Renmark
Murray
Horsham
Ararat
Colac
Portland
Port Fairy
Warrnambool
Wilson's Prom.

Bass Strait
King I.
Furneaux Group
Flinders
C. Barren
TASMANIA
C. Grim
Smithton
Burnie
Devonport
Queenstown
Launceston
St Mary's
Mt Ossa 1617
Hobart
Geeveston
South West C.
South East C.

110 120 130 140 150

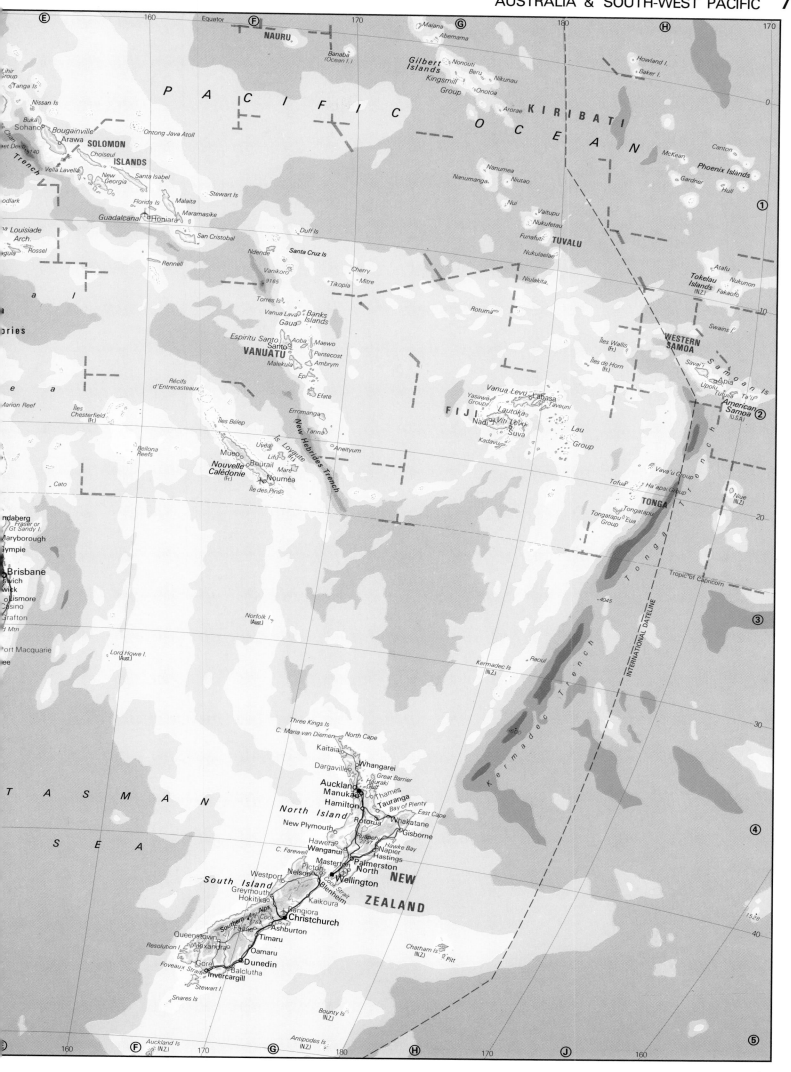

PACIFIC OCEAN

NAURU

Banaba
(Ocean I.)

Gilbert
Islands

Maiana
Abemama

Nonouti
Beru
Nikunau
Onotoa

Kingsmill
Group

Arorae

KIRIBATI

Howland I.

Baker I.

McKean

Canton

Phoenix Islands

Gardner

Hull

Lihir
Group

Tanga Is

Nissan Is

Buka
Sohano
Bougainville
Arawa

SOLOMON

Choiseul

ISLANDS

Vella Lavella
New
Georgia

Santa Isabel

Florida Is
Malaita

Guadalcanal
Honiara

Maramasike

San Cristobal

Duff Is

Ndende

Santa Cruz Is

Rennell

Vanikoro
9165

Cherry

Tikopia
Mitre

Torres Is

Vanua Lava
Banks
Islands

Gaua

Espiritu Santo
Santo
Aoba
Maewo

VANUATU
Pentecost
Malekula
Ambrym

Epi

Efate

Récifs
d'Entrecasteaux

Erromanga

Îles Bélep

Tanna

Aneityum

New Hebrides Trench

Nouvelle
Calédonie
(Fr.)

Mueo
Bourail
Nouméa

Île des Pins

Uvéa
Lifu
Maré

Loyaute
Is
(Fr.)

Nanumea
Niutao

Nanumanga

Nui

Vaitupu

Nukufetau

Funafuti
TUVALU

Nukulaelae

Niulakita

Rotuma

Atafu
Nukunon

Tokelau
Islands
(N.Z.)
Fakaofo

Swains I.

WESTERN
SAMOA

Îles Wallis
(Fr.)

Îles de Horn
(Fr.)

Savai'i
Apia
Upolu
Tutuila
Ta'ū

American
Samoa
(U.S.A.)

FIJI

Vanua Levu
Labasa
Taveuni

Yasawa
Group
Lautoka
Nadi
Viti Levu
Suva

Kadavu

Lau
Group

Vava'u Group

Tofua
Ha'apai Group

TONGA

Tongatapu
Group
Tongatapu
'Eua

Niue
(N.Z.)

0

10

20

Tropic of Capricorn

INTERNATIONAL DATELINE

Tonga Trench

.4045

Kermadec Is
(N.Z.)

Raoul

.9600

Kermadec Trench

30

40

Marion Reef

Îles Chesterfield
(Fr.)

Bellona
Reefs

Cato

ndaberg
Fraser or
Gt Sandy I.
Maryborough
Gympie

Brisbane
swich
Lismore
Casino
Grafton
d Mtn

Port Macquarie
ee

Norfolk I.
(Aust.)

Lord Howe I.
(Aust.)

T A S M A N

S E A

P A C I F I C   O C E A N

Three Kings Is
C. Maria van Diemen
North Cape

Kaitaia

Dargaville

Whangarei

Great Barrier
Hauraki
Gulf
Auckland
Manukau
Thames
Hamilton
Tauranga
Bay of Plenty
East Cape

North Island

Rotorua
Whakatane

New Plymouth

Gisborne

Ruapehu
2797

Hawera
Wanganui

Hawke Bay
Napier
Hastings

Masterton

C. Farewell

Picton
Nelson
Westport
Palmerston
North
Wellington

Greymouth
Hokitika

Blenheim
Cook Strait
Kaikoura

South Island

NEW

ZEALAND

Alps
Cook
3764

Rangiora
Christchurch
Ashburton

Southern
Fairlie
Timaru

Queenstown
Alexandra
Oamaru

Resolution I.
Gore
Balclutha
Dunedin

Foveaux Strait
Invercargill

Stewart I.

Snares Is

Chatham Is
(N.Z.)
Pitt

1528

Bounty Is
(N.Z.)

Auckland Is
(N.Z.)

Antipodes Is
(N.Z.)

160
170
180
170
160

1:5M

50 100 150 200 km
50 100 mils

Three Kings Is.

B

C. Maria van Diemen
North Cape

Ninety Mile Beach
Rangaunu B.
Doubtless B.
Ahipara B.
Kaitaia
Tauroa Pt
Kaikohe
Bay of Islands
C. Brett
Russell
Kawakawa
Hikurangi
Hokianga Har.
Whangarei
Hen & Chickens Is.
Dargaville
Bream B.
Little Barrier I.
Great Barrier I.
Wellsford
Kaipara Har.
C. Colville
Manly
Takapuna
Hauraki Gulf
Mercury Is
Mercury Bay
Coromandel Peninsula
Auckland
Papatoetoe Manukau Papakura
Pukekohe Thames
Waiuku
Paeroa Waihi
Mayor I.

NORTH ISLAND

Huntly Te Aroha
Glen Afton Matakana I.
Ngaruawahia Morrinsville Tauranga Har.
Hamilton Cambridge Tauranga
Te Awamutu Te Puke Bay of Plenty
Kawhia Putaruru Rotorua Whakatane
Otorohanga Rotorua Kawerau Opotiki Tangatua
Waitomo Taupo Raukumara Ra.
Te Kuiti Tokomaru Bay
Mangakino
Murupara Tolaga Bay
C. Runaway
Hicks Bay
White I.

N. Taranaki Bight
Waitara Ohura Taumarunui
New Plymouth Taupo
Inglewood Ngauruhoe Makorako Gisborne
C. Egmont Mt Egmont 2518 Stratford Mt Ngauruhoe 2291 Mohaka Poverty Bay
Opunake Eltham Mt Ruapehu 2797 Ohakune Tarawera Wairoa
Hawera Raetihi Waiouru Eskdale Hawke Bay
S. Taranaki Bight Patea Taihape Taradale Napier Mahia Peninsula
Wanganui Hastings Portland I.
Marton C. Kidnappers
Havelock North
Feilding Danevirke
Palmerston N. Woodville Waipukurau
Foxton Pahiatua C. Turnagain
Levin Herbertville
Otaki Masterton
Carterton

C. Farewell Farewell Spit
Collingwood Golden Bay
Rocks Pt Separation Pt COOK
Takaka C. Stephens
Tasman D'Urville I.
Mts Tasman Bay Paraparaumu
Karamea The Twins Motueka C. Jackson Porirua
Bight 1826 Nelson Tawa Upper Hutt
Seddonville Richmond Wellington Lower Hutt
Westport Richmond Ra. Wairau Blenheim Martinborough
C. Foulwind Murchison Mt Ross 983
Buller Wairau C. Campbell
Reefton Victoria L. Rotoroa Awatere C. Palliser
Ra. L. Rotoiti Kaikoura Palliser Bay
Spenser Ra. Tapuaenuku
Runanga Mts Mt Travers 2865
Greymouth Grey 2338 Kaikoura Ra. Clarence Kaikoura
Lewis Hanmer Kaikoura Pen.
Hokitika Pass Springs Waiau
L. Brunner Waiau
Ross L. Sumner Culverden Hurunui Cheviot

SOUTH ISLAND

Abut Hd Arthurs Pass Waipara
Franz Josef Gl. Puketeraki Ra. Rangiora Pegasus Bay
Coleridge Waimakariri Kaiapoi
Mt Cook 3764 Hornby Christchurch
Mt Sefton 3157 Methven Lyttelton
Jackson Hd Hermitage L. Tekapo Rakaia Lincoln Banks Peninsula
Cascade Pt Geraldine Akaroa
Pollux 2542 Young Ra. L. Ohau Ellesmere
Awarua Pt Mt Aspiring Pukaki Fairlie Ashburton
3027 Wanaka L. Pukaki Temuka
Milford Sd Hawea L. Benmore Canterbury Bight
Milford Sd Wanaka Omarama Timaru
Mt Pyramid 2326 L. Aviemore
George Sd Homer Tunnel Kurow Waimate
Caswell Sd Arrowtown Waitaki
Secretary Cromwell Ranfurly Oamaru
Fiordland Queenstown Clyde
Nat. Park Te Anau Alexandra Hampden
Doubtful Sd L. Te Anau Kingston Roxburgh
Breaksea Sd Lumsden Palmerston
Resolution Manapouri Riversdale Waikouaiti
Dusky Sd L. Hauroko Ohai Heriot Port Chalmers
Mt Ward Gore Clutha Otago Peninsula
Ohai Winton Mataura Lawrence Dunedin
Puysegur Pt Cameron Mts Milton
Tuatapere Edendale Balclutha
Te Waewae Bay Riverton Owaka Kaitangata
Invercargill

Foveaux Strait
Solander I.
Bluff
Codfish I.
Oban
Stewart Island
Paterson Inlet
Mt Allen 730 Shelter Pt
Port Pegasus

TASMAN SEA

SOUTH ISLAND

SOUTHERN ALPS

Canterbury Plains

PACIFIC OCEAN

170 175
35
40
45

Northern Polar Region

CHINA
RUSSIAN FEDERATION
CANADA
ALASKA (U.S.A.)
Mt McKinley 6194
North Pole
N. Magnetic Pole (1990)
Greenland (Kalaallit Nunaat) (Den.)
ICELAND
Svalbard (Spitsbergen) (Nor.)
Novaya Zemlya
Severnaya Zemlya
Novosibirskiye Ostrova
Zemlya Frantsa Iosifa
Kara Sea
Barents Sea
Laptev Sea
E. Siberian Sea
Chukchi Sea
Beaufort Sea
Baffin Bay
Baffin I.
Ellesmere I.
Queen Elizabeth Islands
Victoria I.
Banks I.
Hudson Bay
Foxe Basin
Southampton I.
Greenland Sea
Norwegian Sea
Denmark Strait
Davis Str.
ATLANTIC OCEAN
Arctic Circle
Bjørnøya (Bear I.) (Nor.)
Jan Mayen (Nor.)
Watkins Bjerge 3700
Greenland Sea
average minimum extent of sea ice
Tree Limit

Places: Seattle, Vancouver, Vancouver I., Prince Rupert, Juneau, Fairbanks, Anchorage, Teller, Vankarem, Prudhoe Bay, Barrow, Dawson, Norman Wells, Inuvik, Yellowknife, Calgary, Edmonton, Saskatoon, Flin Flon, Winnipeg, Churchill, Chisasibi, Inukjuak, Resolute, Eureka, Alert, Thule, Nord, Pond Inlet, Upernavik, Godhavn, Søndre Strømfjord, Godthåb (Nuuk), Angmagssalik, Julianehåb, K. Farvel, Scoresbysund, Reykjavik, Tromsø, Narvik, Murmansk, Arkhangel'sk, Nordkapp, Oulu, Umeå, Yaroslavl, Sankt-Peterburg (Leningrad), Nizhniy Novgorod, Kazan', Samara, Ufa, Perm', Yekaterinburg, Magnitogorsk, Orsk, Aktyubinsk, Tselinograd, Omsk, Novosibirsk, Barnaul, Krasnoyarsk, Noril'sk, Turukhansk, Dudinka, Dikson, Salekhard, Vorkuta, Nadym, Berezovo, Tobol'sk, Serov, Syktyvkar, Kirov, Kotlas, Mezen', Sev. Dvina, Yakutsk, Aldan, Verkhoyansk, Zhigansk, Tiksi, Nordvik, Khatanga, Ust'Kut, Irkutsk, Ulan-Ude, Oz. Baykal, Chita, Skovorodino, Blagoveshchensk, Ayan, Ust'Nera, Kolyma, Indigirka, Lena, Yenisey, Amur, Chul'man, O. Vrangelya, Pevek, Ambarchik, Polyarn'yy, Kazach'ye, Tree Limit, Gt Bear L., Gt Slave L., L. Athabasca, Hudson Str., G. of Boothia, Nares Str., Lincoln Sea, McClure Str., Mackenzie, Yukon, Bering Str., Newfoundland, Gander, Schefferville, Hebron, Nain, Qurlurtuuq, Vaduz, KAZAKHSTAN, NORWAY, SWEDEN, FINLAND, ROCKY MTS, Uralskiy Khrebet

Southern Polar Region (Antarctica)

ATLANTIC OCEAN
PACIFIC OCEAN
INDIAN OCEAN
Antarctic Circle
Weddell Sea
Ross Sea
Ross Ice Shelf
GREATER ANTARCTICA
LESSER ANTARCTICA
Dronning Maud Land
Enderby Land
Mac. Robertson Land
Queen Mary Land
Wilkes Land
Victoria Land
Marie Byrd Land
Ellsworth Land
Palmer Land
Antarctic Peninsula
Graham Land
Coats Land
American Highland
Transantarctic Mts
South Pole
Amundsen-Scott (U.S.)
Vostok (Rus. Fed.)
Vinson Massif 5140
Mt Sidley 4181
Mt Seelig 3022
Mt Kirkpatrick 4528
Mt Markham 4351
Q. Maud Mts
Pensacola Mts
Ronne Ice Shelf
Amery Ice Shelf
Shackleton Ice Shelf
Berkner I.
Roosevelt I.
Alexander I.
Charcot I.
Thurston I.
Siple I.
Peter I Øy (Nor.)
Bellingshausen Sea
Amundsen Sea
Scotia Sea
Drake Passage
Falkland Is (U.K.)
S. Orkney Is (U.K.)
S. Shetland Is (U.K.)
Tierra del Fuego
ARGENTINA
Heard I. (Aust.)
Lambert Gl.
Pt. Charles Mts 3355
C. Darnley
C. Poinsett
Knox Coast
Walgreen Coast
Oates Land
George V Land
Terre Adélie
Dumont d'Urville (Fr.)
S. Magnetic Pole (1990)
C. Adare
C. Colbeck
Sturge I.
Scott I.
Balleny Is
average minimum extent of sea ice

Stations and labels: Orcadas (Arg.), Signy (U.K.), Georg von Neumayer (Germany), Sanae (S.A.), Maitri (India), Prinsesse Astrid Kyst, Prinsesse Ragnhild Kyst, Asuka (Jap.), Novolazarevskaya (Rus. Fed.), Syowa (Jap.), Molodezhnaya (Rus. Fed.), Mawson (Aust.), Zhongshan (China), Davis (Aust.), Mirnyy (Rus. Fed.), Casey (Aust.), Halley (U.K.), Grl Belgrano (Arg.), Gral San Martin, McMurdo (U.S.), Scott (N.Z.), C. Norvegia

Antarctic Research Stations
1 Artigas (Uruguay)
2 Teniente Rodolfo Marsh Martin (Chile)
3 Bellingshausen (Rus. Fed.)
4 Chang Cheng (Great Wall) (China)
5 Comandante Ferraz (Brazil)
6 Henryk Arctowski (Poland)
7 Teniente Jubany (Arg.)
8 King Sejong (Korea)
9 Capitán Arturo Prat (Chile)
10 General Bernardo O'Higgins (Chile)
11 Esperanza (Arg.)
12 Vicecomodoro Marambio (Arg.)
13 Palmer (USA)
14 Farady (UK)
15 Rothera
16 General San Martin (Arg.)
17 Václav Voytěch (Czech Rep.)

Abbreviations

Abbreviations used in Reference Map Section

	Full Form	English Form	Language
A			
a.d.	an der	on the	German
Akr.	Ákra, Akrotírion	cape	Greek
Appno	Appennino	mountain range	Italian
Arch.	Archipelago	archipelago	English
B			
B.	1. Baai, Bahía, Baía, Baie, Bay, Bucht, Bukhta, Bugt	bay	Dutch, Spanish, Portuguese, French, English, German, Russian, Danish
	2. Ban	village	Indo-Chinese
	3. Barrage	dam	French
Bol.	Bol'sh/aya, -oy, -oye	big	Russian
Br.	1. Branch	branch	English
	2. Bridge, Brücke	bridge	English, German
	3. Burun	cape	Turkish
Brj	Baraj,-i	dam	Turkish
C			
C.	Cabo, Cap, Cape	cape	Spanish, French, English
Can.	Canal	canal	English
Cd	Ciudad	town	Spanish
Chan.	Channel	channel	English
Ck	Creek	creek	English
Cord.	Cordillera	mountain range	Spanish
D			
D.	1. Dağ, Dägh, Daği, Dağlari	mountain, range	Persian, Turkish
	2. Daryächeh	lake	Persian
Dj.	Djebel	mountain	Arabic
E			
E.	East	east	English
Emb.	Embalse	reservoir	Spanish
Escarp.	Escarpment	escarpment	English
Estr.	Estrecho	strait	Spanish
F			
F.	Firth	estuary	Gaelic
Fj.	1. Fjell	mountain	Norwegian
	2. Fjord, Fjorður	fjord	Norwegian, Icelandic
Ft	Fort	fort	English
G			
G.	1. Gebel	mountain	Arabic
	2. Göl, Gölü	lake	Turkish
	3. Golfe, Golfo, Gulf	gulf	French, Italian, Portuguese, Spanish, English
	4. Gora, -gory	mountain, range	Russian
	5. Gunung	mountain	Malay, Indonesian
Gd, Gde	Grand, Grande	grand	English, French
Geb.	Gebirge	mountain range	German
Gl.	Glacier	glacier	French, English
Grl	General	general	Spanish
Gt, Gtr	Great, Groot, -e, Greater	greater	English, Dutch
H			
Har.	Harbour	harbour	English
Hd	Head	head	English
I			
I.	Ile, Ilha, Insel, Isla, Island, Isle, Isola, Isole	island	French, Portuguese, German, Spanish, English, Italian
In.	1. Indre, Inner	inner	Norwegian, English
	2. Inlet	inlet	English
Is	Iles, Ilhas, Islands, Isles, Islas	islands	French, Portuguese, English, Spanish
Isth.	Isthmus	isthmus	English
J			
J.	Jabal, Jebel, Jibal	mountain	Arabic
K			
K.	1. Kaap, Kap, Kapp	cape	Dutch, German, Norwegian, Swedish
	2. Koh, Kuh, Kuhha	mountain	Persian
	3. Kolpos	gulf	Greek
Kep.	Kepulauan	islands	Indonesian
Khr.	Khrebet	mountain range	Russian
Kör.	Körfez, -i	gulf, bay	Turkish
L			
L.	1. Lac, Lago, Lagoa, Lake, Liman, Limni, Loch, Lough	lake	French, Italian, Spanish, Portuguese, English, Russian, Greek, Gaelic
Lag.	Lagoon, Laguna, -e, Lagôa	lagoon	English, Spanish, French, Portuguese
Ld	Land	land	English
Lit.	Little	little	English
M			
M.	1. Muang	town	Thai
	2. Mys	cape	Russian
m	metre, -s	metre(s)	English, French
Mal.	Mali, -o, -yy	small	Russian
Mf	Massif	mountain group	French
Mgne	Montagne(s)	mountain(s)	French
Mont	Monument	monument	English
Mt	Mont, Mount	mountain	French, English
Mte	Monte	mountain	Italian, Portuguese, Spanish
Mti	Monti	mountain, range	Italian
Mtn	Mountain	mountain	English
Mts	Monts, Mountains, Montañas, Montes	mountains	French, English, Spanish, Italian, Portuguese
N			
N.	1. Neu, Ny	new	German
	2. Nevado	snow capped mtns	Spanish
	3. Noord, Nord, Norte, Nørre, North	north	Danish, French, Portuguese, Spanish, Danish, English
Nat.	National	national	English
Nat. Pk	National Park	national park	English
Ndr	Neder, Nieder	lower	Dutch, Swedish, German
N.E.	North East	north east	English
N.M.	National Monument	national monument	English
N.P.	National Park	national park	English
N.W.	North West	north west	English
O			
O.	1. Oost, Ost	east	Dutch, German
	2. Ostrov	island	Russian
Ø	Øy	island	Norwegian
Oz.	Ozero, Ozera	lake(s)	Russian
P			
P.	1. Pass, Passo	pass	English, German, Italian
	2. Pic, Pico, Pizzo	peak	French, Portuguese, Spanish, Italian
	3. Pulau	island	Malay, Indonesian
P.P.	Pulau-pulau	islands	Indonesian
Pass.	Passage	passage	English
Peg.	Pegunungan	mountains	Indonesian
Pen.	Peninsula, Peninsola	peninsula	English, Italian
Pk	1. Park	park	English
	2. Peak, Pik	peak	English, Russian
Plat.	Plateau, Planalto	plateau	English, French, Portuguese
Pov	Poluostrov	peninsula	Russian
Pr.	Prince	prince	English
Pres.	President, Presidente	president	English, Spanish, Portuguese
Promy	Promontory	promontory	English
Pt	Point	point	English
Pta	1. Ponta, Punta	point	Portuguese, Italian, Spanish
	2. Puerta	pass	Spanish
Pte	Pointe	point	French
Pto	Porto, Puerto	port	Spanish
R			
R.	1. Rio, River, Rivière,	river	Portuguese, Spanish, English, French
	2. Ría	river mouth	Spanish
Ra.	Range	range	English
Rap.	Rapids	rapids	English
Res.	Reserve, Reservation	reserve, reservation	English
Resr	Reservoir	reservoir	English
Résr	Réservoir	reservoir	French
S			
S.	1. Salar, Salina	salt marsh	Spanish
	2. San, São	saint	Spanish, Portuguese
	3. See	sea, lake	German
	4. South, Sud	south	English, French
s.	sur	on	French
Sa	Serra, Sierra	mountain range	Portuguese, Spanish
Sd	Sound, Sund	sound	English, German, Swedish
S.E.	South East	south east	English
Sev.	Sever, Severnaya	north	Russian
Sp.	Spitze	peak	German
Spr.	Spring,(s)	spring(s)	English
St	Saint	saint	English
Sta	Santa	saint	Spanish
Sta.	Station	station	English
Ste	Sainte	saint	French
Sto	Santo	saint	Portuguese, Spanish
Str.	Strait	strait	English
S.W.	South West	south west	English
T			
T.	Tall, Tel	hill, mountain	Arabic, Hebrew
Tg	Tanjong, Tandjong	cape	Malay, Indonesian
Tk	Têluk, Télok	bay	Indonesian
Tr.	Trench, Trough	trench, trough	English
U			
U.	Uad	wadi	Arabic
Ug	Ujung	cape	Malay
Upr	Upper	upper	English
V			
V.	1. Val, Valle	valley	French, Italian, Spanish
	2. Ville	town	French
Va	Villa	town	Spanish
Vdkhr.	Vodokhranilishche	reservoir	Russian
Vol.	Volcán, Volcano	volcano	Spanish, English
Vozv.	Vozvyshennost'	upland	Russian
W			
W.	1. Wadi	wadi	Arabic
	2. Water	water	English
	3. Well	well	English
	4. West	west	English
Y			
Yuzh.	Yuzhnaya, Yuzhno, Yuzhnyy	south	Russian
Z			
Z.	Zaliv	gulf, bay	Russian
Zap.	Zapadnyy, -aya, -o, -oye	western	Russian
Zem.	Zemlya	country, land	Russian

Index

Introduction to the index

In the index, the first number refers to the page, and the following letter and number to the section of the map in which the index entry can be found. For example, 38C2 **Paris** means that Paris can be found on page 38 where column C and row 2 meet.

Abbreviations used in the index

Afghan	Afghanistan	Hung	Hungary	Par	Paraguay	Arch	Archipelago
Alb	Albania	Ind	Indonesia	Phil	Philippines	B	Bay
Alg	Algeria	Irish Rep	Irish Republic	Pol	Poland	C	Cape
Ant	Antarctica	Kirgh	Kirghizia	Port	Portugal	Chan	Channel
Arg	Argentina	Leb	Lebanon	Rom	Romania	Gl	Glacier
Aust	Australia	Lib	Liberia	Russian Fed	Russian Federation	I(s)	Island(s)
Bang	Bangladesh	Liech	Liechtenstein	S Africa	South Africa	Lg	Lagoon
Belg	Belgium	Lux	Luxembourg	S Arabia	Saudi Arabia	L	Lake
B-H	Bosnia-Herzegovina	Mac	Macedonia	Scot	Scotland	Mt(s)	Mountain(s)
Bol	Bolivia	Madag	Madagascar	Sen	Senegal	O	Ocean
Bulg	Bulgaria	Malay	Malaysia	Sl	Slovakia	P	Pass
Camb	Cambodia	Maur	Mauritania	Switz	Switzerland	Pass	Passage
Can	Canada	Mor	Morocco	Tanz	Tanzania	Pen	Peninsula
CAR	Central African Republic	Mozam	Mozambique	Thai	Thailand	Plat	Plateau
Cz. R	Czech Republic	Neth	Netherlands	Turk	Turkey	Pt	Point
Den	Denmark	Nic	Nicaragua	USA	United States of America	Res	Reservoir
Dom Rep	Dominican Republic	Nig	Nigeria	Urug	Uruguay	R	River
El Sal	El Salvador	N Ire	Ireland, Northern	Ven	Venezuela	S	Sea
Eng	England	Nor	Norway	Viet	Vietnam	Sd	Sound
Eq Guinea	Equatorial Guinea	NZ	New Zealand	Yugos	Yugoslavia	Str	Strait
Eth	Ethiopia	Pak	Pakistan	Zim	Zimbabwe	V	Valley
Fin	Finland	PNG	Papua New Guinea				

A

42B2 **Aachen** Germany
36C1 **Aalst** Belg
32K6 **Äänekoski** Fin
37C1 **Aarau** Switz
37B1 **Aare** *R* Switz
52A3 **Aba** China
71H4 **Aba** Nig
72D3 **Aba** Zaïre
63B2 **Ābādān** Iran
63C2 **Ābādeh** Iran
70B1 **Abadla** Alg
29C2 **Abaeté** Brazil
29C2 **Abaeté** *R* Brazil
27J4 **Abaetetuba** Brazil
52D1 **Abagnar Qi** China
71H4 **Abaji** Nig
19E3 **Abajo Mts** USA
71H4 **Abakaliki** Nig
49L4 **Abakan** Russian Fed
70C3 **Abala** Niger
70C2 **Abalessa** Alg
26D6 **Abancay** Peru
63C2 **Abarqū** Iran
53E3 **Abashiri** Japan
53E3 **Abashiri-wan** *B* Japan
22C1 **Abasolo** Mexico
51H7 **Abau** PNG
72D3 **Abaya** *L* Eth
72D2 **Abbai** *R* Eth
72E2 **Abbe** *L* Eth
38C1 **Abbeville** France
17D4 **Abbeville** Louisiana, USA
15C2 **Abbeville** S Carolina, USA
37C2 **Abbiategrasso** Italy
18B1 **Abbotsford** Can
12A2 **Abbotsford** USA
60C2 **Abbottabad** Pak
67F4 **Abd-al-Kuri** *I* Yemen
44J5 **Abdulino** Russian Fed
72C2 **Abéché** Chad
71F4 **Abengourou** Ivory Coast
32F7 **Åbenrå** Den
42B1 **Åbenra** Den
71G4 **Abeokuta** Nig
72D3 **Abera** Eth
35C5 **Aberaeron** Wales
20C2 **Aberdeen** California, USA
13D3 **Aberdeen** Maryland, USA
15B2 **Aberdeen** Mississippi, USA
74C3 **Aberdeen** S Africa
34D3 **Aberdeen** Scot
8D2 **Aberdeen** S Dakota, USA

8A2 **Aberdeen** Washington, USA
6J3 **Aberdeen L** Can
34D3 **Aberfeldy** Scot
35D6 **Abergavenny** Wales
35C5 **Aberystwyth** Wales
44L2 **Abez'** Russian Fed
66D3 **Abha** S Arabia
63B1 **Abhar** Iran
71H4 **Abia** *State* Nigeria
66C4 **Abi Adi** Eth
71F4 **Abidjan** Ivory Coast
17C2 **Abilene** Kansas, USA
16C3 **Abilene** Texas, USA
35E6 **Abingdon** Eng
12C3 **Abingdon** USA
7K4 **Abitibi** *R* Can
7L5 **Abitibi,L** Can
45G7 **Abkhazskaya** Respublika, Georgia
36A2 **Ablis** France
60C2 **Abohar** India
71G4 **Abomey** Benin
72B3 **Abong Mbang** Cam
57E9 **Aborlan** Phil
72B2 **Abou Deïa** Chad
67E1 **Abqaiq** S Arabia
39A2 **Abrantes** Port
72D1 **'Abri** Sudan
76A3 **Abrolhos** *Is* Aust
8B2 **Absaroka Range** *Mts* USA
67F2 **Abu al Abyad** *I* UAE
67E1 **Abū 'Ali** *I* S Arabia
66D3 **Abu Arish** S Arabia
66B3 **Abu Deleiq** Sudan
67F2 **Abū Dhabi** UAE
66B3 **'Abu Dom** *Watercourse* Sudan
65C3 **Abū el Jurdhān** Jordan
66B3 **Abu Fatima** Sudan
72D2 **Abu Hamed** Sudan
68E7 **Abuja** Nigeria
65A3 **Abu Kebir Hihya** Egypt
26E5 **Abunã** Brazil
26E6 **Abuna** *R* Bol
64D3 **Abū Sukhayr** Iraq
65B3 **Abu Suweir** Egypt
78B2 **Abut Head** *C* NZ
66B1 **Abu Tig** Egypt
72D2 **Abu'Urug** *Well* Sudan
72D2 **Abuye Meda** *Mt* Eth
72C2 **Abu Zabad** Sudan
72D3 **Abwong** Sudan
42B1 **Åby** Den

65C3 **Aby 'Aweigîla** *Well* Egypt
72C3 **Abyei** Sudan
13F2 **Acadia Nat Pk** USA
21B2 **Acambaro** Mexico
23B5 **Acandi** Colombia
21B2 **Acaponeta** Mexico
21B3 **Acapulco** Mexico
27L4 **Acaraú** Brazil
26E2 **Acarigua** Ven
21C3 **Acatlán** Mexico
22C2 **Acatlan** Mexico
22C2 **Acatzingo** Mexico
22D2 **Acayucan** Mexico
71F4 **Accra** Ghana
28E2 **Aceguá** Urug
60D4 **Achalpur** India
25B6 **Achao** Chile
53B2 **Acheng** China
37D1 **Achensee** *L* Austria
36E2 **Achern** Germany
33A3 **Achill** *I* Irish Rep
49L4 **Achinsk** Russian Fed
40D3 **Acireale** Italy
11D3 **Ackley** USA
23C2 **Acklins** *I* Caribbean
26D6 **Acobamba** Peru
25B4 **Aconcagua** *Mt* Chile
27L5 **Acopiara** Brazil
68B4 **A'cores** *Is* Atlantic O
A Coruna = La Coruna
37C2 **Acqui** Italy
75A2 **Acraman,L** Aust
26D5 **Acre** *State*, Brazil
20C3 **Acton** USA
22C1 **Actopan** Mexico
71G4 **Ada** Ghana
17C3 **Ada** USA
39B1 **Adaja** *R* Spain
10C6 **Adak** *I* USA
67G2 **Adam** Oman
72D3 **Adama** Eth
29B3 **Adamantina** Brazil
72B3 **Adamaoua** Region, Nig/Cam
71J4 **Adamawa** State, Nigeria
37D1 **Adamello** *Mt* Italy
14D1 **Adams** USA
72D3 **Adams L** Can
8A2 **Adams,Mt** USA
62C3 **Adam's Peak** *Mt* Sri Lanka

67E4 **'Adan** Yemen
45F8 **Adana** Turk
45E7 **Adapazari** Turk
66B3 **Adarama** Sudan
79F7 **Adare,C** Ant
57D4 **Adaut** Indon
75B1 **Adavale** Aust
37C2 **Adda** *R* Italy
67E1 **Ad Dahna'** Region, S Arabia
66D4 **Ad Dāli'** Yemen
67F1 **Ad Damman** S Arabia
66D3 **Ad Darb** S Arabia
66D2 **Ad Dawādimi** S Arabia
67E1 **Ad Dibdibah** Region, S Arabia
67F3 **Ad Dikākah** Region, S Arabia
67E2 **Ad Dilam** S Arabia
67E2 **Ad Dir'iyah** S Arabia
66C4 **Addis Zeman** Eth
64D3 **Ad Dīwaniyah** Iraq
64D3 **Ad Duwayd** S Arabia
11D3 **Adel** USA
76C4 **Adelaide** Aust
6J3 **Adelaide Pen** Can
51G8 **Adelaide River** Aust
20D3 **Adelanto** USA
Aden = 'Adan
58C4 **Aden,G of** Yemen/Somalia
70C3 **Aderbissinat** Niger
65D2 **Adhra** Syria
51G7 **Adi** *I* Indon
40C1 **Adige** *R* Italy
72D2 **Adigrat** Eth
66C4 **Adi Kale** Eth
60D5 **Adilābād** India
18B2 **Adin** USA
13E2 **Adirondack Mts** USA
72B3 **Ādīs Ābeba** Eth
72D2 **Adi Ugai** Eritrea
64C2 **Adıyaman** Turk
41F1 **Adjud** Rom
10G1 **Admiralty B** USA
6E4 **Admiralty I** USA
7K2 **Admiralty Inlet** *B* Can
76D1 **Admiralty Is** PNG
57B4 **Adonara** *I* Indon
62B1 **Ādoni** India
38B3 **Adour** *R* France
70A2 **Adrar** Region, Maur
70C2 **Adrar** Alg
70A2 **Adrar** *Mts* Alg
70A2 **Adrar Soutouf** Region, Mor
72C2 **Adré** Chad

69A2 **Adri** Libya
37E2 **Adria** Italy
12C2 **Adrian** Michigan, USA
16B2 **Adrian** Texas, USA
40C2 **Adriatic S** Italy/Yugos
72D2 **Adwa** Eth
49P3 **Adycha** *R* Russian Fed
71F4 **Adzopé** Ivory Coast
44K2 **Adz'va** *R* Russian Fed
44K2 **Adz'vavom** Russian Fed
41E3 **Aegean** *S* Greece
58E2 **Afghanistan** Republic, Asia
72E3 **Afgooye** Somalia
66D2 **'Afif** S Arabia
71H4 **Afikpo** Nig
32G6 **Åfjord** Nor
71C2 **Aflou** Alg
72E3 **Afmado** Somalia
70A3 **Afollé** Region, Maur
14C1 **Afton** New York, USA
18D2 **Afton** Wyoming, USA
65C2 **Afula** Israel
45E8 **Afyon** Turk
65A3 **Aga** Egypt
72B2 **Agadem** Niger
70C3 **Agadez** Niger
70B1 **Agadir** Mor
60D4 **Agar** India
61D3 **Agartala** India
18B1 **Agassiz** Can
10A6 **Agattu** *I* USA
10A5 **Agattu Str** USA
71H4 **Agbor** Nig
71F4 **Agboville** Ivory Coast
64E1 **Agdam** Azerbaijan
54C3 **Agematsu** Japan
38C3 **Agen** France
63B2 **Agha Jāri** Iran
45G8 **Ağn** Turk
37D2 **Agno** *R* Italy
66C3 **Agordat** Eth
37E1 **Agordo** Italy
71G4 **Agou,Mt** Togo
38C3 **Agout** *R* France
60D3 **Agra** India
64D2 **Ağri** Turk
40D2 **Agri** *R* Italy
40C3 **Agrigento** Italy
41E3 **Agrínion** Greece
28A3 **Agrio** *R* Chile
40C2 **Agropoli** Italy
44J4 **Agryz** Russian Fed
7N3 **Agto** Greenland
29B3 **Agua Clara** Brazil

1

Aguada de Guerra

Al Qalībah

28B4 **Aguada de Guerra** Arg
23D3 **Aguadilla** Puerto Rico
28B4 **Aguado Cicilio** Arg
22B1 **Aguanava** *R* Mexico
5J3 **Aguanish** Can
5J3 **Aguanus** *R* Can
28D1 **Aguapey** *R* Arg
21B1 **Agua Prieta** Mexico
29A3 **Aguaray Guazu** Par
21B2 **Aguascalientes** Mexico
22B1 **Aguascalientes** State, Mexico
29D2 **Aguas Formosas** Brazil
25G1 **Agua Vermelha, Barragem** *Res* Brazil
39A1 **Agueda** Port
70C3 **Aguelhok** Mali
70A2 **Agüenit** *Well* Mor
39B2 **Aguilas** Spain
22B2 **Aguililla** Mexico
xxviiiC7 **Agulhas Basin** Indian O
73C7 **Agulhas,C** S Africa
xxviiiC6 **Agulhas Plat** Indian O
57G9 **Agusan** *R* Phil
Ahaggar = Hoggar
45H8 **Ahar** Iran
78B1 **Ahipara B** NZ
36D1 **Ahlen** Germany
60C4 **Ahmadābād** India
62A1 **Ahmadnagar** India
72E3 **Ahmar** *Mts* Eth
15D1 **Ahoskie** USA
36D1 **Ahr** *R* Germany
36D1 **Ahrgebirge** Region, Germany
22B1 **Ahuacatlán** Mexico
22B1 **Ahualulco** Mexico
32G7 **Åhus** Sweden
63C1 **Āhuvān** Iran
63B2 **Ahvāz** Iran
23A4 **Aiajuela** Costa Rica
37B1 **Aigle** Switz
28E2 **Aiguá** Urug
37B2 **Aiguille d'Arves** *Mt* France
37B2 **Aiguille de la Grand Sassière** *Mt* France
53B1 **Aihui** China
54C3 **Aikawa** Japan
15C2 **Aiken** USA
52A5 **Ailao Shan** *Upland* China
28B1 **Aimogasta** Arg
29D2 **Aimorés** Brazil
37A1 **Ain** *R* France
71D1 **Aïn Beïda** Alg
71B2 **Ain Beni Mathar** Mor
69B2 **Ain Dalla** *Well* Egypt
39C2 **Aïn el Hadjel** Alg
72B2 **Aïn Galakka** Chad
71C1 **Aïn Oussera** Alg
71B2 **Aïn Sefra** Alg
64B4 **'Ain Sukhna** Egypt
11C3 **Ainsworth** USA
71B1 **Aïn Temouchent** Alg
54B4 **Aioi** Japan
70B2 **Aioun Abd el Malek** *Well* Maur
70B3 **Aïoun El Atrouss** Maur
26E7 **Aiquile** Bol
70C3 **Aïr** *Desert Region* Niger
3F3 **Airdrie** Can
36B1 **Aire** France
35E5 **Aire** *R* Eng
36C2 **Aire** *R* France
7L3 **Airforce I** Can
37C1 **Airolo** Switz
6E3 **Aishihik** Can
10L3 **Aishihik L** Can
36B2 **Aisne** Department, France
38C2 **Aisne** *R* France
76D1 **Aitape** PNG
43F1 **Aiviekste** *R* Latvia
52B2 **Aixa Zuogi** China
38D3 **Aix-en-Provence** France
37A2 **Aix-les-Bains** France
61C3 **Aiyar Res** India
41E3 **Aíyion** Greece
41E3 **Aíyna** *I* Greece
61D3 **Āīzawl** India
73B6 **Aizeb** *R* Namibia
53E4 **Aizu-Wakamatsu** Japan
40B2 **Ajaccio** Corse
22C2 **Ajalpan** Mexico
69B1 **Ajdabiyak** Libya
37E2 **Ajdovščina** Slovenia, Yugos
53E3 **Ajigasawa** Japan
65C2 **Ajlūn** Jordan
67G1 **Ajman** UAE
60C3 **Ajmer** India
19D4 **Ajo** USA
41F2 **Ajtos** Bulg
22B2 **Ajuchitan** Mexico
41F3 **Ak** *R* Turk
54D2 **Akabira** Japan
54C3 **Akaishi-sanchi** *Mts* Japan
62B1 **Akalkot** India
65B1 **Akanthou** Cyprus
78B2 **Akaroa** NZ
66B2 **Akasha** Sudan
54B4 **Akashi** Japan
71C1 **Akbou** Alg
45K5 **Akbulak** Russian Fed
64C2 **Akçakale** Turk
70A2 **Akchar** *Watercourse* Maur
41F3 **Ak Dağ** *Mt* Turk
57C2 **Akelamo** Indon
72C3 **Aketi** Zaïre
64D1 **Akhalkalaki** Georgia
64D1 **Akhalsikhe** Georgia
41E3 **Akharnái** Greece
10H4 **Akhiok** USA
64A2 **Akhisar** Turk
43F1 **Akhiste** Latvia
69C2 **Akhmîm** Egypt
45H6 **Akhtubinsk** Russian Fed
45E5 **Akhtyrka** Ukraine
54B4 **Aki** Japan
7K4 **Akimiski I** Can
53E4 **Akita** Japan
70A3 **Akjoujt** Maur
65C2 **'Akko** Israel
10L2 **Aklavik** Can
70B3 **Aklé Aouana** *Desert Region* Maur
72D3 **Akobo** Sudan
72D3 **Akobo** *R* Sudan
60B1 **Akoha** Afghan
60D4 **Akola** India
71G4 **Akosombo Dam** Ghana
60D4 **Akot** India
7M3 **Akpatok I** Can
41E3 **Ákra Kafirévs** *C* Greece
41E4 **Ákra Líthinon** *C* Greece
41E3 **Ákra Maléa** *C* Greece
32A2 **Akranes** Iceland
41F3 **Ákra Sídheros** *C* Greece
41E3 **Ákra Spátha** *C* Greece
41E3 **Ákra Taínaron** *C* Greece
9E2 **Akron** USA
65B1 **Akrotiri B** Cyprus
60D1 **Aksai Chin** *Mts* China
45E8 **Aksaray** Turk
45J5 **Aksay** Kazakhstan
60D1 **Aksayquin Hu** *L* China
64B2 **Akşehir** Turk
64B2 **Akseki** Turk
49N4 **Aksenovo Zilovskoye** Russian Fed
50E1 **Aksha** Russian Fed
59G1 **Aksu** China
66C4 **Aksum** Eth
45J7 **Aktau** Kazakhstan
48J5 **Aktogay** Kazakhstan
45K6 **Aktumsyk** Kazakhstan
45K5 **Aktyubinsk** Kazakhstan
4F1 **Akulivik** Can
71H4 **Akure** Nig
32B1 **Akureyri** Iceland
10E5 **Akutan** USA
10E5 **Akutan** *I* USA
10E5 **Akutan Pass** USA
71H5 **Akwa Ibom** *State* Nigeria
Akyab = Sittwe
48K5 **Akzhal** Kazakhstan
9E3 **Alabama** State, USA
15B2 **Alabama** *R* USA
15B2 **Alabaster** USA
64C2 **Ala Dağlari** *Mts* Turk
45G7 **Alagir** Russian Fed
37B2 **Alagna** Italy
27L5 **Alagoas** State, Brazil
27L6 **Alagoinhas** Brazil
39B1 **Alagón** Spain
64E4 **Al Ahmadi** Kuwait
21D3 **Alajuela** Costa Rica
10F3 **Alakanuk** USA
48K5 **Alakol, Ozero** *L* Russian Fed/Kazakhstan
32L5 **Alakurtti** Russian Fed
64E3 **Al Amārah** Iraq
19B3 **Alameda** USA
22C1 **Alamo** Mexico
19C3 **Alamo** USA
16A3 **Alamogordo** USA
16C4 **Alamo Heights** USA
16A2 **Alamosa** USA
32H6 **Åland** *I* Fin
45E8 **Alanya** Turk
15C2 **Alapaha** *R* USA
44L4 **Alapayevsk** Russian Fed
Alappuzha = Alleppey
56A2 **Alas** *R* Indon
64A2 **Alaşehir** Turk
50D3 **Ala Shan** *Mts* China
6C3 **Alaska** State, USA
6D4 **Alaska,G of** USA
10G4 **Alaska Pen** USA
6C3 **Alaska Range** *Mts* USA
40B2 **Alassio** Italy
37C3 **Alássio** Region, Italy
10H2 **Alatna** *R* USA
44H5 **Alatyr'** Russian Fed
75B2 **Alawoona** Aust
67G2 **Al'Ayn** UAE
59F2 **Alayskiy Khrebet** *Mts* Tajikistan
49R3 **Alazeya** *R* Russian Fed
71E2 **Al'Azīzīyah** Libya
38D3 **Alba** Italy
64C2 **Al Bāb** Syria
39B2 **Albacete** Spain
39A1 **Alba de Tormes** Spain
64D2 **Al Badi** Iraq
41E1 **Alba Iulia** Rom
41D2 **Albania** Republic, Europe
76A4 **Albany** Aust
15C2 **Albany** Georgia, USA
12B3 **Albany** Kentucky, USA
13E2 **Albany** New York, USA
8A2 **Albany** Oregon, USA
4E3 **Albany** *R* Can
7K4 **Albany** *R* Can
66C4 **Albara** *R* Sudan
28B2 **Albardón** Arg
67G2 **Al Batinah** Region, Oman
51H8 **Albatross B** Aust
69B1 **Al Baydā** Libya
67E4 **Al Baydā'** Yemen
65C1 **Al Baylūlīyah** Syria
15C1 **Albemarle** USA
15D1 **Albemarle Sd** USA
37C2 **Albenga** Region, Italy
39B1 **Alberche** *R* Spain
75A1 **Alberga** Aust
36B1 **Albert** France
6G4 **Alberta** Province, Can
51H7 **Albert Edward** *Mt* PNG
74C3 **Albertinia** S Africa
72D3 **Albert,L** Uganda/Zaïre
9D2 **Albert Lea** USA
72D3 **Albert Nile** *R* Uganda
18D1 **Alberton** USA
5J4 **Alberton** Can
38D2 **Albertville** France
38C3 **Albi** France
17D1 **Albia** USA
27H2 **Albina** Suriname
12C2 **Albion** Michigan, USA
11C3 **Albion** Nebraska, USA
13D2 **Albion** New York, USA
64C4 **Al Bi'r** S Arabia
66D3 **Al Birk** S Arabia
67E2 **Al Biyadh** Region, S Arabia
39B2 **Alborán** *I* Spain
32G7 **Ålborg** Den
36E2 **Albstadt-Ebingen** Germany
64D3 **Al Bū Kamāl** Syria
37C1 **Albula** *R* Switz
8C3 **Albuquerque** USA
67G2 **Al Buraymi** Oman
69A1 **Al Burayqah**
69B1 **Al Burdī** Libya
76D4 **Albury** Aust
64E3 **Al Buşayyah** Iraq
34G3 **Albuskjell** *Oilfield* N Sea
67F3 **Al Buzūn** Yemen
39B1 **Alcalá de Henares** Spain
40C3 **Alcamo** Italy
39B1 **Alcaniz** Spain
27K4 **Alcântara** Brazil
39B2 **Alcaraz** Spain
39B2 **Alcázar de San Juan** Spain
39B2 **Alcira** Spain
29E2 **Alcobaça** Brazil
39B1 **Alcolea de Pinar** Spain
39B2 **Alcoy** Spain
39C2 **Alcudia** Spain
68J8 **Aldabra** *Is* Indian O
16A4 **Aldama** Mexico
22C1 **Aldama** Mexico
49O4 **Aldan** Russian Fed
49P4 **Aldan** *R* Russian Fed
49O4 **Aldanskoye Nagor'ye** *Upland* Russian Fed
35F5 **Aldeburgh** Eng
38B2 **Alderney** *I* UK
35E6 **Aldershot** Eng
70A3 **Aleg** Maur
29A2 **Alegre** *R* Brazil
25E3 **Alegrete** Brazil
28C2 **Alejandro Roca** Arg
49Q4 **Aleksandrovsk Sakhalinskiy** Russian Fed
48J4 **Alekseyevka** Kazakhstan
44F5 **Aleksin** Russian Fed
42D1 **Älem** Sweden
29D3 **Além Paraíba** Brazil
38C2 **Alençon** France
20E5 **Alenuihaha Chan** Hawaiian Is
Aleppo = Ḩalab
7M1 **Alert** Can
38C3 **Alès** France
40B2 **Alessandria** Italy
48B3 **Ålesund** Nor
10B5 **Aleutian Is** USA
10G4 **Aleutian Range** *Mts* USA
xxixL2 **Aleutian Trench** Pacific O
6E4 **Alexander Arch** USA
74B2 **Alexander Bay** S Africa
15B2 **Alexander City** USA
79G3 **Alexander I** Ant
78A3 **Alexandra** NZ
25J8 **Alexandra,C** South Georgia
7L2 **Alexandra Fjord** Can
69B1 **Alexandria** Egypt
9D3 **Alexandria** Louisiana, USA
9D2 **Alexandria** Minnesota, USA
9F3 **Alexandria** Virginia, USA
41F2 **Alexandroúpolis** Greece
5K3 **Alexis** *R* Can
3D3 **Alexis Creek** Can
65C2 **Aley** Leb
48K4 **Aleysk** Russian Fed
64D3 **Al Fallūjah** Iraq
67E4 **Al Fardah** Yemen
39B1 **Alfaro** Spain
41F2 **Alfatar** Bulg
64E3 **Al Fāw** Iraq
36E1 **Alfeld** Germany
29C3 **Alfensas** Brazil
41E3 **Alfiós** *R* Greece
37D2 **Alfonsine** Italy
29D3 **Alfonzo Cláudio** Brazil
29D3 **Alfredo Chaves** Brazil
67E1 **Al Furūthi** S Arabia
45K6 **Alga** Kazakhstan
28A1 **Algarrobal** Chile
28B3 **Algarrobo del Águila** Arg
39A2 **Algeciras** Spain
71C1 **Alger** Alg
70B2 **Algeria** Republic, Africa
67F3 **Al Ghaydah** Yemen
40B2 **Alghero** Sardegna
Algiers = Alger
11D3 **Algona** USA
13D1 **Algonquin Park** Can
4F4 **Algonquin Prov Park** Can
28D2 **Algorta** Urug
67G2 **Al Hadd** Oman
64D3 **Al Hadithah** Iraq
64C3 **Al Hadithah** S Arabia
64D2 **Al Haḑr** Iraq
65D1 **Al Haffah** Syria
67G2 **Al Hajar al Gharbī** *Mts* Oman
67G2 **Al Hajar ash Sharqī** *Mts* Oman
64C3 **Al Hamad** *Desert Region* Jordan/S Arabia
64E4 **Al Haniyah** *Desert Region* Iraq
67E2 **Al Harīq** S Arabia
64C3 **Al Harrah** *Desert Region* S Arabia
69A2 **Al Harūj al Aswad** *Upland* Libya
67E1 **Al Hasa** Region, S Arabia
64D2 **Al Hasakah** Syria
64C4 **Al Hawjā'** S Arabia
64E3 **Al Hayy** Iraq
67F2 **Al Hibāk** Region, S Arabia
65D2 **Al Hījānah** Syria
64D3 **Al Hillah** Iraq
67E2 **Al Hillah** S Arabia
71B1 **Al Hoceima** Mor
66D4 **Al Hudaydah** Yemen
67E1 **Al Hufūf** S Arabia
67F2 **Al Humrah** Region, UAE
67G2 **Al Huwatsah** Oman
63B1 **Alīābad** Iran
63D3 **Aliabad** Iran
41E2 **Aliákmon** *R* Greece
64E3 **Alī al Gharbī** Iraq
62A1 **Alībāg** India
71B3 **Alibori** *R* Benin
39B2 **Alicante** Spain
8D4 **Alice** USA
76C3 **Alice Springs** Aust
40C3 **Alicudi** *I* Italy
60D3 **Aligarh** India
63B2 **Aligūdarz** Iran
60B2 **Ali-Khel** Afghan
41F3 **Alimniá** *I* Greece
61C2 **Alīpur Duār** India
12C2 **Aliquippa** USA
67E4 **Al'Irqah** Yemen
64C3 **Al'Īsawiyah** S Arabia
74D3 **Aliwal North** S Africa
69B2 **Al Jaghbūb** Libya
64D3 **Al Jālamīd** S Arabia
69B2 **Al Jawf** Libya
64C4 **Al Jawf** S Arabia
45G8 **Al Jazīrah** Syria
64D2 **Al Jazīrah** *Desert Region* Syria/Iraq
39A2 **Aljezur** Port
67E1 **Al Jubayl** S Arabia
65D4 **Al Kabid** *Desert* Jordan
66D1 **Al Kahfah** S Arabia
67G2 **Al Kāmil** Oman
64D2 **Al Khābūr** *R* Syria
67G2 **Al Khābūrah** Oman
64D3 **Al Khālis** Iraq
66D2 **Al Khamāsīn** S Arabia
67G1 **Al Khasab** Oman
67F1 **Al Khawr** Qatar
69A1 **Al Khums** Libya
67F2 **Al Kidan** Region, S Arabia
65D2 **Al Kiswah** Syria
42A2 **Alkmaar** Neth
69B2 **Al Kufrah Oasis** Libya
64E3 **Al Kūt** Iraq
64C2 **Al Lādhiqīyah** Syria
61B2 **Allahābād** India
65D2 **Al Lajāh** *Mt* Syria
10H2 **Allakaket** USA
55B2 **Allanmyo** Burma
66B2 **'Allaqi** *Watercourse* Egypt
15C2 **Allatoona L** USA
74D1 **Alldays** S Africa
13D2 **Allegheny** *R* USA
9F3 **Allegheny Mts** USA
14A2 **Allegheny Res** USA
15C2 **Allendale** USA
78A3 **Allen,Mt** NZ
13D2 **Allentown** USA
62B3 **Alleppey** India
38C2 **Aller** *R* France
37D1 **Allgäu** *Mts* Germany
11B3 **Alliance** USA
66D2 **Al Līth** S Arabia
67F2 **Al Liwā** Region, UAE
75D1 **Allora** Aust
37B2 **Allos** France
12C2 **Alma** Michigan, USA
16C1 **Alma** Nebraska, USA
59F1 **Alma Ata** Kazakhstan
39A2 **Almada** Port
Al Madinah = Medina
51H5 **Almagan** I Pacific O
67F3 **Al Mahrah** Region, Yemen
67E1 **Al Majma'ah** S Arabia
67F1 **Al Manāmah** Bahrain
64D3 **Al Ma'nīyah** Iraq
19B2 **Almanor,L** USA
39B2 **Almansa** Spain
3C2 **Alma Peak** *Mt* Can
67F2 **Al Māriyyah** UAE
5G4 **Alma** Can
69B1 **Al Marj** Libya
Almaty = Alma Ata
39B1 **Almazán** Spain
36E1 **Alme** *R* Germany
29D2 **Almenara** Brazil
39B2 **Almeria** Spain
29C2 **Almes** *R* Brazil
44J5 **Al'met'yevsk** Russian Fed
42C1 **Älmhult** Sweden
66D1 **Al Midhnab** S Arabia
64E3 **Al Miqdādīyah** Iraq
79G3 **Almirante Brown** *Base* Ant
28A1 **Almirante Latorre** Chile
41E3 **Almirós** Greece
67E1 **Al Mish'ab** A Arabia
39A2 **Almodôvar** Port
60D3 **Almora** India
64D2 **Al Mawşil** Iraq
67E1 **Al Mubarraz** S Arabia
64C4 **Al Mudawwara** Jordan
67G2 **Al Mudaybi** Oman
67F1 **Al Muharraq** Bahrain
67E4 **Al Mukallā** Yemen
66D4 **Al Mukhā** Yemen
64D3 **Al Musayyib** Iraq
66C1 **Al Muwaylih** S Arabia
34C3 **Alness** Scot
64E3 **Al Nu'mānīyah** Iraq
34E4 **Alnwick** Eng
4B3 **Alonsa** Can
57B4 **Alor** *I* Indon
55C4 **Alor Setar** Malay
Alost = Aalst
76E2 **Alotau** PNG
76B3 **Aloysius,Mt** Aust
28C3 **Alpachiri** Arg
37D2 **Alpe di Succiso** *Mt* Italy
12C1 **Alpena** USA
37B1 **Alpes du Valais** *Mts* Switz
37B2 **Alpes Maritimes** *Mts* France
37E1 **Alpi Carniche** *Mts* Italy
40C1 **Alpi Dolomitiche** *Mts* Italy
37B2 **Alpi Graie** *Mts* Italy
19E4 **Alpine** Arizona, USA
16B3 **Alpine** Texas, USA
18D2 **Alpine** Wyoming, USA
37C1 **Alpi Orobie** *Mts* Italy
37B2 **Alpi Penine** *Mts* Italy
37C1 **Alpi Retiche** *Mts* Switz
37D1 **Alpi Venoste** *Mts* Italy
40B1 **Alps** *Mts* Europe
69A1 **Al Qaddāhiyah** Libya
65D1 **Al Qadmūs** Syria
64D3 **Al Qā'im** Iraq
64C4 **Al Qalībah** S Arabia

Al Qāmishlī Arad

64D2 **Al Qāmishlī** Syria
65D1 **Al Qardāhah** Syria
69A1 **Al Qaryah Ash Sharqiyah** Libya
64C3 **Al Qaryatayn** Syria
66D1 **Al Qasīm** Region, S Arabia
67E1 **Al Qātif** S Arabia
69A2 **Al Qatrūn** Libya
67E1 **Al Qayṣāmah** S Arabia
65D2 **Al Quatayfah** Syria
39A2 **Alquera** *Res* Port/Spain
64C3 **Al Qunayṭirah** Syria
66D3 **Al Qunfidhah** S Arabia
64E3 **Al Qurnah** Iraq
65D1 **Al Quṣayr** Syria
64C3 **Al Qutayfah** Syria
67E2 **Al Quwayīyah** S Arabia
42B1 **Als** *I* Den
38D2 **Alsace** Region, France
42B2 **Alsfeld** Germany
34D4 **Alston** Eng
32J5 **Alta** Nor
25D4 **Alta Gracia** Arg
23D5 **Altagracia de Orituco** Ven
50B2 **Altai** *Mts* Mongolia
15C2 **Altamaha** *R* USA
27H4 **Altamira** Brazil
22C1 **Altamira** Mexico
40D2 **Altamura** Italy
50D1 **Altanbulag** Mongolia
49M5 **Altanbulag** Russian Fed
51H7 **Altape** PNG
21B2 **Altata** Mexico
48K5 **Altay** China
49L5 **Altay** Mongolia
48K4 **Altay** *Mts* Russian Fed
37C1 **Altdorf** Switz
36D1 **Altenkirchen** Germany
28B3 **Altiplanicie del Payún** *Plat* Arg
37B1 **Altkirch** France
29B2 **Alto Araguaia** Brazil
73D5 **Alto Molócue** Mozam
12A3 **Alton** USA
13D2 **Altoona** USA
28B2 **Alto Pencoso** *Mts* Arg
29B2 **Alto Sucuriú** Brazil
22C2 **Altotonga** Mexico
22B2 **Altoyac de Alvarez** Mexico
59G2 **Altun Shan** *Mts* China
18B2 **Alturas** USA
16C3 **Altus** USA
67F2 **Al'Ubaylah** S Arabia
66C1 **Al'Ulā** S Arabia
28A3 **Aluminé** Arg
64C4 **Al Urayq** *Desert Region* S Arabia
67F2 **Al'Uruq al Mu'taridah** Region, S Arabia
16C2 **Alva** USA
22C2 **Alvarado** Mexico
17C3 **Alvarado** USA
32G6 **Älvdalen** Sweden
28D1 **Alvear** Arg
17C4 **Alvin** USA
32J5 **Alvsbyn** Sweden
69A2 **Al Wāha** Libya
66C1 **Al Wajh** S Arabia
60D3 **Alwar** India
64D3 **Al Widyān** *Desert Region* Iraq/S Arabia
52A2 **Alxa Yougi** China
64E2 **Alyat** Azerbaijan
32J8 **Alytus** Lithuania
36E2 **Alzey** Germany
22C2 **Amacuzac** *R* Mexico
72D3 **Amadi** Sudan
64D2 **Amādīyah** Iraq
7L3 **Amadjuak L** Can
57C3 **Amahai** Indon
53B5 **Amakusa-shotō** *I* Japan
32G7 **Åmål** Sweden
49N4 **Amalat** *R* Russian Fed
41E3 **Amaliás** Greece
60C4 **Amalner** India
29A3 **Amambai** Brazil
29B3 **Amambai** *R* Brazil
50F4 **Amami** *I* Japan
50F4 **Amami gunto** *Arch* Japan
27H3 **Amapá** Brazil
27H3 **Amapá** State, Brazil
4B3 **Amaranth** Can
61E3 **Amarapura** Burma
16B2 **Amarillo** USA
45F7 **Amasya** Turk
22B1 **Amatitan** Mexico
22C1 **Amaulipas** Mexico
Amazonas = Solimões
27H4 **Amazonas** Brazil
26E4 **Amazonas** State, Brazil
24D4 **Amazonas** *R* Brazil
60D2 **Ambāla** India
62C3 **Ambalangoda** Sri Lanka
73E6 **Ambalavao** Madag
72B3 **Ambam** Cam
73E5 **Ambanja** Madag
49S3 **Ambarchik** Russian Fed
26C4 **Ambato** Ecuador
73E5 **Ambato-Boeny** Madag
73E5 **Ambatolampy** Madag
73E5 **Ambatondrazaka** Madag
42C3 **Amberg** Germany
21D3 **Ambergris Cay** *I* Belize
37A2 **Ambérieu** France
61B3 **Ambikāpur** India
73E5 **Ambilobe** Madag
73E6 **Amboasary** Madag
73E5 **Ambodifototra** Madag
73E6 **Ambohimahasoa** Madag
57C3 **Ambon** Indon
57C3 **Ambon** *I* Indon
73E6 **Ambositra** Madag
73E6 **Ambovombe** Madag
73B4 **Ambriz** Angola
77F2 **Ambrym** *I* Vanuatu
10B6 **Amchitka** USA
10B6 **Amchitka** *I* USA
10C6 **Amchitka Pass** USA
72C2 **Am Dam** Chad
44L2 **Amderma** Russian Fed
21B2 **Ameca** Mexico
22A1 **Ameca** *R* Mexico
22C2 **Amecacameca** Mexico
28C2 **Ameghino** Arg
42B2 **Ameland** *I* Neth
14D2 **Amenia** USA
18D2 **American Falls** USA
18D2 **American Falls Res** USA
19D2 **American Fork** USA
79F10 **American Highland** *Upland* Ant
xxixL5 **American Samoa** *Is* Pacific O
15C2 **Americus** USA
42B2 **Amersfoort** Neth
74D2 **Amersfoort** S Africa
11D2 **Amery** USA
79G10 **Amery Ice Shelf** Ant
11D3 **Ames** USA
14E1 **Amesbury** USA
4E4 **Ameson** Can
41E3 **Amfilokhía** Greece
41E3 **Amfissa** Greece
49P3 **Amga** Russian Fed
49P3 **Amgal** *R* Russian Fed
53D2 **Amgu** Russian Fed
10C2 **Amguema** *R* Russian Fed
53D1 **Amgun'** *R* Russian Fed
72D2 **Amhara** *Region* Eth
Amherst = Kyaikkami Burma
7M5 **Amherst** Can
14D1 **Amherst** Massachusetts, USA
13D3 **Amherst** Virginia, USA
62B2 **Amhūr** India
38C2 **Amiens** France
54C3 **Amino** Japan
65C1 **Amioune** Leb
68K8 **Amirante Is** Indian O
3H3 **Amisk L** Can
16B4 **Amistad Res** Mexico
61C2 **Amlekhgan** Nepal
10D6 **Amlia** *I* USA
64C3 **Amman** Jordan
32K6 **Ämmänsaario** Fin
54A3 **Amnyong-dan** *C* N Korea
63C1 **Amol** Iran
7L5 **Amos** Can
Amoy = Xiamen
57B3 **Ampana** Indon
73E6 **Ampanihy** Madag
29C3 **Amparo** Brazil
39C1 **Amposta** Spain
5H4 **Amqui** Can
66D3 **Amrān** Yemen
60D4 **Amrāvati** India
60C4 **Amreli** India
60C2 **Amritsar** India
42A2 **Amsterdam** Neth
74E2 **Amsterdam** S Africa
13E2 **Amsterdam** USA
72C2 **Am Timan** Chad
48H5 **Amu Darya** *R* Uzbekistan
10D6 **Amukta** *I* USA
10D6 **Amukta Pass** USA
7J2 **Amund Ringnes I** Can
6F2 **Amundsen G** Can
79F4 **Amundsen S** Ant
79E **Amundsen-Scott** *Base* Ant
56E3 **Amuntai** Indon
49O4 **Amur** *R* Russian Fed
66C3 **Amur** *Watercourse* Sudan
57B2 **Amurang** Indon
53D1 **Amursk** Russian Fed
53E1 **Amurskiy Liman** *Str* Russian Fed
53C2 **Amurzet** Russian Fed
49N2 **Anabar** *R* Russian Fed
26F2 **Anaco** Ven
8B2 **Anaconda** USA
18B1 **Anacortes** USA
16C2 **Anadarko** USA
49T3 **Anadyr'** Russian Fed
49T3 **Anadyr'** *R* Russian Fed
49U3 **Anadyrskiy Zaliv** *S* Russian Fed
49T3 **Anadyrskoye Ploskogor'ye** *Plat* Russian Fed
41F3 **Anáfi** *I* Greece
29D1 **Anagé** Brazil
64D3 **'Ānah** Iraq
19C4 **Anaheim** USA
62B2 **Anaimalai Hills** India
62C1 **Anakāpalle** India
10J2 **Anaktuvuk P** USA
73E5 **Analalaya** Madag
71H4 **Anambra** *State* Nig
71H4 **Anambra** *R* Nig
12A2 **Anamosa** USA
45E8 **Anamur** Turk
54B4 **Anan** Japan
62B2 **Anantapur** India
60D2 **Anantnag** India
27J7 **Anápolis** Brazil
63D2 **Anār** Iran
63C2 **Anārak** Iran
63E2 **Anardara** Afghan
51H5 **Anatahan** *I* Pacific O
25D3 **Añatuya** Arg
53B4 **Anbyŏn** N Korea
20C4 **Ancapa Is** USA
28B1 **Ancasti** Arg
6D3 **Anchorage** USA
26E7 **Ancohuma** *Mt* Bol
26C6 **Ancón** Peru
40C2 **Ancona** Italy
14D1 **Ancram** USA
25B6 **Ancud** Chile
36C3 **Ancy-le-Franc** France
26D6 **Andabuaylas** Peru
28A3 **Andacollo** Arg
75A1 **Andado** Aust
28B1 **Andagalá** Arg
32F6 **Andalsnes** Nor
39A2 **Andalucia** Region, Spain
15B2 **Andalusia** USA
59H4 **Andaman Is** Burma
59H4 **Andaman S** Burma
75A2 **Andamooka** Aust
29D1 **Andaraí** Brazil
35B5 **Andee** Irish Rep
36C2 **Andelot** France
32H5 **Andenes** Nor
37C1 **Andermatt** Switz
42B2 **Andernach** Germany
12B2 **Anderson** Indiana, USA
17D2 **Anderson** Missouri, USA
15C2 **Anderson** S Carolina, USA
6F3 **Anderson** *R* Can
62B1 **Andhra Pradesh** State, India
41E3 **Andikíthira** *I* Greece
48J5 **Andizhan** Uzbekistan
48H6 **Andkhui** Afghan
53B4 **Andong** S Korea
39C1 **Andorra** Principality, SW Europe
39C1 **Andorra-La-Vella** Andorra
35E6 **Andover** Eng
14E1 **Andover** New Hampshire, USA
14B1 **Andover** New York, USA
29B3 **Andradina** Brazil
10F3 **Andreafsky** USA
10C6 **Andreanof Is** USA
43G1 **Andreapol'** Russian Fed
64B2 **Andreas,C** Cyprus
16B3 **Andrews** USA
40D2 **Andria** Italy
9F4 **Andros** *I* Bahamas
41E3 **Ándros** *I* Greece
62A2 **Androth** *I* India
39B2 **Andújar** Spain
73B5 **Andulo** Angola
71G4 **Anécho** Togo
70C3 **Anéfis** Mali
77F3 **Aneityum** *I* Vanuatu
28B3 **Añelo** Arg
66C4 **Angareb** *Watercourse* Eth
49M4 **Angarsk** Russian Fed
44A3 **Ånge** Sweden
21A2 **Angel de la Guarda** *I* Mexico
57F7 **Angeles** Phil
32G7 **Angelholm** Sweden
75C1 **Angellala Creek** *R* Aust
20B1 **Angels Camp** USA
51G7 **Angemuk** *Mt* Indon
38B2 **Angers** France
36B2 **Angerville** France
55C3 **Angkor** *Hist Site* Camb
33C3 **Anglesey** *I* Wales
17C4 **Angleton** USA
7P3 **Angmagssalik** Greenland
73E5 **Angoche** Mozam
25B5 **Angol** Chile
12C2 **Angola** Indiana, USA
14A1 **Angola** New York, USA
68F9 **Angola** Republic, Africa
73B5 **Angola** Republic, Africa
xxxJ5 **Angola Basin** Atlantic O
10M4 **Angoon** USA
38C2 **Angoulême** France
70A1 **Angra do Heroismo** Açores
29D3 **Angra dos Reis** Brazil
28C3 **Anguil** Arg
23E3 **Anguilla** *I* Caribbean
23B2 **Anguilla Cays** *Is* Caribbean
61C3 **Angul** India
72C4 **Angumu** Zaïre
42C1 **Anholt** *I* Den
52C4 **Anhua** China
52D3 **Anhui** Province, China
29B2 **Anhumas** Brazil
54A3 **Anhŭng** S Korea
10G3 **Aniak** USA
29C2 **Anicuns** Brazil
71G4 **Anié** Togo
16A2 **Animas** *R* USA
16A3 **Animas Peak** *Mt* USA
11D3 **Anita** USA
36B2 **Anizy-le-Château** France
38B2 **Anjou** Republic, France
73E5 **Anjouan** *I* Comoros
73E5 **Anjozorobe** Madag
53B4 **Anju** N Korea
52B3 **Ankang** China
45E8 **Ankara** Turk
73E5 **Ankaratra** *Mt* Madag
73E6 **Ankazoabo** Madag
73E5 **Ankazobe** Madag
11D3 **Ankeny** USA
42C2 **Anklam** Germany
71H4 **Ankwe** *R* Nig
55D3 **An Loc** Viet
52B4 **Anlong** China
52C3 **Anlu** China
12B3 **Anna** USA
68E4 **Annaba** Alg
71D1 **'Annaba** Alg
64C3 **An Nabk** S Arabia
64C3 **An Nabk** Syria
75A1 **Anna Creek** Aust
69B2 **An Nāfūrah** Libya
64D3 **An Najaf** Iraq
34D4 **Annan** Scot
13D3 **Annapolis** USA
61B2 **Annapurna** *Mt* Nepal
12C2 **Ann Arbor** USA
65D1 **An Nāsirah** Syria
64E3 **An Nāsirīyah** Iraq
37B2 **Annecy** France
37B1 **Annemasse** France
3B2 **Annette I** USA
55D3 **An Nhon** Viet
66D3 **An Nimās** S Arabia
52A5 **Anning** China
15B2 **Anniston** USA
70C4 **Annobon, I** Eq Guinea
38C2 **Annonay** France
37B3 **Annot** France
23J1 **Annotto Bay** Jamaica
52D3 **Anqing** China
52B2 **Ansai** China
42C3 **Ansbach** Germany
23C3 **Anse d'Hainault** Haiti
52E1 **Anshan** China
52B4 **Anshun** China
16C1 **Ansley** USA
16C3 **Anson** USA
51F8 **Anson B** Aust
70C3 **Ansongo** Mali
12C1 **Ansonville** Can
12C3 **Ansted** USA
45F8 **Antakya** Turk
73F5 **Antalaha** Madag
45E8 **Antalya** Turk
45E8 **Antalya Körfezi** *B* Turk
73E5 **Antananarivo** Madag
79G1 **Antarctic Circle** Ant
79G3 **Antarctic Pen** Ant
39B2 **Antequera** Spain
16A3 **Anthony** USA
70B1 **Anti-Atlas** *Mts* Mor
37B3 **Antibes** France
7M5 **Anticosti, Î d'** Can
5J4 **Anticosti Prov Park** Can
12B1 **Antigo** USA
23E3 **Antigua** *I* Caribbean
Anti Lebanon = Jebel esh Sharqi
19B3 **Antioch** USA
77G5 **Antipodes Is** NZ
17C3 **Antlers** USA
25B2 **Antofagasta** Chile
29C4 **Antonina** Brazil
16A2 **Antonito** USA
34B4 **Antrim** County, N Ire
34B4 **Antrim** N Ire
14E1 **Antrim** USA
34B4 **Antrim Hills** N Ire
73E5 **Antseranana** Madag
73E5 **Antsirabe** Madag
73E5 **Antsohiny** Madag
55D3 **An Tuc** Viet
28C1 **Añtuya** Arg
36C1 **Antwerpen** Belg
35B5 **An Uaimh** Irish Rep
54A3 **Anui** S Korea
60C3 **Anupgarh** India
62C3 **Anuradhapura** Sri Lanka
Anvers = Antwerpen
6B3 **Anvik** USA
10B6 **Anvil Pk** *Mt* USA
49L5 **Anxi** China
52C2 **Anyang** China
52A3 **A'nyêmaqên Shan** *Upland* China
49S3 **Anyuysk** Russian Fed
37C2 **Anza** *R* Italy
3F2 **Anzac** Can
48K4 **Anzhero-Sudzhensk** Russian Fed
40C2 **Anzio** Italy
77F2 **Aoba** *I* Vanuatu
53E3 **Aomori** Japan
40B1 **Aosta** Italy
70B3 **Aoukar** *Desert Region* Maur
70C2 **Aoulef** Alg
72B1 **Aozou** Chad
25E2 **Apa** *R* Brazil/Par
9E4 **Apalachee B** USA
15C3 **Apalachicola** USA
15B3 **Apalachicola B** USA
22C2 **Apan** Mexico
26D3 **Apaporis** *R* Colombia
29B3 **Aparecida do Taboado** Brazil
57F7 **Aparri** Phil
41D1 **Apatin** Croatia, Yugos
44E2 **Apatity** Russian Fed
21B3 **Apatzingan** Mexico
42B2 **Apeldoorn** Neth
77H2 **Apia** Western Samoa
29C3 **Apiai** Brazil
22B1 **Apizolaya** Mexico
27G2 **Apoera** Suriname
75B3 **Apollo Bay** Aust
57G9 **Apo,Mt** Phil
15C3 **Apopka,L** USA
27H7 **Aporé** *R* Brazil
12A1 **Apostle Is** USA
22B1 **Apozol** Mexico
9E3 **Appalachian Mts** USA
37D2 **Appenino Tosco-Emiliano** *Mts* Italy
40C2 **Appennino Abruzzese** *Mts* Italy
40B2 **Appennino Ligure** *Mts* Italy
40D2 **Appennino Lucano** *Mts* Italy
40D2 **Appennino Napoletano** *Mts* Italy
40C2 **Appennino Tosco-Emilliano** *Mts* Italy
40C2 **Appennino Umbro-Marchigiano** *Mts* Italy
37C1 **Appenzell** Switz
35D4 **Appleby** Eng
11C2 **Appleton** Minnesota, USA
12B2 **Appleton** Wisconsin, USA
45J7 **Apsheronskiy Poluostrov** *Pen* Azerbaijan
4F5 **Apsley** Can
37A3 **Apt** France
25F2 **Apucarana** Brazil
22C1 **Apulco** Mexico
26E2 **Apure** *R* Ven
26D6 **Apurimac** *R* Peru
64C4 **'Aqaba** Jordan
64B4 **'Aqaba,G of** Egypt/S Arabia
63C2 **'Aqdā** Iran
27G8 **Aqidauana** Brazil
22A1 **Aqua Nueva** Mexico
29A3 **Aquidabán** *R* Par
25E2 **Aquidauana** Brazil
29A2 **Aquidauana** *R* Brazil
22B2 **Aquila** Mexico
61B2 **Ara** India
15B2 **Arab** USA
65C1 **'Arab al Mulk** Syria
58E4 **Arabian** *S* Asia/Arabian Pen
xxviiiE4 **Arabian Basin** Indian O
27L6 **Aracajú** Brazil
25E2 **Aracanguy, Mts de** *Mts* Brazil
29A3 **Aracanguy, Mts de** Par
27L4 **Aracati** Brazil
29D1 **Aracatu** Brazil
27H8 **Araçatuba** Brazil
39A2 **Aracena** Spain
27K7 **Araçuai** Brazil
65C3 **Arad** Israel
45C6 **Arad** Rom

B

Bejaïa **Birch Mts**

71D1 **Bejaïa** Alg
39A1 **Béjar** Spain
63D2 **Bejestān** Iran
43E3 **Békéscsaba** Hung
73E6 **Bekily** Madag
61B2 **Bela** India
60B3 **Bela** Pak
56D2 **Belaga** Malay
14B3 **Bel Air** USA
62B1 **Belamoalli** India
57B2 **Belang** Indon
56A2 **Belangpidie** Indon
xxviiiH4 **Belau** *I* Pacific O
Belau = Palau
74E2 **Bela Vista** Mozam
29A3 **Béla Vista** Par/Brazil
56A2 **Belawan** Indon
44K4 **Belaya** *R* Ukraine
43G3 **Belaya Tserkov'** Russian Fed
7J2 **Belcher Chan** Can
7L4 **Belcher Is** Can
60B1 **Belchiragh** Afghan
44J5 **Belebey** Russian Fed
72E3 **Beled Weyne** Somalia
27J4 **Belém** Brazil
28B1 **Belén** Arg
26C3 **Belén** Colombia
29A3 **Belén** Par
28D2 **Belén** Urug
8C3 **Belen** USA
28B1 **Belén** *R* Arg
34B4 **Belfast** N Ire
74E2 **Belfast** S Africa
5H5 **Belfast** USA
34B4 **Belfast Lough** *Estuary* N Ire
11B2 **Belfield** USA
72D2 **Bēlfodiyo** Eth
34E4 **Belford** Eng
38D2 **Belfort** France
62A1 **Belgaum** India
42A2 **Belgium** Kingdom, N W Europe
45F5 **Belgorod** Russian Fed
45E6 **Belgorod Dnestrovskiy** Ukraine
Belgrade = Beograd
18D1 **Belgrade** USA
69A2 **Bel Hedan** Libya
56C3 **Belinyu** Indon
56C3 **Belitung** *I* Indon
21D3 **Belize** Belize
21D3 **Belize** Republic, C America
49P2 **Bel'kovskiv, Ostrov** *I* Russian Fed
38C2 **Bellac** France
6F4 **Bella Coola** Can
37C2 **Bellagio** Italy
17C4 **Bellaire** USA
37C1 **Bellano** Italy
62B1 **Bellary** India
75C1 **Bellata** Aust
28D2 **Bella Union** Urug
28D1 **Bella Vista** Arg
37B2 **Belledonne** *Mts* France
14B2 **Bellefonte** USA
8C2 **Belle Fourche** USA
11B3 **Belle Fourche** *R* USA
38D2 **Bellegarde** France
15E4 **Belle Glade** USA
7N4 **Belle I** Can
38B2 **Belle-Ile** *I* France
7N4 **Belle Isle,Str of** Can
36A2 **Bellême** France
5K4 **Belleoram** Can
7L5 **Belleville** Can
12B3 **Belleville** Illinois, USA
17C2 **Belleville** Kansas, USA
18D2 **Bellevue** Idaho, USA
12A2 **Bellevue** Iowa, USA
18B1 **Bellevue** Washington, USA
37A2 **Belley** France
75D2 **Bellingen** Aust
8A2 **Bellingham** USA
79G2 **Bellingshausen** *Base* Ant
79G3 **Bellingshausen S** Ant
40B1 **Bellinzona** Switz
26C2 **Bello** Colombia
77E3 **Bellona Reefs** Nouvelle Calédonie
20B1 **Bellota** USA
13E2 **Bellows Falls** USA
7K3 **Bell Pen** Can
40C1 **Belluno** Italy
25D4 **Bell Ville** Arg
4C5 **Belmond** USA
14B1 **Belmont** USA
27L7 **Belmonte** Brazil
21D3 **Belmopan** Belize
53B1 **Belogorsk** Russian Fed
73E6 **Beloha** Madag
27K7 **Belo Horizonte** Brazil
16C2 **Beloit** Kansas, USA
9E2 **Beloit** Wisconsin, USA
44E3 **Belomorsk** Russian Fed
44K5 **Beloretsk** Russian Fed
44D5 **Belorussia**
73E5 **Belo-Tsiribihina** Madag
44F2 **Beloye More** *S*
44F3 **Beloye Ozero** *L* Russian Fed
44F3 **Belozersk** Russian Fed
12C3 **Belpre** USA
75A2 **Beltana** Aust
17C3 **Belton** USA
43F3 **Bel'tsy** Moldova
48K5 **Belukha** *Mt* Russian Fed
44H2 **Belush'ye** Russian Fed
12B2 **Belvidere** Illinois, USA
14C2 **Belvidere** New Jersey, USA
48J2 **Belyy, Ostrov** *I* Russian Fed
73B4 **Bembe** Angola
71G3 **Bembéréke** Benin
9D2 **Bemidji** USA
15B1 **Bemis** USA
32G6 **Bena** Nor
72C4 **Bena Dibele** Zaïre
75C3 **Benalla** Aust
34C2 **Ben Attow** *Mt* Scot
39A1 **Benavente** Spain
34B3 **Benbecula** *I* Scot
76A4 **Bencubbin** Aust
8A2 **Bend** USA
69E3 **Bendarbeyla** Somalia
34C3 **Ben Dearg** *Mt* Scot
43F3 **Bendery** Moldova
76D4 **Bendigo** Aust
71F3 **Bénéna** Mali
42C3 **Benešov** Czech Republic
40C2 **Benevento** Italy
59G4 **Bengal,B of** Asia
69A1 **Ben Gardane** Libya
71E2 **Ben Gardane** Tunisia
52D3 **Bengbu** China
57B3 **Benggai** *I* Indon
69B1 **Benghāzī** Libya
56B2 **Bengkalis** Indon
56B3 **Bengkulu** Indon
73B5 **Benguela** Angola
71A2 **Benguerir** Mor
64B3 **Benha** Egypt
34C2 **Ben Hope** *Mt* Scot
72C3 **Beni** Zaïre
26E6 **Béni** *R* Bol
70B1 **Beni Abbes** Alg
39C1 **Benicarló** Spain
39B2 **Benidorm** Spain
39C2 **Beni Mansour** Alg
69C2 **Beni Mazar** Egypt
71A2 **Beni Mellal** Mor
70C4 **Benin** Republic, Africa
71H4 **Benin City** Nig
71B1 **Beni-Saf** Alg
69C2 **Beni Suef** Egypt
16B2 **Benkelman** USA
34C2 **Ben Kilbreck** *Mt* Scot
33C2 **Ben Lawers** *Mt* Scot
34D3 **Ben Macdui** *Mt* Scot
34C2 **Ben More Assynt** *Mt* Scot
78B2 **Benmore,L** NZ
49R2 **Bennetta, Ostrov** *I* Russian Fed
34C3 **Ben Nevis** *Mt* Scot
13E2 **Bennington** USA
65C2 **Bennt Jbail** Leb
72B3 **Bénoué** *R* Cam
71J4 **Bénoué Nat Pk** Cam
36E2 **Bensheim** Germany
8B3 **Benson** Arizona, USA
11C2 **Benson** Minnesota, USA
72C3 **Bentiu** Sudan
29A2 **Bento Gomes** *R* Brazil
17D3 **Benton** Arkansas, USA
20C2 **Benton** California, USA
12B3 **Benton** Kentucky, USA
12B2 **Benton Harbor** USA
71H4 **Benue** State, Nig
71H4 **Benue** *R* Nig
34C3 **Ben Wyvis** *Mt* Scot
52E1 **Benxi** China
57C2 **Beo** Indon
41E2 **Beograd** Serbia, Yugos
61B3 **Beohāri** India
53C5 **Beppu** Japan
41D2 **Berat** Alb
72D2 **Berber** Sudan
72E2 **Berbera** Somalia
72B3 **Berbérati** CAR
36A1 **Berck** France
43F3 **Berdichev** Ukraine
45F6 **Berdyansk** Ukraine
12C3 **Berea** USA
57C2 **Berebere** Indon
71F4 **Berekum** Ghana
20B2 **Berenda** USA
66C2 **Berenice** Egypt
4C3 **Berens** *R* Can
6J4 **Berens** *R* Can
6J4 **Berens River** Can
75A1 **Beresford** Aust
11C3 **Beresford** USA
43E3 **Berettyoújfalu** Hung
43E2 **Bereza** Belorussia
43E3 **Berezhany** Ukraine
43F2 **Berezina** *R* Belorussia
44G3 **Bereznik** Russian Fed
44K4 **Berezniki** Russian Fed
45E6 **Berezovka** Ukraine
44L3 **Berezovo** Russian Fed
53D1 **Berezovyy** Russian Fed
64A2 **Bergama** Turk
40B1 **Bergamo** Italy
32F6 **Bergen** Nor
14B1 **Bergen** USA
36C1 **Bergen op Zoom** Neth
38C3 **Bergerac** France
36D1 **Bergisch-Gladbach** Germany
4D4 **Bergland** USA
62C1 **Berhampur** India
49S4 **Beringa, Ostrov** *I* Russian Fed
10K3 **Bering Gl** USA
49T3 **Beringovskiy** Russian Fed
xxixK2 **Bering S** Russian Fed/USA
79C6 **Bering Str** Russian Fed/USA
63D3 **Berīzak** Iran
39B2 **Berja** Spain
71B2 **Berkane** Mor
8A3 **Berkeley** USA
14A3 **Berkeley Spring** USA
79F2 **Berkner I** Ant
41E2 **Berkovitsa** Bulg
35E6 **Berkshire** County, Eng
14D1 **Berkshire Hills** USA
3E3 **Berland** *R* Can
42C2 **Berlin** Germany
13E2 **Berlin** New Hampshire, USA
14A3 **Berlin** Pennsylvania, USA
42C2 **Berlin** State, Germany
26F8 **Bermejo** Bol
25E3 **Bermejo** *R* Arg
2M5 **Bermuda** *I* Atlantic O
40B1 **Bern** Switz
16A2 **Bernalillo** USA
29B4 **Bernardo de Irigoyen** Arg
14C2 **Bernardsville** USA
28C3 **Bernasconi** Arg
36A2 **Bernay** France
42C2 **Bernburg** Germany
37B1 **Berner Orberland** *Mts* Switz
7K2 **Bernier B** Can
42C3 **Berounka** *R* Czech Republic
71A2 **Berrechid** Mor
75B2 **Berri** Aust
71C2 **Berriane** Alg
38C2 **Berry** Region, France
20A1 **Berryessa,L** USA
9F4 **Berry Is** Bahamas
14B3 **Berryville** USA
74B2 **Berseba** Namibia
56F6 **Bertam** Malay
16A2 **Berthoud P** USA
72B3 **Bertoua** Cam
77G1 **Beru** *I* Kiribati
13D2 **Berwick** USA
34D4 **Berwick-upon-Tweed** Eng
35D5 **Berwyn** *Mts* Wales
73E5 **Besalampy** Madag
38D2 **Besançon** France
43E3 **Beskidy Zachodnie** *Mts* Pol
3G2 **Besnard L** Can
64C2 **Besni** Turk
65C3 **Besor** *R* Israel
15B2 **Bessemer** Alabama, USA
12B1 **Bessemer** Michigan, USA
73E5 **Betafo** Madag
39A1 **Betanzos** Spain
71J4 **Betaré Oya** Cam
65C3 **Bet Guvrin** Israel
74D2 **Bethal** S Africa
74B2 **Bethanie** Namibia
17D1 **Bethany** Missouri, USA
17C2 **Bethany** Oklahoma, USA
6B3 **Bethel** Alaska, USA
14D2 **Bethel** Connecticut, USA
12C2 **Bethel Park** USA
13D3 **Bethesda** USA
65C3 **Bethlehem** Israel
74D2 **Bethlehem** S Africa
13D2 **Bethlehem** USA
74D3 **Bethulie** S Africa
38C1 **Bethune** France
36A2 **Béthune** *R* France
73E6 **Betioky** Madag
75B1 **Betoota** Aust
72B3 **Betou** Congo
59E1 **Betpak Dala** *Steppe* Kazakhstan
73E6 **Betroka** Madag
7M5 **Betsiamites** Can
12A2 **Bettendorf** USA
61B2 **Bettiah** India
10H2 **Bettles** USA
37C2 **Béttola** Italy
60D4 **Bētul** India
36C1 **Betuwe** Region, Neth
60D3 **Betwa** *R* India
36D1 **Betzdorf** Germany
10G4 **Beverley,L** USA
14E1 **Beverly** USA
20C3 **Beverly Hills** USA
70B4 **Beyla** Guinea
62B2 **Beypore** India
Beyrouth = Beirut
64B2 **Beyşehir** Turk
45E8 **Beysehir Gölü** *L* Turk
65C2 **Beyt Shean** Israel
37C1 **Bezan** Austria
44F4 **Bezhetsk** Russian Fed
38C3 **Béziers** France
63D1 **Bezmein** Turkmenistan
50D1 **Beznosova** Russian Fed
61C2 **Bhadgaon** Nepal
62C1 **Bhadrāchalam** India
61C3 **Bhadrakh** India
62B2 **Bhadra Res** India
62B2 **Bhadrāvati** India
60B3 **Bhag** Pak
61C2 **Bhāgalpur** India
60C2 **Bhakkar** Pak
61E3 **Bhamo** Burma
60D4 **Bhandāra** India
60D3 **Bharatpur** India
60C4 **Bharūch** India
61C3 **Bhātiāpāra Ghat** Bang
60C2 **Bhatinda** India
62A2 **Bhatkal** India
61C3 **Bhātpāra** India
60C4 **Bhāvnagar** India
61B4 **Bhawānipatna** India
60C2 **Bhera** Pak
61B2 **Bheri** *R* Nepal
61B3 **Bhilai** India
60C3 **Bhīlwāra** India
62C1 **Bhīmavaram** India
60D3 **Bhind** India
60D3 **Bhiwāni** India
62B1 **Bhongir** India
60D4 **Bhopāl** India
61C3 **Bhubaneshwar** India
60B4 **Bhuj** India
60D4 **Bhusāwal** India
46F4 **Bhutan** Kingdom, Asia
59H3 **Bhutan** Kingdom, Asia
71F4 **Bia** *R* Ghana
51G7 **Biak** *I* Indon
43E2 **Biala Podlaska** Pol
42D2 **Bialograd** Pol
43E2 **Bialystok** Pol
32A1 **Biargtangar** *C* Iceland
63D1 **Biarjmand** Iran
57C2 **Biaro** *I* Indon
38B3 **Biarritz** France
37C1 **Biasca** Switz
64B4 **Biba** Egypt
53E3 **Bibai** Japan
73B5 **Bibala** Angola
37D3 **Bibbiena** Italy
42B3 **Biberach** Germany
71F4 **Bibiani** Ghana
5H4 **Bic** Can
41F1 **Bicaz** Rom
53D1 **Bichi** *R* Russian Fed
19D3 **Bicknell** USA
71H4 **Bida** Nig
62B1 **Bīdar** India
67G2 **Bidbid** Oman
13E2 **Biddeford** USA
35C6 **Bideford** Eng
35C6 **Bideford B** Eng
70C2 **Bidon 5** Alg
43E2 **Biebrza** Pol
40B1 **Biel** Switz
42D2 **Bielawa** Pol
42B2 **Bielefeld** Germany
37B1 **Bieler See** *L* Switz
40B1 **Biella** Italy
43E2 **Bielsk Podlaski** Pol
55D3 **Bien Hoa** Viet
40C2 **Biferno** *R* Italy
64A1 **Biga** Turk
41F3 **Bigadiç** Turk
5H4 **Big Bald Mt** Can
4D3 **Big Beaver House** Can
16B4 **Big Bend Nat Pk** USA
18D1 **Big Belt Mts** USA
17E3 **Big Black** *R* USA
17C1 **Big Blue** *R* USA
15E4 **Big Cypress Swamp** USA
6D3 **Big Delta** USA
38D2 **Bigent** Germany
3G3 **Biggar** Can
75D1 **Biggenden** Aust
10L4 **Bigger,Mt** Can
18D1 **Big Hole** *R* USA
11A2 **Bighorn** *R* USA
11A2 **Bighorn L** USA
11A3 **Bighorn Mts** USA
55C3 **Bight of Bangkok** *B* Thai
70C4 **Bight of Benin** *B* W Africa
70C4 **Bight of Biafra** *B* Cam
7L3 **Big I** Can
10G4 **Big Koniuji** *I* USA
16B3 **Big Lake** USA
37C1 **Bignasco** Switz
70A3 **Bignona** Sen
19C3 **Big Pine** USA
15E4 **Big Pine Key** USA
20C3 **Big Pine Mt** USA
12B2 **Big Rapids** USA
6H4 **Big River** Can
4B2 **Big Sand L** Can
18D1 **Big Sandy** USA
3H3 **Big Sandy L** Can
11C3 **Big Sioux** *R* USA
20D1 **Big Smokey V** USA
8C3 **Big Spring** USA
16B1 **Big Springs** USA
11C2 **Big Stone City** USA
12C3 **Big Stone Gap** USA
4B3 **Bigstone L** Can
20B2 **Big Sur** USA
18E1 **Big Timber** USA
7J4 **Big Trout L** Can
4D3 **Big Trout Lake** Can
7K4 **Big Trout Lake** Can
40D2 **Bihać** Bosnia-Herzegovina, Yugos
61C2 **Bihār** India
61C3 **Bihar** State, India
72D4 **Biharamulo** Tanz
45C6 **Bihor** *Mt* Rom
62B1 **Bijāpur** India
62C1 **Bījāpur** India
63B1 **Bījār** Iran
61B2 **Bijauri** Nepal
41D2 **Bijeljina** Bosnia-Herzegovina, Yugos
52B4 **Bijie** China
60D3 **Bijnor** India
60C3 **Bijnot** Pak
60C3 **Bikāner** India
65C2 **Bikfaya** Leb
53C2 **Bikin** Russian Fed
53D2 **Bikin** *R* Russian Fed
72B4 **Bikoro** Zaïre
53A2 **Bila He** *R* China
60C3 **Bilara** India
60D2 **Bilaspur** India
61B3 **Bilāspur** India
55B3 **Bilauktaung Range** *Mts* Thai
39B1 **Bilbao** Spain
65A3 **Bilbeis** Egypt
Bilbo = Bilbao
42D3 **Bilé** *R* Czech Republic/Slovakia
41D2 **Bileća** Bosnia-Herzegovina, Yugos
64B1 **Bilecik** Turk
72C3 **Bili** *R* Zaïre
49S3 **Bilibino** Russian Fed
57F8 **Biliran** *I* Phil
8C2 **Billings** USA
72B2 **Bilma** Niger
9E3 **Biloxi** USA
72C2 **Biltine** Chad
71F4 **Bimbita** Ghana
60D4 **Bina-Etawa** India
57F8 **Binalbagan** Phil
73D5 **Bindura** Zim
73C5 **Binga** Zim
73D5 **Binga** *Mt* Zim
75D1 **Bingara** Aust
42B3 **Bingen** Germany
13F1 **Bingham** USA
9F2 **Binghamton** USA
56E1 **Bingkor** Malay
64D2 **Bingöl** Turk
52D3 **Binhai** China
56A2 **Binjai** Indon
56C2 **Binjai** Indon
57B4 **Binongko** *I* Indon
56B2 **Bintan** *I* Indon
56B3 **Bintuhan** Indon
56D2 **Bintulu** Malay
25B5 **Bió Bió** *R* Chile
xxxJ4 **Bioko** *I* Atlantic O
62B1 **Bīr** India
53C2 **Bira** Russian Fed
69B2 **Bīr Abu Husein** *Well* Egypt
69B2 **Bi'r al Harash** *Well* Libya
72C2 **Birao** CAR
61C2 **Biratnagar** Nepal
3F2 **Birch** *R* Can
10J2 **Birch Creek** USA
75B3 **Birchip** Aust
11D2 **Birch L** USA
4C3 **Birch L** Can
6G4 **Birch Mts** Can

xxxJ7 **Bouvet I** Atlantic O
28D2 **Bovril** Arg
3F3 **Bow** *R* Can
11B2 **Bowbells** USA
76D2 **Bowen** Aust
19E4 **Bowie** Arizona, USA
17C3 **Bowie** Texas, USA
3F4 **Bow Island** Can
9E3 **Bowling Green** Kentucky, USA
17D2 **Bowling Green** Missouri, USA
12C2 **Bowling Green** Ohio, USA
13D3 **Bowling Green** Virginia, USA
11B2 **Bowman** USA
13D2 **Bowmanville** Can
75D2 **Bowral** Aust
3D3 **Bowron** *R* Can
52D3 **Bo Xian** China
52D2 **Boxing** China
64B1 **Boyabat** Turk
72B3 **Boyali** CAR
43G2 **Boyarka** Ukraine
6J4 **Boyd** Can
14C2 **Boyertown** USA
3F3 **Boyle** Can
33B3 **Boyle** Irish Rep
35B5 **Boyne** *R* Irish Rep
15E4 **Boynoton Beach** USA
72C3 **Boyoma Falls** Zaïre
18E2 **Boysen Res** USA
41F3 **Bozcaada** *I* Turk
41F3 **Boz Dağlari** *Mts* Turk
8B2 **Bozeman** USA
Bozen = Bolzano
72B3 **Bozene** Zaïre
72B3 **Bozoum** CAR
37B2 **Bra** Italy
40D2 **Brač** *I* Croatia, Yugos
4F4 **Bracebridge** Can
69A2 **Brach** Libya
32H6 **Bräcke** Sweden
16B4 **Brackettville** USA
15E4 **Bradenton** USA
35E5 **Bradford** Eng
14A2 **Bradford** USA
20B3 **Bradley** USA
16C3 **Brady** USA
34E1 **Brae** Scot
34D3 **Braemar** Scot
39A1 **Braga** Port
28C3 **Bragado** Arg
39A1 **Bragana** Port
27J4 **Bragança** Brazil
29C3 **Bragança Paulista** Brazil
61D3 **Brahman-Baria** Bang
61C3 **Brāhmani** *R* India
61D2 **Brahmaputra** *R* India
45D6 **Brăila** Rom
9D2 **Brainerd** USA
74C3 **Brak** *R* S Africa
74D1 **Brak** *R* S Africa
70A3 **Brakna** Region, Maur
6F4 **Bralorne** Can
4F5 **Brampton** Can
26F3 **Branco** *R* Brazil
73B6 **Brandberg** *Mt* Namibia
42C2 **Brandenburg** Germany
42C2 **Brandenburg** State, Germany
74D2 **Brandfort** S Africa
8D2 **Brandon** Can
11C3 **Brandon** USA
74C3 **Brandvlei** S Africa
42C2 **Brandys nad Lebem** Czech Republic
43D2 **Braniewo** Pol
9E2 **Brantford** Can
75B3 **Branxholme** Aust
7M5 **Bras d'Or L** Can
29D2 **Brasíla de Minas** Brazil
26E6 **Brasiléia** Brazil
27J7 **Brasília** Brazil
41F1 **Brasov** Rom
56E2 **Brassay Range** *Mts* Malay
42D3 **Bratislava** Slovakia
49M4 **Bratsk** Russian Fed
43F3 **Bratslav** Ukraine
13E2 **Brattleboro** USA
42C2 **Braunschweig** Germany
70A4 **Brava** *I* Cape Verde
8B3 **Brawley** USA
35B5 **Bray** Irish Rep
7L3 **Bray I** Can
36B2 **Bray-sur-Seine** France
3E3 **Brazeau** *R* Can
3E3 **Brazeau,Mt** Can
24E5 **Brazil** Republic, S America
xxxG5 **Brazil Basin** Atlantic O
8D3 **Brazos** *R* USA
72B4 **Brazzaville** Congo
42C3 **Brdy** *Upland* Czech Republic
78A3 **Breaksea Sd** NZ
78B1 **Bream B** NZ
56C4 **Brebes** Indon
34D3 **Brechin** Scot
36C1 **Brecht** Belg
11C2 **Breckenridge** Minnesota, USA
16C3 **Breckenridge** Texas, USA
42D3 **Břeclav** Czech Republic
35D6 **Brecon** Wales
35D6 **Brecon Beacons** *Mts* Wales
35C5 **Brecon Beacons Nat Pk** Wales
42A2 **Breda** Neth
74C3 **Bredasdorp** S Africa
32H6 **Bredby** Sweden
44B3 **Bredbyn** Sweden
44K5 **Bredy** Russian Fed
74B3 **Breede** *R* S Africa
13D2 **Breezewood** USA
37C1 **Bregenz** Austria
37C1 **Bregenzer Ache** *R* Austria
32A1 **Breiðafjörður** *B* Iceland
36D2 **Breisach** Germany
37C2 **Brembo** Italy
37C2 **Brembo** *R* Italy
15B2 **Bremen** USA
42B2 **Bremen** Germany
42B2 **Bremerhaven** Germany
18B1 **Bremerton** USA
19E3 **Brendel** USA
17C3 **Brenham** USA
38E2 **Brenner** *Mt* Austria
42C3 **Brenner** *P* Austria/Italy
37D2 **Breno** Italy
4F4 **Brent** Can
37D2 **Brenta** *R* Italy
20B2 **Brentwood** USA
40C1 **Brescia** Italy
Breslau = Wrocław
37D1 **Bressanone** Italy
34E1 **Bressay** *I* Scot
38B2 **Bressuire** France
38B2 **Brest** France
43E2 **Brest** Belorussia
38B2 **Bretagne** Region, France
36B2 **Breteuil** France
36A2 **Bretevil** France
15B3 **Breton Sd** USA
14C2 **Breton Woods** USA
78B1 **Brett,C** NZ
15C1 **Brevard** USA
75C1 **Brewarrina** Aust
13F2 **Brewer** USA
14D2 **Brewster** New York, USA
18C1 **Brewster** Washington, USA
15B2 **Brewton** USA
74D2 **Breyten** S Africa
40D1 **Brežice** Slovenia, Yugos
72C3 **Bria** CAR
38D3 **Briancon** France
38C2 **Briare** France
15B2 **Bridgeport** Alabama, USA
19C3 **Bridgeport** California, USA
13E2 **Bridgeport** Connecticut, USA
11B3 **Bridgeport** Nebraska, USA
17C3 **Bridgeport** Texas, USA
20C1 **Bridgeport Res** USA
18E1 **Bridger** USA
16A1 **Bridger Peak** USA
14C3 **Bridgeton** USA
23F4 **Bridgetown** Barbados
5H5 **Bridgetown** Can
7M5 **Bridgewater** Can
14E2 **Bridgewater** USA
35D6 **Bridgwater** Eng
35D6 **Bridgwater B** Eng
35E4 **Bridlington** Eng
75E3 **Bridport** Aust
36C2 **Brienne-le-Château** France
37B1 **Brienzer See** *L* Switz
36C2 **Briey** France
40B1 **Brig** Switz
8B2 **Brigham City** USA
75C3 **Bright** Aust
35E6 **Brighton** Eng
37B3 **Brignoles** France
29A3 **Brilhante** *R* Brazil
36E1 **Brilon** Germany
41D2 **Brindisi** Italy
17D3 **Brinkley** USA
77E3 **Brisbane** Aust
13E2 **Bristol** Connecticut, USA
35D6 **Bristol** Eng
13E2 **Bristol** Pennsylvania, USA
14E2 **Bristol** Rhode Island, USA
9E3 **Bristol** Tennessee, USA
10F4 **Bristol B** USA
35C6 **Bristol Chan** Eng/Wales
6F4 **British Columbia** Province, Can
7K1 **British Empire Range** *Mts* Can
10K2 **British Mts** USA/Can
74D2 **Brits** S Africa
74C3 **Britstown** S Africa
4E4 **Britt** Can
11C2 **Britton** USA
38C2 **Brive** France
42D3 **Brno** Czech Republic
15C2 **Broad** *R* USA
14C1 **Broadalbin** USA
7L4 **Broadback** *R* Can
34B2 **Broad Bay** *Inlet* Scot
34C3 **Broadford** Scot
11A2 **Broadus** USA
11B1 **Broadview** Can
11B3 **Broadwater** USA
6H4 **Brochet** Can
6G2 **Brock I** Can
13D2 **Brockport** USA
14E1 **Brockton** USA
4F5 **Brockville** Can
14A2 **Brockway** USA
7K2 **Brodeur Pen** Can
34C4 **Brodick** Scot
43D2 **Brodnica** Pol
45D5 **Brody** Ukraine
36D1 **Brokem Haltern** Germany
16C1 **Broken Bow** Nebraska, USA
17D3 **Broken Bow** Oklahoma, USA
17D3 **Broken Bow L** USA
76D4 **Broken Hill** Aust
37C2 **Broni** Italy
32G5 **Brønnøysund** Nor
14D2 **Bronx** *Borough* New York, USA
57E9 **Brooke's Point** Phil
17D2 **Brookfield** Missouri, USA
12B2 **Brookfield** Wisconsin, USA
9D3 **Brookhaven** USA
18B2 **Brookings** Oregon, USA
8D2 **Brookings** South Dakota, USA
14E1 **Brookline** USA
11D3 **Brooklyn** USA
14D2 **Brooklyn** *Borough* New York, USA
11D2 **Brooklyn Center** USA
6G4 **Brooks** Can
10G4 **Brooks,L** USA
10E2 **Brooks Mt** USA
6C3 **Brooks Range** *Mts* USA
15C3 **Brooksville** USA
13E2 **Brookton** USA
75D1 **Brooloo** Aust
76B2 **Broome** Aust
34D2 **Brora** Scot
18B2 **Brothers** USA
67F4 **Brothers,The** *Is* Yemen
36A2 **Brou** France
72B2 **Broulkou** *Well* Chad
43G2 **Brovary** Ukraine
11D2 **Browerville** USA
16B3 **Brownfield** USA
3F4 **Browning** USA
8D4 **Brownsville** USA
8D3 **Brownwood** USA
51F8 **Browse** *I* Aust
36B1 **Bruay-en-Artois** France
76A3 **Bruce,Mt** Aust
4E5 **Bruce Pen** Can
36E2 **Bruchsal** Germany
37E1 **Bruck** Austria
42D3 **Bruck an der Mur** Austria
Bruges = Brugge
36B1 **Brugge** Belg
36D1 **Brühl** Germany
29D1 **Brumado** Brazil
36D2 **Brumath** France
18C2 **Bruneau** USA
18C2 **Bruneau** *R* USA
56D2 **Brunei** Sultanate, S E Asia
40C1 **Brunico** Italy
78B2 **Brunner,L** NZ
9E3 **Brunswick** Georgia, USA
13F2 **Brunswick** Maine, USA
17D2 **Brunswick** Mississippi, USA
25B8 **Brunswick,Pen de** Chile
75E3 **Bruny I** Aust
44G3 **Brusenets** Russian Fed
16B1 **Brush** USA
23A3 **Brus Laguna** Honduras
Brussel = Bruxelles
42A2 **Bruxelles** Belg
36D2 **Bruyères** France
8D3 **Bryan** USA
75A2 **Bryan,Mt** Aust
44E5 **Bryansk** Russian Fed
17D3 **Bryant** USA
20D3 **Bryce Canyon Nat Pk** USA
42D2 **Brzeg** Pol
64E4 **Būbīyan** *I* Kuwait/Iraq
72D4 **Bubu** *R* Tanz
74E1 **Bubye** *R* Zim
26D2 **Bucaramanga** Colombia
34E3 **Buchan** *Oilfield* N Sea
70A4 **Buchanan** Lib
16C3 **Buchanan,L** USA
34E3 **Buchan Deep** N Sea
7L2 **Buchan G** Can
33C2 **Buchan Ness** *Pen* Scot
7N5 **Buchans** Can
28C2 **Buchardo** Arg
Bucharest = Bucureşti
20B3 **Buchon, Pt** USA
37C1 **Buchs** Switz
19D4 **Buckeye** USA
35E5 **Buckingham** Eng
10F2 **Buckland** USA
10F2 **Buckland** *R* USA
75A2 **Buckleboo** Aust
13F2 **Bucksport** USA
72B4 **Buco Zau** Congo
5J4 **Buctouche** Can
41F2 **Bucureşti** Rom
43D3 **Budapest** Hung
60D3 **Budaun** India
35C6 **Bude** Eng
17D3 **Bude** USA
45G7 **Budennovsk** Russian Fed
36E1 **Büdingen** Germany
41D2 **Budva** Montenegro, Yugos
72A3 **Buéa** Cam
37A2 **Buech** *R* France
20B3 **Buellton** USA
28B2 **Buena Esperanza** Arg
26C3 **Buenaventura** Colombia
16A4 **Buenaventura** Mexico
16A2 **Buena Vista** Colorado, USA
22B2 **Buenavista** Mexico
13D3 **Buena Vista** Virginia, USA
20C3 **Buena Vista L** USA
28A4 **Bueno** *R* Chile
25E4 **Buenos Aires** Arg
25E5 **Buenos Aires** State, Arg
17D2 **Buffalo** Mississipi, USA
9F2 **Buffalo** New York, USA
11B2 **Buffalo** South Dakota, USA
17C3 **Buffalo** Texas, USA
8C2 **Buffalo** Wyoming, USA
74E2 **Buffalo** *R* S Africa
3E2 **Buffalo Head Hills** *Mts* Can
18C1 **Buffalo Hump** USA
3F3 **Buffalo L** Alberta, Can
3E1 **Buffalo L** Northwest Territories, Can
6H4 **Buffalo Narrows** Can
15C2 **Buford** USA
41F2 **Buftea** Rom
43E2 **Bug** *R* Pol/Ukraine
26C3 **Buga** Colombia
63C1 **Bugdayli** Turkmenistan
44H2 **Bugrino** Russian Fed
53A2 **Bugt** China
44J5 **Bugulma** Russian Fed
44J5 **Buguruslan** Russian Fed
64C2 **Buhayrat al Asad** *Res* Syria
18D2 **Buhl** Idaho, USA
11D2 **Buhl** Minnesota, USA
71F4 **Bui Dam** Ghana
35D5 **Builth Wells** Wales
28A2 **Buin** Chile
37A2 **Buis-les-Baronnies** France
37E2 **Buje** Croatia, Yugos
72C4 **Bujumbura** Burundi
77E1 **Buka** *I* PNG
73C4 **Bukama** Zaïre
72C4 **Bukavu** Zaïre
58E2 **Bukhara** Uzbekistan
56D2 **Bukit Batubrok** *Mt* Indon
56B3 **Bukittinggi** Indon
72D4 **Bukoba** Tanz
57B3 **Buku Gandadiwata** *Mt* Indon
57C2 **Buku Saolat** *Mt* Indon
51G7 **Bula** Indon
57F8 **Bulan** Phil
60D3 **Bulandshahr** India
73C6 **Bulawayo** Zim
41F3 **Buldan** Turk
60D4 **Buldāna** India
10B6 **Buldir I** USA
50D2 **Bulgan** Mongolia
41E2 **Bulgaria** Republic, Europe
57C2 **Buli** Indon
37B1 **Bulle** Switz
78B2 **Buller** *R* NZ
75C3 **Buller,Mt** Aust
76A4 **Bullfinch** Aust
75B1 **Bulloo** *R* Aust
75B1 **Bulloo Downs** Aust
75B1 **Bulloo L** Aust
17D2 **Bull Shoals Res** USA
28A3 **Bulnes** Chile
76D1 **Bulolo** PNG
74D2 **Bultfontein** S Africa
57B4 **Bulukumba** Indon
72C3 **Bumba** Zaïre
56E2 **Bum Bum** *I* Malay
45D8 **Bu Menderes** *R* Turk
55B2 **Bumphal Dam** Thai
72D3 **Buna** Kenya
76A4 **Bunbury** Aust
34B4 **Buncrana** Irish Rep
77E3 **Bundaberg** Aust
75D2 **Bundarra** Aust
60D3 **Būndi** India
75C1 **Bungil** *R* Aust
73B4 **Bungo** Angola
54B4 **Bungo-suidō** *Str* Japan
56C2 **Bunguran** *I* Indon
72D3 **Bunia** Zaïre
17D2 **Bunker** USA
17D3 **Bunkie** USA
15C3 **Bunnell** USA
71H3 **Bunsuru** *R* Nig
56D3 **Buntok** Indon
57B2 **Buol** Indon
65D2 **Burāg** Syria
72C2 **Buram** Sudan
61B1 **Burang** China
72E3 **Burao** Somalia
57G8 **Burauen** Phil
66D1 **Buraydah** S Arabia
19C4 **Burbank** USA
75C2 **Burcher** Aust
63E1 **Burdalyk** Turkmenistan
45E8 **Burdur** Turk
53C1 **Bureinskiy Khrebet** *Mts* Russian Fed
50F2 **Bureya** Russian Fed
53C1 **Bureya** *R* Russian Fed
65B3 **Bûr Fu'ad** Egypt
42C2 **Burg** Germany
41F2 **Burgas** Bulg
15D2 **Burgaw** USA
37B1 **Burgdorf** Switz
5K4 **Burgeo** Can
74D3 **Burgersdorp** S Africa
48K5 **Burgin** China
22C1 **Burgos** Mexico
39B1 **Burgos** Spain
43D1 **Burgsvik** Sweden
41F3 **Burhaniye** Turk
60D4 **Burhānpur** India
57F8 **Burias** *I* Phil
5K4 **Burin Pen** Can
55C2 **Buriram** Thai
29C2 **Buritis** Brazil
3C3 **Burke Chan** Can
76C2 **Burketown** Aust
70B3 **Burkina** Republic, Africa
13D1 **Burk's Falls** Can
8B2 **Burley** USA
4F5 **Burlington** Can
16B2 **Burlington** Colorado, USA
9D2 **Burlington** Iowa, USA
14C2 **Burlington** New Jersey, USA
15D1 **Burlington** North Carolina, USA
9F2 **Burlington** Vermont, USA
18B1 **Burlington** Washington, USA
4D5 **Burlington** Wisconsin, USA
59H3 **Burma** Republic, Asia
16C3 **Burnet** USA
18B2 **Burney** USA
14B2 **Burnham** USA
76D5 **Burnie** Aust
35D5 **Burnley** Eng
18C2 **Burns** USA
6F4 **Burns Lake** Can
59G1 **Burqin** China
75A2 **Burra** Aust
75D2 **Burragorang,L** Aust
34D2 **Burray** *I* Scot
75C2 **Burren Junction** Aust
75C2 **Burrinjuck Res** Aust
51G8 **Burrundie** Aust
45D7 **Bursa** Turk
66B1 **Bur Safâga** Egypt
Bûr Sa'îd = Port Said
65B4 **Bûr Taufiq** Egypt
12C2 **Burton** USA
35E5 **Burton upon Trent** Eng
32J6 **Burtrask** Sweden
75B2 **Burtundy** Aust
57C3 **Buru** Indon
72C4 **Burundi** Republic, Africa
56B2 **Burung** Indon
11C3 **Burwell** USA
49N4 **Buryatskaya** Respublika, Russian Fed
72D2 **Burye** Eth
45J6 **Burynshik** Kazakhstan
35F5 **Bury St Edmunds** Eng
63C3 **Būshehr** Iran
72B4 **Busira** *R* Zaïre
43E2 **Busko Zdrój** Pol
65D2 **Busrā ash Shām** Syria
36D3 **Bussang** France
76A4 **Busselton** Aust
38D2 **Busto** Italy
40B1 **Busto Arsizio** Italy
57E8 **Busuanga** *I* Phil

Buta

Cap Rosso

72C3 Buta Zaïre
28B3 Buta Ranquil Arg
72C4 Butare Rwanda
34C4 Bute I Scot
53A2 Butha Qi China
13D2 Butler USA
8B2 Butte USA
55C4 Butterworth Malay
74D3 Butterworth S Africa
33B2 Butt of Lewis C Scot
7M3 Button Is Can
20C3 Buttonwillow USA
57G9 Butuan Phil
57B4 Butung I Indon
76B1 Butung I Indon
45G5 Buturlinovka Russian Fed
61B2 Butwal Nepal
36E1 Butzbach Germany
72E3 Buulobarde Somalia
72E3 Buurhaakaba Somalia
44G4 Buy Russian Fed
52B1 Buyant Ovvo Mongolia
45H7 Buynaksk Russian Fed
49N5 Buyr Nuur L Mongolia
45G8 Büyük Ağri Daği Mt Turk
53E2 Buyukly Russian Fed
64A2 Büyük Menderes R Turk
41F1 Buzău Rom
41F1 Buzău R Rom
44J5 Buzuluk Russian Fed
14E2 Buzzards B USA
41F2 Byala Bulg
41E2 Byala Slatina Bulg
6H2 Byam Martin Chan Can
6H2 Byam Martin I Can
65C1 Byblos Hist. Site Leb
43D2 Bydgoszcz Pol
16B2 Byers USA
32F7 Bygland Nor
43G2 Bykhov Belorussia
53E2 Bykov Russian Fed
7K2 Bylot I Can
75C2 Byrock Aust
20B2 Byron USA
75D1 Byron,C Aust
49P3 Bytantay R Russian Fed
43D2 Bytom Pol

C

25E3 Caacupé Par
29A4 Caaguazú Par
73B5 Caála Angola
3C3 Caamano Sd Can
29A4 Caapucú Par
29B3 Caarapó Brazil
25E3 Caazapá Par
16A3 Caballo Res USA
57F7 Cabanatuan Phil
13F1 Cabano Can
27M5 Cabedelo Brazil
39A2 Cabeza del Buey Spain
28C3 Cabildo Arg
28A2 Cabildo Chile
26D1 Cabimas Ven
72B4 Cabinda Angola
72B4 Cabinda Province, Angola
18C1 Cabinet Mts USA
23C3 Cabo Beata Dom Rep
39C2 Cabo Binibeca C Spain
71A2 Cabo Cantin C Mor
40B3 Cabo Carbonara C Sardegna
28A3 Cabo Carranza C Chile
39A2 Cabo Carvoeiro C Port
8B3 Cabo Colnett C Mexico
28D3 Cabo Corrientes C Arg
26C2 Cabo Corrientes C Colombia
21B2 Cabo Corrientes C Mexico
23B3 Cabo Cruz C Cuba
39B1 Cabo de Ajo C Spain
39C1 Cabo de Caballeria C Spain
39C1 Cabo de Creus C Spain
25C9 Cabo de Hornos C Chile
39C2 Cabo de la Nao C Spain
39A1 Cabo de Peñas C Spain
39A2 Cabo de Roca C Port
39C2 Cabo de Salinas C Spain
74E2 Cabo de Santa Maria C Mozam
29D3 Cabo de São Tomé C Brazil
39A2 Cabo de São Vicente C Port
39B2 Cabo de Sata C Spain
39A2 Cabo de Sines C Port
39C1 Cabo de Tortosa C Spain
25C6 Cabo Dos Bahias C Arg
39A2 Cabo Espichel C Port
8B4 Cabo Falso C Mexico
39B2 Cabo Ferrat C Alg
39A1 Cabo Finisterre C Spain
39C1 Cabo Formentor C Spain
29D3 Cabo Frio Brazil
29D3 Cabo Frio C Brazil
23A4 Cabo Gracias à Dios Honduras
28A1 Cabo Leones C Chile
27J4 Cabo Maguarinho C Brazil
39A2 Cabo Negro C Mor
75D1 Caboolture Aust
27H3 Cabo Orange C Brazil
19C4 Cabo Punta Banda C Mexico
73D5 Cabora Bassa Dam Mozam
21A1 Caborca Mexico
21C2 Cabo Rojo C Mexico
22C1 Cabos Mexico
28D3 Cabo San Antonio C Arg
23A2 Cabo San Antonio C Cuba
25C8 Cabo San Diego C Arg
26B4 Cabo San Lorenzo C Ecuador
40B3 Cabo Teulada C Sardegna
39A2 Cabo Trafalgar C Spain
39B2 Cabo Tres Forcas C Mor
25C7 Cabo Tres Puntas C Arg
7M5 Cabot Str Can
39B2 Cabra Spain
39A1 Cabreira Mt Port
39C2 Cabrera I Spain
28A3 Cabrero Chile
39B2 Cabriel R Spain
22C2 Cacahuamilpa Mexico
41E2 Čačak Serbia, Yugos
28E2 Cacapava do Sul Brazil
14A3 Cacapon R USA
22C2 C A Carillo Mexico
28E1 Caceoul Brazil
27G7 Cáceres Brazil
39A2 Caceres Spain
17D2 Cache R USA
3D3 Cache Creek Can
20A1 Cache Creek, R USA
18D2 Cache Peak Mt USA
25C3 Cachi Arg
27G5 Cachimbo Brazil
27L6 Cachoeira Brazil
29B2 Cachoeira Alta Brazil
27L5 Cachoeira de Paulo Afonso Waterfall Brazil
25F4 Cachoeira do Sul Brazil
27K8 Cachoeiro de Itapemirim Brazil
20C3 Cachuma, L USA
73B5 Cacolo Angola
73B5 Caconda Angola
16B2 Cactus USA
29B2 Caçu Brazil
29D1 Caculé Brazil
73B5 Caculuvar R Angola
43D3 Čadca Slovakia
35D5 Cader Idris Mts Wales
11A2 Cadillac Can
9E2 Cadillac USA
57F8 Cadiz Phil
39A2 Cadiz Spain
27K6 Caeité Brazil
38B2 Caen France
35C5 Caernarfon Wales
35C5 Caernarfon B Wales
65C2 Caesarea Hist Site Israel
29D1 Caetité Brazil
25C3 Cafayate Arg
64B2 Caga Tepe Turk
57F7 Cagayan R Phil
57F9 Cagayan de Oro Phil
57F9 Cagayan Is Phil
37E3 Cagli Italy
40B3 Cagliari Sardegna
23D3 Caguas Puerto Rico
15B2 Cahaba R USA
35B5 Cahir Irish Rep
35B5 Cahone Pt Irish Rep
38C3 Cahors France
73D5 Caia Mozam
73C5 Caianda Angola
29B2 Caiapó R Brazil
29B2 Caiapônia Brazil
27L5 Caicó Brazil
23C2 Caicos Is Caribbean
9F4 Caicos Pass Bahamas
10G3 Cairn Mt USA
76D2 Cairns Aust
64B3 Cairo Egypt
9E3 Cairo USA
75B1 Caiwarro Aust
26C5 Cajabamba Peru
26C5 Cajamarca Peru
23D5 Calabozo Ven
41E2 Calafat Rom
25B8 Calafate Arg
57F8 Calagua Is Phil
39B1 Calahorra Spain
38C1 Calais France
13F1 Calais USA
25C2 Calama Chile
26D3 Calamar Colombia
57E8 Calamian Group Is Phil
73B4 Calandula Angola
56A2 Calang Indon
69B2 Calanscio Sand Sea Libya
57F8 Calapan Phil
41F2 Calarasi Rom
39B1 Calatayud Spain
20B2 Calaveras Res USA
57F8 Calbayog Phil
17D4 Calcasieu L USA
61C3 Calcutta India
39A2 Caldas da Rainha Port
27J7 Caldas Novas Brazil
25B3 Caldera Chile
8B2 Caldwell USA
74B3 Caledon S Africa
74D3 Caledon R S Africa
12A2 Caledonia Minnesota, USA
14B1 Caledonia New York, USA
5H4 Caledonia Hills Can
22B1 Calera Mexico
25C7 Caleta Olivia Arg
8B3 Calexico USA
6G4 Calgary Can
15C2 Calhoun USA
15C2 Calhoun Falls USA
26C3 Cali Colombia
62B2 Calicut India
20C3 Caliente California, USA
8B3 Caliente Nevada, USA
16A2 Caliente New Mexico, USA
20C3 California Aqueduct USA
8A3 California State, USA
62B2 Calimera,Pt India
28B2 Calingasta Arg
19C4 Calipatria USA
74C3 Calitzdorp S Africa
75B1 Callabonna R Aust
75A1 Callabonna,L Aust
13D1 Callander Can
34C3 Callander Scot
75A1 Callanna Aust
26C6 Callao Peru
22C1 Calles Mexico
14C2 Callicoon USA
3F2 Calling L Can
22C1 Calnali Mexico
15E4 Caloosahatchee R USA
75D1 Caloundra Aust
22C2 Calpulalpan Mexico
40C3 Caltanissetta Italy
73B4 Caluango Angola
73B5 Calulo Angola
73B5 Caluquembe Angola
67E4 Caluula Somalia
3C3 Calvert I Can
40B2 Calvi Corse
22B1 Calvillo Mexico
74B3 Calvinia S Africa
36E2 Calw Germany
29E1 Camacari Brazil
22B1 Camacho Mexico
28E2 Camaguã Brazil
28E2 Camaguã R Brazil
21E2 Camagüey Cuba
21E2 Camagüey,Arch de Is Cuba
29E1 Camamu Brazil
26D7 Camaná Peru
10N5 Camania I Can
29B2 Camapuã Brazil
26E8 Camargo Bol
20C3 Camarillo USA
25C6 Camarones Arg
18B1 Camas USA
73B4 Camaxilo Angola
73B4 Cambatela Angola
55C3 Cambodia Republic, S E Asia
35C6 Camborne Eng
38C1 Cambrai France
20B3 Cambria USA
35D5 Cambrian Mts Wales
12C2 Cambridge Can
35E5 Cambridge County, Eng
35F5 Cambridge Eng
23H1 Cambridge Jamaica
13D3 Cambridge Maryland, USA
13E2 Cambridge Massachussets, USA
11D2 Cambridge Minnesota, USA
78C1 Cambridge NZ
12C2 Cambridge Ohio, USA
6H3 Cambridge Bay Can
51F8 Cambridge G Aust
45F7 Cam Burun Pt Turk
9D3 Camden Arkansas, USA
75D2 Camden Aust
13E3 Camden New Jersey, USA
14C1 Camden New York, USA
15C2 Camden South Carolina, USA
10J1 Camden B USA
37E3 Camerino Italy
17D2 Cameron Missouri, USA
17C3 Cameron Texas, USA
56F6 Cameron Highlands Malay
6H2 Cameron I Can
78A3 Cameron Mts NZ
72B3 Cameroon Federal Republic, Africa
72A3 Cameroun Mt Cam
27J4 Cametá Brazil
57F9 Camiguin I Phil
57F7 Camiling Phil
15C2 Camilla USA
20B1 Camino USA
26F8 Camiri Bol
73C4 Camissombo Angola
27K4 Camocim Brazil
76C2 Camooweal Aust
62E3 Camorta I Indian O
28D2 Campana Arg
25A7 Campana I Chile
3C3 Campania I Can
74C2 Campbell S Africa
78B2 Campbell,C NZ
3C3 Campbell I Can
xxixN7 Campbell I NZ
10M2 Campbell L Can
6E3 Campbell,Mt Can
60C2 Campbellpore Pak
6F5 Campbell River Can
12B3 Campbellsville USA
7M5 Campbellton Can
75D2 Campbelltown Aust
34C4 Campbeltown Scot
21C3 Campeche Mexico
75B3 Camperdown Aust
27L5 Campina Grande Brazil
27J8 Campinas Brazil
29C2 Campina Verde Brazil
57B5 Camplong Indon
20C2 Camp Nelson USA
72A3 Campo Cam
40C2 Campobasso Italy
29C3 Campo Belo Brazil
28C1 Campo del Cielo Arg
29C2 Campo Florido Brazil
25D3 Campo Gallo Arg
25F2 Campo Grande Brazil
27K4 Campo Maior Brazil
25F2 Campo Mourão Brazil
28E1 Campo Novo Brazil
29D3 Campos Brazil
29C2 Campos Altos Brazil
37D1 Campo Tures Italy
19D4 Camp Verde USA
55D3 Cam Ranh Viet
6G4 Camrose Can
73B5 Camucuio Angola
23K1 Canaan Tobago
14D1 Canaan USA
73B5 Canacupa Angola
2F3 Canada Dominion, N America
25D4 Cañada de Gomez Arg
14C2 Canadensis USA
16B2 Canadian USA
8C3 Canadian R USA
45D7 Canakkale Turk
28B3 Canalejas Arg
3E3 Canal Flats Can
14B1 Canandaigua USA
14B1 Canandaigua L USA
21A1 Cananea Mexico
29C4 Cananeia Brazil
xxxG3 Canary Basin Atlantic O
Canary Is = Islas Canarias
22B2 Canas Mexico
21B2 Canatlán Mexico
9E4 Canaveral,C USA
27L7 Canavieriras Brazil
76D4 Canberra Aust
18B2 Canby California, USA
11C3 Canby Minnesota, USA
41F3 Çandarli Körfezi B Turk
3G3 Candle L Can
14D2 Candlewood,L USA
11C2 Cando USA
14B1 Candor USA
25E4 Canelones Urug
17C2 Caney USA
73C5 Cangamba Angola
73C5 Cangombe Angola
28E2 Canguçu Brazil
52D2 Cangzhou China
7M4 Caniapiscau R Can
7M4 Caniapiscau, Réservoir Res Can
40C3 Canicatti Italy
27L4 Canindé Brazil
14B1 Canisteo USA
14B1 Canisteo R USA
22B1 Canitas de Felipe Pescador Mexico
16A2 Canjilon USA
64B1 Çankırı Turk
3E3 Canmore Can
34B3 Canna I Scot
62B2 Cannanore India
38D3 Cannes France
11B2 Cannonball R USA
75C3 Cann River Aust
25F3 Canõas Brazil
3G2 Canoe L Can
29B4 Canoinhas Brazil
16A2 Canon City USA
75B2 Canopus Aust
6H4 Canora Can
75C2 Canowindra Aust
5J4 Canso Can
35B5 Cansore Pt Irish Rep
35F6 Canterbury Eng
78B2 Canterbury Bight B NZ
78B2 Canterbury Plains NZ
55D4 Can Tho Viet
20D3 Cantil USA
28A1 Canto de Augua Chile
Canton = Guangzhou
17E3 Canton Mississippi, USA
12A2 Canton Missouri, USA
9E2 Canton Ohio, USA
14B2 Canton Pensylvania, USA
11C3 Canton S Dakota, USA
77H1 Canton I Phoeniz Is
10J3 Cantwell USA
36A2 Cany-Barville France
16B3 Canyon USA
18C2 Canyon City USA
18D1 Canyon Ferry L USA
19D3 Canyonlands Nat Pk USA
10N3 Canyon Range Mts Can
18B2 Canyonville USA
73C4 Canzar Angola
55D1 Cao Bang Viet
27J4 Capanema Brazil
29C3 Capão Bonito Brazil
37B3 Cap Bénat C France
71D1 Cap Blanc C Tunisia
71E1 Cap Bon C Tunisia
71D1 Cap Bougaron C Alg
38B3 Capbreton France
37B3 Cap Camarat C France
5H4 Cap Chat Can
22A1 Cap Corrientes C Mexico
40B2 Cap Corse C Corse
73E5 Cap d'Ambre C Madag
37B3 Cap d'Antibes C France
5J4 Cap de Gaspé C Can
38B2 Cap de la Hague C France
5G4 Cap-de-la-Madeleine Can
7L3 Cap de Nouvelle-France C Can
39C2 Capdepera Spain
22B2 Cap de Tancitiario C Mexico
71B1 Cap des Trois Fourches C Mor
75E3 Cape Barren I Aust
xxxJ6 Cape Basin Atlantic O
7N5 Cape Breton I Can
71F4 Cape Coast Ghana
13E2 Cape Cod B USA
7M3 Cape Dyer Can
79F7 Cape Evans Base Ant.
15D2 Cape Fear R USA
17E2 Cape Girardeau USA
Cape Horn = Cabo de Hornos
xxviiiH4 Cape Johnston Depth Pacific O
29D2 Capelinha Brazil
10E2 Cape Lisburne USA
73B5 Capelongo Angola
13E3 Cape May USA
73B4 Capenda Camulemba Angola
6F2 Cape Parry Can
74C3 Cape Province S Africa
74B3 Cape Town S Africa
xxxG4 Cape Verde Is Atlantic O
xxxG4 Cape Verde Basin Atlantic O
10K4 Cape Yakataga USA
76D2 Cape York Pen Aust
37B3 Cap Ferrat C France
36A1 Cap Gris Nez C France
23C3 Cap-Haitien Haiti
27J4 Capim R Brazil
29A3 Capitán Bado Par
20D3 Capitol Reef Nat Pk USA
29A2 Capivari R Brazil
5K3 Cap Mécatina C Can
23P2 Cap Moule à Chique C St Lucia
37C2 Capo di Noli C Italy
40D3 Capo Isola de Correnti C Italy
40D3 Capo Rizzuto C Italy
41D3 Capo Santa Maria di Leuca C Italy
40C3 Capo San Vito Italy
40D3 Capo Spartivento C Italy
23P2 Cap Pt St Lucia
40C2 Capri I Italy
73C5 Caprivi Strip Region, Namibia
40B2 Cap Rosso C Corse

Dihang
Dzavhan Gol

61D2 **Dihang** *R* India
Dijlah = Tigris
37A1 **Dijon** France
72B3 **Dik** Chad
72E2 **Dikhil** Djibouti
65A3 **Dikirnis** Egypt
36B1 **Diksmuide** Belg
48K2 **Dikson** Russian Fed
71J3 **Dikwa** Nig
63E2 **Dilaram** Afghan
57C4 **Dili** Indon
55D3 **Di Linh** Viet
36E1 **Dillenburg** Germany
17F4 **Dilley** USA
72C2 **Dilling** Sudan
10G4 **Dillingham** USA
8B2 **Dillon** USA
14B2 **Dillsburg** USA
73C5 **Dilolo** Zaïre
22A1 **Dimas** Mexico
Dimashq = Damascus
72C4 **Dimbelenge** Zaïre
71F4 **Dimbokro** Ivory Coast
41F2 **Dimitrovgrad** Bulg
44H5 **Dimitrovgrad** Russian Fed
65C3 **Dimona** Israel
61D2 **Dimpāpur** India
57G8 **Dinagat** *I* Phil
61C2 **Dinajpur** India
38B2 **Dinan** France
36C1 **Dinant** Belg
64B2 **Dinar** Turk
72D2 **Dinder** *R* Sudan
62B2 **Dindigul** India
52B2 **Dingbian** China
61C2 **Dinggyê** China
33A3 **Dingle** Irish Rep
33A3 **Dingle** *B* Irish Rep
70A3 **Dinguiraye** Guinea
34C3 **Dingwall** Scot
52A2 **Dingxi** China
52D2 **Ding Xian** China
55D1 **Dinh Lap** Viet
11D2 **Dinorwic L** Can
16A1 **Dinosaur** USA
20C2 **Dinuba** USA
10E2 **Diomede Is** Russian Fed/ USA
70A3 **Diouloulou** Sen
61D2 **Diphu** India
72E3 **Diredawa** Eth
76A3 **Dirk Hartog** *I* Aust
72B2 **Dirkou** Niger
75C1 **Dirranbandi** Aust
25J8 **Disappointment,C** South Georgia
18B1 **Disappointment,C** USA
76B3 **Disappointment,L** Aust
75B3 **Discovery B** Aust
xxxJ6 **Discovery Tablemount** Atlantic O
37C1 **Disentis Muster** Switz
66B1 **Dishna** Egypt
7N3 **Disko** *I* Greenland
7N3 **Disko Bugt** *B* Greenland
7N3 **Diskofjord** Greenland
13D3 **Dismal Swamp** USA
43F1 **Disna** *R* Belorussia
29C2 **Distrito Federal** Federal District, Brazil
60C4 **Diu** India
57G9 **Diuat Mts** Phil
36A2 **Dives** *R* France
27K8 **Divinópolis** Brazil
45G6 **Divnoye** Russian Fed
64C2 **Divriği** Turk
20B1 **Dixon** California, USA
12B2 **Dixon** Illinois, USA
18D1 **Dixon** Montana, USA
6E4 **Dixon Entrance** *Sd* Can/ USA
3E2 **Dixonville** Can
64E3 **Diyālā** *R* Iraq
45G8 **Diyarbakir** Turk
63E3 **Diz** Pak
63B2 **Diz** *R* Iran
72B3 **Dja** *R* Cam
71C2 **Djadi** *R* Alg
72B1 **Djado,Plat du** Niger
71D2 **Djamaa** Alg
72B4 **Djambala** Congo
70C2 **Djanet** Alg
71C2 **Djebel Amour** *Mts* Alg
39A2 **Djebel Bouhalla** *Mt* Mor
71D1 **Djebel Chambi** *Mt* Tunisia
71D1 **Djebel Chélia** *Mts* Alg
71E1 **Djebel Zaghouan** *Mt* Tunisia
71D2 **Djebel Zrega** *Mt* Tunisia
71G4 **Djebobo** *Mt* Ghana
71C2 **Djelfa** Alg
72C3 **Djéma** CAR
70B3 **Djenné** Mali
71J4 **Djerem** *R* Cam
71F3 **Djibasso** Burkina
70B3 **Djibo** Burkina
72E2 **Djibouti** Djibouti
72E2 **Djibouti** Republic, E Africa
72C3 **Djolu** Zaïre
71G4 **Djougou** Benin
72D3 **Djugu** Zaïre
32C2 **Djúpivogur** Iceland
39C2 **Djurdjura** *Mts* Alg
44F4 **Dmitrov** Russian Fed
Dnepr = Dnieper
45E6 **Dneprodzerzhinsk** Ukraine
45F6 **Dnepropetrovsk** Ukraine
44D5 **Dneprovskaya Nizmennost'** Region, Belorussia
Dnestr = Dniester
45E6 **Dnieper** *R* Ukraine
45C6 **Dniester** *R* Ukraine
44E4 **Dno** Russian Fed
72B3 **Doba** Chad
43E1 **Dobele** Latvia
28C3 **Doblas** Arg
76C1 **Dobo** Indon
41D2 **Doboj** Bosnia-Herzegovina, Yugos
41F2 **Dobrich** Bulg
45E5 **Dobrush** Belorussia
27K7 **Doce** *R* Brazil
25D2 **Doctor R P Peña** Arg
62B2 **Dod** India
62B2 **Doda Betta** *Mt* India
41F3 **Dodecanese** *Is* Greece
8C3 **Dodge City** USA
3G2 **Dodge L** Can
12A2 **Dodgeville** USA
72D4 **Dodoma** Tanz
34G4 **Dogger Bank** *Sand-bank* N Sea
12B1 **Dog L** Can
12C1 **Dog L** Can
54B3 **Dōgo** *I* Japan
70C3 **Dogondoutchi** Niger
64D2 **Doğubayazit** Turk
67F1 **Doha** Qatar
61D2 **Doilungdêqên** China
66C4 **Doka** Sudan
76C1 **Dolak** *I* Indon
11C3 **Doland** USA
7L5 **Dolbeau** Can
38D2 **Dole** France
66B4 **Doleib** *Watercourse* Sudan
35D5 **Dolgellau** Wales
14C1 **Dolgeville** USA
44K2 **Dolgiy, Ostrov** *I* Russian Fed
53E2 **Dolinsk** Russian Fed
37D1 **Dolomitche** *Mts* Italy
72E3 **Dolo Odo** Eth
25E5 **Dolores** Arg
28D2 **Dolores** Urug
16A2 **Dolores** *R* USA
22B1 **Dolores Hidalgo** Mexico
6G3 **Dolphin and Union Str** Can
25E8 **Dolphin,C** Falkland Is
51G7 **Dom** *Mt* Indon
45K5 **Dombarovskiy** Russian Fed
32F6 **Dombas** Nor
36D2 **Dombasle-sur-Meurthe** France
41D1 **Dombóvár** Hung
28A1 **Domeyko** Chile
38B2 **Domfront** France
23E3 **Dominica** *I* Caribbean
23C3 **Dominican Republic** Caribbean
7L3 **Dominion,C** Can
7N4 **Domino** Can
50E1 **Domna** Russian Fed
40B1 **Domodossola** Italy
28E2 **Dom Pedrito** Brazil
56E4 **Dompu** Indon
25B5 **Domuyo** *Mt* Arg
75D1 **Domville,Mt** Aust
34D3 **Don** *R* Scot
45G6 **Don** *R* Russian Fed
34B4 **Donaghadee** N Ire
22B1 **Donato Guerta** Mexico
Donau = Dunav
42C3 **Donau, R** Austria
42C3 **Donau** *R* Germany
36E3 **Donaueschingen** Germany
42C3 **Donauwörth** Germany
39A2 **Don Benito** Spain
35E5 **Doncaster** Eng
73B4 **Dondo** Angola
73D5 **Dondo** Mozam
62C3 **Dondra Head** *C* Sri Lanka
34B4 **Donegal** County, Irish Rep
33B3 **Donegal** Irish Rep
33B3 **Donegal** *B* Irish Rep
34A4 **Donegal** *Mts* Irish Rep
45F6 **Donetsk** Ukraine
71J4 **Donga** *R* Nig
52C4 **Dong'an** China
76A3 **Dongara** Aust
52A4 **Dongchuan** China
55D2 **Dongfang** China
53B3 **Dongfeng** China
76A1 **Donggala** Indon
50C3 **Donggi Cona** *L* China
53A4 **Donggou** China
52C5 **Donghai Dao** *I* China
52A1 **Dong He** *R* China
55D2 **Dong Hoi** Viet
52C5 **Dong Jiang** *R* China
53C2 **Donglanghong** China
53C3 **Dongning** China
72D2 **Dongola** Sudan
52D5 **Dongshan** China
50E4 **Dongsha Qundao** *I* China
52C2 **Dongsheng** China
52E3 **Dongtai** China
52C4 **Dongting Hu** *L* China
52B5 **Dongxing** China
52D3 **Dongzhi** China
17D2 **Doniphan** USA
40D2 **Donji Vakuf** Bosnia-Herzegovina, Yugos
32G5 **Dönna** *I* Nor
19B3 **Donner** *P* USA
36D2 **Donnersberg** *Mt* Germany
74D2 **Donnybrook** S Africa
38B3 **Donostia** Spain
20B2 **Don Pedro Res** USA
10H2 **Doonerak,Mt** USA
57F9 **Dopolong** Phil
52A3 **Do Qu** *R* China
37B2 **Dora Baltea** *R* Italy
38D2 **Dorbirn** Austria
53A2 **Dorbod** China
35D6 **Dorchester** Eng
7L3 **Dorchester,C** Can
38C2 **Dordogne** *R* France
42A2 **Dordrecht** Neth
74D3 **Dordrecht** S Africa
3G3 **Doré L** Can
3G3 **Doré Lake** Can
14D1 **Dorest Peak** *Mt* USA
70B3 **Dori** Burkina
74B3 **Doring** *R* S Africa
36B2 **Dormans** France
42B3 **Dornbirn** Austria
34C3 **Dornoch** Scot
34C3 **Dornoch Firth** *Estuary* Scot
32H6 **Dorotea** Sweden
75D2 **Dorrigo** Aust
18B2 **Dorris** USA
35D6 **Dorset** County, Eng
36D1 **Dorsten** Germany
42B2 **Dortmund** Germany
72C3 **Doruma** Zaïre
49N4 **Dosatuy** Russian Fed
60B1 **Doshi** Afghan
20B2 **Dos Palos** USA
71G3 **Dosso** Niger
48G5 **Dossor** Kazakhstan
9E3 **Dothan** USA
38C1 **Douai** France
72A3 **Douala** Cam
75D1 **Double Island Pt** Aust
5K3 **Double Mer** *B* Can
16B3 **Double Mountain Fork** *R* USA
20C3 **Double Mt** USA
38D2 **Doubs** *R* France
78A3 **Doubtful Sd** NZ
70B3 **Douentza** Mali
3B2 **Douglas** Alaska, USA
8C3 **Douglas** Arizona, USA
35C4 **Douglas** Eng
15C2 **Douglas** Georgia, USA
74C2 **Douglas** S Africa
8C2 **Douglas** Wyoming, USA
10E2 **Douglas,C** USA
3C3 **Douglas Chan** Can
15C1 **Douglas L** USA
10H4 **Douglas,Mt** USA
36C2 **Doulevant-le-Château** France
36B1 **Doullens** France
35B4 **Doun** County, N Ire
27H8 **Dourados** Brazil
29B3 **Dourados** *R* Brazil
36B2 **Dourdan** France
39A1 **Douro** *R* Port
16A2 **Dove Creek** USA
13D3 **Dover** Delaware, USA
35F6 **Dover** Eng
13E2 **Dover** New Hampshire, USA
14C2 **Dover** New Jersey, USA
12C2 **Dover** Ohio, USA
35E5 **Dover** *R* Eng
35F6 **Dover,Str of** Eng/France
43G2 **Dovsk** Belorussia
14C3 **Downington** USA
35C4 **Downpatrick** N Ire
14C1 **Downsville** USA
3D3 **Downton,Mt** Can
14C2 **Doylestown** USA
54B3 **Dōzen** *I* Japan
70A2 **Dr'aa** *R* Mor
37A2 **Drac** *R* France
29B3 **Dracena** Brazil
14E1 **Dracut** USA
38D3 **Draguignan** France
11B2 **Drake** USA
73D6 **Drakensberg** *Mts* S Africa
74D2 **Drakensberg** *Mt* S Africa
xxxE7 **Drake Pass** Pacific/ Atlantic O
41E2 **Dráma** Greece
32G6 **Drammen** Nor
32A1 **Drangajökull** Iceland
22B1 **Dr Arroyo** Mexico
37E1 **Drau** *R* Austria
40D1 **Drava** *R* Slovenia, Yugos
3F3 **Drayton Valley** Can
38C2 **Dreaux** France
42C2 **Dresden** Germany
36A2 **Dreux** France
18C2 **Drewsey** USA
4E4 **Driftwood** Can
14A2 **Driftwood** USA
41E2 **Drin** *R* Alb
41D2 **Drina** *R* Bosnia-Herzegovina/Serbia, Yugos
43F1 **Drissa** *R* Belorussia
35B5 **Drogheda** Irish Rep
43E3 **Drogobych** Ukraine
37A2 **Drôme** *R* France
37B2 **Dronera** Italy
79F12 **Dronning Maud Land** Region, Ant
26F8 **Dr P.P. Pená** Par
6G4 **Drumheller** Can
18D1 **Drummond** USA
12C1 **Drummond I** USA
5G4 **Drummondville** Can
43E2 **Druskininksi** Lithuania
49Q3 **Druzhina** Russian Fed
10L4 **Dry B** USA
11D2 **Dryberry L** Can
7J5 **Dryden** Can
14B1 **Dryden** USA
23H1 **Dry Harbour Mts** Jamaica
71J4 **Dschang** Cam
55B3 **Duang** *I* Burma
66C1 **Dubā** S Arabia
67G1 **Dubai** UAE
6H3 **Dubawnt** *R* Can
6H3 **Dubawnt L** Can
76D4 **Dubbo** Aust
35B5 **Dublin** County, Irish Rep
35B5 **Dublin** Irish Rep
15C2 **Dublin** USA
44F4 **Dubna** Russian Fed
45D5 **Dubno** Ukraine
18D2 **Dubois** Idaho, USA
13D2 **Du Bois** USA
18E2 **Dubois** Wyoming, USA
3C3 **Dubose,Mt** Can
43F3 **Dubossary** Moldova
43F2 **Dubrovica** Ukraine
41D2 **Dubrovnik** Croatia, Yugos
9D2 **Dubuque** USA
19D2 **Duchesne** USA
15B1 **Duck** *R* USA
3H3 **Duck Mts** Can
20C3 **Ducor** USA
36D2 **Dudelange** Lux
48K3 **Dudinka** Russian Fed
35D5 **Dudley** Eng
49L2 **Dudypta** *R* Russian Fed
70B4 **Duekoué** Ivory Coast
39B1 **Duero** *R* Spain
77F1 **Duff Is** Solomon Is
34D3 **Dufftown** Scot
40C2 **Dugi Otok** *I* Croatia, Yugos
5G2 **Du Gué** *R* Can
42B2 **Duisburg** Germany
74E1 **Duiwelskloof** S Africa
64E3 **Dūkan** Iraq
10M5 **Duke I** USA
72D3 **Duk Faiwil** Sudan
67F1 **Dukhān** Qatar
52A4 **Dukou** China
50C3 **Dulan** China
28C2 **Dulce** *R* Arg
56D2 **Dulit Range** *Mts* Malay
61D3 **Dullabchara** India
36D1 **Dülmen** Germany
9D2 **Duluth** USA
65D2 **Dūmā** Syria
56B2 **Dumai** Indon
57E8 **Dumaran** *I* Phil
8C3 **Dumas** USA
65D2 **Dumayr** Syria
71G4 **Dumbai** Ghana
34C4 **Dumbarton** Scot
34D4 **Dumfries** Scot
34C4 **Dumfries and Galloway** Region, Scot
61C3 **Dumka** India
57B2 **Dumoga Kecil** Indon
13D1 **Dumoine,L** Can
79G8 **Dumont d'Urville** *Base* Ant
69C1 **Dumyât** Egypt
Dunărea = Danube *R* Rom
35B5 **Dunary Head** *Pt* Irish Rep
Dunav = Danube
43F3 **Dunayevtsy** Ukraine
3D4 **Duncan** Can
17C3 **Duncan** USA
4E3 **Duncan,C** Can
4F3 **Duncan L** Can
14B2 **Duncannon** USA
62E2 **Duncan Pass** Andaman Is
34D2 **Duncansby Head** *Pt* Scot
35B4 **Dundalk** Irish Rep
14B3 **Dundalk** USA
35B5 **Dundalk B** Irish Rep
7M2 **Dundas** Greenland
10M5 **Dundas I** Can
6G2 **Dundas Pen** Can
51G8 **Dundas Str** Aust
74E2 **Dundee** S Africa
34D3 **Dundee** Scot
14B1 **Dundee** USA
75B1 **Dundoo** Aust
35C4 **Dundrum** *B* N Ire
77G5 **Dunedin** NZ
15C3 **Dunedin** USA
75C2 **Dunedoo** Aust
34D3 **Dunfermline** Scot
60C4 **Dungarpur** India
35B5 **Dungarvan** Irish Rep
35F6 **Dungeness** Eng
75D2 **Dungog** Aust
72C3 **Dungu** Zaïre
72D1 **Dungunab** Sudan
53B3 **Dunhua** China
50C2 **Dunhuang** China
36B1 **Dunkerque** France
9F2 **Dunkirk** USA
72D2 **Dunkur** Eth
71F4 **Dunkwa** Ghana
33B3 **Dun Laoghaire** Irish Rep
14C2 **Dunmore** USA
23B1 **Dunmore Town** Bahamas
15D1 **Dunn** USA
34D2 **Dunnet Head** *Pt* Scot
11B3 **Dunning** USA
34D4 **Duns** Scot
11B2 **Dunseith** USA
18B2 **Dunsmuir** USA
78A2 **Dunstan Mts** NZ
36C2 **Dun-sur-Meuse** France
52D1 **Duolun** China
11B2 **Dupree** USA
73B4 **Duque de Braganca** Angola
12B3 **Du Quoin** USA
65C3 **Dura** Israel
38D3 **Durance** *R* France
12A2 **Durand** USA
21B2 **Durango** Mexico
39B1 **Durango** Spain
22A1 **Durango** State, Mexico
8C3 **Durango** USA
8D3 **Durant** USA
65D1 **Duraykīsh** Syria
25E4 **Durazho** Urug
74E2 **Durban** S Africa
36D1 **Duren** Germany
61B3 **Durg** India
61C3 **Durgapur** India
34E4 **Durham** County, Eng
34E4 **Durham** Eng
9F3 **Durham** N Carolina, USA
14E1 **Durham** New Hampshire, USA
75B1 **Durham Downs** Aust
41D2 **Durmitor** *Mt* Montenegro, Yugos
34C2 **Durness** Scot
41D2 **Durrës** Alb
75B1 **Durrie** Aust
41F3 **Dursunbey** Turk
78B2 **D'Urville I** NZ
63E1 **Dushak** Turkmenistan
52B4 **Dushan** China
59E2 **Dushanbe** Tajikistan
14B2 **Dushore** USA
78A3 **Dusky Sd** NZ
42B2 **Düsseldorf** Germany
10E5 **Dutch Harbor** USA
19D3 **Dutton,Mt** USA
52B4 **Duyun** China
64B1 **Düzce** Turk
44F2 **Dvinskaya Guba** *B* Russian Fed
60B4 **Dwārka** India
18C1 **Dworshak Res** USA
9E3 **Dyersburg** USA
35C5 **Dyfed** County, Wales
45G7 **Dykh Tau** *Mt* Russian Fed
75B1 **Dynevor Downs** Aust
50C2 **Dzag** Mongolia
50D2 **Dzamīn Uūd** Mongolia
73E5 **Dzaoudzi** Mayotte
50C2 **Dzavhan Gol** *R* Mongolia

Encruzilhada do Sul Fetisovo

28E2 **Encruzilhada do Sul** Brazil
66C4 **Enda Salassie** Eth
76B1 **Endeh** Indon
3E3 **Enderby** Can
79G11 **Enderby Land** Region, Ant
11C2 **Enderlin** USA
13D2 **Endicott** USA
10H2 **Endicott Mts** USA
15D1 **Enfield** USA
37D1 **Engadin** *Mts* Switz
57F7 **Engaño,C** Phil
54D2 **Engaru** Japan
65C3 **En Gedi** Israel
37C1 **Engelberg** Switz
56B4 **Enggano** *I* Indon
33C3 **England** Country, UK
7N4 **Englee** Can
15D1 **Englehard** USA
13D1 **Englehart** Can
16B2 **Englewood** USA
11D1 **English** *R* Can
33C3 **English Channel** Eng/ France
4C4 **English River** Can
17C2 **Enid** USA
54D2 **Eniwa** Japan
70B3 **Enji** *Well* Maur
32H7 **Enkoping** Sweden
40C3 **Enna** Italy
72C2 **En Nahud** Sudan
72C2 **Ennedi** *Desert Region* Chad
10C2 **Ennelen** Russian Fed
75C1 **Enngonia** Aust
11B3 **Enning** USA
33B3 **Ennis** Irish Rep
18D1 **Ennis** Montana, USA
17C3 **Ennis** Texas, USA
35B5 **Enniscorthy** Irish Rep
35B4 **Enniskillen** N Ire
65C2 **Enn Nâqoûra** Leb
42C3 **Enns** *R* Austria
57A3 **Enrekang** Indon
32F8 **Enschede** Neth
21A1 **Ensenada** Mexico
52B3 **Enshi** China
36D3 **Ensisheim** France
72D4 **Entebbe** Uganda
15B2 **Enterprise** Alabama, USA
3E1 **Enterprise** Can
18C1 **Enterprise** Oregon, USA
71H4 **Enugu** Nig
71H4 **Enugu** *State* Nig
10D2 **Enurmino** Russian Fed
36E2 **Enz** *R* w Germ
54C3 **Enzan** Japan
71G4 **Epe** Nig
38C2 **Epernay** France
19D3 **Ephraim** USA
14B2 **Ephrata** Pennsylvania, USA
18C1 **Ephrata** Washington, USA
77F2 **Epi** *I* Vanuatu
38D2 **Épinal** France
65B1 **Episkopi** Cyprus
65B1 **Episkopi B** Cyprus
36E2 **Eppingen** Germany
36A2 **Epte** *R* France
74B1 **Epukiro** Namibia
28C3 **Epu pel** Arg
63C2 **Eqlid** Iran
68D7 **Equator**
72A3 **Equatorial Guinea** Republic, Africa
14D1 **Equinox Mt** USA
14C2 **Equinunk** USA
37C2 **Erba** Italy
36E2 **Erbach** Germany
36D2 **Erbeskopf** *Mt* Germany
28A3 **Ercilla** Chile
64D2 **Erciş** Turk
45F8 **Erciyas Daglari** *Mt* Turk
53B3 **Erdaobaihe** China
52C1 **Erdene** Mongolia
50D2 **Erdenet** Mongolia
72C2 **Erdi** *Desert Region* Chad
25F3 **Erechim** Brazil
64B1 **Ereğli** Turk
64B2 **Ereğli** Turk
50E2 **Erenhot** China
39B1 **Eresma** *R* Spain
36D1 **Erft** *R* Germany
42C2 **Erfurt** Germany
64C2 **Ergani** Turk
70B2 **Erg Chech** *Desert Region* Alg
72B2 **Erg du Djourab** *Desert Region* Chad
70D3 **Erg Du Ténéré** *Desert Region* Niger
64A1 **Ergene** *R* Turk
70B2 **Erg Iguidi** *Region* Alg
43F1 **Ērgli** Latvia
72B2 **Erguig** *R* Chad
50E1 **Ergun** *R* China/ Russian Fed
49O4 **Ergun Zuoqi** China
10C2 **Erguveyem** *R* Russian Fed
72D2 **Eriba** Sudan
9F2 **Erie** USA
9E2 **Erie,L** USA/Can
4B3 **Eriksdale** Can
54D2 **Erimo-misaki** *C* Japan
35C4 **Erin Port** Eng
34B3 **Eriskay** *I* Scot
66C3 **Eritrea** Republic, Africa
36D1 **Erkelenz** Germany
42C3 **Erlangen** Germany
17D3 **Erling,L** USA
74D2 **Ermelo** S Africa
62B3 **Ernākulam** India
62B2 **Erode** India
75B1 **Eromanga** Aust
74B1 **Erongoberg** *Mt* Namibia
71B2 **Er Rachidia** Mor
72D2 **Er Rahad** Sudan
73D5 **Errego** Mozam
33B2 **Errigal** *Mt* Irish Rep
33A3 **Erris Head** *Pt* Irish Rep
77F2 **Erromanga** *I* Vanuatu
72D2 **Er Roseires** Sudan
71C2 **er Rtem** *R* Alg
65C2 **Er Rummān** Jordan
11C2 **Erskine** USA
36D2 **Erstein** France
28E2 **Erval** Brazil
42C2 **Erzgebirge** *Upland* Germany
45F8 **Erzincan** Turk
45G8 **Erzurum** Turk
54D2 **Esan-misaki** *C* Japan
38C3 **Esara** *R* Spain
54D2 **Esashi** Japan
42B1 **Esbjerg** Den
19D3 **Escalante** USA
8C4 **Escalón** Mexico
9E2 **Escanaba** USA
21C3 **Escárcega** Mexico
36C2 **Esch** Luxembourg
19C4 **Escondido** USA
21B2 **Escuinapa** Mexico
21C3 **Escuintla** Guatemala
72B3 **Eséka** Cam
39C1 **Esera** *R* Spain
63C2 **Eşfahān** Iran
74E2 **Eshowe** S Africa
65C3 **Esh Sharā** *Upland* Jordan
37E3 **Esino** Italy
78C1 **Eskdale** NZ
32C1 **Eskifjörður** Iceland
32H7 **Eskilstuna** Sweden
6E3 **Eskimo L** Can
7J3 **Eskimo Point** Can
45E8 **Eskisehir** Turk
39A1 **Esla** *R* Spain
26C3 **Esmeraldas** Ecuador
23B2 **Esmerelda** Cuba
25A7 **Esmerelda** *I* Chile
38C3 **Espalion** France
4E4 **Espanola** Can
16A2 **Espanola** USA
76B4 **Esperance** Aust
28C2 **Esperanza** Arg
79G2 **Esperanza** *Base* Ant
29D2 **Espírito Santo** State, Brazil
77F2 **Espiritu Santo** *I* Vanuatu
73D6 **Espungabera** Mozam
25B6 **Esquel** Arg
18B1 **Esquimalt** Can
28D2 **Esquina** Arg
65D2 **Es Samra** Jordan
71A2 **Essaourira** Mor
71E2 **Es-Sekhira** Tunisia
42B2 **Essen** Germany
27G3 **Essequibo** Guyana
35F6 **Essex** County, Eng
12C2 **Essexville** USA
42B3 **Esslingen** Germany
36B2 **Essonne** France
36C2 **Essoyes** France
27L6 **Estância** Brazil
74D2 **Estcourt** S Africa
37D2 **Este** Italy
26A1 **Esteli** Nic
36B2 **Esternay** France
20B3 **Estero B** USA
22C1 **Esteros** Mexico
25D2 **Esteros** Par
28D1 **Esteros del Iberá** *Swamp* Arg
16A1 **Estes Park** USA
6H5 **Estevan** Can
11D3 **Estherville** USA
15C2 **Estill** USA
36B2 **Estissac** France
44C4 **Estonia**
25B8 **Estrecho de Magallanes** *Str* Chile
20B3 **Estrella** *R* USA
39A2 **Estremoz** Port
43D3 **Esztergom** Hung
75A1 **Etadunna** Aust
7L2 **Etah** Can
36C2 **Etam** France
5K3 **Etamamiou** Can
38C2 **Etampes** France
75A1 **Etamunbanie,L** Aust
36A1 **Etaples** France
60D3 **Etāwah** India
72D3 **Ethiopia** Republic, Africa
22C2 **Etla** Mexico
40C3 **Etna** *Mt* Italy
10M4 **Etolin I** USA
10E3 **Etolin Str** USA
73B5 **Etosha Nat Pk** Namibia
73B5 **Etosha Pan** *Salt L* Namibia
15C2 **Etowah** *R* USA
36A2 **Etretat** France
3D2 **Etsha Plateau** Can
36C2 **Ettelbruck** Lux
77H3 **Eua** *I* Tonga
75C2 **Euabalong** Aust
12C2 **Euclid** USA
75C3 **Eucumbene,L** Aust
75A2 **Eudunda** Aust
17C2 **Eufala L** USA
15B2 **Eufaula** USA
8A2 **Eugene** USA
75C1 **Eulo** Aust
17D3 **Eunice** Louisiana, USA
16B3 **Eunice** New Mexico, USA
36D1 **Eupen** Germany
64D3 **Euphrates** *R* Iraq
17E3 **Eupora** USA
36A2 **Eure** Department, France
38C2 **Eure** *R* France
36A2 **Eure-et-Loir** Department, France
18B2 **Eureka** California, USA
7K1 **Eureka** Can
18C1 **Eureka** Montana, USA
8B3 **Eureka** Nevada, USA
11C2 **Eureka** S Dakota, USA
19D3 **Eureka** Utah, USA
7K2 **Eureka Sound** Can
20D2 **Eureka V** USA
75C3 **Euroa** Aust
75C1 **Eurombah** *R* Aust
73E6 **Europa** *I* Mozam Chan
36C1 **Europort** Neth
42B2 **Euskirchen** Germany
15B2 **Eutaw** USA
3C3 **Eutsuk L** Can
3F3 **Evansburg** Can
7K1 **Evans,C** Can
7L4 **Evans,L** Can
16A2 **Evans,Mt** Colorado, USA
18D1 **Evans,Mt** Montana, USA
7K3 **Evans Str** Can
12B2 **Evanston** Illinois, USA
8B2 **Evanston** Wyoming, USA
9E3 **Evansville** Indiana, USA
11A3 **Evansville** Wyoming, USA
74D2 **Evaton** S Africa
76C4 **Everard,L** Aust
59G3 **Everest,Mt** Nepal/China
14A2 **Everett** Pennsylvania, USA
8A2 **Everett** Washington, USA
14D1 **Everett,Mt** USA
9E4 **Everglades,The** *Swamp* USA
15B2 **Evergreen** USA
35E5 **Evesham** Eng
72B3 **Evinayong** Eq Guinea
32F7 **Evje** Nor
37B1 **Evolène** Switz
39A2 **Évora** Port
38C2 **Evreux** France
41E3 **Évvoia** *I* Greece
72B4 **Ewo** Congo
20C1 **Excelisor Mt** USA
20C1 **Excelisor Mts** USA
17D2 **Excelsior Springs** USA
19C3 **Exeter** California, USA
35D6 **Exeter** Eng
13E2 **Exeter** New Hampshire, USA
35D6 **Exmoor Nat Pk** Eng
35D6 **Exmouth** Eng
39A2 **Extremadura** Region, Spain
21E2 **Exuma Sd** Bahamas
72D4 **Eyasi** *L* Tanz
34D4 **Eyemouth** Scot
69D4 **Eyl** Somalia
76B4 **Eyre** Aust
76C3 **Eyre Creek** *R* Aust
76C3 **Eyre,L** Aust
76C4 **Eyre Pen** Aust
3H2 **Eyrie L** Can
57F8 **Eyte** *I* Phil
22B1 **Ezatlan** Mexico
41F3 **Ezine** Turk
66B3 **Ez Zeidab** Sudan

F

4G3 **Faber L** Can
32F7 **Fåborg** Den
40C2 **Fabriano** Italy
37B2 **Fabrosa** Italy
72B2 **Fachi** Niger
72C2 **Fada** Chad
71G3 **Fada N'Gourma** Burkina
49Q2 **Faddeyevskiy, Ostrov** *I* Russian Fed
40C2 **Faenza** Italy
7N3 **Faeringehavn** Greenland
30E2 **Faeroerne** Is, N Atlantic
72B3 **Fafa** *R* CAR
72E3 **Fafan** *R* Eth
71G3 **Faga** *R* Burkina
41E1 **Făgăraş** Rom
36C1 **Fagnes** Region, Belg
70B3 **Faguibine,L** Mali
67G2 **Fahud** Oman
70A1 **Faiol** *I* Açores
16A3 **Fairacres** USA
6D3 **Fairbanks** USA
12C3 **Fairborn** USA
8D2 **Fairbury** USA
14B3 **Fairfax** USA
19B3 **Fairfield** California, USA
14D2 **Fairfield** Connecticut, USA
18D2 **Fairfield** Idaho, USA
18D1 **Fairfield** Montana, USA
12C3 **Fairfield** Ohio, USA
34B4 **Fair Head** *Pt* N Ire
33C2 **Fair Isle** *I* Scot
78B2 **Fairlie** NZ
11D3 **Fairmont** Minnesota, USA
12C3 **Fairmont** W Virginia, USA
14B1 **Fairport** USA
3E2 **Fairview** Can
16C2 **Fairview** USA
6E4 **Fairweather,Mt** USA
51H6 **Fais** *I* Pacific O
60C2 **Faisalabad** Pak
11B2 **Faith** USA
34E1 **Faither,The** *Pen* Scot
61B2 **Faizābād** India
77H1 **Fakaofo** *I* Tokeau Is
35F5 **Fakenham** Eng
76C1 **Fakfak** Indon
32G7 **Faköping** Sweden
71F3 **Falaise de Banfora** Burkina
61D3 **Falam** Burma
28B4 **Falckner** Arg
21C2 **Falcon Res** USA/Mexico
70A3 **Falémé** *R* Mali/Sen
17F4 **Falfurrias** USA
3E2 **Falher** Can
32G7 **Falkenberg** Sweden
34D4 **Falkirk** Scot
25D8 **Falkland Is** Dependency, S Atlantic
25E8 **Falkland Sd** Falkland Is
20D4 **Fallbrook** USA
8B3 **Fallon** USA
13E2 **Fall River** USA
16A1 **Fall River P** USA
17C1 **Falls City** USA
35C6 **Falmouth** Eng
23H1 **Falmouth** Jamaica
13E2 **Falmouth** Maine, USA
14E2 **Falmouth** Massachusetts, USA
74B3 **False B** S Africa
21A2 **Falso,C** Mexico
42C2 **Falster** *I* Den
41F1 **Fălticeni** Rom
32H6 **Falun** Sweden
64B2 **Famagusta** Cyprus
65B1 **Famagusta B** Cyprus
28B1 **Famatina** Arg
36C1 **Famenne** Region, Belg
43B4 **Family L** Can
20C3 **Famoso** USA
55B2 **Fang** Thai
72D3 **Fangak** Sudan
52E5 **Fang liao** Taiwan
53B2 **Fangzheng** China
40C2 **Fano** Italy
65A3 **Fâqûs** Egypt
79G3 **Faraday** *Base* Ant
72C3 **Faradje** Zaïre
73E6 **Farafangana** Madag
69B2 **Farafra Oasis** Egypt
63E2 **Farah** Afghan
63E2 **Farah** *R* Afghan
51H5 **Farallon de Medinilla** *I* Pacific O
70A3 **Faranah** Guinea
51H6 **Faraulep** *I* Pacific O
35E6 **Fareham** Eng
Farewell,C = Kap Farvel
77G5 **Farewell,C** NZ
78B2 **Farewell Spit** *Pt* NZ
8D2 **Fargo** USA
65C2 **Fari'a** *R* Israel
9D2 **Faribault** USA
61C3 **Faridpur** Bang
63D1 **Farimān** Iran
65A3 **Fâriskûr** Egypt
13E2 **Farmington** Maine, USA
17D2 **Farmington** Missouri, USA
14E1 **Farmington** New Hampshire, USA
8C3 **Farmington** New Mexico, USA
18D2 **Farmington** Utah, USA
20B2 **Farmington Res** USA
34E4 **Farne Deep** N Sea
3E3 **Farnham,Mt** Can
10M3 **Faro** Can
39A2 **Faro** Port
32H7 **Fåro** *I* Sweden
71J4 **Faro** *R* Cam
68K8 **Farquhar** *Is* Indian O
34C3 **Farrar** *R* Scot
12C2 **Farrell** USA
41E3 **Fársala** Greece
63E2 **Farsi** Afghan
16B3 **Farwell** USA
63C3 **Fasā** Iran
45D5 **Fastov** Ukraine
61B2 **Fatehpur** India
27H7 **Fatima du Sul** Brazil
18C1 **Fauquier** Can
74D2 **Fauresmith** S Africa
37B2 **Faverges** France
4C3 **Fawcett L** Can
7K4 **Fawn** *R* Can
32H6 **Fax** *R* Sweden
32A2 **Faxaflóri** *B* Iceland
72B2 **Faya** Chad
15B2 **Fayette** USA
9D3 **Fayetteville** Arkansas, USA
9F3 **Fayetteville** N Carolina, USA
15B1 **Fayetteville** Tennessee, USA
65B3 **Fâyid** Egypt
64E4 **Faylakah** *I* Kuwait
60C2 **Fāzilka** India
70A2 **Fdérik** Maur
9F3 **Fear,C** USA
19B3 **Feather Middle Fork** *R* USA
36A2 **Fécamp** France
28D2 **Federación** Arg
28D2 **Federal** Arg
71H4 **Federal Capital Territory** Nig
51H6 **Federated States of Micronesia** *Is* Pacific O
42C2 **Fehmarn** *I* Germany
26D5 **Feijó** Brazil
52C5 **Feilai Xai Bei Jiang** *R* China
78C2 **Feilding** NZ
73D5 **Feira** Zambia
27L6 **Feira de Santan** Brazil
64C2 **Feke** Turk
36D3 **Feldberg** *Mt* Germany
42B3 **Feldkirch** Austria
28D2 **Feliciano** *R* Arg
33D3 **Felixstowe** Eng
37D1 **Feltre** Italy
32G6 **Femund** *L* Nor
53A3 **Fengcheng** China
52B4 **Fengdu** China
52D1 **Fenging** China
52B3 **Fengjie** China
53A1 **Fengshui Shan** *Mt* China
52B3 **Feng Xian** China
52C1 **Fengzhen** China
52C2 **Fen He** *R* China
10C6 **Fenimore Pass** USA
73E5 **Fenoarivo Atsinanana** Madag
45F7 **Feodosiya** Ukraine
63D2 **Ferdow** Iran
36B2 **Fère** France
36B2 **Fère-Champenoise** France
59F2 **Fergana** Uzbekistan
3J2 **Fergus** *R* Can
11C2 **Fergus Falls** USA
35B4 **Fermanagh** County, N Ire
37E3 **Fermo** Italy
37D1 **Fern** *Mt* Austria
28C1 **Fernandez** Arg
15C2 **Fernandina Beach** USA
xxxG5 **Fernando de Noronha** *I* Atlantic O
29B3 **Fernandópolis** Brazil
70C4 **Fernando Poo** *I* Eq Guinea
18B1 **Ferndale** USA
18C1 **Fernie** Can
19C3 **Fernley** USA
40C2 **Ferrara** Italy
26C5 **Ferreñafe** Peru
17D3 **Ferriday** USA
36B2 **Ferriéres** France
71A2 **Fès** Mor
5G4 **Festubert** Can
17D2 **Festus** USA
41F2 **Feteşti** Rom
64A2 **Fethiye** Turk
45J7 **Fetisovo** Kazakhstan

Fetlar Gabe's

34E1 **Fetlar** *I* Scot
53C1 **Fevral'skoye** Russian Fed
48J6 **Feyzabad** Afghan
28B1 **Fiambalá** Arg
73E6 **Fianarantsoa** Madag
72D3 **Fichē** Eth
74D2 **Ficksburg** S Africa
37D2 **Fidenza** Italy
41D2 **Fier** Alb
37D1 **Fiera Di Primeiro** Italy
34D3 **Fife** Region, Scot
34D3 **Fife Ness** *Pen* Scot
38C3 **Figeac** France
39A1 **Figueira da Foz** Port
39C1 **Figueras** Spain
Figueres = Figueras
71B2 **Figuig** Mor
77G2 **Fiji** *Is* Pacific O
27G8 **Filadelpia** Par
41E2 **Filiaşi** Rom
41E3 **Filiatrá** Greece
40C3 **Filicudi** *I* Italy
19C4 **Fillmore** California, USA
19D3 **Fillmore** Utah, USA
37C2 **Finale Ligure** Italy
34C3 **Findhorn** *R* Scot
9E2 **Findlay** USA
3E3 **Findlay,Mt** Can
13D2 **Finger Lakes** USA
73D5 **Fingoè** Mozam
45E8 **Finike** Turk
76C3 **Finke** *R* Aust
75A1 **Finke Flood Flats** Aust
44C3 **Finland** Republic, N Europe
32J7 **Finland,G of** N Europe
6F4 **Finlay** *R* Can
6F4 **Finlay Forks** Can
75C3 **Finley** Aust
32H5 **Finnsnes** Nor
51H7 **Finschhafen** PNG
37C1 **Finsteraarhorn** *Mt* Switz
42C2 **Finsterwalde** Germany
35B4 **Fintona** N Ire
78A3 **Fiordland Nat Pk** NZ
65C2 **Fiq** Syria
45F8 **Firat** *R* Turk
3F2 **Firebag** *R* Can
20B2 **Firebaugh** USA
40C2 **Firenze** Italy
37D2 **Firenzuola** Italy
3C2 **Fireside** Can
28C2 **Firmat** Arg
60D3 **Firozābād** India
60C2 **Firozpur** India
32H7 **Firspång** Sweden
34C4 **Firth of Clyde** *Estuary* Scot
34D3 **Firth of Forth** *Estuary* Scot
34B3 **Firth of Lorn** *Estuary* Scot
33C2 **Firth of Tay** *Estuary* Scot
63C3 **Firūzābād** Iran
74B2 **Fish** *R* Namibia
74C3 **Fish** *R* S Africa
20C2 **Fish Camp** USA
14D2 **Fishers I** USA
7K3 **Fisher Str** Can
35C6 **Fishguard** Wales
10O3 **Fish L** Can
7N3 **Fiskenaesset** Greenland
36B2 **Fismes** France
13E2 **Fitchburg** USA
34E2 **Fitful Head** *Pt* Scot
15C2 **Fitzgerald** USA
3F2 **Fitzgerald** Can
76B2 **Fitzroy** *R* Aust
76B2 **Fitzroy Crossing** Aust
12C1 **Fitzwilliam I** Can
Fiume = Rijeka
72C4 **Fizi** Zaïre
74D3 **Flagstaff** S Africa
8B3 **Flagstaff** USA
13E1 **Flagstaff L** USA
35E4 **Flamborough Head** *C* Eng
8C2 **Flaming Gorge Res** USA
34B2 **Flannan Isles** *Is* Scot
10N3 **Flat** *R* Can
3F4 **Flathead** *R* USA
8B2 **Flathead L** USA
17D2 **Flat River** USA
51H8 **Flattery,C** Aust
8A2 **Flattery,C** USA
35D5 **Fleetwood** Eng
32F7 **Flekkefjord** *Inlet* Nor
50H4 **Fleming Deep** Pacific Oc
14C2 **Flemington** USA
42B2 **Flensburg** Germany
5K3 **Fleur-de-Lys** Can
37B1 **Fleurier** Switz
36A2 **Fleury-sur-Andelle** France
76C4 **Flinders** *I* Aust
76D5 **Flinders** *I* Aust
76D2 **Flinders** *R* Aust
76C4 **Flinders Range** *Mts* Aust
6H4 **Flin Flon** Can
9E2 **Flint** USA
35D5 **Flint** Wales
9E3 **Flint** *R* USA
36B1 **Flixecourt** France
12A1 **Floodwood** USA
15B2 **Florala** USA
Florence = Firenze
9E3 **Florence** Alabama, USA
19D4 **Florence** Arizona, USA
16A2 **Florence** Colorado, USA
17C2 **Florence** Kansas, USA
18B2 **Florence** Oregon, USA
9F3 **Florence** S Carolina, USA
20C2 **Florence,L** USA
26C3 **Florencia** Colombia
36C2 **Florenville** Belg
21D3 **Flores** Guatemala
70A1 **Flores** *I* Açores
76B1 **Flores** *I* Indon
28D3 **Flores** *R* Arg
51E7 **Flores S** Indon
27K5 **Floriano** Brazil
25G3 **Florianópolis** Brazil
21D2 **Florida** State, USA
25E4 **Florida** Urug
15E4 **Florida B** USA
15E4 **Florida City** USA
77E1 **Florida Is** Solomon Is
9E4 **Florida Keys** *Is* USA
9E4 **Florida,Strs of** USA
41E2 **Flórina** Greece
32F6 **Florø** Nor
16B3 **Floydada** USA
37D1 **Fluchthorn** *Mt* Austria
57C3 **Fluk** Indon
76D1 **Fly** *R* PNG
37E2 **Foci del Po** *Delta* Italy
41F1 **Focsani** Rom
40D2 **Foggia** Italy
37E3 **Foglia** *R* Italy
5L4 **Fogo** Can
5L4 **Fogo I** Can
70A4 **Fogo** *I* Cape Verde
38C3 **Foix** France
4E4 **Foleyet** Can
7L3 **Foley I** Can
40C2 **Foligno** Italy
35F6 **Folkestone** Eng
15C2 **Folkston** USA
40C2 **Follonica** Italy
20B1 **Folsom** USA
14C1 **Fonda** USA
6H4 **Fond-du-Lac** Can
9E2 **Fond du Lac** USA
38C2 **Fontainebleau** France
3D2 **Fontas** *R* Can
17D2 **Fontenac** USA
38B2 **Fontenay-le-Comte** France
41D1 **Fonyód** Hung
Foochow = Fuzhou
10H3 **Foraker,Mt** USA
36D2 **Forbach** France
75C2 **Forbes** Aust
71H4 **Forcados** Nig
37A3 **Forcalquier** France
20C3 **Ford City** USA
32F6 **Forde** Nor
75C1 **Fords Bridge** Aust
17D3 **Fordyce** USA
70A4 **Forécariah** Guinea
7P3 **Forel,Mt** Greenland
18D1 **Foremost** Can
12C2 **Forest** Can
15B2 **Forest** USA
11D3 **Forest City** Iowa, USA
14C2 **Forest City** Pennsylvania, USA
15C2 **Forest Park** USA
20A1 **Forestville** USA
36B2 **Forêt d'Othe** France
34D3 **Forfar** Scot
16B2 **Forgan** USA
36A2 **Forges-les-Eaux** France
18B1 **Forks** USA
40C2 **Forlì** Italy
39C2 **Formentera** *I* Spain
40C2 **Formia** Italy
70A1 **Formigas** *I* Açores
Formosa = Taiwan
25E3 **Formosa** Arg
27J7 **Formosa** Brazil
25D2 **Formosa** State, Arg
52D5 **Formosa Str** Taiwan/China
29C1 **Formoso** Brazil
29C1 **Formoso** *R* Brazil
37D2 **Fornovo di Taro** Italy
34D3 **Forres** Scot
76B4 **Forrest** Aust
9D3 **Forrest City** USA
3G2 **Forrest L** Can
76D2 **Forsayth** Aust
32J6 **Forssa** Fin
75D2 **Forster** Aust
17D2 **Forsyth** Missouri, USA
11A2 **Forsyth** Montana, USA
60C3 **Fort Abbas** Pak
7K4 **Fort Albany** Can
27L4 **Fortaleza** Brazil
34C3 **Fort Augustus** Scot
74D3 **Fort Beaufort** S Africa
18D1 **Fort Benton** USA
19B3 **Fort Bragg** USA
3F2 **Fort Chipewyan** Can
16C2 **Fort Cobb Res** USA
8C2 **Fort Collins** USA
4F4 **Fort Coulonge** Can
13D1 **Fort Coulonge** Can
16B3 **Fort Davis** USA
23E4 **Fort de France** Martinique
15B2 **Fort Deposit** USA
9D2 **Fort Dodge** USA
76A3 **Fortescue** *R* Aust
7J5 **Fort Frances** Can
6F3 **Fort Franklin** Can
6F3 **Fort Good Hope** Can
75B1 **Fort Grey** Aust
34C3 **Forth** *R* Scot
16A3 **Fort Hancock** USA
7K4 **Fort Hope** Can
34F3 **Forties** *Oilfield* N Sea
28B3 **Fortin Uno** Arg
13F1 **Fort Kent** USA
70C1 **Fort Lallemand** Alg
Fort Lamy = Ndjamena
11B3 **Fort Laramie** USA
9E4 **Fort Lauderdale** USA
3D1 **Fort Liard** Can
6G4 **Fort Mackay** Can
6G5 **Fort Macleod** Can
6G4 **Fort McMurray** Can
6E3 **Fort McPherson** Can
12A2 **Fort Madison** USA
8C2 **Fort Morgan** USA
9E4 **Fort Myers** USA
6F4 **Fort Nelson** Can
3D2 **Fort Nelson** *R* Can
6F3 **Fort Norman** Can
15B2 **Fort Payne** USA
11A2 **Fort Peck** USA
8C2 **Fort Peck Res** USA
9E4 **Fort Pierce** USA
11B3 **Fort Pierre** USA
14C1 **Fort Plain** USA
6G3 **Fort Providence** Can
3H3 **Fort Qu'Appelle** Can
10F4 **Fort Randall** USA
6G3 **Fort Resolution** Can
72B4 **Fort Rousset** Congo
6F4 **Fort St James** Can
3D2 **Fort St John** Can
3F3 **Fort Saskatchewan** Can
17D2 **Fort Scott** USA
6E3 **Fort Selkirk** Can
7K4 **Fort Severn** Can
45J7 **Fort Shevchenko** Kazakhstan
6F3 **Fort Simpson** Can
6G3 **Fort Smith** Can
9D3 **Fort Smith** USA
6F3 **Fort Smith** Region, Can
8C3 **Fort Stockton** USA
16B3 **Fort Sumner** USA
16C2 **Fort Supply** USA
18B2 **Fortuna** California, USA
11B2 **Fortuna** N Dakota, USA
5K4 **Fortune B** Can
6G4 **Fort Vermilion** Can
15B2 **Fort Walton Beach** USA
9E2 **Fort Wayne** USA
34C3 **Fort William** Scot
16A2 **Fort Wingate** USA
8D3 **Fort Worth** USA
10K3 **Fortymile** *R* USA
10J2 **Fort Yukon** USA
52C5 **Foshan** China
7K2 **Fosheim** *Pen* Can
37B2 **Fossano** Italy
37E3 **Fossombrone** Italy
11C2 **Fosston** USA
3G2 **Foster L** Can
10L4 **Foster,Mt** USA
72B4 **Fougamou** Gabon
38B2 **Fougères** France
34D1 **Foula** *I* Scot
35F6 **Foulness I** Eng
78B2 **Foulwind,C** NZ
72B3 **Foumban** Cam
38C1 **Fourmies** France
10E5 **Four Mountains,Is of** USA
41F3 **Foúrnoi** *I* Greece
70A3 **Fouta Djallon** *Mts* Guinea
77F5 **Foveaux Str** NZ
35C6 **Fowey** Eng
16B2 **Fowler** USA
12B2 **Fox** *R* USA
3E3 **Fox Creek** Can
7K3 **Foxe Basin** *G* Can
7K3 **Foxe Chan** Can
7L3 **Foxe Pen** Can
10E5 **Fox Is** USA
3F2 **Fox Lake** Can
16A1 **Foxpark** USA
78C2 **Foxton** NZ
3G3 **Fox Valley** Can
73B5 **Foz do Cuene** Angola
25F3 **Foz do Iquaçu** Brazil
22B1 **Fracisco I Madero** Mexico
14B2 **Frackville** USA
28B2 **Fraga** Arg
14E1 **Framingham** USA
27J8 **Franca** Brazil
38C2 **France** Republic, Europe
10N3 **Frances** *R* Can
4D5 **Francesville** USA
38D2 **Franche Comté** Region, France
74D1 **Francistown** Botswana
3C3 **Francois L** Can
18E2 **Francs Peak** *Mt* USA
36E1 **Frankenberg** Germany
12B2 **Frankfort** Indiana, USA
9E3 **Frankfort** Kentucky, USA
14C1 **Frankfort** New York, USA
42B2 **Frankfurt** Germany
74D2 **Frankfurt** S Africa
36E1 **Frankfurt am Main** Germany
42C2 **Frankfurt-an-der-Oder** Germany
42C3 **Fränkischer Alb** *Upland* Germany
18D2 **Franklin** Idaho, USA
12B3 **Franklin** Indiana, USA
17D4 **Franklin** Louisiana, USA
14E1 **Franklin** Massachusetts, USA
15C1 **Franklin** N Carolina, USA
14E1 **Franklin** New Hampshire, USA
14C2 **Franklin** New Jersey, USA
13D2 **Franklin** Pennsylvania, USA
15B1 **Franklin** Tennessee, USA
13D3 **Franklin** Virginia, USA
6F2 **Franklin B** Can
18C1 **Franklin D Roosevelt** *L* USA
6F3 **Franklin Mts** Can
10G1 **Franklin,Pt** USA
6J2 **Franklin Str** Can
14A1 **Franklinville** USA
4E4 **Franz** Can
78B2 **Franz Josef Glacier** NZ
Franz-Joseph-Land = Zemlya Franza Josifa
4F5 **Fraser** *R* Can
74C3 **Fraserburg** S Africa
34D3 **Fraserburgh** Scot
75D1 **Fraser I** Aust
3C3 **Fraser Lake** Can
5J2 **Fraser** *R* Can
37B1 **Frasne** France
37C1 **Frauenfield** Switz
28D2 **Fray Bentos** Urug
33C2 **Frazerburgh** Scot
14C3 **Frederica** USA
42B1 **Fredericia** Den
13D3 **Frederick** Maryland, USA
16C3 **Frederick** Oklahoma, USA
16C3 **Fredericksburg** Texas, USA
13D3 **Fredericksburg** Virginia, USA
10M4 **Frederick Sd** USA
17D2 **Fredericktown** USA
7M5 **Fredericton** Can
7N3 **Frederikshåb** Greenland
32G7 **Frederikshavn** Den
13D2 **Fredonia** USA
32G7 **Fredrikstad** Nor
14C2 **Freehold** USA
20C1 **Freel Peak** *Mt* USA
5L4 **Freels,C** Can
11C3 **Freeman** USA
23B1 **Freeport** Bahamas
5H5 **Freeport** Can
12B2 **Freeport** Illinois, USA
17C4 **Freeport** Texas, USA
17F4 **Freer** USA
70A4 **Freetown** Sierra Leone
42B3 **Freiburg** Germany
36D2 **Freiburg im Breisgau** Germany
28A1 **Freirina** Chile
42C3 **Freistadt** Austria
37B3 **Fréjus** France
76A4 **Fremantle** Aust
20B2 **Fremont** California, USA
17C1 **Fremont** Nebraska, USA
12C2 **Fremont** Ohio, USA
27H3 **French Guiana** Dependency, S America
11A2 **Frenchman** *R* USA
75E3 **Frenchmans Cap** *Mt* Aust
xxixM5 **French Polynesia** *Is* Pacific O
71C1 **Frenda** Alg
21B2 **Fresnillo** Mexico
8B3 **Fresno** USA
20C2 **Fresno** *R* USA
18D1 **Fresno Res** USA
37A1 **Fretigney** France
36E2 **Freudenstadt** Germany
36B1 **Frévent** France
75E3 **Freycinet Pen** Aust
70A3 **Fria** Guinea
20C2 **Friant** USA
20C2 **Friant Dam** USA
28B1 **Frías** Arg
40B1 **Fribourg** Switz
36E1 **Friedberg** Germany
42B3 **Friedrichshafen** Germany
16C4 **Frio** *R* USA
16B3 **Friona** USA
37E1 **Friuli** Region, Italy
7M3 **Frobisher B** Can
7M3 **Frobisher Bay** Can
6H4 **Frobisher L** Can
45G6 **Frolovo** Russian Fed
35D6 **Frome** Eng
75A1 **Frome** *R* Aust
35D6 **Frome** *R* Eng
76C4 **Frome,L** Aust
21C3 **Frontera** Mexico
13D3 **Front Royal** USA
40C2 **Frosinone** Italy
14A3 **Frostburg** USA
16A2 **Fruita** USA
52C5 **Fuchuan** China
52E4 **Fuding** China
21B2 **Fuerte** *R* Mexico
29A3 **Fuerte Olimpo** Brazil
25E2 **Fuerte Olimpo** Par
70A2 **Fuerteventura** *I* Canary Is
52C2 **Fugu** China
50B2 **Fuhai** China
67G1 **Fujairah** UAE
54C3 **Fuji** Japan
52D4 **Fujian** Province, China
53C2 **Fujin** China
54C3 **Fujinomiya** Japan
53D4 **Fuji-san** *Mt* Japan
54C3 **Fujisawa** Japan
54C3 **Fuji-Yoshida** Japan
54D2 **Fukagawa** Japan
48K5 **Fukang** China
53C4 **Fukuchiyima** Japan
54A4 **Fukue** Japan
54A4 **Fukue** *I* Japan
53D4 **Fukui** Japan
53C5 **Fukuoka** Japan
53E4 **Fukushima** Japan
53C5 **Fukuyama** Japan
11C3 **Fulda** USA
42B2 **Fulda** Germany
42B2 **Fulda** *R* Germany
52B4 **Fuling** China
23L1 **Fullarton** Trinidad
20D4 **Fullerton** USA
12A2 **Fulton** Illinois, USA
12B3 **Fulton** Kentucky, USA
13D2 **Fulton** New York, USA
36C1 **Fumay** France
54D3 **Funabashi** Japan
77G1 **Funafuti** *I* Tuvalu
70A1 **Funchal** Medeira
29D2 **Fundão** Brazil
7M5 **Fundy,B of** Can
73D6 **Funhalouro** Mozam
52B5 **Funing** China
52D3 **Funing** China
71H3 **Funtua** Nig
52D4 **Fuqing** China
73D5 **Furancungo** Mozam
54D2 **Furano** Japan
63D3 **Fürg** Iran
37C1 **Furka** *P* Switz
76D5 **Furneaux Group** *Is* Aust
42C2 **Fürstenwalde** Germany
42C3 **Fürth** Germany
54D2 **Furubira** Japan
53D4 **Furukawa** Japan
7K3 **Fury and Hecla Str** Can
53A3 **Fushun** Liaoning, China
52A4 **Fushun** Sichuan, China
53B3 **Fusong** China
42C3 **Füssen** Germany
52E2 **Fu Xian** China
52E1 **Fuxin** China
52D3 **Fuyang** China
53A2 **Fuyu** China
53C2 **Fuyuan** Heilongjiang, China
52E1 **Fuyuan** Liaoning, China
52A4 **Fuyuan** Yunnan, China
50B2 **Fuyun** China
52D4 **Fuzhou** China
42C1 **Fyn** *I* Den

G

72E3 **Gaalkacyo** Somalia
19C3 **Gabbs** USA
20C1 **Gabbs Valley Range** *Mts* USA
73B5 **Gabela** Angola
71E2 **Gabe's** Tunisia

Gloucester

Greenport

35D6 **Gloucester** Eng
14E1 **Gloucester** USA
14C1 **Gloversville** USA
43F1 **Glubokoye** Belorussia
45E5 **Glukhov** Russian Fed
42D3 **Gmünd** Austria
42C3 **Gmunden** Austria
43D2 **Gniezno** Pol
74B2 **Goabeg** Namibia
62A1 **Goa, Daman and Diu** Union Territory, India
61D2 **Goālpāra** India
71F4 **Goaso** Ghana
72D3 **Goba** Eth
74B1 **Gobabis** Namibia
28C2 **Gobernador Crespo** Arg
28B3 **Gobernador Duval** Arg
52B1 **Gobi** *Desert* China/Mongolia
54C4 **Gobo** Japan
43G1 **Gobza** *R* Russian Fed
74B1 **Gochas** Namibia
62B1 **Godag** India
62C1 **Godāvari** *R* India
5H4 **Godbout** Can
20C2 **Goddard,Mt** USA
4E5 **Goderich** Can
7N3 **Godhavn** Greenland
60C4 **Godhra** India
28B2 **Godoy Cruz** Arg
4C2 **Gods** *R* Can
7J4 **Gods L** Can
7N3 **Godthåb** Greenland
Godwin Austen = K2
14E1 **Goffstown** USA
4E4 **Gogama** Can
66C4 **Gogora** Eth
29C2 **Goiandira** Brazil
29C2 **Goianésia** Brazil
29C2 **Goiânia** Brazil
29B2 **Goiás** Brazil
27J6 **Goiás** State, Brazil
29B3 **Goio-Erê** Brazil
72D3 **Gojab** *R* Eth
41F2 **Gökçeada** *I* Turk
45F8 **Goksu** *R* Turk
64C2 **Göksun** Turk
49M5 **Gol** *R* Mongolia
61D2 **Golāghāt** India
64C2 **Gölbaşi** Turk
48K2 **Gol'chikha** Russian Fed
18C2 **Golconda** USA
14B2 **Gold** USA
18B2 **Gold Beach** USA
75D1 **Gold Coast** Aust
3E3 **Golden** Can
78B2 **Golden B** NZ
18B1 **Goldendale** USA
20A2 **Golden Gate** *Chan* USA
17D4 **Golden Meadow** USA
19C3 **Goldfield** USA
4C3 **Goldpines** Can
20D2 **Gold Point** USA
4A2 **Goldsand L** Can
16C3 **Goldthwaite** USA
42C2 **Goleniów** Pol
20C3 **Goleta** USA
40B2 **Golfe d'Ajaccio** *G* Corse
71E2 **Golfe de Gabes** *G* Tunisia
Golfe de Gascogne = Biscay,Bay of
71E1 **Golfe de Hammamet** *G* Tunisia
37B3 **Golfe de la Napoule** *G* France
40B2 **Golfe de St Florent** *G* Corse
38B2 **Golfe de St-Malo** *B* France
38C3 **Golfe du Lion** *G* France
25B6 **Golfo Corcovado** *G* Chile
39B2 **Golfo de Almeira** *G* Spain
25B6 **Golfo de Ancud** *G* Chile
21D2 **Golfo de Batabano** *G* Cuba
23A2 **Golfo de Batano** *G* Cuba
39A2 **Golfo de Cadiz** *G* Spain
40B3 **Golfo de Cagliari** *G* Sardegna
21A1 **Golfo de California** *G* Mexico
21D4 **Golfo de Chiriqui** *G* Panama
21D3 **Golfo de Fonseca** Honduras
23B2 **Golfo de Guacanayabo** *G* Cuba
26B4 **Golfo de Guayaquil** *G* Ecuador
23B5 **Golfo del Darien** *G* Colombia/Panama
26B2 **Golfo de los Mosquitos** *G* Panama
26A1 **Golfo del Papagaya** *G* Nic
39B2 **Golfo de Mazarrón** *G* Spain
26A2 **Golfo de Nicoya** *G* Costa Rica
40B3 **Golfo de Oristano** *G* Sardegna
21E4 **Golfo de Panamá** *G* Panama
21D3 **Golfo de Papagayo** *G* Costa Rica
23E4 **Golfo de Paria** *G* Ven
26F1 **Golfo de Paris** *G* Ven
25B7 **Golfo de Penas** *G* Chile
38D3 **Golfo de St Florent** Corse
39C1 **Golfo de San Jorge** *G* Spain
21C3 **Golfo de Tehuantepec** *G* Mexico
26C3 **Golfo de Torugas** *G* Colombia
26C2 **Golfo de Uraba** *G* Colombia
39C2 **Golfo de Valencia** *G* Spain
37E2 **Golfo de Venezia** *G* Italy
23C4 **Golfo de Venezuela** *G* Ven
40B2 **Golfo di Genova** *G* Italy
40D3 **Golfo di Policastro** *G* Italy
40D3 **Golfo di Squillace** *G* Italy
40D2 **Golfo di Taranto** *G* Italy
37E2 **Golfo di Trieste** *G* Italy
40C1 **Golfo di Venezia** *G* Italy
21D4 **Golfo Dulce** *G* Costa Rica
25C7 **Golfo San Jorge** *G* Arg
25D6 **Golfo San Matías** *G* Arg
50C3 **Golmud** China
72E3 **Golocha** Eth
10F3 **Golovin B** USA
53F3 **Golovnino** Russian Fed
72C4 **Goma** Zaïre
71J3 **Gombe** Nig
71J3 **Gombi** Nig
43G2 **Gomel** Belorussia
70A2 **Gomera** *I* Canary Is
21B2 **Gómez Palacio** Mexico
49O4 **Gonam** *R* Russian Fed
63D1 **Gonbad-e Kāvūs** Iran
61B2 **Gonda** India
60C4 **Gondal** India
72D2 **Gonder** Eth
61B3 **Gondia** India
64A1 **Gönen** Turk
41F3 **Gonen** *R* Turk
35B5 **Goney** Irish Rep
61D1 **Gongbo'gyamba** China
52A4 **Gongga Shan** *Mt* China
52A2 **Gonghe** China
29D1 **Gongogi** *R* Brazil
71J3 **Gongola** *R* Nig
20B2 **Gonzales** California, USA
17C4 **Gonzales** Texas, USA
22C1 **Gonzalez** Mexico
28C3 **Gonzalez Chaves** Arg
74B3 **Good Hope,C of** S Africa
3D3 **Good Hope Mt** Can
18D2 **Gooding** USA
16B2 **Goodland** USA
10F4 **Goodnews Bay** USA
75C1 **Goodooga** *R* Aust
35E5 **Goole** Eng
75C2 **Goolgowi** Aust
75A3 **Goolwa** Aust
76A4 **Goomalling** Aust
75C2 **Goombalie** Aust
75D1 **Goomer** Aust
75D1 **Goomeri** Aust
75D1 **Goondiwindi** Aust
7N4 **Goose Bay** Can
15D2 **Goose Creek** USA
5J3 **Goose** *R* Can
18B2 **Goose L** USA
62B1 **Gooty** India
76D1 **Goraka** PNG
44K3 **Gora Koyp** *Mt* Russian Fed
49M4 **Gora Munku Sardyk** *Mt* Mongolia/Russian Fed
44K3 **Gora Narodnaya** *Mt* Russian Fed
44L2 **Gora Pay-Yer** *Mt* Russian Fed
44K3 **Gora Telpos-Iz** *Mt* Russian Fed
41D2 **Goražde** Bosnia-Herzegovina, Yugos
10K2 **Gordon** USA
3F2 **Gordon L** Can
13D3 **Gordonsville** USA
72B3 **Goré** Chad
72D3 **Gorē** Eth
78A3 **Gore** NZ
49P4 **Gore Topko** *Mt* Russian Fed
63C1 **Gorgān** Iran
37C3 **Gorgona** *I* Italy
36C1 **Gorinchem** Neth
64E2 **Goris** Armenia
40C1 **Gorizia** Italy
Gorki = Novogorod
44M2 **Gorki** Russian Fed
44G4 **Gor'kovskoye Vodokhranilishche** *Res* Russian Fed
42C2 **Gorlitz** Germany
45F6 **Gorlovka** Ukraine
20C3 **Gorman** USA
41F2 **Gorna Orjahovica** Bulg
50B1 **Gorno-Altaysk** Russian Fed
53E1 **Gorno Lopatina** *Mt* Russian Fed
53D2 **Gorno Medvezh'ya** *Mt* Russian Fed
53C3 **Gorno Oblachnaya** *Mt* Russian Fed
53D2 **Gorno Tardoki Yani** *Mt* Russian Fed
53E2 **Gornozavodsk** Russian Fed
53D1 **Gornyy** Russian Fed
44K3 **Goro Denezhkin Kamen'** *Mt* Russian Fed
44G4 **Gorodets** Russian Fed
43G2 **Gorodnya** Ukraine
43F1 **Gorodok** Belorussia
43E3 **Gorodok** Ukraine
43F3 **Gorodok** Ukraine
51H7 **Goroka** PNG
61B2 **Gorokhpur** India
57D3 **Gorong** *I* Indon
73D5 **Gorongosa** Mozam
57B2 **Gorontalo** Indon
71G3 **Goroubi** *R* Burkina
44L4 **Goro Yurma** *Mt* Russian Fed
29D2 **Gorutuba** *R* Brazil
49M4 **Goryachinsk** Russian Fed
45J7 **Gory Akkyr** *Upland* Turkmenistan
49L2 **Gory Byrranga** *Mts* Russian Fed
43F3 **Goryn'** *R* Ukraine
49L3 **Gory Putorana** *Mts* Russian Fed
43E2 **Góry Świętokrzyskie** *Upland* Pol
32H8 **Gorzów Wielkopolski** Pol
20C2 **Goshen** USA
53E3 **Goshogawara** Japan
45F8 **Gosku** *R* Turk
40D2 **Gospić** Croatia, Yugos
41E2 **Gostivar** Macedonia, Yugos
43D2 **Gostynin** Pol
32G7 **Göteborg** Sweden
72B3 **Gotel** *Mts* Nig
16B1 **Gothenburg** USA
32H7 **Gotland** *I* Sweden
53B5 **Gotō-retto** *I* Japan
32H7 **Gotska Sandön** *I* Sweden
53C4 **Gōtsu** Japan
36C1 **Gouda** Neth
72B2 **Goudoumaria** Niger
xxxH7 **Gough I** Atlantic O
75C2 **Goulburn** Aust
70B3 **Goumbou** Mali
70B3 **Goundam** Mali
72B2 **Gouré** Niger
70B3 **Gourma Rharous** Mali
36A2 **Gournay-en-Bray** France
72B2 **Gouro** Chad
18E1 **Govenlock** Can
51G8 **Gove Pen** Aust
45C6 **Goverla** *Mt* Ukraine
29D2 **Governador Valadares** Brazil
28D1 **Governador Virasoro** Arg
61B3 **Govind Ballabh Paht Sāgar** *L* India
14A1 **Gowanda** USA
60B3 **Gowārān** Afghan
28D1 **Goya** Arg
72C2 **Goz-Beïda** Chad
40C3 **Gozo** *I* Medit S
66C3 **Goz Regeb** Sudan
74C3 **Graaff-Reinet** S Africa
13D1 **Gracefield** Can
37E2 **Grado** Italy
75D1 **Grafton** Aust
11C2 **Grafton** N Dakota, USA
12C3 **Grafton** W Virginia, USA
3D2 **Graham** *R* Can
3B3 **Graham I** Can
3F2 **Graham L** Can
19E4 **Graham,Mt** USA
74D3 **Grahamstown** S Africa
27J5 **Grajaú** Brazil
43E2 **Grajewo** Pol
41E2 **Grámmos** *Mt* Greece/Alb
34D3 **Grampian** Region, Scot
34C3 **Grampian** *Mts* Scot
26D3 **Granada** Colombia
26A1 **Granada** Nic
39B2 **Granada** Spain
5G4 **Granby** Can
16A1 **Granby** USA
70A2 **Gran Canaria** *I* Canary Is
25D3 **Gran Chaco** *Region* Arg
12B2 **Grand** *R* Michigan, USA
17D1 **Grand** *R* Missouri, USA
23Q2 **Grand B** Dominica
9F4 **Grand Bahama** *I* Bahamas
36D3 **Grand Ballon** *Mt* France
7N5 **Grand Bank** Can
xxxF1 **Grand Banks** Atlantic O
71F4 **Grand Bassam** Ivory Coast
37B2 **Grand Bérard** *Mt* France
19D3 **Grand Canyon** USA
19D3 **Grand Canyon Nat Pk** USA
23A3 **Grand Cayman** *I* Caribbean
3F3 **Grand Centre** Can
18C1 **Grand Coulee** USA
28B3 **Grande** *R* Arg
27K6 **Grande** *R* Bahia, Brazil
29C2 **Grande** *R* Minas Gerais/São Paulo, Brazil
3E3 **Grande Cache** Can
5H4 **Grande Cascapédia** Can
37A2 **Grande Chartreuse** Region, France
73E5 **Grande Comore** *I* Comoros
3E2 **Grande Prairie** Can
17C3 **Grande Prairie** USA
72B2 **Grand Erg de Bilma** *Desert Region* Niger
70B2 **Grand erg Occidental** *Mts* Alg
70C2 **Grand erg Oriental** *Mts* Alg
5J4 **Grande Rivière** Can
7L4 **Grande Rivière de la Baleine** *R* Can
18C1 **Grande Ronde** *R* USA
19D4 **Gran Desierto** USA
5H4 **Grande Vallée** Can
7M5 **Grand Falls** New Brunswick, Can
7N5 **Grand Falls** Newfoundland, Can
18C1 **Grand Forks** Can
11C2 **Grand Forks** USA
14C1 **Grand Gorge** USA
12B2 **Grand Haven** USA
16C1 **Grand Island** USA
17E3 **Grand Isle** USA
16A2 **Grand Junction** USA
5K4 **Grand L** Can
17D4 **Grand L** USA
5H5 **Grand Manan I** Can
12A1 **Grand Marais** USA
5G4 **Grand Mère** Can
5K3 **Grandois** Can
39A2 **Grândola** Port
6J4 **Grand Rapids** Can
12B2 **Grand Rapids** Michigan, USA
12A1 **Grand Rapids** Minnesota, USA
37B2 **Grand St Bernard** *P* Italy/Switz
8B2 **Grand Teton** *Mt* USA
18D2 **Grand Teton Nat Pk** USA
16A2 **Grand Valley** USA
36A2 **Grandvilliers** France
21D1 **Grangeburg** USA
18C1 **Grangeville** USA
4B5 **Granite Falls** USA
18E1 **Granite Peak** *Mt* Montana, USA
19D2 **Granite Peak** *Mt* Utah, USA
39C1 **Granollérs** Spain
40B1 **Gran Paradiso** *Mt* Italy
37D1 **Gran Pilastro** *Mt* Austria/Italy
35E5 **Grantham** Eng
20C1 **Grant,Mt** USA
34D3 **Grantown-on-Spey** Scot
16A2 **Grants** USA
18B2 **Grants Pass** USA
38B2 **Granville** France
14D1 **Granville** USA
6H4 **Granville L** Can
29D2 **Grão Mogol** Brazil
20C3 **Grapevine** USA
20D2 **Grapevine Mts** USA
74E1 **Graskop** S Africa
38D3 **Grasse** France
18E1 **Grassrange** USA
19B3 **Grass Valley** USA
5L4 **Grates Pt** Can
25F4 **Gravatai** Brazil
6H5 **Gravelbourg** Can
36B1 **Gravelines** France
73D6 **Gravelotte** S Africa
4F5 **Gravenhurst** Can
18D1 **Grave Peak** *Mt* USA
75D1 **Gravesend** Aust
10M4 **Gravina I** USA
37A1 **Gray** France
10F3 **Grayling** USA
4E5 **Grayling** Michigan, USA
18B1 **Grays Harbor** *B* USA
18D2 **Grays L** USA
12C3 **Grayson** USA
12B3 **Grayville** USA
42D3 **Graz** Austria
23H1 **Great** *R* Jamaica
9F4 **Great Abaco** *I* Bahamas
76B4 **Great Australian Bight** *G* Aust
14E1 **Great B** New Hampshire, USA
14C3 **Great B** New Jersey, USA
21E2 **Great Bahama Bank** Bahamas
78C1 **Great Barrier I** NZ
76D2 **Great Barrier Reef** *Is* Aust
14D1 **Great Barrington** USA
19C2 **Great Basin** USA
10O2 **Great Bear** *R* Can
6F3 **Great Bear L** Can
16C2 **Great Bend** USA
65B3 **Great Bitter L** Egypt
14A3 **Great Cacapon** USA
62E2 **Great Coco I** Burma
76D3 **Great Dividing Range** *Mts* Aust
35E4 **Great Driffield** Eng
14C3 **Great Egg Harbor** *B* USA
79F10 **Greater Antarctic** Region, Ant
23B2 **Greater Antilles** *Is* Caribbean
35E6 **Greater London** County, Eng
35D5 **Greater Manchester** County, Eng
21E2 **Great Exuma** *I* Bahamas
18D1 **Great Falls** USA
74D3 **Great Fish** *R* S Africa
34C3 **Great Glen** *V* Scot
61C2 **Great Himalayan Range** *Mts* Asia
9F4 **Great Inagua** *I* Bahamas
74C3 **Great Karroo** *Mts* S Africa
74D3 **Great Kei** *R* S Africa
75E3 **Great L** Aust
73B6 **Great Namaland** Region, Namibia
62E3 **Great Nicobar** *I* Indian O
35D5 **Great Ormes Head** *C* Wales
14E2 **Great Pt** USA
9F4 **Great Ragged** *I* Bahamas
73D4 **Great Ruaha** *R* Tanz
13E2 **Great Sacandaga L** USA
18D2 **Great Salt L** USA
18D2 **Great Salt Lake Desert** USA
69B2 **Great Sand Sea** Libya/Egypt
76B3 **Great Sandy Desert** Aust
8A2 **Great Sandy Desert** USA
Great Sandy I = Fraser I
10C6 **Great Sitkin, I** USA
6G3 **Great Slave L** Can
15C1 **Great Smoky Mts** USA
15C1 **Great Smoky Mts Nat Pk** USA
3D2 **Great Snow Mt** Can
14D2 **Great South B** USA
74C3 **Great Tafelberg** *Mt* S Africa
76B3 **Great Victoria Desert** Aust
52B2 **Great Wall** China
35F5 **Great Yarmouth** Eng
65C1 **Greco,C** Cyprus
41E3 **Greece** Republic, Europe
13D2 **Greece** USA
16B1 **Greeley** USA
7K1 **Greely Fjord** Can
12B3 **Green** *R* Kentucky, USA
19D3 **Green** *R* Utah, USA
12B1 **Green B** USA
12B2 **Green Bay** USA
48H1 **Green Bell, Ostrov** *I* Russian Fed
12B3 **Greencastle** Indiana, USA
14B3 **Greencastle** Pennsylvania, USA
14C1 **Greene** USA
15C1 **Greeneville** USA
20B2 **Greenfield** California, USA
20C3 **Greenfield** California, USA
14D1 **Greenfield** Massachusetts, USA
12B2 **Greenfield** Wisconsin, USA
5G4 **Greening** Can
3G3 **Green Lake** Can
7O2 **Greenland** Dependency, N Atlantic
xxxH1 **Greenland Basin** Greenland S
79B1 **Greenland S** Greenland
34C4 **Greenock** Scot
14D2 **Greenport** USA

Hamburg Hilo

14A1 **Hamburg** New York, USA
14C2 **Hamburg** Pennsylvania, USA
42B2 **Hamburg** Germany
14D2 **Hamden** USA
32J6 **Hämeeninna** Fin
76A3 **Hamersley Range** *Mts* Aust
53B3 **Hamgyong Sanmaek** *Mts* N Korea
53B3 **Hamhŭng** N Korea
50C2 **Hami** China
65C1 **Hamīdīyah** Syria
15B2 **Hamilton** Alabama, USA
75B3 **Hamilton** Aust
4F5 **Hamilton** Can
18D1 **Hamilton** Montana, USA
14C1 **Hamilton** New York, USA
78C1 **Hamilton** NZ
12C3 **Hamilton** Ohio, USA
34C4 **Hamilton** Scot
20B2 **Hamilton,Mt** USA
32K6 **Hamina** Fin
61B2 **Hamirpur** India
54A3 **Hamju** N Korea
42B2 **Hamm** Germany
69A2 **Hammādāh al Hamra** *Upland* Libya
32H6 **Hammerdal** Sweden
32J4 **Hammerfest** Nor
4F5 **Hammond** Can
12B2 **Hammond** Illinois, USA
17D3 **Hammond** Louisiana, USA
11B2 **Hammond** Montana, USA
14C3 **Hammonton** USA
78B3 **Hampden** NZ
35E6 **Hampshire** County, Eng
17D3 **Hampton** Arkansas, USA
11D3 **Hampton** Iowa, USA
14E1 **Hampton** New Hampshire, USA
13D3 **Hampton** Virginia, USA
63D3 **Hāmūn-e Jaz Mūrīan** *L* Iran
60B3 **Hamun-i-Lora** *Salt L* Pak
63E3 **Hamun-i Mashkel** *Salt Plain* Pak
54A3 **Han** *R* S Korea
20E5 **Hana** Hawaiian Is
20E5 **Hanalei** Hawaiian Is
53E4 **Hanamaki** Japan
36E1 **Hanau** Germany
52C2 **Hancheng** China
52C3 **Hanchuan** China
13D3 **Hancock** Maryland, USA
12B1 **Hancock** Michigan, USA
14C2 **Hancock** New York, USA
54C4 **Handa** Japan
52C2 **Handan** China
72D4 **Handeni** Tanz
20C2 **Hanford** USA
52B2 **Hanggin Qi** China
32J7 **Hangö** Fin
52E3 **Hangzhou** China
52E3 **Hangzhou Wan** *B* China
66D4 **Hanīsh** *I* Yemen
11C2 **Hankinson** USA
19D3 **Hanksville** USA
78B2 **Hanmer Springs** NZ
3F3 **Hanna** Can
4E3 **Hannah B** Can
17D2 **Hannibal** USA
42B2 **Hannover** Germany
32G7 **Hanöbukten** *B* Sweden
55D1 **Hanoi** Viet
74C3 **Hanover** S Africa
14B3 **Hanover** USA
25B8 **Hanover** *I* Chile
52B3 **Han Shui** China
52C3 **Han Shui** *R* China
60D3 **Hānsi** India
50D2 **Hantay** Mongolia
52B3 **Hanzhong** China
61C3 **Hāora** India
32J5 **Haparanda** Sweden
54A3 **Hapch'on** S Korea
28D1 **Hapevi** Brazil
61D2 **Hāpoli** India
5J3 **Happy Valley** Can
64C4 **Haql** S Arabia
66D3 **Harad** Yemen
67E2 **Haradh** S Arabia
72E3 **Hara Fanna** Eth
66D3 **Haraja** S Arabia
54D3 **Haramachi** Japan
72E3 **Harar** Eth
73D5 **Harare** Zim
72C2 **Harazé** Chad
53B2 **Harbin** China
12C2 **Harbor Beach** USA
5K3 **Harbour Deep** Can
5L4 **Harbour Grace** Can
60D4 **Harda** India
32F6 **Hardangerfjord** *Inlet* Nor
11A2 **Hardin** USA
36D2 **Hardt** Region, Germany
75A2 **Hardwicke B** Aust
17D2 **Hardy** USA
5K3 **Hare B** Can
72E3 **Harer** Eth
72E3 **Hargeysa** Somalia
65C3 **Har Hakippa** *Mt* Israel
50C3 **Harhu** *L* China
56B3 **Hari** *R* Indon
67E4 **Harīb** Yemen
54B4 **Harima-nada** *B* Japan
12C3 **Harlan** USA
18E1 **Harlem** USA
42B2 **Harlingen** Neth
17F4 **Harlingen** USA
35F6 **Harlow** Eng
18E1 **Harlowtown** USA
65C2 **Har Meron** *Mt* Israel
18C2 **Harney Basin** USA
18C2 **Harney L** USA
32H6 **Härnösand** Sweden
49L5 **Har Nuur** *L* Mongolia
70B4 **Harper** Lib
20D3 **Harper L** USA
10K3 **Harper,Mt** USA
13D3 **Harpers Ferry** USA
65C3 **Har Ramon** *Mt* Israel
66C1 **Harrāt al 'Uwayrid** *Upland* Region, S Arabia
66D2 **Harrāt Kishb** Region, S Arabia
66D2 **Harrat Nawaāsīf** Region, S Arabia
66D2 **Harrat Rahat** Region, S Arabia
7L4 **Harricana** *R* Can
5J2 **Harrigan,C** Can
15C1 **Harriman** USA
14D1 **Harriman Res** USA
14C3 **Harrington** USA
7N4 **Harrington Harbour** Can
34B3 **Harris** *District* Scot
12B3 **Harrisburg** Illinois, USA
14B2 **Harrisburg** Pennsylvania, USA
74D2 **Harrismith** S Africa
17D2 **Harrison** USA
10H1 **Harrison B** USA
13D3 **Harrisonburg** USA
7N4 **Harrison,C** Can
3D4 **Harrison L** Can
17D2 **Harrisonville** USA
34B3 **Harris,Sound of** *Chan* Scot
12C2 **Harrisville** USA
35E4 **Harrogate** Eng
65C3 **Har Saggi** *Mt* Israel
32H5 **Harstad** Nor
10L3 **Hart** *R* Can
74C2 **Hartbees** *R* S Africa
32F6 **Hårteigen** *Mt* Nor
14D2 **Hartford** Connecticut, USA
12B2 **Hartford** Michigan, USA
11C3 **Hartford** S Dakota, USA
32G6 **Hartkjølen** *Mt* Nor
75A2 **Hart,L** Aust
5H4 **Hartland** Can
35C6 **Hartland Pt** Eng
34E4 **Hartlepool** Eng
16B2 **Hartley** USA
15B2 **Hartselle** USA
17C3 **Hartshorne** USA
15C2 **Hartwell Res** USA
74C2 **Hartz** *R* S Africa
50C2 **Har Us Nuur** *L* Mongolia
63E2 **Harut** *R* Afghan
16A2 **Harvard,Mt** USA
11B2 **Harvey** USA
35F6 **Harwich** Eng
60D3 **Haryāna** State, India
65C3 **Hāsā** Jordan
66B4 **Hasaheisa** Sudan
65C2 **Hāsbaiya** Leb
35E6 **Haselmere** Eng
54C4 **Hashimoto** Japan
63B1 **Hashtpar** Iran
63B1 **Hashtrūd** Iran
67G3 **Hāsik** Oman
16C3 **Haskell** USA
62B2 **Hassan** India
42B2 **Hasselt** Belg
70C2 **Hassi Inifel** Alg
70B2 **Hassi Mdakane** *Well* Alg
70C1 **Hassi Messaoud** Alg
71C2 **Hassi R'mel** Alg
32G4 **Hassleholm** Sweden
75C3 **Hastings** Aust
35F6 **Hastings** Eng
11D3 **Hastings** Minnesota, USA
8D2 **Hastings** Nebraska, USA
78C1 **Hastings** NZ
3H2 **Hatchet L** Can
15B1 **Hatchie** *R* USA
75B2 **Hatfield** Aust
10F2 **Hatham Inlet** USA
60D3 **Hāthras** India
55D2 **Ha Tinh** Viet
75B2 **Hattah** Aust
9F3 **Hatteras,C** USA
17E3 **Hattiesburg** USA
43D3 **Hatvan** Hung
55D3 **Hau Bon** Viet
72E3 **Haud** Region, Eth
32F7 **Haugesund** Nor
78C1 **Hauhungaroa Range** *Mts* NZ
3G2 **Haultain** *R* Can
78B1 **Hauraki G** NZ
78A3 **Hauroko,L** NZ
37C1 **Hausstock** *Mt* Switz
71A2 **Haut Atlas** *Mts* Mor
72C3 **Haute Kotto** Region, CAR
36C2 **Haute-Marne** Department, France
5H4 **Hauterive** Can
36C3 **Haute-Saône** Department, France
36C1 **Hautes Fagnes** *Mts* Belg
37A2 **Hauteville-Lompnès** France
36C1 **Hautmont** Belg
36D3 **Haut-Rhin** Department, France
71B2 **Hauts Plateaux** *Mts* Alg
63E2 **Hauzdar** Iran
60A2 **Hauz Qala** Afghan
12A2 **Havana** USA
Havana = Habana
62B3 **Havankulam** Sri Lanka
19D4 **Havasu L** USA
15D2 **Havelock** USA
78C1 **Havelock North** NZ
35C6 **Haverfordwest** West
14E1 **Haverhill** USA
62B2 **Hāveri** India
14D2 **Haverstraw** USA
42D3 **Havlíčkův Brod** Czech Republic
18E1 **Havre** USA
14B3 **Havre de Grace** USA
7M4 **Havre-St-Pierre** Can
41F2 **Havsa** Turk
20E5 **Hawaii** Hawaiian Is
20E5 **Hawaii Volcanoes Nat Pk** Hawaiian Is
71J3 **Hawal** *R* Nig
78A2 **Hawea,L** NZ
78B1 **Hawera** NZ
20E5 **Hawi** Hawaiian Is
34D4 **Hawick** Scot
78A2 **Hawkdun Range** *Mts* NZ
78C1 **Hawke B** NZ
75D2 **Hawke,C** Aust
75A2 **Hawker** Aust
14C2 **Hawley** USA
55B1 **Hawng Luk** Burma
64D3 **Hawr al Habbaniyah** *L* Iraq
64E3 **Hawr al Hammár** *L* Iraq
20C1 **Hawthorne** USA
75B2 **Hay** Aust
6G3 **Hay** *R* Can
36C2 **Hayange** France
6B3 **Haycock** USA
19D4 **Hayden** Arizona, USA
16A1 **Hayden** Colorado, USA
4C2 **Hayes** *R* Can
7J4 **Hayes** *R* Can
7M2 **Hayes Halvø** *Region* Greenland
10J3 **Hayes,Mt** USA
14B3 **Haymarket** USA
67E3 **Haynin** Yemen
6G3 **Hay River** Can
16C2 **Hays** USA
66D4 **Hays** Yemen
17C2 **Haysville** USA
12A1 **Hayward** Wisconsin, USA
12C3 **Hazard** USA
61C3 **Hazārībāg** India
36B1 **Hazebrouck** France
17D3 **Hazelhurst** USA
6F4 **Hazelton** Can
3C2 **Hazelton Mts** Can
10E3 **Hazen B** USA
7M1 **Hazen L** Can
6G2 **Hazen Str** Can
65C3 **Hazeva** Israel
14C2 **Hazleton** USA
75C3 **Healesville** Aust
10J3 **Healy** USA
xxviiiE7 **Heard I** Indian O
17C3 **Hearne** USA
4E4 **Hearst** Can
11B2 **Heart** *R* USA
17F4 **Hebbronville** USA
52D2 **Hebei** Province, China
75C1 **Hebel** Aust
18D2 **Heber City** USA
18D2 **Hebger L** USA
52C2 **Hebi** China
52C2 **Hebian** China
7M4 **Hebron** Can
65C3 **Hebron** Israel
11B2 **Hebron** N. Dakota, USA
17C1 **Hebron** Nebraska, USA
3B3 **Hecate Str** Can
10M4 **Heceta I** USA
52B5 **Hechi** China
36E2 **Hechingen** Germany
6G2 **Hecla and Griper B** Can
78C2 **Hector,Mt** NZ
32G6 **Hede** Sweden
32H6 **Hedemora** Sweden
18C1 **He Devil Mt** USA
42B2 **Heerenveen** Neth
36C1 **Heerlen** Neth
Hefa = Haifa
52D3 **Hefei** China
52B4 **Hefeng** China
53C2 **Hegang** China
54C3 **Hegura-jima** *I* Japan
61E3 **Heho** Burma
65C3 **Heidan** *R* Jordan
42B2 **Heide** Germany
74C3 **Heidelberg** Cape Province, S Africa
74D2 **Heidelberg** Transvaal, S Africa
42B3 **Heidelberg** Germany
49O4 **Heihe** China
74D2 **Heilbron** S Africa
42B3 **Heilbronn** Germany
42C2 **Heiligenstadt** Germany
53B2 **Heilongjiang** Province, China
53A1 **Heilong Jiang** *R* China
32K6 **Heinola** Fin
52B4 **Hejiang** China
7R3 **Hekla** *Mt* Iceland
55C1 **Hekou** Viet
52A5 **Hekou Yaozou Zizhixian** China
52B2 **Helan** China
52B2 **Helan Shan** *Mt* China
17D3 **Helena** Arkansas, USA
18D1 **Helena** Montana, USA
20D3 **Helendale** USA
57D2 **Helen Reef** *I* Pacific O
34C3 **Helensburgh** Scot
65A3 **Heliopolis** Egypt
63C3 **Helleh** *R* Iran
39B2 **Hellin** Spain
18C1 **Hells Canyon** *R* USA
36D1 **Hellweg** Region, Germany
20B2 **Helm** USA
63E2 **Helmand** *R* Afghan
74B2 **Helmeringhausen** Namibia
36C1 **Helmond** Neth
34D2 **Helmsdale** Scot
53B3 **Helong** China
32G7 **Helsingborg** Sweden
Helsingfors = Helsinki
42C1 **Helsingør** Den
32J6 **Helsinki** Fin
35C6 **Helston** Eng
64B4 **Helwân** Egypt
17C3 **Hempstead** USA
32H7 **Hemse** Sweden
52A3 **Henan** China
52C3 **Henan** Province, China
78B1 **Hen and Chicken Is** NZ
54C2 **Henashi-zaki** *C* Japan
12B3 **Henderson** Kentucky, USA
15D1 **Henderson** N. Carolina, USA
19D3 **Henderson** Nevada, USA
17D3 **Henderson** Texas, USA
15C1 **Hendersonville** N. Carolina, USA
15B1 **Hendersonville** Tennessee, USA
74D3 **Hendrik Verwoerd Dam** S Africa
52E5 **Heng-ch'un** Taiwan
50C4 **Hengduan Shan** *Mts* China
42B2 **Hengelo** Neth
52B2 **Hengshan** China
52D2 **Hengshui** China
55D1 **Heng Xian** China
52C4 **Hengyang** China
55A4 **Henhoaha** Nicobar Is
35E6 **Henley-on-Thames** Eng
14C3 **Henlopen,C** USA
14E1 **Henniker** USA
16C3 **Henrietta** USA
7K4 **Henrietta Maria,C** Can
19D3 **Henrieville** USA
17C2 **Henryetta** USA
7M3 **Henry Kater Pen** Can
74A1 **Henties Bay** Namibia
50D2 **Hentiyn Nuruu** *Mts* Mongolia
55B2 **Henzada** Burma
52B5 **Hepu** China
63E2 **Herat** Afghan
6H4 **Herbert** Can
10D5 **Herbert** *I* USA
78C2 **Herbertville** NZ
36E1 **Herborn** Germany
23A4 **Heredia** Costa Rica
35D5 **Hereford** Eng
16B3 **Hereford** USA
35D5 **Hereford & Worcester** County, Eng
36C1 **Herentals** Belg
37B1 **Héricourt** France
17C2 **Herington** USA
78A3 **Heriot** NZ
37C1 **Herisau** Switz
14C1 **Herkimer** USA
37E1 **Hermagor** Austria
34E1 **Herma Ness** *Pen* Scot
74B3 **Hermanus** S Africa
75C2 **Hermidale** Aust
78B2 **Hermitage** NZ
76D1 **Hermit Is** PNG
Hermon,Mt = Jebel ash Shaykh
21A2 **Hermosillo** Mexico
29B4 **Hernandarias** Par
14B2 **Herndon** USA
36D1 **Herne** Germany
42B1 **Herning** Den
4D4 **Heron Bay** Can
63B1 **Herowābad** Iran
29A4 **Herradura** Arg
28C1 **Herrera** Arg
39B2 **Herrera del Duque** Spain
10L2 **Herschel I** Can
14B2 **Hershey** USA
35E6 **Hertford** County, Eng
65C2 **Herzliyya** Israel
36C1 **Hesbaye** Region, Belg
36A1 **Hesdin** France
52B2 **Heshui** China
20D3 **Hesperia** USA
10M3 **Hess** *R* Can
42B2 **Hessen** State, Germany
20C2 **Hetch Hetchy Res** USA
11B2 **Hettinger** USA
35F5 **Heweth** *Oilfield* N Sea
34D4 **Hexham** Eng
52C5 **He Xian** China
74D2 **Heystekrand** S Africa
52C5 **Heyuan** China
75B3 **Heywood** Aust
52D2 **Heze** China
15E4 **Hialeah** USA
11D2 **Hibbing** USA
15C1 **Hickory** USA
78C1 **Hicks Bay** NZ
75C3 **Hicks,Pt** Aust
17C3 **Hico** USA
54D2 **Hidaka-sammyaku** *Mts* Japan
22C1 **Hidalgo** Mexico
22C1 **Hidalgo** State, Mexico
21B2 **Hidalgo del Parral** Mexico
29C2 **Hidrolândia** Brazil
70A2 **Hierro** *I* Canary Is
54D3 **Higashine** Japan
53B5 **Higashi-suidō** *Str* Japan
18B2 **High Desert** USA
4B2 **High Hill** *R* Can
17D4 **High Island** USA
34C2 **Highland** Region, Scot
20D3 **Highland** USA
20C1 **Highland Peak** *Mt* USA
14C2 **Highland Falls** USA
3E2 **High Level** Can
15C1 **High Point** USA
3E2 **High Prairie** Can
6G4 **High River** Can
3G2 **Highrock L** Can
4A2 **Highrock L** Can
15C3 **High Springs** USA
14C2 **Hightstown** USA
35E6 **High Wycombe** Eng
32J7 **Hiiumaa** *I* Estonia
66C1 **Hijaz** Region, S Arabia
54C4 **Hikigawa** Japan
19C3 **Hiko** USA
54C3 **Hikone** Japan
78B1 **Hikurangi** NZ
8C4 **Hildago del Parral** Mexico
42B2 **Hildesheim** Germany
23Q2 **Hillaby,Mt** Barbados
16C2 **Hill City** USA
42C1 **Hillerød** Den
3G1 **Hill Island L** Can
11C2 **Hillsboro** N. Dakota, USA
14E1 **Hillsboro** New Hampshire, USA
16A3 **Hillsboro** New Mexico, USA
12C3 **Hillsboro** Ohio, USA
18B1 **Hillsboro** Oregon, USA
17C3 **Hillsboro** Texas, USA
4D4 **Hillsport** Can
75C2 **Hillston** Aust
12C3 **Hillsville** USA
34E1 **Hillswick** Scot
20E5 **Hilo** Hawaiian Is

Idah
Is-sur-Tille

71H4 **Idah** Nig
18D2 **Idaho** State, USA
18C2 **Idaho City** USA
18D2 **Idaho Falls** USA
16A2 **Idaho Springs** USA
18B2 **Idanha** USA
36D2 **Idar Oberstein** Germany
69A2 **Idehan Marzūg** *Desert* Libya
69A2 **Idehan Ubari** *Desert* Libya
70C2 **Idelés** Alg
50C2 **Iderlym Gol** *R* Mongolia
66B2 **Idfu** Egypt
41E3 **Ídhi Óros** *Mt* Greece
41E3 **Ídhra** *I* Greece
72B4 **Idiofa** Zaïre
10G3 **Iditarod** *R* USA
64C2 **Idlib** Syria
37E2 **Idrija** Slovenia, Yugos
32K7 **Idritsa** Russian Fed
74D3 **Idutywa** S Africa
36B1 **Ieper** Belg
41F3 **Ierápetra** Greece
37E3 **Iesi** Italy
73D4 **Ifakara** Tanz
51H6 **Ifalik** *I* Pacific
73E6 **Ifanadiana** Madag
71G4 **Ife** Nig
70C3 **Iférouane** Niger
56D2 **Igan** Malay
29C3 **Igaranava** Brazil
48K3 **Igarka** Russian Fed
29A3 **Igatimi** Par
71G4 **Igbetti** Nig
64E2 **Igdir** Iran
32H6 **Iggesund** Sweden
28B2 **Iglesia** Arg
40B3 **Iglesias** Sardegna
7K3 **Igloolik** Can
4C4 **Ignace** Can
64A1 **Iğneada Burun** *Pt* Turk
62E2 **Ignoitijala** Andaman Is
41E3 **Igoumenítsa** Greece
44J4 **Igra** Russian Fed
44L3 **Igrim** Russian Fed
22C2 **Iguala** Mexico
25G2 **Iguape** Brazil
29C3 **Iguatama** Brazil
29B3 **Iguatemi** Brazil
29A3 **Iguatemi** *R* Brazil
27L5 **Iguatu** Brazil
72A4 **Iguéla** Gabon
71H4 **Igumale** Nig
71H4 **Ihiala** Nig
73E6 **Ihosy** Madag
53D4 **Iida** Japan
54C3 **Iide-san** *Mt* Japan
32K6 **Iisalmi** Fin
54B4 **Iizuka** Japan
71G4 **Ijebulgbo** Nig
71G4 **Ijebu Ode** Nig
42B2 **IJsselmeer** *S* Neth
28E1 **Ijuí** Brazil
28D1 **Ijui** *R* Brazil
41F3 **Ikaría** *I* Greece
53E3 **Ikeda** Japan
72C4 **Ikela** Zaïre
71H4 **Ikerre** Nig
41E2 **Ikhtiman** Bulg
54A4 **Iki** *I* Japan
71G4 **Ikire** Nig
10H4 **Ikolik,C** USA
73E5 **Ikopa** *R* Madag
71G4 **Ila** Nig
57F7 **Ilagan** Phil
63B2 **Īlām** Iran
50C1 **Ilanskiy** Russian Fed
37C1 **Ilanz** Switz
71G4 **Ilaro** Nig
3G2 **Île à la Crosse** Can
3G2 **Île à la Crosse,L** Can
68G8 **Ilebo** Zaire
36B2 **Île De France** Region, France
71E2 **Île de Jerba** *I* Tunisia
38B2 **Ile de Noirmoutier** *I* France
38B2 **Ile de Ré** *I* France
77F3 **Île des Pins** *I* Nouvelle Calédonie
13E1 **Ile d'Orleans** Can
38A2 **Ile d'Ouessant** *I* France
38B2 **Ile d'Yeu** *I* France
45K5 **Ilek** *R* Russian Fed
22A1 **Ile María Cleofas** *I* Mexico
22A1 **Ile María Madre** *I* Mexico
22A1 **Ile María Magdalena** Mexico
22A1 **Ile San Juanico** *I* Mexico
77F2 **Îles Bélèp** Nouvelle Calédonie
77E2 **Îles Chesterfield** Nouvelle Calédonie
77H2 **Îles de Horn** *Is* Pacific O
38D3 **Îles d'Hyères** *Is* France
71G4 **Ilesha** Nig
71E2 **Iles Kerkenna** *Is* Tunisia
4B2 **Ilford** Can
35C6 **Ilfracombe** Eng
64B1 **Ilgaz Dağları** *Mts* Turk
73D6 **Ilha Bazaruto** *I* Mozam
29C3 **Ilha Comprida** *I* Brazil
29E1 **Ilha de Boipeba** *I* Brazil
27H3 **Ilha De Maracá** *I* Brazil
27H4 **Ilha de Marajó** *I* Brazil
29C4 **Ilha de São Francisco** *I* Brazil
29C3 **Ilha de São Sebastião** *I* Brazil
29E1 **Ilha de Tinharé** *I* Brazil
27H6 **Ilha do Bananal** *Region* Brazil
29C4 **Ilha do Cardoso** *I* Brazil
25F2 **Ilha Grande, Reprêsa** *Res* Brazil
29D3 **Ilha Grande** *I* Brazil
29B3 **Ilha Grande ou Sete Quedas** *I* Brazil
29C3 **Ilha Santo Amaro** *I* Brazil
29B3 **Ilha Solteira Dam** Brazil
70A2 **Ilhas Selvegens** *I* Atlantic O
27L6 **Ilhéus** Brazil
48J5 **Ili** *R* Kazakhstan
10G4 **Iliamna L** USA
10H3 **Iliamna V** USA
36A2 **Iliers** France
57F9 **Iligan** Phil
49M4 **Ilim** *R* Russian Fed
49M4 **Ilimsk** Russian Fed
53E2 **Il'inskiy** Russian Fed
41E3 **Iliodhrómia** *I* Greece
14C1 **Ilion** USA
57F9 **Illana B** Phil
28A2 **Illapel** Chile
28A2 **Illapel** *R* Chile
70C3 **Illéla** Niger
37D1 **Iller** *R* Germany
22B1 **Illescas** Mexico
77H2 **Îlles Wallis** *Is* Pacific O
12B2 **Illinois** State, USA
12A3 **Illinois** *R* USA
70C2 **Illizi** Alg
44E4 **Il'men, Ozero** *L* Russian Fed
26D7 **Ilo** Peru
57F8 **Iloilo** Phil
32L6 **Ilomantsi** Fin
71G4 **Ilorin** Nig
57C4 **Ilwaki** Indon
43G1 **Il'yino** Russian Fed
53D4 **Imabari** Japan
54C3 **Imalchi** Japan
32L5 **Imandra, Ozero** *L* Russian Fed
54A4 **Imari** Japan
44D3 **Imatra** Fin
25G3 **Imbituba** Brazil
29B4 **Imbitura** Brazil
72E3 **Imi** Eth
54A3 **Imjin** *R* N Korea
18C2 **Imlay** USA
37D1 **Immenstadt** Germany
71H4 **Imo** State, Nig
40C2 **Imola** Italy
27J5 **Imperatriz** Brazil
40B2 **Imperia** Italy
16B1 **Imperial** USA
19C4 **Imperial V** USA
72B3 **Impfondo** Congo
61D3 **Imphāl** India
37D1 **Imst** Austria
10F2 **Imuruk L** USA
54C3 **Ina** Japan
70C2 **In Afahleleh** *Well* Alg
54C4 **Inamba-jima** *I* Japan
70C2 **In Amenas** Alg
32K5 **Inari** Fin
32K5 **Inarijärvi** *L* Fin
54D3 **Inawashiro-ko** *L* Japan
70C2 **In Belbel** Alg
45F7 **Ince Burun** *Pt* Turk
64B2 **Incekum Burun** *Pt* Turk
53B4 **Inch'ŏn** S Korea
70B2 **In Dagouber** *Well* Mali
29C2 **Indaís** *R* Brazil
32H6 **Indals** *R* Sweden
35G5 **Indefatigable** *Gasfield* N Sea
20C2 **Independence** California, USA
11D3 **Independence** Iowa, USA
17C2 **Independence** Kansas, USA
17D2 **Independence** Missouri, USA
18C2 **Independence Mts** USA
56B3 **Inderagiri** *R* Indon
45J6 **Inderborskiy** Kazakhstan
59F4 **India** Federal Republic, Asia
12B2 **Indiana** State, USA
13D2 **Indiana** USA
xxviiiF7 **Indian-Antarctic Basin** Indian O
xxviiiF7 **Indian-Antarctic Ridge** Indian O
12B3 **Indianapolis** USA
Indian Desert = Thar Desert
7N4 **Indian Harbour** Can
3H3 **Indian Head** Can
xxviiiE5 **Indian O**
17D1 **Indianola** Iowa, USA
17D3 **Indianola** Mississippi, USA
29C2 **Indianópolis** Brazil
19C3 **Indian Springs** USA
44H2 **Indiga** Russian Fed
49Q3 **Indigirka** *R* Russian Fed
55D2 **Indo China** Region, S E Asia
51F7 **Indonesia** Republic, S E Asia
60D4 **Indore** India
56C4 **Indramayu** Indon
38C2 **Indre** *R* France
60B3 **Indus** *R* Pak
45E7 **Inebdu** Turk
70C2 **In Ebeggi** *Well* Alg
64B1 **Inebolu** Turk
70C2 **In Ecker** Alg
64A1 **Inegöl** Turk
70D2 **In Ezzane** Alg
74C3 **Infante,C** S Africa
70C3 **Ingal** Niger
12C2 **Ingersoll** Can
76D2 **Ingham** Aust
7M2 **Inglefield Land** *Region* Greenland
78B1 **Inglewood** NZ
75D1 **Inglewood** Queensland, Aust
20C4 **Inglewood** USA
75B3 **Inglewood** Victoria, Aust
32B2 **Ingólfshöfði** *I* Iceland
42C3 **Ingolstadt** Germany
61C3 **Ingrāj Bāzār** India
70C3 **In-Guezzam** *Well* Alg
74E2 **Inhaca** *I* Mozam
74E2 **Inhaca Pen** Mozam
73D6 **Inhambane** Mozam
73D6 **Inharrime** Mozam
29C2 **Inhumas** Brazil
26E3 **Inirida** *R* Colombia
34B4 **Inishowen** District, Irish Rep
75C1 **Injune** Aust
3B2 **Inklin** Can
10M4 **Inklin** *R* Can
10G2 **Inland L** USA
37D1 **Inn** *R* Austria
75B1 **Innamincka** Aust
50D2 **Inner Mongolia** Autonomous Region, China
76D2 **Innisfail** Aust
53E2 **Innokent'yevskiy** Russian Fed
10G3 **Innoko** *R* USA
42C3 **Innsbruck** Austria
72B4 **Inongo** Zaïre
43D2 **Inowrocław** Pol
70C2 **In Salah** Alg
54A3 **Insil** S Korea
44L2 **Inta** Russian Fed
37B1 **Interlaken** Switz
77H3 **International Date Line**
11D2 **International Falls** USA
28C1 **Intiyaco** Arg
37C2 **Intra** Italy
56E3 **Intu** Indon
54D3 **Inubo-saki** *C* Japan
7L4 **Inukjuak** Can
6E3 **Inuvik** Can
6E3 **Inuvik** Region, Can
34C3 **Inveraray** Scot
78A3 **Invercargill** NZ
75D1 **Inverell** Aust
3E3 **Invermere** Can
34C2 **Inverness** Scot
34D3 **Inverurie** Scot
75A3 **Investigator Str** Aust
50B1 **Inya** Russian Fed
49Q3 **Inya** *R* Russian Fed
73D5 **Inyanga** Zim
20D3 **Inyokern** USA
20C2 **Inyo Mts** USA
72B4 **Inzia** *R* Zaïre
41E3 **Ioánnina** Greece
17C2 **Iola** USA
63E1 **Iolotan** Turkmenistan
34B3 **Iona** *I* Scot
73B5 **Iôna Nat Pk** Angola
18C1 **Ione** USA
Ionian Is = Iоnίoi Nísoi
41D3 **Ionian S** Italy/Greece
41E3 **Iоnίoi Nísoi** *Is* Greece
10D2 **Ioniveyem** *R* Russian Fed
41F3 **Íos** *I* Greece
44J3 **Iosser** Russian Fed
11D3 **Iowa** State, USA
11D3 **Iowa** *R* USA
12A2 **Iowa City** USA
11D3 **Iowa Falls** USA
29C2 **Ipameri** Brazil
29D2 **Ipanema** Brazil
45G6 **Ipatovo** Russian Fed
26C3 **Ipiales** Colombia
29E1 **Ipiaú** Brazil
29B4 **Ipiranga** Brazil
55C5 **Ipoh** Malay
27H7 **Iporá** Brazil
41F2 **Ipsala** Turk
75D1 **Ipswich** Aust
35F5 **Ipswich** Eng
14E1 **Ipswich** USA
43G2 **Iput** *R* Russian Fed
29C3 **Iquape** Brazil
25B2 **Iquique** Chile
26D4 **Iquitos** Peru
28E1 **Irai** Brazil
41F3 **Iráklion** Greece
58D2 **Iran** Republic, S W Asia
63E3 **Irānshahr** Iran
22B1 **Irapuato** Mexico
64D3 **Iraq** Republic, S W Asia
29B4 **Irati** Brazil
69A2 **Irā Wan** *Watercourse* Libya
65C2 **Irbid** Jordan
44L4 **Irbit** Russian Fed
27G3 **Ireng** *R* Guyana
53B4 **Iri** S Korea
51G7 **Irian Jaya** Province, Indon
72C2 **Iriba** Chad
57F8 **Iriga** Phil
73D4 **Iringa** Tanz
50F4 **Iriomote** *I* Japan
23A3 **Iriona** Honduras
27H5 **Iriri** *R* Brazil
35C5 **Irish S** Eng/Irish Rep
10H2 **Irkillik** *R* USA
49M4 **Irkutsk** Russian Fed
75A2 **Iron Knob** Aust
12B1 **Iron Mountain** USA
76D2 **Iron Range** Aust
12B1 **Iron River** USA
12C3 **Irontown** USA
12A1 **Ironwood** USA
4E4 **Iroquois Falls** Can
54C4 **Iro-zaki** *C* Japan
61E4 **Irrawaddy** *R* Burma
55A2 **Irrawaddy,Mouths of the** Burma
48H4 **Irtysh** *R* Russian Fed
39B1 **Irun** Spain
34C4 **Irvine** Scot
17C3 **Irving** USA
71H3 **Isa** Nig
57F9 **Isabela** Phil
20C3 **Isabella Res** USA
6H2 **Isachsen** Can
6H2 **Isachsen,C** Can
7Q3 **Ísafjörður** Iceland
53C5 **Isahaya** Japan
72C3 **Isangi** Zaïre
37D1 **Isar** *R* Germany
37D1 **Isarco** *R* Italy
34E1 **Isbister** Scot
37D1 **Ischgl** Austria
40C2 **Ischia** *I* Italy
54C4 **Ise** Japan
37D2 **Iseo** Italy
37A2 **Isère** *R* France
36D1 **Iserlohn** Germany
40C2 **Isernia** Italy
54C4 **Ise-wan** *B* Japan
71G4 **Iseyin** Nig
50F4 **Ishigaki** *I* Japan
53E3 **Ishikari** *R* Japan
53E3 **Ishikari-wan** *B* Japan
48H4 **Ishim** Russian Fed
48H4 **Ishim** *R* Kazakhstan
53E4 **Ishinomaki** Japan
54D3 **Ishioka** Japan
60C1 **Ishkashim** Afghan
12B1 **Ishpeming** USA
48J4 **Isil'kul'** Russian Fed
57B2 **Isimu** Indon
72D3 **Isiolo** Kenya
72C3 **Isiro** Zaïre
64C2 **Iskenderun** Turk
64C2 **Iskenferun Körfezi** *B* Turk
64B1 **İskilip** Turk
48K4 **Iskitim** Russian Fed
41E2 **Iskur** *R* Bulg
10M4 **Iskut** *R* Can/USA
22C2 **Isla** Mexico
28D1 **Isla Apipe Grande** Arg
23C3 **Isla Beata** Dom Rep
28C3 **Isla Bermejo** *I* Arg
23E4 **Isla Blanquilla** Ven
26B2 **Isla Coiba** *I* Panama
8B4 **Isla de Cedros** *I* Mexico
25B6 **Isla de Chiloé** *I* Chile
21D2 **Isla de Cozumel** *I* Mexico
23C3 **Isla de la Gonâve** Cuba
23A2 **Isla de la Juventud** *I* Cuba
28D2 **Isla de las Lechiguanas** *I* Arg
2K8 **Isla del Coco** *I* Costa Rica
21D3 **Isla del Maiz** *I* Caribbean
22C1 **Isla de Lobos** *I* Mexico
25D8 **Isla de los Estados** *I* Arg
24F4 **Isla de Marajó** *I* Brazil
xxixO6 **Isla de Pascua** *I* Pacific O
23A4 **Isla de Providencia** *I* Caribbean
23A4 **Isla de San Andres** *I* Caribbean
25G3 **Isla de Santa Catarina** *I* Brazil
27H2 **Isla du Diable** *I* French Guiana
27M4 **Isla Fernando de Noronha** *I* Brazil
25C8 **Isla Grande de Tierra del Fuego** *I* Arg/Chile
23D4 **Isla la Tortuga** *I* Ven
60C2 **Islamabad** Pak
21A2 **Isla Magdalena** *I* Mexico
23E4 **Isla Margarita** Ven
28A3 **Isla Mocha** Chile
15E4 **Islamorada** USA
4C3 **Island L** Can
75A2 **Island Lg** Aust
18D2 **Island Park** USA
5K4 **Islands,B of** Can
78B1 **Islands,B of** NZ
26B1 **Isla Providencia** *I* Colombia
26B4 **Isla Puná** *I* Ecuador
xxxD6 **Isla San Ambrosia** *I* Pacific O
xxxD6 **Isla San Felix** *I* Pacific O
21A2 **Isla Santa Margarita** *I* Mexico
28A3 **Isla Santa Maria** *I* Chile
Islas Baleares = Balearic Is
70A2 **Islas Canarias** *Is* Atlantic O
39C2 **Islas Columbretes** *Is* Spain
21D3 **Islas de la Bahia** *Is* Honduras
23A4 **Islas del Maíz** *Is* Caribbean
26F1 **Islas de Margarita** *Is* Ven
25C9 **Islas Diego Ramírez** *Is* Chile
26N0 **Islas Galapagos** *Is* Pacific O
26Q0 **Islas Juan Fernandez** *Is* Pacific O
26E1 **Islas los Roques** *Is* Ven
Islas Malvinas = Falkland Is
xxixO4 **Islas Revilla Gigedo** *Is* Pacific O
25C9 **Islas Wollaston** *Is* Chile
70A3 **Isla Tidra** *I* Maur
25B7 **Isla Wellington** *I* Chile
34B4 **Islay** *I* Scot
38C2 **Isle** *R* France
xxviiiE6 **Isle Amsterdam** *I* Indian O
13F2 **Isle au Haut** *I* USA
35E6 **Isle of Wight** *I* Eng
12B1 **Isle Royale** *I* USA
12B1 **Isle Royale Nat Pk** USA
xxviiiE6 **Isle St Paul** *I* Indian O
xxviiiD7 **Ísles Crozet** *I* Indian O
xxixM5 **Ísles de la Société** Pacific O
xxixN6 **Ísles Gambier** *Is* Pacific O
73E5 **Ísles Glorieuses** *Is* Madag
xxviiiE7 **Ísles Kerguelen** *Is* Indian O
77F3 **Ísles Loyauté** *Is* Nouvelle Calédonie
xxixN5 **Ísles Marquises** *Is* Pacific O
xxixM5 **Ísles Tuamotu** *Is* Pacific O
xxixM6 **Ísles Tubai** *Is* Pacific O
20B1 **Isleton** USA
64B3 **Ismâ'ilîya** Egypt
66B1 **Isna** Egypt
73E6 **Isoanala** Madag
73D5 **Isoka** Zambia
37C3 **Isola di Capraia** *I* Italy
40C3 **Isola Egadi** *I* Italy
40C2 **Isola Ponziane** *I* Italy
40C3 **Isole Lipari** *Is* Italy
40D2 **Isoles Tremiti** *Is* Italy
54C3 **Isosaki** Japan
64B2 **Isparta** Turk
65C2 **Israel** Republic, S W Asia
39C2 **Isser** *R* Alg
38C2 **Issoire** France
38C2 **Issoudun** France
37A1 **Is-sur-Tille** France

Johannesburg
Karaman

19C3 Johannesburg USA
7L2 Johan Pen Can
10H2 John R USA
18C2 John Day USA
18B1 John Day R USA
3E2 John d'Or Prairie Can
13D3 John H. Kerr Res USA
16B2 John Martin Res USA
34D2 John O'Groats Scot
17C2 John Redmond Res USA
14A2 Johnsonburg USA
14C1 Johnson City New York, USA
15C1 Johnson City Tennessee, USA
15C2 Johnston USA
23N2 Johnston Pt St Vincent
14C1 Johnstown New York, USA
13D2 Johnstown Pennsylvania, USA
55C5 Johor Bharu Malay
38C2 Joigny France
25G3 Joinville Brazil
36C2 Joinville France
44J5 Jok R Russian Fed
32H5 Jokkmokk Sweden
67E4 Jōl Mts Yemen
45H8 Jolfa Iran
9E2 Joliet USA
7L5 Joliette Can
57F9 Jolo Phil
57F9 Jolo I Phil
59H2 Joma Mt China
43E1 Jonava Lithuania
52A3 Jonê China
9D3 Jonesboro Arkansas, USA
17D3 Jonesboro Louisiana, USA
7K2 Jones Sd Can
43E1 Joniškis Lithuania
32G7 Jönköping Sweden
5G4 Jonquière Can
9D3 Joplin USA
64C3 Jordan Kingdom, S W Asia
11A2 Jordan Montana, USA
14B1 Jordan New York, USA
65C2 Jordan R Israel
18C2 Jordan Valley USA
29B4 Jordão R Brazil
61D2 Jorhāt India
44C2 Jörn Sweden
56D3 Jorong Indon
32F7 Jørpeland Nor
71H4 Jos Nig
28E2 José Batlle y Ordoñez Urug
57F8 Jose Pañganiban Phil
28E2 José Pedro Varela Urug
76B2 Joseph Bonaparte G Aust
19D3 Joseph City USA
34G3 Josephine Oilfield N Sea
71H4 Jos Plat Nig
48B3 Jotunheimen Mt Nor
65C2 Jouai'ya Leb
65C2 Jounié Leb
61D2 Jowal India
72E3 Jowhar Somalia
10M3 Joy,Mt Can
27K5 Juàjeiro Brazil
22B1 Juan Aldama Mexico
6F5 Juan de Fuca,Str of USA/Can
73E5 Juan de Nova I Mozam Chan
28D3 Juárez Arg
27L5 Juazeiro do Norte Brazil
72D3 Juba Sudan
72E3 Juba R Somalia
65C1 Jubail Leb
64D3 Jubbah S Arabia
39B2 Jucar R Spain
22C2 Juchatengo Mexico
22B1 Juchipila R Mexico
22C2 Juchitán Mexico
22B1 Juchitlan Mexico
42C3 Judenburg Austria
26D7 Juilaca Peru
52C4 Juiling Shan Hills China
27K8 Juiz de Fora Brazil
25C2 Jujuy State, Arg
16B1 Julesburg USA
26E7 Juli Peru
27G3 Julianatop Mt Suriname
7O3 Julianehåb Greenland
36D1 Jülich Germany
37E1 Julijske Alpen Mts Slovenia, Yugos
28E1 Júlio de Castilhos Brazil
61B2 Jumla Nepal
65C3 Jum Suwwāna Mt Jordan
60C4 Jūnāgadh India
52D2 Junan China
16C3 Junction Texas, USA
19D3 Junction Utah, USA
8D3 Junction City USA
25G2 Jundiaí Brazil
6E4 Juneau USA
76D4 Junee Aust
20C2 June Lake USA
40B1 Jungfrau Mt Switz
14B2 Juniata R USA
25D4 Junín Arg
28A3 Junin de los Andes Arg
20B2 Junipero Serra Peak Mt USA
52A4 Junlian China
25G2 Juquiá Brazil
72C3 Jur R Sudan
34C4 Jura I Scot
38D2 Jura Mts France
34C3 Jura,Sound of Chan Scot
65C3 Jurf ed Darāwīsh Jordan
48K4 Jurga Russian Fed
44C4 Jūrmala Latvia
26E4 Juruá R Brazil
27G6 Juruena R Brazil
53B2 Jusheng China
65D1 Jūsīyah Syria
28B2 Justo Daract Arg
26E4 Jutai R Brazil
21D3 Juticalpa Honduras
Jutland = Jylland
63D2 Jūymand Iran
42B1 Jylland Pen Den
32K6 Jyväskyla Fin

K

59F2 K2 Mt China/India
71H3 Ka R Nig
63D1 Kaakhka Turkmenistan
74E2 Kaapmuiden S Africa
76B1 Kabaena I Indon
70A4 Kabala Sierra Leone
72D4 Kabale Rwanda
72C4 Kabalo Zaïre
72C4 Kabambare Zaïre
72D3 Kabarole Uganda
71H4 Kabba Nig
76B1 Kabia I Indon
12C1 Kabinakagami L Can
4E3 Kabinakagami R Can
72C4 Kabinda Zaïre
65C1 Kabīr R Syria
63B2 Kabir Kuh Mts Iran
73C5 Kabompo Zambia
73C5 Kabompo R Zambia
73C4 Kabongo Zaïre
60B2 Kabul Afghan
57C2 Kaburuang I Indon
66B3 Kabushiya Sudan
60B4 Kachchh,G of India
44K4 Kachkanar Russian Fed
49M4 Kachug Russian Fed
55B3 Kadan Burma
56E3 Kadapongan I Indon
77G2 Kadavu I Fiji
60C4 Kadi India
75A2 Kadina Aust
64B2 Kadınhanı Turk
62B2 Kadiri India
45F6 Kadiyevka Ukraine
11B3 Kadoka USA
73C5 Kadoma Zim
72C2 Kadugli Sudan
71H3 Kaduna Nig
71H3 Kaduna State, Nig
71H3 Kaduna R Nig
62B2 Kadūr India
61E2 Kadusam Mt China
44K3 Kadzherom Russian Fed
54A3 Kaechon N Korea
70A3 Kaédi Maur
20E5 Kaena Pt Hawaiian Is
53B4 Kaesŏng N Korea
71H4 Kafanchan Nig
70A3 Kaffrine Sen
65D1 Kafr Behum Syria
65A3 Kafr Sa'd Egypt
65A3 Kafr Saqv Egypt
65D1 Kafrūn Bashūr Syria
73C5 Kafue Zambia
73C5 Kafue R Zambia
73C5 Kafue Nat Pk Zambia
53D4 Kaga Japan
10C6 Kagalaska I USA
48H6 Kagan Uzbekistan
45K7 Kağizman Turk
66B4 Kagmar Sudan
53C5 Kagoshima Japan
43F3 Kagul Moldova
63D1 Kāhak Iran
72D4 Kahama Tanz
60B3 Kahan Pak
56D3 Kahayan R Indon
73B4 Kahemba Zaïre
36E1 Kahler Asten Mt Germany
63D3 Kahnūj Iran
12A2 Kahoka USA
20E5 Kahoolawe I Hawaiian Is
64C2 Kahramanmaraş Turk
20E5 Kahuku Pt Hawaiian Is
20E5 Kahului Hawaiian Is
78B2 Kaiapoi NZ
19D3 Kaibab Plat USA
27G2 Kaieteur Fall Guyana
52C3 Kaifeng China
78B1 Kaikohe NZ
77G5 Kaikoura NZ
78B2 Kaikoura Pen NZ
78B2 Kaikoura Range Mts NZ
52B4 Kaili China
20E5 Kailua Hawaiian Is
51G7 Kaimana Indon
54C4 Kainan Japan
71G3 Kainji Res Nig
78B1 Kaipara Harbour B NZ
52C5 Kaiping China
71E1 Kairouan Tunisia
20C2 Kaiser Peak Mt USA
38D2 Kaiserslautern Germany
42B3 Kaiserslautern Germany
53B3 Kaishantun China
43E2 Kaisiadorys Lithuania
78B1 Kaitaia NZ
78A3 Kaitangata NZ
60D3 Kaithal India
20E5 Kaiwi Chan Hawaiian Is
52B3 Kai Xian China
52A5 Kaiyuan Liaoning, China
53A3 Kaiyuan Yunnan, China
10G3 Kaiyuh Mts USA
32K6 Kajaani Fin
60B2 Kajaki Afghan
56F7 Kajang Malay
72D4 Kajiado Kenya
60B2 Kajrān Afghan
72D2 Kaka Sudan
12B1 Kakabeka Falls Can
72D3 Kakamega Kenya
54B4 Kake Japan
10M4 Kake USA
10H4 Kakhonak USA
45E6 Kakhovskoye Vodokhranilishche Res Ukraine
63C3 Kākī Iran
62C1 Kākināda India
3E1 Kakiska L Can
54B4 Kakogawa Japan
10K1 Kaktovik USA
54D3 Kakuda Japan
71D1 Kalaa El Khasba Tunisia
Kalaallit Nunaat = Greenland
57B4 Kalabahi Indon
41E3 Kalabáka Greece
56E2 Kalabakan Malay
73C5 Kalabo Zambia
45G5 Kalach Russian Fed
45G6 Kalach-na-Donu Russian Fed
61D3 Kaladan R Burma
20E5 Ka Lae C Hawaiian Is
73C6 Kalahari Desert Botswana
74C2 Kalahari Gemsbok Nat Pk S Africa
63E1 Kalai-Mor Turkmenistan
44C3 Kalajoki Fin
49N4 Kalakan Russian Fed
56A2 Kalakepen Indon
60C1 Kalam Pak
41E3 Kalámai Greece
9E2 Kalamazoo USA
57B4 Kalao I Indon
57B4 Kalaotoa I Indon
20E5 Kalapana Hawaiian Is
43F3 Kalarsh Moldova
60B3 Kalat Pak
20E5 Kalaupapa Hawaiian Is
67G2 Kalbān Oman
64B1 Kalecik Turk
57B4 Kaledupa I Indon
56E3 Kalembau I Indon
72C4 Kalémié Zaïre
44E2 Kalevala Russian Fed
61D3 Kalewa Burma
10H3 Kalgin I USA
76B4 Kalgoorlie Aust
61B2 Kali R India
56C4 Kalianda Indon
57F8 Kalibo Phil
72C4 Kalima Zaïre
56D3 Kalimantan Province, Indon
41F3 Kálimnos I Greece
61C2 Kālimpang India
44F4 Kalinin Russian Fed
32J8 Kaliningrad Russian Fed
45D5 Kalinkovichi Belorussia
43F3 Kalinovka Ukraine
8B2 Kalispell USA
43D2 Kalisz Pol
72D4 Kaliua Tanz
32J5 Kalix R Sweden
73B6 Kalkfeld Namibia
74C1 Kalkfontein Botswana
74B1 Kalkrand Namibia
75A1 Kallakoopah R Aust
32K6 Kallávesi L Fin
41F3 Kallonis Kólpos B Greece
32H7 Kalmar Sweden
45H6 Kalmytskaya Respublika, Russian Fed
57B3 Kalolio Indon
73C5 Kalomo Zambia
12A2 Kalona USA
3C3 Kalone Peak Mt Can
62A2 Kalpeni I India
60D3 Kālpi India
10F3 Kalskag USA
10G3 Kaltag USA
44F5 Kaluga Russian Fed
32G7 Kalundborg Den
43E3 Kalush Ukraine
62A1 Kalyān India
62B2 Kalyandurg India
44F4 Kalyazin Russian Fed
71J4 Kam R Nig
44J3 Kama R Russian Fed
53E4 Kamaishi Japan
60C2 Kamalia Pak
78C1 Kamanawa Mts NZ
73B5 Kamanjab Namibia
49O4 Kamara China
66D3 Kamarān I Yemen
5J2 Kamarsuk Can
60D2 Kamat Mt India
62B3 Kamban India
44J4 Kambarka Russian Fed
70A4 Kambia Sierra Leone
49S4 Kamchatka Pen Russian Fed
43F3 Kamenets Podolskiy Ukraine
44G5 Kamenka Russian Fed
48K4 Kamen-na-Obi Russian Fed
53C3 Kamen' Rybolov Russian Fed
49S3 Kamenskoya Russian Fed
44L4 Kamensk-Ural'skiy Russian Fed
74B3 Kamieskroon S Africa
6H3 Kamilukuak L Can
73C4 Kamina Zaïre
7J3 Kaminak L Can
54D3 Kaminoyama Japan
6F4 Kamloops Can
64E1 Kamo Armenia
54D3 Kamogawa Japan
72D3 Kampala Uganda
55C5 Kampar Malay
56B2 Kampar R Indon
42B2 Kampen Neth
55B2 Kamphaeng Phet Thai
55C3 Kampot Camb
3H3 Kamsack Can
63E3 Kamsaptar Iran
44K4 Kamskoye Vodokhranilishche Res Russian Fed
60D4 Kāmthi India
3H2 Kamuchawie L Can
45H5 Kamyshin Russian Fed
44L4 Kamyshlov Russian Fed
7L4 Kanaaupscow R Can
19D3 Kanab USA
10C6 Kanaga I USA
37E1 Kanal Slovenia, Yugos
72C4 Kananga Zaïre
44H4 Kanash Russian Fed
54C3 Kanayama Japan
53D4 Kanazawa Japan
62B2 Kānchipuram India
60B2 Kandahar Afghan
5J3 Kanairiktok R Can
44E2 Kandalaksha Russian Fed
32L5 Kandalakshskaya Guba B Russian Fed
71G4 Kandé Togo
36D2 Kandel Mt Germany
71G3 Kandi Benin
75C2 Kandos Aust
62C3 Kandy Sri Lanka
13D2 Kane USA
7L1 Kane Basin B Can
72B2 Kanem Desert Region Chad
20E5 Kaneohe Hawaiian Is
44F2 Kanevka Russian Fed
37E2 Kanfanar Slovenia, Yugos
74C1 Kang Botswana
70B3 Kangaba Mali
64C2 Kangal Turk
7N3 Kangâmiut Greenland
63C3 Kangān Iran
55C4 Kangar Malay
76C4 Kangaroo I Aust
7N3 Kangâtsiaq Greenland
63B2 Kangavar Iran
52C1 Kangbao China
59G3 Kangchenjunga Mt Nepal
52A4 Kangding China
7P3 Kangerdlugssuaq B Greenland
7P3 Kangerdlugssuatsaiq B Greenland
72D3 Kangetet Kenya
53B3 Kanggye N Korea
7M4 Kangiqsualujjuaq Can
7L3 Kangiqsujuak Can
7L3 Kangirsuk Can
53B4 Kangnŭng S Korea
72B3 Kango Gabon
50C4 Kanĝto Mt China
52B3 Kang Xian China
55D4 Kanh Hung Viet
73C4 Kaniama Zaïre
62B1 Kani Giri India
44G2 Kanin, Poluostrov Pen Russian Fed
32J6 Kankaanpää Fin
12B2 Kankakee USA
12B2 Kankakee R USA
70B3 Kankan Guinea
61B3 Kānker India
15C1 Kannapolis USA
62B3 Kanniyākuman India
Kannur = Cannanore
71H3 Kano Nig
71H3 Kano State, Nig
71H3 Kano R Nig
16B2 Kanorado USA
53C5 Kanoya Japan
61B2 Kānpur India
8D3 Kansas State, USA
17C2 Kansas R USA
9D3 Kansas City USA
52D5 Kanshi China
49L4 Kansk Russian Fed
54A3 Kansŏng S Korea
71G3 Kantchari Burkina
61C3 Kanthi India
10H3 Kantishna USA
10H3 Kantishna R USA
74D1 Kanye Botswana
50E4 Kao-hsiung Taiwan
73B5 Kaoka Veld Plain Namibia
70A3 Kaolack Sen
73C5 Kaoma Zambia
20E5 Kapaa Hawaiian Is
20E5 Kapaau Hawaiian Is
73C4 Kapanga Zaïre
7O3 Kap Cort Adelaer C Greenland
7Q3 Kap Dalton C Greenland
32H7 Kapellskär Sweden
7O4 Kap Farvel C Greenland
7P3 Kap Gustav Holm C Greenland
73C5 Kapiri Zambia
4E3 Kapiskau R Can
56D2 Kapit Malay
17D3 Kaplan USA
42C3 Kaplice Czech Republic
55B4 Kapoe Thai
73C4 Kapona Zaïre
41D1 Kaposvár Hung
7L2 Kap Parry C Greenland
7Q3 Kap Ravn C Greenland
54A2 Kapsan N Korea
56C3 Kapuas R Indon
75A2 Kapunda Aust
60D2 Kapurthala India
7K5 Kapuskasing Can
12C1 Kapuskasing R Can
75D2 Kaputar Mt Aust
45H8 Kapydzhik Mt Armenia
54A3 Kapyŏng S Korea
7M2 Kap York C Greenland
71G4 Kara Togo
71G4 Kara R Togo
64B1 Karabük Turk
41F2 Karacabey Turk
60B4 Karachi Pak
62A1 Karād India
45F7 Kara Daglari Mt Turk
45D7 Karadeniz Boğazi Sd Turk
50E1 Karaftit Russian Fed
48J5 Karaganda Kazakhstan
48J5 Karagayly Kazakhstan
49S4 Karaginskiy, Ostrov I Russian Fed
62B2 Kāraikāl India
63C1 Karaj Iran
64C3 Karak Jordan
56F7 Karak Malay
48G5 Kara Kalpakskaya Respublika, Uzbekistan
60D1 Karakax He R China
57C2 Karakelong I Indon
60D1 Karakoram Mts India
60D1 Karakoram P India/China
70A3 Karakoro R Maur/Sen
63E1 Karakumskiy Kanal Turkmenistan
48G6 Karakumy Desert Russian Fed
65C3 Karama Jordan
57A3 Karama R Indon
45E8 Karaman Turk

Khatanga
Komsomolets, Ostrov

49M2 **Khatanga** Russian Fed
49N2 **Khatangskiy Zaliv** *Estuary* Russian Fed
49T3 **Khatyrka** Russian Fed
55B3 **Khawsa** Burma
66C1 **Khaybar** S Arabia
66B2 **Khazzan an-Nasr** *L* Egypt
55C2 **Khe Bo** Viet
60C4 **Khed Brahma** India
39C2 **Khemis** Alg
71A2 **Khemisset** Mor
71D1 **Khenchela** Alg
71A2 **Khenifra** Mor
39D2 **Kherrata** Alg
45E6 **Kherson** Ukraine
49N4 **Khilok** Russian Fed
41F3 **Khíos** Greece
41F3 **Khíos** *I* Greece
45D6 **Khmel'nitskiy** Ukraine
43E3 **Khodorov** Ukraine
59E1 **Khodzhent** Taji
60B1 **Kholm** Afghan
43G1 **Kholm** Russian Fed
53E2 **Kholmsk** Russian Fed
74B1 **Khomas Hochland, Mts** Namibia
55D3 **Khong** Laos
63C3 **Khonj** Iran
53C2 **Khor** Russian Fed
53D2 **Khor** *R* Russian Fed
63B2 **Khoramshahr** Iran
67F2 **Khōr Duwayhin** *B* UAE
60C1 **Khorog** Tajikistan
63B2 **Khorramābad** Iran
63D2 **Khosf** Iran
60B2 **Khost** Pak
45D6 **Khotin** Ukraine
10G3 **Khotol** *Mt* USA
71A2 **Khouribga** Mor
45D5 **Khoyniki** Belorussia
49Q3 **Khrebet Cherskogo** *Mts* Russian Fed
53B1 **Khrebet Dzhagdy** *Mts* Russian Fed
49P4 **Khrebet Dzhugdzhur** *Mts* Russian Fed
10C2 **Khrebet Iskamen** *Mts* Russian Fed
49O3 **Khrebet Orulgan** *Mts* Russian Fed
44L2 **Khrebet Pay-khoy** *Mts* Russian Fed
53D2 **Khrebet Sikhote Alin'** *Mts* Russian Fed
59G1 **Khrebet Tarbagatay** *Mts* Kazakhstan
49O4 **Khrebet Tukuringra** *Mts* Russian Fed
53C1 **Khrebet Turana** *Upland* Russian Fed
65B1 **Khrysokhou B** Cyprus
44L3 **Khulga** *R* Russian Fed
61C3 **Khulna** Bang
60D1 **Khunjerab** *P* China/India
63C2 **Khunsar** Iran
67E1 **Khurays** S Arabia
61C3 **Khurda** India
60D3 **Khurja** India
67G3 **Khūryan Mūryān** *Is* Oman
60C2 **Khushab** Pak
65C2 **Khushnīyah** Syria
43E3 **Khust** Ukraine
72C2 **Khuwei** Sudan
60B3 **Khuzdar** Pak
63E2 **Khvāf** Iran
45H5 **Khvalynsk** Russian Fed
63D2 **Khvor** Iran
63C3 **Khvormūj** Iran
45G8 **Khvoy** Iran
60C1 **Khwaja Muhammad** *Mts* Afghan
60C2 **Khyber P** Afghan/Pak
73C4 **Kiambi** Zaïre
17C3 **Kiamichi** *R* USA
10F2 **Kiana** USA
72B4 **Kibangou** Congo
72D4 **Kibaya** Tanz
72C4 **Kibombo** Zaïre
72D4 **Kibondo** Tanz
72D4 **Kibungu** Rwanda
41E2 **Kičevo** Macedonia, Yugos
6G4 **Kicking Horse P** Can
70C3 **Kidal** Mali
35D5 **Kidderminster** Eng
70A3 **Kidira** Sen
78C1 **Kidnappers,C** NZ
42C2 **Kiel** Germany
43E2 **Kielce** Pol
42C2 **Kieler Bucht** *B* Germany
Kiev = Kiyev
58E2 **Kifab** Uzbekistan
70A3 **Kiffa** Maur
68H8 **Kigali** Rwanda
5J2 **Kiglapatt,C** Can
10E3 **Kigluaik Mts** USA
72C4 **Kigoma** Tanz
20E5 **Kiholo** Hawaiian Is
54C4 **Kii-sanchi** *Mts* Japan
53C5 **Kii-suido** *B* Japan
49R4 **Kikhchik** Russian Fed
41E1 **Kikinda** Serbia, Yugos
Kikládhes = Cyclades
76D1 **Kikon** PNG
54D2 **Kikonai** Japan
51H7 **Kikori** PNG
72B4 **Kikwit** Zaïre
20E5 **Kilauea Crater** *Mt* Hawaiian Is
6C3 **Kilbuck Mts** USA
53B3 **Kilchu** N Korea
75D1 **Kilcoy** Aust
35B5 **Kildane** County, Irish Rep
35B5 **Kildare** Irish Rep
17D3 **Kilgore** USA
72E4 **Kilifi** Kenya
72D4 **Kilimanjaro** *Mt* Tanz
73D4 **Kilindoni** Tanz
64C2 **Kilis** Turk
43F3 **Kiliya** Ukraine
35B5 **Kilkenny** County, Irish Rep
35B5 **Kilkenny** Irish Rep
41E2 **Kilkís** Greece
75D1 **Killarney** Aust
33B3 **Killarney** Irish Rep
17C3 **Killeen** USA
10H2 **Killik** *R* USA
34C3 **Killin** Scot
5J1 **Killinek I** Can
41E3 **Killíni** *Mt* Greece
34C4 **Kilmarnock** Scot
44J4 **Kil'mez** Russian Fed
73D4 **Kilosa** Tanz
33B3 **Kilrush** Irish Rep
71J4 **Kilunga** *R* Nig
73C4 **Kilwa** Zaïre
73D4 **Kilwa Kisiwani** Tanz
73D4 **Kilwa Kivinje** Tanz
71J4 **Kim** *R* Cam
75A2 **Kimba** Aust
16B1 **Kimball** USA
10K3 **Kimball,Mt** USA
3E4 **Kimberley** Can
74C2 **Kimberley** S Africa
76B2 **Kimberley Plat** Aust
53B3 **Kimch'aek** N Korea
53B4 **Kimch'ŏn** S Korea
54A3 **Kimhae** S Korea
41E3 **Kími** Greece
54A3 **Kimje** S Korea
44F4 **Kimry** Russian Fed
54A3 **Kimwha** N Korea
56E1 **Kinabalu** *Mt* Malay
56E1 **Kinabatangan** *R* Malay
4E5 **Kincardine** Can
3C2 **Kincolith** Can
17D3 **Kinder** USA
3G3 **Kindersley** Can
70A3 **Kindia** Guinea
72C4 **Kindu** Zaïre
44J5 **Kinel'** Russian Fed
44G4 **Kineshma** Russian Fed
75D1 **Kingaroy** Aust
19B3 **King City** USA
6F4 **Kingcome Inlet** Can
10F4 **King Cove** USA
17C2 **Kingfisher** USA
7L4 **King George Is** Can
76D5 **King I** Aust
3C3 **King I** Can
44C4 **Kingissepp** Estonia
76B2 **King Leopold Range** *Mts* Aust
8B3 **Kingman** USA
72C4 **Kingombe** Zaïre
75A2 **Kingoonya** Aust
20C2 **Kingsburg** USA
19C3 **Kings Canyon Nat Pk** USA
75A3 **Kingscote** Aust
76B2 **King Sd** Aust
12B1 **Kingsford** USA
15C2 **Kingsland** USA
35F5 **King's Lynn** Eng
77G1 **Kingsmill Group** *Is* Kiribati
14D2 **Kings Park** USA
8B2 **Kings Peak** *Mt* USA
15C1 **Kingsport** USA
76C4 **Kingston** Aust
7L5 **Kingston** Can
21E3 **Kingston** Jamaica
13E2 **Kingston** New York, USA
78A3 **Kingston** NZ
14C2 **Kingston** Pennsylvania, USA
23E4 **Kingstown** St Vincent
8D4 **Kingsville** USA
5J2 **Kingurutik** *R* Can
34C3 **Kingussie** Scot
6J3 **King William I** Can
74D3 **King William's Town** S Africa
72B4 **Kinkala** Congo
32G7 **Kinna** Sweden
34D3 **Kinnairds Head** *Pt* Scot
54C3 **Kinomoto** Japan
34D3 **Kinross** Scot
72B4 **Kinshasa** Zaïre
16C2 **Kinsley** USA
15D1 **Kinston** USA
56E3 **Kintap** Indon
34C4 **Kintyre** *Pen* Scot
3E2 **Kinuso** Can
72D3 **Kinyeti** *Mt* Sudan
36E1 **Kinzig** *R* Germany
3H2 **Kipahigan L** Can
41E3 **Kiparissía** Greece
41E3 **Kiparissiakós Kólpos** *G* Greece
13D1 **Kipawa,L** Can
73D4 **Kipili** Tanz
10F4 **Kipnuk** USA
35B5 **Kippure** *Mt* Irish Rep
73C5 **Kipushi** Zaïre
36E2 **Kirchheim** Germany
49M4 **Kirensk** Russian Fed
48J5 **Kirgizia**
59F1 **Kirgizskiy Khrebet** *Mts* Kirgizia
72B4 **Kiri** Zaïre
77G1 **Kiribati** *Is* Pacific O
64B2 **Kırıkkale** Turk
44E4 **Kirishi** Russian Fed
60B3 **Kirithar Range** *Mts* Pak
41F3 **Kirkağaç** Turk
45H8 **Kirk Bulāg Dāgh** *Mt* Iran
35D4 **Kirkby** Eng
34D3 **Kirkcaldy** Scot
34C4 **Kirkcudbright** Scot
32K5 **Kirkenes** Nor
7K5 **Kirkland Lake** Can
64A1 **Kırklareli** Turk
79E **Kirkpatrick,Mt** Ant
9D2 **Kirksville** USA
64D2 **Kirkūk** Iraq
34D2 **Kirkwall** Scot
17D2 **Kirkwood** USA
74D3 **Kirkwood** *R* S Africa
44E5 **Kirov** Russian Fed
44H4 **Kirov** Russian Fed
45H7 **Kirovabad** Azerbaijan
64D1 **Kirovakan** Armenia
44K4 **Kirovgrad** Russian Fed
45E6 **Kirovograd** Ukraine
44E2 **Kirovsk** Russian Fed
49R4 **Kirovskiy** Kamchatka, Russian Fed
53C2 **Kirovskiy** Primorskiykray, Russian Fed
44J4 **Kirs** Russian Fed
64B2 **Kirşehir** Turk
42C2 **Kiruna** Sweden
54C3 **Kiryū** Japan
72C3 **Kisangani** Zaïre
57C4 **Kisar** *I* Indon
56A2 **Kisaran** Indon
54C3 **Kisarazu** Japan
61C2 **Kishanganj** India
60C3 **Kishangarh** India
43F3 **Kishinev** Moldova
54C4 **Kishiwada** Japan
72D4 **Kisii** Kenya
73D4 **Kisiju** Tanz
10B6 **Kiska** *I* USA
4B3 **Kiskitto L** Can
43D3 **Kiskunhalas** Hung
45G7 **Kislovodsk** Russian Fed
72E4 **Kismaayo** Somalia
54C3 **Kiso-sammyaku** *Mts* Japan
70B4 **Kissidougou** Guinea
15C3 **Kissimmee,L** USA
3H2 **Kississing L** Can
72D4 **Kisumu** Kenya
43E3 **Kisvárda** Hung
70B3 **Kita** Mali
48H6 **Kitab** Uzbekistan
54D3 **Kitakami** Japan
54D3 **Kitakami** *R* Japan
54D3 **Kitakata** Japan
53C5 **Kita-Kyūshū** Japan
72D3 **Kitale** Kenya
50H4 **Kitalo** *I* Japan
53E3 **Kitami** Japan
54D2 **Kitami-Esashi** Japan
16B2 **Kit Carson** USA
7K5 **Kitchener** Can
4F3 **Kitchigama** *R* Can
72D3 **Kitgum** Uganda
41E3 **Kíthira** *I* Greece
41E3 **Kíthnos** *I* Greece
65B1 **Kiti,C** Cyprus
6G2 **Kitikmeot** Region, Can
6F4 **Kitimat** Can
32K5 **Kitnen** *R* Fin
54B4 **Kitsuki** Japan
13D2 **Kittanning** USA
13E2 **Kittery** USA
32J5 **Kittilä** Fin
15D1 **Kitty Hawk** USA
73D4 **Kitunda** Tanz
10N4 **Kitwanga** Can
73C5 **Kitwe** Zambia
42C3 **Kitzbühel** Austria
37E1 **Kitzbühler Alpen** *Mts* Austria
42C3 **Kitzingen** Germany
72C4 **Kiumbi** Zaïre
10F2 **Kivalina** USA
43F2 **Kivercy** Ukraine
72C4 **Kivu,L** Zaïre/Rwanda
6B3 **Kiwalik** USA
45E5 **Kiyev** Ukraine
43G2 **Kiyevskoye Vodokhranilishche** *Res* Ukraine
44K4 **Kizel** Russian Fed
44G3 **Kizema** Russian Fed
64C2 **Kizil** *R* Turk
58D2 **Kizyl-Arvat** Turkmenistan
45J8 **Kizyl-Atrek** Turkmenistan
42C2 **Kladno** Czech Republic
42C3 **Klagenfurt** Austria
44C4 **Klaipēda** Lithuania
18B2 **Klamath** USA
8A2 **Klamath** *R* USA
8A2 **Klamath Falls** USA
18B2 **Klamath Mts** USA
3C2 **Klappan** *R* Can
42C3 **Klatovy** Czech Republic
10M4 **Klawak** USA
65C1 **Kleiat** Leb
74B2 **Kleinsee** S Africa
74D2 **Klerksdorp** S Africa
43G2 **Kletnya** Russian Fed
36D1 **Kleve** Germany
43G2 **Klimovichi** Belorussia
44F4 **Klin** Russian Fed
43D1 **Klintehamn** Sweden
45E5 **Klintsy** Russian Fed
74C3 **Klipplaat** S Africa
40D2 **Ključ** Bosnia-Herzegovina, Yugos
42D2 **Kłodzko** Pol
10L3 **Klondike** *R* USA/Can
6D3 **Klondike Plat** USA/Can
42D3 **Klosterneuburg** Austria
10L3 **Kluane** *R* Can
10L3 **Kluane L** Can
10L3 **Kluane Nat Pk** Can
43D2 **Kluczbork** Pol
10L4 **Klukwan** USA
10J3 **Klutina L** USA
10J3 **Knight I** USA
35D5 **Knighton** Wales
40D2 **Knin** Croatia, Yugos
76A4 **Knob,C** Aust
36B1 **Knokke-Heist** Belg
10M5 **Knox,C** Can
79G9 **Knox Coast** Ant
11D3 **Knoxville** Iowa, USA
9E3 **Knoxville** Tennessee, USA
7Q3 **Knud Ramsussens Land** *Region* Greenland
74C3 **Knysna** S Africa
56C3 **Koba** Indon
7O3 **Kobberminebugt** *B* Greenland
53D5 **Kobe** Japan
42C1 **København** Den
37E1 **Kobiard** Slovenia, Yugos
42B2 **Koblenz** Germany
53C1 **Koboldo** Russian Fed
44C5 **Kobrin** Russian Fed
51G7 **Kobroör** *I* Indon
10G2 **Kobuk** *R* USA
41E2 **Kočani** Macedonia, Yugos
54A3 **Kochang** S Korea
54A3 **Kŏch'ang** S Korea
55C3 **Ko Chang** *I* Thai
61C2 **Koch Bihār** India
37D1 **Kochel** Germany
36E2 **Kocher** *R* Germany
7L3 **Koch I** Can
Kochi = Cochin
53C5 **Kōchi** Japan
10H4 **Kodiak** USA
10H4 **Kodiak I** USA
62B2 **Kodiyakkari** India
72D3 **Kodok** Sudan
54D2 **Kodomari-misaki** *C* Japan
43F3 **Kodyma** Ukraine
20D3 **Koehn L** USA
74B2 **Koes** Namibia
74D2 **Koffiefontein** S Africa
71F4 **Koforidua** Ghana
53D4 **Kōfu** Japan
54C3 **Koga** Japan
5J2 **Kogaluk** *R* Can
32G7 **Køge** Den
71H4 **Kogi** *State* Nig
60C2 **Kohat** Pak
60B2 **Koh-i-Baba** *Mts* Afghan
60B1 **Koh-i-Hisar** *Mts* Afghan
60B2 **Koh-i-Khurd** *Mt* Afghan
61D2 **Kohīma** India
60B1 **Koh-i-Mazar** *Mt* Afghan
63E2 **Koh-i-Qaisar** *Mt* Afghan
60B3 **Kohlu** Pak
44D4 **Kohtla Järve** Estonia
54A4 **Kohung** S Korea
54A4 **Kohyon** S Korea
54C3 **Koide** Japan
10K3 **Koidern** Can
55A4 **Koihoa** *Is* Nicobar Is
54A2 **Koin** N Korea
53B5 **Kōje-do** *I* S Korea
54C2 **Ko-jima** *I* Japan
48H4 **Kokchetav** Kazakhstan
32J6 **Kokemaki** *L* Fin
32J6 **Kokkola** Fin
71G3 **Koko** Nig
76D1 **Kokoda** PNG
12B2 **Kokomo** USA
51G7 **Kokonau** Indon
50B2 **Kokpekty** Kazakhstan
54A3 **Koksan** N Korea
7M4 **Koksoak** *R* Can
54A3 **Koksŏng** S Korea
74D3 **Kokstad** S Africa
55C3 **Ko Kut** *I* Thai
44E2 **Kola** Russian Fed
57B3 **Kolaka** Indon
55B4 **Ko Lanta** *I* Thai
62B2 **Kolār** India
62B2 **Kolār Gold Fields** India
70A3 **Kolda** Sen
32F7 **Kolding** Den
53E1 **Kolendo** Russian Fed
44H2 **Kolguyev, Ostrov** *I* Russian Fed
62A1 **Kolhāpur** India
10G4 **Koliganek** USA
42D2 **Kolín** Czech Republic
Kollam = Quilon
42B2 **Köln** Germany
43D2 **Kolo** Pol
20E5 **Koloa** Hawaiian Is
42D2 **Kolobrzeg** Pol
70B3 **Kolokani** Mali
44F4 **Kolomna** Russian Fed
45D6 **Kolomyya** Ukraine
57B3 **Kolono** Indon
57B3 **Kolonodale** Indon
49R4 **Kolpakovskiy** Russian Fed
48K4 **Kolpashevo** Russian Fed
41F3 **Kólpos Merabéllou** *B* Greece
41E2 **Kólpos Singitikós** *G* Greece
41E2 **Kólpos Strimonikós** *G* Greece
41E2 **Kólpos Toronaíos** *G* Greece
44F2 **Kol'skiy Poluostrov** *Pen* Russian Fed
44K2 **Kolva** *R* Russian Fed
32G6 **Kolvereid** Nor
73C5 **Kolwezi** Zaïre
49R3 **Kolyma** *R* Russian Fed
49R3 **Kolymskaya Nizmennost** *Lowland* Russian Fed
49S3 **Kolymskoye Nagor'ye** *Mts* Russian Fed
10D2 **Kolyuchinskaya Guba** *B* Russian Fed
41E2 **Kom** *Mt* Bulg/Serbia
72D3 **Koma** Eth
54D3 **Koma** Japan
71J3 **Komaduga Gana** *R* Nig
71J3 **Komadugu Yobé** *R* Nig
54D2 **Komaga take** *Mt* Japan
49S4 **Komandorskiye Ostrova** *I* Russian Fed
43D3 **Komárno** Slovakia
74E2 **Komati,R** S Africa
74E2 **Komati Poort** S Africa
53D4 **Komatsu** Japan
54B4 **Komatsushima** Japan
71F3 **Kombissiri** Burkina
44J3 **Komi** Respublika, Russian Fed
50B1 **Kommunar** Russian Fed
57A4 **Komodo** *I* Indon
71F4 **Komoé** *R* Ivory Coast
51G7 **Komoran** *I* Indon
54C3 **Komoro** Japan
41F2 **Komotiní** Greece
74C3 **Kompasberg** *Mt* S Africa
55D3 **Kompong Cham** Camb
55C3 **Kompong Chhnang** *Mts* Camb
Kompong Som = Sihanoukville
55D3 **Kompong Thom** Camb
55D3 **Kompong Trabek** Camb
43F3 **Komrat** Moldova
74C3 **Komsberg** *Mts* S Africa
49Li **Komsomolets, Ostrov** *I* Russian Fed

Lucenec Malange

43D3 **Lucenec** Slovakia
Lucerne = Luzern
16A3 **Lucero** Mexico
53C2 **Luchegorsk** Russian Fed
52C5 **Luchuan** China
20B2 **Lucia** USA
42C2 **Luckenwalde** Germany
74C2 **Luckhoff** S Africa
61B2 **Lucknow** India
73C5 **Lucusse** Angola
36D1 **Lüdenscheid** Germany
74B2 **Lüderitz** Namibia
60D2 **Ludhiana** India
12B2 **Ludington** USA
19C4 **Ludlow** California, USA
35D5 **Ludlow** Eng
14D1 **Ludlow** Vermont, USA
41F2 **Ludogorie** *Upland* Bulg
15C2 **Ludowici** USA
41E1 **Luduş** Rom
32H6 **Ludvika** Sweden
42B3 **Ludwigsburg** Germany
42B3 **Ludwigshafen** Germany
42C2 **Ludwigslust** Germany
72C4 **Luebo** Zaïre
72C4 **Luema** *R* Zaïre
73C4 **Luembe** *R* Angola
73B5 **Luena** Angola
73C5 **Luene** *R* Angola
52B3 **Lüeyang** China
52D5 **Lufeng** China
9D3 **Lufkin** USA
44D4 **Luga** Russian Fed
44D4 **Luga** *R* Russian Fed
40B1 **Lugano** Switz
73D5 **Lugela** Mozam
73D5 **Lugenda** *R* Mozam
37D2 **Lugo** Italy
39A1 **Lugo** Spain
41E1 **Lugoj** Rom
52A3 **Luhuo** China
73B4 **Lui** *R* Angola
73C5 **Luiana** Angola
73C5 **Luiana** *R* Angola
Luichow Peninsula = Leizhou Bandao
37C2 **Luino** Italy
72B3 **Luionga** *R* Zaïre
52B2 **Luipan Shan** *Upland* China
44D2 **Luiro** *R* Fin
73C5 **Luishia** Zaïre
50C4 **Luixi** China
73C4 **Luiza** Zaïre
28B2 **Luján** Arg
28D2 **Luján** Arg
52D3 **Lujiang** China
72B4 **Lukenie** *R* Zaïre
19D4 **Lukeville** USA
72B4 **Lukolela** Zaïre
43E2 **Luków** Pol
72C4 **Lukuga** *R* Zaïre
73C5 **Lukulu** Zambia
44C2 **Lule** *R* Sweden
32J5 **Luleå** Sweden
41F2 **Lüleburgaz** Turk
52C2 **Lüliang Shan** *Mts* China
17C4 **Luling** USA
26E8 **Lullaillaco** *Mt* Chile
72C3 **Lulonga** *R* Zaïre
Luluabourg = Kananga
73C5 **Lumbala Kaquengue** Angola
9F3 **Lumberton** USA
56E2 **Lumbis** Indon
44G2 **Lumbovka** Russian Fed
61D2 **Lumding** India
73C5 **Lumeje** Angola
78A3 **Lumsden** NZ
32G7 **Lund** Sweden
11C1 **Lundar** Can
73D5 **Lundazi** Zambia
73D6 **Lundi** *R* Zim
35C6 **Lundy** *I* Eng
42C2 **Lüneburg** Germany
36D2 **Lunéville** France
73C5 **Lunga** *R* Zambia
61D3 **Lunglei** India
73B5 **Lungue Bungo** *R* Angola
43F2 **Luninec** Belorussia
20C1 **Luning** USA
53C2 **Luobei** China
72B4 **Luobomo** Congo
52B5 **Luocheng** China
52C5 **Luoding** China
52C3 **Luohe** China
52C3 **Luo He** *R* Henan, China
52B2 **Luo He** *R* Shaanxi, China
52C4 **Luoxiao Shan** *Hills* China
52C3 **Luoyang** China
72B4 **Luozi** Zaïre
73C5 **Lupane** Zim
73D5 **Lupilichi** Mozam
Lu Qu = Tao He
25E3 **Luque** Par
36D3 **Lure** France
35B4 **Lurgan** N Ire
73D5 **Lurio** *R* Mozam
63B2 **Luristan** Region, Iran
73C5 **Lusaka** Zambia
72C4 **Lusambo** Zaïre
41D2 **Lushnjë** Alb
72D4 **Lushoto** Tanz
50C4 **Lushui** China
52E2 **Lüshun** China
11B3 **Lusk** USA
35E6 **Luton** Eng
45D5 **Lutsk** Ukraine
72E3 **Luuq** Somalia
11C3 **Luverne** USA
73C4 **Luvua** *R* Zaïre
73D4 **Luwegu** *R* Tanz
73D5 **Luwingu** Zambia
57B3 **Luwuk** Indon
36D2 **Luxembourg** Grand Duchy, N W Europe
38D2 **Luxembourg** Lux
36D3 **Luxeuil-les-Bains** France
52A5 **Luxi** China
69C2 **Luxor** Egypt
44H3 **Luza** Russian Fed
44H3 **Luza** *R* Russian Fed
40B1 **Luzern** Switz
14D1 **Luzerne** USA
52B5 **Luzhai** China
52B4 **Luzhi** China
52B4 **Luzhou** China
29C2 **Luziânia** Brazil
57F7 **Luzon** *I* Phil
57F6 **Luzon Str** Phil
43E3 **L'vov** Ukraine
34D2 **Lybster** Scot
32H6 **Lycksele** Sweden
73C6 **Lydenburg** S Africa
3B3 **Lyell I** Can
8B3 **Lyell,Mt** USA
14B2 **Lykens** USA
18D2 **Lyman** USA
35D6 **Lyme B** Eng
35D6 **Lyme Regis** Eng
9F3 **Lynchburg** USA
75A2 **Lyndhurst** Aust
13E2 **Lynn** USA
3A2 **Lynn Canal** *Sd* USA
15B2 **Lynn Haven** USA
3H2 **Lynn Lake** Can
4D3 **Lynx** Can
6H3 **Lynx L** Can
38C2 **Lyon** France
10L4 **Lyon Canal** *Sd* USA
15C2 **Lyons** Georgia, USA
14B1 **Lyons** New York, USA
76A3 **Lyons** *R* Aust
37B2 **Lys** *R* Italy
44K4 **Lys'va** Russian Fed
78B2 **Lyttelton** NZ
3D3 **Lytton** Can
20A1 **Lytton** USA
43F2 **Lyubeshov** Ukraine
44F4 **Lyublino** Russian Fed

M

55C1 **Ma** *R* Viet
65C2 **Ma'agan** Jordan
65C2 **Ma'alot Tarshīha** Israel
64C3 **Ma'an** Jordan
52D3 **Ma'anshan** China
65D1 **Ma'arrat an Nu'mān** Syria
36C1 **Maas** *R* Neth
36C1 **Maaseik** Belg
57F8 **Maasin** Phil
42B2 **Maastricht** Neth
74E1 **Mabalane** Mozam
27G2 **Mabaruma** Guyana
35F5 **Mablethorpe** Eng
73D6 **Mabote** Mozam
43E2 **Mabrita** Belorussia
43F2 **M'adel** Belorussia
29D3 **Macaé** Brazil
8D3 **McAlester** USA
8D4 **McAllen** USA
73D5 **Macaloge** Mozam
52C5 **Macao** Dependency, China
27H3 **Macapá** Brazil
29D2 **Macarani** Brazil
26C4 **Macas** Ecuador
27L5 **Macaú** Brazil
29D1 **Macaúbas** Brazil
72C3 **M'Bari** *R* CAR
3D3 **McBride** Can
18C2 **McCall** USA
16B3 **McCamey** USA
18D2 **McCammon** USA
10K3 **McCarthy** USA
3B3 **McCauley I** Can
35D5 **Macclesfield** Eng
7K1 **McClintock B** Can
6H2 **McClintock Chan** Can
14B2 **McClure** USA
20B2 **McClure,L** USA
6G2 **McClure Str** Can
17D3 **McComb** USA
16B1 **McConaughy,L** USA
14B3 **McConnellsburg** USA
8C2 **McCook** USA
7L2 **Macculloch,C** Can
3D2 **McCusker,Mt** Can
6F4 **McDame** Can
18C2 **McDermitt** USA
4D4 **Macdiarmid** Can
18D1 **Mcdonald Peak** *Mt* USA
76C3 **Macdonnell Ranges** *Mts* Aust
39A1 **Macedo de Cavaleiros** Port
41E2 **Macedonia** *Republic* Europe
27L5 **Maceió** Brazil
70B4 **Macenta** Guinea
40C2 **Macerata** Italy
3G2 **Macfarlane** *R* Can
75A2 **Macfarlane,L** Aust
17D3 **McGehee** USA
19D3 **McGill** USA
6C3 **McGrath** USA
18D1 **McGuire,Mt** USA
29C3 **Machado** Brazil
73D6 **Machaíla** Mozam
72D4 **Machakos** Kenya
26C4 **Machala** Ecuador
73D6 **Machaze** Mozam
62B1 **Mācherla** India
65C2 **Machgharab** Leb
13F2 **Machias** USA
4C2 **Machichi** *R* Can
62C1 **Machilīpatnam** India
26D1 **Machiques** Ven
26D6 **Machu-Picchu** *Hist Site* Peru
73D6 **Macia** Mozam
Macias Nguema = Fernando Poo
11B2 **McIntosh** USA
75C1 **MacIntyre** *R* Aust
16A2 **Mack** USA
76D3 **Mackay** Aust
18D2 **Mackay** USA
76B3 **Mackay,L** Aust
77H1 **McKean** *I* Phoenix Is
13D2 **McKeesport** USA
3D2 **Mackenzie** Can
6F3 **Mackenzie** *R* Can
6E3 **Mackenzie B** Can
6G2 **Mackenzie King I** Can
6E3 **Mackenzie Mts** Can
12C1 **Mackinac,Str of** USA
12C1 **Mackinaw City** USA
10H3 **McKinley,Mt** USA
17C3 **McKinney** USA
7L2 **Mackinson Inlet** *B* Can
20C3 **McKittrick** USA
75D2 **Macksville** Aust
18B2 **Mclaoughlin,Mt** USA
11B2 **McLaughlin** USA
75D1 **Maclean** Aust
74D3 **Maclear** S Africa
6G4 **McLennan** Can
3E3 **McLeod** *R* Can
6G3 **McLeod B** Can
76A3 **McLeod,L** Aust
3D2 **McLeod Lake** Can
6E3 **Macmillan** *R* Can
16B3 **McMillan,L** USA
10M3 **Macmillan P** Can
18B1 **McMinnville** Oregon, USA
15B1 **McMinnville** Tennessee, USA
79F7 **McMurdo** *Base* Ant
3C2 **McNamara,Mt** Can
19E4 **McNary** USA
3E3 **McNaughton L** Can
12A2 **Macomb** USA
40B2 **Macomer** Sardegna
73D5 **Macomia** Mozam
38C2 **Mâcon** France
9E3 **Macon** Georgia, USA
17D2 **Macon** Missouri, USA
73C5 **Macondo** Angola
3H2 **Macoun L** Can
17C2 **McPherson** USA
xxviiiJ7 **Macquarie** *Is* Aust
75C2 **Macquarie** *R* Aust
75E3 **Macquarie Harbour** *B* Aust
75D2 **Macquarie,L** Aust
15C2 **McRae** USA
79F11 **Mac Robertson Land** Region, Ant
71E1 **M'saken** Tunisia
71C1 **M'Sila** Alg
6G3 **McTavish Arm** *B* Can
75A1 **Macumba** *R* Aust
37C2 **Macunaga** Italy
6F3 **McVicar Arm** *B* Can
42D3 **M'yaróvár** Hung
71H4 **Mada** *R* Nig
65C3 **Mādabā** Jordan
72C2 **Madadi** *Well* Chad
68J9 **Madagascar** *I* Indian O
xxviiiD6 **Madagascar Basin** Indian O
72B1 **Madama** Niger
76D1 **Madang** PNG
70C3 **Madaoua** Niger
61D3 **Madaripur** Bang
63C1 **Madau** Turkmenistan
5H4 **Madawaska** USA
13D1 **Madawaska** *R* Can
61E3 **Madaya** Burma
70A1 **Madeira** *I* Atlantic O
26F5 **Madeira** *R* Brazil
7M5 **Madeleine, Îles de la** Can
11D3 **Madelia** USA
21B2 **Madera** Mexico
19B3 **Madera** USA
62A1 **Madgaon** India
61C2 **Madhubani** India
61B3 **Madhya Pradesh** State, India
62B2 **Madikeri** India
72B4 **Madimba** Zaïre
72B4 **Madingo Kayes** Congo
72B4 **Madingou** Congo
9E3 **Madison** Indiana, USA
11C2 **Madison** Minnesota, USA
11C3 **Madison** Nebraska, USA
11C3 **Madison** S Dakota, USA
9E2 **Madison** Wisconsin, USA
18D1 **Madison** *R* USA
12B3 **Madisonville** Kentucky, USA
17C3 **Madisonville** Texas, USA
56D4 **Madiun** Indon
4F5 **Madoc** Can
72D3 **Mado Gashi** Kenya
37D1 **Madonna Di Campiglio** Italy
62C2 **Madras** India
18B2 **Madras** USA
25A8 **Madre de Dios** *I* Chile
26E6 **Madre de Dios** *R* Bol
39B1 **Madrid** Spain
39B2 **Madridejos** Spain
56D4 **Madura** *I* Indon
62B3 **Madurai** India
54C3 **Maebashi** Japan
55B3 **Mae Khlong** *R* Thai
55B4 **Mae Nam Lunang** *R* Thai
55C2 **Mae Nam Mun** *R* Thai
55B2 **Mae Nam Ping** *R* Thai
54A3 **Maengsan** N Korea
73E5 **Maevatanana** Madag
77F2 **Maewo** *I* Vanuatu
74D2 **Mafeking** S Africa
74D2 **Mafeteng** Lesotho
75C3 **Maffra** Aust
73D4 **Mafia** *I* Tanz
25G3 **Mafra** Brazil
64C3 **Mafraq** Jordan
49R4 **Magadan** Russian Fed
26D2 **Magargué** Colombia
71H3 **Magaria** Niger
53B1 **Magdagachi** Russian Fed
28D3 **Magdalena** Arg
8B3 **Magdalena** Mexico
16A3 **Magdalena** USA
23C4 **Magdalena** *R* Colombia
56E2 **Magdalena,Mt** Malay
42C2 **Magdeburg** Germany
26D2 **Magdelena** *R* Colombia
27K8 **Magé** Brazil
56D4 **Magelang** Indon
37C1 **Maggia** *R* Switz
64B4 **Maghâgha** Egypt
34B4 **Magherafelt** N Ire
41D2 **Maglie** Italy
44K5 **Magnitogorsk** Russian Fed
17D3 **Magnolia** USA
53E1 **Mago** Russian Fed
5G4 **Magog** Can
13E1 **Magog** Can
22C1 **Magosal** Mexico
5J3 **Magpie** *R* Can
37C2 **Magra** *R* Italy
3F3 **Magrath** Can
20D2 **Magruder Mt** USA
74E2 **Magude** Mozam
7J3 **Maguse River** Can
Magway = Magwe
55B1 **Magwe** Burma
45H8 **Mahābād** Iran
61C2 **Mahabharat Range** *Mts* Nepal
62A1 **Mahād** India
60D4 **Mahadeo Hills** India
14A2 **Mahaffey** USA
73E5 **Mahajanga** Madag
74D1 **Mahalapye** Botswana
61B3 **Mahānadi** *R* India
73E5 **Mahanoro** Madag
14B2 **Mahanoy City** USA
62A1 **Maharashtra** State, India
61B3 **Māhāsamund** India
55C2 **Maha Sarakham** Thai
73E5 **Mahavavy** *R* Madag
62B1 **Mahbūbnagar** India
71E1 **Mahdia** Tunisia
62B2 **Mahe** India
60D4 **Mahekar** India
61B3 **Mahendragarh** India
73D4 **Mahenge** Tanz
60C4 **Mahesāna** India
78C1 **Mahia Pen** NZ
11C2 **Mahnomen** USA
60D3 **Mahoba** India
39C2 **Mahón** Spain
5J5 **Mahone B** Can
10N2 **Mahony L** Can
71E2 **Mahrés** Tunisia
60C4 **Mahuva** India
26D1 **Maicao** Colombia
37B1 **Maîche** France
66C4 **Maichew** Eth
35F6 **Maidstone** Eng
72B2 **Maiduguri** Nig
44B3 **Maigomaj** *R* Sweden
61B3 **Maihar** India
61D3 **Maijdi** Bang
55B3 **Mail Kyun** *I* Burma
60A1 **Maimana** Afghan
36E2 **Main** *R* Germany
4E4 **Main Chan** Can
72B4 **Mai-Ndombe** *L* Zaïre
9G2 **Maine** State, USA
36A3 **Maine** *Region* France
71J3 **Mainé-Soroa** Niger
34D2 **Mainland** *I* Scot
60D3 **Mainpuri** India
36A2 **Maintenon** France
73E5 **Maintirano** Madag
42B2 **Mainz** Germany
70A4 **Maio** *I* Cape Verde
25C4 **Maipó** *Mt* Arg/Chile
28D3 **Maipú** Arg
26E1 **Maiquetía** Ven
37B2 **Maira** *R* Italy
61D2 **Mairābāri** India
61D3 **Maiskhal I** Bang
76E4 **Maitland** New South Wales, Aust
75A2 **Maitland** S Australia, Aust
79F12 **Maitri** *Base* Ant
38D1 **Maiz** Germany
53D4 **Maizuru** Japan
76A1 **Majene** Indon
26D7 **Majes** *R* Peru
72D3 **Maji** Eth
52D2 **Majia He** *R* China
Majunga = Mahajanga
72D2 **Makale** Eth
57A3 **Makale** Indon
56B3 **Makalo** Indon
61C2 **Makalu** *Mt* China/Nepal
44K2 **Makarikha** Russian Fed
53E2 **Makarov** Russian Fed
40D2 **Makarska** Croatia, Yugos
44G4 **Makaryev** Russian Fed
Makassar Ujung Pandang
56E3 **Makassar Str** Indon
45J6 **Makat** Kazakhstan
70A4 **Makeni** Sierra Leone
45F6 **Makeyevka** Ukraine
73C6 **Makgadikgadi** *Salt* Pan Botswana
45H7 **Makhachkala** Russian Fed
64D1 **Makharadze** Georgia
57C2 **Makian** *I* Indon
72D4 **Makindu** Kenya
Makkah = Mecca
7N4 **Makkovik** Can
43E3 **Makó** Hung
72B3 **Makokou** Gabon
78C1 **Makorako,Mt** NZ
72B3 **Makoua** Congo
60C3 **Makrāna** India
60A3 **Makran Coast Range** *Mts* Pak
53D2 **Maksimovka** Russian Fed
63E3 **Maksotag** Iran
71D1 **Maktar** Tunisia
45G8 **Mākū** Iran
72C4 **Makumbi** Zaïre
53C5 **Makurazaki** Japan
71H4 **Makurdi** Nig
10E5 **Makushin V** USA
57F9 **Malabang** Phil
62B2 **Malabar Coast** India
68E7 **Malabo** Bioko
28D1 **Malabrigo** Arg
55C5 **Malacca,Str of** S E Asia
18D2 **Malad City** USA
26D2 **Málaga** Colombia
39B2 **Malaga** Spain
16B3 **Malaga** USA
73E6 **Malaimbandy** Madag
77F1 **Malaita** *I* Solomon Is
72D3 **Malakal** Sudan
60C2 **Malakand** Pak
57B3 **Malamala** Indon
56D4 **Malang** Indon
73B4 **Malange** Angola

Malanville **Mas'adah**

71G3 **Malanville** Benin
49S3 **Mal Anyuy** *R* Russian Fed
32H7 **Mälaren** *L* Sweden
28B3 **Malargüe** Arg
4F4 **Malartic** Can
10K4 **Malaspina Gl** USA
45F8 **Malatya** Turk
73D5 **Malawi** Republic, Africa
Malawi,L = Nyasa,L
53D2 **Malaya Sidima** Russian Fed
57G9 **Malaybalay** Phil
63B2 **Malāyer** Iran
51D6 **Malaysia** Federation, S E Asia
64D2 **Malazgirt** Turk
43D2 **Malbork** Pol
28C1 **Malbrán** Arg
42C2 **Malchin** Germany
17E2 **Malden** USA
59F5 **Maldives Is** Indian O
xxviiiE4 **Maldives Ridge** Indian O
36A1 **Maldon** Eng
25F4 **Maldonado** Urug
37D1 **Male** Italy
60C4 **Malegaon** India
42D3 **Malé Karpaty** *Upland* Slovakia
77F2 **Malekula** *I* Vanuatu
73D5 **Malema** Mozam
44F3 **Malen'ga** Russian Fed
36B2 **Malesherbes** France
60B2 **Mālestān** Afghan
32H5 **Malgomaj** *L* Sweden
72C2 **Malha** *Well* Sudan
18C2 **Malheur L** USA
70B3 **Mali** Republic, Africa
61E2 **Mali Hka** *R* Burma
57B3 **Malili** Indon
43F2 **Malin** Ukraine
56E2 **Malinau** Indon
72E4 **Malindi** Kenya
Malines = Mechelen
33B2 **Malin Head** *Pt* Irish Rep
61B3 **Malkala Range** *Mts* India
60D4 **Malkāpur** India
41F2 **Malkara** Turk
41F2 **Malko Tŭrnovo** Bulg
34C3 **Mallaig** Scot
69C2 **Mallawi** Egypt
37D1 **Málles Venosta** Italy
39C2 **Mallorca** *I* Spain
32G6 **Malm** Nor
32J5 **Malmberget** Sweden
36D1 **Malmédy** Germany
35D6 **Malmesbury** Eng
74B3 **Malmesbury** S Africa
32G7 **Malmö** Sweden
44J4 **Malmyzh** Russian Fed
57F8 **Malolos** Phil
13E2 **Malone** USA
74D2 **Maloti Mts** Lesotho
32F6 **Måloy** Nor
44J2 **Malozemel'skaya Tundra** *Plain* Russian Fed
22B1 **Mal Paso** Mexico
22D2 **Malpaso** Mexico
24B3 **Malpelo** *I* Colombia
28A2 **Malpo** *R* Chile
60D3 **Mālpura** India
18D2 **Malta** Idaho, USA
8C2 **Malta** Montana, USA
40C3 **Malta** *Chan* Malta/Italy
40C3 **Malta** *I* Medit S
74B1 **Maltahöhe** Namibia
35E4 **Malton** Eng
32G6 **Malung** Sweden
62A1 **Mālvan** India
17D3 **Malvern** USA
74E1 **Malvérnia** Mozam
60D4 **Malwa Plat** India
49Q2 **Malyy Lyakchovskiy, Ostrov** *I* Russian Fed
49M2 **Malyy Taymyr, Ostrov** *I* Russian Fed
45H6 **Malyy Uzen'** *R* Kazakhstan
49N4 **Mama** Russian Fed
44J4 **Mamadysh** Russian Fed
72C3 **Mambasa** Zaïre
76C1 **Mamberamo** *R* Aust
51G7 **Mamberamo** *R* Indon
72B3 **Mambéré** *R* CAR
57A3 **Mamciju** Indon
36A2 **Mamers** France
72A3 **Mamfé** Cam
19D4 **Mammoth** USA
12B3 **Mammoth Cave Nat Pk** USA
20C2 **Mammoth Pool Res** USA
26E6 **Mamoré** *R* Bol
70A3 **Mamou** Guinea
73E5 **Mampikony** Madag
71F4 **Mampong** Ghana
65C3 **Mamshit** *Hist Site* Israel
67G3 **Ma'mūl** Oman
74C1 **Mamuno** Botswana
70B4 **Man** Ivory Coast
20E5 **Mana** Hawaiian Is
73E6 **Manabo** Madag
26F4 **Manacapuru** Brazil
39C2 **Manacor** Spain
57B2 **Manado** Indon
26A1 **Managua** Nic
73E6 **Manakara** Madag
76D1 **Manam** *I* PNG
73E5 **Mananara** Madag
73E6 **Mananjary** Madag
78A3 **Manapouri** NZ
78A3 **Manapouri,L** NZ
61D2 **Manas** Bhutan
59G1 **Manas** China
48K5 **Manas Hu** *L* China
61B2 **Manaslu** *Mt* Nepal
14C2 **Manasquan** USA
27G4 **Manaus** Brazil
45E8 **Manavgat** Turk
64C2 **Manbij** Syria
71J4 **Manbilla Plat** Nig
35C4 **Man,Calf of** *I* Eng
12B2 **Mancelona** USA
62B1 **Mancheral** India
13E2 **Manchester** Connecticut, USA
35D5 **Manchester** Eng
12C3 **Manchester** Kentucky, USA
9F2 **Manchester** New Hampshire, USA
14B2 **Manchester** Pennsylvania, USA
15B1 **Manchester** Tennessee, USA
14D1 **Manchester** Vermont, USA
53B2 **Manchuria** Hist Region, China
63C3 **Mand** *R* Iran
73D5 **Manda** Tanz
29B3 **Mandaguari** Brazil
32F7 **Mandal** Nor
55B1 **Mandalay** Burma
50D2 **Mandalgovī** Mongolia
41F3 **Mandalya Körfezi** *B* Turk
8C2 **Mandan** USA
72E3 **Mandera** Eth
23B3 **Mandeville** Jamaica
73D5 **Mandimba** Mozam
57C3 **Mandioli** *I* Indon
61B3 **Mandla** India
73E5 **Mandritsara** Madag
60D4 **Mandsaur** India
41D2 **Manduria** Italy
60B4 **Māndvi** India
62B2 **Mandya** India
43F2 **Manevichi** Ukraine
66B1 **Manfalût** Egypt
35E5 **Manfield** Eng
40D2 **Manfredonia** Italy
29D1 **Manga** Brazil
71F3 **Manga** Burkina
72B2 **Manga** *Desert Region* Niger
78C1 **Mangakino** NZ
41F2 **Mangalia** Rom
72C2 **Mangalmé** Chad
62A2 **Mangalore** India
56C3 **Manggar** Indon
61E3 **Mangin Range** *Mts* Burma
50C3 **Mangnia** China
73D5 **Mangoche** Malawi
73E6 **Mangoky** *R* Madag
57C3 **Mangole** *I* Indon
60B4 **Māngral** India
29B4 **Manguerinha** Brazil
49O4 **Mangui** China
16C3 **Mangum** USA
45J7 **Mangyshiak, Poluostrov** *Pen* Kazakhstan
8D3 **Manhattan** USA
74E2 **Manhica** Mozam
27K8 **Manhuacu** Brazil
73E5 **Mania** *R* Madag
37E1 **Maniago** Italy
73D5 **Manica** Mozam
7M5 **Manicouagan** *R* Can
7M4 **Manicouagan, Réservoir** *Res* Can
67E1 **Manifah** S Arabia
57F8 **Manila** Phil
18E2 **Manila** USA
75D2 **Manilla** Aust
70B3 **Maninian** Ivory Coast
57C3 **Manipa** *I* Indon
61D3 **Manipur** State, India
61D3 **Manipur** *R* Burma
45D8 **Manisa** Turk
33C3 **Man,Isle of** Irish Sea
12B2 **Manistee** USA
12B2 **Manistee** *R* USA
12B1 **Manistique** USA
6J4 **Manitoba** Province, Can
6J4 **Manitoba,L** Can
3G3 **Manito L** Can
11C2 **Manitou** Can
11D1 **Manitou Falls** Can
12B1 **Manitou Is** USA
7K5 **Manitoulin** *I* Can
16B2 **Manitou Springs** USA
12C1 **Manitowik L** Can
12B2 **Manitowoc** USA
4F4 **Maniwaki** Can
26C2 **Manizales** Colombia
73E6 **Manja** Madag
76A4 **Manjimup** Aust
62B1 **Mānjra** *R* India
9D2 **Mankato** USA
70B4 **Mankono** Ivory Coast
10H3 **Manley Hot Springs** USA
78B1 **Manly** NZ
60C4 **Manmād** India
56B3 **Manna** Indon
75A2 **Mannahill** Aust
62B3 **Mannar** Sri Lanka
62B3 **Mannār,G of** India
62B2 **Mannārgudi** India
42B3 **Mannheim** Germany
3E2 **Manning** Can
15C2 **Manning** USA
75A2 **Mannum** Aust
70A4 **Mano** Sierra Leone
76C1 **Manokwari** Indon
73C4 **Manono** Zaïre
55B3 **Manoron** Burma
37A3 **Manosque** France
5G3 **Manouane** *R* Can
54C3 **Mano-wan** *B* Japan
53B3 **Manp'o** N Korea
60D2 **Mānsa** India
73C5 **Mansa** Zambia
7K3 **Mansel I** Can
17D2 **Mansfield** Arkansas, USA
75C3 **Mansfield** Aust
17D3 **Mansfield** Louisiana, USA
14E1 **Mansfield** Massachusetts, USA
9E2 **Mansfield** Ohio, USA
13D2 **Mansfield** Pennsylvania, USA
29B2 **Manso** *R* Brazil
51G5 **Mansyu Deep** Pacific O
57E9 **Mantalingajan,Mt** Phil
54A2 **Mantap-san** *Mt* N Korea
26C6 **Mantaro** *R* Peru
20B2 **Manteca** USA
15D1 **Manteo** USA
38C2 **Mantes** France
19D3 **Manti** USA
40C1 **Mantova** Italy
32J6 **Mantta** Fin
44G4 **Manturovo** Russian Fed
22C1 **Manuel** Mexico
16B4 **Manuel Benavides** Mexico
29B3 **Manuel Ribas** Brazil
57B3 **Manui** *I* Indon
57F9 **Manukan** Phil
77G4 **Manukau** NZ
51H7 **Manus** *I* Pacific O
39B2 **Manzanares** Spain
21E2 **Manzanillo** Cuba
21B3 **Manzanillo** Mexico
49N5 **Manzhouli** China
65D3 **Manzil** Jordan
73D6 **Manzini** Swaziland
72B2 **Mao** Chad
52A2 **Maomao Shan** *Mt* China
52C5 **Maoming** China
73D6 **Mapai** Mozam
61B1 **Mapam Yumco** *L* China
51G6 **Mapia** *Is* Pacific O
57E9 **Mapin** *I* Phil
6H5 **Maple Creek** Can
74E1 **Mapulanguene** Mozam
74E2 **Maputo** Mozam
74E2 **Maputo** *R* Mozam
Ma Qu = Huange He
52A3 **Maqu** China
61C2 **Maquan He** *R* China
72B4 **Maquela do Zombo** Angola
25C6 **Maquinchao** Arg
27J5 **Marabá** Brazil
26D1 **Maracaibo** Ven
29A3 **Maracaju** Brazil
29D1 **Máracás** Brazil
26E1 **Maracay** Ven
69A2 **Marādah** Libya
70C3 **Maradi** Niger
45H8 **Marāgheh** Iran
30E5 **Marakech** Mor
72D3 **Maralal** Kenya
77F1 **Maramasike** *I* Solomon Is
Maramba = Livingstone
56G7 **Maran** Malay
19D4 **Marana** USA
45H8 **Marand** Iran
29C1 **Maranhão** *R* Brazil
27J4 **Maranhõa** State, Brazil
75C1 **Maranoa** *R* Aust
26C4 **Marañón** *R* Peru
45F8 **Maras** Turk
7K5 **Marathon** Can
15E4 **Marathon** Florida, USA
14B1 **Marathon** New York, USA
16B3 **Marathon** Texas, USA
56E2 **Maratua** *I* Indon
29E1 **Maraú** Brazil
22B2 **Maravatio** Mexico
57F9 **Marawi** Phil
28B2 **Marayes** Arg
67F3 **Mar'ayt** Yemen
39B2 **Marbella** Spain
76A3 **Marble Bar** Aust
19D3 **Marble Canyon** USA
74D2 **Marble Hall** S Africa
14E1 **Marblehead** USA
42B2 **Marburg** Germany
28E1 **Marcelino Ramos** Brazil
42B2 **Marche** Belg
37E3 **Marche** Region, Italy
39A2 **Marchean** Spain
36C1 **Marche-en-Famenne** Belg
15E4 **Marco** USA
28C2 **Marcos Juárez** Arg
10J3 **Marcus Baker,Mt** USA
13E2 **Marcy,Mt** USA
45G8 **Mar Dağlari** *Mt* Turk
60C2 **Mardan** Pak
25E5 **Mar del Plata** Arg
45G8 **Mardin** Turk
77F3 **Maré** *I* Nouvelle Calédonie
72D2 **Mareb** *R* Eritrea/Eth
51H8 **Mareeba** Aust
72E3 **Mareeq** Somalia
16B3 **Marfa** USA
14C1 **Margaretville** USA
28C1 **Margarita** Arg
35F6 **Margate** Eng
41E1 **Marghita** Rom
75E3 **Maria I** Aust
xxviiiJ3 **Mariana** *Is* Pacific O
3F2 **Mariana Lake** Can
xxviiiJ4 **Marianas Trench** Pacific O
61D2 **Mariāni** India
17D3 **Marianna** Arkansas, USA
15B2 **Marianna** Florida, USA
77G4 **Maria Van Diemen,C** NZ
42D3 **Mariazell** Austria
67E3 **Ma'rib** Yemen
40D1 **Maribor** Slovenia, Yugos
74D1 **Marico** *R* Botswana/ S Africa
20C3 **Maricopa** USA
72C3 **Maridi** Sudan
79F5 **Marie Byrd Land** Region, Ant
23E3 **Marie Galante** *I* Caribbean
32H6 **Mariehamn** Fin
36C1 **Mariembourg** Belg
27H2 **Marienburg** Suriname
74B1 **Mariental** Namibia
32G7 **Mariestad** Sweden
15C2 **Marietta** Georgia, USA
12C3 **Marietta** Ohio, USA
17C3 **Marietta** Oklahoma, USA
71H3 **Mariga** *R* Nig
23Q2 **Marigot** Dominica
44C5 **Marijampolė** Lithuania
25G2 **Marilia** Brazil
73B4 **Marimba** Angola
57F8 **Marinduque** *I* Phil
9E2 **Marinette** USA
25F2 **Maringá** Brazil
72C3 **Maringa** *R* Zaïre
17D2 **Marion** Arkansas, USA
12B3 **Marion** Illinois, USA
9E2 **Marion** Indiana, USA
9E2 **Marion** Ohio, USA
15D2 **Marion** S Carolina, USA
9E3 **Marion,L** USA
77E2 **Marion Reef** Aust
19C3 **Mariposa** USA
20B2 **Mariposa** *R* USA
20B2 **Mariposa Res** USA
57B2 **Marisa** Indon
45F6 **Mariupol** Ukraine
45D7 **Marista** *R* Bulg
44H4 **Mariyskaya** Respublika, Russian Fed
65C2 **Marjayoun** Leb
43F2 **Marjina Gorki** Belorussia
65C3 **Marka** Jordan
72E3 **Marka** Somalia
42C1 **Markaryd** Sweden
35D5 **Market Drayton** Eng
35E5 **Market Harborough** Eng
79E **Markham,Mt** Ant
20C1 **Markleeville** USA
49T3 **Markovo** Russian Fed
14E1 **Marlboro** Massachusetts, USA
14D1 **Marlboro** New Hampshire, USA
76D3 **Marlborough** Aust
36B2 **Marle** France
4E5 **Marlette** USA
17C3 **Marlin** USA
14D1 **Marlow** USA
38C3 **Marmande** France
41F2 **Marmara Adi** *I* Turk
64A1 **Marmara,S of** Turk
41F3 **Marmaris** Turk
11B2 **Marmarth** USA
12C3 **Marmet** USA
4C4 **Marmion L** Can
40C1 **Marmolada** *Mt* Italy
10H4 **Marmot B** USA
22D2 **Mar Muerto** *Lg* Mexico
37A1 **Marnay** France
36C2 **Marne** Department, France
36B2 **Marne** *R* France
72B3 **Maro** Chad
73E5 **Maroantsetra** Madag
73D5 **Marondera** Zim
27H3 **Maroni** *R* French Guiana
75D1 **Maroochydore** Aust
57A3 **Maros** Indon
72B2 **Maroua** Cam
73E5 **Marovoay** Madag
9E4 **Marquesas Keys** *Is* USA
9E2 **Marquette** USA
36A1 **Marquise** France
75C2 **Marra** *R* Aust
74E2 **Marracuene** Mozam
70B1 **Marrakech** Mor
76C3 **Marree** Aust
17D4 **Marrero** USA
73D5 **Marromeu** Mozam
73D5 **Marrupa** Mozam
66B1 **Marsa Alam** Egypt
72D3 **Marsabit** Kenya
40C3 **Marsala** Italy
36E1 **Marsberg** Germany
38D3 **Marseille** France
10F3 **Marshall** Alaska, USA
12B3 **Marshall** Illinois, USA
12C2 **Marshall** Michigan, USA
11C3 **Marshall** Minnesota, USA
17D2 **Marshall** Missouri, USA
9D3 **Marshall** Texas, USA
14B3 **Marshall** Virginia, USA
xxixK4 **Marshall Is** Pacific O
11D3 **Marshalltown** USA
17D2 **Marshfield** Missouri, USA
12A2 **Marshfield** Wisconsin, USA
23B1 **Marsh Harbour** Bahamas
17D4 **Marsh I** USA
10M3 **Marsh L** Can
26B4 **Marta** Ecuador
55B2 **Martaban,G of** Burma
56B3 **Martapura** Indon
56D3 **Martapura** Indon
13E2 **Martha's Vineyard** *I* USA
38D2 **Martigny** Switz
43D3 **Martin** Slovakia
11B3 **Martin** S Dakota, USA
15B1 **Martin** Tennessee, USA
78C2 **Martinborough** NZ
28B3 **Martín de Loyola** Arg
22C1 **Martínez de la Torre** Mexico
23E4 **Martinique** *I* Caribbean
15B2 **Martin,L** USA
10K1 **Martin Pt** USA
13D3 **Martinsburg** USA
12C2 **Martins Ferry** USA
13D3 **Martinsville** USA
xxxG5 **Martin Vaz** *I* Atlantic O
38D3 **Martiques** France
78C2 **Marton** NZ
39B2 **Martos** Spain
45G7 **Martvili** Georgia
56D2 **Marudi** Malay
60B2 **Maruf** Afghan
54B4 **Marugame** Japan
19D3 **Marvine,Mt** USA
60C3 **Mārwār** India
48H6 **Mary** Turkmenistan
77E3 **Maryborough** Queensland, Aust
75B3 **Maryborough** Victoria, Aust
6F4 **Mary Henry,Mt** Can
9F3 **Maryland** State, USA
34D4 **Maryport** Eng
5K3 **Mary's Harbour** Can
5K4 **Marystown** Can
19B3 **Marysville** California, USA
17C2 **Marysville** Kansas, USA
18B1 **Marysville** Washington, USA
17D1 **Maryville** Missouri, USA
15C1 **Maryville** Tennessee, USA
69A2 **Marzuq** Libya
65A3 **Masabb Dumyât** *C* Egypt
Masada = Mezada
65C2 **Mas'adah** Syria

Masai Steppe — Mexico

72D4 **Masai Steppe** *Upland* Tanz
72D4 **Masaka** Uganda
64E2 **Masally** Azerbaijan
57B3 **Masamba** Indon
53B4 **Masan** S Korea
73D5 **Masasi** Tanz
21D3 **Masaya** Nic
57F8 **Masbate** Phil
57F8 **Masbate** *I* Phil
71C1 **Mascara** Alg
xxviiiD5 **Mascarene Ridge** Indian O
22B1 **Mascota** Mexico
29E2 **Mascote** Brazil
57C4 **Masela** *I* Indon
74D2 **Maseru** Lesotho
60B2 **Mashaki** Afghan
63D1 **Mashhad** Iran
63E3 **Mashkel** *R* Pak
72B4 **Masi-Manimba** Zaïre
72D3 **Masindi** Uganda
72C4 **Masisi** Zaïre
63B2 **Masjed Soleyman** Iran
73F5 **Masoala** *C* Madag
20C1 **Mason** Nevada, USA
16C3 **Mason** Texas, USA
9D2 **Mason City** USA
67G2 **Masqat** Oman
42B2 **Mass** *R* Neth
40C2 **Massa** Italy
9F2 **Massachusetts** State, USA
13E2 **Massachusetts B** USA
72B2 **Massakori** Chad
37D3 **Massa Marittima** Italy
73D6 **Massangena** Mozam
66C3 **Massawa Chan** Eth
13E2 **Massena** USA
72B2 **Massénya** Chad
3B3 **Masset** Can
12C1 **Massey** Can
38C2 **Massif Central** *Mts* France
71C1 **Massif de l'Ouarsenis** *Mts* Alg
72B3 **Massif de l'Adamaoua** *Mts* Cam
23C3 **Massif de la Hotte** *Mts* Haiti
73E6 **Massif de l'Isalo** *Upland* Madag
72C3 **Massif des Bongo** *Upland* CAR
38D2 **Massif du Pelvoux** *Mts* France
73E5 **Massif du Tsaratanana** *Mt* Madag
12C2 **Massillon** USA
70B3 **Massina** Region, Mali
73D6 **Massinga** Mozam
74E1 **Massingir** Mozam
45J6 **Masteksay** Kazakhstan
77G5 **Masterton** NZ
53C5 **Masuda** Japan
72B4 **Masuku** Gabon
64C2 **Maşyāf** Syria
4E4 **Matachewan** Can
16A4 **Matachie** Mexico
72B4 **Matadi** Zaïre
26A1 **Matagalpa** Nic
7L5 **Matagami** Can
8D4 **Matagorda B** USA
17F4 **Matagorda I** USA
78C1 **Matakana I** NZ
73B5 **Matala** Angola
62C3 **Matale** Sri Lanka
70A3 **Matam** Sen
70C3 **Matameye** Niger
21C2 **Matamoros** Mexico
69B2 **Ma'tan as Sarra** *Well* Libya
7M5 **Matane** Can
21D2 **Matanzas** Cuba
13F1 **Matapédia** *R* Can
28A2 **Mataquito** *R* Chile
62C3 **Matara** Sri Lanka
76A1 **Mataram** Indon
26D7 **Matarani** Peru
29E1 **Mataripe** Brazil
39C1 **Mataró** Spain
74D3 **Matatiele** S Africa
78A3 **Mataura** NZ
21B2 **Matehuala** Mexico
37E3 **Matelica** Italy
23L1 **Matelot** Trinidad
40D2 **Matera** Italy
43E3 **Mátészalka** Hung
71D1 **Mateur** Tunisia
20C2 **Mather** USA
12C1 **Matheson** Can
17F4 **Mathis** USA
60D3 **Mathura** India
57G9 **Mati** Phil
22C2 **Matías Romero** Mexico
56E3 **Matisiri** *I* Indon
35E5 **Matlock** Eng
71D2 **Matmatma** Tunisia
27G6 **Mato Grosso** Brazil
27G6 **Mato Grosso** State, Brazil
27G7 **Mato Grosso do Sul** State, Brazil
74E2 **Matola** Mozam
67G2 **Matrah** Oman
37E1 **Matrel im Osttirol** Austria
64A3 **Matrûh** Egypt
53C4 **Matsue** Japan
53E3 **Matsumae** Japan
53D4 **Matsumoto** Japan
53D5 **Matsusaka** Japan
53C5 **Matsuyama** Japan
7K5 **Mattagami** *R* Can
4F4 **Mattawa** Can
5H4 **Mattawamkeag** USA
40B1 **Matterhorn** *Mt* Switz/Italy
18C2 **Matterhorn** *Mt* USA
23C2 **Matthew Town** Bahamas
4E4 **Mattice** Can
14D2 **Mattituck** USA
12B3 **Mattoon** USA
60B2 **Matun** Afghan
23L1 **Matura B** Trinidad
26F2 **Maturin** Ven
61B2 **Mau** India
73D5 **Maúa** Mozam
38C1 **Maubeuge** France
75B2 **Maude** Aust
xxxJ8 **Maud Seamount** Atlantic O
20E5 **Maui** *I* Hawaiian Is
28A3 **Maule** *R* Chile
12C2 **Maumee** USA
12C2 **Maumee** *R* USA
57B4 **Maumere** Indon
73C5 **Maun** Botswana
20E5 **Mauna Kea** *Mt* Hawaiian Is
20E5 **Mauna Loa** *Mt* Hawaiian Is
6F3 **Maunoir,L** Can
37B3 **Maures** *Mts* France
38C2 **Mauriac** France
70A2 **Mauritania** Republic, Africa
68K10 **Mauritius** *I* Indian O
12A2 **Mauston** USA
37E1 **Mauterndorf** Austria
73C5 **Mavinga** Angola
74E1 **Mavue** Mozam
61D3 **Mawlaik** Burma
Mawlamyine = Moulmein
79G10 **Mawson** *Base* Ant
11B2 **Max** USA
74E1 **Maxaila** Mozam
22C1 **Maxcaltzin** Mexico
56C3 **Maya** *I* Indon
49P4 **Maya** *R* Russian Fed
64D2 **Mayādīn** Syria
9F4 **Mayaguana** *I* Bahamas
23D3 **Mayagüez** Puerto Rico
70C3 **Mayahi** Niger
72B4 **Mayama** Congo
63D1 **Mayamey** Iran
57D4 **Mayanobab** Indon
34C4 **Maybole** Scot
9F3 **May,C** USA
75E3 **Maydena** Aust
36D1 **Mayen** Germany
38B2 **Mayenne** France
19D4 **Mayer** USA
3E3 **Mayerthorpe** Can
67E4 **Mayfa'ah** Yemen
12B3 **Mayfield** USA
16A3 **Mayhill** USA
45G7 **Maykop** Russian Fed
48H6 **Maymaneh** Afghan
55B1 **Maymyo** Burma
6E3 **Mayo** Can
14B3 **Mayo** USA
71J4 **Mayo Deo** *R* Cam
57F8 **Mayon** *Mt* Phil
39C2 **Mayor** *Mt* Spain
28C3 **Mayor Buratovich** Arg
78C1 **Mayor I** NZ
25D1 **Mayor P Lagerenza** Par
73E5 **Mayotte** *I* Indian O
23H2 **May Pen** Jamaica
14C3 **May Point,C** USA
37D1 **Mayrhofen** Austria
53B1 **Mayskiy** Russian Fed
14C3 **Mays Landing** USA
3G2 **Mayson L** Can
12C3 **Maysville** USA
72B4 **Mayumba** Gabon
11C2 **Mayville** USA
16B1 **Maywood** USA
73C5 **Mazabuka** Zambia
22B1 **Mazapil** Mexico
60D1 **Mazar** China
65C3 **Mazār** Jordan
40C3 **Mazara del Vallo** Italy
60B1 **Mazar-i-Sharif** Afghan
21B2 **Mazatlán** Mexico
44C4 **Mazeikiai** Lithuania
65C3 **Mazra** Jordan
73D6 **Mbabane** Swaziland
71J4 **Mbabo,Mt** Cam
72B3 **Mbaïki** CAR
73D4 **Mbala** Zambia
73C6 **Mbalabala** Zim
72D3 **Mbale** Uganda
72B3 **Mbalmayo** Cam
72B3 **Mbam** *R* Cam
73D5 **Mbamba Bay** Tanz
72B3 **Mbandaka** Zaïre
72B4 **Mbanza Congo** Angola
72B4 **Mbanza-Ngungu** Zaïre
72D4 **Mbarara** Uganda
71J4 **Mbé** Cam
71J4 **Mbengwi** Cam
72B3 **Mbènza** Congo
72B3 **Mbére** *R* Cam
73D4 **Mbeya** Tanz
72B4 **Mbinda** Congo
71J4 **Mbouda** Cam
70A3 **Mbout** Maur
72C4 **Mbuji-Mayi** Zaïre
71J3 **Mbuli** *R* Nig
72D4 **Mbulu** Tanz
28D1 **Mburucuyá** Arg
70B2 **Mcherrah** Region, Alg
73D5 **Mchinji** Malawi
4C2 **M'Clintock** Can
55D3 **Mdrak** Viet
16B2 **Meade** USA
10G1 **Meade** *R* USA
8B3 **Mead,L** USA
6H4 **Meadow Lake** Can
12C2 **Meadville** USA
54D2 **Me-akan dake** *Mt* Japan
7N4 **Mealy Mts** Can
75C1 **Meandarra** Aust
6G4 **Meander River** Can
35B5 **Meath** Irish Rep
38C2 **Meaux** France
66C2 **Mecca** S Arabia
19C4 **Mecca** USA
14D1 **Mechanicville** USA
48G2 **Mechdusharskiy, Ostrov** *I* Russian Fed
42A2 **Mechelen** Belg
71B2 **Mecheria** Alg
42C2 **Mecklenburger Bucht** *B* Germany
42C2 **Mecklenburg-Vorpommern** State, Germany
73D5 **Meconta** Mozam
73D5 **Mecuburi** Mozam
73E5 **Mecufi** Mozam
73D5 **Mecula** Mozam
56A2 **Medan** Indon
28C3 **Medanos** Arg
28D2 **Médanos** Arg
71C1 **Médéa** Alg
26C2 **Medellin** Colombia
71E2 **Medenine** Tunisia
8A2 **Medford** USA
41F2 **Medgidia** Rom
28B2 **Media Agua** Arg
41E1 **Mediaş** Rom
18C1 **Medical Lake** USA
11A3 **Medicine Bow** USA
16A1 **Medicine Bow Mts** USA
11A3 **Medicine Bow Peak** *Mt* USA
6G5 **Medicine Hat** Can
16C2 **Medicine Lodge** USA
29D2 **Medina** Brazil
11C2 **Medina** N Dakota, USA
14A1 **Medina** New York, USA
66C2 **Medina** S Arabia
39B1 **Medinaceli** Spain
39A1 **Medina del Campo** Spain
39A1 **Medina de Rio Seco** Spain
16C4 **Medina L** USA
61C3 **Medinīpur** India
68E4 **Mediterranean S** Europe
3F3 **Medley** Can
45K5 **Mednogorsk** Russian Fed
49S4 **Mednyy, Ostrov** *I* Russian Fed
61E2 **Mêdog** China
72B3 **Medouneu** Gabon
45G5 **Medvedista** *R* Russian Fed
49S2 **Medvezh'i Ova** *I* Russian Fed
44E3 **Medvezh'yegorsk** Russian Fed
76A3 **Meekatharra** Aust
16A1 **Meeker** USA
60D3 **Meerut** India
18E2 **Meeteetse** USA
72D3 **Mēga** Eth
41E3 **Megalópolis** Greece
41E3 **Mégara** Greece
61D2 **Meghālaya** State, India
61D3 **Meghna** *R* Bang
65C2 **Megido** *Hist Site* Israel
4F4 **Mégiscane** *R* Can
71C2 **Mehaïguene** *R* Alg
10E3 **Mehoryuk** USA
63C3 **Mehran** *R* Iran
63C2 **Mehriz** Iran
29C2 **Meia Ponte** *R* Brazil
72B3 **Meiganga** Cam
55B1 **Meiktila** Burma
37C1 **Meiringen** Switz
52A4 **Meishan** China
42C2 **Meissen** Germany
52D5 **Mei Xian** China
52D5 **Meizhou** China
26D8 **Mejillones** Chile
72B3 **Mekambo** Gabon
4E4 **Mekatina** Can
71C4 **Mek'elē** Eth
71A2 **Meknès** Mor
Mekong = Lancang
55D3 **Mekong, R** Camb
71G3 **Mekrou** *R* Benin
55C5 **Melaka** Malay
xxviiiJ5 **Melanesia** *Region* Pacific O
56D3 **Melawi** *R* Indon
76D4 **Melbourne** Aust
9E4 **Melbourne** USA
8C4 **Melchor Muźguiz** Mexico
44K5 **Meleuz** Russian Fed
72B2 **Melfi** Chad
6H4 **Melfort** Can
71B1 **Melilla** N W Africa
25B6 **Melimoyu** *Mt* Chile
28C2 **Melincué** Arg
28A2 **Melipilla** Chile
11B2 **Melita** Can
45F6 **Melitopol'** Ukraine
7M2 **Meliville Bugt** *B* Greenland
72D3 **Melka Guba** Eth
71D1 **Mellègue** *R* Tunisia
66D4 **Melli** *R* Eth
74E2 **Melmoth** S Africa
28C2 **Melo** Arg
25F4 **Melo** Urug
29A3 **Melo** *R* Brazil
20B2 **Melones Res** USA
10H2 **Melozitna** *R* USA
11D2 **Melrose** USA
37C1 **Mels** Switz
36E1 **Melsungen** Germany
56E1 **Melta,Mt** Malay
35E5 **Melton Mowbray** Eng
38C2 **Melun** France
6H4 **Melville** Can
23Q2 **Melville,C** Dominica
6F3 **Melville Hills** *Mts* Can
76C2 **Melville I** Aust
6G2 **Melville I** Can
7N4 **Melville,L** Can
7K3 **Melville Pen** Can
73E5 **Memba** Mozam
76A1 **Memboro** Indon
42C3 **Memmingen** Germany
56C2 **Mempawan** Indon
9E3 **Memphis** Tennessee, USA
16B3 **Memphis** Texas, USA
17D3 **Mena** USA
43G2 **Mena** Ukraine
35C5 **Menai Str** Wales
70C3 **Ménaka** Mali
12B2 **Menasha** USA
28B4 **Mencué** Arg
56D3 **Mendawai** *R* Indon
38C3 **Mende** France
72D3 **Mendebo** *Mts* Eth
10E4 **Mendenhall,C** USA
76D1 **Mendi** PNG
35D6 **Mendip Hills** *Upland* Eng
18B2 **Mendocino,C** USA
xxixM3 **Mendocino Seascarp** Pacific O
20B2 **Mendota** California, USA
12B2 **Mendota** Illinois, USA
25C4 **Mendoza** Arg
25C5 **Mendoza** State, Arg
41F3 **Menemen** Turk
36B1 **Menen** Belg
52D3 **Mengcheng** China
56C3 **Menggala** Indon
55B1 **Menghai** China
52A5 **Mengla** China
55B1 **Menglian** China
52A5 **Mengzi** China
5H3 **Menihek Lakes** Can
76D4 **Menindee** Aust
75B2 **Menindee L** Aust
75A3 **Meningie** Aust
12B1 **Menominee** USA
12B2 **Menomonee Falls** USA
12A2 **Menomonie** USA
73B5 **Menongue** Angola
39C1 **Menorca** *I* Spain
10K3 **Mentasta Mts** USA
16A2 **Mentmore** USA
56C3 **Mentok** Indon
37B3 **Menton** France
12C2 **Mentor** USA
36B2 **Ménu** France
52A2 **Menyuan** China
44J4 **Menzelinsk** Russian Fed
42B2 **Meppen** Germany
36A3 **Mer** France
56E2 **Merah** Indon
17D2 **Meramec** *R* USA
40C1 **Merano** Italy
76D1 **Merauke** Indon
8A3 **Merced** USA
20B2 **Merced** *R* USA
25B4 **Mercedario** *Mt* Chile
25C4 **Mercedes** Arg
25E4 **Mercedes** Buenos Aires, Arg
25E3 **Mercedes** Corrientes, Arg
25E4 **Mercedes** Urug
78C1 **Mercury B** NZ
78C1 **Mercury Is** NZ
6F2 **Mercy B** Can
7M3 **Mercy,C** Can
16B2 **Meredith,L** *L* USA
55B3 **Mergui** Burma
55B3 **Mergui Arch** Burma
21D2 **Mérida** Mexico
39A2 **Mérida** Spain
26D2 **Mérida** Ven
9E3 **Meridian** USA
75C3 **Merimbula** Aust
75B2 **Meringur** Aust
16B3 **Merkel** USA
72D2 **Merowe** Sudan
76A4 **Merredin** Aust
34C4 **Merrick** *Mt* Scot
12B1 **Merrill** USA
12B2 **Merrillville** USA
14E1 **Merrimack** *R* USA
11B3 **Merriman** USA
3D3 **Merritt** Can
15C3 **Merritt Island** USA
75D2 **Merriwa** Aust
66D4 **Mersa Fatma** Eth
39B2 **Mers el Kebir** Alg
35D5 **Mersey** *R* Eng
35D5 **Merseyside** County, Eng
45E8 **Mersin** Turk
55C5 **Mersing** Malay
60C3 **Merta** India
35D6 **Merthyr Tydfil** Wales
39A2 **Mertola** Port
72D4 **Meru** *Mt* Tanz
45F7 **Merzifon** Turk
36D2 **Merzig** Germany
8B3 **Mesa** USA
16A2 **Mesa Verde Nat Pk** USA
36E1 **Meschede** Germany
64D1 **Mescit Dağ** *Mt* Turk
10G4 **Meshik** USA
72C3 **Meshra'er Req** Sudan
37C1 **Mesocco** Switz
41E3 **Mesolóngion** Greece
19D3 **Mesquite** Nevada, USA
17C3 **Mesquite** Texas, USA
71C2 **Messaad** Alg
73D5 **Messalo** *R* Mozam
40D3 **Messina** Italy
74D1 **Messina** S Africa
41E3 **Messíni** Greece
41E3 **Messiniakós Kólpos** *G* Greece
Mesta = Néstos
41E2 **Mesta, R** Bulg
40C1 **Mestre** Italy
26D3 **Meta** *R* Colombia
44E4 **Meta** *R* Russian Fed
26E2 **Meta** *R* Ven
7L3 **Meta Incognita Pen** Can
17D4 **Metairie** USA
18C1 **Metaline Falls** USA
25D3 **Metán** Arg
73D5 **Metangula** Mozam
40D2 **Metaponto** Italy
37E3 **Metauro** *R* Italy
66C4 **Metemma** Eth
34D3 **Methil** Scot
14E1 **Methuen** USA
78B2 **Methven** NZ
10M4 **Metlakatla** USA
71D2 **Metlaoui** Tunisia
12B3 **Metropolis** USA
62B2 **Mettūr** India
38D2 **Metz** France
36E2 **Metzingen** Germany
56A2 **Meulaboh** Indon
36A2 **Meulan** France
36A3 **Meung-sur-Loire** France
36D2 **Meurthe** *R* France
36D2 **Meurthe-et-Moselle** Department, France
36C2 **Meuse** Department, France
36C1 **Meuse** *R* Belg
38D2 **Meuse** *R* France
17C3 **Mexia** USA
21A1 **Mexicali** Mexico
19E3 **Mexican Hat** USA
21B2 **Mexico** Federal Republic, Central America

México
Monreal del Campo

21C3 **México** Mexico
22B2 **México** State, Mexico
17D2 **Mexico** USA
21C2 **Mexico,G of** C America
37A2 **Meximieux** France
65C3 **Mezada** *Hist Site* Israel
22C2 **Mezcala** Mexico
22D2 **Mezcalapa** *R* Mexico
44G2 **Mezen'** Russian Fed
44H3 **Mezen'** *R* Russian Fed
43G1 **Mezha** *R* Russian Fed
44J1 **Mezhdusharskiy, Ostrov** *I* Russian Fed
22B1 **Mezquital** Mexico
22B1 **Mezquital** *R* Mexico
53E1 **Mgachi** Russian Fed
60D4 **Mhow** India
22C2 **Miahuatlán** Mexico
19D4 **Miami** Arizona, USA
9E4 **Miami** Florida, USA
17D2 **Miami** Oklahoma, USA
9E4 **Miami Beach** USA
45H8 **Miandowāb** Iran
73E5 **Miandrivazo** Madag
45H8 **Miāneh** Iran
60C2 **Mianwali** Pak
52A3 **Mianyang** China
52C3 **Mianyang** China
52A3 **Mianzhu** China
52E2 **Miaodao Qundao** *Arch* China
52B4 **Miao Ling** *Upland* China
44L5 **Miass** Russian Fed
43E3 **Michalovce** Slovakia
18D1 **Michel** Can
23D3 **Miches** Dom Rep
9E2 **Michigan** State, USA
12B2 **Michigan City** USA
9E2 **Michigan,L** USA
12C1 **Michipicoten** Can
7K5 **Michipicoten I** Can
22B2 **Michoacan** State, Mexico
41F2 **Michurin** Bulg
45G5 **Michurinsk** Russian Fed
47J5 **Micronesia, Fed. States of** Pacific O
xxviiiJ4 **Micronesia** *Region* Pacific O
56C2 **Midai** *I* Indon
xxxF4 **Mid Atlantic Ridge** Atlantic O
36B1 **Middelburg** Neth
18B2 **Middle Alkali L** USA
xxixO4 **Middle America Trench** Pacific O
62E2 **Middle Andaman** *I* Indian O
14E2 **Middleboro** USA
74C3 **Middleburg** Cape Province, S Africa
14B2 **Middleburg** Pennsylvania, USA
74D2 **Middleburg** Transvaal, S Africa
14B3 **Middleburg** Virginia, USA
14C1 **Middleburgh** USA
13E2 **Middlebury** USA
9E3 **Middlesboro** USA
35E4 **Middlesbrough** Eng
5H5 **Middleton** Can
14D2 **Middletown** Connecticut, USA
14C3 **Middletown** Delaware, USA
13E2 **Middletown** New York, USA
12C3 **Middletown** Ohio, USA
14B2 **Middletown** Pennsylvania, USA
14C1 **Middleville** USA
71B2 **Midelt** Mor
35D6 **Mid Glamorgan** County, Wales
66D3 **Mīdī** Yemen
xxviiiE5 **Mid Indian Basin** Indian O
xxviiiE5 **Mid Indian Ridge** Indian O
7L5 **Midland** Can
12C2 **Midland** Michigan, USA
8C3 **Midland** Texas, USA
73E6 **Midongy Atsimo** Madag
xxixK4 **Mid Pacific Mts** Pacific O
18C2 **Midvale** USA
xxixL3 **Midway Is** Pacific O
11A3 **Midwest** USA
17C2 **Midwest City** USA
64D2 **Midyat** Turk
41E2 **Midžor** *Mt* Serbia, Yugos
43E2 **Mielec** Pol
41F1 **Miercurea-Ciuc** Rom
39A1 **Mieres** Spain
14B2 **Mifflintown** USA
22B1 **Miguel Auza** Mexico
22C1 **Miguihuana** Mexico
54B4 **Mihara** Japan
52D1 **Mijun Shuiku** *Res* China
41E2 **Mikhaylovgrad** Bulg
45G5 **Mikhaylovka** Russian Fed
48J4 **Mikhaylovskiy** Russian Fed
65C4 **Mikhrot Timna** Israel
32K6 **Mikkeli** Fin
3F2 **Mikkwa** *R* Can
41F3 **Míkonos** *I* Greece
42D3 **Mikulov** Czech Republic
73D4 **Mikumi** Tanz
44J3 **Mikun** Russian Fed
53D4 **Mikuni-sammyaku** *Mts* Japan
54C4 **Mikura-jima** *I* Japan
11D2 **Milaca** USA
26C4 **Milagro** Ecuador
Milan = Milano
15B1 **Milan** USA
39C2 **Milana** Alg
73D5 **Milange** Mozam
57B2 **Milango** *R* Indon
40B1 **Milano** Italy
45D8 **Milas** Turk
11C2 **Milbank** USA
76D4 **Mildura** Aust
52A5 **Mile** China
64D3 **Mileh Tharthār** *L* Iraq
76E3 **Miles** Aust
8C2 **Miles City** USA
14D2 **Milford** Connecticut, USA
13D3 **Milford** Delaware, USA
13E2 **Milford** Massachusetts, USA
17C1 **Milford** Nebraska, USA
14E1 **Milford** New Hampshire, USA
14C2 **Milford** Pennsylvania, USA
19D3 **Milford** Utah, USA
35C6 **Milford Haven** Wales
35C6 **Milford Haven** *Sd* Wales
17C2 **Milford L** USA
78A2 **Milford Sd** NZ
71C1 **Miliana** Alg
11A2 **Milk** *R* USA
49R4 **Mil'kovo** Russian Fed
3F4 **Milk River** Can
38C3 **Millau** France
14D2 **Millbrook** USA
15C2 **Milledgeville** USA
11D2 **Mille Lacs L** USA
11C3 **Miller** USA
10K3 **Miller,Mt** USA
45G6 **Millerovo** Russian Fed
14B2 **Millersburg** USA
75A1 **Millers Creek** Aust
14D1 **Millers Falls** USA
14D2 **Millerton** USA
20C2 **Millerton L** USA
75B3 **Millicent** Aust
15B1 **Millington** USA
13F1 **Millinocket** USA
75D1 **Millmerran** Aust
37E1 **Millstätter See** *L* Austria
13F1 **Milltown** Can
18D1 **Milltown** USA
20A2 **Mill Valley** USA
13E3 **Millville** USA
7Q2 **Milne Land** *I* Greenland
20E5 **Milolii** Hawaiian Is
41E3 **Mílos** *I* Greece
76D3 **Milparinka** Aust
14B2 **Milroy** USA
15B2 **Milton** Florida, USA
78A3 **Milton** NZ
14B2 **Milton** Pennsylvania, USA
9E2 **Milwaukee** USA
4D3 **Miminiska L** Can
54D2 **Mimmaya** Japan
20C1 **Mina** USA
39C2 **Mina** *R* Alg
64E4 **Mīnā' al Ahmadī** Kuwait
63D3 **Mīnāb** Iran
57B2 **Minahassa Pen** Indon
4C4 **Minaki** Can
53C5 **Minamata** Japan
56B2 **Minas** Indon
25E4 **Minas** Urug
5J4 **Minas Basin** Can
5J4 **Minas Chan** Can
27J7 **Minas Gerais** State, Brazil
29D2 **Minas Novas** Brazil
21C3 **Minatitlan** Mexico
55A1 **Minbu** Burma
55A1 **Minbya** Burma
28A2 **Mincha** Chile
34B3 **Minch,Little** *Sd* Scot
34B2 **Minch,North** *Sd* Scot
33B2 **Minch,The** *Sd* Scot
10H3 **Minchumina,L** USA
37D2 **Mincio** *R* Italy
57F9 **Mindanao** *I* Phil
17D3 **Minden** Louisiana, USA
20C1 **Minden** Nevada, USA
42B2 **Minden** Germany
75B2 **Mindona L** Aust
57F8 **Mindoro** *I* Phil
57F8 **Mindoro Str** Phil
35D6 **Minehead** Eng
27H7 **Mineiros** Brazil
17C3 **Mineola** USA
22C1 **Mineral de Monte** Mexico
16C3 **Mineral Wells** USA
14B2 **Minersville** USA
5J3 **Mingan** Can
75B2 **Mingary** Aust
45H7 **Mingechaurskoye Vodokhranilische** *Res* Azerbaijan
53B2 **Mingshui** China
52A2 **Minhe** China
37D3 **Minialo** Italy
62A3 **Minicoy** *I* India
52D4 **Min Jiang** *R* Fujian, China
52A4 **Min Jiang** *R* Sichuan, China
20C2 **Minkler** USA
75A2 **Minlaton** Aust
52A2 **Minle** China
71H4 **Minna** Nig
9D2 **Minneapolis** USA
6J4 **Minnedosa** Can
9D2 **Minnesota** State, USA
11C3 **Minnesota** *R* USA
4C4 **Minnitaki L** Can
39A1 **Miño** *R* Spain
8C2 **Minot** USA
52A2 **Minqin** China
52A3 **Min Shan** *Upland* China
44D5 **Minsk** Belorussia
43E2 **Mińsk Mazowiecki** Pol
10J3 **Minto** USA
6G2 **Minto Inlet** *B* Can
7L4 **Minto,L** Can
16A2 **Minturn** USA
50C1 **Minusinsk** Russian Fed
52A3 **Min Xian** China
65A3 **Minyael Qamn** Egypt
4F4 **Miquelon** Can
7N5 **Miquelon** *I* France
20D3 **Mirage L** USA
62A1 **Miraj** India
25E5 **Miramar** Arg
5J4 **Miramichi B** Can
60B2 **Miram Shah** Pak
29A2 **Miranda** *R* Brazil
39B1 **Miranda de Ebro** Spain
29A3 **Mirandia** Brazil
37D2 **Mirandola** Italy
60B2 **Mir Bachchen Kūt** Afghan
67F3 **Mirbāt** Oman
37A1 **Mirebeau** France
36C2 **Mirecourt** France
56D2 **Miri** Malay
63E3 **Miri** *Mt* Pak
70A3 **Mirik,C** Maur
28D1 **Mirinay** *R* Arg
63E3 **Mīrjāveh** Iran
37E2 **Mirna** *R* Croatia, Yugos
49K3 **Mirnoye** Russian Fed
49N3 **Mirnyy** Russian Fed
79G9 **Mirnyy** *Base* Ant
3H2 **Miron L** Can
43G3 **Mironovka** Ukraine
60C2 **Mirpur** Pak
60B3 **Mirpur Khas** Pak
41E3 **Mirtoan S** Greece
53B4 **Miryang** S Korea
61B2 **Mirzāpur** India
22C2 **Misantla** Mexico
5J4 **Miscou I** Can
60C1 **Misgar** Pak
53C2 **Mishan** China
12B2 **Mishawaka** USA
10F2 **Misheguk Mt** USA
54B4 **Mi-shima** *I* Japan
61E2 **Mishmi Hills** India
77E2 **Misima** *I* Solomon Is
25F3 **Misiones** State, Arg
43E3 **Miskolc** Hung
65D2 **Mismīyah** Syria
51G7 **Misoöl** *I* Indon
3H2 **Misow L** Can
69A1 **Misrātah** Libya
7K5 **Missinaibi** *R* Can
12C1 **Missinaibi L** Can
3H2 **Missinipe** Can
11B3 **Mission** S Dakota, USA
17F4 **Mission** Texas, USA
18B1 **Mission City** Can
13D2 **Mississauga** Can
9D3 **Mississippi** State, USA
9D3 **Mississippi** *R* USA
17E3 **Mississippi Delta** USA
8B2 **Missoula** USA
71B2 **Missour** Mor
9D3 **Missouri** State, USA
9D3 **Missouri** *R* USA
11C3 **Missouri Valley** USA
5G4 **Mistassini** Can
5G4 **Mistassini** *R* Can
5G3 **Mistassini Provincial Park** Can
5J2 **Mistastin L** Can
26D7 **Misti** *Mt* Peru
5J2 **Mistinibi L** Can
75C1 **Mitchell** Aust
8D2 **Mitchell** USA
76D2 **Mitchell** *R* Aust
9E3 **Mitchell,Mt** USA
51H8 **Mitchell River** Aust
65A3 **Mit el Nasâra** Egypt
65A3 **Mît Ghamr** Egypt
60B3 **Mithankot** Pak
41F3 **Mitilíni** Greece
22C2 **Mitla** Mexico
65B3 **Mitla P** Egypt
77G2 **Mitre** *I* Solomon Is
10G4 **Mitrofania I** USA
41E2 **Mitrovica** Serbia, Yugos
72D2 **Mits'iwa** Eritrea
37E1 **Mittersill** Austria
26D3 **Mitu** Colombia
72C4 **Mitumbar** *Mts* Zaïre
73C4 **Mitwaba** Zaïre
72B3 **Mitzic** Gabon
54C3 **Miura** Japan
52C3 **Mi Xian** China
50G3 **Miyake** *I* Japan
54C4 **Miyake-jima** *I* Japan
50F4 **Miyako** *I* Japan
53C5 **Miyakonojō** Japan
53C5 **Miyazaki** Japan
54C3 **Miyazu** Japan
53C5 **Miyoshi** Japan
52D1 **Miyun** China
54D2 **Mi-zaki** *Pt* Japan
72D3 **Mīzan Teferī** Eth
69A1 **Mizdah** Libya
41F1 **Mizil** Rom
61D3 **Mizo Hills** India
61D3 **Mizoram** Union Territory, India
65C3 **Mizpe Ramon** Israel
79F11 **Mizuho** *Base* Ant
53E4 **Mizusawa** Japan
32H7 **Mjolby** Sweden
73C5 **Mkushi** Zambia
74E2 **Mkuzi** S Africa
42C2 **Mladá Boleslav** Czech Republic
43E2 **Mława** Pol
41D2 **Mljet** *I* Croatia, Yugos
74D2 **Mmabatho** S Africa
60D2 **Mnadi** India
57C4 **Moa** *I* Indon
70A4 **Moa** *R* Sierra Leone
65C3 **Moab** Region, Jordan
8C3 **Moab** USA
74E2 **Moamba** Mozam
72B4 **Moanda** Congo
72B4 **Moanda** Gabon
73C4 **Moba** Zaïre
54D3 **Mobara** Japan
72C3 **Mobaye** CAR
72C3 **Mobayi** Zaire
9D3 **Moberly** USA
9E3 **Mobile** USA
9E3 **Mobile B** USA
15B2 **Mobile Pt** USA
8C2 **Mobridge** USA
73E5 **Moçambique** Mozam
Moçâmedes = Namibe
55C1 **Moc Chau** Viet
74D1 **Mochudi** Botswana
73E5 **Mocimboa da Praia** Mozam
26C3 **Mocoa** Colombia
29C3 **Mococa** Brazil
28D2 **Mocoreta** *R* Arg
22C1 **Moctezulma** *R* Mexico
22B1 **Moctezuma** Mexico
73D5 **Mocuba** Mozam
37B2 **Modane** France
74D2 **Modder** *R* S Africa
40C2 **Modena** Italy
36D2 **Moder** *R* France
8A3 **Modesto** USA
20B2 **Modesto Res** USA
40C3 **Modica** Italy
42D3 **Mödling** Austria
76D4 **Moe** Aust
37C1 **Moesa** *R* Switz
34D4 **Moffat** Scot
60D2 **Moga** India
68J7 **Mogadiscio** Somalia
61E2 **Mogaung** Burma
29C3 **Mogi das Cruzes** Brazil
43G2 **Mogilev** Belorussia
45D6 **Mogilev Podol'skiy** Ukraine
29C3 **Mogi-Mirim** Brazil
73E5 **Mogincual** Mozam
37E2 **Mogliano** Italy
28B2 **Mogna** Arg
50E1 **Mogocha** Russian Fed
48K4 **Mogochin** Russian Fed
61E3 **Mogok** Burma
74D1 **Mogol** *R* S Africa
39A2 **Moguer** Spain
78C1 **Mohaka** *R* NZ
74D3 **Mohale's Hoek** Lesotho
11B2 **Mohall** USA
71C1 **Mohammadia** Alg
71A2 **Mohammedia** Mor
61D3 **Mohanganj** Bang
19D3 **Mohave,L** USA
14C1 **Mohawk** USA
13E2 **Mohawk** *R* USA
73E5 **Mohéli,I** Comoros
10E3 **Mohican,C** USA
73D4 **Mohoro** Tanz
48J5 **Mointy** Kazakhstan
32G5 **Mo i Rana** Nor
5H3 **Moisie** *R* Can
38C3 **Moissac** France
19C3 **Mojave** USA
20D3 **Mojave** *R* USA
8B3 **Mojave Desert** USA
56D4 **Mojokerto** Indon
66C4 **Mokada** *Mt* Eth
61C2 **Mokama** India
78B1 **Mokau** *R* NZ
20B1 **Mokelumne Aqueduct** USA
20B1 **Mokelumne Hill** USA
20B1 **Mokelumne North Fork** *R* USA
74D2 **Mokhotlong** Lesotho
71E1 **Moknine** Tunisia
61D2 **Mokokchūng** India
72B2 **Mokolo** Cam
53B5 **Mokp'o** S Korea
44G5 **Moksha** *R* Russian Fed
22C1 **Molango** Mexico
41E3 **Moláoi** Greece
32F6 **Molde** Nor
45D6 **Moldova**
41E1 **Moldoveanu** *Mt* Rom
71F4 **Mole Nat Pk** Ghana
74D1 **Molepolole** Botswana
36D2 **Molesheim** France
40D2 **Molfetta** Italy
28A3 **Molina** Chile
37E1 **Möll** *R* Austria
26D7 **Mollendo** Peru
44D5 **Molodechno** Belorussia
79G11 **Molodezhnaya** *Base* Ant
20E5 **Molokai** *I* Hawaiian Is
44H4 **Moloma** *R* Russian Fed
75C2 **Molong** Aust
74C2 **Molopo** *R* S Africa/ Botswana
72B3 **Molounddu** Cam
4B3 **Molson L** Can
76B1 **Molucca S** Indon
51F7 **Moluccas** *Is* Indon
73D5 **Moma** Mozam
27K5 **Mombaca** Brazil
72D4 **Mombasa** Kenya
54D2 **Mombetsu** Japan
72C3 **Mompono** Zaïre
42C2 **Mon** *I* Den
34B3 **Monach** *Is* Scot
38D3 **Monaco** Principality, Europe
34C3 **Monadhliath** *Mts* Scot
35B4 **Monaghan** County, Irish Rep
35B4 **Monaghan** Irish Rep
16B3 **Monahans** USA
23D3 **Mona Pass** Caribbean
3C3 **Monarch Mt** Can
16A2 **Monarch P** USA
6G4 **Monashee Mts** Can
33B3 **Monastereven** Irish Rep
54D2 **Monbetsu** Japan
37B2 **Moncalieri** Italy
27J4 **Monção** Brazil
32L5 **Monchegorsk** Russian Fed
42B2 **Mönchen-gladbach** Germany
21B2 **Monclova** Mexico
7M5 **Moncton** Can
39A1 **Mondego** *R* Port
40B2 **Mondovi** Italy
23H1 **Moneague** Jamaica
13D2 **Monessen** USA
4F4 **Monet** Can
17D2 **Monett** USA
40C1 **Monfalcone** Italy
39A1 **Monforte de Lemos** Spain
72C3 **Monga** Zaïre
72C3 **Mongala** *R* Zaïre
72D3 **Mongalla** Sudan
55D1 **Mong Cai** Viet
72B2 **Mongo** Chad
50C2 **Mongolia** Republic, Asia
73C5 **Mongu** Zambia
19C3 **Monitor Range** *Mts* USA
72C4 **Monkoto** Zaïre
35D6 **Monmouth** Eng
12A2 **Monmouth** USA
3D3 **Monmouth,Mt** Can
71G4 **Mono** *R* Togo
19C3 **Mono L** USA
41D2 **Monopoli** Italy
39B1 **Monreal del Campo** Spain

45K6 **Mugodzhary** *Mts* Kazakhstan
64C4 **Mughayra** S Arabia
64A2 **Muğla** Turk
45K6 **Mugodzhary** *Mts* Kazakhstan
61B2 **Mugu** Nepal
52A3 **Muguaping** China
66C2 **Muhammad Qol** Sudan
64D3 **Muhaywir** Iraq
36E2 **Mühlacker** Germany
42C3 **Mühldorf** Germany
42C2 **Muhlhausen** Germany
32K6 **Muhos** Fin
55C4 **Mui Bai Bung** *C* Camb
35B5 **Muine Bheag** Irish Rep
73C5 **Mujimbeji** Zambia
43E3 **Mukachevo** Ukraine
56D2 **Mukah** Malay
54D2 **Mukawa** Japan
50H4 **Muko-jima** *I* Japan
61B2 **Muktinath** Nepal
60B2 **Mukur** Afghan
53B2 **Mulan** China
17D2 **Mulberry** USA
10G3 **Mulchatna** *R* USA
28A3 **Mulchén** Chile
42C2 **Mulde** *R* Germany
11B3 **Mule Creek** USA
16B3 **Muleshoe** USA
51H8 **Mulgrave I** Aust
39B2 **Mulhacén** *Mt* Spain
36D1 **Mülheim** Germany
36D3 **Mulhouse** France
52A4 **Muli** China
53C3 **Muling** China
53C2 **Muling He** *R* China
34C3 **Mull** *I* Scot
62C3 **Mullaitvu** Sri Lanka
75C2 **Mullaley** Aust
76A3 **Mullewa** Aust
36D3 **Müllheim** Germany
14C3 **Mullica** *R* USA
35B5 **Mullingar** Irish Rep
34C4 **Mull of Kintyre** *Pt* Scot
34B4 **Mull of Oa** *C* Scot
75D1 **Mullumbimby** Aust
73C5 **Mulobezi** Zambia
60C2 **Multan** Pak
57C3 **Muluku** *Is* Indon
Mumbai = Bombay
73C5 **Mumbwa** Zambia
45H6 **Mumra** Russian Fed
57B4 **Muna** *I* Indon
42C2 **München** Germany
3C2 **Muncho Lake** Can
54A3 **Munchön** N Korea
12B2 **Muncie** USA
75A1 **Munconnie,L** Aust
14B2 **Muncy** USA
42B2 **Münden** Germany
75D1 **Mundubbera** Aust
75C1 **Mungallala** Aust
75C1 **Mungallala** *R* Aust
72C3 **Mungbere** Zaïre
61B3 **Mungeli** India
61C2 **Munger** India
75C1 **Mungindi** Aust
Munich = München
12B1 **Munising** USA
25B8 **Muñoz Gomero,Pen** Chile
3J2 **Munroe L** Can
54A3 **Munsan** S Korea
36E2 **Münsingen** Germany
36D2 **Munster** France
37C1 **Münster** Switz
42B2 **Münster** Germany
36D1 **Münsterland** Region, Germany
41E1 **Muntii Apuseni** *Mts* Rom
41E1 **Muntii Călimanilor** *Mts* Rom
41E1 **Muntii Carpaţii Meridionali** *Mts* Rom
41E1 **Muntii Rodnei** *Mts* Rom
41E1 **Muntii Zarandului** *Mts* Rom
64C2 **Munzur Silsilesi** *Mts* Turk
48D3 **Muomio** Fin
55C1 **Muong Khoua** Laos
55D3 **Muong Man** Viet
55D2 **Muong Nong** Laos
55C1 **Muong Ou Neua** Laos
55C1 **Muong Sai** Laos
55C2 **Muong Sen** Viet
55C1 **Muong Sing** Laos
55C1 **Muong Son** Laos
32J5 **Muonio** Fin
32J5 **Muonio** *R* Sweden/Fin
66B3 **Muqaddam** *Watercourse* Sudan
72E3 **Muqdisho** Somalia
40C1 **Mur** *R* Austria
53D4 **Murakami** Japan
25B7 **Murallón** *Mt* Chile/Arg
44H4 **Murashi** Russian Fed

64D2 **Murat** *R* Turk
40B3 **Muravera** Sardegna
54D3 **Murayama** Japan
67F4 **Murcanyo** Somalia
63C2 **Murcheh Khvort** Iran
78B2 **Murchison** NZ
76A3 **Murchison** *R* Aust
39B2 **Murcia** Region, Spain
39B2 **Murcia** Spain
11B3 **Murdo** USA
41E1 **Mureş** *R* Rom
41E1 **Muresui** *R* Rom
15B1 **Murfreesboro** USA
15D1 **Murfreesboro** USA
36E2 **Murg** *R* Germany
48H6 **Murgab** *R* Turkmenistan
60B2 **Murgha Kibzai** Pak
75D1 **Murgon** Aust
61C3 **Muri** India
29D3 **Muriaé** Brazil
73C4 **Muriege** Angola
44E2 **Murmansk** Russian Fed
44G4 **Murom** Russian Fed
53E3 **Muroran** Japan
39A1 **Muros** Spain
53C5 **Muroto** Japan
54B4 **Muroto-zaki** *C* Japan
18C2 **Murphy** Idaho, USA
15C1 **Murphy** N Carolina, USA
20B1 **Murphys** USA
12B3 **Murray** Kentucky, USA
18D2 **Murray** Utah, USA
75B2 **Murray** *R* Aust
3D2 **Murray** *R* Can
75A3 **Murray Bridge** Aust
51H7 **Murray,L** PNG
15C2 **Murray,L** USA
74C3 **Murraysburg** S Africa
xxixM3 **Murray Seacarp** Pacific O
36E2 **Murrhardt** Germany
75B2 **Murrumbidgee** *R* Aust
75C2 **Murrumburrah** Aust
75D2 **Murrurundi** Aust
37B1 **Murten** Switz
75B3 **Murtoa** Aust
78C1 **Murupara** NZ
61B3 **Murwāra** India
75D1 **Murwillimbah** Aust
64D2 **Muş** Turk
41E2 **Musala** *Mt* Bulg
53B3 **Musan** N Korea
67G1 **Musandam** *Pen* Oman
Muscat = Masqat
67G2 **Muscat** *Region* Oman
11D3 **Muscatine** USA
76C3 **Musgrave Range** *Mts* Aust
72B4 **Mushie** Zaïre
14E2 **Muskeget Chan** USA
12B2 **Muskegon** USA
12B2 **Muskegon** *R* USA
17C2 **Muskogee** USA
66C3 **Musmar** Sudan
72D4 **Musoma** Tanz
76D1 **Mussau** *I* PNG
18E1 **Musselshell** *R* USA
73B5 **Mussende** Angola
38C2 **Mussidan** France
41F2 **Mustafa-Kemalpasa** Turk
61B2 **Mustang** Nepal
54A2 **Musu-dan** *C* N Korea
75D2 **Muswelibrook** Aust
69B2 **Mut** Egypt
73D5 **Mutarara** Mozam
73D5 **Mutare** Zim
57B4 **Mutis** *Mt* Indon
44K2 **Mutnyy Materik** Russian Fed
73D5 **Mutoko** Zim
73E5 **Mutsamudu** Comoros
73C5 **Mutshatsha** Zaïre
53E3 **Mutsu** Japan
53E3 **Mutsu-wan** *B* Japan
5K3 **Mutton Bay** Can
29C1 **Mutunópolis** Brazil
52B2 **Mu Us Shamo** *Desert* China
73B4 **Muxima** Angola
49N4 **Muya** Russian Fed
44E3 **Muyezerskiy** Russian Fed
72D4 **Muyinga** Burundi
73C4 **Muyumba** Zaïre
59E1 **Muyun Kum** *Desert* Kazakhstan
60C2 **Muzaffarābad** Pak
60C2 **Muzaffargarh** Pak
60D3 **Muzaffarnagar** India
61C2 **Muzaffarpur** India
48H3 **Muzhi** Russian Fed
59G2 **Muzlag** *Mt* China
3B3 **Muzon,C** USA
59F2 **Muztagala** *Mt* China
73D5 **Mvuma** Zim
72D4 **Mwanza** Tanz
73C4 **Mwanza** Zaïre
72C4 **Mweka** Zaïre

73C4 **Mwene Ditu** Zaïre
73D6 **Mwenezi** Zim
72C4 **Mwenga** Zaïre
73C4 **Mweru** *L* Zambia
73C5 **Mwinilunga** Zambia
61E4 **Myanaung** Burma
Myanma = Burma
61E3 **Myingyan** Burma
55B1 **Myingyao** Burma
55B3 **Myinmoletkat** *Mt* Burma
61E3 **Myinmu** Burma
61E2 **Myitkyina** Burma
55B3 **Myitta** Burma
61E3 **Myittha** Burma
61D3 **Mymensingh** Bang
50G3 **Myojin** *I* Japan
54A2 **Myongchon** N Korea
54A2 **Myonggan** N Korea
32F6 **Myrdal** Nor
32B2 **Myrdalsjökur** *Mts* Iceland
15D2 **Myrtle Beach** USA
18B2 **Myrtle Creek** USA
49U3 **Mys Chaplino** *C* Russian Fed
49M2 **Mys Chelyuskin** *C* Russian Fed
10D3 **Mys Chukotskiy** *Pt* Russian Fed
10E2 **Mys Dezhneva** *Pt* Russian Fed
32G7 **Mysen** Nor
44G2 **Mys Kanin Nos** *C* Russian Fed
49S4 **Mys Kronotskiy** *C* Russian Fed
43D3 **Myślenice** Pol
42C2 **Myśliborz** Pol
49R4 **Mys Lopatka** *C* Russian Fed
49T3 **Mys Navarin** *C* Russian Fed
10D2 **Mys Nygchigen** *Pt* Russian Fed
49T4 **Mys Olyutorskiy** *C* Russian Fed
62B2 **Mysore** India
45E7 **Mys Sarych** *C* Ukraine
10D2 **Mys Serdtse Kamen** *Pt* Russian Fed
49T2 **Mys Shelagskiy** *C* Russian Fed
49U3 **Mys Shmidta** Russian Fed
49S4 **Mys Sivuchiy** *C* Kirgizia
44F2 **Mys Svyatoy Nos** *C* Russian Fed
14E2 **Mystic** USA
45J7 **Mys Tyub-Karagan** *Pt* Kazakhstan
49Q4 **Mys Yelizavety** *C* Russian Fed
48H2 **Mys Zhelaniya** *C* Russian Fed
55D3 **My Tho** Viet
18B2 **Mytle Point** USA
73D5 **Mzimba** Malawi
73D5 **Mzuzú** Malawi

N

20E5 **Naalehu** Hawaiian Is
32J6 **Naantali** Fin
35B5 **Naas** Irish Rep
54C4 **Nabari** Japan
44J4 **Naberezhnyye Chelny** Russian Fed
10K3 **Nabesna** *R* USA
71E1 **Nabeul** Tunisia
29A3 **Nabileque** *R* Brazil
65C2 **Nablus** Israel
73E5 **Nacala** Mozam
18B1 **Naches** USA
5H2 **Nachikapau L** Can
73D5 **Nachingwea** Tanz
20B3 **Nacimiento** *R* USA
20B3 **Nacimiento Res** USA
17D3 **Nacogdoches** USA
55A3 **Nacondam** *I* Indian O
21B1 **Nacozari** Mexico
36E1 **Nadel** *Mt* Germany
77G2 **Nadi** Fiji
60C4 **Nadiād** India
39B2 **Nador** Mor
63C2 **Nadushan** Iran
44E3 **Nadvoitsy** Russian Fed
43E3 **Nadvornaya** Ukraine
42C1 **Naestved** Den
54B4 **Nagahama** Japan
61E2 **Naga Hills** Burma
54C3 **Nagai** Japan
10G5 **Nagai** *I* USA
61D2 **Nāgaland** State, India
53D4 **Nagano** Japan
53D4 **Nagaoka** Japan
61D2 **Nagaon** India
62B2 **Nāgappattinam** India
60C4 **Nagar Parkar** Pak
53B5 **Nagasaki** Japan

73B5 **Namutoni** Namibia
53B4 **Namwön** S Korea
3D4 **Nanaimo** Can
53B3 **Nanam** N Korea
75D1 **Nanango** Aust
53D4 **Nanao** Japan
54C3 **Nanatsu-jima** *I* Japan
52B3 **Nanbu** China
53B2 **Nancha** China
52D4 **Nanchang** China
52B3 **Nanchong** China
62E3 **Nancowry** *I* Indian O
38D2 **Nancy** France
61B1 **Nanda Devi** *Mt* India
62B1 **Nānded** India
75D2 **Nandewar Range** *Mts* Aust
60C4 **Nandurbar** India
62B1 **Nandyāl** India
72B3 **Nanga Eboko** Cam
57B4 **Nangahale** Indon
60C1 **Nanga Parbat** *Mt* Pak
56D3 **Nangapinoh** Indon
56D3 **Nangatayap** Indon
36B2 **Nangis** France
54A2 **Nangnim** N Korea
53B3 **Nangnim Sanmaek** *Mts* N Korea
61D2 **Nang Xian** China
62B2 **Nanjangüd** India
52D3 **Nanjing** China
Nanking = Nanjing
54B4 **Nankoku** Japan
52C4 **Nan Ling** Region, China
55D1 **Nanliu** *R* China
52B5 **Nanning** China
7O3 **Nanortalik** Greenland
52A5 **Nanpan Jiang** *R* China
61B2 **Nānpāra** India
52D4 **Nanping** China
7J1 **Nansen Sd** Can
72D4 **Nansio** Tanz
38B2 **Nantes** France
14C2 **Nanticoke** USA
3F3 **Nanton** Can
52E3 **Nantong** China
37A1 **Nantua** France
14E2 **Nantucket** USA
14E2 **Nantucket I** USA
14E2 **Nantucket Sd** USA
14A2 **Nanty Glo** USA
77G1 **Nanumanga** *I* Tuvalu
77G1 **Nanumea** *I* Tuvalu
29D2 **Nanuque** Brazil
52C3 **Nanyang** China
52D2 **Nanyang Hu** *L* China
72D3 **Nanyuki** Kenya
53D4 **Naoetsu** Japan
60B4 **Naokot** Pak
20A1 **Napa** USA
10F3 **Napaiskak** USA
13D2 **Napanee** Can
48K4 **Napas** Russian Fed
7N3 **Napassoq** Greenland
55D2 **Nape** Laos
78C1 **Napier** NZ
Naples = Napoli
15E4 **Naples** Florida, USA
14B1 **Naples** New York, USA
17D3 **Naples** Texas, USA
52B5 **Napo** China
26D4 **Napo** *R* Peru/Ecuador
11C2 **Napoleon** USA
40C2 **Napoli** Italy
63B1 **Naqadeh** Iran
65C3 **Naqb Ishtar** Jordan
54C4 **Nara** Japan
70B3 **Nara** Mali
76D4 **Naracoorte** Aust
22C1 **Naranjos** Mexico
62B1 **Narasarāopet** India
55C4 **Narathiwat** Thai
61D3 **Narayanganj** Bang
62B1 **Nārāyenpet** India
38C3 **Narbonne** France
60D2 **Narendranagar** India
7L2 **Nares Str** Can
43E2 **Narew** *R* Pol
54D3 **Narita** Japan
60C4 **Narmada** *R* India
60D3 **Nārnaul** India
44F4 **Naro Fominsk** Russian Fed
72D4 **Narok** Kenya
43F2 **Narovl'a** Belorussia
60C2 **Narowal** Pak
76D4 **Narrabri** Aust
75C1 **Narran** *L* Aust
75C1 **Narran** *R* Aust
75C2 **Narrandera** Aust
76A4 **Narrogin** Aust
75C2 **Narromine** Aust
12C3 **Narrows** USA
14C2 **Narrowsburg** USA
60D4 **Narsimhapur** India
62C1 **Narsīpatnam** India
7O3 **Narssalik** Greenland

Narssaq **Nissan Is**

7O3 **Narssaq** Greenland
7O3 **Narssarssuaq** Greenland
74B2 **Narubis** Namibia
54D3 **Narugo** Japan
54B4 **Naruto** Japan
44D4 **Narva** Russian Fed
32H5 **Narvik** Nor
60D3 **Narwāna** India
44J2 **Nar'yan Mar** Russian Fed
75B1 **Narylico** Aust
48J5 **Naryn** Kazakhstan
71H4 **Nasarawa** Nig
xxxD5 **Nasca Ridge** Pacific O
14E1 **Nashua** USA
17D3 **Nashville** Arkansas, USA
15B1 **Nashville** Tennessee, USA
41D1 **Našice** Croatia, Yugos
60C4 **Nāsik** India
72D3 **Nasir** Sudan
5J3 **Naskaupi** *R* Can
3C2 **Nass** *R* Can
23B1 **Nassau** Bahamas
14D1 **Nassau** USA
69C2 **Nasser,L** Egypt
71F4 **Nassian** Ivory Coast
32G7 **Nässjö** Sweden
7L4 **Nastapoka Is** Can
4F2 **Nastapoca** *R* Can
73C6 **Nata** Botswana
27L5 **Natal** Brazil
56A2 **Natal** Indon
74E2 **Natal** Province, S Africa
xxviiiC6 **Natal Basin** Indian O
63C2 **Natanz** Iran
7M4 **Natashquan** Can
7M4 **Natashquan** *R* Can
17D3 **Natchez** USA
17D3 **Natchitoches** USA
75C3 **Nathalia** Aust
7Q2 **Nathorsts Land** *Region* Greenland
3D2 **Nation** *R* Can
19C4 **National City** USA
National Republic of China = Taiwan
71G3 **Natitingou** Benin
54D3 **Natori** Japan
72D4 **Natron** *L* Tanz
76A4 **Naturaliste,C** Aust
4D4 **Naubinway** USA
37D1 **Nauders** Austria
42C2 **Nauen** Germany
14D2 **Naugatuck** USA
42C2 **Naumburg** Germany
65C3 **Naur** Jordan
77F1 **Nauru** *I* Pacific O
49M4 **Naushki** Russian Fed
74B2 **Naute Dam** *Res* Namibia
22C1 **Nautla** Mexico
63E2 **Nauzad** Afghan
8C3 **Navajo Res** USA
39A2 **Navalmoral de la Mata** Spain
25C9 **Navarino** *I* Chile
39B1 **Navarra** Province, Spain
28D3 **Navarro** Arg
17C3 **Navasota** USA
17C3 **Navasota** *R* USA
39A1 **Navia** *R* Spain
28A2 **Navidad** Chile
60C4 **Navlakhi** India
45E5 **Navlya** Russian Fed
21B2 **Navojoa** Mexico
41E3 **Návpaktos** Greece
41E3 **Návplion** Greece
71F3 **Navrongo** Ghana
60C4 **Navsāri** India
65D2 **Nawá** Syria
61C3 **Nawāda** India
60B2 **Nawah** Afghan
60B3 **Nawrabshah** Pak
52B4 **Naxi** China
41F3 **Náxos** *I* Greece
22B1 **Nayar** Mexico
22A1 **Nayarit** State, Mexico
63C3 **Nāy Band** Iran
63D2 **Nay Band** Iran
53E3 **Nayoro** Japan
29E1 **Nazaré** Brazil
65C2 **Nazareth** Israel
38B2 **Nazay** France
26D6 **Nazca** Peru
64A2 **Nazilli** Turk
49L4 **Nazimovo** Russian Fed
3D3 **Nazko** *R* Can
58B5 **Nazrēt** Eth
67G2 **Nazwa** Oman
48J4 **Nazyvayevsk** Russian Fed
73B4 **Ndalatando** Angola
72C3 **Ndélé** CAR
72B4 **Ndendé** Gabon
77F2 **Ndende** *I* Solomon Is
72B2 **Ndjamena** Chad
72B4 **Ndjolé** Gabon
73C5 **Ndola** Zambia
71F4 **Ndouci** Ivory Coast
75C1 **Neabul** Aust
75A1 **Neales** *R* Aust
41E3 **Neápolis** Greece
10A6 **Near Is** USA
35D6 **Neath** Wales
75C1 **Nebine** *R* Aust
48G6 **Nebit Dag** Turkmenistan
8C2 **Nebraska** State, USA
17C1 **Nebraska City** USA
3D3 **Nechako** *R* Can
17C3 **Neches** *R* USA
36E2 **Neckar** *R* Germany
28D3 **Necochea** Arg
61D2 **Nêdong** China
19D4 **Needles** USA
12B2 **Neenah** USA
6J4 **Neepawa** Can
36C1 **Neerpelt** Belg
71D2 **Nefta** Tunisia
53E1 **Neftegorsk** Russian Fed
49M4 **Neftelensk** Russian Fed
72D3 **Negelli** Eth
65C3 **Negev** *Desert* Israel
29A3 **Negla** *R* Par
45C6 **Negolu** *Mt* Rom
62B3 **Negombo** Sri Lanka
55A2 **Negrais,C** Burma
26B4 **Negritos** Peru
26F4 **Negro** *R* Amazonas, Brazil
28C4 **Negro** *R* Arg
29A2 **Negro** *R* Mato Grosso de Sul, Brazil
29A3 **Negro** *R* Par
28D2 **Negro** *R* Urug
57F8 **Negros** *I* Phil
41F2 **Negru Voda** Rom
63E2 **Nehbāndan** Iran
53A2 **Nehe** China
52B4 **Neijiang** China
12A2 **Neillsville** USA
52B1 **Nei Monggol** Autonomous Region, China
26C3 **Neira** Colombia
72D3 **Nejo** Eth
72D3 **Nek'emte** Eth
44E4 **Nelidovo** Russian Fed
11C3 **Neligh** USA
62B2 **Nellore** India
53D2 **Nel'ma** Russian Fed
3E4 **Nelson** Can
78B2 **Nelson** NZ
6J4 **Nelson** *R* Can
75B3 **Nelson,C** Aust
10F3 **Nelson I** USA
74E2 **Nelspruit** S Africa
70B3 **Néma** Maur
52A1 **Nemagt Uul** *Mt* Mongolia
53D1 **Nemilen** *R* Russian Fed
41F1 **Nemira** *Mt* Rom
53B2 **Nemor He** *R* China
36B2 **Nemours** France
43E1 **Nemunas** *R* Lithuania
53F3 **Nemuro** Japan
49O5 **Nen** *R* China
33B3 **Nenagh** Irish Rep
10J3 **Nenana** USA
10J3 **Nenana** *R* USA
35E5 **Nene** *R* Eng
56F6 **Nenggiri** *R* Malay
53B2 **Nenjiang** China
17C2 **Neodesha** USA
17D2 **Neosho** USA
49M4 **Nepa** Russian Fed
59G3 **Nepal** Kingdom, Asia
61B2 **Nepalganj** Nepal
19D3 **Nephi** USA
65C3 **Neqarot** *R* Israel
28A3 **Nequén** State, Arg
50E1 **Nerchinsk** Russian Fed
41D2 **Neretva** *R* Bosnia-Herzegovina/Croatia, Yugos
51H5 **Nero Deep** Pacific O
44G2 **Nes'** Russian Fed
32C1 **Neskaupstaður** Iceland
36B2 **Nesle** France
16C2 **Ness City** USA
3B2 **Nesselrode,Mt** Can/USA
5G3 **Nestaocano** *R* Can
41E2 **Néstos** *R* Greece
65C2 **Netanya** Israel
14C2 **Netcong** USA
42B2 **Netherlands** Kingdom, Europe
2M7 **Netherlands Antilles** *Is* Caribbean
49N4 **Net Oktyobr'ya** Russian Fed
61D3 **Netrakona** Bang
7L3 **Nettilling L** Can
42C2 **Neubrandenburg** Germany
37B1 **Neuchâtel** Switz
36C2 **Neufchâteau** Belg
36C2 **Neufchâteau** France
38C2 **Neufchâtel** France
36A2 **Neufchâtel-en-Bray** France
42B2 **Neumünster** Germany
40D1 **Neunkirchen** Austria
36D2 **Neunkirchen** Germany
28B3 **Neuquén** Arg
25B6 **Neuquén** State, Arg
28B3 **Neuquén** *R* Arg
42C2 **Neuruppin** Germany
15D1 **Neuse** *R* USA
36D1 **Neuss** Germany
42C2 **Neustadt** Germany
36E2 **Neustadt an der Weinstrasse** Germany
36E3 **Neustadt im Schwarzwald** Germany
42C2 **Neustrelitz** Germany
36D1 **Neuwied** Germany
8B3 **Nevada** State, USA
17D2 **Nevada** USA
28A3 **Nevada de Chillán** *Mts* Chile/Arg
22B2 **Nevada de Collima** Mexico
22C2 **Nevada de Toluca** *Mt* Mexico
65C3 **Nevatim** Israel
44D4 **Nevel'** Russian Fed
53E2 **Nevel'sk** Russian Fed
53A1 **Never** Russian Fed
38C2 **Nevers** France
75C2 **Nevertire** Aust
64B2 **Nevşehir** Turk
44L4 **Nev'yansk** Russian Fed
12C3 **New** *R* USA
73D5 **Newala** Tanz
12B3 **New Albany** Indiana, USA
17E3 **New Albany** Mississippi, USA
27G2 **New Amsterdam** Guyana
75C1 **New Angledool** Aust
13D3 **Newark** Delaware, USA
9F2 **Newark** New Jersey, USA
14B1 **Newark** New York, USA
12C2 **Newark** Ohio, USA
35E5 **Newark-upon-Trent** Eng
13E2 **New Bedford** USA
3C3 **New Bella Bella** Can
18B1 **Newberg** USA
15D1 **New Bern** USA
15C2 **Newberry** USA
74C3 **New Bethesda** S Africa
23B2 **New Bight** Bahamas
12C3 **New Boston** USA
16C4 **New Braunfels** USA
14D2 **New Britain** USA
76E1 **New Britain** *I* PNG
76E1 **New Britain Trench** PNG
7M5 **New Brunswick** Province, Can
14C2 **New Brunswick** USA
14C2 **Newburgh** USA
35E6 **Newbury** Eng
14E1 **Newburyport** USA
14D2 **New Canaan** USA
75D2 **Newcastle** Aust
5H4 **Newcastle** Can
12B3 **New Castle** Indiana, USA
35C4 **Newcastle** N Ire
12C2 **New Castle** Pennsylvania, USA
74D2 **Newcastle** S Africa
11B3 **Newcastle** Wyoming, USA
34E4 **Newcastle upon Tyne** Eng
76C2 **Newcastle Waters** Aust
20C3 **New Cuyama** USA
60D3 **New Delhi** India
75D2 **New England Range** *Mts* Aust
10F4 **Newenham,C** USA
14A1 **Newfane** USA
35E6 **New Forest,The** Eng
7M4 **Newfoundland** Province, Can
7N5 **Newfoundland** *I* Can
xxxF2 **Newfoundland Basin** Atlantic O
17D2 **New Franklin** USA
34C4 **New Galloway** Scot
77E1 **New Georgia** *I* Solomon Is
7M5 **New Glasgow** Can
76D1 **New Guinea** *I* S E Asia
66C3 **New Haifa** Sudan
10H4 **Newhalen** USA
20C3 **Newhall** USA
9F2 **New Hampshire** State, USA
11D3 **New Hampton** USA
74E2 **New Hanover** S Africa
76E1 **New Hanover** *I* PNG
35F6 **Newhaven** Eng
13E2 **New Haven** USA
3C2 **New Hazelton** Can
77F3 **New Hebrides Trench** Pacific O
17D3 **New Iberia** USA
76E1 **New Ireland** *I* PNG
9F2 **New Jersey** State, USA
16B3 **Newkirk** USA
7L5 **New Liskeard** Can
14D2 **New London** USA
76A3 **Newman** Aust
20B2 **Newman** USA
35F5 **Newmarket** Eng
13D3 **New Market** USA
18C2 **New Meadows** USA
8C3 **New Mexico** State, USA
14D2 **New Milford** Connecticut, USA
14C2 **New Milford** Pennsylvania, USA
15C2 **Newnan** USA
75E3 **New Norfolk** Aust
9D3 **New Orleans** USA
14C2 **New Paltz** USA
12C2 **New Philadelphia** USA
78B1 **New Plymouth** NZ
17D2 **Newport** Arkansas, USA
35E6 **Newport** Eng
12C3 **Newport** Kentucky, USA
14D1 **Newport** New Hampshire, USA
18B2 **Newport** Oregon, USA
14B2 **Newport** Pennsylvania, USA
13E2 **Newport** Rhode Island, USA
13E2 **Newport** Vermont, USA
35D6 **Newport** Wales
18C1 **Newport** Washington, USA
20D4 **Newport Beach** USA
9F3 **Newport News** USA
23B1 **New Providence** *I* Caribbean
35C6 **Newquay** Eng
7L3 **New Quebec Crater** Can
35B5 **New Ross** Irish Rep
35B4 **Newry** N Ire
New Siberian Is = Novosibirskye Ostrova
15C3 **New Smyrna Beach** USA
76D4 **New South Wales** State, Aust
10G4 **New Stuyahok** USA
11D3 **Newton** Iowa, USA
17C2 **Newton** Kansas, USA
14E1 **Newton** Massachusetts, USA
17E3 **Newton** Mississippi, USA
14C2 **Newton** New Jersey, USA
35D6 **Newton Abbot** Eng
34B4 **Newton Stewart** N Ire
34C4 **Newton Stewart** Scot
11B2 **New Town** USA
35D5 **Newtown** Wales
35C4 **Newtownards** N Ire
11D3 **New Ulm** USA
14B2 **Newville** USA
5J4 **New Waterford** Can
6F5 **New Westminster** Can
9F2 **New York** State, USA
9F2 **New York** USA
77G5 **New Zealand** Dominion, SW Pacific O
xxixK7 **New Zealand Plat** Pacific O
44G4 **Neya** Russian Fed
63C3 **Neyrīz** Iran
63D1 **Neyshābūr** Iran
45E5 **Nezhin** Ukraine
72B4 **Ngabé** Congo
71J3 **Ngadda** Nig
73C6 **Ngami** *L* Botswana
71J4 **N'Gaoundéré** Cam
78C1 **Ngaruawahia** NZ
78C1 **Ngaruroro** *R* NZ
78C1 **Ngauruhoe,Mt** NZ
72B4 **Ngo** Congo
55D2 **Ngoc Linh** *Mt* Viet
72B3 **Ngoko** *R* Cam
50C3 **Ngoring Hu** *L* China
72D4 **Ngorongoro Crater** Tanz
72B4 **N'Gounié** *R* Gabon
72B2 **Nguigmi** Niger
51G6 **Ngulu** *I* Pacific O
71J3 **Nguru** Nig
55D3 **Nha Trang** Viet
29A2 **Nhecolandia** Brazil
75B3 **Nhill** Aust
74E2 **Nhlangano** Swaziland
55D2 **Nhommarath** Laos
76C2 **Nhulunbuy** Aust
70B3 **Niafounké** Mali
12B1 **Niagara** USA
13D2 **Niagara Falls** Can
13D2 **Niagara Falls** USA
56D2 **Niah** Malay
70B4 **Niakaramandougou** Ivory Coast
70C3 **Niamey** Niger
72C3 **Niangara** Zaïre
71F3 **Niangoloko** Burkina
72C3 **Nia Nia** Zaïre
53A2 **Nianzishan** China
56A2 **Nias** *I* Indon
21D3 **Nicaragua** Republic, C America
40D3 **Nicastro** Italy
38D3 **Nice** France
23B1 **Nicholl's Town** Bahamas
14C2 **Nicholson** USA
59H5 **Nicobar Is** Indian O
65B1 **Nicosia** Cyprus
21D3 **Nicoya,Pen de** Costa Rica
36E1 **Nidda** *R* Germany
43E2 **Nidzica** Pol
36D2 **Niederbronn** France
37E1 **Niedere Tauern** *Mts* Austria
42B2 **Niedersachsen** State, Germany
72C4 **Niemba** Zaïre
42B2 **Nienburg** Germany
36D1 **Niers** *R* Germany
70B4 **Niete,Mt** Lib
27G2 **Nieuw Amsterdam** Suriname
27G2 **Nieuw Nickeire** Suriname
74B3 **Nieuwoudtville** S Africa
36B1 **Nieuwpoort** Belg
22B1 **Nieves** Mexico
64B2 **Niğde** Turk
70C3 **Niger** Republic, Africa
71H4 **Niger** State, Nig
71H4 **Niger** *R* Nig
70C4 **Nigeria** Federal Republic, Africa
12C1 **Nighthawk L** Can
41E2 **Nigríta** Greece
54D3 **Nihommatsu** Japan
53D4 **Niigata** Japan
53C5 **Niihama** Japan
54C4 **Nii-jima** *I* Japan
54B4 **Niimi** Japan
53D4 **Niitsu** Japan
65C3 **Nijil** Jordan
42B2 **Nijmegen** Neth
44E2 **Nikel'** Russian Fed
71G3 **Nikki** Benin
53D4 **Nikko** Japan
45E6 **Nikolayev** Ukraine
45H6 **Nikolayevsk** Russian Fed
49Q4 **Nikolayevsk-na-Amure** Russian Fed
44H5 **Nikol'sk** Penza, Russian Fed
44H4 **Nikol'sk** Russian Fed
10E5 **Nikolski** USA
45E6 **Nikopol** Ukraine
64C1 **Niksar** Turk
63E3 **Nīkshahr** Iran
41D2 **Nikšić** Montenegro, Yugos
77G1 **Nikunau** *I* Kiribati
57C4 **Nila** *I* Indon
58B3 **Nile** *R* N E Africa
12B2 **Niles** USA
62B2 **Nilgiri Hills** India
22D2 **Niltepec** Mexico
60C4 **Nimach** India
38C3 **Nîmes** France
75C3 **Nimmitabel** Aust
72D3 **Nimule** Sudan
59F5 **Nine Degree Chan** Indian O
xxviiiF5 **Ninety-East Ridge** Indian O
75C3 **Ninety Mile Beach** Aust
53B3 **Ning'an** China
52D4 **Ningde** China
52D4 **Ningdu** China
50C3 **Ningjing Shan** *Mts* China
55D1 **Ningming** China
52A4 **Ningnan** China
52B2 **Ningxia** Province, China
52B2 **Ning Xian** China
52B5 **Ninh Binh** Vietnam
76D1 **Ninigo Is** PNG
10H3 **Ninilchik** USA
29A3 **Nioaque** Brazil
11B3 **Niobrara** *R* USA
72B4 **Nioki** Zaïre
70B3 **Nioro du Sahel** Mali
38B2 **Niort** France
6H4 **Nipawin** Can
7K5 **Nipigon** Can
4D4 **Nipigon B.** Can
7K5 **Nipigon,L** Can
7K5 **Nipissing,L** *R* Can
20B3 **Nipomo** USA
19C3 **Nipton** USA
29C1 **Niquelândia** Brazil
62B1 **Nirmal** India
61C2 **Nirmāli** India
41E2 **Niš** Serbia, Yugos
67E4 **Nisāb** Yemen
53C5 **Nishinoomote** Japan
50G4 **Nishino-shima** *I* Japan
54B3 **Nishino-shima** *I* Japan
54A4 **Nishi-suidō** *Str* S Korea
54B4 **Nishiwaki** Japan
4D2 **Niskibi** *R* Can
10L3 **Nisling** *R* Can
77E1 **Nissan Is** PNG

Nisutlin Oban

10M3 **Nisutlin** *R* Can
7L4 **Nitchequon** Can
27K8 **Niterói** Brazil
34D4 **Nith** *R* Scot
57B4 **Nitibe** Indon
43D3 **Nitra** Slovakia
12C3 **Nitro** USA
77J2 **Niue** *I* Pacific O
77G2 **Niulakita** *I* Tuvalu
56D2 **Niut** *Mt* Malay
77G1 **Niutao** *I* Tuvalu
36C1 **Nivelles** Belg
38C2 **Nivernais** Region, France
32L5 **Nivskiy** Russian Fed
62B1 **Nizāmābād** India
65C3 **Nizana** *Hist Site* Israel
44J4 **Nizhnekamskoye Vodokhranilische** *Res* Russian Fed
50C1 **Nizhneudinsk** Russian Fed
44K4 **Nizhniye Sergi** Russian Fed
44G5 **Nizhniy Lomov** Russian Fed
44G4 **Nizhniy Novgorod** Russian Fed
44J3 **Nizhniy Odes** Russian Fed
44K4 **Nizhniy Tagil** Russian Fed
49L3 **Nizhnyaya Tunguska** *R* Russian Fed
44G2 **Nizhnyaya Zolotitsa** Russian Fed
64C2 **Nizip** Turk
73C5 **Njoko** *R* Zambia
73D4 **Njombe** Tanz
72B3 **Nkambé** Cam
71F4 **Nkawkaw** Ghana
73D5 **Nkhata Bay** Malawi
72B3 **Nkongsamba** Cam
70C3 **N'Konni** Niger
61D3 **Noakhali** Bang
10F2 **Noatak** USA
10G2 **Noatak** *R* USA
53C5 **Nobeoka** Japan
54D2 **Noboribetsu** Japan
29A1 **Nobres** Brazil
37D1 **Noce** *R* Italy
22B1 **Nochistlán** Mexico
22C2 **Nochixtlán** Mexico
17C3 **Nocona** USA
21A1 **Nogales** Sonora, Mexico
19D4 **Nogales** USA
22C2 **Nogales** Veracruz, Mexico
37D2 **Nogara** Italy
54B4 **Nogata** Japan
36C2 **Nogent-en-Bassigny** France
36A2 **Nogent-le-Rotrou** France
36B2 **Nogent-sur-Seine** France
44F4 **Noginsk** Russian Fed
53E1 **Nogliki** Russian Fed
28D2 **Nogoyá** Arg
28D2 **Nogoyá** *R* Arg
60C3 **Nohar** India
54D2 **Noheji** Japan
74C1 **Nojane** Botswana
54C4 **Nojima-zaki** *C* Japan
63E3 **Nok Kundi** Pak
3H2 **Nokomis L** Can
72B3 **Nola** CAR
44H4 **Nolinsk** Russian Fed
14E2 **Nomans Land** *I* USA
22B1 **Nombre de Dioz** Mexico
10E3 **Nome** USA
36D2 **Nomeny** France
52B1 **Nomgon** Mongolia
54A4 **Nomo-saki** *Pt* Japan
6H3 **Nonachol L** Can
53B3 **Nong'an** China
55C2 **Nong Khai** Thai
74E2 **Nongoma** S Africa
77G1 **Nonouti** *I* Kiribati
54A3 **Nonsan** S Korea
74B2 **Noordoewer** Namibia
10F2 **Noorvik** USA
3C4 **Nootka Sd** Can
22C2 **Nopala** Mexico
72B4 **Noqui** Angola
7L5 **Noranda** Can
36B1 **Nord** Department, France
48D2 **Nordaustlandet** *I* Barents S
3E3 **Nordegg** Can
32F6 **Nordfjord** *Inlet* Nor
32F8 **Nordfriesische** *Is* Germany
42C2 **Nordhausen** Germany
32J4 **Nordkapp** *C* Nor
7N3 **Nordre Strømfjord** Greenland
42B2 **Nordrhein Westfalen** State, Germany
32G5 **Nord Stronfjället** *Mt* Sweden
49N2 **Nordvik** Russian Fed
35B5 **Nore** *R* Irish Rep
35F5 **Norfolk** County, Eng
11C3 **Norfolk** Nebraska, USA
13D3 **Norfolk** Virginia, USA
77F3 **Norfolk I** Aust
17D2 **Norfolk L** USA
xxixK5 **Norfolk Ridge** Pacific O
49K3 **Noril'sk** Russian Fed
12B2 **Normal** USA
17C2 **Norman** USA
38B2 **Normandie** Region, France
15C1 **Norman,L** USA
76D2 **Normanton** Aust
10N2 **Norman Wells** Can
44B2 **Norra Storfjället** *Mt* Sweden
15C1 **Norris L** USA
13D2 **Norristown** USA
32H7 **Norrköping** Sweden
32H6 **Norrsundet** Sweden
32H7 **Norrtälje** Sweden
76B4 **Norseman** Aust
53C1 **Norsk** Russian Fed
29A1 **Nortelândia** Brazil
xxxJ2 **North** *S* N W Europe
35E4 **Northallerton** Eng
76A4 **Northam** Aust
74D2 **Northam** S Africa
xxxE3 **North American Basin** Atlantic O
76A3 **Northampton** Aust
35E5 **Northampton** County, Eng
35E5 **Northampton** Eng
13E2 **Northampton** USA
62E2 **North Andaman** *I* Indian O
6G3 **North Arm** *B* Can
15C2 **North Augusta** USA
7M4 **North Aulatsivik I** Can
3G3 **North Battleford** Can
7L5 **North Bay** Can
18B2 **North Bend** USA
34D3 **North Berwick** Scot
14E1 **North Berwick** USA
7M5 **North,C** Can
77G4 **North C** NZ
10D5 **North C** USA
16B2 **North Canadian** *R* USA
4C3 **North Caribou L** Can
9E3 **North Carolina** State, USA
18B1 **North Cascade Nat Pk** USA
4E4 **North Chan** Can
34C4 **North Chan** Ire/Scot
14A1 **North Collins** USA
8C2 **North Dakota** State, USA
35F6 **North Downs** Eng
36A1 **North Downs** *Upland* Eng
13D2 **North East** USA
xxxH1 **North East Atlantic Basin** Atlantic O
10E3 **Northeast C** USA
4B2 **Northern Indian L** Can
33B3 **Northern Ireland** UK
11D2 **Northern Light L** Can
23L1 **Northern Range** *Mts* Trinidad
76C2 **Northern Territory** Aust
34D3 **North Esk** *R* Scot
14D1 **Northfield** Massachusetts, USA
11D3 **Northfield** Minnesota, USA
35F6 **North Foreland** Eng
36A1 **North Foreland** *Pt* Eng
10H3 **North Fork** *R* USA
4E3 **North French** *R* Can
5K3 **North Head** *C* Can
78B1 **North I** NZ
4B2 **North Knife** *R* Can
53B4 **North Korea** Republic, S E Asia
North Land = Severnaya Zemlya
17D3 **North Little Rock** USA
11B3 **North Loup** *R* USA
79B4 **North Magnetic Pole** Can
15E4 **North Miami** USA
15E4 **North Miami Beach** USA
10O3 **North Nahanni** *R* Can
20C2 **North Palisade** *Mt* USA
16B1 **North Platte** USA
8C2 **North Platte** *R* USA
5J4 **North Pt** *C* Can
79A **North Pole** Arctic
23Q2 **North Pt** Barbados
12C1 **North Pt** USA
11D3 **North Raccoon** *R* USA
33B2 **North Rona** *I* Scot
34D2 **North Ronaldsay** *I* Scot
3G3 **North Saskatchewan** *R* Can
33D2 **North Sea** N W Europe
3H2 **North Seal** *R* Can
62E2 **North Sentinel** Andaman Is
10J2 **North Slope** USA
6D3 **North Slope** *Region* USA
75D1 **North Stradbroke** *I* Aust
14B1 **North Syracuse** USA
78B1 **North Taranaki Bight** *B* NZ
14A1 **North Tonawanda** USA
8C3 **North Truchas Peak** *Mt* USA
4F3 **North Twin I** Can
34B3 **North Uist** *I* Scot
34D4 **Northumberland** County, Eng
76E3 **Northumberland Is** Aust
7M5 **Northumberland Str** Can
18B1 **North Vancouver** Can
14C1 **Northville** USA
35F5 **North Walsham** Eng
10K3 **Northway** USA
76A3 **North West C** Aust
60C2 **North West Frontier** Province, Pak
7M4 **North West River** Can
6G3 **North West Territories** Can
11C2 **Northwood** USA
35E4 **North York Moors Nat Pk** Eng
16C2 **Norton** *R* USA
10F3 **Norton B** USA
10F3 **Norton Sd** USA
79F1 **Norvegia,C** Ant
14D2 **Norwalk** Connecticut, USA
12C2 **Norwalk** Ohio, USA
32F6 **Norway** Kingdom, Europe
6J4 **Norway House** Can
7J2 **Norwegian B** Can
xxxH1 **Norwegian Basin** Norewegian S
48B3 **Norwegian S** N W Europe
14D2 **Norwich** Connecticut, USA
35F5 **Norwich** Eng
14C1 **Norwich** New York, USA
14E1 **Norwood** Massachusetts, USA
12C3 **Norwood** Ohio, USA
41F2 **Nos Emine** *C* Bulg
53D3 **Noshiro** Japan
41F2 **Nos Kaliakra** *C* Bulg
44J2 **Nosovaya** Russian Fed
43G2 **Nosovka** Ukraine
34E1 **Noss** *I* Scot
74B1 **Nossob** *R* Namibia
63E3 **Nostrābād** Iran
73E5 **Nosy Barren** *I* Madag
73E5 **Nosy Bé** *I* Madag
73F5 **Nosy Boraha** *I* Madag
73E6 **Nosy Varika** Madag
42D2 **Notéc** *R* Pol
6G4 **Notikewin** Can
40D3 **Noto** Italy
32F7 **Notodden** Nor
54C3 **Noto-hantō** *Pen* Japan
7N5 **Notre Dame B** Can
4E5 **Nottawasaga B** Can
4F3 **Nottaway** *R* Can
35E5 **Nottingham** County, Eng
35E5 **Nottingham** Eng
7L3 **Nottingham I** Can
11A2 **Notukeu Creek** *R* Can
70A2 **Nouadhibou** Maur
70A3 **Nouakchott** Maur
77F3 **Nouméa** Nouvelle Calédonie
71F3 **Nouna** Burkina
74C3 **Noupoort** S Africa
77F3 **Nouvelle Calédonie** *I* S W Pacific O
29C2 **Nova América** Brazil
73B4 **Nova Caipemba** Angola
29B3 **Nova Esperança** Brazil
29D3 **Nova Friburgo** Brazil
73B5 **Nova Gaia** Angola
29C3 **Nova Granada** Brazil
29C3 **Nova Herizonte** Brazil
29D3 **Nova Lima** Brazil
Nova Lisboa = Huambo
29B3 **Nova Londrina** Brazil
73D6 **Nova Mambone** Mozam
37C2 **Novara** Italy
29C1 **Nova Roma** Brazil
57C4 **Nova Sagres** Indon
7M5 **Nova Scotia** Province, Can
20A1 **Novato** USA
29D2 **Nova Venécia** Brazil
45E6 **Novaya Kakhovka** Ukraine
49R2 **Novaya Sibir, Ostrov** *I* Russian Fed
48G2 **Novaya Zemlya** *I* Russian Fed
41F2 **Nova Zagora** Bulg
27K4 **Nove Russas** Brazil
41D1 **Nové Zámky** Slovakia
44E4 **Novgorod** Russian Fed
37E2 **Novigrad** Croatia, Yugos
53E2 **Novikovo** Russian Fed
37C2 **Novi Ligure** Italy
22A1 **Novillero** Mexico
41F2 **Novi Pazar** Bulg
41E2 **Novi Pazar** Serbia, Yugos
41D1 **Novi Sad** Serbia, Yugos
45K5 **Novoalekseyevka** Kazakhstan
45G5 **Novoanninskiy** Russian Fed
53C2 **Novobureyskiy** Russian Fed
45G6 **Novocherkassk** Russian Fed
44G3 **Novodvinsk** Russian Fed
43G2 **Novogorod** Belorussia
45D5 **Novograd Volynskiy** Ukraine
43F2 **Novogrudok** Belorussia
28E1 **Novo Hamburgo** Brazil
48H5 **Novokazalinsk** Kazakhstan
48K4 **Novokuznetsk** Russian Fed
79F12 **Novolazarevskaya** *Base* Ant
40D1 **Novo Mesto** Slovenia, Yugos
43G3 **Novomirgorod** Ukraine
44F5 **Novomoskovsk** Russian Fed
Novo Redondo = Sumbe
45F7 **Novorossiysk** Russian Fed
49M2 **Novorybnoye** Russian Fed
48K4 **Novosibirsk** Russian Fed
49P2 **Novosibirskye Ostrova** *Is* Russian Fed
45K5 **Novotroitsk** Russian Fed
45H5 **Novo Uzensk** Russian Fed
43E2 **Novovolynsk** Ukraine
44H4 **Novo Vyatsk** Russian Fed
45E5 **Novozybkov** Russian Fed
48J3 **Novvy Port** Russian Fed
43E2 **Novy Dwór Mazowiecki** Pol
44L4 **Novyy Lyalya** Russian Fed
44N2 **Novyy Port** Russian Fed
45J7 **Novyy Uzen** Kazakhstan
42D2 **Nowa Sól** Pol
17C2 **Nowata** USA
10H3 **Nowitna** *R* USA
75D2 **Nowra** Aust
63C1 **Now Shahr** Iran
60C2 **Nowshera** Pak
43E3 **Nowy Sącz** Pol
10M4 **Noyes I** USA
36B2 **Noyon** France
71F4 **Nsawam** Ghana
71H4 **Nsukka** Nig
74E1 **Nuanetsi** Zim
74E1 **Nuanetsi** *R* Zim
71G4 **Nuatja** Togo
72D2 **Nuba** *Mts* Sudan
66B2 **Nubian Desert** Sudan
28A3 **Nuble** *R* Chile
8D4 **Nueces** *R* USA
6J3 **Nueltin L** Can
21B1 **Nueva Casas Grandes** Mexico
29A3 **Nueva Germania** Par
23A2 **Nueva Gerona** Cuba
28A3 **Nueva Imperial** Chile
28D2 **Nueva Palmira** Urug
21B2 **Nueva Rosita** Mexico
23B2 **Nuevitas** Cuba
22B1 **Nuevo** State, Mexico
21B1 **Nuevo Casas Grandes** Mexico
22A1 **Nuevo Ideal** Mexico
21C2 **Nuevo Laredo** Mexico
69D4 **Nugaal** Region, Somalia
7N2 **Nûgâtsiaq** Greenland
7N2 **Nûgussuaq** *Pen* Greenland
7N2 **Nûgussuaq** *I* Greenland
77G1 **Nui** *I* Tuvalu
52A5 **Nui Con Voi** *R* Vietnam
36C3 **Nuits** France
61E2 **Nu Jiang** *R* China
75A2 **Nukey Bluff** *Mt* Aust
64D3 **Nukhayb** Iraq
77G1 **Nukufetau** *I* Tuvalu
77G1 **Nukulaelae** *I* Tuvalu
77H1 **Nukunon** *I* Tokelau Is
48G5 **Nukus** Uzbekistan
10G3 **Nulato** USA
76B4 **Nullarbor Plain** Aust
71J4 **Numan** Nig
54C3 **Numata** Japan
72C3 **Numatinna** *R* Sudan
53D4 **Numazu** Japan
51G7 **Numfoor** *I* Indon
75C3 **Numurkah** Aust
10F3 **Nunapitchuk** USA
14A1 **Nunda** USA
10E3 **Nunivak I** USA
60D2 **Nunkun** *Mt* India
10C3 **Nunligran** Russian Fed
53A1 **Nuomin He** *R* China
40B2 **Nuoro** Sardegna
63C2 **Nurābād** Iran
37C2 **Nure** *R* Italy
75A2 **Nuriootpa** Aust
60C1 **Nuristan** *Upland* Afghan
44J5 **Nurlat** Russian Fed
32K6 **Nurmes** Fin
42C3 **Nürnberg** Germany
75C2 **Nurri,Mt** Aust
56E4 **Nusa Tenggara** *Is* Indon
57B4 **Nusa Tenggara Timor** Province, Indon
64D2 **Nusaybin** Turk
10G4 **Nushagak** *R* USA
10G4 **Nushagak B** USA
10G4 **Nushagak Pen** USA
60B3 **Nushki** Pak
7M4 **Nutak** Can
10K3 **Nutzotin Mts** USA
Nuuk = Godthåb
7L3 **Nuvukjuak** Can
61B2 **Nuwakot** Nepal
62C3 **Nuwara-Eliya** Sri Lanka
74C3 **Nuweveldreeks** *Mts* S Africa
45C3 **Nyac** USA
14D2 **Nyack** USA
72D3 **Nyahururu Falls** Kenya
75B3 **Nyah West** Aust
50C3 **Nyaingentanglha Shan** *Mts* China
72D4 **Nyakabindi** Tanz
44L3 **Nyaksimvol'** Russian Fed
72C2 **Nyala** Sudan
61C2 **Nyalam** China
72C3 **Nyamlell** Sudan
73D6 **Nyanda** Zim
44G3 **Nyandoma** Russian Fed
72B4 **Nyanga** *R* Gabon
61D2 **Nyang Qu** China
73D5 **Nyasa L** Malawi/Mozam
55B2 **Nyaunglebin** Burma
44K4 **Nyazepetrovsk** Russian Fed
32G7 **Nyborg** Den
32H7 **Nybro** Sweden
48J3 **Nyda** Russian Fed
7M1 **Nyeboes Land** *Region* Can
61D1 **Nyenchentanglha Range** *Mts* China
72D4 **Nyeri** Kenya
73D5 **Nyimba** Zambia
59H2 **Nyingchi** China
43E3 **Nyíregyháza** Hung
72D3 **Nyiru,Mt** Kenya
32J6 **Nykarleby** Fin
32F7 **Nykøbing** Den
32G8 **Nykøbing** Den
32H7 **Nyköping** Sweden
74D1 **Nyl** *R* S Africa
74D1 **Nylstroom** S Africa
75C2 **Nymagee** Aust
32H7 **Nynäshamn** Sweden
75C2 **Nyngan** Aust
37B1 **Nyon** Switz
72B3 **Nyong** *R* Cam
54A3 **Nyongwol** S Korea
54A3 **Nyongwon** N Korea
38D3 **Nyons** France
42D2 **Nysa** Pol
53E1 **Nysh** Russian Fed
18C2 **Nyssa** USA
44H3 **Nyukhcha** Russian Fed
50F1 **Nyukzha** *R* Russian Fed
49N3 **Nyurba** Russian Fed
72D4 **Nzega** Tanz
70B4 **Nzérékore** Guinea
73B4 **N'zeto** Angola
71F4 **Nzi** *R* Ivory Coast

O

11C3 **Oacoma** USA
11B3 **Oahe,L** *Res* USA
20E5 **Oahu,I** Hawaiian Is
75B2 **Oakbank** Aust
20B2 **Oakdale** USA
11C2 **Oakes** USA
75D1 **Oakey** Aust
19B3 **Oakland** California, USA
11C3 **Oakland** Nebraska, USA
18B2 **Oakland** Oregon, USA
12B3 **Oakland City** USA
12B2 **Oak Lawn** USA
20B2 **Oakley** California, USA
16B2 **Oakley** Kansas, USA
15C1 **Oak Ridge** USA
18B2 **Oakridge** USA
4F5 **Oakville** Can
78B3 **Oamaru** NZ
20D2 **Oasis** California, USA
18D2 **Oasis** Nevada, USA
79F7 **Oates Land** Region, Ant
75E3 **Oatlands** Aust
22C2 **Oaxaca** Mexico
22C2 **Oaxaca** State, Mexico
48H3 **Ob'** *R* Russian Fed
4E4 **Oba** Can
54C3 **Obama** Japan
78A3 **Oban** NZ
34C3 **Oban** Scot

Obanazawa **Ostrava**

54D3 **Obanazawa** Japan
71H4 **Oban Hills** Nig
63E2 **Obeh** Afghan
37D1 **Oberammergau** Germany
37E1 **Oberdrauburg** Austria
36D1 **Oberhausen** Germany
16B2 **Oberlin** USA
36E2 **Obernburg** Germany
37D1 **Oberstdorf** Germany
37E1 **Obervellach** Austria
57C3 **Obi** *I* Indon
27G4 **Obidos** Brazil
53E3 **Obihiro** Japan
53C2 **Obluch'ye** Russian Fed
72C3 **Obo** CAR
72E2 **Obock** Djibouti
42D2 **Oborniki** Pol
45F5 **Oboyan'** Russian Fed
18B2 **O'Brien** USA
45J5 **Obshchiy Syrt** *Mts* Russian Fed
48J3 **Obskaya Guba** *B* Russian Fed
71F4 **Obuasi** Ghana
15C3 **Ocala** USA
22C1 **Ocampo** Mexico
26D2 **Ocana** Colombia
39B2 **Ocaño** Spain
10L4 **Ocean C** USA
13D3 **Ocean City** Maryland, USA
14C3 **Ocean City** New Jersey, USA
6F4 **Ocean Falls** Can
Ocean I = Banaba
20B3 **Oceano** USA
20D4 **Oceanside** USA
17E3 **Ocean Springs** USA
44J4 **Ocher** Russian Fed
34D3 **Ochil Hills** Scot
15C2 **Ochlockonee** *R* USA
23H1 **Ocho Rios** Jamaica
15C2 **Ocmulgee** *R* USA
15C2 **Oconee** *R* USA
12B2 **Oconto** USA
22B1 **Ocotlán** Jalisco, Mexico
22C2 **Ocotlán** Oaxaca, Mexico
22D2 **Ocozocoautla** Mexico
71F4 **Oda** Ghana
54B3 **Oda** Japan
54A2 **Ŏdaejin** N Korea
32B2 **Ódáðahraun** Region, Iceland
53E3 **Odate** Japan
53D4 **Odawara** Japan
32F6 **Odda** Nor
17F4 **Odem** USA
39A2 **Odemira** Port
41F3 **Ödemiş** Turk
74D2 **Odendaalsrus** S Africa
32G7 **Odense** Den
36E2 **Odenwald** Region, Germany
42C2 **Oder** *R* Pol/Germany
37E2 **Oderzo** Italy
16B3 **Odessa** Texas, USA
45E6 **Odessa** Ukraine
18C1 **Odessa** Washington, USA
70B4 **Odienné** Ivory Coast
Odra = Oder
43D2 **Odra, R** Pol
27K5 **Oeiras** Brazil
11B3 **Oelrichs** USA
11D3 **Oelwein** USA
40D2 **Ofanto** *R* Italy
65C3 **Ofaqim** Israel
71G4 **Offa** Nig
35B5 **Offaly** County, Irish Rep
36E1 **Offenbach** Germany
36D2 **Offenburg** Germany
54D3 **Ofunato** Japan
53D4 **Oga** Japan
72E3 **Ogaden** Region, Eth
53D4 **Ogaki** Japan
16B1 **Ogallala** USA
50H4 **Ogasawara Gunto** *Is* Japan
71G4 **Ogbomosho** Nig
11D3 **Ogden** Iowa, USA
18D2 **Ogden** Utah, USA
3B2 **Ogden,Mt.** Can/USA
13D2 **Ogdensburg** USA
15C2 **Ogeechee** *R* USA
10L2 **Ogilvie** Can
6E3 **Ogilvie Mts** Can
15C2 **Oglethorpe,Mt** USA
37D2 **Oglio** *R* Italy
37B1 **Ognon** *R* France
71H4 **Ogoja** Nig
4D3 **Ogoki** Can
4D3 **Ogoki** *R* Can
4D3 **Ogoki Res** Can
72A4 **Ogooué** *R* Gabon
71G4 **Ogou** *R* Togo
43E1 **Ogre** Latvia
70B2 **Oguilet Khenachich** *Well* Mali
40D1 **Ogulin** Croatia, Yugos
71G4 **Ogun** State, Nig
14E1 **Ogunquit** USA
45J8 **Ogurchinskiy, Ostov** *I* Turkmenistan
78A3 **Ohai** NZ
78C1 **Ohakune** NZ
70C2 **Ohanet** Alg
54D2 **Ōhata** Japan
78A2 **Ohau,L** NZ
9E2 **Ohio** State, USA
12B3 **Ohio** *R* USA
36E1 **Ohm** *R* Germany
73B5 **Ohopoho** Namibia
42C2 **Ohre** *R* Czech Republic
41E2 **Ohrid** Macedonia, Yugos
41E2 **Ohridsko Jezero** *L* Macedonia, Yugos/Alb
78B1 **Ohura** NZ
27H3 **Oiapoque** French Guiana
50C2 **Oijiaojing** China
13D2 **Oil City** USA
20C3 **Oildale** USA
49L6 **Oilian Shan** *Mts* China
36B2 **Oise** Department, France
38C2 **Oise** *R* France
53C5 **Ōita** Japan
20C3 **Ojai** USA
21B2 **Ojinaga** Mexico
22C2 **Ojitlán** Mexico
54C3 **Ojiya** Japan
22B1 **Ojocaliente** Mexico
25C3 **Ojos del Salado** *Mt* Arg
22B1 **Ojueloz** Mexico
45F5 **Oka** *R* Russian Fed
74B1 **Okahandja** Namibia
18C1 **Okanagan Falls** Can
3E3 **Okanagan L** Can
18C1 **Okanogan** USA
18C1 **Okanogan** *R* USA
18B1 **Okanogan Range** *Mts* Can/USA
60C2 **Okara** Pak
74B1 **Okasise** Namibia
73B5 **Okavango** *R* Namibia/Angola
73C5 **Okavango Delta** *Marsh* Botswana
53D4 **Okaya** Japan
53C5 **Okayama** Japan
54C4 **Okazaki** Japan
15E4 **Okeechobee** USA
15E4 **Okeechobee,L** USA
15C2 **Okefenokee Swamp** USA
71H4 **Okene** Nig
60B4 **Okha** India
53E1 **Okha** Russian Fed
61C2 **Okhaldunga** Nepal
49Q4 **Okhotsk** Russian Fed
49Q4 **Okhotsk,S of** Russian Fed
50F4 **Okinawa, I** Japan
50F4 **Okinagunto** *Arch* Japan
53C4 **Oki-shoto** *Is* Japan
71G4 **Okitipupa** Nig
8D3 **Oklahoma** State, USA
17C2 **Oklahoma City** USA
17C2 **Okmulgee** USA
74B1 **Okombahe** Namibia
72B4 **Okondja** Gabon
54D2 **Okoppe** Japan
72B4 **Okoyo** Congo
71G4 **Okpara** *R* Nig
44A2 **Okstindan** *Mt* Nor
45K6 **Oktyabr'sk** Kazakhstan
53B1 **Oktyabr'skiy** Amurskaya, Russian Fed
44J5 **Oktyabr'skiy** Bashkirskaya, Russian Fed
50J1 **Oktyabr'skiy** Kamchatka, Russian Fed
49L2 **Oktyabrskoy Revolyutsii, Ostrov** *I* Russian Fed
44M3 **Oktyabr'skoye** Russian Fed
53D3 **Okushiri-tō** *I* Japan
74C1 **Okwa** *R* Botswana
32A2 **Olafsvik** Iceland
20D2 **Olancha** USA
20C2 **Olanch Peak** *Mt* USA
32H7 **Öland** *I* Sweden
75B2 **Olary** Aust
17D2 **Olathe** USA
25D5 **Olavarría** Arg
40B2 **Olbia** Sardegna
14A1 **Olcott** USA
10L2 **Old Crow** Can
42B2 **Oldenburg** Niedersachsen, Germany
42C2 **Oldenburg** Schleswig-Holstein, Germany
14C2 **Old Forge** USA
35D5 **Oldham** Eng
10H4 **Old Harbor** USA
33B3 **Old Head of Kinsale** *C* Scot
14D2 **Old Lyme** USA
3F3 **Olds** Can
13F2 **Old Town** USA
3G3 **Old Wives L** Can
52B1 **Öldziyt** Mongolia
14A1 **Olean** USA
49O4 **Olekma** *R* Russian Fed
49O3 **Olekminsk** Russian Fed
44E2 **Olenegorsk** Russian Fed
49N3 **Olenek** Russian Fed
49O2 **Olenek** *R* Russian Fed
43F2 **Olevsk** Ukraine
53D3 **Ol'ga** Russian Fed
4F4 **Olga L** Can
74C3 **Olifants** *R* Cape Province, S Africa
74B1 **Olifants** *R* Namibia
74E1 **Olifants** *R* Transvaal, S Africa
74C2 **Olifantshoek** S Africa
28E2 **Olimar** *R* Urug
41E2 **Ólimbos** *Mt* Greece
29C3 **Olímpia** Brazil
22C2 **Olinala** Mexico
27M5 **Olinda** Brazil
28C2 **Oliva** Arg
25C4 **Olivares** *Mt* Arg
29D3 **Oliveira** Brazil
3E4 **Oliver** Can
3H2 **Oliver L** Can
11D3 **Olivia** USA
25C2 **Ollagüe** Chile
25C2 **Ollagüe** *Mt* Bol
12B3 **Olney** Illinois, USA
16C3 **Olney** Texas, USA
50E1 **Olochi** Russian Fed
32G7 **Olofstrom** Sweden
72B4 **Olombo** Congo
42D3 **Olomouc** Czech Republic
44E3 **Olonets** Russian Fed
57F8 **Olongapa** Phil
38B3 **Oloron ste Marie** France
50E1 **Olovyannaya** Russian Fed
36D1 **Olpe** Germany
43E2 **Olsztyn** Pol
37B1 **Olten** Switz
41E2 **Olt** *R* Rom
18B1 **Olympia** USA
18B1 **Olympic Nat Pk** USA
Olympus = Ólimbos
65B1 **Olympus,Mt** Cyprus
18B1 **Olympus,Mt** USA
54C3 **Omachi** Japan
54C4 **Omae-zaki** *C* Japan
34B4 **Omagh** N Ire
17C1 **Omaha** USA
18C1 **Omak** USA
67G2 **Oman** Sultanate, Arabian Pen
67G2 **Oman,G of** UAE
74B1 **Omaruru** Namibia
74A1 **Omaruru** *R* Namibia
54D2 **Ōma-saki** *C* Japan
72A4 **Omboué** Gabon
72D2 **Omdurman** Sudan
22C2 **Ometepec** Mexico
72D2 **Om Häjer** Eritrea
54D2 **Ōminato** Japan
3C2 **Omineca** *R* Can
3C2 **Omineca Mts** Can
54C3 **Omiya** Japan
10M4 **Ommaney,C** USA
6H2 **Ommanney B** Can
72D3 **Omo** *R* Eth
71H4 **Omoku** Nig
49R3 **Omolon** *R* Russian Fed
49P3 **Omoloy** *R* Russian Fed
54D3 **Omono** *R* Japan
48J4 **Omsk** Russian Fed
54D2 **Ōmu** Japan
53B5 **Omura** Japan
74C1 **Omuramba Eiseb** *R* Botswana
53C5 **Ōmuta** Japan
44J4 **Omutninsk** Russian Fed
12A2 **Onalaska** USA
13D3 **Onancock** USA
57A3 **Onang** Indon
12C1 **Onaping L** Can
11C3 **Onawa** USA
73B5 **Oncócua** Angola
73B5 **Ondangua** Namibia
43E3 **Ondava** *R* Slovakia
71G4 **Ondo** Nig
71G4 **Ondo** State, Nig
50E2 **Öndörhaan** Mongolia
59F5 **One and Half Degree Chan** Indian O
44F3 **Onega** Russian Fed
44F3 **Onega** *R* Russian Fed
14C1 **Oneida** USA
14B1 **Oneida L** USA
11C3 **O'Neill** USA
50J2 **Onekotan** *I* Russian Fed
72C4 **Onema** Zaïre
14C1 **Oneonta** USA
41F1 **Oneşti** Rom
44F3 **Onezhskaya Guba** *B* Russian Fed
74C3 **Ongers** *R* S Africa
73B5 **Ongiva** Angola
53B4 **Ongjin** N Korea
52D1 **Ongniud Qi** China
62C1 **Ongole** India
13D2 **Onieda L** USA
73E6 **Onilahy** *R* Madag
71H4 **Onitsha** Nig
50D2 **Onjüül** Mongolia
54C3 **Ono** Japan
54C4 **Ōnohara-jima** *I* Japan
53C5 **Onomichi** Japan
77G1 **Onotoa** *I* Kiribati
76A3 **Onslow** Aust
15D2 **Onslow B** USA
54C3 **Ontake-san** *Mt* Japan
20D3 **Ontario** California, USA
18C2 **Ontario** Oregon, USA
7J4 **Ontario** Province, Can
13D2 **Ontario,L** USA/Can
39B2 **Onteniente** Spain
77E1 **Ontong Java Atoll** Solomom Is
54A3 **Onyang** S Korea
20C3 **Onyx** USA
76C3 **Oodnadatta** Aust
76C4 **Ooldea** Aust
17C2 **Oologah L** USA
36B1 **Oostende** Belg
36B1 **Oosterschelde** *Estuary* Neth
62B2 **Ootacamund** India
3C3 **Ootsa L** Can
22B1 **Opal** Mexico
49R4 **Opala** Russian Fed
72C4 **Opala** Zaïre
62C3 **Opanake** Sri Lanka
44H4 **Oparino** Russian Fed
4E4 **Opasatika** Can
4E4 **Opasatika** *R* Can
4C3 **Opasquia** Can
43D3 **Opava** Czech Republic
15B2 **Opelika** USA
17D3 **Opelousas** USA
11A2 **Opheim** USA
10G3 **Ophir** USA
4F3 **Opinaca** *R* Can
4E3 **Opinnagau** *R* Can
43F1 **Opochka** Russian Fed
43D2 **Opole** Pol
Oporto = Porto
78C1 **Opotiki** NZ
15B2 **Opp** USA
32F6 **Oppdal** Nor
78B1 **Opunake** NZ
41E1 **Oradea** Rom
32B2 **Oraefajökull** *Mts* Iceland
60D3 **Orai** India
71B1 **Oran** Alg
25D2 **Orán** Arg
54A2 **Orang** N Korea
75C2 **Orange** Aust
20D4 **Orange** California, USA
38C3 **Orange** France
17D3 **Orange** Texas, USA
74B2 **Orange** *R* S Africa
15C2 **Orangeburg** USA
11C3 **Orange City** USA
74D2 **Orange Free State** Province, S Africa
15C2 **Orange Park** USA
12C2 **Orangeville** Can
42C2 **Oranienburg** Germany
74C2 **Oranje** *R* S Africa
74B2 **Oranjemund** Namibia
74D1 **Orapa** Botswana
57G8 **Oras** Phil
41E1 **Orăştie** Rom
41E1 **Oraviţa** Rom
40C2 **Orbetello** Italy
14B2 **Orbisonia** USA
75C3 **Orbost** Aust
36B1 **Orchies** France
37B2 **Orco** *R* Italy
20B3 **Orcutt** USA
11C3 **Ord** USA
76B2 **Ord** *R* Aust
19D3 **Orderville** USA
76B2 **Ord,Mt** Aust
49M6 **Ordos** *Desert* China
64C1 **Ordu** Turk
16B2 **Ordway** USA
32H7 **Örebro** Sweden
8A2 **Oregon** State, USA
12C2 **Oregon** USA
18B1 **Oregon City** USA
32H6 **Oregrund** Sweden
44F4 **Orekhovo Zuyevo** Russian Fed
45F5 **Orel** Russian Fed
53D1 **Orel, Ozero'** *L* Russian Fed
19D2 **Orem** USA
45J5 **Orenburg** Russian Fed
28D3 **Orense** Arg
39A1 **Orense** Spain
42C1 **Oresund** *Str* Den/Sweden
78A3 **Oreti** *R* NZ
5G5 **Orford** USA
43F3 **Orgeyev** Moldova
41F3 **Orhaneli** *R* Turk
50D2 **Orhon Gol** *R* Mongolia
22C2 **Oriental** Mexico
75B1 **Orientos** Aust
39B2 **Orihuela** Spain
4F5 **Orillia** Can
26F2 **Orinoco** *R* Ven
14C1 **Oriskany Falls** USA
61B3 **Orissa** State, India
40B3 **Oristano** Sardegna
32K6 **Orivesi** *L* Fin
27G4 **Oriximina** Brazil
22C2 **Orizaba** Mexico
29C2 **Orizona** Brazil
34D2 **Orkney** *I* Scot
29C3 **Orlândia** Brazil
15C3 **Orlando** USA
38C2 **Orléanais** *Region* France
38C2 **Orléans** France
14E2 **Orleans** USA
49L4 **Orlik** Russian Fed
63E3 **Ormara** Pak
37B2 **Ormea** Italy
57F8 **Ormoc** Phil
15C3 **Ormond Beach** USA
36C2 **Ornain** *R* France
37B1 **Ornans** France
38B2 **Orne** *R* France
32H6 **Örnsköldsvik** Sweden
54A2 **Oro** N Korea
26D3 **Orocué** Colombia
18C1 **Orofino** USA
5H4 **Oromocto** Can
65C3 **Oron** Israel
Orontes = 'Āsī,R
53A1 **Oroqen Zizhiqi** China
57F9 **Oroquieta** Phil
43E3 **Orosháza** Hung
49R3 **Orotukan** Russian Fed
19B3 **Oroville** California, USA
18C1 **Oroville** Washington, USA
32F6 **Ørsba** Nor
43G2 **Orsha** Belorussia
37B1 **Orsières** Switz
45K5 **Orsk** Russian Fed
38B3 **Orthez** France
39A1 **Ortigueira** Spain
37D1 **Ortles** *Mts* Italy
38E2 **Ortles** *Mt* Italy
23L1 **Ortoire** *R* Trinidad
11C2 **Ortonville** USA
26E7 **Oruro** Bol
44K4 **Osa** Russian Fed
11D3 **Osage** Iowa, USA
11B3 **Osage** Wyoming, USA
17D2 **Osage** *R* USA
54C3 **Osaka** Japan
21D4 **Osa,Pen de** Costa Rica
49P2 **Osbrov Stolbovoy** *I* Russian Fed
17E2 **Osceola** Arkansas, USA
17D1 **Osceola** Iowa, USA
18C2 **Osgood Mts** USA
54D2 **Oshamambe** Japan
4F5 **Oshawa** Can
54C2 **Ō-shima** *I* Japan
54C4 **Ō-shima** *I* Japan
16B1 **Oshkosh** Nebraska, USA
12B2 **Oshkosh** Wisconsin, USA
45H8 **Oshnoviyeh** Iran
71G4 **Oshogbo** Nig
72B4 **Oshwe** Zaïre
41D1 **Osijek** Croatia, Yugos
37E3 **Osimo** Italy
48K4 **Osinniki** Russian Fed
43F2 **Osipovichi** Belorussia
17D1 **Oskaloosa** USA
44B4 **Oskarshamn** Sweden
32G6 **Oslo** Nor
64C2 **Osmaniye** Turk
42B2 **Osnabrück** Germany
25B6 **Osorno** Chile
39B1 **Osorno** Spain
18C1 **Osoyoos** Can
3D2 **Ospika** *R* Can
76D5 **Ossa,Mt** Aust
71H4 **Ossé** *R* Nig
12A2 **Osseo** USA
37E1 **Ossiacher See** *L* Austria
14D2 **Ossining** USA
5J3 **Ossokmanuan L** Can
49S4 **Ossora** Russian Fed
44E4 **Ostashkov** Russian Fed
Ostend = Oostende
32G6 **Østerdalen, V** Nor
32G6 **Östersund** Sweden
32H6 **Östhammär** Sweden
40C2 **Ostia** Italy
37D2 **Ostiglia** Italy
43D3 **Ostrava** Czech Republic

Ostróda
Paropamisus

43D2 **Ostróda** Pol
43E2 **Ostrołęka** Pol
44D4 **Ostrov** Russian Fed
43E2 **Ostrowiec** Pol
43E2 **Ostrów Mazowiecka** Pol
43D2 **Ostrów Wielkopolski** Pol
53C5 **Ōsumi-kaikyō** *Str* Japan
53C5 **Ōsumi-shotō** *Is* Japan
71G4 **Osun** *State* Nigeria
39A2 **Osuna** Spain
14B1 **Oswego** USA
14B1 **Oswego** *R* USA
35D5 **Oswestry** Eng
43D3 **Oświęcim** Pol
54C3 **Ota** Japan
78B3 **Otago Pen** NZ
78C2 **Otaki** NZ
53E3 **Otaru** Japan
26C3 **Otavalo** Ecuador
73B5 **Otavi** Namibia
54D3 **Otawara** Japan
14C1 **Otego** USA
18C1 **Othello** USA
3G2 **Otherside** *R* Can
41E3 **Óthris** *Mt* Greece
71G4 **Oti** *R* Ghana
71G4 **Otiki** *R* Nig
16B1 **Otis** Colorado, USA
14D1 **Otis** Massachusetts, USA
14C2 **Otisville** USA
74B1 **Otjimbingwe** Namibia
73B6 **Otjiwarongo** Namibia
52B2 **Otog Qi** China
54D2 **Otoineppu** Japan
78C1 **Otorohanga** NZ
41D2 **Otranto** Italy
41D2 **Otranto,Str of** *Chan* Italy/Alb
12B2 **Otsego** USA
14C1 **Otsego L** USA
4E5 **Otsego Lake** USA
54C3 **Otsu** Japan
26C2 **Otta** Nor
32F7 **Otta** *R* Nor
4F4 **Ottawa** Can
4F4 **Ottawa** *R* Can
12B2 **Ottawa** Illinois, USA
17C2 **Ottawa** Kansas, USA
7K4 **Ottawa Is** Can
7K4 **Otter Rapids** Can
7K1 **Otto Fjord** Can
74D2 **Ottosdal** S Africa
12A2 **Ottumwa** USA
36D2 **Ottweiler** Germany
71H4 **Otukpa** Nig
71H4 **Oturkpo** Nig
26C5 **Otusco** Peru
75B3 **Otway,C** Aust
43E2 **Otwock** Pol
37D1 **Ötz** Austria
37D1 **Otzal** *Mts* Austria
55C1 **Ou** *R* Laos
17D3 **Ouachita** *R* USA
17D3 **Ouachita,L** USA
17D3 **Ouachita Mts** USA
70A2 **Ouadane** Maur
72C3 **Ouadda** CAR
72C2 **Ouaddai** *Desert Region* Chad
71F3 **Ouagadougou** Burkina
71F3 **Ouahigouya** Burkina
72C3 **Ouaka** CAR
70C3 **Oualam** Niger
71G3 **Oualé** *R* Burkina
70C2 **Ouallen** Alg
72C3 **Ouanda Djallé** CAR
36B3 **Ouanne** *R* France
70A2 **Ouarane** Region, Maur
70C1 **Ouargla** Alg
72C3 **Ouarra** *R* CAR
70B1 **Ouarzazate** Mor
39C2 **Ouassel** *R* Alg
72B3 **Oubangui** *R* Congo
36B1 **Oudenaarde** Belg
74C3 **Oudtshoorn** S Africa
39B2 **Oued Tlělat** Alg
71A2 **Oued Zem** Mor
71F4 **Ouellé** Ivory Coast
72B3 **Ouesso** Congo
71A2 **Ouezzane** Mor
72B3 **Ouham** *R* Chad
71G4 **Ouidah** Benin
4D4 **Ouimet** Can
71B2 **Oujda** Mor
32J6 **Oulainen** Fin
32K5 **Oulu** Fin
32K6 **Oulu** *R* Fin
32K6 **Oulujärvi** *L* Fin
72C2 **Oum Chalouba** Chad
71D1 **Oum el Bouaghi** Alg
71A2 **Oumer Rbia** *R* Mor
72B2 **Oum Hadjer** Chad
72C2 **Oum Haouach** *Watercourse* Chad
32K5 **Ounas** *R* Fin
44C2 **Ounasjoki** *R* Fin
44C2 **Ounastunturi** *Mt* Fin
72C2 **Ounianga Kebir** Chad
36D1 **Our** *R* Germany
16A2 **Ouray** USA
36C2 **Ource** *R* France
Ourense = Orense
36B2 **Ourcq** *R* France
27K5 **Ouricurí** Brazil
29C3 **Ourinhos** Brazil
29D3 **Ouro Prêto** Brazil
36C1 **Ourthe** *R* Belg
35E4 **Ouse** *R* Eng
35F5 **Ouse** *R* Eng
33B2 **Outer Hebrides** *Is* Scot
20C4 **Outer Santa Barbara** *Chan* USA
73B6 **Outjo** Namibia
3G3 **Outlook** Can
32K6 **Outokumpu** Fin
37A2 **Ouvèze** *R* France
75B3 **Ouyen** Aust
37C2 **Ovada** Italy
28A2 **Ovalle** Chile
73B5 **Ovamboland** Region, Namibia
19D3 **Overton** USA
32J5 **Övertorneå** Sweden
16B1 **Ovid** Colorado, USA
14B1 **Ovid** New York, USA
39A1 **Oviedo** Spain
45D5 **Ovruch** Ukraine
49O4 **Ovsyanka** Russian Fed
78A3 **Owaka** NZ
14B1 **Owasco L** USA
54C4 **Owase** Japan
11D3 **Owatonna** USA
14B1 **Owego** USA
20C2 **Owens** *R* USA
12B3 **Owensboro** USA
20D2 **Owens L** USA
4E5 **Owen Sound** Can
76D1 **Owen Stanley Range** *Mts* PNG
71H4 **Owerri** Nig
4C2 **Owl** *R* Can
18E2 **Owl Creek Mts** USA
71H4 **Owo** Nig
12C2 **Owosso** USA
18C2 **Owyhee** USA
18C2 **Owyhee** *R* USA
18C2 **Owyhee Mts** USA
26C6 **Oxampampa** Peru
3H4 **Oxbow** Can
32H7 **Oxelösund** Sweden
35E6 **Oxford** County, Eng
35E5 **Oxford** Eng
14E1 **Oxford** Massachusetts, USA
17E3 **Oxford** Mississippi, USA
14C1 **Oxford** New York, USA
20C3 **Oxnard** USA
53D4 **Oyama** Japan
3F3 **Oyen** Can
72B3 **Oyen** Gabon
34C3 **Oykel** *R* Scot
49Q3 **Oymyakon** Russian Fed
71G4 **Oyo** Nig
37A1 **Oyonnax** France
32F6 **Øyre** Nor
75E3 **Oyster B** Aust
57F9 **Ozamiz** Phil
43F2 **Ozarichi** Belorussia
15B2 **Ozark** USA
17D2 **Ozark Plat** USA
17D2 **Ozarks,L of the** USA
43E3 **Ózd** Hung
53E2 **Ozerskiy** Russian Fed
16B3 **Ozona** USA
22C1 **Ozuluama** Mexico
64D1 **Ozurgeti** Georgia

P

74B3 **Paarl** S Africa
34B3 **Pabbay** *I* Scot
43D2 **Pabianice** Pol
61C3 **Pabna** Bang
43F1 **Pabrade** Lithuania
26C5 **Pacasmayo** Peru
28E2 **Pacheca** Brazil
22B1 **Pacheco** Mexico
22C1 **Pachuca** Mexico
20B1 **Pacific** USA
xxixN7 **Pacific-Antarctic Ridge** Pacific O
20B2 **Pacific Grove** USA
xxixG8 **Pacific O**
56D4 **Pacitan** Indon
29D2 **Pacuí** *R* Brazil
56B3 **Padang** Indon
57B4 **Padang** Indon
56B3 **Padangpanjang** Indon
56A2 **Padangsidempuan** Indon
44E3 **Padany** Russian Fed
42B2 **Paderborn** Germany
6J3 **Padlei** Can
61D3 **Padma** *R* Bang
37D2 **Padova** Italy
8D4 **Padre I** USA
35C6 **Padstow** Eng
75B3 **Padthaway** Aust
Padua = Padova
12B3 **Paducah** Kentucky, USA
16B3 **Paducah** Texas, USA
32L5 **Padunskoye More** *L* Russian Fed
54A2 **Paegam** N Korea
53A4 **Paengnyŏng-do** *I* S Korea
78C1 **Paeroa** NZ
74E1 **Pafuri** Mozam
40C2 **Pag** *I* Croatia, Yugos
57F9 **Pagadian** Phil
56B3 **Pagai Seletan** *I* Indon
56B3 **Pagai Utara** *I* Indon
51H5 **Pagan** *I* Pacific O
56E3 **Pagatan** Indon
19D3 **Page** USA
51F8 **Pago Mission** Aust
41F3 **Pagondhas** Greece
16A2 **Pagosa Springs** USA
4C4 **Paguchi L** Can
4D3 **Pagwa River** Can
20E5 **Pahala** Hawaiian Is
78C2 **Pahiatua** NZ
20E5 **Pahoa** Hawaiian Is
15E4 **Pahokee** USA
71J4 **Pai** *R* Nig
32K6 **Päijänna** *L* Fin
28A4 **Paillaco** Chile
20E5 **Pailola Chan** Hawaiian Is
12C2 **Painesville** USA
19D3 **Painted Desert** USA
12C3 **Paintsville** USA
34C4 **Paisley** Scot
26B5 **Paita** Peru
32J5 **Pajala** Sweden
57B4 **Pajeti** Indon
58E3 **Pakistan** Republic, Asia
55C2 **Pak Lay** Laos
61E3 **Pakokku** Burma
3F4 **Pakowki L** Can
40D1 **Pakrac** Croatia, Yugos
41D1 **Paks** Hung
55C2 **Pak Sane** Laos
55D2 **Pakse** Laos
72D3 **Pakwach** Uganda
72B3 **Pala** Chad
40D2 **Palagruža** *I* Croatia, Yugos
36B2 **Palaiseau** France
Palakhat = Pālghāt
74D1 **Palala** *R* S Africa
62E2 **Palalankwe** Andaman Is
49S4 **Palana** Russian Fed
56D3 **Palangkaraya** Indon
62B2 **Palani** India
60C4 **Palanpur** India
74D1 **Palapye** Botswana
15C3 **Palatka** USA
51G6 **Palau Is** Pacific O
55B3 **Palaw** Burma
57E9 **Palawan** *I* Phil
57E9 **Palawan Pass** Phil
62B3 **Palayankottai** India
32J7 **Paldiski** Estonia
57B2 **Paleleh** Indon
56B3 **Palembang** Indon
39B1 **Palencia** Spain
65B1 **Paleokhorio** Cyprus
40C3 **Palermo** Italy
17C3 **Palestine** USA
61D3 **Paletwa** Burma
62B2 **Pālghāt** India
60C3 **Pāli** India
71G4 **Palimé** Togo
56E1 **Palin,Mt** Malay
16A2 **Palisade** USA
60C4 **Pālitāna** India
62B3 **Palk Str** India/Sri Lanka
45H5 **Pallasovka** Russian Fed
32J5 **Pallastunturi** *Mt* Fin
78B2 **Palliser B** NZ
78C2 **Palliser,C** NZ
73E5 **Palma** Mozam
39C2 **Palma de Mallorca** Spain
27L5 **Palmares** Brazil
28E2 **Palmares do Sul** Brazil
23A5 **Palmar Sur** Costa Rica
29B4 **Palmas** Brazil
70B4 **Palmas,C** Lib
29D1 **Palmas de Monte Alto** Brazil
23B2 **Palma Soriano** Cuba
15C3 **Palm Bay** USA
15E4 **Palm Beach** USA
20C3 **Palmdale** USA
29C4 **Palmeira** Brazil
27L5 **Palmeira dos Indos** Brazil
10J3 **Palmer** USA
79G3 **Palmer** *Base* Ant
79G3 **Palmer Arch** Ant
79F3 **Palmer Land** *Region* Ant
78B3 **Palmerston** NZ
78C2 **Palmerston North** NZ
14C2 **Palmerton** USA
15E4 **Palmetto** USA
40D3 **Palmi** Italy
28E1 **Palmiera das Missões** Brazil
22C1 **Palmillas** Mexico
26C3 **Palmira** Colombia
76D2 **Palm Is** Aust
4E5 **Palms** USA
19C4 **Palm Springs** USA
12A3 **Palmyra** Missouri, USA
14B1 **Palmyra** New York, USA
14B2 **Palmyra** Pennsylvania, USA
61C3 **Palmyras Pt** India
20A2 **Palo Alto** USA
56C2 **Paloh** Indon
72D2 **Paloích** Sudan
22C2 **Palomares** Mexico
19C4 **Palomar Mt** USA
57B3 **Palopo** Indon
57A3 **Palu** Indon
64C2 **Palu** Turk
60D3 **Palwal** India
10B2 **Palyavaam** *R* Russian Fed
71G3 **Pama** Burkina
56D4 **Pamekasan** Indon
56C4 **Pameungpeuk** Indon
38C3 **Pamiers** France
59F2 **Pamir** *Mts* China
48J6 **Pamir** *R* Russian Fed
15D1 **Pamlico** *R* USA
15D1 **Pamlico Sd** USA
16B2 **Pampa** USA
28B2 **Pampa de la Salinas** *Salt pan* Arg
28B3 **Pampa de la Varita** *Plain* Arg
57B3 **Pampanua** Indon
28D2 **Pampeiro** Brazil
26D2 **Pamplona** Colombia
39B1 **Pamplona** Spain
12B3 **Pana** USA
19D3 **Panaca** USA
41E2 **Panagyurishte** Bulg
62A1 **Panaji** India
26C2 **Panamá** Panama
26B2 **Panama** Republic, C America
23B5 **Panama Canal** Panama
15B2 **Panama City** USA
19C3 **Panamint Range** *Mts* USA
20D2 **Panamint V** USA
37D2 **Panaro** *R* Italy
57F8 **Panay** *I* Phil
41E2 **Pancevo** Serbia, Yugos
57F8 **Pandan** Phil
62B1 **Pandharpur** India
75A1 **Pandie Pandie** Aust
43E1 **Panevežys** Lithuania
48K5 **Panfilov** Kazakhstan
55B1 **Pang** *R* Burma
72D4 **Pangani** Tanz
72D4 **Pangani** *R* Tanz
72C4 **Pangi** Zaïre
57A3 **Pangkajene** Indon
56C3 **Pangkalpinang** Indon
7M3 **Pangnirtung** Can
55B1 **Pangtara** Burma
19D3 **Panguitch** USA
57F9 **Pangutaran Group** *Is* Phil
16B2 **Panhandle** USA
60D3 **Panipat** India
60B2 **Panjao** Afghan
63E3 **Panjgur** Pak
10F5 **Pankof,C** USA
71H4 **Pankshin** Nig
53B4 **P'anmunjŏm** N Korea
61B3 **Panna** India
29B3 **Panorama** Brazil
29A2 **Pantanal de São Lourenço** *Swamp* Brazil
29A2 **Pantanal do Rio Negro** *Swamp* Brazil
29A2 **Pantanal do Taquari** *Swamp* Brazil
57B4 **Pantar** *I* Indon
40C3 **Pantelleria** *I* Medit S
22C1 **Pantepec** Mexico
22C1 **Panuco** Mexico
22C1 **Pánuco** *R* Mexico
52A4 **Pan Xian** China
40D3 **Paola** Italy
17D2 **Paola** USA
12B3 **Paoli** USA
42D3 **Papa** Hung
20E5 **Papaikou** Hawaiian Is
78B1 **Papakura** NZ
22C2 **Papaloapan** *R* Mexico
22C1 **Papantla** Mexico
34E1 **Papa Stour** *I* Scot
78B1 **Papatoetoe** NZ
34D2 **Papa Westray** *I* Scot
65B1 **Paphos** Cyprus
76D1 **Papua,G of** PNG
76D1 **Papua New Guinea** Republic, S E Asia
28A2 **Papudo** Chile
55B2 **Papun** Burma
27H4 **Para** State, Brazil
27J4 **Pará** *R* Brazil
76A3 **Paraburdoo** Aust
26C6 **Paracas,Pen de** Peru
29C2 **Paracatu** Brazil
29C2 **Paracatu** *R* Brazil
55E2 **Paracel Is** S E Asia
75A2 **Parachilna** Aust
60C2 **Parachinar** Pak
41E2 **Paracin** Serbia, Yugos
29D2 **Pará de Minas** Brazil
19B3 **Paradise** California, USA
19D3 **Paradise** Nevada, USA
5K3 **Paradise** *R* Can
20D1 **Paradise Peak** *Mt* USA
17D2 **Paragould** USA
26F6 **Paraguá** *R* Bol
26F2 **Paragua** *R* Ven
29D1 **Paraguaçu** *R* Brazil
27G7 **Paraguai** *R* Brazil
29A4 **Paraguari** Par
25E2 **Paraguay** Republic, S America
25E2 **Paraguay** *R* Par
27L5 **Paraiba** State, Brazil
29D3 **Paraíba do Sul** *R* Brazil
22D2 **Paraiso** Mexico
71G4 **Parakou** Benin
75A2 **Parakylia** Aust
62B3 **Paramakkudi** India
27G2 **Paramaribo** Suriname
29D1 **Paramirim** Brazil
49R4 **Paramushir, Ostrov** *I* Russian Fed
29B4 **Paraná** Brazil
25F2 **Paraná** State, Brazil
28C2 **Paraná** Urug
25E4 **Paraná** *R* Arg
27J6 **Paranã** *R* Brazil
29C4 **Paranaguá** Brazil
29B2 **Paranaiba** Brazil
29B2 **Paranaiba** *R* Brazil
29B3 **Paranapanema** *R* Brazil
29B3 **Paranavai** Brazil
57F9 **Parang** Phil
29D2 **Paraope** *R* Brazil
78B2 **Paraparaumu** NZ
29D1 **Paratinga** Brazil
62B1 **Parbhani** India
71G3 **Parc National d'Arly** Burkina
71F4 **Parc National de la Komoé** Ivory Coast
71G3 **Parc National de la Pendjari** Benin
71G3 **Parcs Nationaux du W** Benin
65C2 **Pardes Hanna** Israel
28D3 **Pardo** Arg
29E2 **Pardo** *R* Bahia, Brazil
29B3 **Pardo** *R* Mato Grosso do Sul, Brazil
29C2 **Pardo** *R* Minas Gerais, Brazil
29C3 **Pardo** *R* Sao Paulo, Brazil
42D2 **Pardubice** Czech Republic
50G4 **Parece Vela** *Reef* Pacific O
29A1 **Parecis** Brazil
4G4 **Parent** Can
57A3 **Parepare** Indon
28C3 **Parera** Arg
56B3 **Pariaman** Indon
26F1 **Paria,Pen de** Ven
57B3 **Parigi** Indon
38C2 **Paris** France
12C3 **Paris** Kentucky, USA
15B1 **Paris** Tennessee, USA
17C3 **Paris** Texas, USA
19D4 **Parker** USA
12C3 **Parkersburg** USA
75C2 **Parkes** Aust
14C3 **Parkesburg** USA
12A1 **Park Falls** USA
20B3 **Parkfield** USA
12B2 **Park Forest** USA
11C2 **Park Rapids** USA
11C3 **Parkston** USA
18B1 **Parksville** Can
18D2 **Park Valley** USA
62C1 **Parlākimidi** India
62B1 **Parli** India
37D2 **Parma** Italy
12C2 **Parma** USA
27K4 **Parnaiba** Brazil
27K4 **Parnaiba** *R* Brazil
41E3 **Párnon Óros** *Mts* Greece
44C4 **Pärnu** Estonia
61C2 **Paro** Bhutan
75B1 **Paroo** *R* Aust
75B2 **Paroo Channel** *R* Aust
63E2 **Paropamisus** *Mts* Afghan

Portland Bight **Puri**

23H2 **Portland Bight** *B* Jamaica
35D6 **Portland Bill** *Pt* Eng
75E3 **Portland,C** Aust
3B2 **Portland Canal** *Sd* USA/Can
78C1 **Portland I** NZ
23H2 **Portland Pt** Jamaica
33B3 **Port Laoise** Irish Rep
17F4 **Port Lavaca** USA
36A2 **Port-l'Evêque** France
75A2 **Port Lincoln** Aust
70A4 **Port Loko** Sierra Leone
73F6 **Port Louis** Mauritius
75B3 **Port MacDonnell** Aust
3C3 **Port McNeill** Can
75D2 **Port Macquarie** Aust
5H5 **Port Maitland** Can
14A2 **Port Matilda** USA
5J4 **Port Menier** Can
10F4 **Port Moller** USA
76D1 **Port Moresby** PNG
4C2 **Port Nelson** Can
74B2 **Port Nolloth** S Africa
14C3 **Port Norris** USA
39A1 **Porto** Port
25F4 **Pôrto Alegre** Brazil
Porto Alexandre = Tombula Angola
23A5 **Porto Armuelles** Panama
29A1 **Pôrto Artur** Brazil
29B3 **Pôrto de Novembro** Brazil
29B1 **Pôrto dos Meinacos** Brazil
25F2 **Pôrto E Cunha** Brazil
29A2 **Pôrto Esperança** Brazil
40C2 **Portoferraio** Italy
23E4 **Port of Spain** Trinidad
37E2 **Portogruaro** Italy
29A2 **Porto Jofre** Brazil
28D1 **Porto Lucena** Brazil
37D2 **Portomaggiore** Italy
29B3 **Porto Mendez** Brazil
29A3 **Porto Murtinho** Brazil
71G4 **Porto Novo** Benin
25F2 **Pôrto Primavera, Reprêsa** *Res* Brazil
18B1 **Port Orchard** USA
37E3 **Porto Recanati** Italy
18B2 **Port Orford** USA
70A1 **Porto Santo** *I* Medeira
29B3 **Porto São José** Brazil
27L7 **Pôrto Seguro** Brazil
40B2 **Porto Torres** Sardegna
29B4 **Porto União** Brazil
40B2 **Porto Vecchio** Corse
26F5 **Pôrto Velho** Brazil
78A3 **Port Pegasus** *B* NZ
75B3 **Port Phillip B** Aust
75A2 **Port Pirie** Aust
10P2 **Port Radium** Can
34B3 **Portree** Scot
18B1 **Port Renfrew** Can
23J2 **Port Royal** Jamaica
15C2 **Port Royal Sd** USA
34B4 **Portrush** N Ire
65B3 **Port Said** Egypt
15B3 **Port St Joe** USA
74D3 **Port St Johns** S Africa
7N4 **Port Saunders** Can
74E3 **Port Shepstone** S Africa
3B3 **Port Simpson** Can
23Q2 **Portsmouth** Dominica
35E6 **Portsmouth** Eng
14E1 **Portsmouth** New Hampshire, USA
12C3 **Portsmouth** Ohio, USA
13D3 **Portsmouth** Virginia, USA
75D2 **Port Stephens** *B* Aust
72D2 **Port Sudan** Sudan
17E3 **Port Sulphur** USA
32K5 **Porttipahdan Tekojärvi** *Res* Fin
39A2 **Portugal** Republic, Europe
14A1 **Portville** USA
12B2 **Port Washington** USA
55C5 **Port Weld** Malay
26E6 **Porvenir** Bol
25E3 **Posadas** Arg
39A2 **Posadas** Spain
37D1 **Poschiavo** Switz
63D2 **Posht-e Badam** Iran
57B3 **Poso** Indon
54A4 **Posŏng** S Korea
44M2 **Pos Polvy** Russian Fed
29C1 **Posse** Brazil
16B3 **Post** USA
43F1 **Postavy** Belorussia
74C2 **Postmasburg** S Africa
40C1 **Postojna** Slovenia, Yugos
53C3 **Pos'yet** Russian Fed
57B4 **Pota** Indon
74D2 **Potchetstroom** S Africa
17D2 **Poteau** USA
40D2 **Potenza** Italy
74D1 **Potgietersrus** S Africa
16C4 **Poth** USA
45G7 **Poti** Georgia
71J3 **Potiskum** Nig
18C1 **Potlatch** USA
74C3 **Potloer** *Mt* S Africa
18C1 **Pot Mt** USA
13D3 **Potomac** *R* USA
14A3 **Potomac South Branch** *R* USA
26E7 **Potosi** Bol
25C3 **Potrerillos** Chile
42C2 **Potsdam** Germany
5G5 **Potsdam** USA
16B1 **Potter** USA
14C2 **Pottstown** USA
14B2 **Pottsville** USA
14D2 **Poughkeepsie** USA
29C3 **Pouso Alegre** Brazil
78C1 **Poverty B** NZ
44E3 **Povonets** Russian Fed
45G5 **Povorino** Russian Fed
7L4 **Povungnituk** Can
11A2 **Powder** *R* USA
11A3 **Powder River** USA
18E2 **Powell** USA
76C2 **Powell Creek** Aust
19D3 **Powell,L** USA
3D4 **Powell River** Can
35D5 **Powys** County, Wales
29B2 **Poxoréo** Brazil
52D4 **Poyang Hu** *L* China
53B2 **Poyarkovo** Russian Fed
64C2 **Pozantı** Turk
22C1 **Poza Rica** Mexico
42D2 **Poznań** Pol
25E2 **Pozo Colorado** Par
40C2 **Pozzuoli** Italy
71F4 **Pra** *R* Ghana
55C3 **Prachin Buri** Thai
55B3 **Prachuap Khiri Khan** Thai
42D2 **Praděd** *Mt* Czech Republic
38C3 **Pradelles** France
29E2 **Prado** Brazil
Prague = Praha
42C2 **Praha** Czech Republic
70A4 **Praia** Cape Verde
29A1 **Praia Rica** Brazil
26F5 **Prainha** Brazil
16B3 **Prairie Dog Town Fork** *R* USA
12A2 **Prairie du Chien** USA
17D2 **Prairie Village** USA
55C3 **Prakhon Chai** Thai
29C2 **Prata** Brazil
29C2 **Prata** *R* Brazil
Prates = Dongsha Qundao
37D3 **Prato** Italy
37D3 **Pratomagno** *Mt* Italy
14C1 **Prattsville** USA
15B2 **Prattville** USA
38B1 **Prawle Pt** Eng
56E4 **Praya** Indon
37D1 **Predazzo** Italy
49L4 **Predivinsk** Russian Fed
49Q3 **Predporozhnyy** Russian Fed
43E2 **Pregolyu** *R* Russian Fed
55D3 **Prek Kak** Camb
12A1 **Prentice** USA
42C2 **Prenzlau** Germany
62E2 **Preparis I** Burma
55A2 **Preparis North Chan** Burma
55A3 **Preparis South Chan** Burma
42D3 **Přerov** Czech Republic
22C1 **Presa de les Adjuntas** Mexico
22B2 **Presa del Infiernillo** Mexico
28D2 **Presa de Salto Grande** Urug
22D2 **Presa Netzahualcóyotl** Mexico
19D4 **Prescott** Arizona, USA
17D3 **Prescott** Arkansas, USA
13D2 **Prescott** Can
11B3 **Presho** USA
25D3 **Presidencia Roque Sáenz Peña** Arg
29B3 **Presidente Epitácio** Brazil
79G2 **Presidente Frei** *Base* Ant
22C2 **Presidente Migúel Aleman** *L* Mexico
29B2 **Presidente Murtinho** Brazil
29B3 **Presidente Prudente** Brazil
29B3 **Presidente Venceslau** Brazil
16B4 **Presidio** USA
22A1 **Presidio** *R* Mexico
43E3 **Prešov** Slovakia
41E2 **Prespansko Jezero** *L* Macedonia, Yugos
13F1 **Presque Isle** USA
71F4 **Prestea** Ghana
35D5 **Preston** Eng
8B2 **Preston** Idaho, USA
11D3 **Preston** Minnesota, USA
17D2 **Preston** Missouri, USA
34C4 **Prestwick** Scot
27J8 **Prêto** Brazil
29C2 **Prêto** *R* Brazil
74D2 **Pretoria** S Africa
41E3 **Préveza** Greece
55D3 **Prey Veng** Camb
10E4 **Pribilof Is** USA
19D3 **Price** USA
3C3 **Price I** Can
15B2 **Prichard** USA
45E6 **Prichernomorskaya Nizmennost'** *Lowland* Ukraine
23M2 **Prickly Pt** Grenada
43F3 **Pridneprovskaya Vozvyshennost'** *Upland* Ukraine
43E1 **Priekule** Lithuania
74C2 **Prieska** S Africa
18C1 **Priest L** USA
18C1 **Priest River** USA
Prikaspiyskaya Nizmennost' = Caspian Depression
41E2 **Prilep** Macedonia, Yugos
45E5 **Priluki** Ukraine
28C2 **Primero** *R* Arg
32K6 **Primorsk** Russian Fed
45F6 **Primorsko-Akhtarsk** Russian Fed
3G3 **Primrose L** Can
3G3 **Prince Albert** Can
74C3 **Prince Albert** S Africa
6F2 **Prince Albert,C** Can
3G3 **Prince Albert Nat Pk** Can
6G2 **Prince Albert Pen** Can
6G2 **Prince Albert Sd** Can
7L3 **Prince Charles I** Can
79G10 **Prince Charles Mts** Ant
xxviiiC7 **Prince Edward** *I* Indian O
7M5 **Prince Edward I** Province, Can
3D3 **Prince George** Can
6H2 **Prince Gustaf Adolp Sea** Can
10E2 **Prince of Wales,C** USA
51H8 **Prince of Wales I** Aust
6H2 **Prince of Wales I** Can
3B2 **Prince of Wales I** USA
6G2 **Prince of Wales Str** Can
6G2 **Prince Patrick I** Can
7J2 **Prince Regent Inlet** *Str* Can
3B3 **Prince Rupert** Can
76D2 **Princess Charlotte B** Aust
3C3 **Princess Royal I** Can
23L1 **Princes Town** Trinidad
3D4 **Princeton** Can
12B2 **Princeton** Illinois, USA
12B3 **Princeton** Kentucky, USA
17D1 **Princeton** Missouri, USA
14C2 **Princeton** New Jersey, USA
12C3 **Princeton** W Virginia, USA
10J3 **Prince William Sd** USA
70C4 **Principe** *I* W Africa
18B2 **Prineville** USA
10J2 **Pringle,Mt** USA
7O3 **Prins Christian Sund** *Sd* Greenland
79F12 **Prinsesse Astrid Kyst** Region, Ant
79F12 **Prinsesse Ragnhild Kyst** Region, Ant
48C2 **Prins Karls Forland** *I* Barents S
21D3 **Prinzapolca** Nic
44E3 **Priozersk** Russian Fed
43F2 **Pripet** *R* Belorussia
Pripyat' = Pripet
41E2 **Priština** Serbia, Yugos
42C2 **Pritzwalk** Germany
44G5 **Privolzhskaya Vozvyshennost'** *Upland* Russian Fed
41E2 **Prizren** Serbia, Yugos
56D4 **Probolinggo** Indon
11D2 **Proctor** USA
62B2 **Proddatūr** India
21D2 **Progreso** Mexico
53B2 **Progress** Russian Fed
18B2 **Project City** USA
45G7 **Prokhladnyy** Russian Fed
48K4 **Prokop'yevsk** Russian Fed
45G6 **Proletarskaya** Russian Fed
49P2 **Proliv Dmitriya Lapteva** *Str* Russian Fed
48G2 **Proliv Karskiye Vorota** *Str* Russian Fed
49T2 **Proliv Longa** *Str* Russian Fed
49L2 **Proliv Vilkitskogo** *Str* Russian Fed
Prome = Pyè
29A2 **Promissão** Brazil
43G2 **Pronya** *R* Belorussia
3D2 **Prophet** *R* Can
27L6 **Propriá** Brazil
14C1 **Prospect** New York, USA
18B2 **Prospect** Oregon, USA
76D3 **Prosperine** Aust
42D3 **Prostějov** Czech Republic
7N2 **Prøven** Greenland
38D3 **Provence** Region, France
14E2 **Providence** USA
49U3 **Provideniya** Russian Fed
14E1 **Provincetown** USA
36B2 **Provins** France
19D2 **Provo** USA
3F3 **Provost** Can
29B4 **Prudentópolis** Brazil
10J1 **Prudhoe B** USA
10J1 **Prudhoe Bay** USA
7M2 **Prudhoe Land** *Region* Greenland
43E2 **Pruszkow** Pol
43F3 **Prut** *R* Rom/Moldova
45D6 **Prutul** *R* Rom
43E2 **Pruzhany** Belorussia
17C2 **Pryor** USA
43E3 **Przemyśl** Pol
41F3 **Psará** *I* Greece
44D4 **Pskov** Russian Fed
43F2 **Ptich** *R* Belorussia
41E2 **Ptolemaïs** Greece
54A3 **Puan** S Korea
26D5 **Pucallpa** Peru
52D4 **Pucheng** China
28A3 **Pucón** Chile
32K5 **Pudasjärvi** Fin
44F3 **Pudozh** Russian Fed
62B2 **Pudukkottai** India
39A1 **Puebai de Trives** Spain
22C2 **Puebla** Mexico
22C2 **Puebla** State, Mexico
39A1 **Puebla de Sanabria** Spain
16B2 **Pueblo** USA
28B3 **Puelches** Arg
28B3 **Puelén** Arg
22B2 **Puenta Ixbapa** Mexico
28B2 **Puente del Inca** Arg
26B5 **Puerta Aguja** Peru
26D7 **Puerta Coles** Peru
28B2 **Puerta de los Llanos** Arg
22A1 **Puerta de Mita** Mexico
27L5 **Puerta do Calcanhar** *Pt* Brazil
74E2 **Puerta do Oro** *Pt* S Africa
22C2 **Puerta Galera** Mexico
26D1 **Puerta Gallinas** Colombia
22C2 **Puerta Maldonado** *Pt* Mexico
26B2 **Puerta Mariato** Panama
25C7 **Puerta Médanosa** *Pt* Arg
22B2 **Puerta Mongrove** Mexico
22C2 **Puerta Roca Partida** Mexico
21E4 **Puerta San Blas** *Pt* Panama
22B2 **Puerta San Telmo** Mexico
29B3 **Puerto Adela** Brazil
25B7 **Puerto Aisén** Chile
22C2 **Puerto Angel** Mexico
21D4 **Puerto Armuelles** Panama
27G6 **Puerto Artur** Brazil
26C3 **Puerto Asis** Colombia
26E2 **Puerto Ayacucho** Ven
21D3 **Puerto Barrios** Guatemala
26D2 **Puerto Berrio** Colombia
26E1 **Puerto Cabello** Ven
21D3 **Puerto Cabezas** Nic
26E2 **Puerto Carreńo** Ven
29A3 **Puerto Casado** Brazil
26B1 **Puerto Cavezas** Nic
29A3 **Puerto Cooper** Brazil
21D4 **Puerto Cortes** Costa Rica
21D3 **Puerto Cortés** Honduras
70A2 **Puerto del Rosario** Canary Is
27H8 **Puerto E Cunha** Brazil
22C2 **Puerto Escondido** Mexico
26D1 **Puerto Fijo** Ven
27J5 **Puerto Franco** Brazil
29A3 **Puerto Guarani** Brazil
26E6 **Puerto Heath** Bol
21D2 **Puerto Juarez** Mexico
26F1 **Puerto la Cruz** Ven
39B2 **Puertollano** Spain
23C4 **Puerto Lopez** Colombia
25D6 **Puerto Madryn** Arg
26E6 **Puerto Maldonado** Peru
22C2 **Puerto Marquéz** Mexico
25B6 **Puerto Montt** Chile
24C7 **Puerto Moritt** Chile
27G8 **Puerto Murtinho** Brazil
25B8 **Puerto Natales** Chile
21A1 **Puerto Peñasco** Mexico
29A3 **Puerto Pinasco** Brazil
25D6 **Puerto Pirámides** Arg
23C3 **Puerto Plata** Dom Rep
57E9 **Puerto Princesa** Phil
26C3 **Puerto Rico** Colombia
23D3 **Puerto Rico** *I* Caribbean
23D3 **Puerto Rico Trench** Caribbean
22B2 **Puerto San Juan de Lima** Mexico
27H4 **Puerto Santanga** Brazil
29A3 **Puerto Sastre** Brazil
25E1 **Puerto Suárez** Bol
22A1 **Puerto Vallarta** Mexico
25B6 **Puerto Varas** Chile
26F7 **Puerto Villarroel** Bol
45H5 **Pugachev** Russian Fed
60C3 **Pugal** India
39C1 **Puigcerdá** Spain
54A2 **Pujŏn** N Korea
54A2 **Pujŏn Res** N Korea
78B2 **Pukaki,L** NZ
4D4 **Pukaskwa Nat Park** Can
4A2 **Pukatawagan** Can
54A2 **Pukchin** N Korea
53B3 **Pukch'ŏng** N Korea
78B1 **Pukekobe** NZ
78B2 **Puketeraki Range** *Mts* NZ
44G3 **Puksoozero** Russian Fed
40C2 **Pula** Croatia, Yugos
13D2 **Pulaski** New York, USA
15B1 **Pulaski** Tennessee, USA
12C3 **Pulaski** Virginia, USA
51G7 **Pulau Kolepom** *I* Indon
57D2 **Pulau Pulau Asia** *Is* Indon
57D2 **Pulau Pulau Ayu** *Is* Indon
56A2 **Pulau Pulau Banyak** *Arch* Indon
56A3 **Pulau Pulau Batu** *Is* Indon
76A1 **Pulau Pulau Kangean** *Is* Indon
76B1 **Pulau Pulau Macan** *Is* Indon
57D3 **Pulau Pulau Pisang** *Is* Indon
56A3 **Pulautelo** Indon
43E2 **Pulawy** Pol
62C2 **Pulicat,L** India
60B1 **Pul-i-Khumri** Afghan
62B3 **Puliyangudi** India
36E3 **Pullendorf** Germany
18C1 **Pullman** USA
51G6 **Pulo Anna Merir** *I* Pacific I
57F7 **Pulog,Mt** Phil
32L5 **Pulozero** Russian Fed
43E2 **Pultusk** Pol
25C3 **Puna de Atacama** Arg
61C2 **Punakha** Bhutan
60C2 **Punch** Pak
74E1 **Punda Milia** S Africa
62A1 **Pune** India
22B2 **Punéper** Mexico
54A2 **Pungsan** N Korea
54A2 **Pungso** N Korea
72C4 **Punia** Zaïre
28A2 **Punitaqui** Chile
60C2 **Punjab** Province, Pak
60D2 **Punjab** State, India
26D7 **Puno** Peru
21A2 **Punta Abreojos** *Pt* Mexico
40D3 **Punta Alice** *Pt* Italy
28C3 **Punta Alta** Arg
25B8 **Punta Arenas** Chile
21A2 **Punta Baja** *Pt* Mexico
28C4 **Punta Bermeja** *Pt* Arg
28A2 **Punta Curaumilla** *Pt* Chile
73B5 **Punta da Marca** *Pt* Angola
73D6 **Punta de Barra Falsa** *Pt* Mozam
28E2 **Punta del Este** Urug
37C2 **Punta di Portofino** *Pt* Italy
21A2 **Punta Eugenia** *Pt* Mexico
28A3 **Punta Galera** Chile
21D3 **Punta Gorda** Belize
15E4 **Punta Gorda** USA
28A3 **Punta Lavapié** *Pt* Chile
28A2 **Punta Lengua de Vaca** *Pt* Chile
40C2 **Punta Licosa** *Pt* Italy
28D3 **Punta Norte** *Pt* Arg
28D3 **Punta Piedras** *Pt* Arg
28A1 **Punta Poroto** *Pt* Chile
28C4 **Punta Rasa** *Pt* Arg
26B1 **Puntarenas** Costa Rica
28C4 **Punta Rubia** *Pt* Arg
8B4 **Punta San Antonio** *Pt* Mexico
28D3 **Punta Sur** Arg
28A2 **Punta Topocalma** Chile
57B4 **Puntjak Ranakah** *Mt* Indon
14A2 **Punxsutawney** USA
57D3 **Puper** Indon
52C4 **Puqi** China
46J3 **Pur** *R* Russian Fed
17C2 **Purcell** USA
10G2 **Purcell Mt** USA
3E3 **Purcell Mts** Can
28A3 **Purén** Chile
16B2 **Purgatoire** *R* USA
61C3 **Puri** India

Rawāndiz **Romanche Gap**

64D2 **Rawāndiz** Iraq
25D6 **Rawson** Arg
61E2 **Rawu** China
56D3 **Raya** *Mt* Indon
62B2 **Rāyadurg** India
62C1 **Rāyagada** India
65D2 **Rayak** Leb
7N5 **Ray,C** Can
53B2 **Raychikhinsk** Russian Fed
66D3 **Raydah** Yemen
63D3 **Rāyen** Iran
20C2 **Raymond** California, USA
18D1 **Raymond** Can
14E1 **Raymond** New Hampshire, USA
18B1 **Raymond** Washington, USA
75D2 **Raymond Terrace** Aust
17F4 **Raymondville** USA
10H2 **Ray Mts** USA
22C1 **Rayon** Mexico
67F3 **Raysūt** Oman
63B1 **Razan** Iran
43G3 **Razdel'naya** Ukraine
53C3 **Razdol'noye** Russian Fed
41F2 **Razgrad** Bulg
41F2 **Razim** *L* Rom
35E6 **Reading** Eng
14C2 **Reading** USA
6G3 **Read Island** Can
14D1 **Readsboro** USA
28B2 **Real de Padre** Arg
28C3 **Realicó** Arg
69B2 **Rebiana** *Well* Libya
69B2 **Rebiana Sand Sea** Libya
32L6 **Reboly** Russian Fed
53E2 **Rebun-tō** *I* Japan
76B4 **Recherche,Arch of the** *Is* Aust
43G2 **Rechitsa** Belorussia
27M5 **Recife** Brazil
74D3 **Recife,C** S Africa
29E2 **Recifes da Pedra Grande** *Arch* Brazil
77F2 **Récifs D'Entrecasteaux** Nouvelle Calédonie
36D1 **Recklinghausen** Germany
28D1 **Reconquista** Arg
28C1 **Recreo** Arg
11C2 **Red** *R* Can/USA
17D3 **Red** *R* USA
55C4 **Redang** *I* Malay
14C2 **Red Bank** New Jersey, USA
15B1 **Red Bank** Tennessee, USA
5K3 **Red Bay** Can
3G3 **Redberry L** Can
19B2 **Red Bluff** USA
16B3 **Red Bluff L** USA
35E4 **Redcar** Eng
3F3 **Redcliff** Can
75D1 **Redcliffe** Aust
75B2 **Red Cliffs** Aust
16C1 **Red Cloud** USA
3F3 **Red Deer** Can
3F3 **Red Deer** *R* Can
3H3 **Red Deer** *R* Saskatchewan, Can
3H3 **Red Deer L** Can
18B2 **Redding** USA
11C3 **Redfield** USA
16C2 **Red Hills** USA
9D2 **Red L** USA
7J4 **Red Lake** Can
11C2 **Red Lake** *R* USA
20D3 **Redlands** USA
14B3 **Red Lion** USA
18E1 **Red Lodge** USA
18B2 **Redmond** USA
20D3 **Red Mountain** USA
17C1 **Red Oak** USA
38B2 **Redon** France
20C4 **Redondo Beach** USA
10H3 **Redoubt V** USA
52B5 **Red River Delta** Vietnam
58B3 **Red Sea** Africa/Arabian Pen
10N3 **Redstone** *R* Can
4C3 **Red Sucker L** Can
3F3 **Redwater** Can
3G4 **Redwater** *R* USA
11D3 **Red Wing** USA
20A2 **Redwood City** USA
11C3 **Redwood Falls** USA
12B2 **Reed City** USA
20C2 **Reedley** USA
18B2 **Reedsport** USA
13D3 **Reedville** USA
78B2 **Reefton** NZ
64C2 **Refahiye** Turk
17F4 **Refugio** USA
29E2 **Regência** Brazil
42C3 **Regensburg** Germany
70C2 **Reggane** Alg
40D3 **Reggio di Calabria** Italy
37D2 **Reggio Nell'Emilia** Italy
41E1 **Reghin** Rom
3H3 **Regina** Can
63E2 **Registan** Region, Afghan
22A1 **Regocijo** Mexico
74B1 **Rehoboth** Namibia
13D3 **Rehoboth Beach** USA
65C3 **Rehovot** Israel
26E1 **Reicito** Ven
15D1 **Reidsville** USA
35E6 **Reigate** Eng
36B2 **Reims** France
11D3 **Reinbeck** USA
3H2 **Reindeer** *R* Can
3H2 **Reindeer L** Can
39B1 **Reinosa** Spain
14B3 **Reisterstown** USA
74D2 **Reitz** S Africa
6H3 **Reliance** Can
18E2 **Reliance** USA
71C1 **Relizane** Alg
75A2 **Remarkable,Mt** Aust
56D4 **Rembang** Indon
63D3 **Remeshk** Iran
36D2 **Remiremont** France
36D1 **Remscheid** Germany
14C1 **Remsen** USA
37A2 **Rémuzat** France
12B3 **Rend L** USA
42B2 **Rendsburg** Germany
4F4 **Renfrew** Can
56B3 **Rengat** Indon
28A2 **Rengo** Chile
43F3 **Reni** Ukraine
72D2 **Renk** Sudan
7Q2 **Renland** *Pen* Greenland
75B2 **Renmark** Aust
77F2 **Rennell** *I* Solomon Is
38B2 **Rennes** France
19C3 **Reno** USA
37D2 **Reno** *R* Italy
14B2 **Renovo** USA
14D1 **Rensselaer** USA
18B1 **Renton** USA
57B4 **Reo** Indon
71F3 **Réo** Burkina
63E1 **Repetek** Turkmenistan
43G2 **Repki** Ukraine
29C3 **Reprêsa de Furnas** *Dam* Brazil
29C2 **Reprêsa Três Marias** *Dam* Brazil
18C1 **Republic** USA
16C1 **Republican** *R* USA
33B3 **Republic of Ireland** NW Europe
7K3 **Repulse Bay** Can
4F4 **Réservoir Baskatong** *Res* Can
13D1 **Réservoir Cabonga** *Res* Can
4F4 **Réservoir Decelles** *Res* Can
7L4 **Réservoir de La Grande 2** *Res* Can
7L4 **Réservoir de La Grande 3** *Res* Can
7L4 **Réservoir de La Grande 4** *Res* Can
4F4 **Réservoir Dozois** *Res* Can
7L5 **Réservoir Gouin** *Res* Can
5G4 **Réservoir Pipmouacane** *Res* Can
63C1 **Reshteh-ye Alborz** *Mts* Iran
52A2 **Reshui** China
25E3 **Resistencia** Arg
41E1 **Resita** Rom
7J2 **Resolute** Can
78A3 **Resolution I** NZ
7M3 **Resolution Island** Can
74E2 **Ressano Garcia** Mozam
5H4 **Restigouche** *R* Can
28E1 **Restinga Seca** Brazil
28B2 **Retamito** Arg
36C2 **Rethel** France
41E3 **Réthimnon** Greece
xxviiD6 **Reunion** *I* Indian O
39C1 **Reus** Spain
37C1 **Reuss** *R* Switz
36E2 **Reutlingen** Germany
37D1 **Reutte** Austria
44K4 **Revda** Russian Fed
3E3 **Revelstoke** Can
21A3 **Revillagigedo** *Is* Mexico
10M4 **Revillagigedo I** USA
36C2 **Revin** France
65C3 **Revivim** Israel
61B3 **Rewa** India
60D3 **Rewari** India
18D2 **Rexburg** USA
32A2 **Reykjavik** Iceland
14A2 **Reynoldsville** USA
21C2 **Reynosa** Mexico
38B2 **Rezé** France
43F1 **Rezekne** Latvia
44L4 **Rezh** Russian Fed
37C1 **Rhātikon** *Mts* Austria/Switz
65C1 **Rhazīr** Republic, Leb
36E1 **Rheda Wiedenbrück** Germany
Rhein = Rhine
42B2 **Rheine** Germany
37B1 **Rheinfielden** Switz
38D2 **Rheinland Pfalz** Region, Germany
37C1 **Rheinwaldhorn** *Mt* Switz
42B2 **Rhine** *R* W Europe
14D2 **Rhinebeck** USA
12B1 **Rhinelander** USA
37C2 **Rho** Italy
13E2 **Rhode Island** State, USA
14E2 **Rhode Island Sd** USA
Rhodes = Ródhos
74D1 **Rhodes Drift** *Ford* S Africa
18D1 **Rhodes Peak** *Mt* USA
38C3 **Rhône** *R* France
35D5 **Rhyl** Wales
27L6 **Riachão do Jacuipe** Brazil
39A1 **Ria de Arosa** *B* Spain
39A1 **Ria de Betanzos** *B* Spain
39A1 **Ria de Corcubion** *B* Spain
39A1 **Ria de Lage** *B* Spain
39A1 **Ria de Sta Marta** *B* Spain
39A1 **Ria de Vigo** *B* Spain
60C2 **Riāsi** Pak
39A1 **Ribadeo** Spain
29B3 **Ribas do Rio Pardo** Brazil
73D5 **Ribauè** Mozam
35D5 **Ribble** *R* Eng
29C3 **Ribeira** Brazil
29C3 **Ribeirão Prêto** Brazil
26E6 **Riberala** Bol
37E3 **Riccione** Italy
13D2 **Rice L** Can
12A1 **Rice Lake** USA
29D1 **Richao de Santana** Brazil
74E2 **Richard's Bay** S Africa
10L2 **Richards I** Can
17C3 **Richardson** USA
3F2 **Richardson** *R* Can
10L2 **Richardson Mts** Can
19D3 **Richfield** USA
14C1 **Richfield Springs** USA
20C3 **Richgrove** USA
5J4 **Richibucto** Can
18C1 **Richland** USA
12C3 **Richlands** USA
20A2 **Richmond** California, USA
74C3 **Richmond** Cape Province, S Africa
12C3 **Richmond** Kentucky, USA
74E2 **Richmond** Natal, S Africa
75D2 **Richmond** New South Wales, Aust
78B2 **Richmond** NZ
76D3 **Richmond** Queensland, Aust
13D3 **Richmond** Virginia, USA
78B2 **Richmond Range** *Mts* NZ
14C1 **Richmondville** USA
4F5 **Rideau Lakes** Can
15C2 **Ridgeland** USA
14A2 **Ridgway** USA
11B1 **Riding Mountain Nat Pk** Can
23D4 **Riecito** Ven
37D1 **Rienza** *R* Italy
42C2 **Riesa** Germany
25B8 **Riesco** *I* Chile
74C2 **Riet** *R* S Africa
40C2 **Rieti** Italy
37B3 **Riez** France
39B2 **Rif** *Mts* Mor
16A2 **Rifle** USA
43E1 **Riga** Latvia
44C4 **Riga,G of** Estonia/Latvia
63D3 **Rīgān** Iran
18D2 **Rigby** USA
18C1 **Riggins** USA
7N4 **Rigolet** Can
32J6 **Riihimaki** Fin
40C1 **Rijeka** Croatia, Yugos
54D3 **Rikuzen-Tanaka** Japan
71H3 **Rima** *R* Nig
3F3 **Rimbey** Can
32H7 **Rimbo** Sweden
37E2 **Rimini** Italy
41E1 **Rîmnicu Vîlcea** Rom
5H4 **Rimouski** Can
22B1 **Rincón de Romos** Mexico
32F7 **Ringkøbing** Den
28A3 **Riñihue** Chile
57A4 **Rinja** *I* Indon
72A3 **Rio Benito** Eq Guinea
26E5 **Rio Branco** Brazil
28E2 **Rio Branco** Urug
29C4 **Rio Branco do Sul** Brazil
17F4 **Rio Bravo** Mexico
21B1 **Rio Bravo del Norte** *R* USA/Mexico
29B3 **Rio Brilhante** Brazil
28A4 **Rio Bueno** Chile
26D1 **Riochacha** Colombia
29C3 **Rio Claro** Brazil
23L1 **Rio Claro** Trinidad
28C3 **Rio Colorado** Arg
28C2 **Rio Cuarto** Arg
27L6 **Rio de Jacuipe** Brazil
29D3 **Rio de Janeiro** Brazil
29D3 **Rio de Janeiro** State, Brazil
28D2 **Rio de la Plata** *Estuary* Arg/Urug
25C8 **Rio Gallegos** Arg
25C8 **Rio Grande** Arg
28E2 **Rio Grande** Brazil
22B1 **Rio Grande** Mexico
23A4 **Rio Grande** Nic
21D3 **Rio Grande** *R* Nicaragua
21B2 **Rio Grande** *R* USA/Mexico
17F4 **Rio Grande City** USA
22B1 **Rio Grande de Santiago** Mexico
27L5 **Rio Grande do Norte** State, Brazil
28E1 **Rio Grande do Sul** State, Brazil
xxxG6 **Rio Grande Rise** Atlantic O
23C4 **Riohacha** Colombia
38C2 **Riom** France
26C4 **Riombamba** Ecuador
26E7 **Rio Mulatos** Bol
29C4 **Rio Negro** Brazil
28B4 **Río Negro** State, Arg
25F3 **Rio Pardo** Brazil
28C2 **Rio Tercero** Arg
26F6 **Rio Theodore Roosevelt** *R* Brazil
25B8 **Rio Turbio** Arg
3G2 **Riou L** Can
29B2 **Rio Verde** Brazil
22B1 **Rio Verde** Mexico
29B2 **Rio Verde de Mato Grosso** Brazil
12C3 **Ripley** Ohio, USA
15B1 **Ripley** Tennessee, USA
12C3 **Ripley** West Virginia, USA
35E4 **Ripon** Eng
20B2 **Ripon** USA
53E2 **Rishiri-tō** *I* Japan
65C3 **Rishon le Zion** Israel
14B3 **Rising Sun** USA
36A2 **Risle** *R* France
32F7 **Risør** Nor
62E2 **Ritchie's Arch** Andaman Is
7N3 **Ritenbenk** Greenland
20C2 **Ritter,Mt** USA
18C1 **Ritzville** USA
28B2 **Rivadavia** Arg
28A1 **Rivadavia** Chile
28C3 **Rivadavia Gonzalez Moreno** Arg
37D2 **Riva de Garda** Italy
26A1 **Rivas** Nic
28C3 **Rivera** Arg
28D2 **Rivera** Urug
20B2 **Riverbank** USA
70B4 **River Cess** Lib
20C2 **Riverdale** USA
14D2 **Riverhead** USA
75B3 **Riverina** Aust
71H4 **Rivers** State, Nig
78A3 **Riversdale** NZ
74C3 **Riversdale** S Africa
20D4 **Riverside** USA
3C3 **Rivers Inlet** Can
4B3 **Riverton** Can
78A3 **Riverton** NZ
18E2 **Riverton** USA
37A2 **Rives** France
15E4 **Riviera Beach** USA
7L4 **Rivière aux Feuilles** *R* Can
5G2 **Rivière aux Mélèzes** *R* Can
5H3 **Rivière aux Outardes** *R* Can
7M4 **Rivière de la Baleine** *R* Can
5G4 **Rivière du Lièvre** *R* Can
5H4 **Rivière-du-Loup** Can
7M4 **Rivière du Petit Mècatina** *R* Can
5F2 **Rivière Innuksuac** *R* Can
5G1 **Rivière Lepellé** *R* Can
5H4 **Rivière Pentecôte** Can
5F1 **Rivière Povungnituk** *R* Can
5G1 **Rivière Vachon** *R* Can
36C2 **Rivigny-sur-Ornain** France
54A2 **Riwon** N Korea
67E2 **Riyadh** S Arabia
64D1 **Rize** Turk
52D2 **Rizhao** China
65C1 **Rizokaipaso** Cyprus
32F7 **Rjukan** Nor
7K2 **Roanes Pen** Can
38C2 **Roanne** France
15B2 **Roanoke** Alabama, USA
13D3 **Roanoke** Virginia, USA
13D3 **Roanoke** *R* USA
15D1 **Roanoke Rapids** USA
19D3 **Roan Plat** USA
18D2 **Roberts** USA
19C3 **Roberts Creek Mt** USA
32J6 **Robertsforz** Sweden
17D2 **Robert S Kerr Res** USA
74B3 **Robertson** S Africa
70A4 **Robertsport** Lib
7L5 **Roberval** Can
75B2 **Robinvale** Aust
3H3 **Roblin** Can
3E3 **Robson,Mt** Can
17F4 **Robstown** USA
21A3 **Roca Partida** *I* Mexico
xxxG5 **Rocas** *I* Atlantic O
27M4 **Rocas** *I* Brazil
37D2 **Rocca San Casciano** Italy
28E2 **Rocha** Urug
35D5 **Rochdale** Eng
29B2 **Rochedo** Brazil
38B2 **Rochefort** France
12B2 **Rochelle** USA
6G3 **Rocher River** Can
75B3 **Rochester** Aust
35F6 **Rochester** Eng
11D3 **Rochester** Minnesota, USA
14E1 **Rochester** New Hampshire, USA
14B1 **Rochester** New York, USA
3C1 **Rock** *R* Can
12B2 **Rock** *R* USA
12B2 **Rockford** USA
3G4 **Rockglen** Can
15C2 **Rock Hill** USA
15D2 **Rockingham** USA
12A2 **Rock Island** USA
5H5 **Rockland** Maine, USA
12B1 **Rockland** Michigan, USA
75B3 **Rocklands Res** Aust
15C3 **Rockledge** USA
17F4 **Rockport** USA
11C3 **Rock Rapids** USA
11A3 **Rock River** USA
11A2 **Rock Springs** Montana, USA
16B3 **Rocksprings** Texas, USA
18E2 **Rock Springs** Wyoming, USA
78B2 **Rocks Pt** NZ
75C3 **Rock,The** Aust
14D2 **Rockville** Connecticut, USA
12B3 **Rockville** Indiana, USA
14B3 **Rockville** Maryland, USA
13F1 **Rockwood** USA
16B2 **Rocky Ford** USA
4E4 **Rocky Island L** Can
15D1 **Rocky Mount** USA
3F3 **Rocky Mountain House** Can
16A1 **Rocky Mountain Nat Pk** USA
8B1 **Rocky Mts** Can/USA
10F3 **Rocky Pt** USA
42C2 **Rødbyhavn** Den
5K3 **Roddickton** Can
28B2 **Rodeo** Arg
38C3 **Rodez** France
41F3 **Ródhos** Greece
41F3 **Ródhos** *I* Greece
40D2 **Rodi Garganico** Italy
41E2 **Rodopi Planina** *Mts* Bulg
76A3 **Roebourne** Aust
74D1 **Roedtan** S Africa
36D1 **Roer** *R* Neth
36C1 **Roermond** Neth
36B1 **Roeselare** Belg
7K3 **Roes Welcome Sd** Can
43F2 **Rogachev** Belorussia
17D2 **Rogers** USA
12C1 **Rogers City** USA
20D3 **Rogers L** USA
12C3 **Rogers,Mt** USA
18D2 **Rogerson** USA
4F3 **Roggan L** Can
4F3 **Roggan** *R* Can
74B3 **Roggeveldberge** *Mts* S Africa
18B2 **Rogue** *R* USA
60B3 **Rohn** Pak
60D3 **Rohtak** India
43E1 **Roja** Latvia
29B3 **Rolândia** Brazil
17D2 **Rolla** USA
18D1 **Rollins** USA
75C1 **Roma** Aust
40C2 **Roma** Italy
37D2 **Romagna** Region, Italy
37C2 **Romagnano** Italy
15D2 **Romain,C** USA
5J3 **Romaine** *R* Can
41F1 **Roman** Rom
xxxH4 **Romanche Gap** Atlantic O

Romang St James,C

57C4 **Romang** *I* Indon
45C6 **Romania** Republic, E Europe
15E4 **Romano,C** USA
38D2 **Romans sur Isère** France
10E3 **Romanzof,C** USA
10K2 **Romanzof Mts** USA
57F8 **Romblon** Phil
Rome = Roma
15B2 **Rome** Georgia, USA
14C1 **Rome** New York, USA
13D2 **Rome** USA
38C2 **Romilly-sur-Seine** France
71A2 **Rommani** Mor
13D3 **Romney** USA
45E5 **Romny** Ukraine
42B1 **Rømø** *I* Den
37B1 **Romont** Switz
38C2 **Romoratin** France
56G7 **Rompin** Malay
56G7 **Rompin** *R* Malay
37D2 **Ronco** Italy
39A2 **Ronda** Spain
26F6 **Rondônia** Brazil
26F6 **Rondônia** State, Brazil
29B2 **Rondonópolis** Brazil
52B4 **Rong'an** China
52B4 **Rongchang** China
52E2 **Rongcheng** China
52B4 **Rongjiang** China
52B4 **Rong Jiang** *R* China
55A1 **Rongklang Range** *Mts* Burma
32G7 **Rønne** Denmark
32H7 **Ronneby** Sweden
79F2 **Ronne Ice Shelf** Ant
36B1 **Ronse** Belg
36A1 **Ronthieu** Region, France
8C3 **Roof Butte** *Mt* USA
60D3 **Roorkee** India
36C1 **Roosendaal** Neth
19D2 **Roosevelt** USA
79E **Roosevelt I** Ant
3C2 **Roosevelt,Mt** Can
10O3 **Root** *R* Can
11D3 **Root** *R* USA
76C2 **Roper** *R* Aust
37A3 **Roquevaire** France
26F3 **Roraima** State, Brazil
26F2 **Roraime** *Mt* Ven
4B3 **Rorketon** Can
32G6 **Røros** Nor
37C1 **Rorschach** Switz
32G6 **Rørvik** Nor
43G3 **Ros'** *R* Ukraine
23Q2 **Rosalie** Dominica
20C3 **Rosamond** USA
20C3 **Rosamond L** USA
22A1 **Rosamorada** Mexico
28C2 **Rosario** Arg
27K4 **Rosário** Brazil
22A1 **Rosario** Mexico
29A3 **Rosario** Par
28D2 **Rosario** Urug
28D2 **Rosario del Tala** Arg
28E2 **Rosário do Sul** Brazil
29A1 **Rosário Oeste** Brazil
14C2 **Roscoe** USA
38B2 **Roscoff** France
33B3 **Roscommon** Irish Rep
35B5 **Roscrea** Irish Rep
23E3 **Roseau** Dominica
4B4 **Roseau** *R* Can/USA
75E3 **Rosebery** Aust
5K4 **Rose Blanche** Can
11A2 **Rosebud** USA
18B2 **Roseburg** USA
17C4 **Rosenberg** USA
42C3 **Rosenheim** Germany
3G3 **Rosetown** Can
20B1 **Roseville** USA
41E2 **Rosiorii de Verde** Rom
32G7 **Roskilde** Den
44E5 **Roslavl'** Russian Fed
44G4 **Roslyatino** Russian Fed
78B2 **Ross** NZ
10M3 **Ross** *R* Can
33B3 **Rossan** *Pt* Irish Rep
40D3 **Rossano** Italy
17E3 **Ross Barnet Res** USA
13D1 **Rosseau L** Can
77E2 **Rossel** *I* Solomon Is
79E **Ross Ice Shelf** Ant
18B1 **Ross L** USA
3E4 **Rossland** Can
35B5 **Rosslare** Irish Rep
78C2 **Ross,Mt** NZ
70A3 **Rosso** Maur
35D6 **Ross-on-Wye** Eng
45F5 **Rossosh** Russian Fed
6E3 **Ross River** Can
79F6 **Ross S** Ant
63C3 **Rostāq** Iran
3G3 **Rosthern** Can
42C2 **Rostock** Germany
44F4 **Rostov** Russian Fed
45F6 **Rostov-na-Donu** Russian Fed
15C2 **Roswell** Georgia, USA
16B3 **Roswell** New Mexico, USA
51H5 **Rota** Pacific O
36E1 **Rotenburg** Hessen, Germany
42B2 **Rotenburg** Niedersachsen, Germany
36E1 **Rothaar-Geb** *Region* Germany
79G3 **Rothera** *Base* Ant
35E5 **Rotherham** Eng
5H4 **Rothesay** Can
34C4 **Rothesay** Scot
57B5 **Roti** *I* Indon
75C2 **Roto** Aust
78B2 **Rotoiti,L** NZ
78B2 **Rotoroa,L** NZ
78C1 **Rotorua** NZ
78C1 **Rotorua,L** NZ
36E2 **Rottenburg** Germany
42A2 **Rotterdam** Neth
36E2 **Rottweil** Germany
77G2 **Rotuma** *I* Fiji
36B1 **Roubaix** France
38C2 **Rouen** France
35F5 **Rough** *Oilfield* N Sea
Roulers = Roeselare
73F6 **Round I** Mauritius
20D1 **Round Mountain** USA
75D2 **Round Mt** Aust
18E1 **Roundup** USA
34D2 **Rousay** *I* Scot
38C3 **Roussillon** Region, France
74D3 **Rouxville** S Africa
4F4 **Rouyn** Can
32K5 **Rovaniemi** Fin
37D2 **Rovereto** Italy
37D2 **Rovigo** Italy
40C1 **Rovinj** Croatia, Yugos
43F2 **Rovno** Ukraine
63B1 **Row'ān** Iran
75C1 **Rowena** Aust
7L3 **Rowley I** Can
76A2 **Rowley Shoals** Aust
57E8 **Roxas** Palawan, Phil
57F8 **Roxas** Panay, Phil
15D1 **Roxboro** USA
78A3 **Roxburgh** NZ
18E1 **Roy** USA
35B5 **Royal Canal** Irish Rep
35E5 **Royal Leamington Spa** Eng
12C2 **Royal Oak** USA
35F6 **Royal Tunbridge Wells** Eng
38B2 **Royan** France
36B2 **Roye** France
35E5 **Royston** Eng
43E3 **Rožňava** Slovakia
36B2 **Rozoy** France
45G5 **Rtishchevo** Russian Fed
37E2 **Rt Kamenjak** *C* Croatia, Yugos
73D4 **Ruaha Nat Pk** Tanz
78C1 **Ruahine Range** *Mts* NZ
78C1 **Ruapehu,Mt** NZ
67D3 **Rub al Khālī** *Desert* S Arabia
34B3 **Rubha Hunish** Scot
25F2 **Rubinéia** Brazil
29B3 **Rubinéia** Brazil
48K4 **Rubtsovsk** Russian Fed
10G3 **Ruby** USA
19C2 **Ruby Mts** USA
63D3 **Rudan** Iran
63E2 **Rudbar** Afghan
63B1 **Rūdbār** Iran
53D3 **Rudnaya Pristan'** Russian Fed
43G2 **Rudnya** Russian Fed
53C3 **Rudnyy** Russian Fed
41E2 **Rudoka Planina** *Mt* Macedonia, Yugos
48G1 **Rudol'fa, Ostrov** *I* Russian Fed
52E3 **Rudong** China
12C1 **Rudyard** USA
36A1 **Rue** France
66B4 **Rufa'a** Sudan
38C2 **Ruffec** France
73D4 **Rufiji** *R* Tanz
28C2 **Rufino** Arg
70A3 **Rufisque** Sen
73C5 **Rufunsa** Zambia
35E5 **Rugby** Eng
11B2 **Rugby** USA
32G8 **Rügen** *I* Germany
42B2 **Ruhr** *R* Germany
52D4 **Ruijin** China
41E2 **Rujen** *Mt* Macedonia, Bulg/Yugos
73D4 **Rukwa** *L* Tanz
34B3 **Rum** *I* Scot
41D1 **Ruma** Serbia, Yugos
67E1 **Rumāh** S Arabia
72C3 **Rumbek** Sudan
23C2 **Rum Cay** *I* Caribbean
13E2 **Rumford** USA
37A2 **Rumilly** France
76C2 **Rum Jungle** Aust
54D2 **Rumoi** Japan
73D5 **Rumphi** Malawi
78B2 **Runanga** NZ
78C1 **Runaway,C** NZ
73B5 **Rundu** Namibia
73D4 **Rungwa** Tanz
73D4 **Rungwa** *R* Tanz
73D4 **Rungwe** *Mt* Tanz
59G2 **Ruoqiang** China
50D2 **Ruo Shui** *R* China
56F7 **Rupat** *I* Indon
41F1 **Rupea** Rom
18D2 **Rupert** USA
7L4 **Rupert** *R* Can
36D1 **Rur** *R* Germany
26E6 **Rurrenabaque** Bol
73D5 **Rusape** Zim
41F2 **Ruse** Bulg
12A2 **Rushville** Illinois, USA
11B3 **Rushville** Nebraska, USA
75B3 **Rushworth** Aust
17C3 **Rusk** USA
15E4 **Ruskin** USA
3H2 **Russel L** Can
3H3 **Russell** Can
78B1 **Russell** NZ
16C2 **Russell** USA
4A2 **Russell L** Can
15B2 **Russellville** Alabama, USA
17D2 **Russellville** Arkansas, USA
12B3 **Russellville** Kentucky, USA
19B3 **Russian** *R* USA
44E4 **Russian Federation**
49L2 **Russkiy, Ostrov** *I* Russian Fed
64E1 **Rustavi** Georgia
74D2 **Rustenburg** S Africa
17D3 **Ruston** USA
72C4 **Rutana** Burundi
57B4 **Ruteng** Indon
74E1 **Rutenga** Zim
19C3 **Ruth** USA
36E1 **Rüthen** Germany
22C2 **Rutla** Mexico
13E2 **Rutland** USA
62E2 **Rutland** *I* Andaman Is
60D2 **Rutog** China
Ruvu = Pangani
73E5 **Ruvuma, R** Tanz/Mozam
72D3 **Ruwenzori Range** *Mts* Uganda/Zaïre
73D5 **Ruya** *R* Zim
43D3 **Ružomberok** Slovakia
72C4 **Rwanda** Republic, Africa
44F5 **Ryazan'** Russian Fed
44G5 **Ryazhsk** Russian Fed
32L5 **Rybachiy, Poluostrov** *Pen* Russian Fed
44F4 **Rybinsk** Russian Fed
44F4 **Rybinskoye Vodokhranilishche** *Res* Russian Fed
43F3 **Rybnitsa** Moldova
3E2 **Rycroft** Can
35E6 **Ryde** Eng
35F6 **Rye** Eng
18C2 **Rye Patch Res** USA
45E5 **Ryl'sk** Russian Fed
45H6 **Ryn Peski** *Desert* Kazakhstan
54A3 **Ryoju** S Korea
53D4 **Ryōtsu** Japan
43F3 **Ryskany** Moldova
50F4 **Ryūkyū Retto** *Arch* Japan
43E2 **Rzeszów** Pol
44E4 **Rzhev** Russian Fed

S

63C2 **Sa'ādatābād** Iran
66B2 **Saad el Aali** *Dam* Egypt
42C2 **Saale** *R* Germany
37B1 **Saanen** Switz
36D2 **Saar** *R* Germany
36D2 **Saarbrücken** Germany
36D2 **Saarburg** Germany
32J7 **Saaremaa** *I* Estonia
36D2 **Saarland** State, Germany
36D2 **Saarlouis** Germany
28C3 **Saavedra** Arg
65B3 **Şaba'a** Egypt
41D2 **Šabac** Serbia, Yugos
39C1 **Sabadell** Spain
54C3 **Sabae** Japan
56E1 **Sabah** State, Malay
10A6 **Sabak,C** USA
57B3 **Sabal** Indon
23C4 **Sabanalarga** Colombia
56A1 **Sabang** Indon
57A2 **Sabang** Indon
62C1 **Sabari** *R* India
65C2 **Sabastiya** Israel
26E7 **Sabaya** Bol
64C3 **Sab'Bi'ār** Syria
66C3 **Sabderat** Eth
65D2 **Sabhā** Jordan
69A2 **Sabhā** Libya
73D6 **Sabi** *R* Zim
74E2 **Sabie** *R* S Africa
21B2 **Sabinas** Mexico
21B2 **Sabinas Hidalgo** Mexico
17C3 **Sabine** *R* USA
17D4 **Sabine L** USA
67F2 **Sabkhat Maṭṭi** *Salt Marsh* UAE
65B3 **Sabkhet El Bardawîl** *Lg* Egypt
57F8 **Sablayan** Phil
7M5 **Sable,C** Can
15E4 **Sable,C** USA
7N5 **Sable I** Can
63D1 **Sabzevār** Iran
18C1 **Sacajawea Peak** USA
14C1 **Sacandaga Res** USA
11D3 **Sac City** USA
9D1 **Sachigo** *R* Can
4C3 **Sachigo L** Can
54A3 **Sach'on** S Korea
42C2 **Sachsen** State, Germany
42C2 **Sachsen-Anhalt** State, Germany
6F2 **Sachs Harbour** Can
37E2 **Sacile** Italy
37B1 **Säckingen** Germany
5J4 **Sackville** Can
13E2 **Saco** Maine, USA
11A2 **Saco** Montana, USA
20B1 **Sacramento** USA
20B1 **Sacramento** *R* USA
19B2 **Sacramento** *V* USA
16A3 **Sacramento Mts** USA
66D3 **Sa'dah** Yemen
41E2 **Sadanski** Bulg
67G3 **Sadh** Oman
61E2 **Sadiya** India
39A2 **Sado** *R* Port
53D4 **Sado-shima** *I* Japan
60C3 **Sādri** India
Safad = Zefat
60A2 **Safed Koh** *Mts* Afghan
63E2 **Safer** Afghan
32G7 **Saffle** Sweden
19E4 **Safford** USA
64C3 **Safi** Jordan
71A2 **Safi** Mor
63E2 **Safidabeh** Iran
65D1 **Şāfītā** Syria
43G1 **Safonovo** Russian Fed
44H2 **Safonovo** Russian Fed
64E3 **Safwān** Iraq
61C2 **Saga** China
54B4 **Saga** Japan
55B1 **Sagaing** Burma
54C4 **Sagami-nada** *B* Japan
60D4 **Sāgar** India
10J2 **Sagavanirktok** *R* USA
14D2 **Sag Harbor** USA
12C2 **Saginaw** USA
12C2 **Saginaw B** USA
7M4 **Saglek B** Can
54A3 **Sagō-ri** S Korea
16A2 **Saguache** USA
23B2 **Sagua de Tánamo** Cuba
23B2 **Sagua la Grande** Cuba
7L5 **Saguenay** *R* Can
39B2 **Sagunto** Spain
65D3 **Sahāb** Jordan
39A1 **Sahagún** Spain
70C2 **Sahara** *Desert* N Africa
60D3 **Saharanpur** India
60C2 **Sahiwal** Pak
64D3 **Şahrā al Hijārah** *Desert Region* Iraq
66B1 **Sahra esh Sharqiya** *Desert Region* Egypt
22B1 **Sahuayo** Mexico
65D1 **Sahyun** *Hist Site* Syria
76D1 **Saibai I** Aust
71C2 **Saïda** Alg
65C2 **Saïda** Leb
63D3 **Sa'īdabad** Iran
39B2 **Saidia** Mor
61C2 **Saidpur** India
60C2 **Saidu** Pak
54B3 **Saigō** Japan
Saigon = Ho Chi Minh
61D3 **Saiha** India
50E2 **Saihan Tal** China
54B4 **Saijo** Japan
53C5 **Saiki** Japan
44D3 **Saimaa** *L* Fin
22B1 **Sain Alto** Mexico
63E3 **Saindak** Pak
34D4 **St Abb's Head** *Pt* Scot
5G4 **St Agapit** Can
5G4 **Ste Agathe-des-Monts** Can
5K4 **St Albans** Can
35E6 **St Albans** Eng
13E2 **St Albans** Vermont, USA
12C3 **St Albans** West Virginia, USA
35D6 **St Albans Head** *C* Eng
3F3 **St Albert** Can
36B1 **St Amand-les-Eaux** France
38C2 **St Amand-Mont Rond** France
37A1 **St-Amour** France
73E5 **St André** *C* Madag
36A2 **St-André-de-l'Eure** France
15B3 **St Andrew B** USA
34D3 **St Andrews** Scot
15C2 **St Andrew Sd** USA
11C2 **Ste Anne** Can
5G4 **Ste Anne de Beaupré** Can
5H4 **Ste-Anne-des-Monts** Can
23H1 **St Ann's Bay** Jamaica
7N4 **St Anthony** Can
18D2 **St Anthony** USA
75B3 **St Arnaud** Aust
5K3 **St Augustin** *R* Can
15C3 **St Augustine** USA
5K3 **St Augustin-Saguenay** Can
35C6 **St Austell** Eng
36D2 **St-Avold** France
35D4 **St Bees Head** *Pt* Eng
4B4 **St Boniface** Can
37B2 **St-Bonnet** France
35C6 **St Brides B** Wales
38B2 **St-Brieuc** France
36A3 **St-Calais** France
4F5 **St Catharines** Can
23M2 **St Catherine,Mt** Grenada
15C2 **St Catherines I** USA
35E6 **St Catherines Pt** Eng
38C2 **St Chamond** France
18D2 **St Charles** Idaho, USA
17D2 **St Charles** Missouri, USA
12C2 **St Clair** USA
12C2 **St Clair,L** USA/Can
12C2 **St Clair Shores** USA
38D2 **St Claud** France
11D2 **St Cloud** USA
37B1 **Ste Croix** Switz
23E3 **St Croix** *I* Caribbean
12A1 **St Croix** *R* USA
13F1 **St Croix** *R* USA/Can
12A1 **St Croix Falls** USA
35C6 **St Davids Head** *Pt* Wales
36B2 **St Denis** France
73F6 **St Denis** Réunion
36D2 **St-Dié** France
36C2 **St Dizier** France
10K3 **St Elias,Mt** USA
10L3 **St Elias Mts** Can
38B2 **Saintes** France
38C2 **St Étienne** France
37B2 **St Étienne-de-Tinée** France
13E1 **St-Félicien** Can
5K4 **St Fintan's** Can
36B2 **St-Florentin** France
16B2 **St Francis** USA
17D2 **St Francis** *R* USA
74C3 **St Francis B** S Africa
74C3 **St Francis,C** S Africa
37C1 **St Gallen** Switz
38C3 **St-Gaudens** France
75C1 **St George** Aust
15C2 **St George** South Carolina, USA
19D3 **St George** Utah, USA
10E4 **St George** *I* Alaska, USA
15C3 **St George I** Florida, USA
36E2 **St Georgen im Schwarzwald** Germany
18B2 **St George,Pt** USA
5H4 **St George** Can
13E1 **St-Georges** Can
23E4 **St George's** Grenada
5K4 **St George's B** Can
35B5 **St Georges Chan** Irish Rep/Wales
77E1 **St Georges Chan** PNG
37A1 **St Germain-du-Bois** France
36A2 **St German-en-laye** France
37B2 **St-Gervais** France
37C1 **St Gotthard** *P* Switz
35C6 **St Govans Head** *Pt* Wales
20A1 **St Helena** USA
xxxH5 **St Helena** *I* Atlantic O
74B3 **St Helena B** S Africa
15C2 **St Helena Sd** USA
75E3 **St Helens** Aust
35D5 **St Helens** Eng
18B1 **St Helens** USA
18B1 **St Helens,Mt** USA
38B2 **St Helier** Jersey
37B1 **St Hippolyte** France
36C1 **St-Hubert** Belg
7L5 **St-Hyacinthe** Can
12C1 **St Ignace** USA
12B1 **St Ignace I** Can
35C6 **St Ives** Eng
11D3 **St James** Minnesota, USA
17D2 **St James** Missouri, USA
3B3 **St James,C** Can

5G4 St Jean Can
5J3 St Jean R Can
38B2 St Jean-d'Angely France
37A1 St-Jean-de-Losne France
37B2 St-Jean-de-Maurienne France
4G4 St Jérôme Can
18C1 St Joe USA
37E1 St Johann im Pongau Austria
7M5 Saint John Can
5K3 St John B Can
5K4 St John,C Can
13F1 St John R USA Can
19E4 St Johns Arizona, USA
7N5 St John's Can
12C2 St Johns Michigan, USA
15C3 St Johns R USA
13E2 St Johnsbury USA
14C1 St Johnsville USA
13E1 St-Joseph Can
17D3 St Joseph Louisiana, USA
12B2 St Joseph Michigan, USA
17D2 St Joseph Missouri, USA
23L1 St Joseph Trinidad
12C2 St Joseph R USA
12C1 St Joseph I Can
17F4 St Joseph I USA
7J4 St Joseph,L Can
37B1 St Julien France
38C2 St-Junien France
36B2 St-Just-en-Chaussée France
34A3 St Kilda I Scot
23E3 St Kitts-Nevis I Caribbean
5G4 St Laurent Can
37A1 St-Laurent France
7M5 St Lawrence R Can
7M5 St Lawrence,G of Can
10D3 St Lawrence I USA
13D2 St Lawrence Seaway Can/USA
13F1 St Leonard Can
5K3 St Lewis Sd Can
38B2 St Lô France
3G3 St Louis Can
70A3 St Louis Sen
12A3 St Louis USA
36D3 St-Loup-sur-Semou France
23E4 St Lucia I Caribbean
74E2 St Lucia,L S Africa
34E1 St Magnus B Scot
38B2 St Malo France
37A2 St Marcellin France
5H3 Ste Marguerite R Can
73E6 Ste Marie C Madag
36D2 Ste-Marie-aux-Mines France
18C1 St Maries USA
23E3 St Martin I Caribbean
4B3 St Martin,L Can
37B2 St-Martin-Vésubie France
76D1 St Mary,Mt PNG
75A2 St Mary Peak Mt Aust
75E3 St Marys Aust
13D2 St Marys USA
35B7 St Marys I UK
15C2 St Marys R USA
5L4 St Mary's B Can
5L4 St Mary's,C Can
76E1 Saint Mathias Group Is PNG
10D3 St Matthew I USA
5G4 St Maurice R Can
37A3 St-Maximin France
36C2 Ste-Menehould France
10F3 St Michael USA
14B3 St Michaels USA
37B2 St-Michel France
36C2 St-Mihiel France
37C1 St Moritz Switz
38B2 St-Nazaire France
36C1 St-Niklaas Belg
36B1 St-Omer France
5H4 St Pacôme Can
5H4 St Pascal Can
3F3 St Paul Can
11D3 St Paul Minnesota, USA
16C1 St Paul Nebraska, USA
10D4 St Paul I Can
5K3 St Paul R Can
70A4 St Paul R Lib
71G4 St Paul,C Ghana
5H4 St Paul du Nord Can
11D3 St Peter USA
15C3 St Petersburg USA
7N5 St Pierre I Can
13E1 St Pierre,L Can
36B1 St-Pol-Sur-Ternoise France
42D3 St Pölten Austria
36B2 St Quentin France
38D3 St Raphaël France
73E5 St Sébastien C Madag
5H4 St Siméon Can
15C2 St Simons I USA
5H4 St Stephen Can

15C2 St Stephen USA
5G4 Ste Thérèse-de-Blainville Can
10O3 Ste Thérèse,L Can
4E5 St Thomas Can
37B3 St-Tropez France
36C1 St Truiden Belg
36A2 St-Valéry-en-Caux France
36A1 St-Valéry-sur-Somme France
11C2 St Vincent USA
73E6 St Vincent C Madag
23E4 St Vincent & The Grenadines Is Caribbean
75A2 St Vincent,G Aust
36D1 St-Vith Germany
36D2 St Wendel Germany
51H5 Saipan I Pacific O
60B2 Saiydabad Afghan
26E7 Sajama Mt Bol
74C3 Sak R S Africa
53D5 Sakai Japan
54B4 Sakaidi Japan
54B3 Sakaiminato Japan
64D3 Sakākah S Arabia
11B2 Sakakawea,L USA
4F3 Sakami R Can
73C5 Sakania Zaïre
73E6 Sakaraha Madag
45E7 Sakarya R Turk
43E1 Sakasleja Latvia
53D4 Sakata Japan
71G4 Saketél Benin
53E1 Sakhalin I Russian Fed
53E1 Sakhalinskiy Zaliv B Russian Fed
50F4 Sakishima gunto Is Japan
74C3 Sakrivier S Africa
70A4 Sal I Cape Verde
45G6 Sal R Russian Fed
32H7 Sala Sweden
28D1 Saladas Arg
28D3 Saladillo Arg
28C2 Saladillo R Arg
28D3 Salado R Buenos Aires, Arg
28B3 Salado R Mendoza/San Luis, Arg
25D3 Salado R Sante Fe, Arg
71F4 Salaga Ghana
55C3 Sala Hintoun Camb
72B2 Salal Chad
67F3 Şalālah Oman
28A2 Salamanca Chile
22B1 Salamanca Mexico
39A1 Salamanca Spain
14A1 Salamanca USA
72B3 Salamat R Chad
51H7 Salamaua PNG
65B1 Salamis Hist Site Cyprus
56E2 Salang Indon
32H5 Salangen Nor
25C2 Salar de Arizaro Arg
25C2 Salar de Atacama Salt Pan Chile
26E7 Salar de Coipasa Salt Pan Bol
26E8 Salar de Uyuni Salt Pan Bol
37C2 Salasomaggiore Italy
44K5 Salavat Russian Fed
76C1 Salawati I Indon
57B4 Salayar Indon
xxixD6 Sala y Gomez I Pacific O
28C3 Salazar Arg
38C2 Salbris France
10J3 Salcha R USA
74B3 Saldanha S Africa
65D2 Saldhad Syria
28C3 Saldungaray Arg
43E1 Saldus Latvia
75C3 Sale Aust
71A2 Salé Mor
57C2 Salebabu I Indon
44M2 Salekhard Russian Fed
12B3 Salem Illinois, USA
62B2 Salem India
14E1 Salem Massachusetts, USA
14C3 Salem New Jersey, USA
14D1 Salem New York, USA
18B2 Salem Oregon, USA
12C3 Salem Virginia, USA
56D4 Salembu Besar I Indon
32G6 Salen Sweden
40C2 Salerno Italy
35D5 Salford Eng
41D1 Salgót Hung
43D3 Salgótarjan Hung
27L5 Salgueiro Brazil
16A2 Salida USA
41F3 Salihli Turk
73D5 Salima Malawi
32K6 Salimaa L Fin
17C2 Salina Kansas, USA
19D3 Salina Utah, USA

40C3 Salina I Italy
22C2 Salina Cruz Mexico
26E8 Salina de Arizato Arg
28B3 Salina Grande Salt pan Arg
28B4 Salina Gualicho Salt pan Arg
28B2 Salina La Antigua Salt pan Arg
29D2 Salinas Brazil
22B1 Salinas Mexico
20B2 Salinas USA
20B2 Salinas R USA
28B3 Salinas de Llancaneb Salt Pan Arg
28C1 Salinas Grandes Salt Pan Arg
16A3 Salinas Peak Mt USA
17D3 Saline R Arkansas, USA
16B2 Saline R Kansas, USA
23M2 Salines,Pt Grenada
20D2 Saline V USA
27J4 Salinópolis Brazil
37A1 Salins France
35E6 Salisbury Eng
13D3 Salisbury Maryland, USA
15C1 Salisbury North Carolina, USA
7L3 Salisbury I Can
35E6 Salisbury Plain Eng
32K5 Salla Fin
28C1 Salladillo R Arg
37B2 Sallanches France
17D2 Sallisaw USA
7L3 Salluit Can
61B2 Sallyana Nepal
63A1 Salmas Iran
32L6 Salmi Russian Fed
18C1 Salmo Can
18D1 Salmon USA
18C1 Salmon R USA
3E3 Salmon Arm Can
18C1 Salmon River Mts USA
32J6 Salo Fin
37D2 Salò Italy
38D3 Salon-de-Provence France
Salonica = Thessaloníki
41E1 Salonta Rom
32K6 Salpausselka Region, Fin
28B2 Salsacate Arg
45G6 Sal'sk Russian Fed
65C2 Salt Jordan
74C3 Salt R S Africa
19D4 Salt R USA
25C2 Salta Arg
25C2 Salta State, Arg
21B2 Saltillo Mexico
18D2 Salt Lake City USA
28C2 Salto Arg
28D2 Salto Urug
26D3 Salto Angostura Waterfall Colombia
29E2 Salto da Divisa Brazil
29B3 Salto das Sete Quedas Brazil
26F2 Salto del Angel Waterfall Ven
25E2 Salto del Guaira Waterfall Brazil
26D4 Salto Grande Waterfall Colombia
19C4 Salton S USA
29B4 Saltos do Iguaçu Waterfall Arg
60C2 Salt Range Mts Pak
23H2 Salt River Jamaica
15C2 Saluda USA
57B3 Salue Timpaus Str Indon
62C1 Sālūr India
37B2 Saluzzo Italy
27L6 Salvador Brazil
17D4 Salvador,L USA
22B1 Salvatierra Mexico
67F2 Salwah Qatar
55B1 Salween R Burma
45H8 Sal'yany Azerbaijan
12C3 Salyersville USA
37E1 Salzach R Austria
42C3 Salzburg Austria
37E1 Salzburg Province, Austria
42C2 Salzgitter Germany
37E1 Salzkammergut Mts Austria
42C2 Salzwedel Germany
50C1 Samagaltay Russian Fed
57F9 Samales Group Is Phil
23D3 Samaná Dom Rep
64C2 Samandaği Turk
60B1 Samangan Afghan
54D2 Samani Japan
65A3 Samannûd Egypt
57G8 Samar I Phil
44J5 Samara Russian Fed
76E2 Samarai PNG
56E3 Samarinda Indon
58E2 Samarkand Uzbekistan

64D3 Sāmarrā' Iraq
57F8 Samar S Phil
61B3 Sambalpur India
56C2 Sambas Indon
73F5 Sambava Madag
60D3 Sambhal India
56E3 Samboja Indon
43E3 Sambor Ukraine
36B1 Sambre R France
53B4 Samch'ŏk S Korea
54A4 Samch'ŏnp'o S Korea
54A3 Samdŭng N Korea
72D4 Same Tanz
37C1 Samedan Switz
36A1 Samer France
73C5 Samfya Zambia
67F4 Samhah I Yemen
55B1 Samka Burma
55C1 Sam Neua Laos
77H2 Samoan Is Pacific O
41F3 Sámos I Greece
56A2 Samosir I Indon
41F2 Samothráki I Greece
28C2 Sampacho Arg
57A3 Sampaga Indon
57B3 Sampara R Indon
56D3 Sampit Indon
56D3 Sampit R Indon
17D3 Sam Rayburn Res USA
55C3 Samrong Camb
42C1 Samsø I Den
54A2 Samsu N Korea
64C1 Samsun Turk
57D4 Samulaki Indon
71F3 San Mali
55D3 San R Camb
43E2 San R Pol
66D3 Şan'ā' Yemen
72B3 Sanaga R Cam
25C4 San Agustín Arg
57G9 San Agustin,C Phil
10F5 Sanak I USA
57C3 Sanana Indon
57C3 Sanana I Indon
63B1 Sanandaj Iran
20B1 San Andreas USA
16A3 San Andres Mts USA
21C3 San Andrés Tuxtla Mexico
16B3 San Angelo USA
40B3 San Antioco Sardegna
40B3 San Antioco I Medit S
28C1 San Antonio Arg
28A2 San Antonio Chile
16A3 San Antonio New Mexico, USA
57F7 San Antonio Phil
16C4 San Antonio Texas, USA
20B2 San Antonio R California, USA
17F4 San Antonio R Texas, USA
39C2 San Antonio Abad Spain
21D2 San Antonio,C Cuba
16B3 San Antonio de Bravo Mexico
23A2 San Antonio de los Banos Cuba
28C4 San Antonio Este Arg
20D3 San Antonio,Mt USA
28B4 San Antonio Oeste Arg
20B3 San Antonio Res USA
20B2 San Ardo USA
28D3 San Augustin Arg
28B2 San Augustin de Valle Féril Arg
60D4 Sanawad India
22B1 San Bartolo Mexico
21A3 San Benedicto I Mexico
17F4 San Benito USA
20B2 San Benito R USA
20B2 San Benito Mt USA
20D3 San Bernardino USA
28A2 San Bernardo Chile
19C4 San Bernardo Mts USA
22A1 San Blas Mexico
15B3 San Blas,C USA
28A3 San Carlos Chile
22C1 San Carlos Mexico
26B1 San Carlos Nic
57F7 San Carlos Phil
28E2 San Carlos Urug
19D4 San Carlos USA
25B6 San Carlos de Bariloche Arg
50F4 San-chung Taiwan
44H4 Sanchursk Russian Fed
28A3 San Clemente Chile
20D4 San Clemente USA
19C4 San Clemente I USA
28C2 San Cristóbal Arg
21C3 San Cristóbal Mexico
26D2 San Cristóbal Ven
77F2 San Cristobal I Solomon Is
21E2 Sancti Spíritus Cuba
74D1 Sand R S Africa

56D3 Sandai Indon
56E1 Sandakan Malay
37E1 San Daniele del Friuli Italy
34D2 Sanday I Scot
16B3 Sanderson USA
3G2 Sandfly L Can
19C4 San Diego USA
64B2 Sandikli Turk
61B2 Sandila India
4E4 Sand Lake Can
32F7 Sandnes Nor
32G5 Sandnessjøen Nor
32D3 Sandø Faroes
73C4 Sandoa Zaïre
43E2 Sandomierz Pol
37E2 San Donà di Piave Italy
61D4 Sandoway Burma
10F4 Sand Point USA
18C1 Sandpoint USA
38D2 Sandrio Italy
3B3 Sandspit Can
17C2 Sand Springs USA
76A3 Sandstone Aust
11D2 Sandstone USA
52C4 Sandu China
12C2 Sandusky USA
32H6 Sandviken Sweden
14E2 Sandwich USA
5K3 Sandwich B Can
3H2 Sandy Bay Can
7J4 Sandy L Can
4C3 Sandy Lake Can
28C2 San Elcano Arg
29A3 San Estanislao Par
8B3 San Felipe Baja Cal, Mexico
28A2 San Felipe Chile
22B1 San Felipe Guanajuato, Mexico
23D4 San Felipe Ven
39C1 San Feliu de Guixols Spain
28A2 San Fernando Chile
22C1 San Fernando Mexico
57F7 San Fernando Phil
39A2 San Fernando Spain
23E4 San Fernando Trinidad
20C3 San Fernando Ven
26E2 San Fernando Ven
22C1 San Fernando R Mexico
15C3 Sanford Florida, USA
13E2 Sanford Maine, USA
15D1 Sanford N Carolina, USA
9E4 Sanford USA
10K3 Sanford,Mt USA
28C2 San Francisco Arg
23C3 San Francisco Dom Rep
20A2 San Francisco USA
20A2 San Francisco B USA
21B2 San Francisco del Oro Mexico
22B1 San Francisco del Rincon Mexico
20D3 San Gabriel Mts USA
60C5 Sangamner India
12B3 Sangamon R USA
51H5 Sangan I Pacific O
49O3 Sangar Russian Fed
62B1 Sangāreddi India
56E4 Sangeang I Indon
20C2 Sanger USA
52C2 Sangga He R China
56D2 Sanggau Indon
72B3 Sangha R Congo
60B3 Sanghar Pak
57C2 Sangihe I Indon
37E2 San Giorgio di Nogaro Italy
55B3 Sangkhla Buri Thai
56E2 Sangkulirang Indon
62A1 Sängli India
72B3 Sangmélima Cam
8B3 San Gorgonio Mt USA
16A2 Sangre de Cristo Mts USA
28C2 San Gregorio Arg
28D2 San Gregorio Urug
20A2 San Gregorio USA
60D2 Sangrür India
74E1 Sangutane R Mozam
28A4 Sanico Arg
25E3 San Ignacio Arg
57F8 San Isidro Phil
26D2 San Jacinto Colombia
19C4 San Jacinto Peak Mt USA
28A3 San Javier Chile
28D1 San Javier Misiones, Arg
28D2 San Javier Sante Fe, Arg
28D1 San Javier Ven
53D4 Sanjō I Japan
25H2 São João del Rei Brazil
20B2 San Joaquin R USA
20B2 San Joaquin Valley USA
16B2 San Jon USA
26B1 San José Costa Rica
21C3 San José Guatemala
57F7 San Jose Luzon, Phil
57F8 San Jose Mindoro, Phil

Sawatch Mts Shasta,Mt

16A2 **Sawatch Mts** USA
5H3 **Sawbill** Can
10J2 **Sawtooth Mt** USA
18C2 **Sawtooth Range** *Mts* USA
76B2 **Sawu** *I* Indon
14A2 **Saxton** USA
71G3 **Say** Niger
60B1 **Sayghan** Afghan
67G3 **Sayh Hajmah** Oman
67F2 **Sayhūt** Yemen
45H6 **Saykhin** Kazakhstan
50D2 **Saynshand** Mongolia
16C2 **Sayre** Oklahoma, USA
14B2 **Sayre** Pennsylvania, USA
22C2 **Sayula** Mexico
22A1 **Sayulita** Mexico
45J7 **Say-Utes** Kazakhstan
14D2 **Sayville** USA
3C3 **Sayward** Can
42C3 **Sázava** *R* Czech Republic
39C2 **Sbisseb** *R* Alg
35D4 **Scafell Pike** *Mt* Eng
34E1 **Scalloway** Scot
34D2 **Scapa Flow** *Sd* Scot
13D2 **Scarborough** Can
35E4 **Scarborough** Eng
23E4 **Scarborough** Tobago
34B2 **Scarp** *I* Scot
40B1 **Schaffhausen** Switz
42C3 **Scharding** Austria
36D1 **Scharteberg** *Mt* Germany
7M4 **Schefferville** Can
36B1 **Schelde** *R* Belg
19D3 **Schell Creek Range** *Mts* USA
14D1 **Schenectady** USA
16C4 **Schertz** USA
36C1 **Schiedam** Neth
37D2 **Schio** Italy
36D1 **Schleiden** Germany
42B2 **Schleswig** Germany
42B2 **Schleswig Holstein** State, Germany
14C1 **Schoharie** USA
76D1 **Schouten Is** PNG
36E2 **Schramberg** Germany
7K5 **Schreiber** Can
19C3 **Schurz** USA
14C2 **Schuylkill** *R* USA
14B2 **Schuylkill Haven** USA
42B3 **Schwabische Alb** *Upland* Germany
74B2 **Schwarzrand** *R* Namibia
36E2 **Schwarzwald** *Mts* Germany
42B3 **Schwarzwald** *Upland* Germany
10G2 **Schwatka Mts** USA
37D1 **Schwaz** Austria
42C2 **Schweinfurt** Germany
74D2 **Schweizer Reneke** S Africa
42C2 **Schwerin** Germany
37C1 **Schwyz** Switz
40C3 **Sciacca** Italy
35B7 **Scilly Isles** *Is* UK
12C3 **Scioto** *R* USA
11A2 **Scobey** USA
75D2 **Scone** Aust
7Q2 **Scoresby Sd** Greenland
xxxF7 **Scotia Ridge** Atlantic O
xxxF7 **Scotia S** Atlantic O
34C3 **Scotland** Country, UK
79F7 **Scott** *Base* Ant
74E3 **Scottburgh** S Africa
3C3 **Scott,C** Can
16B2 **Scott City** USA
79G6 **Scott I** Ant
7L2 **Scott Inlet** *B* Can
3G2 **Scott L** Can
18B2 **Scott,Mt** USA
76B2 **Scott Reef** Timor S
11B3 **Scottsbluff** USA
15B2 **Scottsboro** USA
75E3 **Scottsdale** Aust
19D4 **Scottsdale** USA
14C2 **Scranton** USA
11C3 **Scribner** USA
37D1 **Scuol** Switz
Scutari = Shkodër
74C3 **Seacow** S Africa
6J4 **Seal** *R* Can
75B3 **Sea Lake** Aust
4B2 **Seal** Can
5K3 **Seal Bight** Can
45F6 **Sea of Azov** *S* Russian Fed
19D3 **Searchlight** USA
17D2 **Searcy** USA
20D3 **Searles** USA
20B2 **Seaside** California, USA
18B1 **Seaside** Oregon, USA
14C3 **Seaside Park** USA
18B1 **Seattle** USA
57B5 **Seba** Indon
13E2 **Sebago L** USA
56B2 **Sebanga** Indon
20A1 **Sebastopol** USA
58B4 **Sebderat** Eritrea
43F1 **Sebez** Russian Fed
13F1 **Seboomook L** USA
15E4 **Sebring** USA
37D2 **Secchia** *R* Italy
78A3 **Secretary I** NZ
17D2 **Sedalia** USA
36C2 **Sedan** France
10E5 **Sedanka** *I* USA
78B2 **Seddonville** NZ
65C3 **Sede Boqer** Israel
65C3 **Sederot** Israel
70A3 **Sédhiou** Sen
65C3 **Sedom** Israel
19D4 **Sedona** USA
74B2 **Seeheim** Namibia
79E **Seelig,Mt** Ant
36A2 **Sées** France
71B2 **Sefrou** Mor
78B2 **Sefton,Mt** NZ
55C5 **Segamat** Malay
44E3 **Segezha** Russian Fed
39B2 **Segorbe** Spain
70B3 **Ségou** Mali
Segovia = Coco
39B1 **Segovia** Spain
39C1 **Segre** *R* Spain
10D6 **Seguam** *I* USA
10D6 **Seguam Pass** USA
70B4 **Séguéla** Ivory Coast
70A2 **Seguia el Hamra** *Watercourse* Mor
17C4 **Seguin** USA
28C2 **Segundo** *R* Arg
56E2 **Seguntur** Indon
39B2 **Segura** *R* Spain
60B3 **Sehwan** Pak
16C2 **Seiling** USA
36D2 **Seille** *R* France
32J6 **Seinäjoki** Fin
11D2 **Seine** *R* Can
38C2 **Seine** *R* France
36B2 **Seine-et-Marne** Department, France
36A2 **Seine-Maritime** Department, France
72D4 **Sekenke** Tanz
72D2 **Sek'ot'a** Eth
18B1 **Selah** USA
51G7 **Selaru** *I* Indon
56E4 **Selat Alas** *Str* Indon
56C3 **Selat Bangka** *Str* Indon
56B3 **Selat Berhala** *B* Indon
51G7 **Selat Dampier** *Str* Indon
56C3 **Selat Gaspar** *Str* Indon
56E4 **Selat Lombok** *Str* Indon
56A3 **Selat Mentawi** *Str* Indon
56E4 **Selat Sape** *Str* Indon
57B4 **Selat Sumba** *Str* Indon
56C4 **Selat Sunda** *Str* Indon
57C4 **Selat Wetar** *Chan* Indon
57D3 **Selawati** *I* Indon
10F2 **Selawik** USA
10G2 **Selawik** *R* USA
10F2 **Selawik L** USA
35E5 **Selby** Eng
11B2 **Selby** USA
41F3 **Selçuk** Turk
10H4 **Seldovia** USA
74D1 **Selebi Pikwe** Botswana
53C1 **Selemdzha** *R* Russian Fed
53C1 **Selemdzhinsk** Russian Fed
49O3 **Selennyakh** *R* Russian Fed
36D2 **Selestat** France
7Q3 **Selfoss** Iceland
11B2 **Selfridge** USA
72C1 **Selima Oasis** Sudan
43G1 **Selizharovo** Russian Fed
6J4 **Selkirk** Can
34D4 **Selkirk** Scot
3E3 **Selkirk Mts** Can
15B2 **Selma** Alabama, USA
20C2 **Selma** California, USA
15B1 **Selmer** USA
37A1 **Selongey** France
39B2 **Selouane** Mor
10M3 **Selous,Mt** Can
56C3 **Selta Karimata** *Str* Indon
28C1 **Selva** Arg
26D5 **Selvas** Region, Brazil
18C1 **Selway** USA
76D3 **Selwyn** Aust
3H1 **Selwyn L** Can
6E3 **Selwyn Mts** Can
56D4 **Semarang** Indon
44G4 **Semenov** Russian Fed
10A5 **Semichi Is** USA
10G4 **Semidi Is** USA
45F5 **Semiluki** Russian Fed
11A3 **Seminoe Res** USA
17C2 **Seminole** Oklahoma, USA
16B3 **Seminole** Texas, USA
15C2 **Seminole,L** USA
48K4 **Semipalatinsk** Kazakhstan
57F8 **Semirara Is** Phil
63C2 **Semirom** Iran
10B6 **Semisopochnoi** *I* USA
56D2 **Semitau** Indon
63C1 **Semnān** Iran
36C2 **Semois** *R* Belg
22C2 **Sempoala** Hist Site, Mexico
56E2 **Semporna** Malay
26E5 **Sena Madureira** Brazil
73C5 **Senanga** Zambia
17E3 **Senatobia** USA
53E4 **Sendai** Honshū, Japan
53C5 **Sendai** Kyūshū, Japan
60D4 **Sendwha** India
14B1 **Seneca Falls** USA
14B1 **Seneca L** USA
16A3 **Senecu** Mexico
70A3 **Senegal** Republic, Africa
70A3 **Sénégal** *R* Maur/Sen
74D2 **Senekal** S Africa
57B3 **Sengkang** Indon
27L6 **Senhor do Bonfim** Brazil
40C2 **Senigallia** Italy
40D2 **Senj** Croatia, Yugos
50F4 **Senkaku Gunto** *Is* Japan
53C3 **Senlin Shan** *Mt* China
36B2 **Senlis** France
72D2 **Sennar** Sudan
7L5 **Senneterre** Can
36D2 **Senones** France
36B2 **Sens** France
41E1 **Senta** Serbia, Yugos
72C4 **Sentery** Zaïre
3D3 **Sentinel Peak** *Mt* Can
60D4 **Seoni** India
Seoul = Soul
78B2 **Separation Pt** NZ
54A3 **Sep'o** N Korea
55D2 **Sepone** Laos
29A2 **Sepotuba** *R* Brazil
7M4 **Sept-Iles** Can
72B1 **Séquédine** Niger
20C2 **Sequoia Nat Pk** USA
65C1 **Serai** Syria
57C3 **Seram** *I* Indon
56C4 **Serang** Indon
56C2 **Serasan** *I* Indon
41D2 **Serbia** *Republic* Yugos
37D2 **Serchio** *R* Italy
45G5 **Serdobsk** Russian Fed
36B3 **Sereín** *R* France
55C5 **Seremban** Malay
72D4 **Serengeti Nat Pk** Tanz
73D5 **Serenje** Zambia
43F3 **Seret** *R* Ukraine
44H4 **Sergach** Russian Fed
53C3 **Sergeyevka** Russian Fed
48H3 **Sergino** Russian Fed
27L6 **Sergipe** State, Brazil
44F4 **Sergiyev Posad** Georgia
56D2 **Seria** Brunei
56D2 **Serian** Malay
41E3 **Sérifos** *I* Greece
5H2 **Sérigny** *R* Can
37C2 **Serio** *R* Italy
69B2 **Serir Calanscio** *Desert* Libya
36C2 **Sermaize-les-Bains** France
7P3 **Sermilik** Greenland
44J5 **Sernovodsk** Russian Fed
44L4 **Serov** Russian Fed
74D1 **Serowe** Botswana
39A2 **Serpa** Port
44F5 **Serpukhov** Russian Fed
29A3 **Serra Amamba** Par
29B1 **Serra Azul** Brazil
29C3 **Serra da Canastra** *Mts* Brazil
39A1 **Serra da Estrela** *Mts* Port
29C3 **Serra da Mantiqueira** *Mts* Brazil
29B2 **Serra da Mombuca** Brazil
29B2 **Serra das Furnas** *Mts* Brazil
29C1 **Serra de Arrajas** *Mts* Brazil
29B4 **Serra de Fartura** *Mts* Brazil
29A3 **Serra de Maracaju** *Mts* Brazil
29A2 **Serra de São Jeronimo** Brazil
28D1 **Serra do Boquairao** *Mts* Brazil
29D2 **Serra do Cabral** *Mt* Brazil
27G5 **Serra do Cachimbo** *Mts* Brazil
29B2 **Serra do Caiapó** *Mts* Brazil
28E2 **Serra do Canguçu** *Mts* Brazil
29B3 **Serra do Cantu** *Mts* Brazil
29D3 **Serra do Caparaó** *Mts* Brazil
27K7 **Serra do Chifre** Brazil
29D2 **Serra do Espinhaço** *Mts* Brazil
28D1 **Serra do Espinilho** *Mts* Brazil
29C2 **Serra do Jibão** *Mts* Brazil
29C3 **Serra do Mar** *Mts* Brazil
29B3 **Serra do Mirante** *Mts* Brazil
27H3 **Serra do Navio** Brazil
29C3 **Serra do Paranapiacaba** *Mts* Brazil
29D1 **Serra do Ramalho** *Mts* Brazil
29B1 **Serra do Roncador** *Mts* Brazil
27G6 **Serra dos Caiabis** *Mts* Brazil
29B3 **Serra dos Dourados** *Mts* Brazil
29D1 **Serra do Sincora** *Mts* Brazil
26F6 **Serra dos Parecis** *Mts* Brazil
29C2 **Serra dos Pilões** *Mts* Brazil
29B2 **Serra do Taquaral** *Mts* Brazil
29B2 **Serra Dourada** *Mts* Brazil
29C1 **Serra Dourada** *Mts* Brazil
28E2 **Serra Encantadas** *Mts* Brazil
27G6 **Serra Formosa** *Mts* Brazil
29D2 **Serra Geral** *Mts* Bahia, Brazil
29B4 **Serra Geral** *Mts* Parona, Brazil
29C1 **Serra Geral de Goiás** *Mts* Brazil
29C2 **Serra Geral do Parana** *Mts* Brazil
41E2 **Sérrai** Greece
21D3 **Serrana Bank** *Is* Caribbean
39B1 **Serrana de Cuenca** *Mts* Spain
16B4 **Serranias del Burro** *Mts* Mexico
29B2 **Serranópolis** Brazil
26F3 **Serra Pacaraima** *Mts* Brazil/Ven
26F3 **Serra Parima** *Mts* Brazil
27H3 **Serra Tumucumaque** Brazil
36B2 **Serre** *R* France
37A2 **Serres** France
28B2 **Serrezuela** Arg
27L6 **Serrinha** Brazil
29D2 **Serro** Brazil
29B3 **Sertanópolis** Brazil
52A3 **Sêrtar** China
57D4 **Serua** *I* Indon
74D1 **Serule** Botswana
56A2 **Seruwai** Indon
56D3 **Seruyan** *R* Indon
53B1 **Seryshevo** Russian Fed
4D3 **Seseganaga L** Can
73B5 **Sesfontein** Namibia
73C5 **Sesheke** Zambia
37B2 **Sestriere** Italy
37C2 **Sestri Levante** Italy
53D3 **Setana** Japan
38C3 **Sète** France
29D2 **Sete Lagoas** Brazil
71D1 **Sétif** Alg
66C4 **Setit** *R* Sudan
54C3 **Seto** Japan
54B4 **Seto Naikai** *S* Japan
71A2 **Settat** Mor
35D4 **Settle** Eng
39A2 **Sètúbal** Port
37A1 **Seurre** France
45H7 **Sevan, Ozero** *L* Armenia
45E7 **Sevastopol'** Ukraine
7K4 **Severn** *R* Can
35D5 **Severn** *R* Eng
44G3 **Severnaya Dvina** *R* Russian Fed
49L1 **Severnaya Zemlya** *I* Russian Fed
44L3 **Severnyy Sos'va** *R* Russian Fed
44K3 **Severnyy Ural** *Mts* Russian Fed
49M4 **Severo-Baykalskoye Nagorye** *Mts* Russian Fed
45F6 **Severo Donets** *R* Ukraine
44F3 **Severodvinsk** Russian Fed
48H3 **Severo Sos'va** *R* Russian Fed
44L3 **Severoural'sk** Russian Fed
19D3 **Sevier** *R* USA
19D3 **Sevier Desert** USA
19D3 **Sevier L** USA
39A2 **Sevilla** Spain
Seville = Sevilla
41F2 **Sevlievo** Bulg
70A4 **Sewa** *R* Sierra Leone
10J3 **Seward** Alaska, USA
17C1 **Seward** Nebraska, USA
10E2 **Seward Pen** USA
3E2 **Sexsmith** Can
68K8 **Seychelles,Is** Indian O
32C1 **Seyðisfjörðor** Iceland
32C1 **Seyðisfjörður** Iceland
64C2 **Seyhan** Turk
45F5 **Seym** *R* Russian Fed
49R3 **Seymchan** Russian Fed
75C3 **Seymour** Aust
14D2 **Seymour** Connecticut, USA
12B3 **Seymour** Indiana, USA
16C3 **Seymour** Texas, USA
37B2 **Seyne** France
37E2 **Sežana** Slovenia, Yugos
36B2 **Sézanne** France
71E2 **Sfax** Tunisia
41F1 **Sfînto Gheorghe** Rom
42A2 **'s-Gravenhage** Neth
52B3 **Shaanxi** Province, China
72C4 **Shabunda** Zaïre
59F2 **Shache** China
79G9 **Shackleton Ice Shelf** Ant
60B3 **Shadadkot** Pak
63C2 **Shādhām** *R* Iran
20C3 **Shafter** USA
35D6 **Shaftesbury** Eng
71G4 **Shagamu** Nig
4D2 **Shagamu** *R* Can
25J8 **Shag Rocks** *Is* South Georgia
63B2 **Shāhabād** Iran
56F7 **Shah Alam** Malay
65D2 **Shahbā** Syria
63D2 **Shahdap** Iran
61B3 **Shahdol** India
63B1 **Shāhīn Dezh** Iran
63D2 **Shāh Kūh** Iran
63E2 **Shahrak** Afghan
63D2 **Shahr-e Bābak** Iran
Shahresa = Qomisheh
63C2 **Shahr Kord** Iran
45J8 **Shahsavār** Iran
44L3 **Shaim** Russian Fed
62B1 **Shājābād** India
60D3 **Shājahānpur** India
60D4 **Shājāpur** India
53E2 **Shakhtersk** Russian Fed
45G6 **Shakhty** Russian Fed
44H4 **Shakhun'ya** Russian Fed
71G4 **Shaki** Nig
11D3 **Shakopee** USA
54D2 **Shakotan-misaki** *C* Japan
10F3 **Shaktoolik** USA
44K4 **Shamary** Russian Fed
72D3 **Shambe** Sudan
14B2 **Shamokin** USA
16B2 **Shamrock** USA
14C1 **Shandaken** USA
20B3 **Shandon** USA
52D2 **Shandong** Province, China
52C5 **Shangchuan Dao** *I* China
52C1 **Shangdu** China
52E3 **Shanghai** China
52C3 **Shangnan** China
73C5 **Shangombo** Zambia
52D4 **Shangra** China
52B5 **Shangsi** China
52C3 **Shang Xian** China
53B2 **Shangzhi** China
33B3 **Shannon** *R* Irish Rep
3H2 **Shannon L** Can
52D3 **Shanqiu** China
53B3 **Shansonggang** China
50G1 **Shantarskiye Ostrova** *I* Russian Fed
52D5 **Shantou** China
52C2 **Shanxi** Province, China
52D3 **Shan Xian** China
52C5 **Shaoguan** China
52E4 **Shaoxing** China
52C4 **Shaoyang** China
34D2 **Shapinsay** *I* Scot
65D2 **Shaqqā** Syria
67E3 **Shaqqat aj Kharitah** Region, S Arabia
67E1 **Shaqra'** S Arabia
67E4 **Shaqrā'** Yemen
67E3 **Sharawrah** S Arabia
52A1 **Sharhulsan** Mongolia
54D2 **Shari** Japan
63D1 **Sharifābād** Iran
67G1 **Sharjah** UAE
76A3 **Shark B** Aust
63D1 **Sharlauk** Turkmenistan
65C2 **Sharon,Plain of** Israel
14B3 **Sharpsburg** USA
44H4 **Sharya** Russian Fed
72D3 **Shashamenē** Eth
74D1 **Shashani** *R* Zim
74D1 **Shashe** *R* Botswana
52C3 **Shashi** China
18B2 **Shasta L** USA
18B2 **Shasta,Mt** USA

Sisak Spjelkavik

40D1 **Sisak** Croatia, Yugos
55C2 **Sisaket** Thai
4A2 **Sisipuk L** Can
55C3 **Sisophon** Camb
20B3 **Sisquoc** USA
20C3 **Sisquoc** *R* USA
11C2 **Sisseton** USA
71F3 **Sissili** *R* Burkina
36B2 **Sissonne** France
63E2 **Sistan** Region, Iran/Afghan
38D3 **Sisteron** France
49L4 **Sistig Khem** Russian Fed
61B2 **Sītāpur** India
41F3 **Sitía** Greece
29C1 **Sitio d'Abadia** Brazil
6E4 **Sitka** USA
10H4 **Sitkalidak I** USA
10H4 **Sitkinak** *I* USA
55B2 **Sittang** *R* Burma
36C1 **Sittard** Neth
61D3 **Sittwe** Burma
56D4 **Situbondo** Indon
53B1 **Sivaki** Russian Fed
64C2 **Sivas** Turk
64C2 **Siverek** Turk
64B2 **Sivrihisar** Turk
69B2 **Siwa** Egypt
60D2 **Siwalik Range** *Mts* India
61B2 **Siwalik Range** *Mts* Nepal
44G3 **Siya** Russian Fed
52D3 **Siyang** China
42C1 **Sjaelland** *I* Den
32G7 **Skagen** Den
32F7 **Skagerrak** *Str* Nor/Den
18B1 **Skagit** *R* USA
18B1 **Skagit Mt** Can
6E4 **Skagway** USA
14B1 **Skaneateles** USA
14B1 **Skaneateles L** USA
32G7 **Skara** Sweden
43E2 **Skarzysko-Kamlenna** Pol
6F4 **Skeena** *R* Can
3C2 **Skeena Mts** Can
6D3 **Skeenjek** *R* USA
35F5 **Skegness** Eng
44B2 **Skellefte** *R* Sweden
32J6 **Skellefteå** Sweden
41E3 **Skíathos** *I* Greece
6E4 **Skidegate** Can
43E2 **Skiemiewice** Pol
32F7 **Skien** Nor
71D1 **Skikda** Alg
53C5 **Skikoku** *I* Japan
35E5 **Skipton** Eng
41E3 **Skíros** *I* Greece
32F7 **Skive** Den
42B1 **Skjern** Den
7O3 **Skjoldungen** Greenland
12B2 **Skokie** USA
41E3 **Skópelos** *I* Greece
41E2 **Skopje** Macedonia, Yugos
32G7 **Skövde** Sweden
49O4 **Skovorodino** Russian Fed
13F2 **Skowhegan** USA
74E1 **Skukuza** S Africa
6C3 **Skwentna** USA
42D2 **Skwierzyna** Pol
33B2 **Skye** *I* Scot
32G7 **Slagelse** Den
35B5 **Slaney** *R* Irish Rep
41E2 **Slatina** Rom
56D4 **Slaung** Indon
41D1 **Slav Brod** Yugos
6G3 **Slave** *R* Can
3F2 **Slave Lake** Can
43G2 **Slavgorod** Belorussia
48J4 **Slavgorod** Russian Fed
43F2 **Slavuta** Ukraine
45F6 **Slavyansk** Ukraine
34C3 **Sleat,Sound of** *Chan* Scot
4F2 **Sleeper Is** Can
10G3 **Sleetmute** USA
35B5 **Sleeve Bloom** *Mts* Irish Rep
17E3 **Slidell** USA
14C2 **Slide Mt** USA
33B3 **Sligo** Irish Rep
33B3 **Sligo** *B* Irish Rep
41F2 **Sliven** Bulg
19C3 **Sloan** USA
41F2 **Slobozia** Rom
3E4 **Slocan** Can
43F2 **Slonim** Belorussia
35E6 **Slough** Eng
20B2 **Slough** *R* USA
43D3 **Slovakia** *Republic* Europe
58C1 **Slovenia** *Republic* Europe
42C2 **Slubice** Pol
43F2 **Sluch'** *R* Ukraine
42D2 **Słupsk** Pol
43F2 **Slutsk** Belorussia
43F2 **Slutsk** *R* Belorussia
33A3 **Slyne Head** *Pt* Irish Rep
49M4 **Slyudyanka** Russian Fed
7M4 **Smallwood Res** Can
70A2 **Smara** Mor
41E2 **Smederevo** Serbia, Yugos
41E2 **Smederevska Palanka** Serbia, Yugos
45E6 **Smela** Ukraine
14A2 **Smethport** USA
53C2 **Smidovich** Russian Fed
53E2 **Smirnykh** Russian Fed
3F2 **Smith** Can
20C1 **Smith** USA
10O2 **Smith Arm** *B* Can
10H1 **Smith B** USA
3C3 **Smithers** Can
15D1 **Smithfield** N Carolina, USA
74D3 **Smithfield** S Africa
18D2 **Smithfield** Utah, USA
7L3 **Smith I** Can
3C2 **Smith River** Can
3C3 **Smith Sd** Can
4F5 **Smiths Falls** Can
75E3 **Smithton** Aust
3E2 **Smoky** *R* Can
16B2 **Smoky** *R* USA
75D2 **Smoky C** Aust
16C2 **Smoky Hills** USA
3F3 **Smoky Lake** Can
18D2 **Smoky Mts** USA
32F6 **Smøla** *I* Nor
44E5 **Smolensk** Russian Fed
41E2 **Smólikas** *Mt* Greece
41E2 **Smolyan** Bulg
3G3 **Smoothstone L** Can
43F2 **Smorgon'** Belorussia
14C3 **Smyrna** Delaware, USA
15C2 **Smyrna** Georgia, USA
35C4 **Snaefell** *Mt* Eng
32B2 **Snafell** *Mt* Iceland
18C1 **Snake** USA
18D2 **Snake** *R* USA
8B2 **Snake River Canyon** USA
18D2 **Snake River Plain** USA
77F5 **Snares** *Is* NZ
42B2 **Sneek** Neth
20B2 **Snelling** USA
42D2 **Sněžka** *Mt* Pol/Czech Republic
32F6 **Snøhetta** *Mt* Nor
18B1 **Snohomish** USA
18B1 **Snoqualmie P** USA
55D3 **Snoul** Camb
3H1 **Snowbird L** Can
35C5 **Snowdon** *Mt* Wales
35C5 **Snowdonia Nat Pk** Wales
6G3 **Snowdrift** Can
19D4 **Snowflake** USA
6H4 **Snow Lake** Can
14B2 **Snow Shoe** USA
75A2 **Snowtown** Aust
18D2 **Snowville** USA
75C3 **Snowy Mts** Aust
16B3 **Snyder** USA
53B5 **Soan-kundo** *I* S Korea
54A3 **Sobaek Sanmaek** *Mts* S Korea
72D3 **Sobat** *R* Sudan
27K4 **Sobral** Brazil
43E2 **Sochaczew** Pol
45F7 **Sochi** Russian Fed
54A3 **Söch'on** S Korea
69A2 **Socna** Libya
16A3 **Socorro** USA
21A3 **Socorro** *I* Mexico
28A2 **Socos** Chile
67F4 **Socotra** *I* Yemen
20C3 **Soda L** USA
32K5 **Sodankylä** Fin
18D2 **Soda Springs** USA
32H6 **Soderhamn** Sweden
32H7 **Södertälje** Sweden
72C2 **Sodiri** Sudan
72D3 **Sodo** Eth
14B1 **Sodus Point** USA
57B4 **Soë** Indon
36E1 **Soest** Germany
Sofala = Beira
Sofia = Sofiya
41E2 **Sofiya** Bulg
53C1 **Sofiysk** Russian Fed
44E2 **Sofporog** Russian Fed
50H4 **Sofu Gan** *I* Japan
26D2 **Sogamoso** Colombia
53C1 **Sogda** Russian Fed
32F6 **Sognefjorden** *Inlet* Nor
54A4 **Sögwi-ri** S Korea
59H2 **Sog Xian** China
66B1 **Sohâg** Egypt
77E1 **Sohano** PNG
60D3 **Sohīpat** India
36B1 **Soignies** Belg
36B2 **Soissons** France
60C3 **Sojat** India
53A4 **Söjosŏn-man** *B* N Korea
54A3 **Sokcho** S Korea
64A2 **Söke** Turk
71G4 **Sokodé** Togo
44G4 **Sokol** Russian Fed
43E2 **Sokołka** Pol
70B3 **Sokolo** Mali
7Q3 **Søkongens Øy** *I* Greenland
71H3 **Sokoto** Nig
71H3 **Sokoto** State, Nig
71G3 **Sokoto** *R* Nig
78A3 **Solander I** NZ
57F7 **Solano** Phil
62B1 **Solapur** India
57B4 **Solar** *I* Indon
37D1 **Solbad Hall** Austria
37D1 **Sölden** Austria
10H3 **Soldotna** USA
23C4 **Soledad** Colombia
20B2 **Soledad** USA
28E1 **Soledade** Brazil
35E6 **Solent** *Sd* Eng
36B1 **Solesmes** France
43F2 **Soligorsk** Belorussia
44K4 **Solikamsk** Russian Fed
45J5 **Sol'Iletsk** Russian Fed
26D4 **Solimões** Peru
36D1 **Solingen** Germany
74B1 **Solitaire** Namibia
32H6 **Sollefteå** Sweden
37B3 **Solliès-Pont** France
36E1 **Solling** Region, Germany
53D1 **Solnenechnyy** Russian Fed
36A3 **Sologne** *R* France
56B3 **Solok** Indon
77E1 **Solomon Is** Pacific O
12A1 **Solon Springs** USA
37B1 **Solothurn** Switz
44F2 **Solovetskiye, Ostrova** *I* Russian Fed
53A1 **Solov'yevsk** Russian Fed
32F8 **Soltau** Germany
20B3 **Solvang** USA
14B1 **Solvay** USA
34D4 **Solway Firth** *Estuary* Scot/Eng
73C5 **Solwezi** Zambia
54D3 **Sōma** Japan
41F3 **Soma** Turk
58C5 **Somalia** Republic, E Africa
xxviiiD4 **Somali Basin** Indian O
41D1 **Sombor** Serbia, Yugos
62E3 **Sombrero Chan** Indian O
22B1 **Sombretete** Mexico
76D2 **Somerset** Aust
35D6 **Somerset** County, Eng
12C3 **Somerset** Kentucky, USA
14E2 **Somerset** Massachusetts, USA
13D2 **Somerset** Pennsylvania, USA
74D3 **Somerset East** S Africa
7J2 **Somerset I** Can
14D1 **Somerset Res** USA
14C3 **Somers Point** USA
14E1 **Somersworth** USA
14C2 **Somerville** USA
17C3 **Somerville Res** USA
41E1 **Somes** *R* Rom
36B2 **Somme** Department, France
36B2 **Somme** *R* France
36C2 **Sommesous** France
26A1 **Somoto** Nic
61B3 **Son** *R* India
53A4 **Sönch'ön** N Korea
74D3 **Sondags** *R* S Africa
32F8 **Sønderborg** Den
7N3 **Søndre Strømfjord** Greenland
7N2 **Søndre Upernavik** Greenland
37C1 **Sondrio** Italy
55D3 **Song Ba** *R* Viet
55D3 **Song Cau** Viet
54A3 **Söngch'on** N Korea
73D5 **Songea** Tanz
54A2 **Songgan** N Korea
53B2 **Songhua Jiang** *R* China
52E3 **Songjiang** China
54A3 **Songjŏng** S Korea
55C4 **Songkhla** Thai
53B4 **Songnim** N Korea
55C5 **Sông Pahang** *R* Malay
52A3 **Songpan** China
54A4 **Söngsan-ni** S Korea
53B3 **Sonhue Hu** *L* China
52C1 **Sonid Youqi** China
55C1 **Son La** Viet
60B3 **Sonmiani** Pak
60B3 **Sonmiani Bay** Pak
19D4 **Sonoita** Mexico
20A1 **Sonoma** USA
20B2 **Sonora** California, USA
19D4 **Sonora** State, Mexico
16B3 **Sonora** Texas, USA
21A2 **Sonora** *R* Mexico
8B3 **Sonoran Desert** USA
20C1 **Sonora P** USA
21D3 **Sonsonate** El Salvador
51G6 **Sonsorol** *I* Pacific O
9E2 **Soo Canals** USA/Can
3D4 **Sooke** Can
43D2 **Sopot** Pol
42D3 **Sopron** Hung
5K4 **Sop's Arm** Can
20B2 **Soquel** USA
40C2 **Sora** Italy
65C3 **Sored** *R* Israel
5G4 **Sorel** Can
75E3 **Sorell** Aust
37C2 **Soresina** Italy
64C2 **Sorgun** Turk
39B1 **Soria** Spain
32J5 **Sørkjosen** Nor
48C2 **Sørksop** *I* Barents S
45J6 **Sor Mertvyy Kultuk** *Plain* Kazakhstan
29C3 **Sorocaba** Brazil
44J5 **Sorochinsk** Russian Fed
51H6 **Soroi** *I* Pacific O
43F3 **Soroki** Moldova
54D2 **Soroma-ko** *L* Japan
51G7 **Sorong** Indon
57D3 **Sorong** Province, Indon
72D3 **Soroti** Uganda
32J4 **Sørøya** *I* Nor
40C2 **Sorrento** Italy
32K5 **Sorsatunturi** *Mt* Fin
32H5 **Sorsele** Sweden
57F8 **Sorsogon** Phil
44E3 **Sortavala** Russian Fed
53B4 **Sösan** S Korea
43D2 **Sosnowiec** Pol
37B3 **Sospel** France
44L4 **Sos'va** Russian Fed
71G3 **Sota** *R* Benin
22C1 **Soto la Manna** Mexico
72B3 **Souanké** Congo
70B4 **Soubré** Ivory Coast
14C2 **Souderton** USA
23P2 **Soufrière** St Lucia
23N2 **Soufrière** *V* St Vincent
38C3 **Souillac** France
71D1 **Souk Ahras** Alg
71A2 **Souk Larbat Gharb** Mor
53B4 **Soul** S Korea
39C2 **Soummam** *R* Alg
Sour = Tyr
74D2 **Sources,Mt aux** Lesotho
11B2 **Souris** Manitoba, Can
5J4 **Souris** Prince Edward I, Can
11B2 **Souris** *R* USA/Can
27L5 **Sousa** Brazil
71E1 **Sousse** Tunisia
73C7 **South Africa** Republic, Africa
14C2 **South Amboy** USA
4E5 **Southampton** Can
35E6 **Southampton** Eng
14D2 **Southampton** USA
7K3 **Southampton I** Can
62E2 **South Andaman** *I* Indian O
7M4 **South Aulatsivik I** Can
76C3 **South Australia** State, Aust
xxviiiH6 **South Australian Basin** Indian O
17E3 **Southaven** USA
16A3 **South Baldy** *Mt* USA
15E4 **South Bay** USA
12C1 **South Baymouth** Can
12B2 **South Bend** Indiana, USA
18B1 **South Bend** Washington, USA
13D3 **South Boston** USA
4E5 **South Branch** USA
14E1 **Southbridge** USA
South Cape = Ka Lae
9E3 **South Carolina** State, USA
51E5 **South China S** S E Asia
8C2 **South Dakota** State, USA
14D1 **South Deerfield** USA
35E6 **South Downs** Eng
75E3 **South East C** Aust
10E3 **Southeast C** USA
xxixO7 **South East Pacific Basin** Pacific O
78A2 **Southen Alps** *Mts* NZ
3H2 **Southend** Can
35F6 **Southend-on-Sea** Eng
77F5 **Southern Alps** *Mts* NZ
76A4 **Southern Cross** Aust
4B2 **Southern Indian L** Can
6J4 **Southern Indian L** Can
15D1 **Southern Pines** USA
23H2 **Southfield** Jamaica
xxixK6 **South Fiji Basin** Pacific O
35F6 **South Foreland** *Pt* Eng
16A2 **South Fork** USA
10H3 **South Fork** *R* Alaska, USA
20B1 **South Fork** *R* California, USA
20B1 **South Fork American** *R* USA
20C3 **South Fork Kern** *R* USA
24G9 **South Georgia** *I* S Atlantic O
35D6 **South Glamorgan** County, Wales
12B2 **South Haven** USA
6J3 **South Henik L** Can
13D3 **South Hill** USA
xxviiiJ3 **South Honshu Reige** Pacific O
78A2 **South I** NZ
14D2 **Southington** USA
4B2 **South Knife** *R* Can
53B4 **South Korea** Republic, S E Asia
19B3 **South Lake Tahoe** USA
xxviiiD6 **South Madagascar Ridge** Indian O
79G8 **South Magnetic Pole** Ant
15E4 **South Miami** USA
14B3 **South Mt** USA
6F3 **South Nahanni** *R* Can
23G1 **South Negril Pt** Jamaica
xxxF8 **South Orkney** *Is* Atlantic O
24B5 **South Pacific O**
16B1 **South Platte** *R* USA
79E **South Pole** Ant
12C1 **South Porcupine** Can
35D5 **Southport** Eng
23Q2 **South Pt** Barbados
14C2 **South River** USA
34D2 **South Ronaldsay** *I* Scot
xxxG7 **South Sandwich Trench** Atlantic O
20A2 **South San Francisco** USA
3G3 **South Saskatchewan** *R* Can
4B2 **South Seal** *R* Can
34E4 **South Shields** Eng
78B1 **South Taranaki Bight** *B* NZ
4F3 **South Twin I** Can
34B3 **South Uist** *I* Scot
South West Africa = Namibia
76D5 **South West C** Aust
10D3 **Southwest C** USA
xxviiiD6 **South West Indian Ridge** Indian O
xxixM6 **South West Pacific Basin** Pacific O
xxxD5 **South West Peru Ridge** Pacific O
35E5 **South Yorkshire** County, Eng
74D1 **Soutpansberg** *Mts* S Africa
43E1 **Sovetsk** Russian Fed
44H4 **Sovetsk** Russian Fed
53E2 **Sovetskaya Gavan'** Russian Fed
44L3 **Sovetskiy** Russian Fed
74D2 **Soweto** S Africa
54D1 **Sōya-misaki** *C* Japan
73B4 **Soyo Congo** Angola
43G2 **Sozh** *R* Belorussia
36C1 **Spa** Belg
39 **Spain** Kingdom, Europe
Spalato = Split
35E5 **Spalding** Eng
12C1 **Spanish** *R* Can
19D2 **Spanish Fork** USA
23B3 **Spanish Town** Jamaica
19C3 **Sparks** USA
12A2 **Sparta** USA
15C2 **Spartanburg** USA
41E3 **Spartí** Greece
53C3 **Spassk Dal'niy** Russian Fed
11B3 **Spearfish** USA
16B2 **Spearman** USA
23Q2 **Speightstown** Barbados
10J3 **Spenard** USA
11C3 **Spence** Iowa, USA
12B3 **Spencer** Indiana, USA
7J3 **Spencer Bay** Can
75A3 **Spencer,C** Aust
75A2 **Spencer G** Aust
7L3 **Spencer Is** *Is* Can
78B2 **Spenser Mts** NZ
34B4 **Sperrin** *Mts* N Ire
36E2 **Spessart** Region, Germany
34D3 **Spey** *R* Scot
42B3 **Speyer** Germany
23K1 **Speyside** Tobago
37B1 **Spiez** Switz
10K2 **Spike Mt** USA
37E1 **Spilimbergo** Italy
18C1 **Spirir Lake** USA
6G4 **Spirit River** Can
Spitsbergen = Svalbard
48C2 **Spitsbergen, I** Barents S
42C3 **Spittal** Austria
37E1 **Spittal an der Drau** Austria
32F6 **Spjelkavik** Nor

Split L
Swale

4B2 Split L Can
40D2 Split Croatia, Yugos
37C1 Splügen Switz
18C1 Spokane USA
12A1 Spooner USA
18C2 Spray USA
42C2 Spree R Germany
74B2 Springbok S Africa
5K4 Springdale Can
17D2 Springdale USA
16B2 Springer USA
19E4 Springerville USA
16B2 Springfield Colorado, USA
12B3 Springfield Illinois, USA
14D1 Springfield Massachusetts, USA
11C3 Springfield Minnesota, USA
17D2 Springfield Missouri, USA
12C3 Springfield Ohio, USA
18B2 Springfield Oregon, USA
15B1 Springfield Tennessee, USA
13E2 Springfield Vermont, USA
74D3 Springfontein S Africa
5J4 Springhill Can
19C3 Spring Mts USA
74D2 Springs S Africa
14A1 Springville New York, USA
19D2 Springville Utah, USA
14B1 Springwater USA
18D2 Spruce Mt USA
35F5 Spurn Head C Eng
33D3 Spurn Head Pt Eng
18B1 Spuzzum Can
3D4 Squamish Can
49R3 Sredhekolymsk Russian Fed
49S4 Sredinnyy Khrebet Mts Russian Fed
44F5 Sredne-Russkaya Vozvyshennost' Upland Russian Fed
49M3 Sredne Sibirskoye Ploskogorye Tableland Russian Fed
44K4 Sredniy Ural Mts Russian Fed
55D3 Srepok R Camb
50E1 Sretensk Russian Fed
55C3 Sre Umbell Camb
62C1 Srīkākulam India
59G5 Sri Lanka Republic, S Asia
60C2 Srīnagar Pak
62A1 Srīvardhan India
42D2 Sroda Wielkopolski Pol
34C2 Stack Skerry I Scot
42B2 Stade Germany
34B3 Staffa I Scot
35D5 Stafford County, Eng
35D5 Stafford Eng
14D2 Stafford Springs USA
Stalingrad = Volgograd
3D2 Stalin,Mt Can
74B3 Stallberg Mt S Africa
7J1 Stallworthy,C Can
43E2 Stalowa Wola Pol
14D2 Stamford Connecticut, USA
14C1 Stamford New York, USA
16C3 Stamford Texas, USA
74B1 Stampriet Namibia
74D2 Standerton S Africa
12C2 Standish USA
18D1 Stanford USA
74E2 Stanger S Africa
20B2 Stanislaus R USA
41E2 Stanke Dimitrov Bulg
75E3 Stanley Aust
25E8 Stanley Falkland Is
18D2 Stanley Idaho, USA
11B2 Stanley N Dakota, USA
62B2 Stanley Res India
Stanleyville = Kisangani
21D3 Stann Creek Belize
50F1 Stanovoy Khrebet Mts Russian Fed
37C1 Stans Switz
75D1 Stanthorpe Aust
34B3 Stanton Banks Sand-bank Scot
16B1 Stapleton USA
43E2 Starachowice Pol
41E2 Stara Planiná Mts Bulg
44E4 Staraya Russa Russian Fed
41F2 Stara Zagora Bulg
42D2 Stargard Szczecinski Pol
17E3 Starkville USA
42C3 Starnberg Germany
43D2 Starogard Gdanski Pol
43F3 Starokonstantinov Ukraine
35D6 Start Pt Eng
45F5 Staryy Oskol Russian Fed
14B2 State College USA
14C2 Staten I USA
15C2 Statesboro USA
15C1 Statesville USA
13D3 Staunton USA
32F7 Stavanger Nor
36C1 Stavelot Belg
45G6 Stavropol' Russian Fed
75B3 Stawell Aust
42D2 Stawno Pol
18B2 Stayton USA
16A1 Steamboat Springs USA
10F3 Stebbins USA
10K3 Steele,Mt Can
14B2 Steelton USA
3E2 Steen R Can
3E2 Steen River Can
18C2 Steens Mt USA
7N2 Steenstrups Gletscher Gl Greenland
6H2 Stefansson I Can
74E2 Stegi Swaziland
37D1 Steinach Austria
4B4 Steinbach Can
44A3 Steinkjer Nor
74B2 Steinkopf S Africa
3D3 Stein Mt Can
74C2 Stella S Africa
5J4 Stellarton Can
74B3 Stellenbosch S Africa
22C2 Stemaco Mexico
36C2 Stenay France
42C2 Stendal Germany
45H8 Stepanakert Azerbaijan
11C2 Stephen USA
78B2 Stephens,C NZ
75B2 Stephens Creek Aust
12B1 Stephenson USA
10M4 Stephens Pass USA
7N5 Stephenville Can
16C3 Stephenville USA
10F4 Stepovak B USA
74D3 Sterkstroom S Africa
16B1 Sterling Colorado, USA
12B2 Sterling Illinois, USA
16C2 Sterling Kansas, USA
11B2 Sterling N Dakota, USA
16B3 Sterling City USA
12C2 Sterling Heights USA
44K5 Sterlitamak Russian Fed
3F3 Stettler Can
12C2 Steubenville USA
4B3 Stevenson L Can
12B2 Stevens Point USA
6D3 Stevens Village USA
3B2 Stewart Can
19C3 Stewart USA
10L3 Stewart R Can
10L3 Stewart Crossing Can
78A3 Stewart I NZ
77F1 Stewart Is Solomon Is
6E3 Stewart River Can
14B3 Stewartstown USA
11D3 Stewartville USA
74D2 Steyn S Africa
74D3 Steynsburg S Africa
42C3 Steyr Austria
74C3 Steytlerville S Africa
37D3 Stia Italy
10L4 Stika USA
3B2 Stikine R Can
10M4 Stikine Ranges Mts Can
11D2 Stillwater Minnesota, USA
17C2 Stillwater Oklahoma, USA
19C3 Stillwater Range Mts USA
4E4 Stimson Can
16B2 Stinett USA
75A2 Stirling Aust
34D3 Stirling Scot
36E3 Stockach Germany
14D1 Stockbridge USA
42D3 Stockerau Austria
32H7 Stockholm Sweden
35D5 Stockport Eng
20B2 Stockton California, USA
35E4 Stockton Eng
16C2 Stockton Kansas, USA
17D2 Stockton L USA
35D5 Stoke-on-Trent Eng
4E4 Stokes Bay Can
32A2 Stokkseyri Iceland
32G5 Stokmarknes Nor
49P2 Stolbovoy, Ostrov I Russian Fed
32K8 Stolbtsy Belorussia
43F2 Stolin Belorussia
14C3 Stone Harbor USA
34D3 Stonehaven Scot
17C3 Stonewall USA
10H3 Stony R USA
5K3 Stony I Can
3J2 Stony L Can
4E3 Stooping R Can
32H5 Storavan L Sweden
32G6 Støren Nor
75E3 Storm B Aust
11C3 Storm Lake USA
34B2 Stornoway Scot
43F3 Storozhinets Ukraine
14D2 Storrs USA
32G6 Storsjön L Sweden
32H5 Storuman Sweden
11A3 Story USA
3H4 Stoughton Can
14E1 Stoughton USA
36A1 Stour R Eng
35F5 Stowmarket Eng
53C1 Stoyba Russian Fed
34B4 Strabane N Ire
75E3 Strahan Aust
42C2 Stralsund Germany
74B3 Strand S Africa
32F6 Stranda Nor
32H7 Strängnäs Sweden
34C4 Stranraer Scot
38D2 Strasbourg France
13D3 Strasburg USA
20C2 Stratford California, USA
4E5 Stratford Can
14D2 Stratford Connecticut, USA
78B1 Stratford NZ
16B2 Stratford Texas, USA
35E5 Stratford-on-Avon Eng
75A3 Strathalbyn Aust
34C4 Strathclyde Region, Scot
3F3 Strathmore Can
13E1 Stratton USA
12B2 Streator USA
37C2 Stresa Italy
40D3 Stretto de Messina Str Italy/Sicily
40D3 Stroboli I Italy
28C4 Stroeder Arg
34D2 Stromness Scot
32D3 Strømø Faroes
17C1 Stromsburg USA
32H6 Stromsund Sweden
32G6 Ströms Vattudal L Sweden
34D2 Stronsay I Scot
35D6 Stroud Eng
14C2 Stroudsburg USA
41E2 Struma R Bulg
35C5 Strumble Head Pt Wales
41E2 Strumica Macedonia, Yugos
43E3 Stryy Ukraine
43E3 Stryy R Ukraine
75B1 Strzelecki Creek R Aust
15E4 Stuart Florida, USA
11C3 Stuart Nebraska, USA
3D3 Stuart R Can
10F3 Stuart I USA
3D3 Stuart L Can
37D1 Stubaier Alpen Mts Austria
32H8 Stubice Pol
55D3 Stung Sen Camb
55D3 Stung Treng Camb
4C2 Stupart R Can
40B2 Stura R Italy
79G7 Sturge I Ant
12B2 Sturgeon Bay USA
4F4 Sturgeon Falls Can
4C4 Sturgeon L Can
12B3 Sturgis Kentucky, USA
12B2 Sturgis Michigan, USA
11B3 Sturgis S Dakota, USA
76B2 Sturt Creek R Aust
75B1 Sturt Desert Aust
74D3 Stuttemeim S Africa
17D3 Stuttgart USA
42B3 Stuttgart Germany
32A1 Stykkishólmur Iceland
43F2 Styr' R Ukraine
49M4 Styudyanka Russian Fed
29D2 Suaçuí Grande R Brazil
66C3 Suakin Sudan
54A3 Suan N Korea
52E5 Su-ao Taiwan
28C2 Suardi Arg
56C2 Subi I Indon
41D1 Subotica Serbia, Yugos
45D6 Suceava Rom
22C2 Suchixtepec Mexico
26E7 Sucre Bol
29B2 Sucuriú R, Brazil
72C2 Sudan Republic, Africa
4E4 Sudbury Can
35F5 Sudbury Eng
72C3 Sudd Swamp Sudan
27G2 Suddie Guyana
65B4 Sudr Egypt
72C3 Sue R Sudan
10M4 Suemez I USA
64B4 Suez Egypt
64B3 Suez Canal Egypt
64B4 Suez,G of Egypt
14C2 Suffern USA
35F5 Suffolk County, Eng
13D3 Suffolk USA
13E2 Sugarloaf Mt USA
75D2 Sugarloaf Pt Aust
3H3 Suggi L Can
49R3 Sugoy R Russian Fed
67G2 Suhār Oman
50D1 Sühbaatar Mongolia
60B3 Sui Pak
53C2 Suibin China
52C2 Suide China
53C3 Suifenhe China
53B2 Suihua China
53B2 Suileng China
52B3 Suining China
36C2 Suippes France
33B3 Suir R Irish Rep
52C3 Sui Xian China
52E1 Suizhong China
60C3 Sujāngarh India
56C4 Sukabumi Indon
56D3 Sukadana Borneo, Indon
56C4 Sukadana Sumatra, Indon
53E4 Sukagawa Japan
56D3 Sukaraya Indon
44F5 Sukhinichi Russian Fed
44G4 Sukhona R Russian Fed
45G7 Sukhumi Georgia
7N3 Sukkertoppen Greenland
7N3 Sukkertoppen Isflade Gl Greenland
32L6 Sukkozero Russian Fed
60B3 Sukkur Pak
62C1 Sukma India
53D2 Sukpay R Russian Fed
73B6 Sukses Namibia
54B4 Sukumo Japan
3D2 Sukunka R Can
45F5 Sula R Russian Fed
60B3 Sulaiman Range Mts Pak
34B2 Sula Sgeir I Scot
57B3 Sulawesi I Indon
57B3 Sulawesi Sulatan Prov, Indon
57B3 Sulawesi Tengah Prov, Indon
57B3 Sulawesi Tenggara Prov, Indon
57B3 Sulawesi Utara Prov, Indon
71H4 Suleja Nig
34C2 Sule Skerry I Scot
41F1 Sulina Rom
32H5 Sulitjelma Nor
26B4 Sullana Peru
17D2 Sullivan USA
3C3 Sullivan Bay Can
3F3 Sullivan L Can
36B3 Sully-sur-Loire France
40C2 Sulmona Italy
17D3 Sulphur Louisiana, USA
17C3 Sulphur Oklahoma, USA
17C3 Sulphur Springs USA
4E4 Sultan Can
45E8 Sultan Dağlari Mts Turk
61B2 Sultānpur India
57F9 Sulu Arch Phil
51E6 Sulu S Philip
36E2 Sulz Germany
25D3 Sumampa Arg
56A2 Sumatera I Indon
57B4 Sumba I Indon
56E4 Sumbawa I Indon
56E4 Sumbawa Besar Indon
73D4 Sumbawanga Tanz
34E2 Sumburgh Head Pt Scot
56D4 Sumenep Indon
45H7 Sumgait Azerbaijan
73B5 Sumbe Angola
50H3 Sumisu I Japan
3E4 Summerland Can
5J4 Summerside Can
3B2 Summer Str USA
6F4 Summit Lake Can
19C3 Summits Mt USA
78B2 Sumner,L NZ
54B4 Sumoto Japan
15C2 Sumter USA
45E5 Sumy Ukraine
18D1 Sun R USA
54D2 Sunagawa Japan
54A3 Sunan N Korea
14B2 Sunbury USA
28C2 Sunchales Arg
28C1 Suncho Corral Arg
53B4 Sunch'ŏn N Korea
53B5 Sunch'ŏn S Korea
11B3 Sundance USA
61B3 Sundargarh India
61C3 Sunderbans Swamp India
34E4 Sunderland Eng
3F3 Sundre Can
13D1 Sundridge Can
32H6 Sundsvaall Sweden
56E3 Sungaianyar Indon
56B3 Sungaisalak Indon
56F6 Sungai Siput Malay
56F6 Sungei Petani Malay
57A4 Sungguminasa Indon
18C1 Sunnyside USA
19B3 Sunnyvale USA
12B2 Sun Prairie USA
49N3 Suntar Russian Fed
63E3 Suntsar Pak
18D2 Sun Valley USA
53B2 Sunwu China
71F4 Sunyani Ghana
44E3 Suojarvi Russian Fed
54B4 Suō-nada B Japan
32K6 Suonejoki Fin
61C2 Supaul India
19D4 Superior Arizona, USA
17C1 Superior Nebraska, USA
12A1 Superior Wisconsin, USA
12B1 Superior,L USA/Can
55C3 Suphan Buri Thai
64D2 Süphan Dağ Turk
51G7 Supiori I Indon
57C2 Supu Indon
66D3 Sūq 'Abs Yemen
64E3 Suq ash Suyukh Iraq
65D1 Suqaylibīyah Syria
52D3 Suqian China
Suqutra = Socotra
67G2 Sūr Oman
44H5 Sura R Russian Fed
56D4 Surabaya Indon
54C4 Suraga-wan B Japan
56D4 Surakarta Indon
65D1 Sūrān Syria
75C1 Surat Aust
60C4 Sūrat India
60C3 Sūratgarh India
55B4 Surat Thani Thai
60C4 Surendranagar India
14C3 Surf City USA
48J3 Surgut Russian Fed
62B1 Suriāpet India
38D2 Sürich Switz
57G9 Surigao Phil
55C3 Surin Thai
27G3 Surinam Republic, S America
20B2 Sur,Pt USA
35E6 Surrey County, Eng
37C1 Sursee Switz
69A1 Surt Libya
32A2 Surtsey I Iceland
56B3 Surulangan Indon
37B2 Susa Italy
54B4 Susa Japan
54B4 Susaki Japan
19B2 Susanville USA
37D1 Süsch Switz
10J3 Susitna R USA
14C2 Susquehanna USA
14B3 Susquehanna R USA
14C2 Sussex USA
35E6 Sussex West Eng
3C2 Sustut Peak Mt Can
74C3 Sutherland S Africa
16B1 Sutherland USA
60C2 Sutlej R Pak
19B3 Sutter Creek USA
12C3 Sutton USA
4E3 Sutton R Can
54D2 Suttsu Japan
10G4 Sutwik I USA
77G2 Suva Fiji
53D4 Suwa Japan
43E2 Suwałki Pol
15C3 Suwannee R USA
65C2 Suweilih Jordan
53B4 Suwŏn S Korea
52D3 Su Xian China
54C3 Suzaka Japan
52E3 Suzhou China
53D4 Suzu Japan
54C4 Suzuka Japan
54C3 Suzu-misaki C Japan
48C2 Svalbard Is Barents S
43E3 Svalyava Ukraine
7N2 Svartenhuk Halvø Region Greenland
32G5 Svartisen Mt Nor
55D3 Svay Rieng Camb
32G6 Sveg Sweden
32G7 Svendborg Den
7J1 Sverdrup Chan Can
6H2 Sverdrup Is Can
53D2 Svetlaya Russian Fed
43E2 Svetlogorsk Russian Fed
32K6 Svetogorsk Russian Fed
41E2 Svetozarevo Serbia, Yugos
41F2 Svilengrad Bulg
43F2 Svir' Belrussia
44E3 Svir' R Russian Fed
42D3 Švitavy Czech Republic
53B1 Svobodnyy Russian Fed
32G5 Svolvaer Nor
77E3 Swain Reefs Aust
77H2 Swains I American Samoa
15C2 Swainsboro USA
74B1 Swakop R Namibia
74A1 Swakopmund Namibia
35E4 Swale R Eng

Swallow Reef **Taurage**

56D1 **Swallow Reef** *I* S E Asia
62B2 **Swāmihalli** India
21D3 **Swan** *I* Honduras
35E6 **Swanage** Eng
75B3 **Swan Hill** Aust
3E3 **Swan Hills** Can
3E3 **Swan Hills** *Mts* Can
23A3 **Swan I** Caribbean
4A3 **Swan L** Can
6H4 **Swan River** Can
35D6 **Swansea** Wales
35D6 **Swansea B** Wales
74C3 **Swartberge** *Mts* S Africa
74D2 **Swartruggens** S Africa
4E4 **Swastika** Can
Swatow = Shantou
74E2 **Swaziland** Kingdom, S Africa
32G7 **Sweden** Kingdom, N Europe
71F4 **Swedru** Ghana
18B2 **Sweet Home** USA
16B3 **Sweetwater** USA
11A3 **Sweetwater** *R* USA
74C3 **Swellendam** S Africa
42D2 **Świdnica** Pol
42D2 **Świdwin** Pol
42D2 **Swiebodzin** Pol
43D2 **Świecie** Pol
3G3 **Swift Current** Can
11A1 **Swift Current Creek** *R* Can
3B1 **Swift River** Can
35E6 **Swindon** Eng
42C2 **Świnoujście** Pol
38D2 **Switzerland** Federal Republic, Europe
35B5 **Swords** Irish Rep
32D3 **Sydero** Faroes
75D2 **Sydney** Aust
7M5 **Sydney** Can
11D1 **Sydney L** Can
5J4 **Sydney Mines** Can
44J3 **Syktyvkar** Russian Fed
15B2 **Sylacauga** USA
32G6 **Sylarna** *Mt* Sweden
61D3 **Sylhet** Bang
42B1 **Sylt** *I* Germany
12C2 **Sylvania** USA
3D2 **Sylvia,Mt** Can
22B1 **Symon** Mexico
79G11 **Syowa** *Base* Ant
Syracuse = Siracusa
16B2 **Syracuse** Kansas, USA
14B1 **Syracuse** New York, USA
13D2 **Syracuse** USA
48H5 **Syr Darya** *R* Kazakhstan
64C2 **Syria** Republic, S W Asia
44L4 **Sysert'** Russian Fed
44H5 **Syzran'** Russian Fed
42C2 **Szczecin** Pol
42D2 **Szczecinek** Pol
43E2 **Szczytno** Pol
43E3 **Szeged** Hung
43D3 **Székesfehérvar** Hung
43D3 **Szekszard** Hung
43D3 **Szolnok** Hung
42D3 **Szombathely** Hung
42D2 **Szprotawa** Pol

T

74D3 **Tabankulu** S Africa
76E1 **Tabar Is** PNG
63D2 **Tabas** Iran
22B1 **Tabasco** Mexico
22D2 **Tabasco** State, Mexico
26E4 **Tabatinga** Brazil
70B2 **Tabelbala** Alg
55C3 **Tabeng** Camb
3F4 **Taber** Can
57F8 **Tablas** *I* Phil
74B3 **Table Mt** S Africa
10K2 **Table Mt** USA
17D2 **Table Rock Res** USA
56C3 **Taboali** Indon
42C3 **Tábor** Czech Republic
72D4 **Tabora** Tanz
44L4 **Tabory** Russian Fed
70B4 **Tabou** Ivory Coast
71D1 **Taboursouk** Tunisia
63B1 **Tabrīz** Iran
64C4 **Tabūk** S Arabia
22B2 **Tacámbaro** Mexico
59G1 **Tacheng** China
57G8 **Tacloban** Phil
26D7 **Tacna** Peru
19D4 **Tacna** USA
8A2 **Tacoma** USA
14D1 **Taconic Range** USA
28E2 **Tacuan** *R* Urug
28D2 **Tacuarembó** Urug
29A3 **Tacuati** Par
72E2 **Tadjoura** Djibouti
66D4 **Tadjoura,G of** Djibouti
4B2 **Tadoule L** Can
5H4 **Tadoussac** Can
62B2 **Tādpatri** India
53B4 **Taebaek Sanmaek** *Mts* S Korea
54A3 **Taech'on** S Korea
54A3 **Taedong** *R* N Korea
54A3 **Taegang-got** *Pen* N Korea
53B4 **Taegu** S Korea
53B5 **Taehŭksan** *I* S Korea
54A2 **Taehung** N Korea
53B4 **Taejŏn** S Korea
56G7 **Taesek Dampar** *L* Malay
39B1 **Tafalla** Spain
70C2 **Tafasaset** *Watercourse* Alg
35D6 **Taff** *R* Wales
65C3 **Tafila** Jordan
20C3 **Taft** USA
45F6 **Taganrog** Russian Fed
70A3 **Tagant** Region, Maur
61E3 **Tagaung** Burma
57F9 **Tagbilaran** Phil
3B2 **Tagish L** Can
37E1 **Tagliamento** *R* Italy
70B2 **Taguenout Hagguerete** *Well* Maur
77E2 **Tagula** *I* Solomon Is
57G9 **Tagum** Phil
Tagus = Tejo
70C2 **Tahat, Mt** Alg
xxixM5 **Tahiti** *I* Pacific O
63E3 **Tahlab** *R* Iran
17C2 **Tahlequah** USA
19B3 **Tahoe City** USA
19B3 **Tahoe,L** USA
16B3 **Tahoka** USA
70C3 **Tahoua** Niger
66B1 **Tahta** Egypt
57C2 **Tahulandang** *I* Indon
57C2 **Tahuna** Indon
52D2 **Tai'an** China
52B3 **Taibai Shan** *Mt* China
52D1 **Taibus Qi** China
52E5 **T'ai-chung** Taiwan
78B3 **Taieri** *R* NZ
52C2 **Taihang Shan** China
78C1 **Taihape** NZ
52E3 **Tai Hu** *L* China
54D2 **Taiki** Japan
53A2 **Tailai** China
56A3 **Taileleo** Indon
75A3 **Tailem Bend** Aust
34C3 **Tain** Scot
52E5 **T'ai-nan** Taiwan
29D2 **Taiobeiras** Brazil
52E5 **T'ai pei** Taiwan
55C5 **Taiping** Malay
54D3 **Taira** Japan
56B3 **Tais** Indon
54B3 **Taisha** Japan
25B7 **Taitao,Pen de** Chile
52E5 **T'ai-tung** Taiwan
32K5 **Taivelkoski** Fin
50F4 **Taiwan** Republic, China
Taiwan Haixia = Formosa Str
65C3 **Taiyiba** Jordan
52C2 **Taiyuan** China
52D3 **Taizhou** China
66D4 **Ta 'izz** Yemen
59E2 **Tajikistan**
39B1 **Tajo** *R* Spain
55B2 **Tak** Thai
53D4 **Takada** Japan
54B4 **Takahashi** Japan
78B2 **Takaka** NZ
53C5 **Takamatsu** Japan
53D4 **Takaoka** Japan
78B1 **Takapuna** NZ
53D4 **Takasaki** Japan
54C3 **Takayama** Japan
66C4 **Takazie** *R* Eth
53D4 **Takefu** Japan
56A2 **Takengon** Indon
55C3 **Takeo** Camb
54B4 **Takeo** Japan
Take-shima = Tok-do
63B1 **Takestān** Iran
54B4 **Taketa** Japan
54D2 **Takikawa** Japan
54D2 **Takinoue** Japan
6G3 **Takiyvak L** Can
72D2 **Takkaze** *R* Eth
3C2 **Takla L** Can
3C2 **Takla Landing** Can
10F3 **Takslesluk L** USA
3B2 **Taku** *R* Can
10M3 **Taku Arm** *R* Can
3B2 **Taku Gl** USA
71J4 **Takum** Nig
22B1 **Tala** Mexico
43D3 **Talabanya** Hung
57C3 **Talaga** Indon
60C2 **Talagang** Pak
28A2 **Talagante** Chile
62B3 **Talaimannar** Sri Lanka
70C3 **Talak** *Desert,* Region, Niger
56B3 **Talangbetutu** Indon
26B4 **Talara** Peru
76E1 **Talasea** PNG
65B3 **Talata** Egypt
39A1 **Talavera de la Reina** Spain
28A3 **Talca** Chile
28A3 **Talcahuano** Chile
61C3 **Tālcher** India
53A1 **Talden** Russian Fed
59F1 **Taldy Kurgan** Kazakhstan
57B3 **Taliabu** Indon
60B1 **Taligan** Afghan
72D3 **Tali Post** Sudan
56E4 **Taliwang** Indon
10H3 **Talkeetna** USA
10J3 **Talkeetna Mts** USA
65A3 **Talkha** Egypt
15B2 **Talladega** USA
64D2 **Tall 'Afar** Iraq
15C2 **Tallahassee** USA
37B2 **Tallard** France
65D1 **Tall Bīsah** Syria
44C4 **Tallinn** Estonia
64C3 **Tall Kalakh** Syria
17D3 **Tallulah** USA
50B1 **Tal'menka** Russian Fed
45E6 **Tal'noye** Ukraine
43E2 **Talpaki** Russian Fed
25B3 **Taltal** Chile
75C1 **Talwood** Aust
11D3 **Tama** USA
56E2 **Tamabo Range** *Mts* Malay
71F4 **Tamale** Ghana
70C2 **Tamanrasset** Alg
70C2 **Tamanrasset** *Watercourse* Alg
14C2 **Tamaqua** USA
Tamatave = Toamasina
22A1 **Tamazula** Durango, Mexico
22B2 **Tamazula** Jalisco, Mexico
22C2 **Tamazulapán** Mexico
22C1 **Tamazunchale** Mexico
70A3 **Tambacounda** Sen
28D2 **Tambores** Urug
45G5 **Tambov** Russian Fed
39A1 **Tambre** *R* Spain
57B3 **Tambu** Indon
72C3 **Tambura** Sudan
70A3 **Tamchaket** Maur
39A1 **Tamega** *R* Port
22C1 **Tamiahua** Mexico
62B2 **Tamil Nādu** State, India
55D2 **Tam Ky** Viet
15C3 **Tampa** USA
15E4 **Tampa B** USA
32J6 **Tampere** Fin
22C1 **Tampico** Mexico
56G7 **Tampin** Malay
50E2 **Tamsagbulag** Mongolia
37E1 **Tamsweg** Austria
61D3 **Tamu** Burma
22C1 **Tamuis** Mexico
75D2 **Tamworth** Aust
35E5 **Tamworth** Eng
44D1 **Tana** Nor
72D2 **Tana** *L* Eth
72E4 **Tana** *R* Kenya
32K5 **Tana** *R* Nor/Fin
54C4 **Tanabe** Japan
32K4 **Tanafjord** *Inlet* Nor
10C6 **Tanaga** *I* USA
56E3 **Tanahgrogot** Indon
57B4 **Tanahjampea** *I* Indon
51G7 **Tanahmerah** Indon
57A4 **Tanakeke** *I* Indon
10H2 **Tanana** USA
10J3 **Tanana** *R* USA
Tananarive = Antananarivo
10C6 **Tananga Pass** USA
37C2 **Tanaro** *R* Italy
53B3 **Tanch'ŏn** N Korea
28D3 **Tandil** Arg
56C2 **Tandjong Datu** *Pt* Indon
51G7 **Tandjung d'Urville** *C* Indon
56A1 **Tandjung Jambuair** *C* Indon
56E3 **Tandjung Layar** *C* Indon
56C3 **Tandjung Lumut** *C* Indon
56E2 **Tandjung Mangkalihet** *C* Indon
56D3 **Tandjung Sambar** *C* Indon
56D2 **Tandjung Sirik** *C* Malay
51G7 **Tandjung Vals** *C* Indon
60B3 **Tando Adam** Pak
60B3 **Tando Muhammad Khan** Pak
75B2 **Tandou L** Aust
62B1 **Tāndūr** India
78C1 **Taneatua** NZ
53C5 **Tanega-shima** *I* Japan
55B2 **Tanen Range** *Mts* Burma/Thai
70B2 **Tanezrouft** *Desert Region* Alg
63D3 **Tang** Iran
72D4 **Tanga** Tanz
77E1 **Tanga Is** PNG
72C4 **Tanganyika,L** Tanz/Zaïre
71A1 **Tanger** Mor
59H2 **Tanggula Shan** *Mts* China
Tangier = Tanger
54A3 **Tangjin** S Korea
56B2 **Tangjungpinang** Indon
56G7 **Tangkak** Malay
59G2 **Tangra Yumco** *L* China
52D2 **Tangshan** China
57F9 **Tangub** Phil
50D1 **Tanguy** Russian Fed
53B2 **Tangwang He** *R* China
53B2 **Tangyuan** China
Tanintharyi = Tenasserim
57F9 **Tanjay** Phil
56D4 **Tanjong Bugel** *C* Indon
56C4 **Tanjong Cangkuang** *C* Indon
56F7 **Tanjong Malim** Malay
56D3 **Tanjong Puting** *C* Indon
56D3 **Tanjong Selatan** *C* Indon
56E3 **Tanjung** Indon
56A2 **Tanjungbalai** Indon
57C3 **Tanjungbaliha** Indon
56B3 **Tanjung Jabung** *Pt* Indon
57A4 **Tanjung Karossa** Indon
57A2 **Tanjung Manimbaya** *Pt* Indon
56C3 **Tanjungpandan** Indon
56C4 **Tanjung Priok** Indon
56E2 **Tanjungredeb** Indon
76A1 **Tanjung Selatan** *Pt* Indon
56E2 **Tanjungselor** Indon
57B2 **Tanjung Torawitan** *C* Indon
76C1 **Tanjung Vals** *Pt* Indon
60C2 **Tank** Pak
77F2 **Tanna** *I* Vanuatu
50C1 **Tannu Ola** *Mts* Russian Fed
71F4 **Tano** *R* Ghana
70C3 **Tanout** Niger
22C1 **Tanquián** Mexico
52E4 **Tan-shui** Taiwan
61B2 **Tansing** Nepal
69C1 **Tanta** Egypt
70A2 **Tan-Tan** Mor
6B3 **Tanunak** USA
54A3 **Tanyang** S Korea
72D4 **Tanzania** Republic, Africa
53A2 **Tao'an** China
53A2 **Tao'er He** *R* China
52A3 **Tao He** *R* China
73E6 **Taola168naro** Madag
52B2 **Taole** China
16A2 **Taos** USA
71B2 **Taounate** Mor
71B2 **Taourirt** Mor
44D4 **Tapa** Estonia
21C3 **Tapachula** Mexico
56F6 **Tapah** Malay
27G4 **Tapajós** *R* Brazil
56A2 **Tapaktuan** Indon
28C3 **Tapalquén** Arg
56B3 **Tapan** Indon
22D2 **Tapanatepec** Mexico
78A3 **Tapanui** NZ
26E5 **Tapauá** *R* Brazil
28E2 **Tapes** Brazil
60D4 **Tapi** *R* India
61C2 **Taplejung** Nepal
71G3 **Tapoa** *R* Burkina
13D3 **Tappahannock** USA
78B2 **Tapuaeniku** *Mt* NZ
29C3 **Tapuaritinga** Brazil
57F9 **Tapul Group** *Is* Phil
26F4 **Tapurucuara** Brazil
29B2 **Taquari** *R* Brazil
75D1 **Tara** Aust
48J4 **Tara** Russian Fed
48J4 **Tara** *R* Russian Fed
41D2 **Tara** *R* Bosnia-Herzegovina/Montenegro, Yugos
71J4 **Taraba** *R* Nig
71J4 **Taraba** *State* Nig
26F7 **Tarabuco** Bol
Tarābulus = Tripoli
39B1 **Taracón** Spain
78C1 **Taradale** NZ
56E2 **Tarakan** Indon
57B4 **Taramana** Indon
34B3 **Taransay** *I* Scot
40D2 **Taranto** Italy
26C5 **Tarapoto** Peru
38C2 **Tarare** France
78C2 **Tararua Range** *Mts* NZ
44H2 **Tarasovo** Russian Fed
70C2 **Tarat** Alg
78C1 **Tarawera** NZ
39B1 **Tarazona** Spain
34D3 **Tarbat Ness** *Pen* Scot
60C2 **Tarbela Res** Pak
34C4 **Tarbert** Strathclyde, Scot
34B3 **Tarbert** Western Isles, Scot
38B3 **Tarbes** France
15D1 **Tarboro** USA
76C4 **Tarcoola** Aust
75C2 **Tarcoon** Aust
48H4 **Tarda** Russian Fed
53D2 **Tardoki Yani, Gora** *Mt* Russian Fed
75D2 **Taree** Aust
70A2 **Tarfaya** Mor
18D2 **Targhee P** USA
69A1 **Tarhūnah** Libya
67F2 **Tarīf** UAE
26F8 **Tarija** Bol
62B2 **Tarikere** India
67E3 **Tarīm** Yemen
72D4 **Tarime** Tanz
59G1 **Tarim He** *R* China
59G2 **Tarim Pendi** *Basin* China
60B2 **Tarin Kut** Afghan
74D3 **Tarkastad** S Africa
17C1 **Tarkio** USA
44J3 **Tarko Sale** Russian Fed
71F4 **Tarkwa** Ghana
57F7 **Tarlac** Phil
26C6 **Tarma** Peru
38C3 **Tarn** *R* France
43E2 **Tarnobrzeg** Pol
43E3 **Tarnów** Pol
37C2 **Taro** *R* Italy
76D3 **Taroom** Aust
70B1 **Taroudannt** Morocco
39C1 **Tarragona** Spain
75E3 **Tarraleah** Aust
39C1 **Tarrasa** Spain
14D2 **Tarrytown** USA
64B2 **Tarsus** Turk
34E2 **Tartan** *Oilfield* N Sea
37D2 **Tartaro** *R* Italy
44D4 **Tartu** Estonia
64C3 **Tartūs** Syria
29D2 **Tarumirim** Brazil
56A2 **Tarutung** Indon
37E1 **Tarvisio** Italy
13D1 **Taschereau** Can
58D1 **Tashauz** Turkmenistan
61D2 **Tashigang** Bhutan
59E1 **Tashkent** Uzbekistan
63E1 **Tashkepri** Turkmenistan
48K4 **Tashtagol** Russian Fed
49K4 **Tashtyp** Russian Fed
56C4 **Tasikmalaya** Indon
65C2 **Tasīl** Syria
5H2 **Tasiujaq** Can
7N2 **Tasiussaq** Greenland
72B2 **Tasker** *Well* Niger
78B2 **Tasman B** NZ
76D5 **Tasmania** *I* Aust
78B2 **Tasman Mts** NZ
75E3 **Tasman Pen** Aust
77E4 **Tasman S** NZ Aust
64C1 **Taşova** Turk
70C2 **Tassili du Hoggar** *Desert,* Region, Alg
70C2 **Tassili N'jjer** *Desert,* Region, Alg
70B2 **Tata** Mor
71E2 **Tataouine** Tunisia
48J4 **Tatarsk** Russian Fed
53E2 **Tatarskiy Proliv** *Str* Russian Fed
44H4 **Tatarstan** Respublika, Russian Fed
54C3 **Tateyama** Japan
3E1 **Tathlina L** Can
66D3 **Tathlith** S Arabia
10J3 **Tatitlek** USA
3D3 **Tatla Lake** Can
7J4 **Tatnam, Cape** Can
43D3 **Tatry** *Mts* Pol/Slovakia
54B4 **Tatsuno** Japan
60B4 **Tatta** Pak
29C3 **Tatuí** Brazil
16B3 **Tatum** USA
64D2 **Tatvan** Turk
77H2 **Ta'u** *I* American Samoa
27K5 **Tauá** Brazil
29C3 **Taubaté** Brazil
36E1 **Taufstein** *Mt* Germany
78C1 **Taumarunui** NZ
74C2 **Taung** S Africa
55B2 **Taungdwingyi** Burma
55B1 **Taung-gyi** Burma
55A2 **Taungup** Burma
60C2 **Taunsa** Pak
35D6 **Taunton** Eng
14E2 **Taunton** USA
36E1 **Taunus** Region, Germany
78C1 **Taupo** NZ
78C1 **Taupo,L** NZ
43E1 **Taurage** Lithuania

Tauranga Tione

78C1 Tauranga NZ
78C1 Tauranga Harbour B NZ
78B1 Tauroa Pt NZ
7J3 Tavani Can
48H4 Tavda R Russian Fed
77H2 Taveuni I Fiji
39A2 Tavira Port
35C6 Tavistock Eng
55B3 Tavoy Burma
55B3 Tavoy Pt Burma
64A2 Tavsanli Turk
78B2 Tawa NZ
17C3 Tawakoni,L USA
12C2 Tawas City USA
56E2 Tawau Malay
72C2 Taweisha Sudan
57F9 Tawitawi I Phil
57F9 Tawitawi Group Is Phil
22C2 Taxco Mexico
22C2 Taxcoco Mexico
34D3 Tay R Scot
56D3 Tayan Indon
72E3 Tayeeglow Somalia
10F2 Taylor Alaska, USA
3D2 Taylor Can
12C2 Taylor Michigan, USA
17C3 Taylor Texas, USA
16A2 Taylor,Mt USA
12B3 Taylorville USA
66C1 Taymā' S Arabia
49L3 Taymura R Russian Fed
49M2 Taymyr, Ozero L Russian Fed
49L2 Taymyr, Poluostrov Pen Russian Fed
55D3 Tay Ninh Viet
22A1 Tayoltita Mexico
49L4 Tayshet Russian Fed
50C2 Tayshir Mongolia
34D3 Tayside Region, Scot
57E8 Taytay Phil
63E2 Tayyebāt Iran
71B2 Taza Mor
54D3 Tazawako Japan
54D3 Tazawa-ko L Japan
3G2 Tazin L Can
69B2 Tazirbu Libya
10J3 Tazlina L USA
48J3 Tazovskiy Russian Fed
45G7 Tbilisi Georgia
71G4 Tchaourou Benin
72B4 Tchibanga Gabon
72B1 Tchigai,Plat du Niger
70C3 Tchin Tabaradene Niger
72B3 Tcholliré Cam
43D2 Tczew Pol
22A1 Teacapán Mexico
78A3 Te Anau NZ
78A3 Te Anua,L NZ
78C1 Te Aroha NZ
78C1 Te Awamutu NZ
71D1 Tébessa Alg
56A2 Tebingtinggi Indon
22B2 Teboman Mexico
22B2 Tecailtlān Mexico
19C4 Tecate Mexico
22B1 Tecclotlán Mexico
44L4 Techa R Russian Fed
22B2 Tećpan Mexico
22A1 Tecuala Mexico
41F1 Tecuci Rom
17C1 Tecumseh USA
58E2 Tedzhen Turkmenistan
48H6 Tedzhen R Turkmenistan
35E4 Tees R Eng
26F4 Tefé Brazil
56C4 Tegal Indon
56C4 Tegineneng Indon
21D3 Tegucigalpa Honduras
20C3 Tehachapi USA
20C3 Tehachapi Mts USA
19C3 Tehachapi P USA
6J3 Tehek L Can
57C3 Tehoru Indon
63C1 Tehrān Iran
22C2 Tehuacán Mexico
22C2 Tehuantepec Mexico
22C2 Tehuitzingo Mexico
35C5 Teifi R Wales
39A2 Tejo R Port
20C3 Tejon P USA
22B2 Tejupilco Mexico
11C3 Tekamah USA
78B2 Tekapo,L NZ
59F1 Tekeli Kazakhstan
64A1 Tekirdağ Turk
41F2 Tekir Dağlari Mts Turk
61D3 Teknaf Bang
57B3 Teku Indon
78C1 Te Kuiti NZ
21D3 Tela Honduras
45H7 Telavi Georgia
65C2 Tel Aviv Yafo Israel
3B2 Telegraph Creek Can
28B3 Telén Arg
19C3 Telescope Peak Mt USA
27G5 Teles Pires R Brazil
37D1 Telfs Austria
49K4 Teli Russian Fed
45F9 Telkalakh Syria
65C3 Tell el Meise Mt Jordan
10E2 Teller USA
62B2 Tellicherry India
55C5 Telok Anson Malay
57C2 Tĕlok Buli B Indon
56E2 Tĕlok Darvel Malay
57B2 Tĕlok Dondo B Indon
51G7 Tĕlok Flamingo B Indon
57C2 Tĕlok Kau B Indon
56D3 Tĕlok Kumai B Indon
56E1 Tĕlok Labuk B Malay
56C4 Tĕlok Pelabuanratu B Indon
56E4 Tĕlok Saleh B Indon
56D3 Tĕlok Sampit B Indon
56C3 Tĕlok Sukadona B Indon
22C2 Teloloapán Mexico
43E1 Telšiai Lithuania
56D3 Telukbatang Indon
51G7 Teluk Berau B Indon
56C4 Telukbetung Indon
57B3 Teluk Bone B Indon
51G7 Teluk Cendrawasih B Indon
56A2 Telukdalam Indon
57A3 Teluk Mandar B Indon
57B3 Teluk Tolo B Indon
57B3 Teluk Tomini B Indon
57C2 Tĕluk Weda B Indon
71F4 Tema Ghana
4E4 Temagami,L Can
22C2 Temascal Mexico
56B3 Tembesi R Indon
56B3 Tembilahan Indon
23E5 Temblador Ven
20B3 Temblor Range Mts USA
55C5 Temerloh Malay
48G5 Temir Kazakhstan
48J4 Temirtau Kazakhstan
13F1 Témiscouata,L Can
4F4 Témiscaming Can
75C2 Temora Aust
19D4 Tempe USA
17C3 Temple USA
35B5 Templemore Irish Rep
20B3 Templeton USA
22C1 Tempoal Mexico
28A3 Temuco Chile
78B2 Temuka NZ
26C4 Tena Ecuador
62C1 Tenāli India
22C2 Tenancingo Mexico
55B3 Tenasserim Burma
35C6 Tenby Wales
25D2 Tenco R Par
66D4 Tendaho Eth
37B2 Tende France
37B2 Tende P Italy
62E3 Ten Degree Chan Indian O
71B2 Tendrara Mor
72B2 Ténéré Desert Region Niger
70A2 Tenerife I Canary Is
71C1 Ténès Alg
16A2 Tenessee P USA
55B1 Teng R Burma
48H4 Tengiz, Ozero L Kazakhstan
56E3 Tenggarong Indon
52A2 Tengger Shamo Desert China
62B3 Tenkāsi India
73C5 Tenke Zaïre
71F3 Tenkodogo Burkina
37E3 Tenna R Italy
76C2 Tennant Creek Aust
9E3 Tennessee State, USA
17E2 Tennessee R USA
28A2 Teno Chile
56E1 Tenom Malay
21C3 Tenosique Mexico
71A2 Tensift R Mor
57B3 Tentena Indon
75D1 Tenterfield Aust
15E4 Ten Thousand Is USA
22B1 Teocaltiche Mexico
29D2 Teófilo Otôni Brazil
22C2 Teotihiucan Hist Site, Mexico
22C2 Teotitlan Mexico
57C4 Tepa Indon
22B1 Tepatitlan Mexico
21B2 Tepehuanes Mexico
22C2 Tepeji Mexico
22B1 Tepic Mexico
42C2 Teplice Czech Republic
78C1 Te Puke NZ
22B1 Tequila Mexico
22C2 Tequistepec Mexico
39C1 Ter R Spain
70C3 Téra Niger
54C3 Teradomari Japan
40C2 Teramo Italy
70A1 Terceira I Açores
43F3 Terebovlya Ukraine
29B2 Terenoz Brazil
27K5 Teresina Brazil
29D3 Teresópolis Brazil
62E3 Teressa I Indian O
56G7 Teriang Malay
64C1 Terme Turk
58E2 Termez Uzbekistan
40C2 Termoli Italy
57C2 Ternate Indon
53D3 Terney Russian Fed
40C2 Terni Italy
43F3 Ternopol Ukraine
20C3 Terra Bella USA
3C3 Terrace Can
12B1 Terrace Bay Can
40C2 Terracina Italy
73C6 Terrafirma S Africa
79G8 Terre Adélie Region, Ant
17D4 Terre Bonne B USA
12B3 Terre Haute USA
17C3 Terrell USA
5L4 Terrenceville Can
11A2 Terry USA
42B2 Terschelling I Neth
39B1 Teruel Spain
6C2 Teshekpuk USA
71G4 Teshi R Nig
54D2 Teshikaga Japan
53E3 Teshio R Japan
54D2 Teshio dake Mt Japan
50C2 Tesiyn Gol Mts Mongolia
10M3 Teslin Can
10M4 Teslin R Can
10M3 Teslin L Can
49L5 Teslyn Gol R Mongolia
70C2 Tessalit Mali
70C3 Tessaoua Niger
71A2 Tessaout R Mor
66C3 Tessenei Eth
73D5 Tete Mozam
22B2 Tetela Mexico
43F2 Teterev R Ukraine
18D1 Teton R USA
18D2 Teton Range Mts USA
71A1 Tetouan Mor
44H5 Tetyushi Russian Fed
26F8 Teuco R Arg
22B1 Teúl de Gonzalez Ortega Mexico
57C4 Teun I Indon
54D2 Teuri-tō I Japan
40C2 Tevere R Italy
34D4 Teviot R Scot
48J4 Tevriz Russian Fed
78A3 Te Waewae B NZ
56D3 Tewah Indon
75D1 Tewantin Aust
52A3 Têwo China
17D3 Texarkana USA
17D3 Texarkana,L USA
75D1 Texas Aust
8C3 Texas State, USA
17D4 Texas City USA
42A2 Texel I Neth
16B2 Texhoma USA
17C3 Texoma,L USA
74D2 Teyateyaneng Lesotho
60A2 Teyuarah Afghan
22C2 Teziutlán Mexico
29B2 Tezouro Brazil
61D2 Tezpur India
55C1 Tha Laos
74D2 Thabana Ntlenyana Mt Lesotho
74D2 Thaba Putsoa Mt Lesotho
74D1 Thabazimbi S Africa
55B3 Thagyettaw Burma
55D1 Thai Binh Viet
55C2 Thailand Kingdom, S E Asia
55C3 Thailand,G of Thai
55D1 Thai Nguyen Viet
55D2 Thakhek Laos
60C2 Thal Pak
Thalassery = Tellicherry
55C4 Thale Luang L Thai
75C1 Thallon Aust
67F3 Thamarit Oman
78C1 Thames NZ
35F6 Thames R Eng
67E3 Thamūd Yemen
62A1 Thāne India
55D2 Thanh Hoah Viet
62B2 Thanjavur India
Thanlwin = Salween
36D3 Thann France
60C3 Thar Desert India
75B1 Thargomindah Aust
61E4 Tharrawaddy Burma
41E2 Thásos I Greece
55B2 Thaton Burma
55A2 Thayetmyo Burma
61E3 Thazi Burma
11B3 Thedford USA
67F1 The Gulf S W Asia
3G1 Thekulthili L Can
6H3 Thelon R Can
36A1 The Naze Eng
76E3 Theodore Aust
19D4 Theodore Roosevelt L USA
41E2 Thermaïkós Kólpos G Greece
18E2 Thermopolis USA
6F2 Thesiger B Can
4E4 Thessalon Can
41E2 Thessaloníki Greece
35F5 Thetford Eng
5G4 Thetford Mines Can
74D2 Theunissen S Africa
17D4 Thibodaux USA
6J4 Thicket Portage Can
11C2 Thief River Falls USA
18B2 Thielsen,Mt USA
38C2 Thiers France
70A3 Thiès Sen
72D4 Thika Kenya
61C2 Thimphu Bhutan
38D2 Thionville France
41F3 Thíra I Greece
35E4 Thirsk Eng
Thiruvananthapuram = Trivandrum
32F7 Thisted Den
41E3 Thívai Greece
38C2 Thiviers France
3G1 Thoa R Can
20C2 Thomas A Eddison,L USA
15C2 Thomaston Georgia, USA
13F2 Thomaston Maine, USA
35B5 Thomastown Irish Rep
15B2 Thomasville Alabama, USA
15C2 Thomasville Georgia, USA
15D1 Thomasville N Carolina, USA
7J2 Thom Bay Can
6J4 Thompson Can
17D1 Thompson USA
18C1 Thompson Falls USA
6G3 Thompson Landing Can
3D3 Thompson R Can
14D2 Thompsonville USA
15C2 Thomson USA
76D3 Thomson R Aust
55C3 Thon Buri Thai
55B2 Thongwa Burma
37B1 Thonon-les-Bains France
16A2 Thoreau USA
34D4 Thornhill Scot
38B2 Thouars France
13D2 Thousand Is Can/USA
18D1 Three Forks USA
3F3 Three Hills Can
77G4 Three Kings Is NZ
12B1 Three Lakes USA
55B2 Three Pagodas P Thai
20C2 Three Rivers California, USA
12B2 Three Rivers Michigan, USA
17F4 Three Rivers Texas, USA
18B2 Three Sisters Mt USA
7M2 Thule Greenland
37B1 Thun Switz
4D4 Thunder Bay Can
10F2 Thunder Mt USA
37B1 Thuner See L Switz
55B4 Thung Song Thai
37C1 Thur R Switz
42C2 Thüringen State, Germany
42C2 Thüringen Wald Upland Germany
35B5 Thurles Irish Rep
51H8 Thursday I Aust
34D2 Thurso Scot
79F4 Thurston I Ant
37C1 Thusis Switz
75B1 Thylungra Aust
52B5 Tiandong China
52B5 Tian'e China
52D2 Tianjin China
52B5 Tianlin China
53B3 Tianqiaoling China
52B3 Tianshui China
52A2 Tianzhu China
71C1 Tiaret Alg
29B3 Tibagi R Brazil
71J4 Tibati Cam
65C2 Tiberias Israel
65C2 Tiberias,L Israel
Tiber,R = Tevere,R
18D1 Tiber Res USA
72B1 Tibesti Mountain Region Chad
59G2 Tibet Autonomous Region, China
75B1 Tibooburra Aust
61B2 Tibrikot Nepal
21A2 Tiburón I Mexico
70B3 Tichitt Maur
70A2 Tichla Mor
37C2 Ticino R Italy/Switz
13E2 Ticonderoga USA
21D2 Ticul Mexico
70A3 Tidjikja Maur
37C1 Tiefencastel Switz
36C1 Tiel Neth
53B2 Tieli China
53A3 Tieling China
36B1 Tielt Belg
36C1 Tienen Belg
36E3 Tiengen Germany
48J5 Tien Shan Mts China/Kirgizia
52D2 Tientsin China
32H6 Tierp Sweden
28A1 Tierra Amarilla Chile
16A2 Tierra Amarilla USA
22C2 Tierra Blanca Mexico
22C2 Tierra Colorada Mexico
25C8 Tierra del Fuego Territory, Arg
24C9 Tierra del Fuego I Chile/Arg
29C3 Tietê Brazil
29B3 Tiete R Brazil
12C2 Tiffin USA
15C2 Tifton USA
57C3 Tifu Indon
10F5 Tigalda I USA
49R4 Tigil Russian Fed
71J4 Tignere Cam
5J4 Tignish Can
26C4 Tigre R Peru
26F2 Tigre R Ven
64E3 Tigris R Iraq
22C1 Tihuatlán Mexico
19C4 Tijuana Mexico
60D4 Tikamgarh India
44E4 Tikhin Russian Fed
45G6 Tikhoretsk Russian Fed
77F2 Tikopia I Solomon Is
64D3 Tikrīt Iraq
49O2 Tiksi Russian Fed
57B2 Tilamuta Indon
36C1 Tilburg Neth
35F6 Tilbury Eng
25C2 Tilcara Arg
75B1 Tilcha Aust
55A1 Tilin Burma
70C3 Tillabéri Niger
18B1 Tillamook USA
62E3 Tillanchong I Indian O
70C3 Tillia Niger
41F3 Tílos I Greece
75B2 Tilpa Aust
26C3 Tiluá Colombia
44H2 Timanskiy Kryazh Mts Russian Fed
78B2 Timaru NZ
45F6 Timashevsk Russian Fed
41E3 Timbákion Greece
17D4 Timbalier B USA
70B3 Timbédra Maur
Timbuktu = Tombouctou
70B3 Timétrine Monts, Mts Mali
70C3 Timia Niger
70C2 Timimoun Alg
41E1 Timiş R Rom
41E1 Timişoara Rom
4E4 Timmins Can
76B1 Timor I Indon
76B2 Timor S Aust/Indon
28C3 Timote Arg
65B3 Timsâh,L Egypt
15B1 Tims Ford L USA
57G9 Tinaca Pt Phil
23D5 Tinaco Ven
62B2 Tindivanam India
70B2 Tindouf Alg
37B2 Tinée R France
20C2 Tinemaha Res USA
70B2 Tinfouchy Alg
70C2 Tin Fouye Alg
10F2 Tingmerkpuk Mt USA
7O3 Tingmiarmiut Greenland
26C5 Tingo Maria Peru
70B3 Tingrela Ivory Coast
61C2 Tingri China
51H5 Tinian Pacific O
28B1 Tinogasta Arg
41F3 Tínos I Greece
61E2 Tinsukia India
35C6 Tintagel Head Pt Eng
70C2 Tin Tarabine Watercourse Alg
75B3 Tintinara Aust
70C2 Tin Zaouaten Alg
11B2 Tioga USA
14B2 Tioga R USA
20C2 Tioga P USA
55C5 Tioman I Malay
4E4 Tionaga Can
37D1 Tione Italy

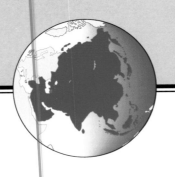

ASIA

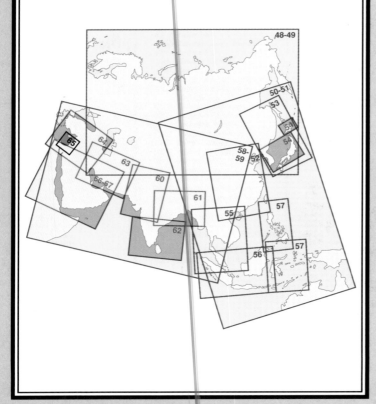

AFRICA

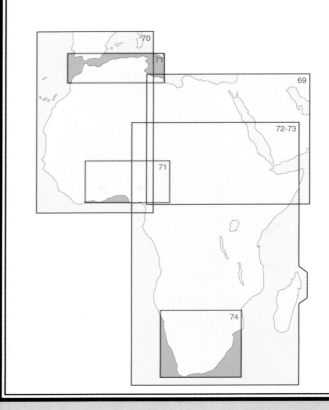